My Works and Days

Books by Lewis Mumford

Lewis Mumford

My Works and Days: *A Personal Chronicle*

Harcourt Brace Jovanovich

New York and London

"East Side Education" and "West Side Love" (as "Tennis, Quadratic Equations, and Love"), "Vincent Van Gogh" (as "Autobiographies in Paint"), "The Taste of New England," "Fantasia on Time," "Consolation in War," "Excursions Abroad" (as "European Diary") appeared originally in *The New Yorker*. "Address on the Vietnam Holocaust" and "On Receiving an Honor in Literature" were first published in the *Proceedings* of the American Academy of Arts and Letters and National Institute of Arts and Letters, Second Series, Numbers 16 (1966) and 21 (1971) respectively. Excerpts from letters written by Lewis Mumford and Van Wyck Brooks to each other are from *The Van Wyck Brooks Lewis Mumford Letters,* edited by Robert E. Spiller, copyright © 1970 by E. P. Dutton, and are reprinted by permission of E. P. Dutton. The quotation from Lewis Mumford's *Art and Technics* is reprinted by permission of Columbia University Press.

Library of Congress Cataloging in Publication Data

Mumford, Lewis, 1895–
My works and days.

1. Mumford, Lewis, 1895–
2. Social reformers—United States—Biography.
3. City planners—United States—Biography.
4. Architects—United States—Biography.   I. Title.
CT275.M734A35   818'.5'209   [B]   78-53893
ISBN 0-15-164087-4

B C D E

To Sophia

Still the best of my Findings,
The most enduring of my Keepings

Contents

Perhaps our works and days are all we shipmates
have. . . . To feel the smart sea spray and ride
the waves a while is all a sailor needs for
happiness. A minute is a sample of Eternity.

—*The Little Testament of Bernard Martin*

My Works and Days

1: Prologue to Our Time

I was born in October 1895, five years before the turn of the century, and the trumpet fanfare on which that wonderful and terrible century died still echoes faintly in my ears. But though, with the aid of family photographs, I can fish up from the depths of infancy sights and smells and fears and dreams, my conscious life dates from the twentieth century. Being a child of my time, I expected much of the new century. This period was destined, almost everyone then confidently supposed, to produce even greater wonders than the steam engine, the electric telegraph, the Hoe printing press, the dynamo, for daring inventors and even more daring prophets, such as H. G. Wells, were already proclaiming that the airplane, the ancient dream of Flying Man, was just around the corner. And, indeed, these one-eyed prophecies came true.

Events of another kind, unfortunately, were also lurking in the same dark alleys of the future. For in the year after my birth Antoine Henri Becquerel, by a happy accident—or was it really so happy?—discovered the radioactive rays emanating from uranium, which were named after him, and when I was three years old the Curies, following his trail, had isolated the first particles of that active but so long unnoticed element —radium. This was but one of many shattering transformations. The very December of the year of my birth, Roentgen had announced his discovery of X-rays, which, penetrating once seemingly impenetrable objects, broke down the wall between the inside and the outside of 'solid' bodies. We had begun, whether we liked it or not, to live in a porous, permeable, increasingly translucent world, whose walls and boundaries, if not altogether illusions, existed mostly in the mind.

But at the turn of the century, everyone still hoped for the best; only benighted souls or disturbed minds furtively suspected the worst. Even

3

a child of five, thanks to his insecurities and anxieties and confusions, was better prepared—had he only remained young—than was any adult for the events that would follow in his own lifetime. Witches, ogres, malignant demons, imbecile giants were still real to him, and when, in the pride of adolescence, he would learn to dismiss these frightening images, along with Santa Claus, fairies, and angels, he would deprive himself for much of his life of any clue to the satanic realities that already threatened him.

In most departments, and not least in science, a certain blind assurance prevailed, distorting observation and undermining judgment. The physicists, the guild whose later discoveries would shake the foundations of civilization, were wide of the mark in their neat assumptions about the nature of the physical world: they did not, as Henry Adams soon discovered, accept radium easily. Having forgotten the enlightening intuitions of Michael Faraday, who from the beginning had rejected their too tidy conception of atomism, the exponents of the exact sciences were convinced that they had already staked out the ultimate boundaries of the material universe and that no new discoveries of radical importance would be made; their ideology found no place for invisible internal activities or unfathomable depths. The physicists' chief anxiety before Haber discovered how to extract nitrogen from the air was that our planet's wheat supply might fall short. The fabric of nineteenth century thought seemed so tightly woven and so durable that the editors of the British periodical 'The Nineteenth Century' refused to change its name to honor the new century: they bowed to the calendar only to the extent of retitling their magazine 'The Nineteenth Century and After.'

Now we know better. We have found out what "and After" means. So far from having reached their ultimate goal, the physical sciences were preparing for a gigantic leap forward, and comparable advances would shortly be made in the life sciences. But meanwhile those aspects of civilization which most closely reflected the human condition and carried with them all the tragic decisions and defeats of history would, for lack of any self-alerting sense of danger, experience a sudden jolt and shudder. In time, we would find that an ancient geological fault which runs through every stratum of recorded history had opened, sending great nations and empires hurtling backward—backward and downward —into an abyss of barbarism that the nineteenth century could not even imagine. But the Industrial Revolution—or, at least, the Scientific Revolution—had changed all that, had it not? When people were faced with any unpleasant contradictory evidence, they refuted it decisively, as one of the characters in Wilkie Collins' 'The Moonstone' did, with "But this is

4

the Nineteenth Century!" Only a few desolate men, such as Jakob Burckhardt, Herman Melville, and the even more sinister Dostoevski, had been prescient enough to glimpse even a fraction of the evils that the First World War would disclose. While at its end most of the superstructure of civilization was left standing, somewhat battered but repairable, the foundations that had long been crumbling were visibly sinking—and kept on sinking.

At the dawn of the twentieth century, the illusion of stability and solidity still prevailed. And yet, and yet . . . Am I not playing down the underlying anxiety? More than once, H. G. Wells, in the midst of his exuberant scientific fantasies about the future, expressed forebodings of disaster. While it was typical of the period that as late as 1919 the historian F. S. Marvin could call the passing era the Century of Hope, Wells as early as 1895, in 'The Time Machine,' saw in the growing pile of civilization "a foolish heaping that must inevitably fall back upon and destroy its makers in the end." Yet his conclusion was even more typical—and irrational—than anything Marvin had to say. "If that is so," Wells wrote, "*it remains for us to live as though it were not so.*" Was that security blanket what the cold, unblinking rationality of modern science actually shivered under?

"Ta-ra-ra-boom-de-ay: did you see my wife today? No, I saw her yesterday: ta-ra-ra-boom-de-ay." That seemed the smartest and naughtiest of retorts when it was sung in the music halls of London and New York, but one now finds a curious innocence about its sophistication. My infant ears also heard another song, even more innocent in content, which now has a somewhat more ominous sound than anyone who heard it then could have guessed: "There'll be a hot time in the old town tonight!"

Even yesterday—that is, two generations ago—the events that were to divorce the twentieth century from the glories and triumphs of the nineteenth were visible in cautionary samples. The convulsive weakness of imperialism as it was practiced by the greatest of the colonial powers, England, was disclosed in the fumbling, amateurish conduct of the Boer War, in which, incidentally, the presumably civilized British leaders employed that instrument of massive political coercion, the civilian concentration camp, and almost at the same moment treason and anti-Semitism joined hands in the French Dreyfus case. Thus, Nazism and Stalinism and Nixonism, as one may now call the corresponding American mode—indeed, all the variants of an oppressive totalitarianism—were already being incubated. Yes, political botulism was spreading, and my country's soil was not immune. At the beginning of the new century, the systematic infliction of torture upon war prisoners, in what was politely termed the 'water cure,' by the American Army in the Philippines, and the wanton sacking of Peking by the combined international forces that put down the Boxer Rebellion set the stage for the epoch we now confront, with its steadily augmenting horrors, from Buchenwald to Vietnam. All the historic collective evils—war, genocide, lawless government—which went into mass production after 1914 a knowing eye might have detected much earlier in these samples.

Had I known the state of the historical weather at the time I emerged from the womb, I might well have been tempted, like a prudent woodchuck in February, to return to my tunnel and await a change of season. But I should have had to wait a long time; in fact, I would still be waiting. As for interpreting those high, thin streaks of cloud which indicate to the weather-wise eye that a great storm is coming, to herald, in turn, a cyclic change in the climate itself, only a handful of those who were then alive could have been capable of it. The majority, whether in Europe or America, were encased in bulletproof ideological vests, which protected them not merely against other systems of ideas but against the direct impact of their own contradictory experiences. And that was even worse, for those experiences might have led them to modify the premise underlying this whole age: the doctrine of Progress.

This doctrine reflected the high humanitarian hopes of the eighteenth century philosophers—impulses that eventually brought about certain happy political and social innovations, among them constitutional government, universal suffrage, and free public education. But the even more rapid advances in exploiting coal and steam and automatic machines overshadowed these human gains, for they conveyed the notion that mankind's improvement could be brought about by the continued invention of ever more powerful man-displacing mechanisms. This belief was reinforced by the Darwinian interpretation of biological evolution through 'natural selection'—fostering the "preservation of Favored Races in the Struggle for Life" (Darwin's words). This curious reading of the will to live applied not merely to races and species but to nations and classes, and embellished the brute fact of survival with a smug eulogy of the survivors. What self-flattery for the ruling classes! What consolation for their predestined victims!

On this theory of human development, Progress meant man's increasing success in overcoming his physical limitations so as to impose his own machine-conditioned fantasies upon nature. By definition, technological change and human improvement were now coupled together, and, also by definition, the forces that made for progress were inevitable, inviolable, irresistible. The latest discovery, the latest invention, the latest fashion was *ipso facto* the best, and the more ruthlessly our in-dustrial advances erased the monuments, and even the happy memories, of the past, the more acceptable (progressive) were the results. Thus, even Modern Man would become "obsolete," one American contemporary observed when the first atomic bomb was exploded. On the same pro-gressive principle, democracy must yield place to totalitarianism, for, as Anne Lindbergh remarked, Nazism was "the Wave of the Future."

'Good' and 'bad' had nothing at all to do with Progress, for they belonged to the platonic world of values, which science had flatly ex-cluded from the area of verifiable knowledge. No longer were self-knowl-edge, and discrimination between good and evil, the beginning of wisdom. This bias is still known in the scientific world as 'objectivity.' These battered clichés still linger today along with others based on scientific and technological notions, in the slogans of the ad writer, the industrial designer, the avant-garde artist, and the go-go professors—all shining brightly against their 'up-to-date' Jules Verne background. If this con-ception of Progress had any substance, no part of man's past experience was worth examining or evaluating for preservation and possible future use on a higher level of culture ("history is bunk"). Progress was a tractor that laid its own roadbed and left no permanent imprint of its own tracks, nor did it move toward an imaginable or a humanly desirable destination. "The going is the goal," a pragmatic philosopher said; past and future had both been swallowed in the void of a meaningless now.

Such are still the pious beliefs of the futurologist, whose inflated expectations, like the inflated values of our dubious financial-credit sys-tem, are based on the supposition that the day for casting up a balance between assets and liabilities can be indefinitely postponed. Are not the losses in fact gains? he asks, like his predecessors, since only through constant waste and war can the megamachine keep on expanding. That this limitless mechanical progress carried with it the possibility of an equally indefinite human regression did not occur, as late as the nineteen-sixties, to the faithful disciples of Marshall McLuhan, Daniel Bell, or Arthur Clarke—those giant minds whose private dreams all too quickly turned into public nightmares.

Progress indeed! That the March of Progress would in fact lead to worldwide calamity and catastrophe was something the Age of Con-fidence never saw as the most remote eventuality. Even while the bridge to the Brave New World of technology was visibly buckling and break-ing apart, my friend Van Wyck Brooks, steeped in humane tradition as he was, clung to the comforting dogma of Progress and reproved me for not bowing to the idols he and Charles Beard accepted. In this one respect, the Old Guard and the Advance Guard were almost indistinguishable. A century earlier, Emerson himself had shared with Mark Twain the belief that the great mechanical inventions, from the cotton mill to the electric telegraph, had decisively established the reality of human progress. And those who march to this tune are, alas, still in fashion. Did not the president of a great university the other day publicly salute Buckminster Fuller, that interminable tape recorder of 'salvation by technology,' as another Leonardo da Vinci, another Freud, another Einstein?

This popular conception of Progress dismissed as unreal the possibility of arrest, reversal, discontinuity, or regression, no matter how often history had demonstrated the occurrence of all four. Yet the physical world itself, for all its regularities and uniformities, has its ups and downs, its contractions and expansions, even its total extinctions. Indeed, the entire universe, astronomers now darkly suspect, may someday coalesce into a ponderous, impenetrable mass, as hostile to all dynamic and dispersed forms of 'matter' as to life itself. At all events, nothing is more certain about our earthly habitat and its denizens than the fact that the processes of building up and breaking down continue, at varying rates of speed, in every organism, in every ecological group, in every society. As long as the tissue-building, self-regenerating, growth-promoting functions provide a margin of free energy, life goes on. But what monsters would walk the streets—what stumbling giants, what mountains of obesity! —if organic vitality meant limitless growth!

I find it hard to believe, I confess, that for more than a century some of the best minds of the West could have operated so long on that faulty premise of Progress. Meanwhile, during this last half century we have seen that the most startling advances in scientific technology have by their very success hurled great nations and empires into a morass of political and moral depravity. For have not supposedly civilized governments countenanced or committed scientifically organized tortures and massacres indistinguishable from the unbridled collective sadism of an Ashurbanipal or a Genghis Khan?

The age of "the men who are ten years old," long ago predicted in the Pali Buddhist texts, had arrived before my adolescence ended: ten-year-old minds enclosed in a ten-year-old culture with only a ten-year future—if that. In an editorial in The Freeman in 1921, I described my generation's fate as 'The Collapse of Tomorrow.' But the Buddhists had peered deeper into the future, for they said of "the men who are ten years old" that "their violent hatred against each other will predominate, with violent enmity, violent malevolence, violent lust for wholesale killing." A world picture that omitted all values except those fostered by science and technology was left with only a blank (nihilism) in our proper human realm. Homer, Herodotus, and Shakespeare were far better equipped to interpret man's condition and arm him to face the future than the latest clutch of futurologists.

Even now, perhaps a majority of our countrymen still believe that science and technics can solve all human problems. They have no suspicion that our runaway science and technics themselves have come to constitute the main problem the human race has to overcome. Only a handful of sensitive scientists, such as Max Born, were ready to admit that this lay at the bottom of our difficulties. Strangely, the palpable rationality of the scientific method within its own accredited area gave rise in the great majority of its practitioners to a compulsive irrationality —an uncritical faith in science's godlike power to control the destinies of the human race. Those who have studied the ancient Mesopotamian and Egyptian religious texts know how cruel, destructive, and inhumane man's godlike faculties actually can be. Only mammalian tenderness and human love have saved mankind from the demented gods that rise up from the unconscious when man cuts himself off from the cosmic and earthly sources of his life.

Very late in my own development, I discovered what any number of more gifted minds should have discovered long before; namely, that the basic ideology which pervaded the Western mind at the beginning of the century was only a scientifically dressed-up justification for the immemorial practices of the ruling classes—historically attested in Egypt, Babylonia, Assyria, Peru, and, indeed, wherever the archetypal megamachine was in control. The dominant institutions of our time, far from being new, were all in the thrall of a myth that was at least five thousand years old. Only one value was acknowledged, and that one was taken for granted: the reality of power in all its forms, from sun power to military power, from manpower to steam power, from cannon power to money power, from machine power and computer power to sex power.

This simplistic formula for Progress created the overriding imperative that the very victims of the power complex meekly accepted: one must go with the tide, ride the wave of the future—or, more vulgarly, keep moving. The meaning of life was reduced to accelerating movement and change, and nothing else remained. Behold the ultimate religion of our seemingly rational age—the Myth of the Machine! Bigger and bigger, more and more, farther and farther, faster and faster became ends in themselves, as expressions of godlike power; and empires, nations, trusts, corporations, institutions, and power-hungry individuals were all directed to the same blank destination. The going was the goal—a defensible doctrine for colliding atoms or falling bodies, but not for men.

Half a century before my own time, Tennyson, in 'Locksley Hall,' had captured the Victorian faith in Progress, with all its comforting emptiness, in "Let the great world spin forever down the ringing grooves of change." For most people, to increase the pace of change by every kind of invention and innovation became nothing less than the whole duty of man. At least, it was the duty of the New Man, and, of course, of the New Woman. Implicitly, the progressives followed the reactionary principle of Jean-Jacques Rousseau: "Reverse all that is now done and you will be right." Particularly if the people who had been doing it were one's elders, one's parents, those in authority.

And now I smile a wintry smile. That was the doctrine I grew up on, and my earliest patron saints were Bernard Shaw and H. G. Wells. Even the master of my youth, Patrick Geddes, who now seems to many people one of the great minds of the period, would write me, "It is time to be getting on with our ideas," and, despite his warm relations with the poet Rabindranath Tagore and the physicist Jagadis Chandra Bose, he criticized Gandhi's program for achieving freedom from Britain and its machine-driven capitalism on the ground that Gandhi's belief in spinning by hand, without even the use of an electric motor, was only Ruskin, 1850; that his belief in passive political resistance was Thoreau, also 1850; and that his militant nationalism was Mazzini, 1848—just as if these dates deprived similar later proposals of validity. Still, what was Geddes's own belief in "getting on" but the progressive ideas of Condorcet, 1789; of Auguste Comte, 1840; and of Frédéric Le Play, circa 1870? By now, they are all just as dust-covered by the March of Progress as those of Gandhi himself. So even Geddes's understanding of biological time in Bergson's sense—as duration in a present that could not exist even in the mind without a bonding together of the past and the future—was tarnished by the fallacious doctrine common to the whole age. At bottom, when he was immersed in the actualities of contemporary history, Geddes himself knew better; his lapses only show what a hold the doctrine of Progress had maintained.

For the first twenty years of my life, or even longer, I shared most of the naïve hopes of these leaders and rallied to the movements and projects that promoted them; in fact, my first definite inclination to a vocation was to that of an engineer, and the most progressive kind of engineer, too—an electrical engineer. I need not apologize for that part of my past, and I am not sorry about it, for this early acceptance of— indeed, high excitement over—the doctrine of Progress has given me a vivid understanding of my 'progressive,' power-infatuated contemporaries. But this early commitment had likewise enabled me to winnow out what was valid in the concept of human progress from the purely mechanical metaphors that so largely had been motivated by the man-devouring ambitions of Bronze Age gods, and incited further by the demented fantasies of absolute rulers.

For all this, there actually was a vital human core in the doctrine of Progress which those who prated most about Progress had lost. What was significant—more than that, sacred and forever memorable—was the slow accretion, though unsteady and intermittent, of meanings and forms and values, those tiny radioactive particles that each generation separates from the gross ore of human experience. To the extent that this precious residue has been extracted and treasured, every part of life—every constructive or creative achievement, every active expression of love—has the aura, however faint, of divinity. To mine and crush tons of pitchblende so that a few grams of radium may become available, metaphorically speaking, is the worthiest conceivable task for mankind, no matter what the penalties and sacrifices: a true fulfillment of emergent evolution and human destiny, though there is no quantitative measure for this kind of creativity or this kind of achievement. But, in a strict sense, this is transcendence, not progress—a change of levels from the human to the divine.

Even when viewed from a less exalted position, there was something to be said for the belief in Progress as it suddenly bloomed in the eighteenth century: the Age of Enlightenment confidently proposed to achieve on earth the equality and justice and love that the Christian Church had dared to promise only in Heaven—and then, quaintly, only after the righteous were segregated from the sinners. As Albert Schweitzer pointed out, Western civilization in the eighteenth century honorably, if belatedly, began to carry out the more universal ethical precepts of Christianity. As a result of this newly affirmed faith in the natural goodness of man, sundry improvements were actually made. Here and there, imprisoned people were treated with more humanity and kept in more sanitary quarters; the insane were no longer shackled and whipped; little children were treated with more understanding and valued in their own right; and for the first time the deplorable condition of the great mass of workers became a matter of open public concern and, fitfully, of amelioration. Many of these departures were pushed further in the nineteenth century. Rousseau's and Froebel's new principles for educating the child and Diderot's acute observations on aiding the deaf, dumb, and blind carried into the daily life of millions the basic precepts of the New Testament, and effected miracles, too: witness Helen Keller. But none of the great projects of the eighteenth century was pushed far enough to alter radically the basis of civilization; and when they went furthest—as with the egalitarian programs of Socialism—they disclosed unsuspected flaws in their conception.

If I have mocked the doctrine of Progress, I have done so only to attack the simpleminded notion that human improvements are guaranteed by purely scientific and technological advances—that they are the predictable outcome of today's panacea, 'research and development.' The genuine achievements, however fragile or fitful, do not deserve to be ignored. Nor have I any notion of belittling these generous visions of human improvement because they were so easily mistaken for the dawn of even better days. The fault was that those who regarded faith in Progress as a moral imperative mistakenly assumed, on the basis of only a century's experience, that the forward movement was continuous, inevitable, and in most respects benign, and, as well, that it could not be retarded, much less opposed or reversed.

"You can't turn the hands of the clock back," people would say, with an owlish air of finality. As if society were not as much of a human artifact as the clock, as if anyone would harbor a clock whose mechanism made no provision for turning its hands forward or backward so that it would keep correct time, as if clocks and communities were as immune to human regulation as the solar system! On the same principle, one might design motorcars whose speed could not be regulated, whose destination could not be altered, cars that lacked brakes to halt them when there was danger of collision. People should talk more carefully about machines, for machines wouldn't be of much use if they did not embody many organic principles unrecognized by the doctrine of automatic Progress.

Yet all things considered, it was to my advantage that the hopes and expectations of the Enlightenment were still vivid in the days of my youth. Those cheerful thoughts entered my bloodstream and today, in whatever dilution, continue to circulate through my body. Indeed, they provide a certain almost physiological sustenance, which those who were born even half a generation later fatally lack. Without that deep animal faith, I could not now review the events of my life and times.

Fortunately, the clouds that soon began to efface all color and light from our sky did not also remove the sun. Some of us still have minds sufficiently immersed in the living stream of human history, and buoyed up by its accumulation of values and meanings in language, art, religion, and science ever since the emergence of man as a recognizable species, to enable us to retain some measure of the emotional energy that has kept the human race alive through an endless series of frustrations, crippling injuries, and disasters—not only natural disasters but even more disheartening man-made ones. Those whose minds were formed in that better day still do not regard all human communication as gibberish, all beautiful form as no better than a child's mud pie.

Even as I put this contrast into words, the reader will mark my hostility to the fashionable nihilist doctrine of our day: the cult of anti-life, with all its psychotic violence and its infantile debasements. That hostility applies equally, of course, to those who seek salvation by giving their energies to quickening, through science and technics, the destructive forces that are now released from their natural limitations and cultural restraints, and are overrunning the habitat and degrading it. I have not lived for three-quarters of a century without some understanding of both aggression and regression—for the irrational avant-garde of the arts and the meticulously 'rational' avant-garde of computerdom are heading toward the same goal. They reinforce each other and converge upon a zero point, where their juncture will signal a self-obliterating explosion.

Plainly, this hostility of mine marks me as still a child of an earlier period, who is increasingly at odds with the world he has faced as an adult, and is even more remote from the world his grandchildren may have to face.

Yes, at the turn of the century the climate of the world was changing; and part of my vocation was to interpret that change, to become acutely aware of its menacing possibilities while I worked, within my range, to forfend them. For those of us who have been awake to realities, this has been a lonely role. But more than half of my life went by before I realized how lonely. There are plenty of people today who view what has been happening in the twentieth century as an entirely normal manifestation of man's nature and destiny. They have no notion of how many dearly bought achievements of human culture (those particles of radium!) have now been buried in irredeemable rubbish heaps or swept out to sea in violent floods.

Most of our contemporaries, perhaps, still see only the endless bounties and benefits resulting from that part of our culture which has been changing most rapidly, and have closed their eyes to the varieties of dehumanization and extermination that twentieth century men—not just the Nazis and the Stalinists—have practiced on a colossal scale. They prefer not to think about the millions who met premature death in war or were gassed in extermination camps, or the countless men, women, and children who are being killed or maimed for life in automobile accidents, week after week, year after year. Even if our contemporaries hide these facts from themselves, there are others, too palpable to be overlooked, in "great" cities, where horrors in the form of mugging, rape, murder, and torture are practiced alike by criminals and by putative guardians of the law. Inoculated against any evidence that is contrary to their basic assumptions, these desensitized minds still believe that "science will find the answer," or that if worst comes to worst, a saving minority of mankind will escape to some other planet in a spaceship. This, incidentally, was the scenario of a play I outlined in 1914 or 1915—only in my version, I am proud to record, the more human residue of mankind remained behind.

By now, the myth of the machine, the basic religion of our present culture, has so captured the modern mind that no human sacrifice seems too great provided it is offered up to the insolent Marduks and Molochs of science and technology. Those who are in the grip of this myth imagine that with an increasing budget for scientific R. and D., with a more voluminous productivity, augmented by almost omniscient computers and a wider range of antibiotics and inoculations, with a greater control over our genetic inheritance, with more complex surgical operations and transplants, with an extension of automation to every form of human activity, mankind will achieve—what? "Happiness," people used to say, wistfully. But do they now not mean anesthesia? These processes are being directed by those who conceive happiness purely in terms of their ability to foster their own favored activities, and to execute plans that would, with the aid of sufficient State or Foundation grants, give them almost complete authority over the destiny of the human race. Life so misconceived and so misdirected can produce only mindless nonentities, incapable of performing as autonomous beings any organic or human functions.

One dare not smile in reflecting what happened to these soaring post-nineteenth century hopes at the very blast-off. The best one can say about them is that most of the scientifically organized imbecilities predicted by Aldous Huxley for the Brave New World in "the Seventh Century After Ford" have already become realities. But in my youth, as a zealous reader of Hugo Gernsback's monthly Modern Electrics, I shared my generation's pious belief in our future; and I still entertain as a valid possibility the slowing down of the pace of automation and depersonalization great enough to permit us to safeguard the immense treasuries of knowledge and technical facility now at our command. There is hardly an invention, a method, or a process produced by the institutions that now work in such a dismally negative fashion which might not in future prove humanly valuable, sometimes highly desirable, if it were applied at the right moment, in the right quantity, for the right purpose—that is, if it were under constant human evaluation and control, if it were directed to higher goals than the expansion of the megamachine and the exaltation of those who command it, and profit by a virtual monopoly of its rewards.

But even at their best all these improvements, however helpful, remain peripheral: they fail to do justice to man's central concern, his own

14

self-humanization. In letting depersonalized organizations and automatic contraptions take charge of our lives, we have been forfeiting the only qualities that could justify our existence: sensitiveness, consciousness, responsiveness, expressive intelligence, human-heartedness, and (alas, one cannot use this word now without wincing) creativity. And love! Yes, love above all. When, more than a century ago, Emerson observed that "things are in the saddle and ride mankind," he identified the conditions we now face in their full-grown form. And as man himself, he who was once—in all his self-sustaining racial, tribal, regional, national, civic, and ultimately personal varieties—potentially an autonomous being, shrinks and disappears, a new kind of creature, infrahuman, fabricated to make our complex megamachine workable, has come into existence: the bureaucratic personality, punched and coded for the machine. As Max Weber predicted over fifty years ago, that under-dimensioned personality has become the all but universal type.

Now this inexorable regimentation, in its fabrication of such a rigid and sterile personality, has given rise to a counter-adaptation, for the bureaucratic type has been compensated for and secretly aided by its negative counterpart: the beatnik, the hippie, the gangster, and their later underground successors, who have rejected the dehumanized order of bureaucratic automation by rejecting as well those humanized modes of behavior by means of which man emerged from his original animal limitations. Indeed, they reject even such orderly routines, such life-sustaining activities, as animals themselves exhibit in acts of grooming, mating, food gathering, and nurturing of the young; and, in order to live at their chosen subanimal level, they destroy their minds and do violence to their bodies with drugs. Year by year, they ingeniously invent more sophisticated modes of disorder and perpetrate them on defenseless communities.

On the bureaucratic side, Adolf Eichmann, the man who faithfully carried out orders from above, is the veritable Hero of Our Time; and a thousand other Eichmanns stand ready to wipe out not just the Jews but the larger part of the human race as soon as the order comes through from the Pentagon or the Kremlin. There are Hitlers in every war office, and Eichmanns in every rocket center, in every aircraft carrier and submarine, in every nuclear and chemical and bacterial laboratory, as the consistently atrocious practices of the American military forces in Vietnam demonstrated.

Those of us who have lived to see this last transformation know the worst about our own countrymen—and so about the human race. The better world my generation grew up in was not wholly a complacent illusion, but we were scarcely equipped to reckon with the massive potentialities for evil that civilization, by its own dynamism and cold audacity, had expanded. Yet did not Giovanni Battista Vico warn us at the beginning of the enlightened eighteenth century that there was no barbarism more savage than that of 'civilized' man? Now 'The Age of Monsters' is here.

Obviously, I have, not without inner resistance, come to a vision of the world different from that which comforts—or, at best, only slightly discomforts—many of my contemporaries. It seems to me that, on the basis of rational calculations, derived from what must admittedly be incomplete evidence, *if the forces that now dominate us continue on their present path* they must lead to collapse of the whole historical fabric, not just this or that great nation or empire. Unfortunately, if we continue to act upon the premises that have increasingly automated all human activities, there will be no stopping point before the ultimate terminus: total destruction. Already, languages show signs of slithering into incoherence and confusion, with vocabularies so limited and a semantic structure so primitive that beside them the most elementary tribal language must count as a delicate work of art. H. G. Wells's dire prediction that "mind is at the end of its tether" can no longer be lightly dismissed as mere senile despair, as it could be in 1945.

To flinch now from facing these realities and evaluating them is to me an act of intellectual cowardice. But because I have dared to face and evaluate them I have often been dismissed as a 'prophet of doom.' This is no more intelligent than to say of a physician who diagnoses a possibly fatal disease and applies his skill to curing it that he is a willing ally of the undertaker. On the contrary, every fibre of my being revolts against the fate that threatens our civilization, and revolts almost equally against those supine minds that accept it as inevitable, or, even worse, seek treasonably to justify its 'inevitability.'

From first to last, my own beliefs challenge those who think there is no turning back on the road that mankind is now travelling, no possibility of changing our minds or altering our course, no way of arresting or redirecting the forces that, if they are not subdued, will bring about the annihilation of man. For the last thirty years, then, I have been forced, much against my native interests and talents, to confront the suicidal nihilism of our civilization, for I believe that only those who are sufficiently awake to the forces that menace us and who have taken the full measure of their probable consequences will be able to overcome them. It is not as a prophet of doom but as an exponent of the Renewal of Life that I have faced the future: not by accident do the books I wrote between 1930 and 1950 bear that phrase for their common title. That title

16

may seem, in the light of what has followed since, almost wantonly hopeful; certainly it did not spring from discouragement or despair. For those who share this vision, life itself is the central good and the source of all other goods: life in all its organic manifestations, and even in its dismaying contradictions, its ultimate tragedies—life embracing not alone love, courage, human-heartedness, and joy but alienation, frustration, and pain.

Now, what I mean by "life" cannot be packed into a single sentence or even a single book. Jeffery Smith, my onetime professorial colleague at Stanford, used to tell of a simple farmhand who had battled against odds all his life, raising a large family while barely able to keep his head above water. If any man had a right to be disheartened or bitter over his fate, it would seem to have been that man, yet he had never despaired. Then, a little while before he died, a visitor found him in a grievous condition, with an ailment that could no longer be fought off or grimly concealed. "Yes, my boy," he said. "My time has come. The feast of life will soon be over."

The feast of life! This phrase, uttered by a man who had faced more than his share of the burdens and miseries of life and seemed to have had too little of its rewards, is an affirmation that should confound a thousand nihilisms. The spirit is at one with the faith Whitman proclaimed, in his acceptance of evil as well as good, in his readiness to count no aspect of life too mean, too vile, too repulsive to be reckoned as part of its meaning and value. And did not Plotinus say that it was better for even an animal to have lived and suffered than never to have lived at all? This, I take it, is what a contemporary witness, Solzhenitzyn, has declared, with equal conviction, about his own experience of cancer, made doubly unbearable by his harsh imprisonment.

In the Second World War, "the feast of life" was snatched from our son at the age of nineteen—all too soon. But when, a little earlier, he was recalling with his sweetheart some of the most disruptive episodes in their association at school, he remarked, "I'm damned if it wasn't fun." Grievous though such an early death was, he had nevertheless known many moments of fulfillment. Far more lamentable is the kind of mental decomposition that takes place in those who have never consciously savored life's feast, for their unlived life takes its revenge, now sinking into docile acceptance of their prisonlike routine, now erupting in fantasies and acts of insensate violence. These victims are the real proponents of doom.

As the twentieth century approached, there was some popular debate as to when the old one came to an end, many holding that 1900 was the veritable beginning, in the face of those who could prove by the calendar that January 1, 1901, marked the true turning point, since the next century was not in existence until the nineteenth had completed its course. Little children are just as puzzled by the fact that when they are five years old they are in their sixth year. My wife remembers that as a child she always resented this premature advance of her age. But this debate is about an abstraction. In terms of events, the nineteenth century began in 1815, as my history teacher, Professor Salwyn Schapiro, used to point out, for it was then that the Napoleonic Wars came to an end; and the nineteenth century terminated in 1914, when the cycle of conflicts and calamities through which we are now living began.

Assuredly there were many signs that were a good augury for the twentieth century. In an effort to head off the coming war, the czar of Russia, no less an advocate of peace (and no more!) than his latter-day successors, Khrushchev and Brezhnev, had in 1899 convoked the first great international peace conference, at The Hague; and even before that, at the World's Columbian Exposition, in Chicago, in 1893, an equally remarkable World Congress of Religions and their churches—bodies harder to disarm and unite than the more openly belligerent nations—had taken place. One might multiply these favorable instances. When the Paris Universal Exposition of 1900 opened, one of its features was the Rue des Nations, an effort (promoted by Patrick Geddes, who was an indefatigable internationalist) to give a concrete expression to the ideas of peace and cooperation by getting each nation to contribute a building in its own characteristic style, as an integral part of the larger whole, safeguarding variety while promoting the unity that the railroad, the steamship, the telegraph, and the telephone had already made possible—indeed, almost imperative. Such, at least, was the intention of this symbolism. Geddes was unable to get backing for his proposal to make this demonstration a permanent one, but, as it happened, the idea was superficially carried out in Paris only a generation later, in the new students' quarter, the Cité Universitaire.

All over the planet, national barriers were breaking down. The risks on a fire-insurance policy in Chicago might be covered by organizations in London, Budapest, and Hamburg, just as Lloyd's still breaks up such risks among its share-takers. Banditry and piracy had ceased everywhere, except in petty strongholds like Sicily, and only a token force of soldiers and battleships was needed to hold vast empires in Africa and Asia, thus supplying at least outward order and security in partial atonement for the malign and callous exploitation that Joseph Conrad was soon to portray in his classic story 'Heart of Darkness.' For the first time in history, as the Italian historian Guglielmo Ferrero pointed out, "the freedom of the seas" actually prevailed throughout the world. Something better than the ancient Pax Romana seemed definitely established. Such conflicts as the Boer War and the Spanish-American War and the Balkan Wars appeared to be little more than a final trickle of bellicosity and savagery, dripping from a faucet that had been turned off.

There was further room for hope because more people than ever, beginning with the socialists and communists, were conscious of the many measures that needed to be taken to repair the inequities and injustices left over from the past. The democratic, egalitarian spirit seemed on the march everywhere: did not the liberal British Prime Minister Sir Henry Campbell-Bannerman proclaim that "good government" was no satisfactory substitute for self-government? And yet one must never forget that there remained a deep morass of human misery, for the margin of capitalist profits was still widened by the ancient method of grinding the face of the poor and calling in the police or the soldiery when the working class or the conquered tribes staged a rebellion. That underlying poverty remains today in supposedly affluent countries, such as the United States, and it is accentuated, rather than lessened, by doles, not to mention corruption, theft, and other impromptu modes of equalization.

Yet even the working class had a freedom then that no one now confidently enjoys. At the beginning of the twentieth century, anyone could travel anywhere he wished, except in Turkey and Russia, without a passport. Workers could move about freely on this planet if they were willing to face the hardships of steerage transportation. They sometimes moved seasonally from one country to another—say, from Italy to the Argentine. My wife's father and mother, thanks to such bribes as even poor people could bestow on the official wretches who guarded the frontiers, escaped from Russia early in the nineties, in order to avoid the long separation that military service would have imposed upon this just married Jewish couple. They had it hard when they reached America, but they stayed; even anti-Semitism was a little less virulent here. As for the proliferating middle classes, never before had such an abundance of material goods and so much cheap human service been at their disposal. For the first time in history, the whole planet was well policed—a precondition for any other kind of comity and unity. And the old moralities were still so studiously respected that—to take a trivial but significant example—newsstands were left unguarded in New York, permitting the buyers to make their own change.

It is only now, when these conditions have ceased to exist, that we can fully realize how much had actually been accomplished in establishing a more benign law and order, in lessening the more outrageous forms of injustice and violence. In many areas, there had been genuine improvements, so the representative figures of the Victorian Age had a right to crow loudly over their political achievements. But there were even surer signs that the tides of life were running high again. Auguste Rodin, the greatest sculptor of his time—probably the greatest since Michelangelo—became a commanding symbol of this vitality. He towered above his contemporaries almost as much because of his feeling for life as for his translation of that feeling into the animated forms, the fluent solids, of his sculptures. A benign deity was he, half Pan, half Jove, whose dancing bodies and passion-entwined lovers celebrated all the qualities left out of the cold Newtonian world picture that had fostered only science and technics. Ranged alongside Rodin were the many mighty spirits of the nineteenth century—scientists no less than artists—who were equally exalted by a fresh vision of life emerging from the primordial slime to dominate the planet and leave the imprint of organic form over every part of the environment, while the inner life of man had been animated and intensified by the works of Delacroix and Van Gogh and Cézanne, of Goethe and Tolstoi and Dostoevski, of Herman Melville and Walt Whitman.

Quite aside from the two-faced triumphs of technology, there was a great outpouring of energy in all the arts, first expressed in music, from the eighteenth century of Haydn and Mozart on, and this ultimately found its way into the remotest channels. To forget all these positive manifestations would be to repeat the howler made by Mark Twain when, on Whitman's seventieth birthday, in 1889, he congratulated Whitman on having lived long enough to behold the invention of the steam engine and the printing press, and thereby to have had a glimpse of man "at his full stature at last." If all the technical triumphs since 1815 had been wiped out the instant they occurred, the exuberant creativity of the Western mind would still have made this one of the most notable moments in human culture. The outlines of man's life were being redrawn, and large segments of his past, which had left only a faint impression on his customs and traditions, and a still fainter one on the written record, became visible. The discovery of man's origins, as archeologists raked among the bones and the stones buried in ancient geological strata, threw a fresh light on the human psyche. And when Picasso and his fellow-artists came into contact with primitive art they recognized vitalities that spoke directly to them. The rediscovery of the meaning of African and Polynesian art was also a rediscovery, parallel with Freud's 'Interpretation of Dreams,' of the dark continent of the psyche, and a recognition of the fact that no part of man's nature or his history could be buried or ignored without reducing his potentialities.

For those of us who came to maturity at the end of this period, Isadora Duncan, creating an imaginary Greek world out of our own twentieth century consciousness, more primitive than archaic, more archaic than archeological, will always remain a symbol of these ideal potentialities. Let us spare ourselves any ironic afterthoughts we might have today, for we might realize how little she represented anything that could be called Greek—as little as Winckelmann's white plaster cast admiration for Hellenistic sculpture. What mattered in Isadora's Hellenic dances and dramatic presentations was not the Greek themes or the gauzy costumes but the uninhibited vitality, the sense of a glorious nakedness about to be affirmed, not only in the rituals of lovers but in every part of life. That illusion threw a veil over the more sordid aspects of the period that followed.

This upsurge of living ideas, this embrace of living organisms, this realization of life itself through time, continuous but never more capturable than water is in a net, was expressed to perfection in the metaphysics of Henri Bergson. At the beginning of the twentieth century, he replaced the grim Malthusian picture of life as a lethal struggle for domination and survival with the picture of creative evolution, forever inventing new organs, building new forms, exploring new possibilities, intuitively finding new meanings, to be understood only by further acts of living. This was the underlying faith of the best minds of the period; and, allowing for differences of method and temperament, this is what links me to Samuel Butler and Henri Bergson, to Kropotkin and Whitehead, and to my own master, Patrick Geddes. For all of them life, human life, and the highest product of human life, the increasingly conscious mind, widening and deepening, conscious even of its unconscious treasure hoard, came first.

Some of this vitality was an integral part—often a major part—of the inheritance of my generation, and for a while it tided us over the most threatening moments of the new century. For, as a healthy body does not usually register the first symptoms of a disease except in some purely local manifestations, so we did not recognize the more insidious forces within our culture that were attacking us. And when we finally became aware of our actual state, we fastened all too easily upon one single manifestation, war, as if it were not a symptom but the main cause. This sense of abundant vitality belonged to our youth; it was the reservoir upon which the prewar generation continued to draw; and even in old age some of us, having sufficient memory of that primordial energy, still derive from it courage in Shelley's words to "wage contention with the times' decay"—no matter how impossible the odds.

By altering the angle of vision, by turning away from our knowledge of the pustulating evils of the last half century and dwelling only on the goods that still beckoned the Western World in the year I was born, I could, I realize, draw another picture, equally true—to the point where it became smudged and then obliterated by our actual experience. To draw that hopeful picture, I need only suppose that the First World War did not in fact break out—that instead there was a postponement, and that the tensions and hostilities which brought it about dissolved themselves in a gale of cosmic laughter, while all the instruments of war passed into obsolescence in a double sense, never to be replaced, never to be improved. The world we would be facing now would still not be any blithering utopia, but the meaning of life would no longer be reduced to the evasion of premature death, and we could cultivate new flowers without augmenting the crop of nettles. But such happy endings cannot be faked.

Both the highest creative possibilities of the twentieth century and its tragic eventualities emerged symbolically in the life and thought of Dr. Sigmund Freud. His career tells both the best and the worst about the period we are now living in. It was Freud who reintroduced, in the guise of science, the very world that science had turned its back on at the beginning of the modern period: the world of dreams, of potentialities and ideal goals, if also the world of repressed desires and demonic impulses, often too morbid to be exposed to view and too life-threatening or life-debasing to be translated directly into action. This was a darker continent than Africa, and one penetrated it at one's peril, on the heels of this daring explorer. Freud, by uncovering the Unconscious, had enlarged the boundaries of man's conscious life; and, much against his own medical training and expertness, he had given man's teeming fantasies, rejected by exact science, a status and a function equal to those of the objective world. To forget that man is a dreaming animal, who had perhaps dreamed himself into consciousness, was to ignore the very conditions of his emergence from animalhood.

This radical insight into the nature of man's whole inner life, as symbolized by but not restricted to his dreams, has not yet been generally accepted, since it challenges more primitive notions about the nature of the external world—views no less naïve than the wanton subjectivity of earlier religions. Yet 'The Interpretation of Dreams' helped open up theretofore impenetrable areas of reality as decisively as radium and the other invisible rays had done in physics. Freud himself was too much a man of the nineteenth century to throw off its own materialistic premises; on that score, Jung, with a more adequate metaphysical background, went deeper than Freud, and remained closer to the sources of man's actual development. Though Freud in the end was to speak for disintegration and death more than for life, as the cancer that killed him penetrated every part of his being, he deepened our sense of reality and unwittingly prepared our minds for the dire events that were to follow. Ironically, when the First World War came, Freud's fine analytic intelligence, so sensitive and so subtle, was overlaid by uncritical hatred of The Enemy, which was supported by a pathetically puerile emotional identification with his own Germanic tribe. He who spoke so contemptuously of the irrationality of early religions bowed to the no less primitive idols of Nationalism. So if in his younger days Freud had helped to liberate the forces of life, he later, in turning from Eros to Thanatos, and thus canonizing the death 'instinct,' helped to undermine resistance to the forces of disintegration; in effect, he enfeebled us and disarmed us. When Albert Einstein consulted Freud about the nature of man, as bearing upon the possibility of eventually eliminating war, Freud spoke with the same naïve confidence in his competence to give an answer that he did when he dismissed religion as an obsolete illusion close to the classic manifestation of a neurosis.

That Black Hole of Freud's ultimate pessimism anticipated the scientific theory of the Black Hole in the universe—the Black Hole that astrophysicists now interpret as the fateful implosion and recoalescence of all the stars and planets and asteroids of the currently expanding universe into a solid, impenetrable lump, duplicating one whose explosion, perhaps six billion years ago, created the starry sky itself and ultimately all the little pockets of life that possibly found a niche on this or that remote planet. The coincidence of these two varieties of Black Hole is of course an accident, indeed only an accident of metaphor, and the metaphor in both cases may be as willfully subjective as the visions of archangels and seraphim and thrones which buoyed up the waning energies of earlier ages. Yet no matter how these Black Holes are read, they remain an awful challenge; and at a lively luncheon of astrophysicists which I attended at M.I.T. one of their number irritably wondered how anyone could go on living from day to day without exhibiting any concern over this astronomical prospect, more lethal than the Black Hole of Calcutta, which threatens to bring an end to all cosmic existence—at least for the time being.

But are we sure that we are looking at the universe? Or is this ultimate black lump, like Freud's final orientation toward death, an image we find in our own demonic mirror, by closing our eyes and reading only what we see within? The astrophysicists are daringly open-minded fellows, and, like the good mathematicians they are, they must reckon with the paradox of the Möbius ring, and the possibility that their outer world is only our inner world turned inside out. So, perhaps, with a further twist of the ring, the impenetrable Black Hole might prove the shadow of a brighter sun. Even the notion of an Explosion and an Implosion, a 'beginning' and an 'ending,' may be only a very human metaphor, which the universe, for reasons of its own, neither recognizes nor exhibits. On that ultimate skepticism my own faith blithely flourishes. Let the curtain rise on the twenty-first century—*and After!*

Note: The first draft of this Prologue was written in 1962, as the opening chapter of my Autobiography. Even in its briefer early form, I felt that it struck the wrong note for the rest of the book and discarded it. The present lengthier version was written in 1974 and published in The New Yorker, March 10, 1975.

2: A Mind in the Making

In a sense this whole book draws the picture of a mind in the making: so it seems appropriate to begin with the first glimmers of intellectual and literary consciousness in the series of random notes begun in 1914, long before my flitting intuitions were seasoned by actual experience. What surprises me, in going over these notes, is that some of the earliest jottings reveal ideas about nature and human culture that it has taken the better part of my life to substantiate and develop. Without these early notes one of the keys to my later work would be missing.

In this early recording of my mind, Samuel Butler's writings, particularly his 'Notebooks,' played an active part. Butler's wide range of interests, which extended from Darwin to Homer and Handel, preceded and complemented Patrick Geddes's influence somewhat later. Some of Butler's Darwinian 'Lucubrations,' while a New Zealand sheep rancher, on the relation of organisms to machines, planted ideas I was later to carry further: indeed he prepared me long in advance to recognize—in 'The Pentagon of Power'—the threatening end-products of both automation and cybernation. Most of our contemporaries are still too blind, too frightened, or too committed to the naive belief in the finality and infallibility of the scientific method to acknowledge these consequences.

What is more immediately to the point, Butler prompted me to capture my ideas on the wing, by always keeping a pencil and a four-by-six pad within easy reach, indoors or outdoors. I rarely drew directly on such notes, even when I carried them further, still less did I conceive until now of assembling any of them in print. Fewer notes are available after 1930 because I kept the same spontaneity and freedom in the letters I wrote my friends. Later on all such notes are labelled RN.

Random Notes: 1914–1921

I have begun these notes, partly in imitation of Samuel Butler, and partly because I stand aghast at the fund of gristy material I have wasted in the past. At best one's most vivid memories are only memories; they are flighty, unaccountable, and never around when you are really in need of them. And then, they are ever so much more pallid than the real materials of sense that you wish to recover. I would give anything for a ten reel moving picture of my life during the last four years, with copious inserts to register the ever-changing succession of mental states, philosophies, dreams, desires, plans, aspirations, and what not. It might grieve me, of course, to learn how pitifully foolish a young man can be; but it would give my present self a more solid foundation. On the other hand, I am not sure whether too great a degree of self-consciousness might not over-balance the worth of such a record. To be neither completely self-conscious, nor completely unconscious is the trick. My last three years have been wasted if I have not acquired it.   (1914)

I think every person of sensibility feels that he has been born "out of his due time." Athens during the early sixth century B.C. would have been more to my liking than New York in the twentieth century after Christ. It is true, this would have cut me off from Socrates, who lived in the disappointing period that followed. But then, I might have been Socrates. (1914)

You may speak of Plato (if you know anything about him) as a conservative, but at any rate he was a hearty feminist, and one of the first who urged woman to leave her dolls, just as Ibsen later urged her to leave her Doll's House. His plan for having girls and women exercize naked along with the men and boys, is about the only sensible proposal I am aware of for bringing the sexual reflexes under control: as it undoubtedly would. What is especially alluring about a beautiful woman is not her beauty, but the veils you wish to remove. Once they are gone you have the chance of developing people who appreciate physical passion without being obsessed by it. And if you can't develop such people you must give the race over to the prudes and the prostitutes: those who avoid sex completely, and those who avoid everything but sex.   (1915)

FIRST AND LAST THINGS. Every religion and every philosophy is an attempt to make sense out of this seemingly nonsensical spectacle of life: this

26

Shakespearian tragedy with a porter who says funny things before a doomed man's crime gets found out.

Each religion is a brave guess at the authorship of Hamlet. Yet, as far as the play goes does it make any difference whether Shakespeare or Bacon wrote it? Would it make any difference to the actors if their parts happened out of nothingness, if they found themselves acting on the stage because of some gross and unpardonable accident? Would it make any difference if the playwright gave them the lines or whether they composed them themselves, so long as the lines were properly spoken? Would it make any difference to the characters if 'A Midsummer Night's Dream' was really a dream? Would it make any difference if it could be proved with mathematical exactitude that happiness was not dealt out 'Measure for Measure'?

Is not our problem in life to say our lines properly, and 'to suit the action to the word and the word to the action'? Why should we bother whether our performance is reported in silly newspapers for the benefit of posterity. In the language of the stage, let us have art for art's sake. Or, as I would put it let us live life for life's sake. Does it really make any difference whether we get our salary on the next payday or whether there isn't any money in the box office—or any box office?   (1915)

What we call "the World" has always implied a relationship between man and the world—it was so much of the hypothetical totality as man, with his necessities and urgencies, had found useful to himself. To call this world "the" world and to assume none other exists is a human provincialism—the world that the swallow sees as it darts after insects in the sunset sky is quite another thing. What is the ultimate reality of all these worlds? Perhaps there is none. What we call eternal verities may be merely shadows passing over the face of some enigmatic deity—and by the very words in which I speak of the verities it is obvious that my deity, with his enigmatic face, is a very human fellow, perhaps not very different from myself. . . . (1921)

THE BANE OF REAL EDUCATION is the encyclopedia and the textbook. Too often they become simply means of supplying students with so-called knowledge at third hand. To take any kind of knowledge at third hand is like taking milk that has been watered three times: what one method fails to give the stomach, the other fails to give the mind. We have substituted knowledge about facts for direct, active acquaintance with them. As a result we know verbally about a thousand things that other people have seen, done, thought, painted, and fought for without necessarily having for a moment had any direct contact with the actual experiences. The best thing my temporary release from formal education at City College has done for me is to show me the futility of a merely formal and superficial education. A man's education is tested not by what he knows but by what he is capable of learning from and using.   (1916)

The materials for education are much like those by means of which a plant grows: the arts and sciences may be compared to earth, air and water. But whereas it is now commonly held that the materials themselves are the education, so that a person who has stored up certain facts and ideas is thereby educated, the truth is that they are no more the education than the air and earth and water are the growth of the plant. The analogy between plant nourishment and what we call education would hold if plants could store up large chemical supplies while remaining shriveled, wizened, small, undeveloped: a thing unknown in botany. We must realize that education is a process of growth, lasting throughout life and coeval with life. If we are wise we shall not try to force it or hasten it. We will give up the whole medal-awarding, diploma-bestowing, scholarship-granting, pupil-pushing rigmarole: and we will direct our efforts toward seeing that the environment is so ordered that the natural processes may be carried on in the most favorable way.   (1916)

THE GREAT TASK OF THE SUPERMAN is to prevent the human race from committing suicide. And it must be admitted that the task is becoming more difficult every day. The number of methods of doing away with life has been extended by leaps and bounds; while life itself is being reproduced with greater fecundity than ever before imagined. From this it follows that life is becoming less precious; that the disrespect for life is increasing; and that unless we look very sharply after our industrial and military systems they will between them reduce life to such a low ebb that it is doubtful if even the Superman will be able to maintain himself in a world of such diminished vitality. The preservation of life is the most urgent business of the human race; without the lives of our domestic animals, our wild animals, our insects, our plants, even of our bacteria, humanity— with all its magnificent pretensions in the realm of synthetic chemistry —would perish. And just as the human race is dependent upon all these lesser forms, it is probably also necessary for the Supermen, who do not yet exist in sufficient quantities to propagate their stock, to keep Homo faber from shooting himself, starving himself, asphyxiating himself, and inoculating himself with disease: in short, from by one means or another committing suicide.   (1915)

28

Note: In 1915 the term 'Superman' referred to a superior type of human being. See Nietzsche's 'Also Sprach Zarathustra' and Shaw's 'Man and Superman.' Today this use has become meaningless: 'Superman' now refers to the vulgar science fiction hero of a comic strip.

Pre-1970 Ecology

ENVIRONMENTAL DEGRADATION: 1921. Some memory of old times drew me over to Staten Island the other day. The shore that I sought was the only one in my recollection which was at once within easy reach of the city, spacious, and set with its face toward the open sea. Presently, after passing through a waste of slum-villages, I found myself on a beach. I remembered it of old as consisting of a little 'amusement park' with a sprinkling of rickety bath houses, separated from a similar park by a long strip of virgin sand. On the landward side, in the old days, stretched a wide sweep of salt marsh, more or less inundated by a tidal river that broke one's passage along the sea front, except at low tide. The amusement park I found had not ceased to exist; on the contrary, in the course of some half-dozen years it had solidly entrenched itself in the landscape; and its length now seemed interminable. Where the Japanese ball games and the bath houses and the refreshment palaces came to an end, a new kind of architectural obscenity, the beach bungalow, had come into existence, and the view of the salt marsh was cut off by rows and rows, sometimes two or three deep, of what looked like Brobdingnagian rabbit hutches.

What had happened to the open beach I used to know? A thousand people who liked sunlight and salt air had purchased building sites and had put up bungalows; and thousands more were drawn to their vicinity every week, in search of surcease from the daily round and trivial task. Finding, however, neither salt air nor shelter nor sunlight nor solitude altogether to their taste, these people—visitors or residents—drifted into the scenic railways and dance halls, ate frankfurters, and generally comported themselves in the attitudes that are popularly supposed by our citizenry to induce happiness and good cheer. What a travesty, not merely of the good life, but of the patent joys, of mere animality! Sadly I turned away from this picture of teeming decay to the hard, narrow margin of the beach, but alas! the sands seemed as wretched as the rest of the landscape: the flotsam and jetsam washed up by the waves spoke less of the sea and its mysteries than of the dump heap.

There is a beach I know on the coast of Maine, a long, noble beach that, with the ocean, forms one of the pillars upon which the great arch of the sky is supported; and the wreckage one finds on that shore after a storm—perhaps a shark driven up by the breakers, or a school of hake—seems only to be sweetened by the wind and the sunlight, and never to decay. The island strand upon which I was walking was once that kind of a beach; but it was so no longer. I picked my way among blackened grapefruit and bananas; here a leg of putrid salt beef; there a dead sea bird with a long beak and dirty, bedraggled feathers; and, of course, everywhere piles and piles of driftwood. I warped my steps toward the trolley track which spans the two amusement parks. Here there were no disappointments. The trolley was the same old trolley that has long subsisted by collecting a feudal revenue from people who wish to cross the tidal stream and cannot do so except by riding in the car over a precarious trestle. The same old trestle and the same old car that I had known so many years ago! Privilege, at least, seemed to know the secret of self-preservation.

Wrapped in a double thickness of solitude, I sat down on a bench by the trolley track, but in spite of myself I shortly found myself in conversation with a vacant-faced young man who affected brazen hair and sunburned, khaki clothes. This idle individual added a few more items to my list of environmental casualties; first, by remarking that he had decided not to swim because the water was too dirty and thick with oil; second, by correlating this defilement with the disappearance of weakfish and bluefish in the Bay; and third—well, he began to drivel, in a sort of shorthand, about the diminution, in contrast with previous years, of erotic encounters along the beach on recent Saturdays and Sundays and the probable diversion of the traffic to Coney Island. This sickly lout, with his dull chatter of obscenity, put a final touch to the unhappy spectacle of waste and dreariness and decay.

This devastated strip of beach, these disastrous bungalows, these dismal amusement parks, this dreary youth and the complaisant doxies he gabbled about; these things and people are not part of a settled, cultivated community; they are the offal of a civilization which is perpetually 'on the make,' and therefore perpetually 'on the move': a civilization which is as impermanent as that of the pioneer, though lacking the pioneer's excuse for existence. Puritanism indeed! The word that describes the crudeness of the greater part of our civilization is not 'puritanism,' but 'barbarism'; and it is a barbarism of which even the Australian aborigine would be ashamed. Miscellany. The Freeman. 1921

Knowledge does not consist in knowing the things you know: it consists in knowing the things you don't know. (1915)

To be moral is to conform to other people's habits of acting; to be immoral is to obey your own impulses when they conflict with the accustomed. The thoroughly moral man is a humbug: the thoroughly immoral man is a fool. And the way to avoid being one or the other is courageously to decide on being a great deal of both. (n.d.)

The attempt to describe life in chemico-physical terms is like an attempt to describe Da Vinci's 'The Last Supper' by publishing the chemical formulae of every square inch of pigment; and the first gives no greater understanding of life than the second does of the picture. Each is an organic synthesis, about which the material composition is, in view of the artist's purpose, the least significant part. (1916)

The danger of a mechanized industrial regime is not that the population will press upon the supply of food (for energized agriculture has not yet sighted the limits of food production): the danger is that population will press upon the supply of intelligence. And it holds good, alike with food or with Vision, that without it the people perish. (1916)

All matter and energy is a gift. No one has created it, no one has earned it, no one 'deserves' it, and therefore no individual or institution should be allowed to appropriate it selfishly. Man's economic function is simply to wrap Nature's gift in convenient parcels for wider distribution. His own ability to do this cleverly and effectively and the tradition of doing this cleverly and effectively, is also a gift. To assert that the producer or the manager or the inventor has a major part in this process is like saying that the cock which heralds the dawn has made the sun rise. (1918)

It is impossible to examine the biographies of the leaders in Victorian science and art without coming to the conclusion that they owed some part of their vigor and originality to the fact that they escaped a formal education. Tyndall, Mill, Spencer, Dalton, Faraday, Dickens, and Shaw were none of them university bred. For that matter neither were Plato and Aristotle! (1918)

Nothing that exists is unnatural. Superstitions, creeds, conventions, cruelties, vices, morbidities—all these are characteristic of man: they are 'natural' to him. A person too rational to be superstitious, too free to observe conventions, too humane to practice cruelty, too healthy to relapse into viciousness, would be a person who could result only from an arduous system of culture, and in one sense would be as unnatural as it is possible for a man to be. But mind culture is as natural to man as

31

'primitivism,' and this statement is therefore utterly false. The greatest artificiality is to seek to do away with artificialities; the unnatural thing is to seek to return to 'nature.' (1916)

Death was one of the great inventions life discovered for keeping itself lively. (n.d.)

Modern industrial civilization releases woman for work and then gives her no work to do. Automatically she becomes a consumption machine. (1917)

The efficiency of an economic system depends upon the adjustment of the means of living to the needs of life: it is not a quantity but a ratio, and there is no indication at all that the amount of work or goods can be expanded without limit as capitalist economics proposes. In terms of life, a social scheme that produces a handful of olives and dates and bread may be more effective than one rich enough to produce a Roman banquet and a special chamber called a vomitorium to take care of the results of gluttony. (n.d.)

Humor is our way of defending ourselves from life's absurdities by thinking absurdly about them. It is a mild antitoxin of the same nature as the disease it seeks to combat. Occasionally it gets the upper hand and becomes the disease itself. (1919)

Education is not *one* of man's activities: it comprises all of them; it is man singing, painting, wondering, feeling, dreaming, working, loving in that terrible comedy we call life. It is man experimenting with fire, in the stone age, or at the kitchen stove; it is man carving the first hieroglyphics, or writing his first ABC's, man wondering at the stars, or plotting them and forecasting their returns; man cackling in the treetops, or spreading the good word through the printed page. (1915)

Religion in the Middle Ages was a dominant factor in determining men's views; today politics plays the same part. May not sex be the determinant tomorrow? May not the lineup—tory or liberal—be over the amount of latitude observed in sex relations—or something of the sort? (1917)

The Call of Tomorrow

Much of the work in a civilized community rests upon the assumption that the show is good for a long run. The drama of the present tends to move in a given direction only when it receives the double impact of the past and the future; and if the past be too frightful for remembrance or the future too cloudy for anticipation, the present ceases to move in any particular direction, and teeters fitfully about from point to point.

If this seems a rather too abstract way of expressing the part that is played by the assurance of continuity in our lives, let the reader consider some concrete examples of its absence. Almost any country that has acutely felt the effects of the war would furnish instances of the empty inconsecutiveness of a present that is divorced from a past and a future. Trustworthy observers who have been abroad during the last two years bring back disheartening reports to the effect that science, art, and scholarship among the younger generation have been steadily on the wane. Perhaps a little too much has been made of the fact that in many parts of Europe artists and students are literally starving; and it is possible that we have not taken sufficiently into account the condition of uncertainty which is making the younger generation turn aside from work the benefits of which may not be immediately realized in order to spend their energies on trifles that promise a speedy return—even if it be only a day's respite from hunger or a night of forgetfulness.

Eat, drink, and be merry, for tomorrow we die, is what the last seven years of 'preserving civilization' has written on the wall. Doubtless Mr. Bernard Shaw's 'Back to Methuselah' owes something to his observations of the attitude of his contemporaries toward wars and rumors of wars. Human life, says Mr. Shaw, must be vastly lengthened before people will have the grace to take it seriously. In that century of fitful peace which followed the Napoleonic Wars the expectation of life for a healthy European male was small enough in all conscience; but today the expectation is so precarious, with armaments piling up and diplomacy festering and home-guards drilling and privilege-hunting rampant, that one cannot even count upon continuity in the life of any particular community, to say nothing of any particular individual. As a result, all work that depends for its sustenance upon a heritage from the past, and is lured forward, through swamp and thicket and jungle, by the gleam of the future, is failing and dying.

The day that does not carry the seed of tomorrow in its womb is sterile and fit only for eating and drinking: the measured, disciplined, purposeful life depends upon the promise of continuity. Is it any wonder, then, that the holocaust in Europe has not merely decreased the amount of arable ground under cultivation but has also, for similar reasons, diminished the area of cultured and civilized life? Art, literature, and science are almost meaningless if their development promises to cease with the life of the particular persons for whom they have a meaning. If there is to be no future there can be no way of differentiating between one kind of activity and another—for the ultimate basis of differentiation must rest upon the capacity for producing a "life more abundant"—and one might equally well, on Bentham's advice, play pushpins instead of writing poetry.

Those of the older generation who have survived the years of the war and the peace will carry on their work, out of habit, as the bees build their honeycombs with no thought for the bee-keeper who will some day pillage their communities; but the younger people whose habits of work have been disrupted by war, who have never tasted the life of plain living and high thinking, who have never given themselves up to any consecutive purpose except that of "defending their country"—what can one expect of these young people except that they will seek out whatever directly promises to give them enjoyment and satisfaction? Scarcely anyone will take the trouble to be an artist or scientist when he may so speedily cease to be even a man.

Does not this account a little for the lassitude, the febrility, the spurious gaiety that a good many competent observers have noted in Europe today? What we call the future is in a sense always an illusion, and the greatest disillusion that Europe possibly suffers from is the loss of something that never existed outside the minds of those who molded their activities in terms of it—the loss of a tomorrow. Statesmen who talk in a loud, guilty way about preserving the fabric of civilization might pause long enough in their clamor to realize that they are talking about something that actually exists. Civilization is the magic instrument by which men live in a world of time that has three dimensions: the past, the present, and the future. When neither security of life nor continuity of works is maintained, civilization must necessarily collapse. It has done so before; and it has taken hundreds of years to weave a new fabric; and it may do so again. A pretty prospect for the encouragement and discipline of adolescents!   —The Freeman. July 13, 1921

THE FUNCTION OF THE PHILOSOPHIC MIND. Faith and the Word are the two prime foundations of philosophy; no philosopher can begin to cogitate intelligibly without words, and he cannot open his mouth without believing that the sounds he utters have that peculiar quality called

34

meaning. So it might be more accurate to say, not that faith and the word are the foundations of philosophy, but that faith *in* the word is the foundation. Without the word this universe presents itself to us as what William James called a booming, buzzing confusion; but with that modicum of faith in the word which a child needs in beginning to talk, it soon becomes an orderly, regular, and on the whole comfortable place to live in. We must admire the deep metaphysic insight of the Greek who began the Gospel according to St. John with the declaration: In the beginning was the Word.

The universe that man exists in (as distinct from the universe which cows or bumblebees live in) has been built up in small increments by our faith in the word. When at night I look up at the blue dome of space all I can see are myriad points of light. All I *know* about that blue dome of space is that occasionally after it has gotten dark (as we say) these tiny twinkling patches begin to appear; that they are sometimes very numerous; and that they always seem to dissolve as soon as a light begins to break in the east. Yet were a child to ask me about these ethereal illuminations he would find me in confident possession of an amazing amount of information, which I would impart to him without scruple. I would tell him that these light-spots were planets and stars; that they were worlds, some of which were bigger and some smaller than our world; that they were all, except our moon, many millions of miles away; that the darkness which brought them into view was caused by the fact that *our* planet (in its daily revolution) had so far revolved that our particular portion of it was now turned away from the sun; and that this sun (which seemed in the morning to pop out of the housetops on the East River, and which in the evening seemed to drop down behind the Palisades) was in reality a center about which this earth of ours was moving.

But if the child was so staggered by this information that he asked me how I knew all these amazing facts to be so, I should either have to tell him foolishly to stop asking sensible questions, or else admit that he would have to take all these facts from me on the same assurance that I took them from other people; namely, on faith. And then, if this precocious youngster wanted to know whether these assumptions were true or not, I should be compelled (in a further riot of frankness) to assure him that I was incompetent then, and probably always would be incompetent to decide for myself on the subject. Having granted this much, I should advise him to accept the universe which has been constructed about these points of light without further ado, until he finds that such a belief is impractical or perturbing; at which time he could try to make head or tail out of it by himself.

Were he a nasty, rationalist infant, he would smile pityingly and ask me: "Then this wonderful universe, with its stars and planets and comets describing their different courses, has in fact so little foundation as far as you are concerned that its very existence rests on an act of faith, without which those little points of light would be not stars but only little points of light?" To this I would of course firmly answer "Yes." And if then he added maliciously: "What would happen to this silly universe if your faith in other people were to vanish, and other people's faith in their logarithms and telescopes and spectroscopes, were to vanish likewise?" I could only shudder and say: "God only knows. Without faith the human race would die, and the beasts of the field and the fowls of the air likewise, and there would be left no one on what we call the earth to bother his head about philosophy."

For as far as I have been able to plumb the matter rightly this precious world of ours is literally almost a castle in air, created by and through man's crude vocalisms. Our science and philosophy is a system of credit resting on capital that most of us have neither seen, heard, tasted, smelt, nor touched; and accordingly our science and philosophy (which give us the universe man lives in, as distinct from the universe which cows or bumblebees live in) would collapse as swiftly as would our monetary system, were our constantly reiterated faith in it somehow to be shattered.

Since such an abundance of faith is needed before one can get the most simple grasp of man's position in the world, his antecedents, and his probable destination, it is not surprising that this faith has amounted very often to pure gullibility. Hence the business of the philosophic mind is to examine with such critical resources as it commands, all the most dubious articles of man's faith. The old articles (such as a belief in the necessity of eating and mating) which have been so long tried and so well remembered that we call them instincts may well be neglected: the person who has any serious doubts on the subject will have them speedily pacified in the dissolution of death. The new articles of faith, however, under which head come most of our religious, philosophic, scientific and esthetic beliefs, have again and again to be examined, and re-corrected on the basis of new evidence. This is the signal function of the philosophic mind. (1916)

Note: The date is almost as significant as the contents.

3: A New York Adolescence

The New Yorker magazine in the thirties, when I was an active contributor, was still closely focussed on the New York milieu; and one of its occasional features came under the head of 'A New York Childhood.' With no thought in those days of ever writing a biography, I embroidered a picture of my native city: dealing, in a lighthearted and highhanded fashion, with the scenes of my childhood, combining in a single character some of my relatives and not hesitating to overcolor even my own colorful memories—though Harold Ross, the editor, drew the line at my first draft, in which the narrator himself was disguised as a prissy young Episcopal clergyman. Enough of my real childhood remained to make these memories still useful for my future biography. But heaven keep any serious researcher from being tempted to draw on this childhood for the unvarnished facts.

When I wrote the first 'A New York Adolescence' three years later, feeling that the 'Childhood' piece broke off too soon, I took fewer liberties with the raw data, and produced a sketch I might almost use unaltered in the final story of my life. I was still near enough to my adolescence to report its details clearly, while far enough away to single out its essential pattern and give an honest judgment. Perhaps the picture is a little too favorable, for it gives no account of the inner tensions, the pangs of love, the humiliations of poverty, not least the insidious assaults of ill-health which began with malaria at sixteen and slid for a while into tuberculosis. But after all, this was a picture of the effect of a great city, New York, upon a growing boy, not a clinical study of adolescence: so it deserves an honorable place in the crazyquilt of my life I am here piecing together.

The Sense of Myself

Before plunging into my maturity, let me try to recall the phases of my early growth, which seem to fall roughly in five or six year periods.

Behold me as a baby, some eight and a half pounds at birth, with a sufficiency of my mother's milk to get me through my first year. The photographs show a 'long-clothes' baby, chubby and bright; and, when I am two, dressed in a piqué dress and bonnet, with gold, pink-enamelled safety pins, not the blue that should have been allotted to a boy, I might be mistaken for the girl my mother had counted on, so placid and docile. Most of my memories before five are in little fleeting patches, of rooms, like the 'music room' in West Sixty-fifth Street, between the front and the back parlor, where my mother and I slept. I recall the sense of waking up early and beginning to chant, insistently, monotonously, "I want my toast and coffee." The coffee was of course warm milk with a teaspoon or so of coffee in it.

In this same room, late one afternoon, I underwent—I was then three—my first great transformation: my mother came home from Altman's with a sailor suit, a brown check with a red dickey that I adored. A real boy at last—with my curls cut off, too. But I have other mainly physical memories before this: eating in a high chair in the downstairs kitchen, resisting its squeezing, sometimes the pinching of the tray top as it came down over my head. With this goes the taste of the fried lamb chop and toast that used to be a standard dinner for me: also the taste of canned corn, freshly opened, which I loved to eat raw.

Tastes and smells: the smell of onions on Nana's fingers, always a constant one, and the delicate, rather sweet smell from under my mother's arm-pits, a pleasant animal odor which in sufficient dilution I have never lost my fondness for: indeed, a touch of this wild gamey quality entered later into the best moments of spontaneous sexual intercourse, giving it a special animal intensity without the more specious perfumed antisepsis that too often sacrifices on the altar of Hygeia the prerogatives of Aphrodite. (On that subject Alfred Stieglitz and I, comparing notes, had independently come to the same conclusion!)

Here, in the Sixty-fifth Street brownstone, playing on the stairs with my cousin Edwin, whose whole family for a while boarded with us, I have my first sense of myself as attached to a name, Lewis Charles, I did not altogether like. His first names were Edwin Baron; and I remember challenging him with the assertion that *my* name was Lewis Baron: the Baron, even at three, seemed to me more appropriate. Legally and physically the argument went in his favor, for he was a year older and much stronger than I, and had the grown ups' word to back him. In my rage, I remember chanting in derision: "Ed, Ed, a Great Big Bed." To which he retorted with equal felicity, "Lew, Lew, a Bottle of Glue." His older sister, Tessie, once experimentally shoved a piece of raw potato up my nostril. I remember that scene because of my mother's way of taking me firmly in her arms and removing the stoppage with the aid of a hairpin. But this left no traumatic effects: indeed I had a special affection for Tessie.

All too suddenly, I am five, with my hair parted on the side, and brushed in the indescribable style of the period: somewhat sober, perhaps a bit snooty, caught in a photo at my little roll-top desk, as if interrupted while writing. Now, or just a little before this, one of my mother's boarders takes me with him to the saloon not far away run by the brother of John L. Sullivan; and I shake the hand of the great prize fighter, big and portly John L. himself. But it is not his face that I remember: rather, I recall the big pictures on the walls, showing naked men and women playfully disporting themselves with an abandon that fascinated me, though somehow I suspected that my eyes were not supposed to linger too intently on these images. These naked people, particularly these naked girls, will accompany me thenceforward, usually in daydreams just after an early waking. Sometimes a girl my own age will appear and join me in ritualistic exposures of nakedness that cause my penis to stiffen, though without any other sensation than this awkward stiffness. Not until I am thirteen does this bring a tantalizing, secret reward: at once delightful and disgusting, shy-making, guilt provoking, too private for words.

Meanwhile, I have ceased to be visited by the one dream I can truly recall from infancy, a dream that was almost a nightmare, which came recurrently and yet in its familiarity was almost welcome: the sense of existing in the midst of empty space, with infinity pressing in upon me from every direction: that unbearable pressure of emptiness was distinctly part of it. This is what psychoanalysts have called, as I remember, the oceanic dream: they find in it a direct reminiscence of the prenatal life one spent surrounded by the amniotic fluid in the womb. I shall never forget this dream: yet it is only verbally that I can recapture the sensation.

My first insensate childhood fear was the fear of death: so intense that though I enjoyed the nurserybook rhyme about Cock Robin, I insisted on skipping the page which showed Cock Robin's funeral. That fear was accompanied by an anxiety which should have given me greater insight into my children's approach to bedtime than, in my forgetfulness as an adult, I actually showed: for until I was seven or eight, I never went to sleep without an adult lying down beside me. This was not an unusual practice then. Patrick Geddes gratefully recorded the way that his father, almost two generations before, a stern but kindly old soldier, had held his hand when he, as a child, went to sleep. Even when they did not hold my hand, I made sure of their presence by calling out good night or asking what time it was. The real horrors, the well-grounded fears, that the present generation faces were not part of our waking life: we went through no air raid or atomic disaster drills. At most, partly because of the famous disappearance of Charlie Ross, we were warned against kidnappers, mysterious beings who offered candy to little children on the street and spirited them away. But when, riding my bike on the sidewalk, I was rudely pushed aside by a grim woman, I identified her, not as a witch or a kidnapper, but as a "stepmother." (I had never actually identified or met a stepmother!)

Our anxieties and fears sprang out of a deeper source in the psyche that psychoanalysis has still hardly plumbed, still less exorcized. And while our own son, from infancy, had accepted the stoic discipline of going to bed by himself, after a final story and a final pat, so that my wife and I thought he was quite immune to such fears as I had experienced, we learned from him, at sixteen, that as a child he used to hide his head under the pillow, to fend off the witches that threatened him when we left. Our daughter knew those witches, too, and made a magic to ward them off.

And now I am nine or ten; rather slight in build, medium height for my age, with a wide mouth, slightly twisted for the next dozen years, probably from chewing on the side of my mouth where the teeth were less decayed: eager for games, but without any stamina: with a weak, receding chin, and a low forehead, for the frontal cranium was then far from being as rounded as it became in maturity. Almost never ill, yet never exuberantly healthy: with a heart so sensitive, so wildly rapid, that the visiting physician at school would soothingly reassure me, after making the usual examination with his ear directly placed against my chest. No removal of clothing, no stethoscope in 1904!

By the time I was fourteen I had shot up in height to five feet seven or so—in maturity I reached five feet ten and a half inches—and was already taller than my mother or my Uncle Charley: an ugly adolescent, with a disproportionately big nose, a scrawny neck, loose limbs, stooping shoulders, face splotched with beady acne: an altogether unattractive creature, even to myself, with hardly a redeeming feature except a sense of humor always verging on the wry and cynical. Hand-me-downs, or ill-fitting clothes bought at random by my mother (usually at Altman's!) often without my presence, did not improve my general style: so my first brown tweed suit with a Norfolk jacket, at nineteen, marked a turning point in both the inward and the outward youth.

Now it is the inward youth I would like to recapture, between fourteen and twenty, with both his night dreams and day dreams intact: that strange elusive creature should tell me more about myself than I will ever be able to tell the reader. But he is almost beyond recall: the one thing I know clearly is that daydreams swarmed through his entire waking life, displaced only by books and occasional human companionship: dreams of heroism, dreams of erotic adventure badly handicapped by sheer ignorance, dreams such as James Thurber translated for all time—and why did no one do half so well before him?—in his picture of 'The Secret Life of Walter Mitty.' Wild dreams and vague frustrations, ambitions and inhibitions: paralyzing disintegration and sedulous order. Out of all this a new creature emerges, outwardly at least: vehement, almost choking with ideas, trying on new thoughts as he might try on costumes, one day a pragmatist, next a Spinozaist, now an anarchist, now a socialist, now a Ruskinian Tory, now a Shavian, now a Platonist, now a disciple of Samuel Butler, a Whitmanite, a Geddesian, or a Tolstoian.

But the scars that accompanied this growth remain: the sense of being physically unattractive to girls, with its self-protective aloofness and simulated disdain, in order to avoid the possibility of rejection.

And now I am nineteen: still under the threat of tuberculosis, with monthly checkups by the family doctor, who happily dismisses the notion of treatment in a sanatorium. Going to Ogunquit alone for a month at his suggestion, I get a new sense of myself: for now I am filled out, normal in weight for my size, bronzed in the sun, almost handsome, reading Plato's 'Phaedrus' and feeling very much like an ancient pagan when I stride along the beach, just behind the skittering sandpipers, or when, in my bathing suit, I practice half mile runs and shorter sprints for the joy of it.

On those lonely morning walks I give lectures on my new found subject, geography, to imaginary classes, or I work as an assistant to my newly discovered master, Geddes, or—because nothing is impossible—I am reading Bernard Hart's 'The Psychology of Insanity,' and have become a practicing psychiatrist, giving advice to a fellow boarder, a neurotic young woman, who shows symptoms of an approaching breakdown. (I tremble guiltily in retrospect over that impudence, that rashness!) Yes: nothing is impossible. Young women—but more often, alas! older young women, five or ten years too old—smile at me and make friendly advances. Part of me—I can tell it from a sheaf of notes—still is vividly aware of his recent callow past: another part is shrewdly, intently, consistently laying out a fresh territory to explore. The sense of invalidism is beginning to lift: I have already made my departure in a one-act play, called 'The Invalids,' in which the real invalid, my other self, dares to fall in love with an enchanting nurse and propose their elopement.

Except for the fact that the scarifying mortifications of the flesh (acne) are spreading from my face to my back, this new youth has no bodily embarrassments: even his nose, though it will always be big, no longer seems preposterous; and the very set of his chin has changed: some thrust of determination has modified his lower jaw. Seemingly his metabolism is unstable: every once in a while, with too heavy a diet, his face will round out into a moon, only to return, just as swiftly, to a decent leanness. With his Byronic collar and his crew cut turning to a wavy pompadour, he looks 'poetic' in an older romantic fashion: almost to the point of casting a doubt upon his masculinity. It is this image on one old snapshot that his son, twenty years later, will turn away from in disdain, as having no relation whatever to the father he knows and acknowledges.

But these soft outlines can be deceiving: underneath, a well-articu-lated armature of iron has been forming. By the time he is thirty-five the effect of the iron will be visible on the outward form, too: then not merely the body but its posture will bear testimony to its achievement, in all the smiling confidence of maturity. There are only a handful of such snapshots and no formal portraits to record this transformation objec-tively. Agnes Tait's romantic glorification of the youthful 'poet'—with a Scots plaid over his shoulders, and his parted lips full of sensual yearning —doesn't tell even half of the story; but the complementary portrait head she did very hastily twenty years later to fill out an exhibit of her paint-ings, is too smoothly in the same tradition to mark the inner growth. Certainly, somewhere between 1924 and 1930 the last outward traces of the larval adolescent form disappeared: a tough, firm-muscled, broad-shouldered figure took over. But maturity was still to come! —Memo-randum for L.M. 1962

MEMORIES OF MY FIRST LOVE AFFAIR IN VERMONT. AET. 11. Bertha and I exchanged exactly seven kisses before I departed for New York! The last took place early in the morning, before seven o'clock. The rest of the house was hardly roused, and for a few minutes Annie, the cook, was absent from the kitchen. It was there, in the end as in the beginning, that with a last kiss I bade Bertha formal good-bye. We promised to be friends forever, and write ever so often. . . .

All that gritty railroad journey home from Vermont my thoughts dwelt on Bertha. Next morning, which was Sunday, before anyone was stirring, I wrote a hot, impassioned letter to Bertha. I sentimentally informed her why I should consider seven my lucky number. Maybe I told her something about my plans [for our future]. I sneaked downstairs to mail it. Lucky for me I was in the habit of rising early and my stealthy deed passed unnoticed.

The letter was never answered, and I have often wondered what happened to it—did Bertha actually get it, or was it intercepted or lost? Would the course of my life have been changed if she *had* answered it? Well, she didn't. And suddenly, overcome by shame and disgust, I ceased to think about the chestnut haired girl in Vermont. Study *is* an excellent antidote for what crass-minded elders are wont to call puppy love. But always she lingered in the back of my mind, for the time as a lofty ideal; and then she became involved in furtive dreams. . . .   —RN. 1915

PORTRAIT OF THE ARTIST AS A YOUNG MAN. The living room on the second floor of a certain brownstone dwelling on the upper West Side: a sombre reminder of the architectural crimes that were rampant in the middle eighties. The furniture is essentially modern, of the better Grand Rapids type, although here and there remain vestiges of the days that chafed the tender soul of Oscar Wilde. With one's back toward the windows that face the street one has on the right a fumed oak typewriter desk, a swivel chair, and a set of Century Encyclopedias. (The books have been used.) Between the bookstand and the hall door in the rear is a window which opens on the court of an apartment house; it embraces a cozy, leather cushioned window seat. On the left a flowered sofa, and the stony crayon portrait of a Deceased Male, mar the esthetic victory gained by the few harmonious rugs, the hardwood floor, and the warm, tan-tinted walls. All the chairs are comfortable beyond the dreams of laziness.

Regius is a thin, slightly stooped youth of nineteen or twenty, with a full forehead, a Napoleonic nose, and persistent, anxious eyes. He is a product of his mother's tender care, his aunt's devotion, his nurse's solicitude, his teacher's coddling, his schoolfellows' toleration, and the protection from any vital contact with the world that has been provided by an ample bourgeois income. Measured by the standards of the society he lives in, he has been excellently brought up: or, as his aunt would probably say, "He has been given every advantage." This means that ever since he learned his ABC's he has been exposed to the most vicious institution of present-day civilization: our so-called educational system. The barrenly intellectualized training he has been given in that system has ingrained in him the habit of living at second hand; with the result that though he has apparently a vast knowledge about art, industry, science, love, friendship, and so forth, he has never had the least direct acquaintance with any of these things. He is emotionally starved, and volitionally frustrate, while intellectually he is prodigious. A modern college president would think him a very promising young man: but according to the ideals of an Athenian in the age of Pericles, he is a hopeless idiot; a nuisance to himself; a burden to his family; and a total loss in manhood to the state.

Note: This is the setting of a one-act play, 'The Invalids,' written in 1916, and accepted by The Baltimore Players in 1918, but never staged: perhaps because the company disbanded during the war.

East Side Education

Toward the end of the first decade of the century, the horizons of New York visibly widened for me. Adolescence and high school advanced together, although I don't think my voice broke or my legs became gangly till at least a year after I had left grammar school. When I was graduated from grammar school, we had sung a song at commencement about our eternal loyalty to dear old 166, but in our hearts we knew that in our part of the West Side one school was practically identical with another, whereas the high schools we had to choose from had names, not numbers, and each one had a collective character. Townsend Harris was almost collegiate in its standards, but, despite its playing fields on Convent Avenue, was terrible in sports. Commerce, at Sixty-fifth Street near Broadway, had a fine baseball team, and it turned out fellows who became bookkeepers, accountants, and male secretaries. De Witt Clinton, at Fifty-ninth Street near Tenth Avenue, was just literary, while Stuyvesant, which had a good basketball team and a new building, prepared people for engineering.

At the time the choice came to me, I was making clumsy models of airplanes on the lines of the Wright plane—models that would never fly in the air and would hardly even stay glued together in repose on my bedroom table. With the help of an old instrument-maker to whom Dr. Phillips, our family doctor, had introduced me, I had begun to rig up feeble little wireless sets with which I purposed to communicate with another ingenious lad in the next block, if either of us ever had the patience to master the Morse code. So I chose Stuyvesant. I think the good basketball team erased any lingering doubts I may have had about it.

Emerson used to say that the essence of a college education was having a room of one's own, with a fire, in a strange city. Going to high school on East Fifteenth Street, between Stuyvesant Square and First Avenue, gave me essentially the same sort of shock. In those days, the upper West Side had a fairly homogeneous population; there was the typical New York mixture of German and Irish stocks, interspersed with older branches of the American. Our fathers and mothers, at least, had usually been born in the United States, and in a class of forty boys, only eight or ten would be identifiably Jewish, while the newer Russo-Polish migration was so sparsely represented that I can still remember the name of Malatzky, the bright, beady-eyed son of a glazier on Columbus Avenue.

Except for Broadway, which was very spottily built up until the opening of the subway in 1904 defined its new character, this part of the West Side had taken shape in the late eighties and nineties. The poorer classes lived in flats on Amsterdam and Columbus Avenues: the cabmen and the clerks and the mechanics and the minor city employees. The rich lived in the big apartments on Central Park West or in the heavy, stone-encrusted mansions on Riverside Drive; between them, on the cross streets, and more sumptuously on West End Avenue, was the connecting tissue of the bourgeoisie, in brownstone rows whose dinginess was sometimes graced by some of the lighter-yellow, brick-and-limestone houses designed by Stanford White and his imitators. A boy growing up in such a neighborhood took middle-class comfort to be the dominant pattern of life, and except for an occasional twist of Irish, everyone spoke plain Manhattanese.

Suddenly I was thrown into a remote quarter of the city, and surrounded by a group of boys with foreign faces and uncouth, almost undecipherable accents and grubby, pushing manners: boys who ate strange food whose flavors pervaded their breath and seemed to hang about their clothes; boys whose aggressive vitality left me feeling like a sick goldfinch among a flock of greedy sparrows. One had to fend for oneself among people who had learned the art of survival in a far more difficult environment than I had come from, and in the lunch hour I would inevitably find myself near the tag end of the line that filed past the cafeteria counter, never capable of making decisions fast enough to get what I wanted before I was pushed beyond reach.

My school comrades were mostly the first American-born generation of the great Russian and Polish Jewish immigration that had swept into the East Side after the assassination of Czar Alexander II. They had names like Moscowitz and Lefkowitz and Pinsky, and they had not merely learned in the Settlement Houses how to play circles round most of us in basketball or track sports, but they had an equally strenuous grip on the academic subjects. Indeed, most of them also excelled in the use of their hands, not having had so many of their manual opportunities shorn from them by solicitous parents and nursemaids. All in all, these boys were good stuff, but for one who had lived a more pallid existence, they were, during the first year, a little overwhelming.

My new schoolfellows brought the raw facts of life home to me with a rush. My own family knew the pinch of genteel poverty, but here was poverty on a grand scale, massive, extensive, blighting vast neighborhoods, altering the whole character of life, a poverty that, instead of shrinking submissively behind a false front, reached out into the city, creating its own forms, demanding, arguing, asserting, claiming its own, now busy with schemes for making money, now whispering the strange word Socialism as a key that would open the door. My political views were extremely conservative in those days; the rights of property seemed axiomatic; and I remember how shocked I was when I found out that one of my pals named Stamer, whose father was a Greenpoint cigarmaker of the old '48 German stock, was a Socialist. Stamer jarred my middle-class complacency with his scornful descriptions of what had hitherto seemed a reasonable and well-balanced world, and I was gradually unsettled in all my views, not so much through the strength of his arguments as through the obvious feebleness of my replies. Even a couple of teachers, quiet, upright men, were Socialists and would occasionally explain their views in class. I might have lived and died in my part of the upper West Side without realizing that neither the Democratic nor the Republican Party had ever recognized the Class Struggle.

Fourteenth Street, too, was something of an education for a provincial West Side boy. Tammany Hall still reigned in its dingy building near Third Avenue, embracing the old Tony Pastor's theatre, and almost across the way was Tom Sharkey's saloon, with a wide glass front, and the Dewey Theatre, painted white, where lurid posters of obese beauties, who did the belly dances that preceded strip tease, were spread before our gaze. "Don't do that dance I tell you Sadie, that ain't no business for a lady" was one of the popular songs of the period, and all of us knew, at least at second hand, how much farther Fourteenth Street went than Broadway's Sadie. My usual route to school was through Irving Place and along Fifteenth Street, because I discovered in my second year that a beautiful girl with austere white cheeks and black hair would pass me almost every morning on her way to the Quaker school at the corner of Stuyvesant Square. I can still see her graceful figure, in a blue serge dress, topped by a black hat with a jaunty feather, her poised, unhurried walk, and her slightly archaic inward smile, which was at once in-penetrable and yet not indifferent, and I wonder now if I played anything of the part in her secret dream life that she did in mine.

When school was out, one would encounter in the same street, nearer Third Avenue, white-faced and heavily rouged prostitutes, no longer young, already on patrol. We knew what these ladies were, in a vague way; some of the boys, who lived on Forsythe or Chrystie Street, had even encountered them closer at hand in the halls of their own tenements; and we held a certain resentment against them because they were mainly responsible for the fact that we were not permitted to go out on the streets for lunch, but had to remain cooped in our building. The year after I was graduated, however, a new social ferment began to work in school. A group of boys rushed the teacher who was guarding the main door and broke for liberty during the lunch hour; this precipitated a school strike, and when the matter was settled the boys had won the right to eat outdoors. The squirrels in Stuyvesant Square benefited more by this arrangement, I am sure, than the painted ladies.

Often I preferred to spend my carfare on candy and walked home, usually with a couple of other lads. The path led diagonally across the city, sometimes up Broadway, sometimes around the open New York Central yards and across the Central Park. I watched the Public Library and the Grand Central Terminal during their building, and remember parts of Fifth Avenue below Fifty-ninth that were still lined with brown-stone dwellings and plushy-looking mansions before which victorias and hansoms would stop, and the stages—as my mother still calls the buses—would roll by. Yet visually these walks remain dim, because so much of them, particularly when a sallow, evangelical boy named Harold Bush was along, was spent in talks about God and immortality and True Christianity. The openness of the midtown district then, its low buildings and the vast unbuilt spaces on Park Avenue, of course remain with me, for they were still visible when the Shelton was erected as late as 1924, but I dearly wish some heavenly stenographer would transcribe one of those theological debates for me. Both Bush and I were still pious lads. Could it be that we spent all those hours comparing the practices of the Baptists and the Episcopalians? Or were we battling with the Higher Criticism? I can't remember.

In grammar school, most of the male teachers were aged men, who had grown old in a profession they conducted with dignity untouched by inspiration—men who could remember the draft riots, or the black-walled city that celebrated Lincoln's funeral. In high school, there were a lot of young teachers who brought into the place the contemporary flavor of Cornell, Chicago, or Wisconsin, as well as nearer universities, people who were stirred up over their subjects and who would break into their routine demonstrations in physics with hints of exciting scientific news that would not for a decade or more penetrate the textbooks—Einstein's first theory of relativity, or the electronic theory of matter, which made the old-fashioned doctrine of the indivisible atom look silly except as a convenience in writing chemical equations. Our principal, a sweet, portly man with a gray Vandyke beard and a bald head, was excited about science, too; he kept a class in physics for himself all through his principalship, and he would beam on us when he had made a good demonstration. Some of the more menial subjects in engineering, like mechanical drawing, seemed to attract routineers, but to make up for it, there were teachers in pattern-making or metal-turning who had worked with the Yale & Towne lock company or in the Baldwin Locomotive Works, and who were not tethered to the profession of teaching out of mere ineptitude for worldly tasks or for the sake of premature repose. As for the man who taught us forging, he was a German blacksmith of the old school, and his iron roses and scrolly leaves were our envy.

That a school so strenuously dedicated to science and the mechanical arts should have had a good English department was extremely fortunate for a lad whose mathematical aptitude waned shortly after he wrote his first love letter. The English teachers worked against odds, too, because the Board of Regents had chosen a lot of pretty stale literature for our edification, and it didn't help matters that, by some oversight, we had already gone through 'The Lady of the Lake' and 'Julius Caesar' in grammar school. But my teacher in freshman English, Thomas Bates, a rapt, brooding young man with a freckled face and a huge mop of carroty hair, encouraged a group of us to write a play, and from his lips I first heard the name of Bernard Shaw. That was what was important, as one looks back on it, in all the classes. Not the lesson itself, but the overflow— a hint, a pat on the shoulder, the confession of a secret ambition, a fragment of unposed life as someone had actually lived it.

I wasn't overly fond of mechanical drawing, but high school had none of the close-packed boredom that remains the chief impress of my earlier education. It was a big chunk of life to swallow, and maybe we were stretched a little too hard at study during a period when our bodies demanded a larger share of idleness and relaxation than we gave them. But there was no lack of intellectual stimulus in this new milieu. By the time we had visited foundries on the East River, practiced tennis on courts in Staten Island, travelling two hours for the sake of playing one, cheered baseball games in the Bronx, and dickered with one-horse job printers on John Street, we knew our way about the city and we knew a lot about what life had to offer ourselves and our fellows.

When I left high school my ambitions had changed. I wanted to be a newspaperman as a first step toward becoming a novelist. Shep Friedman was then the city editor of the Morning Telegraph, and since he was a friend of the family, I kept on politely nagging him for a job for the next year or two. I would usually drop in around 6:00 P.M., before he had started the heavy business or the heavy drinking of the day, and although I was palpably a callow and ratty adolescent, he was always decent enough to drag me down to the corner bar for a friendly beer. After this he would give me a note of introduction to the most recent occupant of the Evening Journal's city desk. Being idiotic as well as honorable, I never examined these notes. I suspect now that they said, "For God's sake dump this kid somewhere or drown him." At the end of six months I compromised with my ambitions and went on the Evening Telegram as copy boy for the lobster trick. My feelings were a little like those of a broken-down gentleman I once knew who was finally reduced to taking a job as dishwasher in a big hotel. But, he proudly explained to his friends, he was not an ordinary dishwasher; he washed only the dishes of the guests who were served privately in their rooms. It was understood that I was to become a cub reporter the first time someone moved up or out.

The job forced me to get up at 2:50 A.M., make my own breakfast, and catch a Sixth Avenue L to Herald Square. The back of our flat faced Columbus Avenue, and I could tell by leaning out the kitchen window and noting whether the passing train had green or white lights how much time I had left for finishing my cocoa. It made one feel slightly superior to be abroad in the city at that hour, before the milkman started on his rounds. The cold white flare of the arc lights intensified one's feeling of aloofness, and an occasional light in the bedroom of an otherwise darkened tenement house might even add a touch of mystery, hinting of someone in pain, someone quarrelling, someone dying or being born. But often I would be oblivious of the sleeping city because I was reading, with an indescribable priggish elation, a few pages in Plato or William James. Reading 'A Pluralistic Universe' at 3:25 in the morning almost wiped away the humiliation of sweeping the floor and setting out the flimsy in the stale air of the city room half an hour later. If I happened to catch a train ten minutes earlier, I would encounter the last of the reporters, winding up their poker game in a corner of our common city room.

The Telegram was even in 1913 a pretty seedy sheet, but James Gordon Bennett was still alive, and some faint, ridiculous spark of his vindictive energy would cause an editor or a reporter suddenly to jump out of his skin. (Bennett was the same insolent devil who offered Stanley his old job on the Herald after he had found Livingstone and made himself famous.) At this time, the name Roosevelt was taboo; he could be referred to only as the Third Termer. Among other examples of Bennett's crotchets, there was an ice chest in one corner of the city room, which was duly filled with ice every day, supposedly because the Old Boy himself might suddenly appear and want ice for his champagne. Bennett's alpaca coat, too, hung on a hook in his private office, waiting. I rushed the beer and sandwiches and coffee while the night city editor was marking up the morning papers for the rewrite men. Even at that hour, the saloon on the northeast corner of Thirty-fifth Street would have a few stragglers in it. The rewrite men, who averaged around thirty-five dollars a week then—the night city editor got only fifty—used to tip me, too, even if I did read William James and sometimes do a stick or two of rewrite myself when one of the men got in late. If any small story broke in the neighborhood, I would be sent out to cover it, but a sewer explosion and a burning mattress were about all that came my way, and my pride suffered as my boredom grew, so I chucked the job after a couple of months. It was a cheap and harmless inoculation. I never looked for Life in newspaper offices any more, and thenceforward I read newspapers with a scorn and a skepticism born of intimacy. Had I not, when a freighter without a wireless sank near Halifax, seen a big front-page story manufactured in three-quarters of an hour out of a rewrite man's stinking clay pipe and his otherwise unaided imagination?

From 1912 to the end of 1914 I was studying in the evening session of City College, from 7:30 to 10:20. In every way that was a remarkable experience, and one that only New York could have offered. Even New York could offer it only once, for the college I knew, with some five hundred students and a close, intimate life, disappeared—under mere pressure of congestion—within half a dozen years after its inception. It was one of those important experiments that the City College began before it went the way of other metropolitan institutions by succumbing to giantism. Dr. Stephen Duggan was the director and Dr. Frederick B. Robinson (he of umbrella memory) was then his assistant, an affable, clever man who was yet to disclose his remarkable talent for disingenuously setting a whole institution by the ears.

The students were mostly mature men, and they spoiled me for any other kind of undergraduate. One of them was a well-established maritime lawyer, with an argumentative Scotch tongue; another was a South

American consul; and there were doctors, brokers, accountants, engineers, as well as people almost as infirmly established as myself. Being under no obligations to regularity, I took my college education backward, skipping most of the freshman subjects and plunging into junior and senior courses in politics, philosophy, and English. In all the new plans for revising curricula that I have examined, not even Dr. Hutchins seems to have hit on this particular dodge, but perhaps it would work no worse for others than it did for me.

There is something amoeboid about the ordinary undergraduate, but we night students had a shape and a backbone and a definite point of view. Our discussions were battles, and though we often lived to change sides, there was nothing tentative or hesitating in our espousals; we did not suffer from the academic disease of evasive 'open-mindedness.' Our professors were men of character—men like Morris Cohen, who thought and taught out of a passion for things of the mind as pure as that of a Socrates or a Spinoza. There was Alfred Compton, a slim, sardonic gentleman with a touch of Robert Louis Stevenson about him. There was John Pickett Turner, a handsome man with a massive dark head, a wart on his cheek, and shoulders of Platonic dimensions; he spoke with a Southern deliberation and enlivened his course on psychology with case histories drawn undisguised from his own life and marital experience. Even-handed and tolerant, he didn't quiver a hairbreadth when a sharp little Rumanian, Jallyer, in the ethics class, declared that the *summum bonum* would be to die at the height of an orgasm in the arms of a beautiful woman. There was J. Salwyn Schapiro, one of J. H. Robinson's brilliant disciples, who filled the air with epigrams and paradoxes, one of which seems even more startling in 1937 than it did in 1913—"The Constitution might be overthrown, but it could not be amended." And then there was Earle Palmer, a little man with a drawn white face, hunched shoulders, and dark eyes that smoldered behind his glasses. He took us through Pancoast's anthology of poetry, living and enacting the poems, with an acrid humor in commentary that sprang out of passion rather than bitterness—a frail but ageless figure, half pixie, half demon, with the sudden dark touch of one who had not lightly triumphed over terror and wrath and pain. My Harvard friends have overfilled me with tales about their famous Copey, but none of them has ever made me feel the least regretful that I missed the histrionic Harvard professor. One touch of Palmer's ruthless sincerity was at least half a college education.

The Trustees of City College had chosen a grand site for their new buildings when the college moved up from Twenty-third Street, and the architecture had a powerful effect when one climbed the hill past the

Hebrew Orphan Asylum through the deepening October twilight and saw the college buildings, in their dark stone masses and white terra-cotta quoins and moldings, rising like a collection of crystals out of the formless rocks on the crest. Below, the plain of Harlem spread, a vapor of light beneath the twinkle and flood of a large beer sign. In the afterglow, or on a dark night, these buildings could awaken nostalgic memory as easily as those of Brasenose or Magdalen. Often we would accompany one of our professors to his home, along Convent Avenue or Broadway, or sometimes a group of us, heady with the discussions started in the classroom, would stalk down Riverside Drive, matching outrageous puns, arguing about free will and determinism, bursting into irrelevant song. It had the intimacy that only a small college can give, plus the variety and intensity of stimulus that come in a great city. —The New Yorker. December 4, 1937

West Side Love

The other part of my adolescence, particularly in the earlier years, centered chiefly around the old tennis courts in Central Park on the south side of the transverse at Ninety-sixth Street. The courts were then covered with grass, and the most popular court, half-denuded by constant playing, was called the dirt court. An aged keeper, with a gray beard spattered with tobacco juice, had charge of the marking of the courts and the stowing away of the nets. He was probably one of those Civil War pensioners who were still favored on the public payrolls, and we called him 'Captain,' but he had a vile temper and carried on an uncivil war of his own with most of the people who played there. He was often drunk, and the white lines he marked with his sprinkler showed no disposition to follow the straight and narrow path, but this crusty character gave the place a certain flavor which contrasts with the colorless, antiseptic courtesy of today. We couldn't start playing till the Captain raised the flag on the flagpole.

It was a queer gang that hung around the courts in those days—a few newspaper reporters on the American and the Press; a theatrical agent whom we called Ted; a little hunchback with no visible occupation, whom we called Dirty Ferdie; a few semi-professional loafers who used to play for stakes; and a handful of young women who were usually attached to the older men, ancients who might be at least thirty years old, as well as a few boys of my own age who took tennis very seriously. Day after day through the muggy summer we would lounge around on the hill behind the dirt court, and play, and lounge, and play again till we could scarcely drag our feet around the court. This was a complete, self-contained world; even on a rainy day, we would come over to the courts with our racquets, sprawling on benches beneath the trees toward the reservoir, speculating on the weather. When the males were alone, the conversation would often descend to basement level, and I would go home with new words I couldn't find in my ten-volume Century Dictionary, sometimes with lickerish hints about aspects of life I hadn't the faintest clue to till I studied abnormal psychology. On the whole, perhaps it was a good thing we played so much tennis.

I don't know if I can convey the precise flavor of the city that one inhaled on those Central Park courts in my day. It was perhaps closest to what one feels on a clean, sunny beach onto which the ocean periodically washes stale watermelon rinds, mildewed oranges, and discarded paper boxes. There was nothing particular in my immediate life to make me look naturally for meanness or sordidness or dishonesty, but constant hints of these things seeped in from the world around me. By the time I was fifteen, I had acquired a layer of protective cynicism that would have honored the proverbial cub reporter, and my tennis coach in high school, an excellent English teacher named Quimby, once said in perfectly justifiable horror, "You talk like a disillusioned man of sixty." Yet with all my early knowingness, I went through the first experience of being in love at fifteen—with Sybil, a girl I met at the tennis courts—as if all my life had been spent among the innocents of Arcadia. The other day I attended a singing festival given by the girls in one of our municipal colleges, a charming mass of hussies whose dance routines would have done credit to Broadway. In the very alluring performance they put on, in the songs they had made up, I detected the same combination of virginity and cynicism, of chastity and shamelessness—the curious patina of hardness that forms over youth in the big city. They were exquisitely young and fresh, yet already they were a little cheapened, a little soiled.

My own girl was one of those ruthless beauties who are never at ease unless they put five or six men simultaneously in a state of torture. With one, she danced for tango prizes in the footsteps of Irene Castle; with another, she swam; with another, she went to football games. She had us all, in fact, pretty well specialized and subordinated, and it was usually for one of the older lads that she reserved her emotional complications. If I began earlier and remained on the scene longer than any of her other young admirers, it was because I served as a sort of fixed spar to mark the height of the incoming or the ebbing tide. Every once in a while she would cling to me to get her bearings. My specialty was playing tennis on the courts near Morningside Park, a few blocks from her apartment, at six in the morning, before she started her day as artist's model. It was perhaps the only time in my life, except in the Navy, that I visibly profited by my gift of waking up easily.

I can't pretend that there was anything very typical of New York in this relationship. The closest it came to taking on the color of the city was one hot summer night, on a street swarming with children and inundated by a hurdy-gurdy thumping out Cavalleria Rusticana, when I told her I wanted to marry her. She was very self-possessed about that. She sent me round the corner for some ice cream, which the dealers then used to heap up in flimsy paper boxes, and then she took me up to the roof of her apartment house, a flight higher than the elevator went, so that we could talk matters over while we dipped, turn and turn, into the ice-cream box. The thick summer sky flared to the east with the lights of Harlem, and on this high roof one had a sense of separation from the rest of the world one usually doesn't achieve in Nature at a level lower than five thousand feet. But nobody ever succeeded in making love convincingly when his hands were all sticky from ice cream. Perhaps Sybil knew that when she complained about the heat. On her telling me what good friends we would always be—pals, in fact—I abruptly left her, and went down onto the steamy pavement, on which big raindrops were beginning to spatter, feeling dramatically solemn. The same tune—probably from the same hand organ—was still clanging in the distance. And I was already sketching in my mind the first act of a play to be called 'Love on Morningside Heights.'   —The New Yorker. December 4, 1937

Note: In this Memoir I have given a brief glimpse of Beryl Morse, the focus of all my youthful dreams, 'platonic' but passionate, of bodily beauty and feminine charm. In my Autobiography I have devoted a whole chapter to Beryl—and with some reason—for my falling in love with her at fifteen left a mark on my later life in more than one way. My almost daily letters to her during the first stage of our friendship did as much as anything else, perhaps, to turn my mind away from technology to literature—all the more because she at first was my literary superior with a background which ranged from Lewis Carroll and the Bab Ballads to French and Russian writers I had then barely heard of. Though Beryl under various names keeps on popping up at different points in my later Notes and plays, she belongs mainly to my adolescence.

"The Escort of Friends"

At some point I must give an account of my early friendships; and on that topic I know neither where to begin nor where to end. For me, as for the ancient Greeks, friendship is one of the ultimate rewards of life; and friendship with members of one's own sex was immune in my generation and my circle from the illusions and magnifications and inordinate imperatives of erotic love: so that there never lurked behind it the suspicion that one was deviously seeking, or perhaps anxiously evading, another, more sexual kind of intimacy. I have been friends, yes, and close friends, with the widest variety of people, men and women; but none of my early friendships persevered till I encountered the group I came to know at the Evening Session of the City College. Some of these friends weave in and out of the picture: but others, who played an equal part in my life, will not be relevant to the themes I will pick up and embroider. So now perhaps is the moment when I should talk about my early friends.

Until I was twelve, the nearest approach I had to a friend who counted more than my other playmates was Paul Brown, who lived on the same block. He loved to draw horses and became, I suspect, the artist whose sporting prints were once famous in the sports world—and even beyond. He was followed by a rather handsome, slightly older, sleepy-faced lad who lived up the block on Ninety-fourth Street, who helped to persuade me that Stuyvesant was the High School I wanted to go to. About this time, a somewhat older lad, named Will Robertson, attracted me: English born, with red hair and a hot but well-controlled temper, his speech was full of crisp consonants our slovenly New Yorkese softened or spoiled, while his sense of humor, enlivened by a literary background that included Kipling and the Bab Ballads, was adequate to every occasion, and kept him unruffled when his soft, somewhat overweight body and his polite ways made other youngsters at the Tennis Courts, the only place we met, set him down as sissy.

But I had no close friend until I met John Tucker: a lean, narrow-shouldered, freckled, sandy-faced young man, always bespectacled, who was already studying to be an engineer at Stevens Institute and who, though I was a good three years younger than he, used to seek my company, increasingly, as my own studies in philosophy led us into long arguments in the best Scots style: for his father was English and his mother a Scot, and John himself was as dogmatic in his skepticisms and his rejections as a Scots dominie would have been about Predestination and Eternal Damnation, though it was Pearson's 'The Grammar of Science' and Mach's logical positivism he was advancing as science's last demolishing word on philosophy.

He served for me as an abrasive stone on which I could sharpen my own ideas; and he used to regard me as an endless source of amusement, marked by loud guffaws of appreciation, because of all the ways in which my reactions to life were different from his own and from those around him. We had two girl friends in common—Beryl and Sarita—and though we kept such friendships in private compartments, we enjoyed comparing notes on their views and their conduct. Beneath his scientifically immaculate mind, devoted to the rational, the calculable, the observable, was a much more emotional personality that never manifested itself except in a stilted, somewhat embarrassed form. Our typical intercourse was full of calculated insults and disparagements: his didacticism—"Well, you see, Fish, *it's like this*"—was in itself somewhat insulting. But we both learned from each other; and one day I even won his respect by my irreproachable answer to a question he posed about Einstein's first relativity theory: a subject that the scientifically educated young were already discussing *circa* 1916.

At Tucker's invitation I went to the Bureau of Standards Laboratory in Pittsburgh in 1917, as a temporary laboratory helper without Civil Service status, in his own cement testing laboratory. We lived in the same boarding house on North Craig Street and usually walked back and forth to work together. Though our friendship never became closer, and our wives never met, we exchanged jibes, wisecracks, and insults by letter, along with occasional meetings, to within a few years of his untimely death after a gallant struggle against his arthritically immobile limbs.

Of all the other friendships of those early days, the two that sustained me most were those of Herbert Feis and Jerome Lachenbruch: but the first was almost entirely epistolary, when he was studying at Harvard, and it hardly outlasted our student days. Feis, with his natural talents and his well-disciplined mind, had at an early moment achieved a place within intellectual circles, like that of 'The New Republic,' where I lingered hungrily on the outside; he was even, as economist, an assistant to Ordway Tead, on a Joint Dress and Waist Board investigation where, in 1916, I worked for two months as a lowly investigator. Herbert early became an ensign in the Navy, on active service, whereas I remained on shore, training as a mere radio operator, and an inactive one at that. But he was a generous spirit, full of irrepressible gaiety in actual life, a gaiety that sometimes gave way to thoughtful, sobering admonitions in his letters to me, for I often distressed him by letting my own gaiety and spontaneity break forth in those affairs of the mind that he looked upon as too sacred for such levity. I can still feel, in retrospect, the touch of his steadying hand.

As for Jerome Lachenbruch, he too was older than I by seven years or so: a sensitive, thoughtful, earnest young man, sober beyond his years because he had early taken on the burden of earning his own living without the college preparation his younger brothers were to have. We must have been in some of the same classes at City College—except for Advanced German we both have forgotten which ones—and with our common literary interests, our common German background, there was much that we could take for granted. We even went together to the German theater in Yorkville to see 'Alma Wo Wohnst Du?' He was both a friend and a badly needed older brother, aware of the inner tensions that accompanied my sexual immaturity, properly critical of the effects of this upon my stories and plays: but full of good hope and cautious counsel, in letters that often sounded the very depths of my situation. In all my life I have received just two letters that were to have a profound effect upon my literary and intellectual development, and one of them was written by Lachenbruch.

Most of the casual friendships I made in the Navy vanished quickly, but the crowded barracks at Newport brought me close to another one of the few friends who, like Lachenbruch, seasoned with me into old age: David Liebovitz. His career as a playwright and a novelist was never rounded out with the success it deserved—perhaps because his first, and most successful book, a picaresque novel called 'Youth Dares All,' was published anonymously. Accident brought us together: Liebovitz by height was in the same tall squad as I, and by alphabetic order his cot was near mine. My hacking cough in fact used to ruin his sleep, but he conquered his irritation when he found that we both took literature seriously. Though we parted when he went in for an ensignship, we had lived actually within half a dozen blocks of each other in Manhattan, and came together again when the war was over. His emotional intensity and unsparing critical honesty accompanied me through his last forty-five years, sometimes close, sometimes distant: yet always there.

The degree of intimacy under which a friendship prospers and the degree of influence it exercises has little to do with time or the possibility of regular meetings: both these friendships flourished at a distance, with only occasional meetings: though Lachenbruch and I have seen each other only at intervals of ten years or more, none of the old sense of our closeness has disappeared. With the other great friendship of my early manhood the same rule holds. Geroid Robinson and I met as rivals for the same post on the fortnightly Dial: instead of fighting for primacy we shared the job and drew closer together; and though we had hoped to continue this relation on The Freeman, it was he who, perhaps because his sober literary style or his turn of mind pleased Nock, the principal editor, more, got that coveted post. For a time we were neighbors on Brooklyn Heights; for another while, neighbors again in Leedsville. But our friendship was so tightly cemented at the beginning that neither closeness nor distance affected it—until our acute differences over the Vietnam holocaust made that subject unutterable, *at his earnest request,* even in our letters. Each of us had a private life he felt no need to share with the other: yet each of us knew—at least until this final breach!— that, came a moment of personal crisis or anguish, the other would be there.

Out of this gathering of early friends I have lifted these five as representative samples: but I am sad to leave out all the others who played an active part in my life before I was thirty. My life would have been poor and empty without these people.   —Fragment from my Autobiography, 1963

4: Young Man in Love

Though the chapter on my courtship and my eventual marriage to Sophia Wittenberg is possibly the best chapter of my still unfinished Auto-biography, only a limited number of the following notes could be fitted into it without breaking the more formal pattern of that book. If the reader finds that some of these notes—and still more the omissions—tease his imagination, that was exactly my intention. My mother's prudish criticism of some of the more realistic novels she had read half a century ago was that the authors "left nothing to the imagination." Ordinarily I prefer to err in the opposite direction: so here and elsewhere I have left room for the mature reader to fill in the blank spaces out of his own experiences. If he should need a little help he will find it in 'The Little Testament of Bernard Martin,' in which actual facts play hide-and-seek with fantasies; for in the first draft the heroine was a liberated but pru-dent Tanya, halfway through the story she turned into the naughtier Eunice, modeled on my first love, only to return to Sophia's proper self in time to have a baby and send Bernard off to Geneva. At a deeper level, though more fully disguised, the reader will find even more about my own character and our married life in 'The Builders of the Bridge,' a play written in 1927, which demanded facilities in production that the motion pictures did not provide until the early thirties. Because of its length it was impossible to include it in the present volume—though not from any doubts of mine as to its suitability for production on film. Until my Autobiography can be published, these glimpses in 'Findings and Keep-ings' must suffice.

None but the Brave Deserves to Escape the Fair

Now Beryl got my verses first:
She taught me how to write;
And bound my metre's crippled feet
And cheered my muse's flight.

She held me half a dozen years
We smiled at parting—through our tears!

To Phyllis went a single sheaf
(I worshipped from afar)
And sent my poems *sans* my name:
Good Lord! That started war.

The vixen sank her claws in me
For hiding my identity.

My next verse came more easily
For I was Elsie's poet.
I sent her some of Beryl's stuff—
Don't tell! She'll never know it!

Well, Elsie liked my efforts. I
Liked Elsie's salads, tea, and pie.

A Titian blonde who loved Rossetti,
Maggie I tried with sonnets:
Her reading sounded like a wail
Stifled in woolen bonnets.

Her pictures had more life than she,
More power, lust, diversity.

When Sophy asked for comic verse
I met the challenge like a jay
And butchered all my erstwhile loves
To make a sophic holiday.

Beware! Some dark philosophy
Lurks behind this treachery.

Note: Sophy had complained that none of her admirers had ever yet written a
poem to her; and so, mockingly, though already more than dimly aware I was
falling in love with her, I wrote this jingle in 1919.

60

MY FIRST AND FINAL MISTRESS . . . I do not understand, mother, what you mean by your allusion to my 'marriage.' I repeat, that event is as unlikely as a German victory. The reasons are brief but sufficient: first, I am not acquainted with a single feminine soul I would under any circumstance get wedded to, and second I am not in a position which would permit me to marry the most lovely and eligible soul. You may retort that before tomorrow dawns I may become acquainted with my future wife. I reply, alas for her! if that is the case, for unless she knows how to support both herself and me, and has sufficient audacity to attempt to overcome my objections to that sort of thing, hers will be a lonely spinsterhood these next ten years; for I am already married to my work, and until I establish a position in society for *that* mistress, I can harbor no thoughts of any other. —Letter to my mother, Elvina C. Mumford. October 4, 1918

Confound Sophy: I am falling in love with her, and the only satisfaction I get out of this fact is the fun of watching the spectacle. Love is a sort of local anesthetic that gets one ready for the ordeal of marriage: and marriage in my present position is such a remote and unimaginable condition that the anesthetic is almost as terrifying as the operation. It is not that I am altogether losing my wits: Sophy does not appear to me in a rosy blur. In fact, I can look upon her in a steady mood of lucid aloofness and watch every movement of her mind and body through a lens of crystalline dispassionateness.* But for all that I cannot get rid of an intense biological conviction that someday we will be thrown into each other's arms as mates. I feel that there is a wonderful completeness in Sophy that I have never encountered before in any other girl, as though she were an embodiment of the three graces and each were dancing in vital unison. A sort of Sophy reverie pervades what would otherwise be vacant moments —a sure sign of the divine madness! And I wonder, in a baffled, irritated way what she is thinking about me. . . .

What an incriminating folly this business of falling in love is. I ought to read Pycraft's courtship among the animals in order to restore my sense of humor. When I am not keeping close watch I find myself ruffling my feathers and strutting on parade. Does the game cock or the young buck find a challenging familiarity and invitation in his mate's eyes? . . . It occurs to me that there is some truth in Graham Wallas's belief that the dissociation of the biological man from the spiritual man is a dominant and quite modern trait. Marie tells the story of a doctor she knows. This girl had attended a medical lecture on a certain disease of the heart, and

* Oh! Can you? [Author: 1974]

she returned home from the theater at night accompanied by a male friend of hers, who kissed her and embraced her in good Southern fashion at parting. In the midst of the embrace she diagnosed his heart palpitation as indicative of the very disease she had been sutdying. "Honey," she said, "you have a systolic murmur," and she told him for farewell that he must consult a physician immediately. . . . —RN. 1919

. . . The metaphor of 'The Research Magnificent' has been running through my head ever since old Geddes's letter came, and I cannot get rid of it. The comparison isn't altogether flattering: for I remember reading 'The Research Magnificent' when it first came out and pouring scorn upon Benham for being such an arrant prig. I could not stomach his white-faced earnestness: it stripped life of decoration and left it knobby and starved. The lamentable failure to tie the research to his Amanda, to recognize their personal and their impersonal interests, interested me because Wells didn't seem to have a clue to answer the question it inevitably provoked. He shirked the problem altogether when he made Benham so stiffly obtuse and Amanda so gracefully trivial. What he should have asked was: suppose they have the best intentions in the world, and the completest sympathy, under what terms could their marriage and the research be pursued without one cutting out the other? —Letter to Sophy Wittenberg. February 8, 1920

. . . We both prided ourselves on our common sense, and yet we can see how easy it is to lose hold of it. My original fear that it would spoil altogether the possibilities of any intimate relations between us was absurdly wide of the mark: how easy it was for me, for example, to abandon my common sense convictions about the impossibility of marriage, and that sort of thing. The danger, as anyone but a conceited prig like myself ought have known, lay just the other way: for rationality and common sense and all those kindred instruments of sweetness and light are in constant danger of being dazed and diverted by more primitive impulses, and one shortly discovers, as does Regius' mother in 'The Invalids,' that having a level head is of no use at all when you have lost it. I think I lost mine rather more completely than you did, for your doubts were probably nothing more nor less than a symptom of a reluctantly dissipated rationality. —Letter to Sophy Wittenberg. May 1920

. . . Last night I was walking with James Henderson along the South Bank of the Thames opposite the Houses of Parliament. We had had supper together in a very good little restaurant, The Ship's Grill, one of the best that I have found, all things considered, in Whitehall, and we were watching the towers of Westminster change in color and aspect against the clear sunset sky. It was about nine o'clock. Suddenly I seized Henderson by the shoulders and looked into his rather heavy, good-humored face. "My dear Henderson," I exclaimed, "I should be perfectly happy this moment if instead of walking with you I was walking here with Sophy." "I often have such thoughts," Henderson replied mildly, "b-b-b-ut I never have the nerve to express them." —Letter to Sophy Wittenberg. June 10, 1920

. . . Branford is trying to arrange a conference with Geddes and Farquharson down at New Milton next Sunday, and since I have not been invited I gather that I am to be the principal subject of discussion. [But Geddes did not come to England that summer.] Indeed Farquharson said as much. Sooner or later at any rate such a conference will be held and I shall cable you the results as soon as possible. The future of the Sociological Society, Farquharson said yesterday to Miss Loch, depends upon whether we have enough money to buy Mr. Mumford. I am glad I put my price up reasonably high and made a three years' stay the limit, because to tell the truth Sophy I don't want to be bought. If I am to get the work and study done that it is in me to do during the next three years I ought to stick to literature, pure literature, and shun anything that looks like a sufficient and lucrative job. This may mean something like a starvation diet at first; it does not *necessarily* mean that, but I am sure that it is the condition of my doing any permanently respectable work. I hate like the devil to go back to the parsimonious habit of life that I cultivated in the days of my early apprenticeship: but short of doing this I don't see any way of escaping a mechanical routine as editor, literary hack, or what not that will stunt my development during a period in which I am still capable of growing. I don't mean by this that I have any visions of living in a garret. (Of course that is where I live now!) I mean only that I shan't attempt to make more than the minimum, say twelve hundred dollars a year, [too low?] which will enable me to keep going by myself. This assumes, then, Soph, that should we live together during the next three or four years we would do so independently, except for the matter of helping each other out, like two good chums, as occasion demanded. After that I shall be prepared, I'm pretty sure (if we are agreed) to make decently heroic efforts to provide for any children you may care to have . . .   —Letter to Sophy Wittenberg. July 4, 1920

Sophy: I like you better and better each time I see the way you behave in a crisis. Your letter of June 28 wasn't an easy one to write: indeed it wasn't an easy one to read: but if you had any notion that it was going to wreck our comradeship you are damned well mistaken. I shouldn't be able to think passionately of comradeship (or love or marriage or anything else for that matter) with you if you didn't see each occasion so clearly and rise to it so bravely: you *are an equal*, Sophy, and if we never met again in our lives I should feel that somehow the whole adventure of existence was justified by my having met you. God help the rest of us if you are low and common and vulgar. I like you, Sophy, and I will be comrades with you as long as we have anything to share. I love you and I will be your mate if affection ever deepens enough between us to make our mating happy. But one or the other, as mate or comrade, I count on you: and if ever I find you falling away from our comradeship and sinking into triviality I shall jolly well up and wring your silly neck before you have the opportunity to degrade either of us . . . —Letter to Sophy Wittenberg. July 10, 1920

. . . Misunderstandings rarely arise from the things you say; they arise from what you've neglected to say. Keeping things back is a form of lying, and much more than any other form it hurts the person who does it. I'm not a pattern of heavenly virtues, goodness knows, but at any rate you've had opportunities in my letters to take peeks at moods and emotions that wouldn't always reveal themselves even in the closest daily intercourse, since they come out of the inner life and don't play about obviously on the surface. I've only had one or two peeks at your inner life: but each time I was happy and satisfied: and even though at the time you thought you were hurting me (and you were) they made me feel nearer to you and more deeply in love with you than you could have made me feel by exercising the utmost care. Like the Norseman in Chesterton's fine poem I get as much keen joy out of disdain as other people do out of their sweetheart's complaisance. You aren't distant when you explain how distant you feel, Soph: you're only genuinely distant when you don't explain it. It isn't pain that makes life unbearable but the absence of sensation: it's better to be tortured than to be ignored. —Letter to Sophy Wittenberg. September 1, 1920

. . . . I don't see why we shouldn't talk as unreservedly as is necessary about sexual matters, since if we are going to be mates (and even if we aren't) it is only by knowing the ins and outs of ourselves that we shall be able to get through life without hurting each other and everyone around us. Thank heaven you conquered your priggishness (or thank heaven the mailboat sailed on the morrow!) and didn't tear up your last letter in order to write about "politer matters." At any rate, though our letters crossed at sea, I gave you the lead last Monday, and if you hadn't had the good sense and the candor to talk about your most intimate desires you might be shocked to find out what a nonchalant scalpel I was using on your interior being.

Do you know, Soph, what the thought was that kept on sobering me and forcing me to see straight each time I read over your letter. Knowing how violent my own sexual desires are, in spite of the fact that my conduct would pass for A-1 in a Y.M.C.A. secretary, and knowing that those of a normal girl may be even deeper and more overwhelming, I wondered what chance I would have had of remaining in the state of virginity if someone had been wooing *me*. Precious little! My outward impeccability is simply a reflex of the sheltered and solitary life I've so long been leading, and though this had made deep channels of habit which in a sense "protect" me, I simply wouldn't give tuppence for the sort of chastity and purity this signifies. The only period since early adolescence when I've had any real sexual balance or health was curiously enough during my service in the Navy: the sort of monastic discipline and communal solidarity that prevailed in the barracks squeezed sex out of existence without one's even noticing it. I know that this is a different version of barracks life than that which you generally hear; but this wasn't my own experience alone; and the viciousness of barracks life, about which there is no doubt, is the product of an idleness and boredom which during our training we never had time to suffer from.

Now, Sophy, I crave a full life just as passionately as you do: half the savor has been taken out of my trip over here because I hadn't you to share it with, and half the impulse to venture and roam and explore was dissipated because it made me so irritable to have to absorb all the joy of this by myself. In postponing Geddes's offer until we at least had had the *chance* to mate I did not feel that I was giving up one career for another: it seemed to me simply that two equally desirable activities conflicted for the moment and that I was choosing to give preference, while the conflict lasted, to that which most vitally mattered. Think of all the crippled, neurotic people in the world: people who have made all manner of mess and meanness out of their lives because they would not face the facts of their sex or because they would not act in terms of their deepest desires and preferred money or security or fame or what not instead of success in life *in terms of life.*   —Letter to Sophy Wittenberg. September 10, 1920

. . . My philosophy doesn't have any place for the idea of trying to live in a Paradise where "falls not hail nor rain nor any snow, nor ever wind blows loudly." And since I object to the best of Paradises it is obvious that I detest fool's paradises most of all.   —Letter to Sophy Wittenberg. September 29, 1920

[On Sophy's birthday] . . . The usual wishes for happiness are always a little banal, because people do not know what they mean when they talk about happiness; they think it is pleasure, or comfort, or 'having all you want in the world,' and they are disappointed when they find that these things have as much capacity for producing misery as for creating anything else. When I say that I wish you happiness, I mean that I hope as you grow older you will become more intensely alive.   —Letter to Sophy Wittenberg. London, October 8, 1920

The Moral Honesty of Sophy. I vow this makes up for all the bitterness and the sadness of my part of our relationship. Last night was, I think, the most painful evening I ever spent in her company, and I have the memory of some pretty painful evenings, like the Sunday before my departure for London; and yet, with Sophy's essential frankness and decency I can bear the pain of such encounters as bravely as a soldier carries an honorable wound. There is a temptation even to prize the wound on account of the caliber of the person who inflicted it.

In some matter or other our talk had wound around to a point where, with no little reluctance, I told Sophy how the poignant cause of my unhappiness during the past couple of weeks was the thought that, in her new developments and experiments, she might drift apart from me in the same way that Beryl had drifted. (I recollect now how I came to make this confession: Sophy had said that perhaps one of the reasons for her reluctance to enter marriage was her dissatisfaction with the state of most of the family relationships she had experienced or observed.)

I pointed out that she was not being "free" by refusing to go along my road, she was simply making the choice of another kind of road; she wasn't merely escaping my set of influences. She agreed to this and said—wisely enough—that she couldn't tell what kind of person she was until she at least experimented in another direction. Her old life had not been a satisfactory one: the new one she was playing with had made her a good deal happier, and if that was the sort of nature she had she was bound to develop in that direction. "I don't think I am spoiled by admiration," she said, "but I like it and want it. I am level-headed enough and it won't make me do anything I don't want to do. I think my case is something like Lou's: I am going through a second adolescence. Perhaps I wouldn't want all these things now if I had had them when I was

66

younger. I am just inclined to let things take their course now and see how they turn out. Sometimes I hope that I won't keep going this way, that I'll return somehow to my old self. But I don't know. I was wondering whether you would understand. I had thought myself that maybe I was repeating the same course Beryl had taken and wondered whether you would see it." —RN. November 8, 1920

Were the last three months wasted? My thoughts again and again come back to that question. I cannot answer. Has my whole life been wasted? Without doubt the greater part of it has, half my potentialities undeveloped, half my opportunities missed, half my energies frittered away. The business of finding a mate, and of achieving success in life in terms of philosophy, is doubtless as important as any of the things I have missed in pursuing it; but of course this leaves unanswered the question as to whether I have found my mate, and time and chance and experiment will alone tell me that. —RN. 1920

After I have spent an evening with Sophy my sleep is filled with dreams of Beryl. What is the Freudian significance of this? Do I want to escape Sophy? Do I seek recompense for all that I missed with Beryl? Is Sophy Beryl in continuation? I find myself occasionally behaving toward Sophy the way Beryl would have liked me to behave toward her: I exaggerate politenesses and formalities and conventions which in the old days I spent most of my time in contentiously resisting. Beryl used to correct my lack of convention, Sophy slices away an overplus: both of them taming me and making me something different. —RN. 1920

In me, Athens and Corinth are perpetually at war; and the intellectual life and the sexual life dominate by turns: they have not yet been able to adjust their difficulties and live harmoniously. To achieve a "peace without victory" is my problem. —RN. 1922

5: London and LePlay House

Vague plans for travel crossed my mind as early as 1914, and as my modest inheritance drew nearer they were at first directed toward Germany. So it was my early interest in Patrick Geddes that drew my mind toward Edinburgh with the wistful notion of studying at Geddes's almost deserted Outlook Tower. This eventually brought me to England in 1920 in response to an invitation from Victor Branford, Geddes's old friend and colleague in the Sociological Society, to come over to London and become acting editor of the newly founded Sociological Review. My sending Branford my appreciative criticism in The Dial of one of Geddes and Branford's books in their 'Making of the Future' series had prompted the invitation.

Branford's plans for me did not come to fruition; but my five months spent mainly in London, meeting many lively minds of the older generation, opened up the world for me in many directions and left an imprint on the rest of my life. Except for a few articles in The Freeman, most of my on-the-spot notes were in letters to Sophy, my future wife: it is only from memory that I can tell about my lecturing on 'Reconstruction' at the Summer School of Civics in High Wycombe—my first initiation as lecturer—or my visit to Shaftesbury and Glastonbury with Branford, or my attending a Labor Conference at Scarborough, where I beheld all the bigwigs of the Labor Movement, from Ramsay MacDonald to Beatrice and Sidney Webb, and even had lunch at the home of one of the Rowntrees, those enlightened Quaker industrialists whose numbers include the Frys and the Cadburys.

ABOARD THE S.S. ADRIATIC. I have been listening to the insular chatter of three Britishers next to me who have been explaining at great length among themselves what is wrong with America and what is particularly right with the Old Country. Confound their silly prejudices: they dislike our genuine virtues! The lack of pro-per discipline. The absence of domestic affection. And so on, *ad mal de mer.* . . . Fuller, indeed, warned me about the British Islander. He emphasized particularly his shyness and reticence. Until this morning I had not discovered much of it, albeit my companions on deck and at mess, are all John Bullish in one degree or another. Yesterday a spare old gentleman, an engineer, in tweeds, with a white Vandyke and a soft meticulous voice, wasted a whole morning which I had intended to devote to sweet, silent reflection in telling me all the weaknesses and ineptitudes he had discovered in America; as for example, item one, how altogether improper it was for the Americans to depart from the elegant orthodoxy of the true mother tongue; item two, what incomprehensible perversity it was for Americans to call the letter zed a zee; item three, what bad taste it was to permit negro railway porters and waiters to greet one familiarly instead of following the genuine British fashion of making niggers mind their place and keep their distance . . .

. . . My first example of Fuller's Englishman was the radio operator. I hung around his shack for a few minutes this morning, examining his instruments and waiting for him to say a civil word. After a few minutes he looked at me. "Do you want anything?" I replied affably that I was just an old radio man who was interested in the works for old time's sake. "Aouw!" he exclaimed, and turned his back on me. I don't know whether to label this British phlegm or British impudence or British shyness: but I am sure it is British. An American would at least have explained to me that his set was the best piece of apparatus in the Mercantile Marine, and before we had been five minutes together he would have clapped his receivers over my ears to prove it. I was not tempted to stay five minutes with this frigid Britisher. (The Britishers on my left have just begun to praise the climate of the British Isles. They have proved to their satisfaction, for the fifth time, that it is incomparably superior to the American climate. Its very dampness keeps the grass from being burned away in the summertime, you know: and that is why English meadows are so green and English lanes so lovely. And so on, in large expressive spatters.) —Letter to Sophy Wittenberg. May 1920

Note: Before I sailed for England Walter Fuller, the first managing editor of The Freeman, and a Manchester man, had earnestly begged me to say to myself, each night before I went to bed: "The English don't mean to be rude; the English don't mean to be rude."

LONDON ARRIVAL. The rich grime of Waterloo Station and a high, sensible old taxi taking me deviously through Westminster to Pimlico, with glimpses of the green Embankment, the playing field of the Westminster School, the helmetted policemen with chin-straps, the black uniformed be-medalled messengers, the towers of the Abbey and the House of Parliament, till, after turning through Churton Street, with its dreary little shops, we finally halted at the headquarters of the Sociological Society, LePlay House.

In effect LePlay House was a New York brownstone with an English basement, newly done over with a coat of muddy stucco. The reek of soft coal fires, still omnipresent then, hung in the air: an odor I used to find as pleasantly haunting as the dim aroma of a skunk—when inhaled from a sufficient distance. There were two rooms to a floor, except at the top, where my narrow room allowed three: but however austere the furnishings of my cell were, it was bright and cheerful, for it faced west, and there was a glass of flowers—five narcissus and a tulip!—with a note on the mantelshelf. The young woman who had left them, Branford's part time secretary, began with that gesture a lifelong friendship. —From first draft of my Autobiography. 1956

In preparation for this immersion in London I had my early saturation in Dickens: the Dickens of 'Pickwick Papers,' 'Nicholas Nickleby,' 'Great Expectations,' and 'David Copperfield,' and not least the young Dickens, avidly picking up material in the byways and dark alleys of London for his 'Sketches by Boz.' As a member by adoption of a learned society, somewhat of an upstart among learned societies, unwilling on principle to accept the domination of the temporal authority through incorporation by royal charter, perhaps it was as well that I also had under my belt the memory of Dickens' farcical papers depicting the meeting of the 'Mudfog Association for the Advancement of Everything.' Besides Dickens, I had H. G. Wells, who was still for me the observant novelist who wrote 'Tono-Bongay' and 'The New Machiavelli'; for both those books took one close to modern London; and I was to find, in the post-war London of 1920, much of Dickens' London still left in the very heart of the city, while the suburbs along with South Kensington were much as Wells had described them. —RN. 1956

. . . When I hear the way the rest of the American Horde is rushing around, seeing this Nabob and interviewing that Sultan, I feel altogether

70

out of it: it doesn't give me the faintest pleasure to meet a big Nobody or a little Somebody and hold my head passively under a drenching of platitudes for half an hour; and I had much rather sit in the gutter and shy stones at them and stick out my tongue than have to go through the painful ritual of taking them seriously. As for the real somebodies (Old Bob Smillie for example) I feel toward them the way that Walt Whitman felt toward Lincoln: he wished that their circumstances would bring them a little closer together but he was amply content to get just a bare friendly nod from Lincoln as he passed by on horseback. I hate to go after people. If one comes upon them by accident, well and good: and if one doesn't come upon them at all, well and good also: all the richest experiences of life, from birth onward, come by chance, and if they come more deliberately they are rarely worth the pains of seizing. . . . —Letter to Sophy Wittenberg. July 20

POLICE MORALITY. One of the particularly pleasing things in a London park is the shamelessness of young lovers. In the long twilight of the summer's evening one may encounter scores of couples tenderly discovering each other, with no fear of being leered at by the passers by, for the spectacle is too common to provoke even wretches who leer, or of being rudely jostled out of their ecstasy by some dogged brute in a blue coat.

The great disability of the American policeman is that he has become a censor of morals, and in our parks and at our bathing beaches he exhibits a sense of delicacy which would make the very angels in heaven seem prurient. I hesitate to think how many arrests would be made, and incidentally, how many recalcitrant heads would be broken, were a New York policeman let loose in a London park with the instructions and moral predilections that we now operate under. At tea time in Kensington Gardens a patrol wagon would back up under the trees around the teahouse, to make away with all the ladies who were shamelessly smoking cigarettes in the open air, and on its way toward Bow Street it would doubtless stop along the banks of the Serpentine to pick up a batch of urchins that had stripped in public view and were taking an afternoon swim. (I am not quite sure whether the London County Council permits children to bathe in the Serpentine during the more exposed hours of the day; but I have seen them do so more than once; and nobody thought it worth while to protest.) Contrast this with the experience of a young lady of my acquaintance who happened to stop before the fountain in Washington Square to see some jolly and almost naked children splashing around in the water, and was told to move on by a policeman who asked her if "she didn't have no shame." —RN. 1921

71

Victor Branford and the 'Soso'

VICTOR BRANFORD. Patrick Geddes's old friend and colleague was one of the active founders of the Sociological Society in 1904. It was he who invited me to London to become editor of the Sociological Review, prompted more or less by quixotic hopes awakened by a single review I had written in The Dial of a little book he and Geddes had brought out in 1919. My association with him, in LePlay House, the Pimlico headquarters of the society, in walks around Westminster and South Kensington, and at his summer home in the New Forest served as the best possible introduction to fresh thinking about society, especially English society. Though this experiment did not fulfill Branford's hopes, since I returned to New York after less than six months, it gave me more than a traveller's entry into the British intellectual scene, for my Pimlico reached out to Bloomsbury, Westminster, and South Kensington.

When the members of the society met at intervals for dinner at the nearby Belgravia, a small but ungenial restaurant, it was certainly not the watery soup, the desiccated slices of roast beef, or the rubbery tarts that drew us there. But around this meager board I had my first opportunity to become acquainted with townplanners like Adshead and Raymond Unwin, with an old-fashioned positivist like S. H. Swinny, who could always be relied upon to say a few words at the end of any discussion to correct any neglect or disparagement of Auguste Comte, with Sir Martin White, old Geddes's sturdy friend and financial sponsor, or with Edward Westermarck, the Finnish sociologist. It was at the Sociological Society's meetings, too, that I had occasion to talk with Frederick Soddy, whose little book on 'Matter and Energy' in 1912 was one of my earliest acquisitions. (I still have it.)

Soddy was then turning from his original researches on radioactivity under Rutherford, to concern himself with the economic and social problems this new source of energy might raise. The fact that Soddy was deserting the field for which he was professionally prepared to devote himself thereafter to political and social problems was perhaps the first example—and for a long time the only one—of a long-delayed awakening by scientists to the possible social consequences of liberating atomic energy. At the time I met him in 1920, Soddy was bringing out a revised edition of his earlier treatise on atomic energy in which, now that Rutherford had split the atom, he pointed out the possibly devastating effect of this new power upon society. This fact shows that later scientists who protested in the 1940's that no one could possibly have anticipated these consequences, were speaking out of indifference or ignorance, not knowledge.

Brief though my contacts with the members of the Sociological Society then were, they played an essential role in my development in more than one field. But the deepest imprint of all was that which Victor Branford himself made upon me.

Victor Branford was a unique combination of the man of affairs and the speculative thinker, a type England has so often produced from the time of Sir Walter Raleigh and Sir Francis Bacon. By profession, he belonged to the abstemious guild of certified accountants, the medical diagnosticians, as he used to say, of business; by interest and attainment, he was a sociologist, a historian, and a philosopher; and in his character were mingled a worldly shrewdness, an ability to appraise all the mischief and madness of his fellows, with a wild devotion to threatened causes and remote ideals. He looked the Elizabethan, too: the long narrow head, the pointed beard, the trim body, the high forehead and the thin nervous lips; so it was easier to imagine him in doublet and hose than it was to accept him in the conventional top hat and morning coat of the City. This combination of aristocrat and adventurer, gentleman and scholar, which was the peculiar attribute of the Renaissance in England, was in his very marrow; and if he knew all the weaknesses of this upper-class culture, brought up, as he used to put it, in the dregs of it, he belonged by heart and manner to the Olympians.

Walking with Branford through Westminster or Oxford or the New Forest was one of the liveliest of pleasures: every stone came to life, and the very advertisements on the hoardings became pregnant commentaries upon our venal and life-starved civilization. His conversation had something his books lacked: a certain spice of worldly observation that might have become cynicism in a less generous soul, or have led to despair in a less hopeful one. He would gleefully point out some sinister exhibition of the social process, as in the combination of a bank with a religious meeting hall in the new Methodist center in Westminster, or the juxtaposition of the bust of Cecil Rhodes with the new examination buildings in Oxford, which sorted out student brains for an imperial bureaucracy: and though Branford loved Oxford, he would repeat with delight the two comments of a young girl, just fresh from Paraguay, with whom he had walked along High Street; "How beautiful these young men are!" . . . Pause. "And how stupid they look!" He delighted in ritual and all manner of beauty, from the curve of a girl's leg to the grand interior of the Roman Catholic Westminster Cathedral; but his own life was an abstemious one, and the bed that he slept on so often in his LePlay House study might have served in the penitential cell of an austere monastery. —The New Republic. August 27, 1930

BRANFORD TAKES ME TO LORD BRYCE. Today I spent the greater part of my time interviewing respectable or eminent persons. The first one was Lord Bryce. Branford and I went round to his apartment shortly after breakfast, in order to solicit his blessing for our project for an international cooperation in sociology, and we found him living in a large and seedy apartment overlooking Buckingham Palace and Green Park. The furnishings of the big room into which we were shown were mid and late Victorian: the walls were plastered with water colors and there was miscellaneous china on the mantel and rows of yellowed nineteenth century books housed in intermittent bookcases. Bryce entered: a solid-boned, athletic-looking youngster of eighty-two, with more energy in carriage and conversation than either Branford or myself. His face was curtained in white hair, and even the patch of nose which protruded from the bushy whiteness was not innocent of a number of white hair stalks which my eyes simply couldn't leave, not even when Bryce was firing questions at me with the astuteness of a lawyer in a criminal court and making me feel like a mouse trying to get away from the paw of a very resolute and dexterous cat. I found that he knew 'Harvey Robinson,' and that this was safe ground: but he also liked 'Murray Butler,' and *that* was dangerous ground. Also, like a good British Islander, he was suspicious of theories and formulae, and as a good Victorian, he thought sociology had something to do with slum expeditions. I felt that there were enormous gulfs between us, in spite of his sprightly way of carrying his eighty-two years, and I perceived that the fact that he knew Harold Laski, who corresponded with him, did not so much bring him nearer to me as put Laski further away. For all that, of course, he was a man of great sageness and discernment, with an experience and record of scholarship that are both to be envied. In other words, he blessed our project. . . . —Letter to Sophy Wittenberg. July 21, 1920

Our morning breakfasts at nine in the little back room on the ground floor of LePlay House with its musty Victorian furniture—originally an office or a music room, I suppose—remain quite as vivid as my evening talks with Victor Branford. Coffee and cigarettes with him, later with Alexander Farquharson as a third participant, had a savor I can never recall without a nostalgic pang. If only I had been apt enough to transcribe Branford's Table Talk! Some of his observations were as astute as Martin Luther's, but out of them all I remember only one conversation.

We somehow had started talking about Egypt and began speculating on all that Flinders Petrie and his colleagues had discovered about that still enigmatic civilization. "By Jove," Branford exclaimed: "that would be a fine place to spend a winter's vacation; it's strange one hasn't thought of looking around there before." At that moment Farquharson, the sharp-witted Scot whom Branford had taken on when he saw that I would not remain as editor, shook with silent but irrepressible mirth. When at last he found breath he said admiringly: "There, my dear Branford, is the difference between us! When you think of Egypt, you think immediately of seeing for yourself; whereas, while you were talking, I was saying to myself—you see the effects of my Scot's education!—how nice it would be to spend a whole winter at the British Museum *reading* about Egypt." Yes, that was the difference, though Branford, once he started on his surveys, never forgot that records and documents and books, to say nothing of studious meditation, would often bring to light much that does not immediately meet the eye. —Fragment from my Autobiography. 1963

YESTERDAY AFTERNOON IN WESTMINSTER ABBEY. The Housing Congress delegates had a section allotted them and I knew that I would feel a little less like a lost sheep that had accidentally strayed into the fold if I sat among them. It was ten years since I had been inside a religious edifice: good Lord! ten years. I must have been about fifteen then, I remember, and I had abandoned all devout observances for a whole year, and I was lured into the house of God not out of piety but out of a pathetic desire to be in Beryl's company. She used to entice young men into church with her every Sunday; she liked the atmosphere of it and said it was better than tramping around the streets on a cold Sunday afternoon, but that was the first and last time that she inveigled me into the thickets of religious orthodoxy. And I remember going back with her to the dingy little apartment in which she and her mother lived on Eighth Avenue and 113 Street, and reading her one of my first short stories, the very first, I think, that was based on my own experience of life. Ten years! What have I learned in the interval? Many things, no doubt; some beyond anticipation. What equipment I had I've developed to perhaps sixty per-cent efficiency, and as far as observation goes this is a relatively high level. Where I've failed vitally is in this: that I haven't been able to add a single element to my equipment. Hence my disastrous ineptitude as an animal; hence my lack of a mate. Beryl admired me and respected me, I know: she said so repeatedly and for once I could believe her. Damn you, Soph, I suppose you admire and respect me too—but am I a piece of statuary? Hath not a man ears, eyes, nose, dimensions? —Letter to Sophy Wittenberg. June 7, 1920

COFFEE WITH A. R. ORAGE. The afternoon was sacred to the presence and person of Orage, the editor of The New Age. After a search for the passageway that leads to his office, and an interview with a young man lodged therein who welcomed me with true British effusiveness (irony) I found Orage seated with another man in the cellar of the Kardomah Cafe, a coffee house in which real coffee is served at tuppence a cup. Major Douglas came in later, and a couple of other Americans; and I listened for three hours to a steady stream of conversation from Orage and Douglas, three quarters of which was a dull and frequently metaphysical discussion of the social credit proposals which The New Age is fostering and the remainder of which was the weirdest nonsense (coming from Orage) on the world contest now taking place between the bureaucracy of Jesuitism, acting through the League of Nations, and the financial manipulations of the Jews, acting through the banking system. Orage spoke of this as the two party system in world politics, and he intimated that the general election which should decide the issue between the two parties was still being held. If Orage were alone in uttering his gibberish I should have promptly sent for a padded ambulance at the first outbreak: but this sort of thing is as virulent here as spiritualism and theosophy and astrology, and the contagion has spread through the whole community. . . . —Letter to Sophy Wittenberg. June 1920

A WALK IN THE CHILTERNS. Yesterday was a sad disappointing day for most British Islanders: a holiday drenched in rain. But the weather couldn't take the edge off the appetite for life which this amazingly lovely little town stimulates in me five minutes after I've set foot in it. It rained buckets all through the afternoon, but for all that I set out for a tramp around five o'clock with a new acquaintance I had struck up slowly during the past week at High Wycombe, a highly reputed old dog of a London surgeon named Parker. . . . Parker proved to be a remarkable specimen of the best sort of Briton. Shrewd, kindly, rational, good-humored. He is about the finest that his country and his profession can offer. He embodies a type: the radical doctor, the same sort of doctor that Meredith pictures in 'Beauchamp's Career.' He is intimate with the local trade union leaders, is a secretary of the local branch of the Workers Educational Association, publicly advocates the establishment of a Preventive Public Health Service (to the consternation of his colleagues on Harley Street) and spends his evenings and holidays as a quiet, unpretentious citizen in an unfashionable little town. He traces his ancestors back on his father's side to the keeper of one of the King's parks in the early Middle Ages, and he has a fund of interesting stories to tell about some of them. One, for example, was a New England colonist, and as a youth led a rebellion in Harvard College against the faculty in the days before that institution was called Harvard. Another, who lived in the early eighteenth century, was a woman who had married a drunken husband and who bequeathed to posterity a remarkably minute and faithful picture of her times, embalmed in a diary. Parker told me some of the things she recorded. As for example, in illustration of the hygienic standard of the time, this: "My dear son Robert is going to be married tomorrow, and this evening, in preparation, he bathed his whole body." Apparently the only time a bath was thought necessary was immediately after birth and immediately before marriage. . . . —Letter to Sophy Wittenberg. August 5, 1920

Blake and Turner

THE TATE GALLERY IN WESTMINSTER is no longer host to the red tape-worm from Whitehall that settled in its entrails during the war. It is now possible for the visitor in London to leave the rumbling lorries on Mill-bank Road, to turn his back to the red-winged barges that lie like clumsy water birds on the Thames, to forget the fustian ugliness of the pottery works across the river in Lambeth, and to immerse himself in the stream of art that flowed onwards from Reynolds and Wilson to Blake, Turner, the Pre-Raphaelites and their issue. In such a retrospect it is important not to get the social and the esthetic characteristics of a period mixed up.

The tendency of a school of art, on the other hand, a tendency frequently shared by people who are not conscious of their place in that school, becomes wellnigh meaningless when lifted out of its social context, and the habit of judging the works of schools purely by an esthetic criterion, leads to the opposite kind of error. It is easy enough, for example, to demolish the Pre-Raphaelites by bombarding them with the canons of the Post-Impressionists: but why should anyone take the trouble? It is quite as fair for some lingering Pre-Raphaelite to point out that the art-for-art's-sake of the modernists is a mechanical result of the specialization in tasks which is enforced by the machine process and which has been accompanied by the breaking up of our spiritual life into distinct and unrelated compartments labelled Work, Thought, Art, and so forth; whilst the Personalism which has more recently come to the front can be socially interpreted, in the same way, as an attempt to compensate for the indignities, denials and repressions to which in these modern times the human personality is exposed. . . .

Through the morass of Victorian painting there ran a clear stream of true art, the work of water-colorists like DeWint and Cotman; and above the swamp of fashionable work, fit for Belgravia drawing rooms, there drifted across the sky, like streamers of Northern Lights, the solitary brilliance of Turner and Blake.

Men like Turner and Blake, it is needless to say, make all the academic canons look silly. The bare suggestion of a sketch like that of Blake's Dante in the 'Empyrean Drinking from a River of Light' is worth a whole studio cupboard of finished essays. Blake defies the Academicians by constructing a human anatomy of his own; he scoffs at the art-for-art's-sakers by making every picture point a moral or adorn a tale; and he outrages the picture buyer by hurling visions on his paper that would make the most excited after-dinner chatter seem more than usually vapid—and in spite of all these high crimes and misdemeanors he holds a place in British art today which no passing trick of craft can unsettle or reduce in importance.

The art of Turner is just as remote from conventional standards. He began as a workmanlike painter who followed the classic fashion and sought to give value for money promised or received. With sober regard for his standing as a craftsman, Turner never got over the habit of giving his pictures a homely, attractive title; and even when, about 1830, he entered the second stage of his career and devoted himself chiefly to experiments in pure light, he clung to the bit of descriptive nomenclature which kept him anchored to the external world. 'Sunrise Between Headlands,' and 'Norham Castle, Sunrise,' are identical but for a slight difference in the spotting of blue and yellow masses, and in spite of the quaintly prosaic titles it is plain that both pictures were meant only to express the transfiguring wonder of light. No one apparently has ever taken so much pleasure as Turner in putting the effects of light on canvas; he was the solitary pupil of his own school and the tradition he created was not carried on until Whistler discovered in fogs and twilights the ecstasy that Turner found in radiance.   —The Freeman. September 22, 1920

A VERY ROYAL ACADEMY.   Just before tea time every day the Summer Exhibition of the British Royal Academy at Burlington House is thronged with visitors. The scene is impressive by contrast with the American Academy's display. The primary distinction between the official art of the two countries lies in the fact that in America it is only the opening which can be called in newspaper slang a social event, whereas the whole season at Burlington House preserves a titillation of popular interest. This does not mean, I hasten to add, that there is a higher level of esthetic appreciation in England. Apart from the small independent exhibitions, and the folk who welcome and understand the work of the independents, the state of the fine arts in this island seems to be appreciably lower than in America. Esthetics have simply nothing to do with the popularity of Burlington House. The British Academy is at bottom a delicate social barometer.

A tour of Burlington House gives happy evidence that the British Empire is back on the old stand of business as usual. There was a period during the war when we were assured that this relapse into the slovenly habits of the Victorian peace was impossible. With a little pain one may recall the time when the world was so uncalloused to murder and starvation as to think that the war must inevitably compensate its filthy necessities by effecting splendid social transformations. We were assured on every side that the world could never, never be the same again. Society was going to be—oh! so different, and in anticipation of this happy issue the young imperialists of the Round Table school began to talk with sanguine rationality about the future of the British Commonwealth.

The British Academy of 1920 has a different story to tell. The war is over, and the war itself intrudes in the galleries with just a few pictures of audacious puerility. The dominant feature of the exhibition is a monster portrait of their Royal Majesties, attended by a couple of clerical dignitaries. The subjects indicate by their modest and affable pose, and the help of a few corroborative words kindly limned by the artist, that the success of British arms had been achieved not by their Majesties—as had been fondly supposed—but by God. As a painting this particular achievement is a masterpiece of ineptitude; but more serious interest attaches to the fact that it is shown without the faintest note of dubiety or apology. A community which had achieved an esthetic revolution would no doubt have kept such a picture from being painted: but a State that was on the verge of a social revolution would, in order to reduce the provocation to riot, keep this massive tablet from ever being hung. The mere presence of this picture is profoundly relevant to the political observer, for it gives the mood of the whole exhibition and demonstrates what its visitors are thinking. Other countries have been raked by war and riddled by famine; other countries have lost territories, principalities, and potentates; other countries have slowly subsided into a condition of barbarism. In the British Islands nothing has changed but the prices. Hard by Burlington House, in Trafalgar Square, the veteran beggars, and the beggared veterans, swarm as thickly as ever they did in the post-African War days. The world has been made a little safer for bureaucracy. —The Freeman. June 16, 1920

One of the lasting benefits I owe to our sociological gatherings at LePlay House came through the opportunity to meet Edward Westermarck, the anthropologist who wrote what was in its day the classic 'History of Human Marriage.' This bluff, genial Finn, with none of the usual English reserves, promptly invited me to lunch with him at his favorite little restaurant in New Oxford Street, whose cellar pleased him; and in the course of our luncheon he drew his own conclusions about my life. At that period I was wrestling with all the slippery possibilities that my own sexual urges and my desire to live with Sophia had conjured up. Every time I lingered for a few furtive moments before the window display of a contraceptive shop—vaginal syringes, condoms, the works of Aristotle and Paul de Koch!—or caught the eye of a pretty girl pausing to scan the street before she entered her door, my heart beat quicker. Westermarck must have sensed what was going on beneath the surface of his young guest: and I am sure it was not by accident that he called my attention to a new book by Dr. Marie Stopes, 'Married Love,' one of the first to dwell in some detail on the choice of contraceptives and the desirability of simultaneous orgasms—though on the latter subject her advice was all too delicately allusive and reserved. As a result of our talk, I went back to America equipped, theoretically, for any possible erotic encounter, though I was far from equipped for an actual one, and even less for the give-and-take of marriage itself in all its baffling complexities. Doubtless I might have profited more from reading Ovid rather than Marie Stopes; but I am still grateful for Westermarck's shrewd and kindly insight. —Note for Autobiography. 1964

BACK IN MANHATTAN. I wish I could trust this deceitful brain of mine to store up accurately all the impressions I have been receiving during the last six months. That of Jacques Loeb, a benign, sallow-faced German, in a long frock coat, in his study at the Rockefeller Institute overlooking the East River one late afternoon in January, and his mingled arrogance and sweetness. The gaping forehead and distorted mouth of Franz Boas in a room looking north from the School of Journalism over the campus; the bulging eye that seemed to focus upon one like a magnifying glass. Albert Jay Nock, at lunch with me in the Lafayette; an averted profile with a hand playing uneasily over his teeth. Walter Fuller, bursting into the Old Chelsea tearoom, expressing beatification and apologies in words that ran together like drops of mercury. Clarence Britten and I, very assured, very quiet, very genial, very sophisticated, in the dining room of the Hotel Seymour; good napery and silver, excellent service, serenity; and a long walk through Central Park with the moonlight shining over the snowy meadows and frosted trees, Clarence limping a little and answering my questions about Chicago. With Robby [Geroid Robinson] in a cafeteria near Columbia, batting the world back and forth between us to the clatter of unseemly crockery and the vapid suggestions of lukewarm tea. The fortnightly gatherings in Harold Stearns's basement room, with Jesus Christ [Ernest Boyd] in a brown suit and baritone voice talking atheism above the whispers of this or that clique. Around Washington Square with Sophy—but Sophy is worth a whole note for herself, and even then I shan't recapture all the separate impressions that keep on drifting into composites. —RN. 1921

6: The Maze of Marriage

No small part of this chronicle is concerned with married love: its expectations, its immediate rewards, its impediments, its deep fulfillments, its tensions, its extra-marital threats or ruptures, its renewals, its ultimate blessings. Sexually liberated though our generation was, both Sophia and I still firmly believed in marriage; but at the beginning she and I were both unsure, for somewhat different reasons, about our marriage. I was concerned over the effect this commitment might have on my work, both immediately and when we should have children; while Sophia felt uneasy during the early years lest my jealous notions of marital sexual loyalty should keep her, if occasion arose, from exploring sex with a more rewarding lover, before she settled down for good. She perhaps feared, not without reason I admit, that even a single brief encounter might cause us to break apart for good. A later chapter on 'Amor Threatening' will present life's ironic resolution of this problem; but the underlying reality of such a union as ours is beyond telling, even were it rounded out with an equally searching self-inquisition by Sophia. So the last word on our marriage must be left to the calendar! We have lived together in sickness and health, in sorrow and in joy, in delight and despair and sudden ecstasy for over half a century. And though we know love in both its heights and its depths, it is from the heights at the end of our lives that we now dare to behold it.

Dear Madame: I don't think you had better come up. School opened today in earnest, and I find that I have fallen in love with at least five young ladies, varying in age from eight to fifteen: so what chance have you against this battery, this galaxy, this harem? . . . There is at least one of these witches in each class, and there are four classes, so that you can see how terribly complex life has become for me. I resolved to cut my dilemma by asking Mrs. Johnson about your coming up; so this afternoon, on our way home from a visit to the Colums—I had broken the ice a couple of days ago by telling her I was married—I said you were green with envy (you are, old darling?) and asked if I could arrange for your visit; and she replied: "Why yes!" and also "Certainly," and likewise "At any time," and she said this in such a cordial and matter-of-course manner that I felt relieved from some nameless anxiety. I have no injunctions with respect to your visit except that you must be sure to wear your wedding ring on the correct finger and remember that one is not to discuss art, religion, science, philosophy or morals with the instructor in science, Brother Wilson. I only await the announcement of the month and day of your coming. That's that; and I am glad it *is* that. —Letter to Sophy Wittenberg. Peterboro, N.H. July 5, 1921

You will remember Sophy as the beautiful dark-haired secretary who used to have the adjacent office to mine at The Dial, and by a deliberate act of the imagination you will try to conceive a young female person who is my opposite in almost every quality: musical where I am deaf, slow where I am quick, hard where I am soft, and yet beneath all these antitheses genial and sympathetic. —Letter to J.L. May 1920

. . . It isn't our senses of humor that are so far apart; it is our taste in literary style: you incline to understatement and I to emphasis, and I am always expecting you to thump the drum and blow the trombone the way I do—*because I am I*—while you doubtless dislike the fact that I don't give any chance to the piccolo and the clarinet, and when the big moments come can only go on pounding and blowing and making a beastly noise. For you to begin a letter with "Dear" is enough to throw me into raptures, whereas when I want to express in this letter more than I have expressed in any others, and there is a geyser of emotion swirling around inside of me, I find myself without a vocabulary. So in the end you have the advantage. . . . —Letter to Sophy Wittenberg. July 8, 1921

Damndest Darling: When the rain lifted this morning I plowed up and down the roads to Peterboro at a rate something better than four miles an hour—for I reached there in fifty minutes—so eager was I to glimpse a word from you, since I had heard from nobody the whole week. Eight letters were waiting for me, and your letter was among them. I walked back along Main Street to a little park alongside a waterfall, and as soon as I had read your letter, written (I "charitably" understand) in the office, I fell to cursing with such vigor that the air got blue around me and I had to let up for fear that it would rain again: I swore at you, darlint, and at your ancestors, and at The Dial, and at the Brevoort, and at all the other places and people that unaccountably intervened between me and you and caused you to write the deadliest of duty notes. Only my anticipation of the look of sad reproach on Jones's [the butler's] face if I had not returned for dinner kept me from jumping immediately into the Deadly Mill-race and shuffling off this immorkle coil. (Dear Jones: tiny hands will live to smile sweetly and whisper with grateful eyes thy simple name.) —Letter to Sophy Wittenberg. July 2, 1921

The great drawback of this idyllic little school is that I, in the midst of all these physical delights, am mentally quite alone. I discovered that tonight as we sat in the twilight on the porch and continued a dinner table conversation about religion. The Johnsons, as becomes the owners of Heartbreak House, do not take religion seriously: but all the rest of the instructors do, and religion for them is but a symbol for a hundred other conventionalities and inhibitions, so that I have to keep a close guard on my wayward tongue, lest they discover that I am seditious, anarchistic, and so forth and so forth, and cast me out from their midst or—which would be worse—attempt tediously to convert me to their intellectual solecisms. I am so used to the company of a nice, sophisticated heathen like you, Soph, that I had forgotten that there is a world in which people go to church, believe in the efficacy of prayer, think the Greeks wicked, worship the American flag, and in short behave in their sanctimonious way like the very devil. Now I know better, however, and—"Oh, the difference to me!" —Letter to Sophy Wittenberg. July 3, 1921

END OF A CLOUDED PRE-MARITAL HONEYMOON. Dearest: The beginning of melancholy days! Back again in a lonesome room. An empty bed. No flimsy, silken things lying sleekly around. A stiff, starchy, monastic air over everything: the typewriter my only temptation and work my only amusement. That is what you left behind you, dear and beloved hussy. I wonder if your day yesterday began like mine in a drowsy solitude, and gradually stretched and yawned and pulled until at about five o'clock in the afternoon, up at Colum's *new* hut, with Max Bodenheim and Padraic and Hervey Allen, poets all—seated in a circle, it found itself at length wide awake. An evening back again on the hill, which now reminds me of nothing so much as an old-fashioned stage setting for heaven at the

Metropolitan Opera House, and which, now that the demon-angel-vampire has run away, is as monotonous as only painted canvas and fake foliage can be. Morning. Alone. No heavy-lidded eyes to greet me with a teasing smile; no breasts to fondle. An unrumpled white spread to glare cool virginities at me . . . Oh hell! —Letter to Sophy Wittenberg. July 25, 1921

. . . Well was it said that a man's worst enemies shall be those of his own household. It is just like you and Jerry to decide that I am a sociologist, and not one of the fifty-seven other things that I want to be. So Leonardo's friends all doubtless used to say that he had the bent and the skill of an engineer and a geologist, but as for painting pictures . . . ! I think what I object to most of all is not the epithet sociologist but the use of it as a means of pigeonholing me and duly separating me from that holy circle of Larpoorlarers that swing about The Dial. (Can't the lad conceal his envy? He exposes it most vulgarly.) I insist that I am not so far from being the artist as they are distant from being fully developed and completely sentient men. It is only an illusion to think that you increase a person's artistic capacities by limiting the rest of his life; what happens is simply ocular magnification. . . . —Letter to Sophy Wittenberg. July 25, 1921

SOPHY AND I. The paradox in our relations is this: except for a short flurry or two, Sophy has never been deeply in love with me, and yet the chief thing that holds us together and makes our intercourse significant and gives us both high moments of satisfaction is our sexual comradeship. So the stability of our relationship rests upon a passion which, though it sometimes runs swiftly, has never thoroughly irrigated every part of Sophy's being.

My dreams and Sophy's dreams, it appears from a talk we had the other night, are complementary: mine are anxiety dreams which picture her flouting me and leaving me; hers are wish dreams which begin with dissatisfaction and misery and end with her flight to some other partner. When this discovery hit me full in the face my equilibrium was upset for twenty-four hours. By themselves those dreams would be bad enough; but since they are accompanied, on Sophy's part, with a decided preference for other people's company—which, for example, expresses itself in a fit of 'contrariness' or sullenness when we go out on a pleasure jaunt to the theater—they make me decidedly uneasy about the future. If I don't capture Sophy, someone else will; and so far I have not captured all of

Sophy—at best I have made fragmentary conquests, and soon enough lose my grip on these. —R.N. January 23, 1922

I LOVE LEWIS MUMFORD

The above declaration typed in capitals is Sophy's, and it expresses a mood—a very intense mood—that has prevailed more or less during the past fortnight, and especially during the last few days. Is it the spring and the absence of physical anxieties and a sudden flare of sympathy that has given us both the feeling that our comradeship is a real and abiding thing? If we had felt this way in January we should now be starting for Europe; at present we content ourselves with being on the way to Elysium. Sophy's eyes dance continually and—oh, but what's the use of talking about it. Sophy summed it up when she said: Thank heaven we didn't part when everything seemed so black. In the midst of our embrace the other night she said with delight: You *have* conquered me. —RN. April 8, 1922

. . . Dr. Schapiro's letter today pleased me because he sees in me something that everybody else neglects and affronts and hoity-toitily passes by, to my great chagrin. But as Carlyle says, with a single adherent to one's beliefs one can hold one's own against the world, and so the world, including you, dearie, had better beware. What Schapiro said was this: "I think you were wise in not specializing in any field. If you had done so, you would today be active as head of a Bronx League of Progressive Citizens, agitating for a new sewer system. Given your temperament and your abilities"—mark this, O best beloved—"given your temperament and your abilities, the only thing that you should specialize in is beauty." But, Lewis, you *are* a sociologist! . . .

SILENCE Woman! Hereafter I pray that you consider me as much a devotee of what Irwin Granich used to call Larpoorlar as any damned Dial critic. As for specializing in beauty, have I not been doing that the last two years, and is not the upshot of it that we are mated? I take back the first sentence, or rather, the second, in this paragraph, down to critic. Larpoorlar be switched. I have specialized in the art of being alive, and 'art' is only one of the manifestations of life, and all the other things that the Larpoorlarers neglect in their cribbed and cabined estheticism are just as fascinating and exciting, in their own fashion, as the things that the sociologists, and their ilk, neglect. The result of this attitude is, of course, that I am an Ishmael in both camps, and am about as popular as a corpse that has lain too long in no man's land between the trenches. —Letter to Sophy Wittenberg. August 4, 1921

. . . Dinner at Robbie's last night. Helen Marot was there, and an anonymous girl, and we discussed mother complexes and the significance of prostitution and the infantilism of the human race in a manner which, I am afraid, made Robbie and Clemens, bland hosts though they were, a little irritated. Helen resents the way in which many men treat their wives as mothers, and then run away to find their sweethearts in other women, all the while protesting that they love their wives dearly and irrevocably; and she wants women to stop permitting their maternal instinct to get the better of them and so undermine their love relationships. In fact, she wants me to write a play about the theme: she says it is what every woman ought to know. Helen's leading idea now is that people must make a conscious attempt to control their relationships; they must learn to thrash out their difficulties in conference, instead of attempting to make an individual one-sided adjustment . . . We talked about jealousy, too, and I asked Helen how the devil we were going to get rid of that. She said that it rested on misunderstanding, and that one must tackle it from that point of view. I protested; because I have found that jealousy is a curiously physical phenomenon which operates in the very teeth of knowledge and reason; and when I began to describe the boiling inside and the thumping of one's heart and the red curtain that falls in front of one's eyes, she was moved to cry, "Enough," for she knew the experience herself. —Letter to Sophy Wittenberg. April 25, 1921

How far this generation has travelled from the dirty prudery of the last century. Sophy was telling me about an operation that one of her friends had undergone and she said that the surgeons feared at first that the ovaries had been infected. Twenty years ago Sophy's prototype would have had the sense of having committed an awful shocker to have mentioned even the ovaries of a fish in a conversation with a young man, and fifty years ago Sophy probably would not have known that ovaries existed. The world is moving along very nicely thank you: we shall soon be so healthy minded and so unrepressed then that we will look back to the age of smut with the sort of bewilderment with which a New York City plumber would greet a Constantinople latrine. What the devil will happen to the risky farce when that day arrives? What will happen to the underdrawer school of humor? [P.S. 1974. We know now!] —RN. 1921

Belated Confession. How profoundly my views of sexual relations have changed during the last year—not that my conduct has been altered very greatly—and yet I have scarcely written a line which would show the gap between my confident and dogmatic earlier self and the quizzical person who is now in the saddle. For the last year Sophy has been the most profound influence in my life—and has shaken and twisted me to the very foundations—and yet no one who read my notes on our relation would begin to suspect what she has meant.   —RN. April 1, 1921

Tonight, our housewarming. Two rooms that defy the northern exposure with warm browns, yellows, and dull oranges; and on the edge of these hospitable chambers, like the tattered edge of a modern city, are the kitchen, bathroom, and storeroom. The minima of creature comforts are scattered about, and as one looks about the rooms one sees the modern equivalent, in a vile and dilapidated tenement, of the earlier beauties of medieval architecture and decoration. It is the best that we could do with our means; and the best is not so bad; indeed it is much to my liking, for I relish the stripped clean, athletic style and the sort of life that goes with it. I hate luxury, not because I am tempted by it, but because it tempts other people out of my society. . . . Tonight, I say, our housewarming. How long will the fires stay lighted? Who knows? Will I get burned? Yes. Will it be worth it? Yes. What of the wound? Where the blood flows there is life.   —RN. October 27, 1921

Last night we were tired and wan and solemn. We discussed the aches and futilities of married life, and Sophy wept—a little. There were moments when she thought that some of our difficulties were due to shallownesses in her, to shallownesses which her more enjoyable contacts with other men during the last couple of years had emphasized. Still, she wanted something more than frivolity, and realized that frivolity alone would leave her quite as cold and dissatisfied as her present life. We were tender and sympathetic; we were very sorry for each other; and in the realization of all the gaps that lay between us we felt oddly drawn together and at one.   —RN. February 6, 1922

. . . Sophy and I are the talk of the ship. The gossips are speculating eagerly—one of our acquaintances tells us—as to whether or not we are married; we seem to enjoy each other's company too much to be regularly and properly joined, unless we were on our honeymoon—and we have loudly and resolutely denounced that notion. It's great fun. One spinster, a Y.M.C.A. worker, who was reading 'Civilization in the United States,' and when told that I had written the chapter on The City, refused to believe it. She said she was sure I was a Greenwich Village poet or a futurist painter and wouldn't possibly be interested in cities!"   —Letter to my mother, Elvina C. Mumford. 30 July 1922

88

MARITAL RECKONINGS. I have been weighing from time to time the last few days how much marriage has tied me down and how much it has released me; and I see clearly that it has done both in great measure; but, on the whole, it has permitted me to do more work than I had ever been able to do before; so that, by marriage, I have gained a little and lost nothing, in the final balance. This is a crude calculation, of course; for one marries, as one comes into the world, because one must; because, given oneself and the dear other self that fate brings within hailing distance, the desire for more or less permanent association and intercourse scores itself on every fibre of one's being.

Our first year and our second year have been as different as if they were transmigrations into another world or metamorphoses into another kind of being. During the first year we were inexperienced, blind, unimaginative, cruel; and I myself added to all these quarrels and dissidences by being evilly jealous and by being perpetually stimulated to jealousy, partly by the rivalry of other people and partly by my own sense of incapacity. During this second year I've acquired a little skill in the art of love, and a very firm and decided sense of capacity; so all my old fears and frustrations and self-reproaches have vanished; and for this reason our relations have been much more easy and intimate, and, in every sense of the word, broad; and at quite frequent times they reach the very pitch of sensuous ecstasy and love.

With this has gone a larger measure of kindliness and understanding on both our parts. . . . We had a vast and almost overwhelming breach last January, when the earth seemed in travail and the streets seemed to tremble and gape beneath our feet; but after lasting a fortnight it vanished as quickly as it came, and except for very short periods of coldness, indifference, or boredom our life together has been a smooth sailing under a steady wind, always within hailing distance of each other, if not actually beam to beam.

Our circle of acquaintances is a little narrow; and chance and decision have to some extent cut Sophy off from old acquaintances and new rivals, so that I really do not know whether my serenity and lack of foreboding is due to the firmness of my mind and our relations, or to the infirmness of Sophy's other relations; and if Sophy should be drawn toward someone else it may be that we should find ourselves roasting and sputtering on the fires of a new little hell. The disintegration and frustration that oppressed me so keenly last year have almost completely vanished; I have a sense of a personal life which does not depend upon the success or failure of my relations with Sophy; and although a break with Sophy would cause a terrible wound, I have a feeling that this time it would not be a septic one, for there would not be an inferiority complex to fester in it, beyond the mild one of having another person preferred to oneself, and this would have its antidote in my easy conviction now of being able to attract and conquer someone else! Now that the basis of our relations seems pretty well settled, now that there are no deep undercurrents of resentment and antagonism, we shall each of us, perhaps, be able to develop a fuller sense of individuality without the constant fear of breaking the tenuous thread of hope that once upon a time was all that held us together.   —RN. June 1923

Love's Paradoxes (After Blake)

When lovers quarrel they agree
With a new sincerity.
When lovers fret and lovers doubt
They keep belief from going out.
When lovers are agrieved and mourn
A Hope and Joy are being born:
When lovers part they meet again
Doubly one because they're twain.

—Geneva, August 1925

To Sophy, Expectant

I loved the wild and virgin stalk
That flung its youth against the sky
In arrows of unflinching green
Whose leaves were banners held on high.

I loved the all-revealing flower
That opened wide the perfumed lips
Between whose dizzy velvet walls
The amorous bee not vainly slips.

In stalk and flower was delight:
Yet more, my love, they are to me
Now that the ripening seed will fall
To make love's happy Trinity.

—Lewis, Christmas 1924

Vain Journeys

Why should I go travel?
Adventure lies at home:
My sweetheart is the planet
Whose surface I would roam.
She is the tangled forest
Where buried cities lie:
She is the starlit cranny
Where only eagles pry.
And when I climb her mountains
Or wander on her plain
I discover wonders
Unknown on land or main.
Her eyes are pools far deeper
Than any Alpine lake
Within her jungle balsam grows
To cure a lover's ache.
Her temple holds a secret
Not found in Thibet tome—
Why should I go travel?
Adventure lies at home.

              —Parc de Mon Repos, Geneva,
                 September 3, 1925

7: Geneva Openings

My visit to Geneva came about through Van Wyck Brooks's recommending me as a lecturer for Alfred Zimmern's newly inaugurated Summer School of International Studies in Geneva in 1925. Brooks had become friends with Zimmern in the brief post-graduate period when he sampled Grub Street in London and taught a group in the new Workers Educational League. The opportunity to work with Zimmern and to meet some of the pick of educated European youth, from France, Sweden, Germany, Poland, Czecho-Slovakia, came at a favorable moment in my own still unsettled career; and the lectures I gave laid the basis for my more original interpretations in 'The Golden Day.' Despite Zimmern's eagerness to have me back, no funds were available until 1929, when he invited me to stay for a week en famille at the Maison Necker, an historic building he had rented at number 10 Rue Jean Calvin, on a hillside of the old medieval city.

During the next twenty years, though we met infrequently, Zimmern's insight into my work deepened our friendly ties, as Victor Branford's encouragement had done at an earlier moment. In September 1940 he wrote me: "You say in 'Men Must Act' that you hold that 'total personality is involved in every situation.' That belief or attribute has enabled you to put the quintessence of specialized knowledge and observation from a dozen or more fields into every page." It was Zimmern's respect for the total personality that had led to his own break with the prudent conventions of academic scholarship—though his early classic study 'The Greek Commonwealth' was both a product of that scholarship and a bold departure from it.

PRELUDE TO GENEVA LECTURES: 1925. . . . Zimmern happily reduced the course to six lectures; so as it now stands, the first lecture will deal with the background of American culture, on which I have nothing to add to the familiar criticism, except a more detailed analysis of the breakdown of Europe. The next two lectures deal with American literature; and on looking over my first draft I am a little frightened at the fact that one is tempted to read a mission into, to give a special logical function to, our literature as a whole, which only a very few writers, perhaps only Whitman, can claim. The other danger that comes from dealing with literature before a foreign audience is that one is tempted to emphasize the importance of writers who deal with patently American themes, and to neglect those who don't fit so well in the general picture; whereas we've always had our Poes and our T. S. Eliots, who, whatever their faults and neuroses, have had as much significance as the Landors and Baudelaires in Europe.

Then comes a lecture on philosophy: its only particular virtue is that it treats John Dewey and Santayana at the same time, and indicates that something like a living synthesis of their philosophies would, for the first time perhaps, embrace the values of science and of humanism. In formulating the first lecture I found myself enormously helped by Santayana; and I think it's a mistake to consider the pragmatists the sole spokesmen of the American spirit. This lecture almost looks to me as if it might have the germs of that book you suggested to me three or four years ago; but I shan't be able to tell until I'm a little more deeply saturated in it. The fifth lecture is in some ways the hardest; for it is on architecture, and it demands that I think freshly on a subject on which I've already, I think, been writing far too extensively, in proportion to my knowledge and preoccupations; but somehow, perhaps, I shall manage it; for I find, consolingly, that my standards in architecture and literature are one, so that the good life that hovers in the background has, at all events, a unity of interior and exterior. I come now to the sixth lecture; which is to deal with the prospects of American culture, with the criticism and appraisal of the last generation, and with such relevant issues as I myself can muster out of the void and make real; at present this lecture remains the sketchiest and most uncertain of the whole lot, and I can only hope that the holy spirit will descend upon me and enlighten me before I step on the platform in Geneva . . . —Letter to Van Wyck Brooks. July 22, 1925

EN ROUTE TO GENEVA. . . . I have for neighbor on deck a horny yellow faced man, who plainly has a large and excessively active, or inactive (which is it?) liver; he is accompanied by a yellow haired harridan who is his wife, and her sister; and in his company I become banal and youthfully cynical, and speak evil of the medical profession, of dentists, of prohibitionists, of bootleggers, of women, of the current food, and am aware that the world has very little goodness or virtue in it. He has already tested my sophistication by remarking that the fat woman, who was practicing her voice in the library, had "got the clap," when she was applauded by her kindly neighbors; and I replied to this with a leering right eye, to show how thoroughly I had assimilated this fine piece of wit; but fortunately, when he is not occupied with his women, I am with Tristram Shandy, and so I manage to escape some of his doubtless finer repartee, and may even, someday, be able to turn out two or three real good smutty jokes of my own. Yes: and there is a blowsy Englishwoman with black hair who looks as if she had stepped out of a Belcher cartoon; and there is the clean-cut young American who likes to explain his country and make large and ample comparisons with an Englishwoman and— oh, the usual menagerie. There is not even a pretty face to draw me out of myself! . . .

The Swiss may be a nation of hotel keepers, but at least they know their business. My French has fallen off dreadfully, but I'm getting used to the sound of other people's; and at times I can understand whole patches of it in a lecture. Mrs. Zimmern is all worked up about my lectures; she wants me to wallop the Europeans hard; and since the new lot of students will contain many English ones, about a hundred students altogether, perhaps I shan't find it difficult. Now you know everything. I detest 'service,' I detest tipping, I detest officialdom; and when I get back to America I won't want to leave it or you for years; why, the two days I spent at the Exposition des Arts Décoratifs have made me actually admire American architecture!

. . . I laughed like a little child when I saw the snow-capped mountains again from the train; and something inside of me has been laughing since. The Rhone rushes out of the Lake of Geneva so fast that the swans have to paddle with all their might to hold their own against it; I saw one this morning who breasted the stream and kept pecking at a bit of floating weed which clung to his bosom, whilst he was swept backward. The water near the shore shows every pebble, but as it sweeps under the bridges the green becomes as dark and rich as that we've used on our screen; and on the Embankment the sycamores are pollarded and turned into huge umbrellas.   —Letter to Sophy. August 7, 1925

NOTES ON GENEVA. . . . The more completely the shock of travel wears off, the more completely you are mine. What does Alfred Kreymborg say?

"When I left you
You were you
But I was not
Quite me. Now I am me
And you are me—
And doubly you."

I've had such an afternoon as I hope lies in front of us. It all began with a lunch at Herbert Feis's villa. I mustn't say too much about that villa: it has a garden that no one would want to leave; a garden with choruses of marigolds and asters and zinnias, singing against a background of young bamboo-trees and mossy oaks; a garden walled, and the walls covered with ripe apricots, a garden nooked and shaded and in the deepest shade the black luster of holly leaves. But that's enough. . . . Herbert is always Herbert: inscrutably merry, but no longer, in his serious intervals, so pontifical. Well, lunch ended; Herbert whizzed me away in his Ford; I sat through a lecture, and then, with one of my new acquaintances, Longuet, whom I already call Alfred, a young California don, keen on puns and literature, I wandered around the courts and alleys and steep narrow streets of the old city. I wanted you there; you must do that with me, you old dear. Age hangs over the stones; the smells are unaltered since the fifteenth century; there are sudden open spaces with trees and fountains; and at the end of dank passageways the blackness heaves abruptly against a garden, such a garden as lovers must have sat in at twilight for hundreds of years, and I daresay they still do today. It took one's breath away again and again; but my breath was taken away in more than one fashion. In a second-hand shop we espied two silver globes, about the size of tennis balls, obviously old, engraved and enameled with a map of the world. We were both curious about them, and went in to find the price; and as I entered the door, thinking again of 'Littleness,' I wondered whether, if they were really silver-plated one mightn't pay as much as ten dollars. The price was—and I daren't put it in numerals lest you think my typewriting has gone wrong—the price was fourteen hundred dollars. Sweet smiles of embarrassment, saved a little by the fact that the shopkeeper was obviously a little proud at having stumped and flabbergasted two Americans. And so up and down and in and out, along streets where the gutters were still in the middle, as they were in the fifteenth century, until we reached the modern town again— that is, the town that dates since 1750 or thereabouts! Neither Oxford nor Innsbruck has anything quite like Geneva; although Innsbruck, I still think, is the more beautiful city. . . . —Letter to Sophy. August 31, 1925

A DAY IN GENEVA. . . . I'll spend the day in the usual way, which includes a swim in the lake, two or three ices, lunch with the Zimmerns and a great galaxy of young or prominent people at the Hotel Russie, and discussion. Mrs. Zimmern is as loquacious and vivacious as ever: she spits and coughs in English as I, in my best moments, have never yet achieved in French: but, as someone said the other day, at least half the things she says are important and interesting. Music is her religion: we have musical evenings at least every other night: but she hates jazz, and as much as told a group of the students in the first term that if they wanted to live in that kind of a world they had no business here. The school is an autocracy, governed with a velvet glove: one hears rumors of discontent and reproach, but there is something to be said for the autocracy. . . .

The Zimmerns are afflicted with the noble idea of rallying together an elite from all the countries, and making them conscious of each other. They've treated me, the Zimmerns, in a way that would make my head reel with immodesty, if I were younger; but the only thing that makes my head reel here is Chianti wine, and I have really mastered that by now. In the meanwhile, the Zimmerns have decided to hold my second three lectures over until the week after next; so I shan't be able to leave here, I am afraid, until the first of September. The disappointment of some of the students at my not continuing immediately is a consolation: my lectures have occasionally been jumbled, but they have had meat in them, and in some ways have taken the haughty and condescending foreigner off his feet. And whom have I met? And whom do I lecture to? A mixed group, with the English and Americans preponderating, but with Hindus, Belgians, French, Germans, Swedes, Norwegians, all mixed up, and both girls and boys—about eighty altogether. The morning after my lecture an amazing young man, Jean de Menasce, partly Jewish partly Egyptian, who speaks French as they speak it in Paris, and English as they do in Oxford, gives my lecture again in French, to those who haven't been able to understand it; and after that follows the usual discussion with Jean for interpreter. He has French elegance and Oxford superiority: I hated the combination at first; but he is really very nice. He has just translated 'The Wasteland' into French; and if he weren't so confoundedly erudite and brilliant he would probably have a great career ahead of him. . . .
—Letter to Sophy. August 15, 1925

Note: Jean de Menasce turned out to be perhaps the most luminous and beautiful spirit I have ever known—though never intimately. I hope to find words worthy of him in my Autobiography.

AND WHAT IS MY REAL WORK? It has been coming over me ever since I delivered the Geneva lectures; on the steamer it crystallized more definitely, and now I am well started on it: nothing less than an attempt, of which certain parts of the Story of Utopias were only the faintest sketches, to describe what has happened to the Western European mind since the breakdown of the medieval synthesis, and to trace out the effects of this in America. Likewise my job is to pick up the one or two threads in our American writers, particularly Emerson and Whitman, which seem to me to lead toward more profitable conclusions than the work of any of the great Europeans of the nineteenth century, although the great Europeans had, individually, reached a more perfect development. A hundred people have gone over this ground before; but unless *I* am blind, they have never seen anything.

The writers who have dealt with the development of the modern mind have had a bias against Romanticism, or against Rousseau, or against Science, or in favor of the Catholic Church, or in favor of Protestantism, or in favor of Liberal Reform or the Communist Revolution. My distinction, I think, is that I am reasonably free from any sort of prepossession for or against these things: I am not a Romantic nor a Catholic nor a follower of Rousseau; but I see what these things have meant in the life of the spirit, and I know a little about their insufficiencies, too.

If we are to have a vision to live by again, it will have to be different from all these efforts; and yet, it will have to learn from them and contain them; it will have to be a synthesis, not of knowledges, for that is impossible in anything but an abstract form, but a synthesis of attitudes, which will lead out toward the knowledge and the life in which we can find satisfaction. To tell the truth, I am a little frightened when I contemplate the size of my task. If it is to be done at all, it will have to call forth every particle of energy and experience I possess; and I will have to venture forth on uncharted waters, in the teeth of an adverse gale—that is to say, in directly the opposite quarter from that of my own generation, whose more sensitive members all say that we must swallow chaos, and may never know order again. Well, I am shoving off, convinced that someone must try to make this undiscovered port. . . . —Letter to Dorothy Cecilia (Delilah) Loch. December 8, 1925

Note: When in 1926 I wrote 'The Little Testament of Bernard Martin,' I fused Geddes and Branford into a single personality, that of James McMaster, who replaces the actual Zimmern. In this account, in describing McMaster's summer school in Geneva, I had pictured, almost clairvoyantly, the very house the Zimmerns occupied in 1929—and even the basement room I was to stay in three years later, looking out on a garden which "dropped onto the rooftops of the street below."

After Geneva: With P. G. in Edinburgh

Geddes drives me to tears, almost he does. I have been with him since Monday; and though I anticipated the worst, the first night and day were happy. He took me about the city, showed me the hundred improvements that he had made or initiated; waste spaces become gardens, courts tidied, tenements renovated, student hostels built, splashes of color introduced by red blinds on windows; fountains designed: a great achievement in itself, all these things. On the second day Mabel Barker came, and some other visitors arrived; and then we were back again in the old cruel mess and chaos: engagements broken, time wasted on trivial idiots, and in the interim an unceasing volume of anecdotes, suggestions, and diagrammatic soliloquy.

The weaknesses and strength, the steadfastness and the impatience, the effacement of himself and the ruthless arrogance of this great man emerged from all this with an effect upon me that is still mingled. He is perfectly lovable in his human moments; in fact he is enchanting; a portrait of him at thirty—a bad portrait but a sufficing one—showing a black-bearded rather chubby man with red cheeks, almost choked me with emotion. Here was a man I might have worked with and merged myself with. But what can I do with a self-absorbed old man whose muffled soliloquy spreads over the hours, a man who is caught in his thinking machines, as one who had invented decimal notation might perhaps spend his life by counting all possible objects in tens: what am I to do with the pathetic tyrant who asks for a collaborator and wants a secretary, who mourns the apathy and neglect of a world that he flouts by his failure to emerge from his own preoccupations and to take account of other peoples' interests, this man who preaches activity and demands quiescence or at least acquiescence; who requires that one see the world completely through his spectacles, and share, or make a murmur as if sharing, every particular and personal reaction. *I have still to have an hour's conversation with him.*

What an affectionate, loyal relation we could have, if Geddes would permit it to exist! How much one would get out of him if he did not try to give one so much! But he wants all or nothing, and without seeking to get more deeply into one's actual life, he sets before one the thwarted ambitions and ideas of his own. Once and again he returned to the notion of my getting a *doctorat étranger* at Montpellier with a year's residence; for he wants me to be active in the universities. He would like me to be a professor, a college president; he even, amazingly, hinted something about my becoming an American ambassador like James Russell Lowell! In short, everything but what I myself, consciously and unconsciously, have been driving at. I squirmed out of his presence to get into the train: I wouldn't let him and Mabel Barker stay to see me off. The incessant soliloquy like the insistent noise of a radio I simply had to run away from. And yet I love him; I respect him; I admire him; he still for me is the most prodigious thinker in the modern world. His arrogance and his weakness have frustrated him; he lacks some internal stamina in spite of all his strength and energy; and is not merely a discouraged old man, but, as I found out from things he has dropped, he fell often into black discouragement as a young man. What is responsible for all these incomplete endeavors, all these unverified hypotheses, whose rejection irritates him and whose proof, when others have given it, does not interest him? Why is there such a streak of feebleness in that greatness? For all that, the greatness is indisputable; and if I have perhaps seen him for the last time—but how sadly incomplete these days were, how fine they might have been—I shall retain of him, not the memory of the stern, sorrow-laden old man, interminably talking, demanding what one cannot give and forgetful of all one could; no, I shall retain the memory of the older comrade I found too late.   —RN., Waverley Station, Edinburgh. September 11, 1925

8: Imprint of Patrick Geddes

From the time I first encountered Patrick Geddes's writing in my biology course at the City College of New York in 1914, he exerted a pervasive influence on my thinking, and even more on my direct relations with the whole environment, cosmic, earthly, and human. So often and so openly have I acknowledged this personal debt that superficial interpreters have sometimes taken for granted that my more significant contributions can all be traced back to Geddes, and have even imputed to me an attachment to the very parts of his graphic synthesis that I questioned in a letter to him as early as 1921, and inwardly rejected as stultifying after he had personally demonstrated his graphic 'thinking machines' to me.

In his old age, Geddes had come to regard his 'Chart of Life'—a kind of intellectual chess on a board of thirty-six squares, played strictly by his own rules with pieces he himself had carved—as his crowning achievement in systematically coordinating knowledge and human experience. Unfortunately, this graphic system left out the very aspects of Geddes's living example that most influenced me. In privately devaluating Geddes's claims for his abstract shortcuts to all-embracing knowledge I was closer to his essential vision than he was: for I embraced without reserve his favorite motto, Vivendo discimus: We learn by living. *The true Geddesian knows there are no shortcuts in this process.*

In his final will Geddes designated me as his biographer: but even after his death I was unwilling to undertake that task; for I had work of my own to do. In time this would validate what was sound in Geddes's audacious career, expose the ideological weaknesses of his system, and explore realms not charted or chartable on his graphs. Though Geddes and I were in correspondence from 1917 to the month of his death in 1932, this friendly tie did no more than our actual meeting in 1923 to narrow the gap between us. That story forms a long, at times somewhat painful chapter in my Autobiography, part of which came out in Encounter in September 1966. Some of the amplifications and corrections needed for a fuller assessment may be found in the four published biographies of Geddes by Amelia Defries, Philip Boardman, Philip Mairet, and Paddy Kitchen.

Biographical and Critical

PATRICK GEDDES WAS BORN IN 1854, two years before Bernard Shaw. One of Shaw's biographers, Auguste Hamon, rated Geddes the only contemporary whose conversation equalled Shaw's in brilliance and range; but apart from that, the life and work of the two men stand in striking contrast: so much so that the qualities of one bring into relief those of the other. Shaw was a man of letters who sought to startle his contemporaries by a new formula for originality: common sense disguised as perversity and perversity parading as common sense. Geddes was primarily a scientist, shy of committing his thoughts to writing, lest the provisional and dynamic and tentative should become static and absolute. Since his was a truly original mind he was more ready to embrace a healthy truism than a meretricious originality: he valued truth itself rather than the vanity of its authorship. From the first, Shaw fell in love with his own image and spent the greater part of his life erecting a pedestal for it and laying wreaths around it. Geddes, on the other hand, had no concern with his own advancement and no skill in the Shavian art of publicity: his last pathetic bid for influence, his acceptance of a knighthood, an honor he had spurned in middle life, was indirectly responsible for his death.

For all Shaw's verbal audacity he was by nature a Fabian: a prudent man, with an essentially middle-class mind, concealing his inability to come to grips with the ultimate matters of human existence, birth or death, love or marriage or man's destiny, by contriving witty arguments, with a legalistic turn, about the more peripheral aspects of these subjects. Geddes was by instinct and intention the opposite type of personality: a Scipian, if I may use the term, as different from Shaw as the bold Scipio Africanus was from Fabius. Geddes was committed to the frontal attack and to direct action, not because he coveted power, but because he put the needs of life first. Even when Shaw was most verbally revolutionary, he usually played the game and sought the rewards of the game; while even when Geddes was most loyal to tradition he refused to play the game. Geddes sought to become a university teacher, but refused to qualify for a degree; and though the Martin White Chair of Sociology at the University of London was founded for his occupancy, he did so little in his probationary lecture to win the approval of the University Committee that they turned him down.

Once Shaw, on the other hand, was well started as dramatist his career was engulfed by success; whereas Geddes's life was, superficially, a long succession of failures: crowned by the final failure of his last decade, the heap of stone buildings and exotic gardens at Montpellier which he called the Collège des Ecossais: an attempt, in defiance of his own philosophy, to transmit living ideas through static structures, buildings, and graphs, instead of giving first place to the activities of other dynamic personalities.

Yet these contrasts and antagonisms between Shaw and Geddes need not wipe out all the essential qualities they had in common, little though that brought them together. They shared high spirits, a gift for satiric criticism, and a savage contempt for sham; and if any single philosophy threads through Shaw's work it is that of evolutionary vitalism; a doctrine of the primacy of life both men derived from a scientific source, Darwin, and a humanistic source, John Ruskin. The preface to 'Man and Superman,' and the Metabiological Pentateuch of 'Back to Methusaleh,' even parts of 'Major Barbara,' float on the same stream of ideas that carried Geddes along: both men were vitalists, rather than mechanists, in that they gave to the internal activities of the organism a role that the negative theory of natural selection attributed mainly to accidental variations, external forces, and environmental pressures.

In an ideal world, Geddes and Shaw, who encountered each other from time to time, at least at the meetings of the Sociological Society in the first decade of this century, should have been allies and co-partners, lending each to the other his own special strength. But, as so often happens with contemporaries, they were hardly close enough to graze each other as rivals, to say nothing of becoming friends. So each lost what the other might have given him: if Geddes had studied the arts of winning an audience as carefully as Shaw, and if Shaw had acquired any of Geddes's gift for detachment and impersonality, they both might have left a deeper mark on their age. —The Architectural Review, London. August 1950

GEDDES AND OUR MARRIAGE. Even when Geddes wanted me to join him as his assistant in Bombay, he nevertheless put my marriage with Sophia and our having children first. His influence came out sometimes in quite unexpected ways. In 1923, Sophia, a loyal 'Lucy Stoner,' still retained her maiden name and wore no wedding ring. Geddes, imbued with the feminism of late Victorian society, could swallow this, but said: "How then does one know she is a married woman?—Oh! there's the ring." Almost blushing, Sophia remembers, she instinctively hid her ringless hand behind her back. And next day we asked my Uncle Charlie, still a jeweler at Tiffany's, to make us both wedding rings. Geddes approved of mine when he noticed it because, he observed, this sign of marriage would warn away unattached girls who might otherwise put my faithfulness to the test. But, alas! I found he was speaking, if he spoke truly, only about the ways of an earlier generation.   —RN. 1963

Paradoxically, I was closest to Geddes when we were spatially far apart and had to communicate by letter. By its nature, correspondence happily is a two-sided affair, whereas when Geddes found a listener, he left little room for the latter to express himself on equal terms even though verbally he would call for 'criticism' and allowed (theoretically!) for dissent. If I came to write more freely about my personal and family affairs in my letters to him after 1925 than about the ideas and projects and memoranda he would keep tossing into my lap, it was because I remained defensively silent about his pleas for assent and 'cooperation.' While I profited by many of Geddes's bold sallies and systematizations, I remained skeptical of the validity of his graphic method, with its fixed categories, and even more dubious about his effort to extend his abstract system far beyond its natural limits or its vital uses. Even as a young man, I had gathered my eggs from many intellectual nests, and had no notion of dumping them out in order to fill a purely Geddesian basket. Though many of Geddes's more valid original perceptions had become part and parcel of my own thinking, as I have often gratefully acknowledged, the fixations of Geddes's increasing age widened our unspoken differences. Geddes answered my first letter to him in 1917, the year he lost his older son Alisdair. We kept up our correspondence until 1932, the year of his death; but we did not actually meet face to face until he spent the summer of 1923 at The New School in New York.   —RN. 1975

ENTER THE RADIO. . . . There is little real news about America, except that we are now in the throes of another huge technological jump. The success of the radio-telephone in long distance communication has now reached a point where it is a distinct rival to radio-telegraphy: and as a result thousands of people are buying radio-receiving sets, from twenty dollars to two hundred in cost, for the purpose of getting the weather reports, sermons, lectures, health advice, stock market reports, and what not that are broadcasted by central stations in Newark, Pittsburgh, Chicago, etc. The whole countryside is now in direct communication with the city: even in the remotest districts it will soon be possible for the farmer to get storm warnings at much shorter notice than the present service. Will not this probably give a new turn to rural life? . . . —Letter to Patrick Geddes. March 29, 1922

THE STORY OF UTOPIAS. . . . Among other things I have discovered a remarkable Utopia by J. V. Andreae, a friend of Comenius, which I think ranks much higher for sociological insight and constructive criticism than the work of either Bacon or Campanella. This 'Christianopolis' was exhumed from Latin by a young American Ph.D. in 1916, and it is about time that it was more widely noticed. Andreae seems to have been responsible, through his correspondence with Samuel Hartlib, for the founding of the Royal Society; and it is interesting that he warned his colleagues against the dissociation of literature from science, a warning which the hard-headed English physicists alas! failed to heed.

In the treatment of Coketown and the Country House I am going to suggest that each great historic period has a real, and to a certain extent, a realized Utopia, implicit in its habits and its institutions and its experiments; a Utopia which is, so to say, the pure form of its actual institutions, and which may therefore be abstracted from them and examined by itself. To write a history of these pragmatic Utopias would be to present the historical "world-within" and thus supplement the conventional historian's account of the world-without. Until psychoanalysis claimed the field we did not sufficiently realize the importance of the world-within; or at any rate, we did not see that it had a directive function. (I realize that *you did* see this; what I mean is that psychoanalysis gave us the tools to explore this field more fully.) So it comes about that a great many of our Utopias are infantile, in that they seek to entrench what Freud calls the pleasure-principle, and deny the reality-principle. —Letter to Patrick Geddes. March 29, 1922

RIEHL AS FORERUNNER. . . . My chief intellectual experience these last few months has been the finding of Wilhelm Heinrich Riehl, the German historian. Gooch mentions him in his 'History and the Historians of the Nineteenth Century' as one of the main culture historians; and his

'Natural History of the German People,' written in the forties and fifties, is a masterly application of the regional method to History. Treitschke once dismissed Riehl as a "historian of the salon," and the reason is plain, for with Riehl the place, the people, the work, the home, the industries, the arts, the folk-music, and so forth are in the foreground, and the political organization enters no more into his history than it does in the life of anyone who is not a functionary of the State. . . . As early as 1850 Riehl saw that the effect of the railroad was to join city to city, and to depress the countryside by draining it into the railway capitals, whereas the old system of roads enabled the city to get out into the country, and preserved an economic balance. He also predicted that freedom would be gone in America when the forests were destroyed; and the beginnings of imperialism here do indeed date from the passing of the frontier, in 1890, and the exhaustion of the Appalachian forests. . . . —Letter to Patrick Geddes. February 25, 1924

CRITIQUE OF GEDDES's GRAPHS. As for the IX to 9 diagram. Once it is laid out I have a difficulty in presenting it to others as a picture of the existing order and of the possibility of its antithetical alternative. The difficulty lies in the manner in which it is built up, particularly with the initial terms.

IX	$\dfrac{\text{Military}}{\text{Theological}}$	$\dfrac{\text{Political}}{\text{Abstractional}}$	$\dfrac{\text{Mechanical}}{\text{Physical Sc.}}$

Comte generalized these terms from history; the ordinary student can grasp them in sequence, but fails, for the most part, to grasp their interaction and cumulative effect. Even if IX is not challenged on the grounds of failing to represent the historic process, there is a further difficulty with the 9. [This was my fundamental criticism: these graphs did not represent the flow of time or do justice to the simultaneity of past, present and future in the human mind.] Are the three corresponding terms also to follow in order? Or are the general elements of the 9 to develop more or less coordinately? If we roughly date the Military Order at 1200, the Political at 1600 and the Mechanical at 1800, are we to date the Biological at 19–, the Geotechnic at 20–, and the Eupsychic at 22–: or are they all to be resolved at an indefinite point in the future? This last point has never been clear in my own mind. How would you answer it? I hold entirely with your thesis that if we could work out the *logical* antithesis we should have a key to the *pragmatic* antithesis and by *acting upon our hypothesis* would ensure its success. It is on this viewpoint however that most of our dispersed modern minds will be in rebellion; for they do not recognize any inherent connection between logical order and the world of fact. This point occurs in the initial explanation of the diagram, too. One can either say, taking one's three terms as granted, that theology reacted upon abstractionism and created the myth of the Powers; or one can say, logically, theologize your abstractions and you get a Theologized Abstraction, i.e. the Sovereign State.

Similarly one can say that the hunter's military tradition, reinforced by machine industry, causes war; or that if you mechanize the military order you get mechanized militarism, i.e. modern war. The first set of statements is historical, the second is logical. In verbal explanation you get the benefit of alternatively using one or the other, as seems more profitable; but in a rational description one cannot slip so easily from one category to another. Quite apart from this, I have only one or two suggestions to, tentatively, make. The first is that the spiritual symbol of the financial order is not $, the theory of money, but the Prospectus or Advertisements, and that the antithesis of this, under social finance, is [Social] Policy. Likewise the antithesis to the Ballot seems to me not to be the Transition, but Group-Direction. These are, of course, minor points; possibly inevitable ones, for if the prime elements are given, the values which will be substituted for their combinations will be different ones for different thinkers until divergent interpretations are brought together and reconciled. Thus, using Good, True, and Beautiful, I got an entirely different set of institutions and states for Good-truth, True-good, etc., than you had given. This is obviously because Good, True, and Beautiful are only counters, or tokens, for a whole variety of things. How can this be made more rigorous? That is, I think, your capital problem. Otherwise the diagrams tend to remain as personal as the more chaotic philosophies they replace. Is this not one of the reasons you sometimes lose adherents? they are not convinced of the impersonality of the logical method: it seems neutral, *but what comes out of it is Geddes!* Some way must be found to show that there are no strings, that anyone who takes pains can manipulate the same instrument, to his own advantage! —Letter to Patrick Geddes. April 9, 1924

REGIONAL PLANNING. . . . We had an Appalachian revival meeting at the Hudson Guild farm in October; we danced and walked over part of the Trail and spent long hours threshing out the contents of the Regional Planning number; and again and again some memory connected with you and your visit there would fall from our lips: so you remained with us and were among us. Let me describe briefly the number as it stands—or rather, as it is projected, for only a few of the articles are ready. It is to be a special number of The Survey Graphic: thirty thousand words; numerous diagrams and illustrations. About ten articles.

The first one is on the Fourth Migration. Each great migration in America has spelled a new kind of opportunity: first the covering of the continent and seizing the land: second, the migration into the industrial town: third, into the financial centers, New York and the ten sub-metropolises. Now, we point out, the community is on the eve of a fourth migration. The occasion is electric power and auto transportation, which, plus the radio and the telephone, tend to equalize advantages over a great area and thus rob the centralized city of much of its attraction. On top of this is the fact that industry, housing, transportation, and so forth, must no longer operate automatically: their automatic growth tends to pile up embarrassing conditions, so that no industry, for example, can afford to pay for the urban housing of its unskilled workers. Since planning is necessary, why should we not plan so as to reap advantages from the Fourth Migration?

. . . Stein, by the way, has been working ever since you came over here on the Garden City, and he and Wright have just made an interesting discovery: they are quite confident of being able to plan a beautiful shell: they are completely at sea as to what sort of *community* to provide for. I quoted to them Branford's notion that the townplanner needs the aid of the poet; and they agreed; and having succeeded so far, I told them a little about regionalism in Europe, and suggested regionalism must be made the cultural motive of regional planning, if it isn't to relapse into an arid technological scheme. Stein pretty well saw the point: I had waited patiently these last three years for an opportunity to make it. I think that in one way or another I shall be able to inject a little regionalism into the Regional Planning number! That may give it a strange distinction   —Letter to Patrick Geddes. December 4, 1924

. . . My lack of a degree has become a valuable distinction in America. The Ph.D. is such an inevitable sign of mediocrity here that when the Carnegie Foundation for the Advancement of Art wanted someone to examine and report upon the various schools of art in America they tried to get hold of me—and this in the face of the fact that with their resources they had all the academic young men in the universities at their beck and call. I was lured by the prospect of touring all over the United States; and almost accepted for that reason: but I countered with an offer to write a critical history of the development of the arts and crafts in America *when I got around to it*—and at that stage we both left it. . . .
—Letter to Patrick Geddes. May 22, 1926

Next week I go to the University of Virginia to attend a conference on Regionalism. The Southerners, particularly the younger intellectuals, have lately become conscious of themselves as the repositories of the agricultural and regional traditions of the country: a group of them recently published a book, 'I'll Take My Stand,' to uphold these traditions against the financial and mechanical standardization of the rest of the country; and though they tend to be slightly reactionary, still dreaming of the past instead of shaping a more integrated future, they may prove valuable allies. John Gould Fletcher, whom you may have met in London, will be there: our New York group, Stein, Wright, MacKaye, are engineering it. We shall miss you.

In Oklahoma a group at the University have published these last two years a Regional Miscellany, chiefly literary, called Folk-Say: an interesting straw in the wind. The writer of the article on Meiklejohn's college, which I enclose, is another one of the young people who have studied you well: he did a study of the French bastides last summer, but unfortunately missed you in London, though he saw Farquharson. Your disciples are coming along now rapidly; the younger generation, that is, those now under twenty-five, are much more concrete-minded than their elders were: architecture begins to share place with literature in the critical journals: Miss Catherine Bauer, the girl who is going to write a history of the House, is a very adept pupil: she has gotten much out of your Biology. These young people are more ready for Graphics than you perhaps realize.   —Letter to Patrick Geddes. June 27, 1931

With P.G.: 1923

'HE' came last week. I speak of Him in capital letters; for now that I have seen a little of him I am more convinced than ever that he is one of the Olympians. Of course *that* is the difficulty. Jove never walked among the sons of men without the sons of men getting the worst of it, and I find that all the warnings and reservations I have put into my letters have had precisely no effect upon P.G.; for he is a terrible and determined old man, and now that he is ready to set down his philosophy, he wants to make use of me to the full. . . .   —Letter to Delilah Loch. May 12, 1923

PRELIMINARY QUANDARIES. . . . Do you remember that walk we had together up in Richmond, Delilah, when I confessed to you that I felt that I was not primarily a sociologist but after all another kind of animal? During the last year that feeling has been growing upon me, and it accounts to some extent, I think, for my difficulty in writing to Geddes at present. . . . I should be much more enthusiastic about writing a biography of Geddes than I am about cooperating with him on the new Opus. I have enough knowledge about the Opus to write a good biography, and I could not have obtained this without drinking long at the fountain from which things Geddesian flow; but the biography attracts me as a piece of creative work, in which one might by good fortune sum up and crystallize all that was good and permanent in Geddes's philosophy (that which is best and most permanent being, I believe, Geddes's life itself) whilst putting together the Opus, has no more fascination for me than the articulation of a skeleton—the poor remnants of a body which once had life. This last sentence of course does not quite do justice to my respect for Geddes's work apart from the man; but it does show where my essential interests lie. . . . —Letter to Delilah Loch. May 13, 1921

RESPECTFUL DISSENT. . . . There have been times when I have thought that Branford spent a little too much time, perhaps, in laying the Geddesian pieces on the board and neglected the opportunity of opening the game, and in particular, of encouraging younger men, and specialists in particular fields, to make their own moves. It seems to me much more important that particular researches and lines of investigation should be *infused* with the sound sociological method, and illumined by the general outlook that you have developed, than that they should begin with an acceptance of the entire schemata. A great many people, who have neither the experience nor the background nor the mental bent for taking over the system as it stands, are nevertheless sympathetic enough to do valuable work along the right lines if they were once put on the right track. Instead of searching for a general preliminary agreement among sociologists as to scope, method, aim, and so forth, it seems to me more expedient to center attention upon getting work done in particular fields— following [as far as may be possible] the broad lines that you have laid down—and then trust to obtaining a general agreement after the efficacy of the Edinburgh school had been demonstrated. . . . —Letter to Patrick Geddes. May 12, 1921

SHOWDOWN WITH GEDDES. . . . In one sense, I have the feeling that we have yet to *meet*. We both have been aware of the obstacles to meeting: but it is rather hard to climb over them, partly because of the gap between our generations and our varieties of secular experience, and partly because my respect for you is so great that it reduces my mental reactions in your presence to those I used to feel in the presence of my teacher when I was twelve years old—that is, complete paralysis! Putting this last matter aside, there is a real barrier to understanding between us in the fact that you grew to manhood in a period of hope, when people looked forward with confidence to the "great world spinning forever down the ringing grooves of time"; whereas I spent my whole adolescence in the shadow of war and disappointment, growing up with a generation which, in large part, had no future.

Your pessimism about the existing state of civilization as portrayed in IX does not prevent you from still working eagerly at the problem of the transition to 9 [These numerals refer to Geddes's sociological graphs: Roman numerals indicating the past, Arabic the future] because your own career still has a momentum acquired under an earlier period of hope and activity; and so perhaps you don't realize the paralyzing effect of that pessimism, which is inherent in the situation, upon those of us whose personal careers had not yet acquired any momentum [before 1917]. Rationally speaking, there is as much chance of doing good work as there ever was; rationally speaking, a work that is worth doing is worth doing for itself without regard to the possible mischances of war, famine, or what not; rationally speaking, all the interests that we had acquired before the war are just as important and as valuable as they ever were. True enough: but something of the impulse has gone; whatever one's conscious mind accepts is not enough to stir the unconscious; our efforts are no longer, as the saying is, whole-souled.

If I found this bitter sense of futility in myself alone I should be tempted to attribute it to an unsatisfactory personal experience; quite the contrary, however, my own career has on the whole been a happy and eventful one; and the forces which undermine its satisfaction are at work in almost every intelligent and sensitive person I know between the ages of twenty-five and forty. Those who are younger than I am differ from my generation in the sense that they are "realists" who have no hope for the morrow whatever and no faith or interest in the polity at large; whilst those who are over forty are still living, as it were, on the capital acquired during the days of hope, and if their store is rapidly running out they manage to scrape on from day to day. Our sense of a 'calling,' our sense of any one task to which we could profoundly dedicate ourselves, is gone; and until we can recover this sense a certain intensity of devotion to our professions is the only thing that prevents our lives from being altogether inconsecutive and dispersed. I have fought against this drift of things from the very moment I detected it; but it is like trying to relieve one's bosom of the pressure of the enveloping air; and I see no way of relieving the crippled psyche except by trusting to some slow and obscure process of cure. It is no use saying, be different: for we are like the sick man that Saadi mentions whose only desire was that he might be well enough to desire something.

You came over to America without, I suppose, any sufficient awareness of this change which, apart from any mere difference of age, separates a large part of the younger generation from the older: you came over, too, with a somewhat over-idealized portrait of me in your mind, as a vigorous young apprentice who might work at the same bench with you for a while, and keep on at the task when you had gone back from America. You are naturally disappointed to find me bound up with literary vocations, and to find that by natural bent and by training I am of the tribe of Euripides and Aristophanes rather than of Pythagoras and Aristotle; a trait which is, possibly, a little obscured by the fact that mere necessity and convenience oblige me to get my living, from day to day, with the Sophists of journalism. Faced with an actual me, you have naturally tried to make me over into the idealized portrait, whose aims and interests and actions were more congruent with your own; and, instinctively, I find myself resisting these frontal attacks, although my defences have again and again fallen down before unpremeditated movements on my flank! In the light of this difficult adjustment between the Ideal and the Actual, it would not be at all surprising if the original portrait had turned into a Caricature—that of a clever young hack writer, rather sullen in temperament and unamenable to conversation, who had no other interests in life than those of turning out a certain number of sheafs of copy per diem. The inability of this creature to follow your talk for more than a couple of hours at a sitting you could, in the light of caricature, attribute to a lack of interest or worse still! to a general lack of synthetic intelligence, whereas it is only the obvious reaction of another thorough visual to an auditive method of presentation. And so on.

Plainly neither the ideal nor the caricature corresponds to the real creature; and one of the things that has hindered our work together is, perhaps, that you began with one and shifted to the other, without our ever having (except in passing moments quickly forgotten) the chance to meet. If instead of thinking of me as a quack journalist you'd conceive of me rather as a young scholar who publishes his notes and lectures instead of speaking to a class: and if you'd see that I have chosen to get a living in this manner because it is for me the one means by which I can work at my own pace and keep at least a third of my time free for thinking and studying of a different sort, there might still be a little exaggeration in the picture, but it would be an exaggeration toward the truth. Eutopitects build in vain unless they prepare the mind as well as the ground for the

New Jerusalem; and nothing you have said has shaken in me the belief that the best part of my work must be in the first field rather than in the second, although it may be true that I shall do the first task more sanely and adroitly if I have had a little direct experience of the second; and I have so far admitted this as to go ahead with the plans of the Mohegan Colony. . . . —Letter to Patrick Geddes. July 6, 1923

Geddes asked me if I had seen the plans for a huge building in New York with a great dome capped on it. "It looked," he said, "as if the Devil had farted into Saint Paul's and raised the dome three hundred feet into the air." He is not afraid of these Rabelaisian touches. Harry Dana was defending himself against Geddes's strictures on Professors of Literature, by complaining that he did not perhaps have enough of the bard or poet in him to fulfill Geddes's notion of a good one, and Geddes answered: "Nonsense: let us speak with biological plainness. Every man is at least passively sexual; and in moments of passion or lust or call it what you will he knows what it is to have an erection. Well, the brain, when you look at it in section, is plainly enough an erectile tissue: there is an apparatus now that measures the amount of erection when you ask a man what six times nine is; and every brain has a poet in it or a scientist; and it can have an erection under the proper conditions: People marvel at the Darwins and the Einsteins, and talk about the biological inheritance; when to me the marvel is that everybody is not a Darwin or an Einstein. What you call genius is to me only a habit of work." Again: he was contrasting the life of the meanest peasant, with its great variety of occupations and tasks from season to season, against the life of those who work in the factories and offices. "These poor devils," he exclaimed, "spend all their lives on a nightstool, with a wastebasket alongside of them to take care of the excrement." At another time he was speaking about the public schools of England. "How the devil can anyone regard England as a pure and Christian country when it boasts of public schools where the pupils learn chiefly two things, masturbation and sodomy, and where the masters have the privilege of unlimited sadism through the system of flogging." —RN. July 7, 1923

Geddes lectured before the Russell Sage Foundation, and he mystified and irritated the city planners like Thomas Adams by talking about New York as a second Rome. They dined him in Chinatown in the midst of the vast slums of the East Side, and pointing to the city around him Geddes asked Adams and Frank Backus Williams what they would do about planning it. They confessed that they were at a loss for a solution; where-upon Geddes said: "Plan it as if you were in the service of a Labour

Government. Your problem is to provide homes for the next generation."
—RN. 1923

Did I mention Whitehead's 'Science and the Modern World' to you? It's a book of first importance. He has an ingenious solution of the problem of mechanism versus vitalism; by showing that the categories of mechanism are useless to further modern explanations in mathematico-physics, and suggesting that even the electron is modified by the properties of its environment—so that iron in a stone is one thing, and iron in the human body is quite another, although the laboratory analysis may reveal identity—i.e. identity in the laboratory. It indicates the important modification of the old physical concepts by biology; and is quite in the line of all your own thinking—unless I have misunderstood both Whitehead and yourself! Do look at it.   —Letter to Patrick Geddes. September 1926

. . . My week at Dartmouth gave me hope; for Ernest Hopkins, the President, has slowly transformed, and is still transforming, the institution from a country club for young barbarians into a serious place of work, and in doing this he is breaking down the barriers between the various departments, and re-integrating the whole curriculum. They have asked me to spend a whole semester with them; and though I cannot do it this spring, I shall try to set aside time next year to do so. They are limited in numbers to 1,600 students; and the President has been cutting away the red tape, as fast as those in authority under him will permit him. Hopkins is capable of unusual strokes; as, for example, he found a great Russian organist on his uppers in Europe and imported him, without further authorization, to Dartmouth, to head a non-existent department of music, which now has a symphony orchestra which draws members from all over the local region. Or again, a painter [Adelbert Ames] who had become interested in the physics of light and color asked him for a laboratory in which to conduct further experiments. Hopkins gave him the laboratory, and the man has during the past six or eight years made very important contributions to optics, to say nothing of furthering the life of the college by his presence, although he has no official position in the university, and does not teach. Then, too, Hopkins prides himself on the number of teachers who do *not* have Ph.D.'s on his faculty: he seeks out his younger men before they become dis-specialized and useless. As for Meiklejohn, he defended his college brilliantly against the rest of the university—his defense taking the form of criticizing its shortcomings harder than his worst opponents would have dared. There are now plans afoot to extend the Experimental College to the rest of the university; plans which, as I told Branford, I hope will be deferred, since

Meiklejohn's curriculum and method need to be shaken down a little further before they are applied on a large scale. Still, he survives and flourishes! . . . —Letter to Patrick Geddes. January 27, 1930

. . . This brings me back to an old point of mine: the economy of writing books, as compared with publication in any periodical form. For books alone are reviewed; and books alone remain in circulation long enough to be discussed by a succession of readers at different times, and so slowly gather their audience. C. K. Ogden has had an influence far out of proportion to Victor Branford or yourself, considering not merely the quality of his contributions but the amount of energy he has spent on disseminating his ideas: and this was because his main efforts have gone into a series of publications, rather than into the Cambridge Magazine with which he originally started. The original idea for 'The Making of the Future' Series was a good one: but the series weakened as it progressed, because Branford's energies and money went to the Sociological Society, and instead of using the series to gather around new writers and to build up a school of thought, he let it finally peter out.

For the sake of the ideas that both you and Branford had to give to the world, I could wish that you both had either gone into a lay monastery in 1920 or been imprisoned by the civil authorities, with nothing other than pen and ink and a library to keep you company! A garden would have kept you both in good health, and instead of communicating with a few poor disciples like myself, scattered at the ends of the earth, you would presently have found yourselves surrounded by a school. Surely, it was contrary to your own teachings, to build the buildings first and then seek to attract the pupils. That is our own weak American method: the method that produces palatial buildings, and fills them with vacant minds. . . . —Letter to Patrick Geddes. May 3, 1931

. . . Did I ever tell you the story of 'simultaneous thinking'? Perhaps Millie Defries tells it in her awful book, 'Geddes the Interpreter.' But I am afraid she doesn't. Geddes, when he was studying under Haeckel in Jena, lived in a boarding house, and there was a remarkable man there, brilliant, witty, intelligent, scholarly. The very ideal of the thinking man, who attracted Geddes very much. They became good friends, and one day this man took Geddes aside and told him he must tell him a secret. The truth was that he was crazy: he had spent years attempting the art of 'simultaneous thinking,' and just as he was on the point of achieving it, he had broken down. Geddes mustn't tell anyone! When Geddes finally evolved his diagrams on squared paper he remembered the talented lunatic, and saw that he, too, was engaged in simultaneous thinking. Madame Zimmern's name for it, polyphonic thinking, is even better; but perhaps one ought to call it contrapuntal or even better symphonic thinking. One ought to coin a word which would describe its opposition to linear thinking. Our present day notion of coordination—which explains why nothing ever really gets coordinated—is that of keeping linear thinking in parallel rows at the same rate of movement, whereas simultaneous thinking involves reciprocal action and [timely] modifications of the whole.   —Letter to Catherine Bauer. September 4, 1931

GEDDES THE URBAN ECOLOGIST.   By both training and general habit of mind Geddes was an ecologist, long before that branch of biology had attained the status of a special discipline; he had come directly into contact with the three men, Ernst Haeckel, Ray Lankester, and Peter Kropotkin, who—after Darwin—had laid the foundation for study of the cooperative activities of all organisms. And it is not as a bold innovator in urban planning, but as an ecologist, the patient investigator of historic filiations and dynamic biological and social interrelationships that Geddes's most important work in cities was done. Geddes distrusted sweeping innovations and clean slates; as a biologist he knew that small quantities, as in traces of minerals in the diet, might be as important for urban life as large ones, and could be far more easily overlooked by stupid wholesale planning, done at a distance by people who over-valued T-squares and tidiness.

Characteristically, one of Geddes's first innovations toward improving the congested slums of Edinburgh was not to map out an ideal system of open spaces, but to get hold of every small patch of unusable or unused vacant land, and, with volunteer help, turn that into a tiny patch of garden or park. The process of 'conservative surgery,' as Geddes called it in one of his Indian reports, was essentially what he stood for: a process that respected the native style of life and sought to recapture and further its best intentions. He felt that if the right method were established, one which enlisted the interest and services of the plain man and woman, even of the school-child, a little leaven would in time leaven the whole loaf.

What Geddes's outlook and method contribute to the planning of today are precisely those elements that the administrator, the bureaucrat, and the businessman in the interest of economy or efficiency, or profit, are tempted to leave out: time, patience, loving care of detail, a watchful interrelation of past and future, an insistence upon establishing the human scale and the human purpose above conforming to merely

115

mechanical requirements: finally a willingness to leave an essential part of the process to those who are most intimately concerned with it—the ultimate users, consumers, or citizens.

"The resorption of government," to use a phrase Geddes and Branford coined, was an integral part of the development of citizenship, and so of the improvement of cities. Like William James, Geddes was against all bigness, and against all the obvious manifestations of success. "On pain of economic waste, of practical failure no less than artistic futility, or even worse, each true design," Geddes noted, "each valid scheme should and must embody the full utilization of local and regional conditions and be the expression of local and regional personality. 'Local character' is thus no mere accidental old world quaintness, as its mimics think and say. It is attained only in course of adequate grasp and treatment of the whole environment, and in active sympathy with the essential and characteristic life of the place concerned." This insistence upon sympathy and human-heartedness as the mark of a right attitude and relationship is one of the distinguishing marks of Geddes's planning philosophy. —The Architectural Review, London. August 1950

Note: Jaqueline Tyrwhitt's selections from Geddes's notable reports on the Planning of Cities, in 'Patrick Geddes in India' give some measure of his essential contributions.

THE YEARS PASS. Old Geddes's letters grow more and more urgent; for he is afflicted with diabetes and sees his time limited; but his mind keeps on spinning in the old grooves and I fear his grandiose plans and projects are more a sign of senility than of his real greatness. The old devil has wantonly poured about $90,000 into his collection of more or less empty buildings at Montpellier, because, dreaming at seventy-seven of a new college with himself as planner, architect, and educator, he has found it easier to gather the stones than the students. The whole business makes one profoundly sad: it shows the old flaw of his wilfullness, a stubborn refusal to embrace any other reality than his own, which is doubtless in part the secret of his genius; but it also explains his failures, too. If I went to him I could only wring my hands and shake my head despairingly; and it seems safer, cheaper, easier, kinder, to do this at a distance. —Letter to Dr. Henry A. Murray. May 12, 1931

Patrick Geddes's Influence on My Thought

P.G. exemplified the basically ecological doctrine of organic unity in his manifold activities: though at the end this dynamic conception was to be frozen in a series of graphic charts that mocked the flow of events, ignoring the dynamism of language, and the essential inner act. His more pious followers memorized and mimicked these static categories, instead of living the life. P.G.'s philosophy helped save me from becoming a one-eyed specialist: but even better, after I had achieved competence in more than one field, it gave me the confidence to become a generalist—one who sought to bring together in a more intelligible pattern the knowledge that the specialist had, by over-strenuous concentration, sealed off in separate compartments. Not that he or I would disparage the work of the specialist. Like Pierre Dansereau I accept it and seek to use it—except when it mistakes the part for the whole, or renounces any effort to understand and utilize the whole. For me, as first for Geddes, specialism and generalism were complementary activities and effective thought must necessarily fuse them together.

Though Geddes was fertile in vivid concrete illustrations—often extremely stimulating, not least because of his satiric, even savage wit—it was his more basic personal insights and responses that have remained with me and partly guided my life. I never accepted C. P. Snow's division of the 'two cultures'—though I find it ironic that even American critics who discuss this thesis never refer to various contemporaries like myself who had already dissolved that false dichotomy in practice. Just the other day, in a seminar of the Jung Institut, in Zürich, I was asked by a young man with an exceptionally high I.Q.—in fact one of the self-satisfied members of the 'Mensa' group—if I considered my work 'literature.' The question was meaningless to me: it covertly assumed that if it was literature it was not 'science'—or at least not scientifically respectable. But I consider Henri Poincaré's 'Science and Hypothesis' notable as fine writing; and I am ashamed of my own writing when it sometimes slips into technical jargon, the 'secret language' of science. Mathematicians are notoriously proud of achieving 'elegant' solutions; and in my ideal world of thought I would gladly forfeit quick results for statements that would be as esthetically satisfying and humanly as attractive as Plato's dialogues, even if it required more time and effort to achieve this result.

Geddes's living example influenced me in many other ways. But this general personal orientation was his most fundamental and lasting contribution, whereas certain other phases of his thought to which he attached great value, like his adhesion to Comte and Le Play, played only a minor part in my thinking, even in my youth, and have left only residual traces. His Comtean sociological division of a society into chiefs and people, emotionals and intellectuals, has indeed its parallel in Jung's later division of personality types. But unfortunately both schemes tacitly accept the rigidities of ancient caste societies and overlook the interplay of types, their changing roles in new situations—as when the butler, in Barrie's 'The Admirable Crichton' becomes the true leader (Chief) of the castaways. The feat of personality is to escape these fixations and transcend these categories. Jung himself saw this when he said it was necessary to reinforce and develop the weak side of the personality in the interest of balance.   —RN. June 14, 1967

DISCIPLESHIP. The tragedy of the relation between teacher and pupil is that every disciple who is worth his salt betrays his master. It is only the spiritual Judas who remains completely loyal to the word and form of the master's statement. Thus treason to the teacher is really loyalty to life, and to every part of his teaching that adequately expresses life. But it is better for the disciple to be aware of the extent of his departures and additions, and to assume the duty of facing facts freshly and re-evaluating them, than to substitute his thought for the master's without making this plain, or to repeat the formulas and words which, even if they reproduce the very letter of the Master's thought, no longer can mean to even his most loyal continuators what they meant to him, since time and experience have changed both parties since their utterance.   —RN. March 24, 1935

Every country poisons itself with its great men. Whitman declares the virtues of democracy to a country that should have read Nietzsche: Nietzsche emphasizes the bellicose brusqueness of the Prussians, who should, instead have learned a little mystic humility from Tolstoi. So England, the land of work, creates a Carlyle who preaches the gospel of work: a salutary gospel, perhaps, for the Hindu. The Master preaches the doctrine of saving opposites.   —RN. For the unwritten 'Great Testament of James McMaster' [Patrick Geddes]. February 1935

9: The Little Testament of Bernard Martin

Nothing I had mulled over or written before 1926 serves to explain the sudden effusion of 'The Little Testament.' Both its form and its contents were gifts of my unconscious, which, to my surprise came forth immediately I had turned 'The Golden Day' over to my publisher. One small incident in New York that summer was perhaps responsible for releasing this gush of memories and fantasies. A year before his death when Van Wyck Brooks began work on a study of my life and work, I feared he might draw too freely on this testament for biographic details in making one of his characteristic pastiches. There was reason for my anxiety, for I found later that even the first two pages of this unfinished manuscript were mottled with bad guesses. To safeguard my old friend, whose health was rapidly failing, I agreed to provide an annotated commentary on 'The Little Testament.' Woe to some future critic who overlooks that document in order to jump the gun before my authentic biography finally is published!

The first draft of 'The Little Testament' was written as free verse; but on revision I turned these lines into paragraphs of rhythmic prose. Horace Liveright, my adventurous first publisher, was generously ready to publish 'The Little Testament' as a book, but predicted a meager sale. So instead I submitted it to my fellow editors of The American Caravan. As a special form of the novella, 'The Little Testament' remained sui generis, imitated only by myself, till in 1939 I began an even more intimate probing of marital and extra-marital love in 'Victor'—an unfinished novel in verse.

Part One

1

Of the first five years nothing remains except goldfish spinning around a slippery jar, and the furtive light of a back-parlor window against the white faces that crept around upon the red carpet that concealed a carpet beneath a wardrobe that was really a bed: that and the figure of Bernie's Granmer grimacing in haste before a pier glass as she perched a black bonnet upon a head that had once been beautiful. Silence follows. One must be silent at play: Granmer is sick: Granmer is very sick: Granmer is not. Black ribbons and black veils and trickling eyes are all that remain of Granmer: black veils are mourning but mourning is not the beginning of day: mourning is the red rim of sunset about tired eyes. Goldfish gasp softly against the translucent boundaries of their existence. Goldfish spin eternally around a glass jar.

2

The days do not hurry: the days come slow: one peels the hours off as Nornie peels a mushroom. The days creep: the minutes clatter with emptiness: an hour with Granper in Central Park rattles like seeds in a gourd, the gourd of empty days. Pine needles do not prick: darning needles do not darn: policemen eat little boys: bugaboos do not scare policemen. Granper is a head waiter at Delmonico's: he brings home detachable noses and false faces. When Granper wears a false face he is the devil: false faces and policemen are not bugaboos but they are even worse than bugaboos. Granper is foxy: and when he bunches his breasts up they are like a woman's.

3

Seven goldfish play wavy hide and seek in wavy weeds. Granper mates yellow birds with green birds: on a spring morning cinnamon birds crack through the speckled eggs. Little boys have no business in the pantry where the yellow birds and the green birds sing. When a little boy leaves the pantry door open the cat eats the goldfish as well as the yellow birds the green birds and the weeny cinnamon birds. Little boys dream of false faces and policemen. Mamadear lights the light and holds the little boy's hands. Morning comes: the cage is empty: the cat is fat. The little boy smiles. Bernie left the pantry door open: the policeman did not eat Bernie: the policeman never even rang the doorbell and asked: Have you a bad little boy named Bernie here? But the goldfish and the birdies are dead: Granmer is dead too. The eternal goldfish will never spin around any more in a glass jar.

4

The hands of the clock turn around. Tick lives: tock dies: tick lives: tock dies. Bong-bong-bong is the voice of doom. The clock never turns backwards: six says wake Bernie: seven says eat Bernie: eight says school Bernie: nine says classroom Bernie. Present: present early: late: present: present. Absent never answers for itself: present never answers for anyone else except when present is naughty. Blang goes the big bell: pling, pling, pling go the classroom bells. Home for lunch: back for school: present: present: tardy: late. The schoolyard is bare: school has begun: loitering is a crime. Little boys cry when their names are put in a black book but loitering is a crime: crimes are punished. Big boys make little boys show their penis in the lavatory: little boys go home at the end of the week with a certificate for good conduct. Five hours five days five certificates make an elementary education: there is also reading writing and arithmetic: drawing is nice but faces are not allowed. Sixty seconds make a minute: sixty minutes make an hour: six years make a little boy who knows that alcohol is bad for the health that trees are deciduous and evergreen that G.C.D. means greatest common divisor that all day suckers are poisonous unless consumed to the last layer that one hundred dollars at six per cent for one year is seven goldfish spinning around a glass jar.

5

Sally is seven: she is a jockey's daughter. Her white face has been kicked in by a horse: her distorted beauty awakens six masculine summers. She cuts up her own food in the Children's Dining Room: she rides to the races in her uncle's buggy. A word from Sally is a golden ball dancing on top of a fountain: the touch of her hand is a glass of cold seltzer at the Spa. Kiss Sally: kiss Sally: hide behind the sofa: hide and seek: spring at her: kiss the hair of Sally's pigtail. But the cuff of Sally's hand behind the sofa is the splintering of a sun into sordid stars. Six masculine years long for Sally: they play with Sally before anyone else is awake: they show everything to Sally: she shows everything to them: but she is not the real Sally with the oily pigtail and the white knuckles that stung like marble against pink jelly.

6

The smell of stale onions on Nornie's cracked fingers means winter. When Granper's frock coat opens on a gold watch chain it is spring. In spring goats ramp for bock beer in front of swinging doors: behind the paving stone in the backyard parsley, pansies, geraniums, and flaxseed left over from poultices grow into flowers, green, purple, red, blue. Hot potatoes in a fire beneath mummied sunflower stalks is autumn: but marbles are always spring. Push wagons in the twilight with a cigarbox lantern are summer. Mamadear getting excited and saying: Isn't the air beautiful and what are the odds on Waterboy in the Brighton Handicap with a sip of beer at a smeary table on the lap of a boney man with yellow finger tips, Mamadear lifting her brown veil and drinking, too, is spring, is summer, is fall.

7

Tick-tock: tick-tock: tick lives: tock dies. Nornie buttons the last button and pulls the muffler higher. Mamadear says don't play with naughty boys in the lavatory. Tick-tock: man is in the nominative case, subject to the verb do: do good: do lessons: do memory work: present participle doing: doing this: doing that: doing nothing: negative particle not: not doing what one wants: not telling what one dreams: not saying what one thinks: not arguing with the teacher: not looking around in class: not throwing boardrubbers: not making spitballs: not speaking out of turn. Tick-tock: report cards: A is excellent: Bernie's A's make a pattern of the months: Bernie is a grind: Bernie is the teacher's pet. When Granper walks with Bernie along Riverside Drive he shows him the ships and the freight trains and he tells him about his life in Paris, Munich, Copenhagen: when Nornie cooks she tells Bernie about the Holy Virgin and Ireland and how the nuns made a Novena and what one found on the strand of Youghal: Mamadear lets Bernie play with her embroidery silks and when she wants some thread she sends Bernie to the store and tells him to mind the change. Granper and Nornie and Mamadear show Bernie the rudiments of geography, ethics, mathematics, art: but Bernie shames them with his school knowledge. Granper can't do fractions like Bernie and he never knew how many states are in South America.

8

Portia's plea closes the Morning Assembly: Bernie wants to be a lawyer. But Shakespeare was a very great poet: Bernie wants to be a poet, too. But electricity is more fun than anything: if one had five dollars one could get a wireless set: a tuning coil and a detector bring musical dash-dots, and if one were rich and had ten dollars one could have a loose-coupler and a variable condenser and get louder music from remoter dash-dots. Barney is Bernie's best friend: Barney and Bernie share candy: Barney will buy a wireless outfit. Bernie is poor and will make his. The dash-dots are declarations of love in a foreign language. Wire and binding posts become exciting pieces of statuary. Bernie decides to be an engineer: Barney will be an engineer, too, and manage a sugar plantation in Cuba.

9

Summer is warm in the city: summer glows on the sear green of Central Park. Bernie meets a Princess: she tells Bernie he is her sweetheart. She is a real Russian Princess with a pug nose and blonde hair. He is convinced but not ravished. Summer is warm. Granper's flabby flesh falls over grayblear mournful eyes: Granper's flabby skin droops from lean shanks where the sheet parts. Kiss me Goodbye, Bernie: be good to Mamadear: be a brave man! You will not see me again. Goodbye Granper: but I shall be back soon. And I shall go soon, says Granper. Twelve years are troubled: six times twelve are putting trouble far behind them. Bernie leaves the doubtful pleasure of a Princess's espousal to meet Betty. Betty helps with the dishes on the farm. To dry the dishes when Betty washes them is to smell the perfume of ferns in her hair and see the down on her neck fall into the hollow of a perfect back. One night Betty says: Kiss me! Jacob the smelly hired man laughs many laughs. Betty has her kiss. Granper dies whilst Betty calmly engages Bernie with more kisses. Bernie does not return till Granper is buried with his griefs and loves: Bernie still dares to dream of love that knows no grief or burial. Back in the city Bernie writes Betty fevered letters, exploding with passion like a milkweed pod in autumn. Betty never gets or never heeds them. Autumn is dank with vegetation and disappointment.

10

Russian faces: German faces: Italian faces: Jewish faces: a thousand faces cloud and scatter in the halls: smudgy faces: keen faces: blubber faces. In the lunchroom they munch and shout in Bernie's ear: Bernie eats his roll alone in the dark corridor. Faces leer at Bernie and call him sweetie: false faces: but old faces are kind faces: kind faces keep school. A patient face with a blind blue eye teaches geometry as if Pythagoras and Euclid were still alive: a black sardonic face above broad shoulders utters the words Philosophy—Descartes—cogito ergo sum. A long bearded face recites his Milton like a prayer: a pink solemn face beneath a carrot pompadour sits down with Bernard, Solomon, and Freddy to write a play. The hours do not crawl: the hours are not empty: the clock says neither tick nor tock. The moments become monuments: each monument shelters a memory. Happy faces turning wood into unbelievable chair legs that never get attached to chairs: anxious faces pouring white lead into green sand molds: blurred faces following the mystery of electrons into test-tubes placed over anode and cathode: wild faces describing elegant parabolae with basketballs: jolly faces twisting in the pageant of a Christmas dance: serious faces walking home along Fifth Avenue, talking about God: these faces made Bernard's face: they translated passive tick-tock into the imperative mood and the active voice.

11

Engines are buckets and shovels dressed up for adults. Science is abracadabra and fie-fy-fo-fum. Electricity is interesting but not so interesting as love. Smooth binding posts are dull beside the frail throbbing fountain that leaps into the sunshine of Annabel's face: alternating currents do not reverse polarity so quickly as the heart that beholds Annabel. Engines are buckets and shovels dressed up for adults who have never known Annabel. Dynamos generate electricity: but Annabel generates the dynamo that generates the dynamo that generates the electricity.

12

The trees of West End Avenue drip warm steam. Annabel's body curls like a white mist against the sullen recess of an August afternoon. Thunder booms in the air: lightning darts gigantic butterflies. Annabel listlessly hovers over a book, her shoulder hunching near to Bernard's. Bernard scarcely dares to sigh on Annabel's neck: a lock of her hair on Bernard's cheek dances shivered sparks within his breast. Embraces that do not touch linger longer in the arms that do not hold: manhood shudders in mid-air on a swinging beam, swinging, swaying, slipping, sliding, edging into nothingness. The soft gloom of Annabel's passion reveals green eyes dew-honeyed with expectancy. The pavements spatter with wild rain: two bodies tremble on the verge of an apocalyptic revelation. Bernard quivers with frightened dizzy joy: the lips of Annabel are sultry with a kiss that is not taken. Like taut elastic all the tension breaks when Why are you sitting in the dark? comes from a portly gray solicitous bosom with an umbrella blocking a doorway that once held at bay a fugitive and unreal world.

13

The love of Bernard and Annabel evaporates into billets of white and blue paper that come every morning laden with philosophy, adoration, and reproach. Autumn lifts the leaves of West End Avenue into crackled nervous heaps. Autumn leaves Bernard with the agony of a reluctant surrender to a lackadaisical youth not keyed to hesitate before an obvious embrace. Engines are shovels and buckets dressed up for adults. Love is interesting but not so interesting as electricity. Without contact or induction electricity does not travel. When sparks jumped across the electrodes of Bernard and Annabel that August afternoon, what mysterious terror became the insulator?

14

Dreams are the color left in the water when acts are wrung out: dreams are blind arrows that never leave the bow: dreams are the remembrance of a courage that never went into battle. One ounce of distilled dreams would provide the plots of five hundred moving pictures or the reality of seven murders, eighteen rapes, fifty-five suicides, a hundred Carnegie medals, and the blushes of many bridesmaids. From a day's dreams one might stock a department store with chemises or get enough courage to quench a fire in a powder plant. The dreams of fifteen would create a menagerie and overflow the house of reptiles: a medical museum could be filled with the pre-natal reminiscences enveloped in dreams, and surgical skill could not unravel the physiological intricacy of the chimeric women known to sleeping adolescents. Dreams are the color left in the water: when life leaves dreams behind life is sad dirty white. Maturity is a white sad dirtiness without the dreams of fifteen: maturity means that the courage which quenches fires will stand by a principle: maturity means that the distillation which would produce a movie will build a home: it means that wild rapes and impossible copulations become the delicious commonplaces of connubiality. But at fifteen Dionysos has a wry neck. Dreams are the color left behind by a sad white dirty life.

Part Two

15

Why is the city sober gray? Why are the stones white sober cold? Rocks crumble into parallelograms against a geometric sky. Black creatures run back and forth in the crevices thinking that civilization is composed of subways, traffic signals, and right angles. If right angles and subways are emblems of civilization how wonderful are the tracks of a cow and the ways of a grasshopper!

16

What will Bernard be: what will Bernard be? In Broad Street white coats clack figures on a July morning: flicker-eyes watch tickers through the sickish atmosphere of desiccated cigars. American Can at 87 is another way of saying tick-tock. Everyday Wall Street goes to school at ten and is dismissed at three: Wall Street has never gotten beyond fractions and elementary arithmetic. Five certificates make a gold star: five gold stars make a tip that almost came from Mr. Morgan and almost made a fortune. Good conduct means that little boys can get to the golflinks by five: good little boys can have bad little girls in nice little flats as soon as they can afford them. Begin at the bottom and work your way up is the rule of Wall Street. But even when Bernard dreams of undies he doesn't want bad little girls. Bernard does not like being a messenger in Wall Street. What shall Bernard do? What shall Bernard do?

17

What shall Bernard be: what shall Bernard be? At three-fifteen in the morning hot cocoa with malted milk is a plausible substitute for interrupted sleep. Ferryboats sound like the snores of nightwatchmen in the green corridors of a hospital: in the Herald Building, stale paper gives dirty mop water the smell of a bad cigar in a Pullman smoking compartment. When Bernard appears the boys in the corner scoop up the cards and go down to Nelligans for a last drink. Bernard lays out eight stacks of paper, buys egg sandwiches, balances three cans of beer, sweeps up the floor around the copy desk, and listens to the tedious sagacity of Rogan the night city editor labeling the morning's columns: Neb Gov: T R: Sex Fed: Pat Murd. Old news is wood pulp macerated and rolled into new news: Ships sink: men murder: wars wax: every day ships sink: men murder: wars wax. But reporters do not always remember that the verb must agree with the subject in number; and the drama of arising at three-fifteen is belittled by the fact that the sun reveals a dozen stale faces in a dirty office. To get up at three-fifteen: to report a fire: to write a stick—oh joy! but a thousand fires: a thousand sticks is tick-tock all over again. If Bernard remains a copy boy he will become a reporter. Bernard will not become a reporter—and what shall Bernard do?

18

Buckets of gold on a chain curve over the hill on an autumn evening: in the solitude of an affected antiquity Gothic pinnacles gleam whitely into fading purple. The diminished roar of the distant El creeps out under a blanket of patchwork silence. In the distance golden beer pours from electric bottles: flash signs display cheap jewelry on the bosom of Harlem: remote lamps melt into the feebleness of foggy stars. Bernard does odd jobs by day: Bernard reads by day: at night he seeks the company of students within walls of an affected antiquity.

19

Dim graygreen corridors swerve in solemn arcs: faces beautiful with thought make thought beautiful. How shall men behave in society and on what Ionic shore did men begin to wing their way above the matted forest of their daily life into the rarefied clarity of philosophic thought? Psychology deals with human behavior. The last entrail of a dissected grasshopper increases the wonder of life. If life is a tree, let us smell the flower and dig at the roots: if Annabel is worth embracing, so is the hypothesis of evolution: the organ that pries into the body of a woman is the instrument that drives excitedly into the womb of Nature: the brain is composed of erectile tissue: every living thought is a divine orgasm.

20

Brother Schapiro wields over Politics a knife that cuts with unguents and balm: man is by nature a political animal and by ill-nature a dangerous one: monogamy is as valuable for the family as it is tedious for the parents: war is inevitable while men believe in the inevitability of war. The inarticulate passion of Selwin over a slide on the microscope beatifies the rosary of great names: Linnaeus, Buffon, Darwin, Mendel, Huxley, with a special prayer for the heretics, Oken, Goethe, Butler, Driesch, Jennings, Geddes, and nameless men who forever storm against the true Church and save it. Palmer who makes literature as familiar as the smile of a beloved mouth is a white ember of happiness: the happiness of Chaucer, Spenser, Shelley, Keats. His eyes are exhausted volcanoes peering over the winter landscape of a wistful smile. The Holy Ghost descends when Adonais beacons from his abode in Palmer's sanctuary: there is religion enough in his classroom to curse a hundred churches for their blasphemy. No word is too often profaned for Palmer to redeem it: no emotion so frail but it becomes a shaft of crystal dancing on his tongue. Palmer disturbs Bernard with the joy of elevated thoughts. Life is neither Annabels nor Dynamos: life is not was not cannot won't be more than the point of calm in the moving whirlwind of God.

21

Palmer brings Bernard to the core of the whirlwind: it is the core of Plato: it is form: it is the core of Aristotle: every living thing fulfills its inner shape: it is the core of Spinoza: the intellectual love of the Universe: it is the core of Berkeley, that man and God have begotten the same reality. When Bernard thinks about Berkeley in the moonlight the dark bulk of almost antique buildings becomes the shadow of his own thought: the solidity of the ground is the exhalation of an ancient dream. There is not was not cannot won't be more matter and bottom to man's life than the ruffle of a passing thought on the brow of God. Man is a thought: cities are a thought: Bernard is a thought: and if the thought perished, what would remain? The universe is an idiot: man is God's first gleam of an idea. The world is a step in the equation of an incalculable theorem. If God knew the answer he would not bother to work it out.

22

This is life! This is learning! Bernard wants to drain it dry. But by day college is tick-tock on a useless metronome. Dull faces crawl through the iniquity of tortured lessons. Massed monkeys are the sport of inane tropisms called hazing, games, and college spirit. Fill out the form: sign the dotted line: report promptly: do not live with a thought lest the thought keep you from turning over memorizable papers and acquiring insignificant marks. Do this: do that: learn this: learn that: all goes toward a degree except the active use and exploration of the outer scene, the city, or the fruitful ground within where bean sprouts of ideas put forth their radicals. Never dwell on anything for more than fifty minutes at a time if you can help it: credits are credits! White worms gnaw at Bernard's soul: this is not meditation. White worms creep through Bernard's mind: this is not learning. White worms tear at Bernard's vitals: this is not living! White worms sallow nervous too much girls or what? Fever's irritation indicates a prolonged rest. The undertaker's shop leers like a pimp at a carnival: white worms are the silent partners of black undertakers.

23

The hours come slowly: the day is wide: the city spreads before Bernard's feet like a gleaming map. Health is a matter of slow deliberate motions, warm baths, clean clothes, and walks along unending avenues, various with economics, sociology, biology, literature, drama, and art in the guise of people. People tell everything. The full waters of the East River are an invitation to explore brown barges with dingy good natured men. From the lower docks the bridges are plutonic fountains, meeting midway between the shores. Two months making systematic tabulations among the garment workers bring Bernard face to face with the blind drama of an industry seeking to achieve stability out of spasmodic and irrelevant enterprises that ebb and flow with fashion.

24

Michael Marx rises to hatred of the bourgeoisie out of a bed illegitimately soiled with bedbugs beyond the usual number: he knows the hey-nonny-nonny of finding the family furniture on the street, and in the handspring of adolescence he leaves behind I pledge allegiance to the flag and to all tick-tock at six per cent. He and Bernard stamp envelopes in a Second Avenue basement where twenty Wobblies proclaim the immediate revolution of doing bad work worse. Mike and Bernard dream of education for the masses from soapboxes. Bernard writes an ABC of economics: Mike never forgets the bedbugs nor the soapboxes nor the verbal duties of class consciousness. Mike and Bernard hate the capitalist oppressors. Bernard equally hates the workers for being oppressed. But Bernard belongs to the bourgeoisie because he has an income of four hundred dollars a year and enjoys the luxury of gentlemanly indigence. Mike writes Bernard loving letters of excommunication.

25

Patches of iridescence on dull and slimy waters: the Art Museum is a patch of iridescence: plaster casts of Greek gods are iridescent on the flats of Yorkville: the Library of spacious catalogues pointing to all necessary books is an iridescence on the smutty night of Broadway. The towers of Manhattan gleaming across the upper Bay on a summer afternoon are iridescent: the Mall is iridescent with a hundred colors on a June Sunday joyblazing brightness. The meadows in Prospect Park on a misty April day are an iridescence hedged with phantom trees: the Westchester hills in October are petrified sunsets. In May the Croton Viaduct leads into Yonkers like a carpet unrolled for a dryad's wedding. Salt odors creeping along the Hudson on an August night uncage seagulls of memory. The smell of roasting coffee in Franklin Street brings perfumes from distant bazaars. The craggy face of Carl Schurz against a lavender night is a stark finger raised against oblivion. Dull and slimy waters creep around the city. Iridescent patches hide the slimy waters. Youth is an iridescence.

26

When the guns bluster with belligerency in 1914 Bernard says: This finishes my career! Bernard does not know what his career is but feels that a great war will finish it. When the cackle of insane apologetics breaks out like the tea-table gossip of Bedlam: when Thomas Mann and Henri Bergson and H. G. Wells share honors for being speciously dishonorable Bernard says: We must keep out of it—may no one win! By 1917 Bernard still hates the war but is carried away by the paper strategy of pragmatists and New Republicans: he whoops for Woodrow Wilson till Memorial Day. . . . Then he knows for sure his world is blasted. Cackles of insanity become requisites for polite intercourse.

27

Bernard's generation goes in for Social Service. They do not particularly care what Society does so long as the technique is good and whatever is done is done efficiently with a minimum wage for hired persons, examinations for the official caste, and well-designed badges of self-righteousness for those who do the thinking and direction. Universal compulsory voluntary pacifistic military service is the sum of liberal aspirations in 1917: this shibboleth will save an autocratic world for democratic unity. The dictatorship of war brings echoes of Armageddon where people who believe in the eight-hour day and the recall of judges battle for the Lord. War is inevitable, and the more we have of it the sooner will pragmatists make wise regulations for instituting a Chatauqua of machine guns. In matters of instrumental technique, conscientious scruples about killing or doubts about the purpose for which one kills are out of place. Randolph Bourne knows better than the pragmatists; with him for rocket, the Seven Arts ascends in glory-fire. He sees that chains are chains though called Democracy and Service that Hell is Hell, though called the vestibule of Heaven. How many paper warriors have said penance to the shade of Randolph Bourne?

28

Men are fighting: men are gasping: men are dying. Bernard smiles at his doctor and answers the undertaker's leer with a wink. Bernard is dying, too, but he does not die so fast as the young men who die in Flanders or in Picardy. The dread of dying excites the pugnacity of clerks and financiers who sit on stools all day and suffer from a constipation that only fear can relieve. Prepare for ripping guts out says the soldier: prepare for safety first and steen per cent says the financier: prepare for more preparedness say the clerks: prepare for the defense of Honor say the politicians, who know of Honor by reputation. Prepare to leave your wastebaskets and your vain motions says a tired God who knows that a hundred million efforts at divinity are already much more dead than they suppose. Living wastebaskets and white tape is the deafness of never hearing life's music. War is the attempt to squelch life's music in the imitative cacophony of brutal valor. In a world that is governed by tick-tock, War is a reasonable and beautiful mode of life.

29

Bernard is not dominated by his overt convictions: Bernard wants to live. But why should Bernard live? Twenty-one is a good time to die. Bernard can remember summer afternoons paddling in the White River of Vermont with heron passing overhead and the slippery flicker of trout in the shadows of aqueous stones: Bernard can remember shrews playing in the woodlot and kisses in the rose garden where Bertha sought white petals and concealment: Bernard can remember the austere divinity of a condescending Annabel, arguing about the basis of ethical conduct in a tawdry Morningside Apartment: no kisses will ever satisfy him like that chastity: no surrender will ever thrill like that aloofness! Bernard can remember walks in the Westchester Hills with Agnes whose milky skin was the nectar offered at a feast of virgins, whose red hair was the last glow of the sun on russet walls. Bernard can remember the tender intimacy of Mamadear when they talked beside an open window above the rumble of the Elevated, domestically fomented with the smell of baking bread. Bernard had known grief without irreparable bitterness and joy without tedious responsibility. Bernard dear: think well: you are twenty-one. The clerks, the preachers, the politicians, the soldiers do not realize it: but perhaps this is your opportunity: twenty-one is a good time to die. Bernard alas! is not governed by philosophic arguments and appraisals: Bernard wants to live—and why should Bernard die?

30

At six in the morning the Flatiron Building shows yellow lights against a green April sky. Sleepy recruits summoned for inspection are told to return at ten for medical examination. At sunset Mamadear and Nornie become the faceless shadows of irretrievable years and it would not matter if Annabel had as many as ten lovers. Nightmares gallop convulsively through tedious days of shorn heads, weakly brackish coffee, steam-trickling clammy naked bodies, and inspection from medical gold-stripers who could learn human decency from veterinaries that handle hydrophobic dogs. Sleep is peace if you do not get bumped out of your hammock to mount guard for two hours over unassailable quarters girdled in quarantine. Sleep is peace, and under ordinary circumstances belly inspection would be funny.

31

Gruff seadogs who spit salt aren't always hardboiled. Even the little Greek C.P.O. grows husky when he tells how a man buried at sea leaves no enemies behind and all are shipmates. The mystery of the uniform of the day is that the sun always shines on overshoes and peajackets and the wind from Narragansett Bay whips icy rain on leggins and no peajackets. Seventy men in a shack cease to be Ohio, Mississippi, Kansas, to become Jim, Bill, and Jack. A squareknot, a figure-of-eight knot, and a clove-hitch can easily be untied but nothing will untie the knot in Bernard's throat on a Sunday afternoon when he sprawls on the crest of Strawberry Hill and watches the train steam-hooting around a distant curve. Men are court-martialed and sent to the brig for little offenses everyone has committed. The Catholic priest never asks Bernard whether he has any religion but gets him the impossible dispensation of a furlough and visits him in the hospital when the measles side with the commandant against God's ministers. At the Knights of Columbus Hut and the J.W.B. you can have plenty of writing paper: at the Y.M.C.A. it is doled out piece by piece, and go-getting business men preach Sunday sermons with enthusiasm for clean guts.

32

A morning on Narragansett Bay in a whale-boat takes the sting out of the Chief's nervous oaths. Sunset over the mainland makes evening muster a stale prayer in a magnificent cathedral. An hour before dawn on a rainy night wafts the perfume of lilacs and newmown hay from the misty ledge of Jamestown. Ratlike boats creep over the water in the faint lemon bleakness of sunrise. Magnolia petals make Bernard think of Agnes's bosom. The sea that surges against the cliffs is the whisper of an old friend who says: Never mind: you and I will be here when they are gone. O World! O Life! O Time! is a good poem for sentry duty on a quiet night.

33

Jerry and Bernard become friends: Jerry works in an office in New York. When the C.P.O. says: So you're wise guys from Toid Avenoo and Toity-toid Street Jerry and Bernard look at each other and smile. Jerry has read Strindberg and Ibsen too: Jerry has gone to City College too: Jerry has been disappointed in love too: Jerry is going to be a radio operator too. Jerry and Bernard recite Dehmel and Rilke to each other: they laugh at the maudlin fevers of patriotism. They would like to talk to a Hun and find out whether anyone had taken Hauptmann's place.

34

Monday roast beef: Tuesday seagull: Wednesday sou-oup: all American mothers, we wish the same to you! Da-dit-da-da: da-da-dit-dit-dit: da-dit-

dit-da. In the clamorous gloom of Austin Hall in Cambridge Bernard wonders what it would be like to hear the signal of the flagship coming from a battle formation in the North Sea. Twenty-one is a good time to die. Captains and radio operators die first. The Heinies sat on their keys and beat the Limies with their radios in the Jutland fight, and if this was a good war we'd be fighting the Limies. In Hong-kong or Guantanamo or Manila we're always fighting the Limies. Perhaps when we've finished with the Huns we'll fight the Limies, too. The Navy's been waiting a long time for a good fight. Dit-dit: dit-dit: dit-dit: stand by for a weather report, Arlington broadcasting.

35

The days become a vacancy of soft lassitude, yellowsoft in the haze of September. Nature has found a rival to poison gas: Nature has found that influenza can turn streets into trenches quicker than an army. On Harvard Field the gobs sprawl around in friendly games or stand at rest. Every once in a while someone falls in a heap and gets a free ride in the hurry-up. Harry awakes in the bunk below Bernard with a chill: Bernard gives Harry his blanket and in the morning draws his arm around Harry's tired neck and walks him to the Sick Bay. When Harry comes back the first rumor of the Armistice has turned the campus into a wild auction room where men offer ditty bags to each other and trample upon white hats hurled against a gray sky.

36

The clerks, the financiers, and the politicians have had a movement! College professors have become as important as overnight ensigns: they have worn iron mittens: at their command coal has got tangled up in the Jersey meadows. Millionaires have made the supreme sacrifice of becoming godalmighty for a dollar a year: a hundred iron ships are floating like paper boats in the Delaware. Irascible men with disordered glands have become patriots by the simple method of spying on their neighbors and selling other people's sacrifices in job-lots: woolen manufacturers, carpenters, riveters, the daughters of the best families have had their fill of money, lust, and glory. Bernard has lost his chance of dying, of dying gloriously, at any rate of dying.

37

When the grinning clerks empty wastepaper baskets and the remains of the candy the boss gave the stenographer upon the white-capped radio-boys who march through State Street, Bernard remembers that the Navy was a decent place after all. When spy-hunting and witch-baiting go on after the Armistice, when patriotic people declare that little Huns should be boiled in oil, when investigators from political boobyhatches discover that Godwin's 'Political Justice,' Marx's 'Kapital' and the plays of Bernard Shaw can be bought at bookstores: when Red Flags take the place of foreign enemies and Blasto for constipation—Bernard remembers that the Navy was a good place after all. The Navy does its job without throwing moral spasms over the enemy: the Navy would like a wallop at the Limies, maybe, but everything else is part of the day's work.

38

Slush lies on the fields of Pelham Bay when Bernard checks out with his seabag and an honorable discharge. Amsterdam Avenue is a queer place to walk with a seabag. When a liberated gob marches along Eighty-third Street life is life is no longer a nightmare. Mamadear says: I knew you'd never have to go across after I visited you last summer in Cambridge. Normie says: "You've been gone a long time and everything's different: we eat toast instead of rolls in the morning my back hasn't gotten any better do you still wear your heavy woolen sox? Mamadear says there's been a letter here from Annabel I didn't forward. Annabel was married a fortnight ago and lives in Pittsburgh with Fred who believes in the Saturday Evening Post, flaked breakfast foods and oral antiseptics. Everything is different; and we eat toast instead of rolls in the morning.

Part Three

39

Bernard is a radio operator: if the worst comes he can try a turn at sea. Bernard can pound a typewriter fast and if the very worst comes he might become a male secretary. Bernard writes better than college graduates usually write at first: but when Bernard asks for books to review at the office of Chronos he feels like a thief and a perjurer when he walks away with four of them. Reviewing books is the summit of Bernard's dreams. With the love he puts into a book review he might write three sonnets or seduce a young lady. The cordiality of Richard Velvet has the hopefulness of Micawber tinctured by worldly wisdom: when Richard Velvet says Would you care for a half-time job as editor? the white fireplace capers behind a desk in time with the unexpected eructations of Bernard's heart. If Bernard knew what swooning was, Bernard would swoon.

40

To have a desk . . . to write an article . . . to offer an opinion! To pore through piles of books! to deliver more opinions! To offer the concealed cleverness of adolescence as the spontaneous breath of maturity! Pinch yourself, Bernard, is this real? Are you real? Are Velvet, Miss Herriott, Welsh, the slim impresario Harrison Martyn real? Is the Brotherhood of Man real? Is the Triumph of Labor real? Is the Russian Revolution real? Is Universal Peace real? Yes: it is all real. The peace treaty has not been signed yet: the revolution has not been choked by military oppression yet: the socialist cause has not died of infantile paralysis and hardening of the arteries yet: you are in the Reconstruction Period, Bernard. You are undertaking the Reconstruction of the Social Order. You know a great deal about it, Bernard: you have been thinking about it for at least five years: every day you are learning more. The ashen Veblen dreams of a heaven fabricated by logical engineers: the blobby Slosson dreams of a heaven concocted by poison gases beneficently used: Miss Herriott has not so much faith in engineers or chemistry as in Shop Committees and the creative impulse: Sam McGinnis, the dour young Irishman, thinks to reach Heaven, like China, by boring through the A.F. of L. There are twenty different kinds of heaven being offered in the streets in 1919, Bernard. Each heaven is a clear, chemically pure distillation of a sample from the present hell.

41

Beer provides good amber tickles in a clean dark saloon. Velvet and Welsh discuss ladies and Dostoevsky and what Copey said to the graduating class after Lowell had abolished Eliot's fraternal keg and substituted the iniquity of compulsory Freshman dorms. The lean curves of Welsh's face are the edges of a thought that evades platitude: the slight failure of focus in Velvet's green eye is the distraction of dance-music among old men in a smoking-room. When Welsh talks about women Bernard realizes he is a very virgin: when Welsh talks about women Bernard affects the boredom of satiety. At twenty-three young men should not be virgins.

42

In November, 1919, Bernard's world goes to sudden smithereens. Chronos, Reconstruction, Revolution, Socialism falter into rheumatic palpitations: youth becomes grizzled: illuminated hopes burst into bitter drops of soapy water: White Guards beat Red Guards: poverty beats revolution: safety beats adventure: doubt beats certainty: the almost goes along with the never-was: and the program of the British Labor Party no longer rises as the sound of birds in a still forest. 'Chronos' slides into oblivion, and into the same but different oblivion slides Bernard.

43

Above Bernard's oblivion something shimmers and shivers as the sun shimmers through green crystal water to a rising diver: something is Eunice: Eunice is everything: Eunice is the perfection of an April day before the edge of winter has gone: hyacinth and daffodil: the shock of lavender and sunny gold: white trickle of anemone through dead leaves: the tinge of scarlet on the beech-boughs: a spring of many clustered possibilities is Eunice: she paints pictures: she is a girl: and the kisses of men have left her as untouched as the spring sun leaves the cold flanks of the April hills: the snow of inner chastity remains through many outer meltings. She is a tease to Bernard: she meets his earnestness with in-difference and his passion with disdain. When 'Chronos' crumbles, Eunice alone is left, a phantom for a ruin, a jackalantern toward which Bernard stumbles, just to find a hot breath whispering in his ear. Eunice fills Bernard's days: she makes wan and desperate the long hours of the night: but Bernard gets no nearer to the heart of Eunice than a mote gets to the eye: lodging there, he has a place of irritation: claiming place he spoils the trifling gallantries of other men but has no larger part in her himself. Bernard lives in happy torment: Bernard is a worshipful-wanting ecstatic coward, hanging between the desire for Eunice and the desire to remain free: the desire to avoid tragic complexes with Mamadears and the desire to mind his own affairs. When Bernard vacillates Eunice is miles away: when Bernard becomes resolute, Eunice is still miles away.

44

Letters from Hong-kong: letters come from Calcutta: they come from Jerusalem: Cairo: Marseilles: Paris: Brussels: Amsterdam: London, the New Forest: the letters are scraps of James McMaster: when Bernard reads them he partakes of the sacrament of discipleship: one of McMaster's ideas thrills Bernard like the touch of Eunice's arm: an in-vitation to collaborate on a book with McMaster causes shivers of frightened delight to run up and down Bernard's spine: to be a spoke in McMaster's wheel would be a short way of traveling far. Jerusalem and Hong-kong and the Sea of Japan are but suburban boroughs in James McMaster's realm: letters are dated there but the thoughts they bear

136

edge slantwise toward infinity: a counter-love to Eunice plays in Bernard: if she is a warm sun, McMaster is the whole vault of sky: letters come from Aberdeen: letters come from Bergen: a letter from Pimlico invites Bernard to become a fellow in Comte House: a letter from Pimlico is a very hard letter to resist.

45

When Bernard and Eunice trudge through a soft mist of snow on Park Avenue, he tells her: I am going to London for a year. If I were not going away so long—the snowmist becomes a fuzzy carpet—the flakes cling to red wisps of Eunice's hair, unmelted, and flicker on her lashes—if I were not going to be away so long, says Bernard . . . If and if and if, mocks Eunice. If time in buckets, and gallons and gallons of ocean were not to part us, says Bernard firmly, I'd say I love you. That is very sweet says Eunice: did it take a visit to the passport office to find this out? I love you, says Bernard stubbornly: if you will marry me I'll not go off to join McMaster. If I loved you, says Eunice, I'd have to bid you go *because* I loved you: it makes no difference: I bid you go because I don't. Don't shake me so: I am not mocking now: I don't love you, but gee oh gee: I wish I did. I'll paint your picture and keep it near to me: if I say yes to it, there's hope for you. There's something deep between us: I don't think we're going to part: but Bernard, you are very young, and I am twice as old as you already: so hurry up. My wild oats are nearly ready to be gathered: but yours are scarcely planted yet. Let's sow and reap together, cries Bernard. That's marriage, says Eunice: but marriage needs more love than I can muster for anyone: so let's be friends. I am not the girl you dream about: one never is: and you are what I want a friend to be, but nothing more. That night Bernard kisses Eunice: his warmth is far too courteous: it jeers at his illusion. The Sunday before Bernard sails is icy blank with jealous despair. Eunice's kisses have a mocking reserve, and Bernard's passion is too dispersed and fretful to convince anyone, even a virgin of eighteen. Virgins of eighteen know what love is without previous demonstration.

46

A hundred pounds a year in London is better than nothing at all a year in New York. Butter and sugar require ration cards in 1920 but Pimlico recovers from the effects of invalid soldiers by the application of paint to the gentlemanly grayness of houses that might have been friends with Colonel Newcome. Sociology was made by Comte the mistress of the sciences: but the concubines of science refuse to recognize the first wife of the Prophet. Comte House in Pimlico preaches the mistress-ship of

sociology to spinsters who are looking for something useful to do as well
as to the passionate souls who have watched the dawn of James
McMaster's thought upon a gray world solemn with wheels, six per cent,
and tick-tock.

47

Alighting from a donkey cart by a brick farmhouse whose thatched roof
brightens to the gorse-gold moor at the edge of the New Forest Bernard
beholds the man he has begun to call his master. Age has achieved the
victory of a red beard beneath a spreading crown of silver hair. Gray eyes
leap to Bernard with a friendly kiss: a knotted hand that seems a tough
old root holds Bernard's hand and claps him on the shoulder: and
through the beard a trickle of impatient questions run off without an
answer. The cuckoo calls across the moor. Bernard puts down his hand-
bag. So this is he!

48

We do not dress for dinner says McMaster: but note the gorse Linnaeus
worshiped when first he trod upon these shores: ticker fools with country
estates hoard their gold in banks and turn their backs to the gorse; of
course you ride? New Forest ponies are perhaps too small for your six
feet: my five-foot-six still finds them helpful: do you want to wash? or
shall we climb that little rise and look the country over: don't bother
about toilets: cockneys pollute the rivers and deplete the land in the
interest of sanitation while China keeps her civilization and her health by
watching her stools: I hope you got your sea-legs quickly? a thermometer
dropped into the water as Franklin did is a good way to study oceanog-
raphy: did you remember? This is the common that keeps the widow's
cow and some of Hampshire's yeomen independence: black days for
England when enclosures broke up old folkways and prosperity: poor
moles in London libraries now laugh at Goldsmith for picturing deserted
villages they might find for themselves by leaving London for a day. You
found Comte House and Mrs. Long? The place is a little bleak perhaps
but tidy: a fine figure of a woman: they breed well in Inverness: but ay
de mi! gray London will take away her scarlet cheeks: the clear thought
of us Scots has all it can to penetrate the beer and fog that cover London
from dawn to closing time: our bodies suffer: Henry the first—

49

Bernard's head bobs like a groggy bottle in a mountain torrent. The
perpetual energy of McMaster's mind bulges the brain itself into a forehead that becomes him like a crown. Bernard longs for the slow digestion

of solitude but is relieved to find a master looking like a master. . . .
Stuffed furniture and stuffy coals hem in the night. McMaster says
abruptly: What have your days been like? What have you done and
seen? What have you thought? What have you got for me? What can I
give you? Begin at your beginning not later than your grandfather. When
Bernard puts himself and all he's been before the kindly sternness of
those eyes he feels like children who in manhood still take their dolls to
be the proof of their fecundity. The days have been crowded with emptiness; the days are the black embers of a letter with an irretrievable
message.

50

A stew of paper! is McMaster's epithet. The brief diurnal flickers of your
journalism have neither light nor heat enough to shame a candle. The
worming through of books experience does not season is scarcely worth a
worm's life, still less yours: the poor preservative of abstention is all that's
kept your life from rotting utterly. You live like clerks and academic
dunces who, wound in paper cocoons, prepare to metamorphose into
dead butterflies. Soldiers, though stupid, have the discipline of drill: but
you have neither discipline nor the strength that can forego it. Brace up,
my lad, you're twenty-four and you have scarce as yet begun to live. Now
look you here—

51

A panic sobs in Bernard's bosom. It is true. His days bear the imprint of
tick-tock: they bear the imprint of escaping tick-tock: but little else is
there. In the forest of Bernard's bewilderment McMaster spreads a map
that diminishes the impenetrable confusion of the landscape: each contour is a shrunken reproduction of life's explored terrain. Life active and
passive, now dominating circumstance by dreams, thoughts, and inventions, now submitting like soft wax to circumstance's mold: sea-shell and
house, antheap and city, tropism and full-fledged idea march into an
organic unity: nothing exists as by itself, but always reacting and being
reacted upon as Life's pendulum swings from not-being into being and
back again. Priapic beasts and the seven gods and goddesses of Greece
reveal man's biological aspiration: at every stage the ideal is but the
hidden uttermost of Life's own reality.

52

The natural history of life and life's environment, portrayed by Kepler,
Newton, Boyle and Kelvin, by Chambers, Lyell, Darwin, Pasteur,
Faraday, reveals a truncated panorama in which the foreground is for-

gotten—which is man. Upon the empty destiny of things man flings the challenge of himself: Pythagoras married mathematics and music to make the stars dance: Plato, Buddha, the Nine Muses and Shakespeare brought forms into existence that Nature, unfulfilled by man, did not suspect. Jesus Christ is just as real as Plato's Socrates: dead, each achieved a new life in the mind more powerful than any Alexander knew on earth. How many men have followed Christ who would not recognize divinity in flesh? By idea, image, an ideal man makes new bestiaries: he dreamed himself out of some blinder shape: his thought imposes destinies and ends upon a formless world that chases its own tail. Man is the chimera and the centaur and all the devils in hell and all the gods above!

53

The donkeys from whose backs young Bernard had painfully unloaded their damaged wares had made of science something hostile and averse to life; and all that smelled of life became a wanton idleness and imbecility. Truth and beauty were at war among the donkeys: dead science was the counterfeit of endless externalities which might be turned to the practical account of tick-tock: literature and art were phantom faces dancing in non-existent fires. Good-truth is gospel! Truth beautiful is life's highest symmetry! But donkeys purposely kept truth in calico and curl-papers lest she be raped by ambushed admirers, whilst esthetic donkeys emptied out beauty's brains, because sawdust had been found more satisfactory for dolls. Among the tough and tender donkeys the real and the ideal could never meet: they gave each other the cold shoulder and the cut direct: the grounds for their divorce were science's frigidity, slightly aggravated by imagination's impotence.

54

Science and art were separate loads upon the backs of donkeys: but in James McMaster's thought Life had begot them both: they were the modes in which Life's rhythm, now turning ego-ward for sustenance, now turning toward the world for mastery, achieved that harmony of acts and facts and dreams and deeds without which life does not dance or leap at all but moves in palsy or droops in a paralysis, now overwhelmed by facts it cannot master or by acts it can't direct, now breaking out in wishful dreams that come from nowhere, lead to nothing, now galloping in vain achievements like the conquests of Napoleon or the misplaced ingenuity of printing presses whose precise and utmost excellence makes yellow journals spawn more easily each hour. Euclid and Plato are not at war: the reality of conic sections or electrons cannot deny the other life-reality of Goethe, Michelangelo, or Blake. Life spans all categories in its movement and reconciles all verbal contradictions: we move in spite of Zeno! Our being is what makes the difference to an indifferent universe!

55

Living, men break through all the husks that keep them safe but undeveloped: the husk of status and profession: the husk of empty creed: the husk of brainless actions and inactive brains: the husk of fixed environments and habits: the husk of righteousness that clings to well-established evils lest it meet greater ones: the husk of comfort and security. Donkeys live on husks: they gorge themselves to sleep and balkiness. Their daily diet is a bag of husks, the husk of politics and mediocre letters, the husk of invention, business, scientific inquiry directed to the greater glory of card-indexes and tick-tock: the husk of acting, moving, thinking, planning, feeling with a minimum of discomfort and disarrangement: the husk of preparing for eventualities that never arrive and discoursing at length about unimportant contingencies so that stuffed donkeys may earn glass cases in museums. . . . *Vivendo discimus!* If appetites are ready, food will follow. To be alive means clear eyes and a good digestion: a readiness to risk one's neck or lose one's sleep: a willingness to work at anything one needs for bread or knowledge from catching fish to measuring an atom's dance: the will to be incorporated with others in a family, union, shop or city, and yet to keep one's proper self intact. A life well-keyed will find its way with equal ease about a landscape or a library. To be a man at all means sharing in the modes of life that men have found a help to sheer existence or to ecstasy.

56

These were McMaster's thoughts. They broke through many husks young Bernard had built up and labeled Education, Wisdom, Culture. They robbed his idols of their forehead's jewels: Bernard Shaw became a cockney limping on a crutch whose shape denied his limb's deformity: he proclaimed the Life-Force but forgot its main activities. Old Berkeley's ego-begotten world was the mooniness of lonely nights. Dear William James seemed but a half-philosopher whose appetite for life was what alone gave life to his philosophy. Dewey kept close to acts and facts but dared not embrace dreams and deeds, lest he be smothered: his better world was generated in an experimental vacuum. The socialists were cockneys, too, who took machines to be prime-movers, and forgot the sun, and what the sun does to the leaf, and how the leaf spreads through man's life. Science used Cartesian dialectics to despise philosophy: philosophy was cowed into forgetting it had forged the weapon for its defeat. Whitman, Emerson, Wordsworth, and Plato kept their seats in Bernard's pantheon: Tolstoi and Goethe joined them: most of the rest were called upon for kitchen duty or for music at vacant intervals. Rabelais and Dickens were the chief factotums in this refurbished household; but there were others. Bernard began to worship trees, because he found in them the vital harmony McMaster sought. If men were sycamores or beeches they'd know less movement and more growth.

57

Temples are built of solid stones: idols do not fall at once. The night McMaster talks till dawn with Bernard finds Bernard shrinking into a chaos of complicated resistances, half paralyzed by worship, weariness, and fear. He shrinks chamberwise with a trickling taper and cannot find the outer door of sleep, aghast at that great pride and energy of mind which takes life for its province and falters at nothing between the autonomy of distant stars and the aspirations of religion or the physiology of our inmost cells, but has a place for all, and an appetite to master more. The furious iteration of McMaster's voice, the gray eyes that look past sorrow and love into the core of the Whirlwind, become the image of the dreadful God that Gustave Doré had set up in Bernard's skies at five or seven. Eventually Bernard sleeps. Eventually Bernard awakes. Eventually the reality of his own sapless days is mixed with the memory of a conversational dream that ended in an intangible triumph. India rubber tubs chill the spine: Americans are not used to bathing in a can of hot water.

58

In London dreams evaporate and intellectual discourse is difficult after a breakfast at nine that includes oatmeal, kippers, eggs, marmalade, and toast. Men worship Mammon: but McMaster plays with him and Moloch: thrice each month he meets with financiers who build railways in remote provinces of India in order to bring the curse of Manchester's dirt to a civilization that has long enjoyed its own ordure. On other days, McMaster plans museums and cities, plows through the muck of learned discourses to seize jettisoned diamonds, exhibits ideas like specimens in cases to the willing few who make Comte House their intellectual home, throws pearls to swine and goldpieces to beggars who achieve academic respectability and a modicum of fame out of the remains of McMaster's breakfast cogitations. Bernard does not rise at five. New Yorkers bred with perpetual janitors and steam do not like to arise in a cold room at five. Bernard's day with McMaster begins when the stuff of McMaster's thinking has already shaped itself in many folded wads of paper, each teasing symbol leading to a book perhaps that's still unwritten. Sanderson shares their quarters: a grizzled cherub whose pink skin is like his own translucent thought: whose blue eyes burst in merriment over entertaining ideas. When Bernard talks with Sanderson and McMaster all ideas are entertaining. Even Bernard learns to spend a whole day in discussion without feeling that breakfast dinner supper are more important. It is a great victory for an American to forget breakfast, lunch, and dinner—but even Sanderson and McMaster remember tea!

59

Twilight hours on the Chelsea Embankment: twilight mist: the snaily creep of smoke from distant chimneys: the words of Eunice's letters that never deepen beyond the twilight of scattered friendship into firm and starry night. Red Chelsea pensioners blotted against the green twilight of remote gardens: red Chelsea houses against the purple twilight of the afterglow. Human twilight! The white twilight of Carlyle's pain: the blue twilight of Whistler's sentimental cynicism: the dusky mottled twilight of the stones that whisper ancient titles to Henry James: the greasy twilight that swims around a Crosby Hall no nearer to Eutopia than Thomas More himself was! To strain for Eunice's words through the twilight of a summer's night: to find the words no warmer and no brighter than the evening: to drop one's hopes in the muddy slime of the receding Thames: to find no rest in the creaky twilight of a deserted house. . . .

60

Verhaeren and Van Gogh went mad in London: who would not? Miles of dull streets are miles of dull streets. Where does Whitechapel Road end and has anybody ever found Tooting or tried to walk through Clapham Junction or get a drink at the Elephant and Castle? To survive a beef stew in a yellowgreasy Lyons is to earn the Order of the Iron Stomach with bars: the sound of a coster hawking fresh filberts or white heather would make harsh the faint murmur of distant winds: but the English of Oxford is worse than the French of Stratford-atte-Bowe. Innocent foreigners have been stabbed at the heart by an icy Euooh? aimed at the indecency of their candor. But a bus-conductor may be a friend in need: a weaver from Nottingham may turn a weekend labor conference at Morley College into an assembly of dignified and helpful men. Snout, Bottom, and Starveling have more humanity than the prigs, false faces, uniforms, and worldly wisemen—and the crowd always feeds the pigeons in front of St. Paul's.

61

The red fog of a September morning by Green Park successfully counterfeits Joseph Mallord William Turner. When the barges slide past the Doulton potteries on a dank afternoon, they are better than almost anything in the Tate Galleries. Saturday night market on Churton Street has a levity that finds only feeble echoes in colossal music halls—and God never made a June day for anything but a walk up the tow path from Kew Gardens to Richmond. The shade of William Morris saunters under the willows to Richmond meditating news from nowhere: Bernard and Charlotte follow the shade, two friendly people drawn into the friendly world that Morris pictured, under willow, over stile, past a grass bank, by a lock, till Richmond Bridge and many punts and picnickers close up the vista.

62

Charlotte came from Aberdeen to help fallen women before she knew exactly what fallen women were. That was seven years before she found a post in Comte House and left a posey of tulips over the fireplace in Bernard's room when he arrived. Charlotte plumbed the depths of other people's tragedies so successfully she made them forget her own was deeper: but love, despair, suicide, jealousy had singed the hem of every garment that she wore. She had watched her youngest friends go bitterly and unconvinced to death in France: she had worked with labor men and conscientious objectors in the face of a family that took comfort in the editorial certitudes of the Morning Post: her sweetness tartened as one side of her clutched loyalty, the other love. . . . She says: Oh dear: I thought so! when Bernard tells her about Eunice. She says: Remember to wear your evening clothes, when he almost goes to a dinner in Notting Hill Gate without a dinner coat. She says: They have Maids of Honor tarts some people call nice at Richmond: and there is an old tree in the park that was meant to shelter lovers or conversation. We have plenty to talk about she adds firmly. Charlotte dresses with the ambiguous primness of a private secretary. Her tweeds are a little too heavy and her shirtwaists not less serviceable than ugly. Her voice is a clear Northern voice. Her face and her body are a fine landscape, shorn by a November storm: her mind is a lake in the midst of the landscape, agitated but deep. When one sees her mind gleaming through a copse of hazel eyes one finds that her face is beautiful. Like a blindman, poor young Bernard

144

plucks at the heavy tweeds and the assertiveness of metallic dress supporters, and takes a long time to discover that her face is beautiful.

63

Charlotte gently wipes clear the foggy patches in Bernard's mind. Charlotte smiles at Bernard's rages against old England: she finds the southern English funny, too, and likes the gaunt dank air of Edinburgh, drinking terror in black closes, more than the slatternly complacence of London. A Sunday spent discussing Eunice in the greenwet silence of the Chiltern beeches almost removes the thought of Eunice from Bernard's heart. When Charlotte recites patches of Chaucer from a northern Downtop near the grassy Pilgrim's Way, Bernard swoops with her to Canterbury, quite forgetting ties of Franco-German-American ancestry. The smell of marjoram and mignonette: the blush of Charlotte's prim-dancing face: almost make England a possibility if ten years and many customs did not come between their pairing. In complementary qualities, Bernard and Charlotte are well-married: but the parish register does not recognize marriages made in Heaven unless they come down to earth. Charlotte feels too tender toward Bernard to let him come down to earth. She has an uncle who was a general in Afghanistan, and her father retired from the Hong-kong Customs Service with honors: Oxford, Cambridge, Eton, or Cheltenham are the prerequisites for marriage in her family. Charlotte has five equally maiden sisters.

64

The days are wrung by the dry torture of desire: the days crawl with the slow crawl of a thirsty man over a desert. . . . The days do not bring Eunice and the days do not bring peace. Ideas are gadflies that add to the sting of unslaked thirst. When Bernard proposes to Eunice again by letter she answers tardily that she prefers to keep her pastels fresh without such fixatives. She is a little diverted by the snorting raptures of a Spanish sculptor who has asked her to be his mistress: she disdains the fetters of such minor titles, too, but likes the bulky power that would impose them. She hopes that Bernard will remain her friend in any case: she does not love Bernard yet: his portrait made her brush go mushy: she's turned it to the wall: and she is rather overpowered by the Spanish bull.

65

Five ships go back and forth across the Atlantic before Bernard is reasonably sure that the bull has not immediately succeeded. When McMaster

says: Come to Palestine to plan the New Jerusalem this fall, Bernard
replies: I am going back to America: I want a terrestrial girl more than I
want the City of God itself. McMaster says: Ask her to join you there!
Bernard fuzzes a mournful and despairing reply. Ideas and sweethearts
do not mix: marriage comes first or never. McMaster says: But girls are
everywhere: so why turn back? And Bernard says: Such rootlets as
Americans have they must preserve. Eunice was born in Brooklyn, I in
Staten Island: we both know what a walk along the Palisades is like.
Having no deeper roots, I keep those that I have: I'm going back. Sometimes I think that Eunice is only America: I need America too. Tough
French and Scottish roots are French and Scotch wherever they may be:
but what is an American but a hope that has not taken root? Old stocks
may rove: we pioneers must settle down. If you would understand it,
read 'The Ordeal of Mark Twain.' You have given me all that I can
take—a thousand thoughts still wait to be digested. I'll give them a sea-
change and set them out in an American garden. Bear with me! And
McMaster says: Marriage sometimes wrecks philosophy: but a married
philosopher thinks with a double mind: one such in Athens stirred up
Plato—all hail Xantippe! My thoughts must stand the biological test: if
marriage brings oblivion to philosophy the fault's not marriage's. An old
angler never blames the fish. Good luck! my lad. When you come back,
bring Eunice with you. Don't mind if there's a bairn or two: we'll find a
bit for all. Unless young folks live dangerously they'll only have skeletons
for thoughts and rabbits for progeny.

66

Up and down goes the boat: back and forth ply the waves. At Tillbury
Docks McMaster tosses a cheery beard that almost rivals Charlotte's
coster-handkerchief. Bernard's thoughts lurch through dim corridors.
Back and forth: up and down. Nothingness is just about as good as
Eunice no meat thank you but a little soup and crackers. Americans that
slobber over the Statue of Liberty are capable of evading customs duties
and clamoring about unnecessary public expenditures upon health and
education. Seagulls swoop up and down: slowsteadily the boat glides
past the lower skyline. Tugs tediously nuzzle the ship into the pier;
portholes snap the dinginess of grimy docks. In the dim crowd at the end
of the pier Eunice's face lifts a sudden white peony out of a garden of
dusky zinnias. Eunice's kiss is pertly intimate. The first five minutes are
pleasant. By the time lunch is over Bernard and Eunice have quarreled.
She promised ages ago to go to the opera next night with Lopez. . . .
Also—there is more than one Lopez.

146

67

O Life: Life: Life: why do you torture Bernard: O Love: Love: Love: why do you torture Bernard? The more the tawny heifer frolics the harder the stags and bulls follow her. Moo! Moo! Moo! moans Bernard. The heifer is skittish: the Spanish bull is persistent. Bernard's pocketbook is empty: Bernard's face cracks wry smiles. The heifer and the bull dance together: the heifer and the bull drink cocktails in ostentatious restaurants: Bernard does not know how to dance: Bernard cannot pay for cocktails. Moo! Moo! moans Bernard every time he sees the tawny heifer. Can't you say anything but Moo! asks the heifer. Spanish bulls do not say Moo. When Spanish bulls ask for something they act as if they were going to get it. O Life: Life: Life: why do you torture Bernard. Moo: Moo: Moo sounds more pathetic than passionate.

68

Dying of a broken heart has been physiologically demonstrated. A smile can alter the pressure of the blood; jealousy may upset the balance of the endocrines: but if Love could be reduced to its physical basis the mystery would merely be translated into another language. When the daffodils at last come out in Thorley's window, Bernard makes his will and commits himself to a physician and a dental surgeon. The pain inflicted in ferreting around Bernard's root canals is diverting anesthetic. By the time Eunice takes Bernard on a long weekend walk and says: Let's get married: spring is here! Bernard wonders whether he has not been a damned fool all along. What on earth made him think he wanted to get married? Eunice's huffled virginity when Bernard alludes to the antithesis of having babies makes him wonder if the prowess of Spanish bulls and the wantonness of girls have not been over-rated. Eunice warmsmiles a didn't-you-know-I-loved-you-all-the-time? Bernard whispers to Bernard Doesn't life beat hell?

69

Blow hot! blow cold! blow warm breezes of spring: blow through the leaf-dimmed windows: blow away dress, camisole and shift: blow against the dusk of reticent pink marble: the marble of firm trunk and rapid flanks. Blow orange fragrance from that Hymettus where no flower has withered, where no bee has sipped: blow twilight on the kiss whose shadow hovered hawklike over Venusberg: blow hot! blow hot! . . . Blow cold! blow cold! blow cold poison of embraces that others have taken: blow poison of often indifferent kisses: blow icebergs of aimless

boredom and indifference: blow northeaster of manifold disappointments: blue-coldness of inadequacy and misapprehension: gray-coldness
of recessive passion. Blow cold! blow hot! blow cold! . . . The rains
scud: the sun comes out: the wind shifts again and yet again. In squall or
calm or in somewhat between, Bernard and Eunice share a bed together
and within a month or two accept a legal durance for their love lest
reproaches and hysterics should disfigure too many family meetings.
Blow tepid winds of legalized reality!

Part Four

70

Pygmalion worshiped Galatea but found that marble was impenetrable:
eager lovers do not easily unlock secrets that tired experience may disclose at a glance. When young men are too hotly eager, girls get colds
and bad tempers: when the ardor of young men is dampened by colds
and bad tempers, it is hard to live happily for more than a few hours at a
time. Bernard's thoughts about the future of civilization become gloomy:
Eunice's portraits become caricature and her still lifes are taunting and
unabashed symbols of defeated fruit: nothing is more amiss than usual
with civilization or vegetables, but something is deeply amiss with Eunice
and Bernard. Eunice dreams of triumphant bulls and awakes with a
satisfied quiver until she sees Bernard's head lying black and white-wan
in the next room. Bernard also dreams of triumphant bulls and awakes
with a nasty temper. The winter Bernard and Eunice spend on Washington Place is a winter of quarrels about nocturnal bulls. Daylight bulls
often have a date or a family to provide for but non-existent bulls are
always victorious. Eunice hates Bernard when she dreams of bulls.

71

The cheery urgency of McMaster's letters makes Bernard want to go into
a corner and howl. Bernard and Eunice buffet themselves through a
succession of impasses: when spring comes again they decide to separate
from a tangled past by sharing their kindred miseries in Europe. They
dream of a hilltop in France where bliss may be properly consummated
under the approval of a burning sun and understanding but indifferent
peasants: they dream of a winter in Prague, a spring in Florence, a
summer in Budapest: Bernard dreams of an obscure village in the Tyrol
beyond the reach of McMaster's letters: Eunice dreams of a gala

promenade at Lido and grand balls where she may dance with many men and stray from Bernard without rousing his jealousy. They compromise with their dreams: their money will take them as far as Paris if they are careful. Bernard is still Bernard: Eunice is still Eunice. His love has frayed into a jealous exacerbation: her response is tenderly indifferent. They are bound together by a common disappointment. They are bound by the fear of acknowledging their disappointment.

72

Footfree in Europe, Bernard and Eunice still limp upon American soil: the common ground of their dissension. He wants a closer loyalty than she can give: she wants a firmer mastery than he has taken: she'd chuck her pictures and all her claim on other men if once he'd lose the balky tone of a defeated but jealous male. She welcomes Bertha on the steamer: Bertha's tall Northern limbs, a trunk that rises like a figurehead into defiant breasts and prowlike chin, her open, forthright ways, awaken something new in Bernard: Eunice leans in friendship toward Bertha, a firmer counterpart of Bernard, and Bernard leans toward Bertha too. Bertha and Eunice discuss the inwardness of sex and what experience is: when Bernard shyly joins them they continue: within a day both Bernard and Eunice have made her common confidante of half their bed and boudoir secrets. The trio share the railway ride to Paris, and at intervals exchange their feelings over lingual diffidence and love and unaccustomed beverages through several weeks of vague exploration in the Louvre and the Musée Rodin, not forgetting their disgust over the sick smell of candied lust that haunts the Boulevards and plies about the urinals which line the stately avenues as if the dogs of Paris were constrained by regulations to avoid all doorways.

73

In London, Bernard feels his competence more keenly: the streets nudge him with memories: he shares his friends with Eunice and Bertha and marvels both at English warmth, once friendship is established, and that iron ring of time which keeps one fettered to a skeleton whose spirit only offers calcareous satisfactions. Comte House is closed for summer holidays: the dust falls in tidy layers upon disordered papers: maps, diagrams, charts, photographs, left by McMaster before another intellectual jaunt to India. Bernard walks through it as through a cemetery, noting new graves of McMaster's progeny and the faint mounds of his own dead selves. What gaps! What gaps between a tea in Bertha's maisonette in Torrington Square and lonely suppers in a chophouse, followed by dull-tossing long libidinous nights and days of agitated thought, uneasy reckonings, muffled uncertainties!

74

Bernard is restless and Bernard is without decision: if mastering Eunice is a man's business, he is almost ready to leave it to some other man. Once Bernard wanted Eunice here in London: Eunice is here: he wants his Eunice still and has her less than ever: and this is gall that lechery can only make more bitter. He wonders, too, if Eunice is his deepest want: or is that want illusion? Then what is real? To find one's work and bend one's back to it! Men leave their women for a polar desert to cross or a look at the stars; no woman ever had a soldier, a scientist, an explorer until he was too tired to go on with his work. A man says, that is over, now for the work: a girl says: that is over, now for the baby: and if no baby comes, she fashions substitutes. Now for the work, says Bernard: but what work? Tick-tock says Piccadilly: Tick-tock says Broadway: Tick-tock says the Boulevard des Italiens: tick-tock, under the present circumstances, is the best we can offer. Bernard goes back to Eunice, vexed, fretful, sad: Eunice is not very much of a comfort: but Eunice is better than tick-tock.

75

Release from amorous nettles comes unexpectedly to Bernard: he gains in age and wisdom in a single night. In Bertha's maisonette, Eunice makes excited epigrams with her eyes for the benefit of a young Dane who haunts the company to curse profoundly the Anglicanism of the English and have a taste of freedom. Bernard, broiling beefsteak in the kitchen, faces a sudden flame of interest in Bertha's face, and throws his bosom on her, like a rug, to quench the fire, only to find it catching on himself. They clasp and kiss as lovers, they who a little while before had talked of sex and love as if life were a textbook with sub-headings for each paragraph: head to head and chest to breast their strength and weakness make a unity of equals: in an instant, Bernard is unfaithful and forgetful: never can he give again to Eunice that jealous and unswerving love that had been his to give through all their quarrels, sorties, fears, remonstrances. A spurt of flaming fat and broiling stench is all that keeps these two from being taken in adultery, platonic but complete.

76

Beneath a fog that smothers the policeman's lamp, Bernard carries Eunice off in an embrace that makes her think the port-wine stronger than it was and Bernard much more drunk—only to find in bed completer mastery than he had ever made her feel before. You lovely dear: where have you learned all this?—In Bertha's arms, he grimly whispers to himself.—Stop: stop: you glorious one: go on: you leave me breathless. Damn all the Danes and Spaniards, says Bernard: I've conquered you. And I'll be yours forever says Eunice. And now: says Bernard: and now goodbye. You cannot leave me now says Eunice. I'm yours. We shall have a thousand and one days of happiness before us and a thousand and one nights. But suppose says Bernard, stabbed by both jealousy and guilt, not all the other thousand are for me!

77

In mastery Bernard feels a shock of indifference: Bernard awakes to find himself a thousand miles apart from the Bernard who married Eunice. Balloonlike, all the cords that held him to her cut, he bounces into rarer atmospheres. He triumphs with his indifference: she is jealous of Bertha: he mystifies her with his indifference: she is irritated with herself. When Eunice dabbles in paints he writes: when, to rouse him up once more she dabbles in love, he writes more seriously: when she challenges his indifference by assuming her own indifference he takes a boat back to America and smiles at the icy flames that follow in his wake. Eunice writes that he is totally heartless and that he has wantonly destroyed a beautiful thing. Bernard answers that he hopes her purse holds out but if it doesn't she can call on him.

78

Hopeless, Bernard feeds on hopelessness: faithless, he holds to empty faith: thoughtless, he spends his days on transient journalism—that treadmill where flayed oxen turn a wheel that grinds no grain: unsociable, he feeds upon the gregarious triviality of teas and dinners where conversation is strained through the stomach and laughter is an irritation in the throat. How clever is young Bernard: how wedded to urbane existence: how easily he bears his emptiness: how complacently he plumbs his shallows for a weekly cheque or a weekend invitation! For quite six months he hides from Eunice behind this front which is not Bernard but the shriveled ghost of Bernard, the mummied wraith of what was once a vehement young man. How do live animals accept such empty days? How do they call such costiveness of spirit animation and all that makes it possible, success?

79

The girls that Bernard meets are all that make him run away from Eunice without the charm that keeps him turning back. The girls that Bernard meets are windfalls, dropped too quickly from the tree, bruised a little, mealy from lying on the ground: easy to pick up and scarcely worth the picking, the cidery smell of fermentation attending all too dankly on their scarlet charm: bruised apples, speckled apples, wormy apples, frost-bitten apples, green apples, sour apples, stunted apples, apples all, but all a little less than apples ripened on the trees. When apples lie too freely on the ground one picks them up and takes a bite and tries another and takes another bite—and tries another. The girls that Bernard meets are windfalls. He bites them gingerly.

80

Queasy with dissatisfaction, Bernard spends a summer fortnight rambling slowly through the Hudson Highlands. Too many weekends: too many girls: too many articles: too many glib opinions: too many bad dinners: too many sallow mornings: damn: damn: trees are not empty: they grow: the sun is not empty: it warms: railroad gangs are not empty: they pry with a crowbar and hammer with a sledge: mothers are not empty: they give mammalian nourishment to the young: damn: damn: damn: drifting is empty: flirtation is empty: incoherent cleverness is empty: bottles of disastrous liquor are always empty: the things that make people find you an agreeable dinner partner, or an affable lover are the emptiest things of all—denials of the fullness that might be within were it not for the emptiness that—damn! damn! damn!—occupies one without. In the midst of Bernard's damns he remembers that the fortnight is over: he must catch the next deadline of the Causeur with an editorial, and Beatrice has asked him to a party the same night.

81

He who has bedded in the grass and thrown ascetic arms around a birch tree is not prepared to face Fifth Avenue in August. Fifth Avenue in August steams like a Turkish bath in haze: the breasts and flanks of maidens under a gauzy negligence of dress assault rusticated young men like an opened seraglio: the buildings swell the mood: the narrow entrances are amorous caverns: the towers are erections: the city is tumescent in the August haze: the girls walk with dangling breasts and insolent thighs: in another hour: in another minute: in another second the brief allurements of dress will be cast off: the orgy will begin.

82

Beatrice's parties are like a thousand parties that begin with sodden men who want their soberness to cease and dead girls who want their deadness to live: five dead people, with Bernard tanned and almost quick, pour a flame or two of gin upon their tired ashes: dry underbrush of food will feed the fire: wine sputters up like dripping bacon fat: more wine makes the fire sing and mount. Let us kiss, my slut: that joke, like wormy Roquefort spreads a giggle with its smell: how many lovers have you had this week? The wine is warm: the air is warmer: the light is giddy warm: in darkness outer dresses slip from languid shoulders. That is better: let us drink again: the lamplight in the street's a summer moon: ha! ha! these little moons are hidden by the thinnest cloud. Gunpowder-black shadows on candle-white faces: the cordials sting the lips like kisses: kisses pour like cordials down to the nether parts. You love me and have loved me since the day I spent five minutes in your office? How strange, says Bernard to himself, to use that word for such a mood: yes: this is hell and all of us are damned: those lips are mine: they were not mine till she was dispossessed by liquor: with that same stint of liquor any other male would do. She sinks: she sinks upon the blackened floor: that tired amorousness is scarcely fit for love: it needs bicarbonate of soda and some peppermint. If this be called a gay and merry life, a free audacious life, let me be bound and prisoned. Good gods: she sleeps: black shadows entwine upon white carcasses that writhe in sleep and nausea. Out: out: follow the pavement cracks: turn west at Thirty-fourth Street: the bleary lights will clarify in time: walk on: hell opens for the dead: the damned are damned: the living damned are damned indeed to think such frantic corpses are alive.

83

That leprous taste within the mouth must go away. Naked, Bernard lies between white sheets and loves their whiteness: through the fumes of his disgust, clearing slowly, a polar radiance enfolds his being. This is he, who was a boy and played, who grew beyond a boy's age and wandered and was vexed: who married and fled from marriage, who found no work to do that called him forth until a drunken stupor sounded desperate revolt: this is he at last: readier to starve than write of servile nothings, readier to transmute his lust in work than spend himself half-heartedly: this is he, who finds no pleasure but in the unity of deed with purpose and of purpose with life: this is the sayer of Yes who denies the maudlin affirmations of the lamed, the weary, the diseased. The leprous taste is gone: baptized in light and water, Bernard turns to Shelley, reading 'Adonais' till the white radiance of eternity shines through the sullied darkness of the night.

84

The blankness of painless blank days, the spirit healing into unity: the furore of uneasy nights: the spirit dividing into seven devils married to incompatible desires: the ebb and flow of breakfast lunch and supper: the up and down of sunrise and sunset: uneasy dark suspensions before mirrors mirroring mirrors: the listening to sounds that echo sounds: attending to memories that remember memories. Disattached from Eunice, Bernard holds a womb where Eunice grows in him beyond indifference and the blankness of painless blank days.

85

The days pass: the days pass: the lone days pass. Eunice grows within Bernard's womb and Bernard grows within Eunice. Each wonders whom the other has taken for a lover: Eunice does not know that Bernard has taken her: Bernard does not know that Eunice has softly drawn him back into her: a part of each has sought to live on parts of other lives and finds it hard to be dismembered: the wholeness of Eunice wants the wholeness of Bernard: they want the disappointment of each other as well as the gladness of each other: they want what lover cannot give to lover if haste or parting be near. When Bernard proposes that they take steps toward a divorce, he really means: I love you still: why should we live apart? When Eunice says: Of course we must: she doesn't mean, I hope we're going to separate. She adds: But I must see you first, and Bernard steels himself against her bittersweet reproaches.

86

The gravity of Eunice has the pixie awe of a little girl who has learned a lesson: Bernard's heart beats fast and loud with love whilst his words utter remembered defiance. I do not need you now, says Bernard: I have found my work and can keep going quite a while alone. I don't need you, you silly wretch, says Eunice: I have found no work worth doing and no man worth caring for beyond a day or two: but both of us might be the better for a child, I think. You've come to motherhood? mocks Bernard. Another life to breed instead of suicide? My ego was a bad, bad eggo, says Eunice: I ought to hate you but I don't. My experience was just as empty as your ignorance: it ditched us both. You've never been a mate to me: why did you leave me once you learned the art of holding me completely? Let's not recriminate says Bernard. I'm happy in my work: but you need straightening out: a baby or divorce? Let's both forget the past, says Eunice: I want a future not bounded by your you-ness or my me-ness. My Eunice! says Bernard tenderly: you cancel out my mean-ness: I need you too. Don't—don't pun when you embrace me! murmurs Eunice. There are no don'ts between us, answers Bernard, only do's. Let go: let go you brute: the dress unbuttons from the shoulder: besides: perhaps you want divorce? Nonsense, says Bernard: you're mine forever. Why did you put the thought of fatherhood in me?

Part Five

87

Safety razors make it hard to grow beards in America: America would be a better place if there were a few bearded, savage, terrible old men. The old men Bernard loves are mostly in Europe: Bernard loves McMaster, Ellis, A. E., Geddes, and Shaw: he loves the passion of Unamuno and the sweet scorn of Tagore. The good die early in America: there are few splendid and terrible old men. The old men in America have slick faces and slack skins: their wisdom consists in saying: Boys will be boys: I am an old boy, too. Bernard likes the bitter steadfastness of Stieglitz: but he does not respect most American old men: nor does he learn much from his tired contemporaries. John Miel's quick spasms of exhausted da-da are realistic photographs of chaotic metal rubbish, little better than the revolutionary catchwords of Michael Marx, whose generosity and passion exhaust themselves in exclamations that do not lead to coherent actions. American minds are slot machines waiting for a penny to disgorge them: the mumbo-jumbo of behaviorist philosophy shows how little material is necessary for a successful textbook or an American mind. Jacques Loeb was stimulated to his researches on tropisms in the infusoria by watching an American crowd perhaps. The intellectuals are also infusorians who go in for the higher esthetics of advertising or burlesque, when they are not engaged in deeply proving that a two-penny candle from Paris boule-vards is the incandescence of super-Tungsten lamps. The group that wrote 'Civilization in the United States' scratched their backs before they turned over to go to sleep. There are perhaps twenty quiet fellows in the laboratories and studies who would make one sit up and think. Twenty is generous.

88

The days are empty husks: but something grows and stirs within. When wars are brutalizing, when laws are oppressing, when civilizations are decaying, when stupid men are governing, when empty heads are thinking, when tired bodies are starving, these things are sure: the trees will grow and the grass will fill up the chinks in the pavement: the sky will redden at sunset on a clear day, and in the evening the stars will shine and the clouds will march like banners or linger like smoke: animals will be happy in the sun: hens will cluck: chicks will peep: cubs will whimper for their mothers: the rain will fall and the droplets will become runnels, the runnels brooks, the brooks rivers, and the rivers will widen to the sea. Men will dig and delve and if necessary invent fish-hooks and bows-and-arrows all over again: the juncture of a man and a maid will be fruitful: the sperm and the ovum will form a blastula: the blastula will become a gastrula: the gastrula an embryo: and the embryo will become a child. The days are empty husks. One hates brutal wars, defies stupid laws, doubts civilizations, resents puny men governing and empty hearts flourishing: but the sun and the grass and man's social ingenuity and the wisdom of having babies—these things remain. Only those who prefer cemeteries to cities and burial mounds to tilled fields may doubt them.

89

Autumn days are sadglad days: the shoots of next spring are hidden in autumn. The flowers of spring are already planted. Eunice's body is proud with the pride of a baby: Eunice's eyes sing with sadglad anticipation: Eunice's cross-tender aches are the aches of a plowed field open to the sun. Winter days are full days. Eunice's body swells with a great pride. Bernard is fretful over the virgin reluctance of pregnancy, but he realizes why men once worshiped the Virgin Mother. Bernard moans to Eunice's sadglad anticipation as the windharp to the wind. Bernard hopes it will be a girl like youngest Eunice: Bernard wants Eunice's first twenty years to leap proudly out of Eunice's body. Spring days are gladglad days. The knitting together of the life in Eunice is the knitting together of Bernard-and-Eunice's life. Bernard wants to see Eunice's baby and kiss Eunice goodbye and go wandering for a year by himself over the earth. Bernard wants to have a baby begotten by Eunice. The children of the body are the pledge of the children of the spirit. The children of the spirit are the pledge of the children of the body. June days are gladglad days. Girls meant for motherhood make easy mothers.

90

The indifference of Bernard's intellectual preoccupations quivers into sudden exaltation over the exquisite ugliness just three quarters of an hour old. Sharp agony leaves a solemn face mewed in pre-natal sleep. After the dizzy irresponsibility of gas Eunice takes everything calmly.

The first week in the hospital brings strained faces to the bedside daily: after a while Eunice's breasts prevail over Little James's callous regrets at embryonic lassitude. Bernard's sense of fatherhood surprises Eunice quite as much as himself. For a fortnight he clucks old-hennishly over James's bassinette. The wrench of leaving to join McMaster in Geneva drives Bernard and Eunice into an appreciation of the inevitable dearness and reality of their love. If love be not dead, parting is perhaps the tenderest form of union.

91

In the middle of the ocean Bernard has a bottle of Pommery to celebrate his thirtieth birthday with a young lady whose intense white face wears spectral glasses. Eunice radios him electric love. When the steward brings around the broth at ten-thirty Bernard regularly starts to think about life—at thirty it is now or never! At thirty one does not take deck flirtations as seriously as the old women who pretend to be asleep. At thirty the porters at Cherbourg could throw an epileptic fit without getting a double tip. At thirty La Vie Parisienne and Le Rire have nothing new to say. At thirty you cash your cheques at a little bank and keep away from the American Express Company. At thirty you do not feel singularly flattered when young ladies lean with an expression of innocuous indifference against your shoulder. At thirty you suddenly realize that you are capable of looking after yourself where porters, hotel proprietors, and girls are concerned. At thirty it is now or never. At thirty life is harmonized or hopeless.

92

The Lake of Geneva is green like the cavern of a glacier: the plane trees are clipped umbrellas throwing orderly shadows: the white swans by the Ile de Rousseau quarrel like stage beauties over morning breakfast. Geneva has the sleepy tidiness of a man who combs his hair while yet in his pyjamas. I come to Geneva, says McMaster, to redd my plans and thoughts: a city washed and swept each morning provokes the bourgeois virtues in the mind. The very weakness of the League incites reflection: it might be pitiful, were great States not far worse, mere pusbags of irritated pride, pretense, and power, ready to burst. I keep a school upon the medieval pattern: some fifty students come from every part of Europe to dust away the cobwebs I've forgotten: I stir them up to manhood's task: they keep me from a fixed senescence, fastened to garrulity. How is the bairn and Mrs. Bernard? You took a long time man: I'm glad you're back.

93

McMaster's garden drops from an old close near Calvin's house onto the rooftops of the street below. The cobbled hill raps sharply to the feet that climb it: the sudden flame of dahlias at the end of a dank passage is the burst of a beautiful solution at the end of a day's darkness. In eager knots the students talk with Sanderson, with Mrs. Sanderson, or with McMaster, or between their british-german-franco-celtic-hindu-danish selves. The French and Germans continue a battle of incompatible ideas that fight on different planes: Urdeutschland is a cobweb left on cellared bottles put down before Hans Sachs or Martin Luther: French thought is like the Place Vendôme, so lucid and correct that it seems cruel to thoughts that never find a uniform in speech. When an American from Wesleyan College says: Where is this talk getting us? let's do something! McMaster answers: thought must lead to life without short-circuits. You strive for action first, as most Americans do, because you do not like to sweat in silence: your paradise, as Bernard says, is the tick-tock of a succession of alarm-clocks. Squat on your hams in isolation for seven days: resist all food and action: you'll learn as much about the East as seven trips to India would teach, and find perhaps where you Americans fall short: you'll learn, my lad, that two and two is four. Without the fertile abstract mode of mathematics even pawnbrokers would not have customers. Thoughts that divert from action are sometimes gay: but actions that lead away from thoughts, or pluck them still unripe, are the worst form of futility and idleness.

94

Bernard sees that these young men and girls have much to learn and much to teach: the Germans talk of Fritz von Unruh, Wefel, and a medievalism much renewed: the French of Jules Romains, Drieu la Rochelle, the Cahiers of L'Esprit—a renaissance that brings to weary staleness last year's stale prophets—Gide, Maurras, the brilliant Marcel Proust: the tired men of twenty tired years that brought and fought and lived beyond the War. The sickish cleverness of Morand is Tzara's da-da for the bourgeoisie: they have a match in England: poor T. E. Hulme deceased and Aldous Huxley who mocks at all he'd like to worship and worships jeeringly all that he hates. Yes: yes: says Bernard: we in America have known that mawkish liquid, too. But Eugene O'Neill begins to find himself: there's meat in Sandburg, Robinson, Brooks, Fletcher, Rosenfeld, and Frank: Kreymborg can make us dance and Frost lies like November's crystals on New England's fields. Mencken and

Lewis ply their whips on Main Street: the smiles of pained self-accusation shriek to heaven. There's promise in all this. I see it better here than in America. New students and new teachers may call a tune for life, once whiskey flasks give out. When youth begins to swarm to an idea, beekeepers who want honey will find that masks are not enough to keep them off. We've energy to burn: once we can give it form, we'll make machines use handkerchiefs to blow their noses, and not speak in company until they're spoken to. We'll break the shells of cities that are rotten eggs, set free the gas, and build a hundred new ones in their place. Your German Siedlungen and prudent English efforts are just beginnings, don't you think? Our architecture will hug the land and dance with color and drink the sun again, instead of making murky setback canyons like imitations of bad cubist pictures. Electric power talks of culture, not subsistence, for the worker: I smell a hundred changes once workingmen have victory in their bones. You Danish lads can give us hints of this and that: you Germans too: if there were Russians here, we'd learn from them as well. This is not all a dream. The American you dread is just as much a dream. Radium disintegrates into lead! Once tick-tock begins to disintegrate it may become a rainbow—who can tell?

95

In the Geneva sun America is beautiful: in the Geneva sun Bernard approaches America as a confident bridegroom approaches a bride: in Geneva Bernard forgets about fundamentalism, poison gas, armored money wagons, aimless miles of aimless motor cars, the clownish religion of one hundred per centers. Geneva is a good place to think about America in. Mid the vast poplars of the Parc de Mon Repos Bernard thinks about America and Eunice: he is excited about America: he is excited about Eunice. He throws a verse for Eunice to the seagulls that hover over Lake Leman in early September: he says: Bring it back to Eunice in Brooklyn Heights: ask any seagull near the Battery where Brooklyn Heights is.

96

The irony of overshoes and peajackets in the sun, and leggins and no peajackets in the rain is the recurrent mystery of life. When Bernard has spent three months in Europe he can think of nothing but Eunice: the mornings begin with Eunice and the nights end with Eunice. When Bernard was twenty young girls were not so reckless nor himself so confident: he thirsted for adventure: but now his desire is muted in an ironic aloofness. At twenty Bernard used to wear his knuckles down beating at formidable editorial doors: a thirty he crumples polite editorial notes with a gesture that might garrot a neck, and goes about his own business. Desire and fulfillment do not synchronize: life should stand still, or dreams should gallop! The self that finally achieves the dream is not the self that dreamed it: disillusion may be the fulfillment of an illusion—five years too late. Bernard has achieved all he ever wanted to achieve—five years too late. To flout this with a grin is thirty's last achievement.

97

When Bernard faces Charlotte in a restaurant in Greek Street, Charlotte's eyes snuggle into Bernard's broad shoulders. Three years ago I knew what hell was like, says Charlotte: I'm past that now: I'm thirty-nine. But you look strong and confident. I've danced on fiery stones and had my fill of nettles too, says Bernard: my letters about Eunice and myself did not begin to tell you half of it. The baby and my being thirty have made me feel mature: having lived through a first day in the Navy, a first year of marriage, and a first hour of childbirth, I'm fit for anything. Do I look strong? You do, says Charlotte: and you, says Bernard suddenly, are beautiful: how is it that I've never kissed you yet? At thirty happy married lads, though anchored fast, begin to realize another woman's worth. I'm glad you came and glad you're going, says Charlotte. A month of seeing you might bring an ache.

98

The shuffle of water against the side of the Aquitania, hovering at slowest speed in thickest fog, accentuates the intolerable loneliness: within a fog a man has nothing but his memories and his dreams. The distant hooting of ships is the passing of days: the jog of the propeller is the incessant reminder of action: when the gong sounds for lunch tick-tock recovers. Wrapped in a cape, a blanket, and impenetrable loneliness, Bernard hovers in the Atlantic: fog abaft and fog abeam. The slush of water slapping at the sides, the noisy gape between the gusts of sound, make Bernard lean upon the rail and strain to see the ship that faintly threatens. When fog descends, the captain shares the landsman's helplessness: the passengers and the crew grow almost chummy: the lookout and the man who shines the brightwork are no farther from land than those who pay their passage. One works or dances, dines or goes to bed: but sometimes fog creeps through the portholes of the cabins and takes the crinkle out of even wavy hair. Electric lights and stars are both bedimmed with fog: it lifts—upon blank ocean and blank sky. The ship recovers speed. Voices speak easily. Thank you! I like two lumps in tea: no cookies, but a bread-and-butter sandwich. But when the steward folds the chairs back in the night, we find the sprinkled sky is but another fog, the fog of distance and eternity. Life insurance and boat drill are the mumbled security of saying one's prayers with tick-tock. When fog drops down we see the unreality of all we hold most real: even ourselves are evanescent. But fog and loneliness are not the worst. If each man had to bear a hand there mightn't be so many idiots to go to Europe! A little honest work about the ship is good for bellyaches and Weltschmerz. Perhaps our works and days are all we shipmates have: perhaps the fog will never lift completely, nor even Aquitanias get to port. It will not matter much. To feel the smart sea spray and ride the waves a while is all a sailor needs for happiness. A minute is a sample of eternity. —Published in The Second American Caravan. New York, 1928

10: Letters in Friendship

Part of my life as a writer, perhaps the most liberated and enjoyable part, has been the writing of letters to my friends; and though I dare not guess how many of these letters have been preserved, a considerable number of them have already come back to me from a convoy of dear people, most of them now dead, who had kept them faithfully. Some day, possibly, a rigorous selection from my entire correspondence might be made—unless my name crumble more rapidly than the paper these letters were written upon.

While some of these Letters in Friendship deal with quite intimate aspects of my life, I have chosen most of them mainly for their literary vitality, which is another way of saying, their high spirits and their range of mind. On mature consideration, I find that I have fewer doubts about my letters than about any other phase of my work. If at some ultimate day of judgment I were asked, "What sort of things have you written?" it might suffice for me to reply, nonchalantly: "Oh, I've written a few letters: don't bother to read my books now. What is worth saving you'll find in the letters."

Besides the four correspondents I have mainly drawn on here, there are various other friends whom I might have called in more freely. Doubtless many of their letters to me, as in the case of Delilah Loch, Henry Murray, Roderick Seidenberg, Carlludwig Franck, David Liebovitz, Paul Rosenfeld, and Franklin Donaldson, would often prove more rewarding than my own to them. But some of the most interesting letters from my friends cannot be used except by quotation within the frame of my formal Autobiography.

Van Wyck Brooks

Who can say when my friendship with Van Wyck Brooks began? In the spring of 1920 Walter Fuller, the Managing Editor of The Freeman, brought us together for a hasty lunch in a white-tiled Child's to discuss the possibility of my writing reviews for Brooks's department. But that meeting mingles with an even dimmer memory of our being briefly introduced a little earlier in The Freeman's first office, in the brownstone building on West Fifty-eighth Street which that weekly briefly occupied before its removal to Thirteenth Street. If those early meetings remain shadowy, it is perhaps because I had already had a more vivid mental encounter with Brooks in the pages of The Seven Arts, if not also in 'America's Coming of Age.'

But in spite of Brooks's constitutional shyness, which neither of us ever quite overcame, I can recall the original impression he made upon me: alert, diffidently humorous, aloofly genial, with his close-cut hair, his ruddy cheeks, his compact body, and the air of spiritual tautness, which one still finds in his early prose. Brooks, almost ten years older than I, was already an established critic, who always knew he was 'a writer born,' while I, despite my brief editorship of the fortnightly Dial, was still uncertain as to whether I would become a sociologist, a dramatist, a critic, or a philosopher until I found the coat of many colors that actually fitted me. Quite spontaneously we became fellow workers in the task of reclaiming our American literary heritage, too long neglected, or apologetically depreciated. In contrast to the disillusioned expatriates of the 'lost generation' who were travelling in the opposite direction, we felt—as did Randolph Bourne, Waldo Frank, and Paul Rosenfeld—that this was an essential preparation for America's cultural 'Coming of Age.' For Brooks this remained a lifelong mission; and between 1921 and 1931, partly under his influence, I made it my concern, too.

Immediately after our meeting, I sailed for London, and during the next half-year was faced with a momentous decision, whether to settle down permanently in the post I was then occupying, as acting editor of The Sociological Review, or return to America. Many factors entered into this decision; and not the least of them was the appeal of Brooks, in 'A Reviewer's Notebook,' his weekly column in The Freeman. That quiet but vibrant voice of his was one of the contemporary voices that called me home.

What with short encounters in his cubbyhole of an office—the rear 'hall bedroom' of a typical old red brick house—and occasional lunches, the ice between us thinned and melted: partly because we then shared many ideas, partly just because we liked each other in the inexplainable way that governs loves and friendships. With my marriage to Sophy Wittenberg the following year, our opportunities for meeting increased, for since The Dial, where she served at that time as editorial assistant, was on the same block, there were many occasions for casual meetings, all the more because in the fall of 1921 we set up a flat 'around the corner,' on West Fourth Street. I can't remember the details; and Brooks and I saw each other too often during his literary editorship of The Freeman for letters of any consequence to pass: but by the winter of 1921 we were on solid ground together.

One animated and memorable night stands out—when Brooks and Fuller dined with us to discuss in detail plans we three had already sketched for publishing a new series of books, modeled after the French *Cahiers de Quinzaine*, with a subscription list, to ensure support for new work. This was only one of a series of similar projects that Brooks played with from time to time: like his earlier notion, startlingly like that which Leonard and Virginia Woolf actually brought to pass, for setting up "a small printing press, like Yeats's Cuala Press, to bring out essays and translations of writers whom we liked."

In this early period I saw more of Brooks because of our propinquity, than I did later when he was in Carmel or Westport, writing his 'Mark Twain' or his 'Henry James.' During the winter of 1920–1921 we met every fortnight, too, in the basement of Harold Stearns's house in Great Jones Street, also around the corner, to discuss art and letters and scholarship and life in general: a real symposium, usually accompanied by a gallon of domestic Marsala Stearns would manage to wangle from a neighborly Italian bootlegger; and if I remember the scene faithfully, the conversations were better, at least gayer and wittier, than the book we finally published, 'Civilization in the United States.' It was during this same period, too, that Joel Spingarn invited Brooks, Ernest Boyd, and myself to take part in a more intimate weekend symposium at Troutbeck: an occasion I later translated into 'Aesthetics: A Dialogue.'

These meetings laid the foundation for our friendship, despite the differences in temperament, family background, and education. Brooks, as the readers of his autobiography know, came from a financially solid, if eventually shaky, upper middle-class background, established in one of the remote Jersey suburbs, Plainfield. He had lived for a year in Europe before he reached high school age, and he had haunted the art galleries of Dresden: even so early he had drunk almost too deeply at the heady fountain that lured Henry James's desperate spinsters to Europe.

By contrast, I came from a very mixed family, the New York branch of which had sunk to the lower middle class. But I was emphatically a child of our great, multinational metropolis, inoculated at birth against the glamor of Europe by feeling its vulgar but vital presence all about me. What was lacking in my immediate family pattern was abundantly supplied by my urban environment. Unlike Brooks, I was not, even as a lonely child, passionately bookish; and I never shared his exclusive, all-absorbing interest in the literary life alone.

Our temperamental and ideological differences of course underlay our specific literary judgments. Whereas Brooks admired the 'healthier' early American stories of Henry James, notably 'The Bostonians,' I delighted in James's equally penetrating English studies, 'Brooksmith,' 'The Shrine,' 'The Turn of the Screw,' 'What Maisie Knew,' and not least of course his incomparable European insights in 'Portrait of a Lady.' Those stories had led me in 'The Golden Day' to describe James as an 'esthetician of corruption,' for his report on the state of civilization in the Nineteenth Century, despite his preoccupation with the thin Upper Crust, was as insidiously devastating as Jacob Burckhardt's or Henry Adams's more open judgments on the future of our whole civilization.

Brooks, revolting against his genteel moneyed background, though fatally embrangled in it to the end of his days, admired his Plainfield friend, Randolph Bourne, who labored under no such handicap; and after Bourne died he transferred some of this feeling to me, as symbol of the monkish regimen and intransigent approach he felt proper to the writer's vocation. Though my own poverty was somewhat softened by a small inheritance that fell to me when I was twenty, I was never thwarted by a plethora of bourgeois comforts, neither did my widowed mother feel it incumbent upon me to engage, for her benefit, in a more profitable vocation than the writing of books. In a word, I had no standard either to live up to or to live down. Brooks, on the other hand, was harried by his outer faithfulness to bourgeois traditions and by his inner need to escape them. For him poverty meant spiritual emancipation.

While Brooks was exacerbated by his financial difficulties, even after he was a well-established writer, he was unwilling to achieve security by swerving ever so slightly from his life course, as the acceptance of the many offers of an editorship, after the Freeman days, would have caused him to do. That primal integrity, that inviolability, was I think what drew me most closely to Brooks, in the days when our friendship was forming: and it remained the basis of our lifelong mutual respect. This overcame our original differences in character and background, and offset those later divergences, occasionally sharpening into quarrels, which our correspondence discloses. If our friendship, however loving, never became deeply intimate, if some reserve and reticence always remained, we nonetheless could not part until death itself parted us. —From 'The Van Wyck Brooks–Lewis Mumford Letters.' New York, 1970

My head has again been busy with our old pamphlet scheme: and as soon as I can get my own bearings straight again I should like to discuss it with you at greater length. Did you see Pierre de Lanux's article on the founding of 'La Nouvelle Revue' in the Evening Post last week? I am quite sure that we could establish a fertile center of ideas in America, too, if we could only find two or three capable people who are not afraid to live on short commons and look physical destitution in the face. The American notion that nothing can be done without a gross financial subsidy is a superstition: what we need is a spiritual subsidy, and there is not quite enough capital in our Musical Banks to supply us with that! Fortunately, Sophy is quite willing to cramp our living quarters a little and wear some of the skin off her fingers if there is anything like the incentive of an adventure in letters to work for; and I think that within the next couple of years we might make a start, trying in the meanwhile to gather a group together and get it in focus. —Letter to Van Wyck Brooks. June 17, 1922

JUNCTURE OF BROOKS'S 'EMERSON' AND MY 'GOLDEN DAY.' [For four months I have been living in a dream, writing a life of Emerson. It has been a sort of religious experience: I never before knew anything like it; and it has kept me at my table, eight, ten, twelve, sometimes fourteen hours a day, reading when I was not writing. But why should I say any more?—I shall have so much to say when I see you. You may know that I had a bad breakdown last spring—it really lasted about two years; and when it came to a head & burst—on May 20th, when I woke up—I felt as if I had expelled from my system the gathering poisons of years. I feel ten years older and ten years younger at the same time, and so conscious, deep down, of the value and meaning of all the things you have been turning over (in your letter, lectures, etc.)—about the "good life," and the "mission"—what other word is there?—of literature, and the necessity of re-asserting the idealistic point of view, with an energy and a faith our good country has not *known* for many years—though the *patter* too has a dim breath of life in it. Everything I have done so far has been a kind of exploration of the *dark* side of our moon, and this blessed Emerson has led me right out into the midst of the sunny side.] —Van Wyck Brooks to L. M. September 13, 1925

Young Geddes kept his temper for a long week at a time, and thereby earned (for the household) a twenty-two calibre rifle: we went on our first murderous expedition against nature today, taking pot-shots at derisive crows and finally—thanks to Geddes's good eye—intercepted a woodchuck, that grubby little vegetarian Cain, in his effort to reach home plate. Some lurking savage in me shrinks at nothing about this but the final scene of slaughter; as for Geddes, the savage in that hardy bosom dances rather than lurks: and I try to keep myself from wondering openly whether this innocent rapine is but the preparation for such strife as is taking place in Spain—which at least has an element of human reason in it—or perhaps for the emptier and more dastardly strife that would mark another World War.

Really: you and I grew up in an innocent world. Soldiers then were all of the tin variety: they liked drums and music and such innocent displays of brass buttons as colored people used to like in a cakewalk: they still thought of war in terms of manly encounters on galloping horses, indeed, only as a more spectacular exhibition than a hunt or a horseshow. Now war is as grim as the assembly line of a Ford factory and as relentless as a financier: the morals of the rattlesnake are everywhere. Sometimes I am tempted to stand up on my two legs and preach one last desperate sermon to my friends and brothers: one frantic gesticulation toward safety before some putrid fool touches off the dynamite. When we were young we could ask ourselves: What can we conquer? Now we can only ask: What can we save? That shrinkage of ambition is not due to age but to the times we live in. —Letter to Van Wyck Brooks. July 24, 1936

My life in New York these last few weeks has achieved an almost monastic simplicity, which harmonizes very well with the work I am doing at the library not alone on the Middle Ages, but on the period of confusion, so much like our own, which preceded them. I have been deep in the early Church fathers; and found myself full of admiration for Tertullian, who felt about Roman amphitheaters pretty much the way I feel about modern ones. I would like to enter a monastery for a few days in retreat, just to get the savor of the life; but not in America; it would have to be some little known place, mossy with the past, on some high hill overlooking the Adriatic! Meanwhile, my due feet never fail to walk to the Forty-second Street library almost in time for the opening each morning; and I keep right at my table till two or three in the afternoon, not even pausing for lunch. (I have something to learn about fasting!) I am struck by the fact that I am haunted by fewer demons, visible ones at least than St.

Anthony or St. Jerome; all of us seem to have capacities for concentration that those holy characters lacked. Their diet may have made them irritable: at all events I can't imagine plucking the feathers off a bothering little sparrow because I was sure he was a demon sent by the devil. A sparrow is a sparrow for us, which is a comforting thought, especially for sparrows.   —Letter to Van Wyck Brooks. February 1, 1940

Another book I have been reading is 'Joseph in Egypt,' and I must say I am still as aloof from this as I was at the beginning: it does not seem to me the masterpiece everyone has been proclaiming it; alas not! There is something irretrievably wooden about this resurrection of an ancient time; the same sort of woodenness one finds in Flaubert's Salammbo. Plenty of archaeological detail; even an excess; but the characters are at once too much and too little like us to be convincing; and when Joseph, to show his pretty intellect, talks Einstein I am incredulous. One can deal with an ancient mind by allusion and suggestion, as happened in the case of such a relatively contemporary account as in the Bible itself: but as soon as one becomes explicit, one tends to describe, willy-nilly, one's own contemporaries, one's own state of mind. Try as he will, Mann does not escape this: indeed, half the time one believes that Joseph is just Hans Castorp, he of 'The Magic Mountain,' in Egyptian fancy dress.   —Letter to Van Wyck Brooks. April 26, 1938

What nonsense is this about your being upset over Farrell's attack upon you in The New Republic? . . . I haven't read the attack itself and I don't intend to. He is not one of those enemies that one can learn from, as for example, I have occasionally learned something from De Voto. Every once in a while God sends one out of the blue a gadfly to keep one from being lazy or complacent; some unidentifiable correspondent will discover a soft spot one had kept concealed from oneself; and one always does well to heed such messengers, because they do what they do without guile, even when they want actually to hurt the recipient. Even more rarely one gets a painful criticism of one's work from someone who thoroughly understands it! This is sometimes harder to take when it probes one's weaknesses; but in the long run such criticisms are deeply encouraging and one is a stronger man for having wrestled with this particular angel of the Lord. Farrell is neither kind of critic.   —Letter to Van Wyck Brooks. December 22, 1944

How much your chapters on Cooper in 'The World of Washington Irving' evoked passages of my boyhood. There was a horribly printed series of books, back around 1905, done on grey paper, pinched in type, drab in looks, definitely non-lasting: but it included a large share of the classics and cost only ten cents. That was within my purse; and on Saturdays I used to go to an uptown department store, long since vanished, to buy Cooper, in either this or a somewhat more lasting twenty-five cent edition. 'The Spy' and 'The Pilot' were both favorites of mine; and among the Leatherstocking Tales I think I liked 'The Pioneers' best. I had my own trick for evading Cooper's long-winded descriptions of scenery and for fastening upon and re-reading his more humorous scenes. He was not perhaps a humorist, but he had, at times, a salty comic touch, an eye for quirks and revealing gestures, as with Dickens. That comic aspect of his genius is too easily overlooked; but I think that this, no less than his familiarity with the sea, must have endeared him to Melville. —Letter to Van Wyck Brooks. June 28, 1944

ON A POPULAR STYLE. The problem you raise in connection with Upton Sinclair's work is one of the hardest in all literature to solve; but I think it a different one from that raised by the gap between popular and esoteric literature today. In the great periods more was expected of the people than we expect today: they were expected to make more of an effort to reach the highest level, and evidently had enough of an inward life to respect it and reach it. Perhaps the gap was already widening in Shakespeare's time; but the man in the street nevertheless stayed through the whole performance, even if he didn't understand it completely, instead of demanding that all of it be on the level of the clowns; and this was true in Pepys' time, or in Haydn's, when the chambermaids or the serfs could share the same music, and like it.

But with Upton Sinclair's work something else is involved: the fact that he really has a decent, but commonplace mind, which is reflected in the quality of his prose, even in books above the Lanny Budd level, like his book on Jesus. Because he was once a 'great' figure, and perhaps because the very commonplaceness of expression makes him more readily understood by a European like Einstein or Jung, he has a way of drawing out from such people more favorable responses than his books deserve: indeed, he extracts praise in the way a broken down actor, known to everybody in his palmy days, extracts dollars from people who once knew him at least by reputation. His subject matter is indeed of the greatest importance and I honor him for sticking so resolutely to his guns over such a long period, but his method of treatment does not do justice to the substance and therefore doesn't work any profound changes in the reader. This is of course at the opposite end of the scale from having nothing to say and saying it exquisitely; but in the end is it not equally barren? "I and mine do not convince by arguments, we convince by our presence." Is it not just the absence of 'presence' in Whitman's sense that makes Sinclair, though so virtuous, so well-meaning, so palpably on the side of the angels, a writer of minor rank? —Letter to Van Wyck Brooks. February 20, 1955

. . . This is the height of fame, dear Van Wyck: in a single mail I was coupled with Tallulah Bankhead and Boris Pasternak! As for the Saturday Evening Post article on The Origins of War, apart from the kind words you and one other friend wrote, the sole outcome of it was to stir up all the crackpots in the United States. Reading my article they said to themselves: "Here's someone just as crazy as we are: maybe he'll listen to us." Two of them have found *the secret of the universe* (not the same secret), but one of them needs a little help with his 'grammer' (sic). . . . What a world! —Letter to Van Wyck Brooks. April 1959

Babette Deutsch and Avrahm Yarmolinsky

As with many other friendships in the twenties, I can't remember exactly when and how my friendship with Babette Deutsch and her husband Avrahm Yarmolinsky began. A passing image of Babette at The Dial office floats into my mind: but nothing else is attached to it. As for Avrahm, who became head of the Slavonic Language Department at the New York Public Library, my second home, we early took to lunching together at the Russian Tea Room, then in the West Thirties. After Sophia and I settled in to Sunnyside Gardens in 1925, the Yarmolinskys moved into a more commodious house a block away: and from then on, our family intercourse, chiefly at evening parties, became more frequent.

Paradoxically, it was our distance apart in recurrent summers that brought Babette and me closer together—by letter of course. In their acute and vivacious observations her letters more than match mine. From the fact that Babette was my interlocutor in 'A Dialogue on Contemporary Disillusion,' printed by The Nation in 1924, it is plain that our friendship had thickened even before we became neighbors in Sunnyside, nourished as it was by our differences as well as our agreements; for though I shared Babette's admiration for Yeats, we parted over Wallace Stevens, only to be united by Josephine Strongin, that elfin friend to all of us. As

170

for Avrahm, the incorruptible scholar, the even-handed biographer of Turgenev and Dostoevski, I postponed my praise for his funeral Eulogy.

. . . I am now reading a book that I have not read since my very early childhood—when I probably only looked at the pictures—'Robinson Crusoe,' and I am entranced with it. Its limitations are honest, the prose is supple and masculine, as supple as George Moore and as masculine as Cobbett—one can't think of anybody later than Cobbett who is really masculine; and short of being able to outpass all limitations, having honest ones is next best, and I honor Defoe for the result. He is better than Fielding: there is a touch of the judicial humorist in Fielding: the ponderous trifling with the classics and with the reader: whilst Defoe has both feet on the ground. What a paean he writes to the Middle Station in Life—such a paean that from this time on every person who has got past his abc's has attempted to achieve it, lured by that plain, manly voice, with his hoarse sigh of regret of having so long bereft himself of the comforts of that middle station, and his sly pride at achieving it by his own hands on the desert island. We doubtless have Defoe to thank for running water and postage stamps and electric washing machines, all because he praised the middle station. He is the siren voice of the modern age, leading us on, on, on. But there: I am already giving you extracts from my next book plus two—'Defoe: A Study of Eighteenth Century Saws and Twentieth-Century Practices'; or some such title. Still, I confess that I am surprised at 'Robinson Crusoe.' It is quite as good as the world has always said; and I have long since given up hoping that this would be true about anything. . . . —Letter to Babette Deutsch. July 6, 1928

. . . I read long and lazily. 'The Red and the Black' has been my most extended adventure; and to speak frankly, I don't like it. Were I a Frenchman, I daresay I might see the whole history of my country embodied in it; but I'm not, and though the story carried me along with it, I felt as though I was irresistibly being conducted along a long passage which scraped my shins and shoulders, and which bruised my spirit, without offering me a single vista—or, what is worse, a single depth. It is an arid book; and it has remained for an arid age to resurrect it and to find its virtues admirable. They are admirable: but they are not sufficient. I have begun to re-read 'War and Peace,' with the sensation one gets on going to Switzerland, when one passes out of the tunnel and suddenly sees the great ice peaks hanging over one in the distance. Glad to get the smoke out of my lungs and leave the tunnel behind! —Letter to Babette Deutsch and Avrahm Yarmolinsky. July 27, 1927

. . . I find that after a day's work I have no better desire than to do something frivolous; and I can understand Herbert Spencer's habit of playing pool—or was it billiards? The village library hath a room in our cottage; and it is a prize, a great prize. It contains Sherlock Holmes and George Borrow and Mr. Dooley and Ouïda and Florence Barclay and Ethel M. Dell, and best of all, it contains 'The Woman Who Did,' one of a series of books, gotten out in the year I was born—wasn't it nice to be *Fin de siècle* and to hear Ta-ra-ra-ra-boom-de-ay in one's crib, Babette?— with a frontispiece by Aubrey Beardsley. Haven't you alawys wanted to read 'The Woman Who Did'? I have. It is a funny and pathetic book: the author was a scientific hack named Grant Allen; and in his dedication he confesses that this is the first book he had written for his own pleasure in twenty years. The heroine renounces the iniquitous institution of marriage; and with heroism, moral courage, and blushes that no flapper today could even imagine, much less imitàte, she has a baby without enchaining the only too-willing-to-be-chained father. The upshot of this great pioneer step is incredible, in the light of what has actually happened in our own generation. The girl grows up, turns against her mother for not having been respectable, and says that she will never be able to marry the man she wants until her mother is dead!!! (No asterisk on my typewriter.) And the heroine, Hermione, being no amateur in the way of martyrdom, swallows a little convenient prussic acid, in one last heroic vindication of herself. But life is more astonishing than the boldest and most progressive of books: the actual sequel today would have astonished and I have no doubt outraged Grant Allen much more than the suicide. . . . —Letter to Babette Deutsch and Avrahm Yarmolinsky. June 1928

. . . I have been reading precious little since coming up here; in fact, for the first three weeks I drugged myself with manual labor: writing was like the struggle of a young child to awaken from deep sleep; and it is only for the last couple of days that I begin to realize that, despite appearances, I still have a mind, and it can be made to function if I am firm and insistent enough about it, and remember to carry about a pencil and a pad of paper! My sole spiritual nourishment, in fact, has been a single chapter of the Bhagavad Gita every night, as the sun is tinting the last clouds in the West, and the swallows are darting overhead.

How little of that Scripture remains alive! The wonder and awe at the multitudinous universe: yes: that lived there as it was not fully to live again until Newton and Darwin. Also the feeling that life matters in the process, not in the result: "Counting gain or loss as one prepare for battle!" That's fine. Finally the notion—in a sense it suggests what is best in Dewey, only he sees but half of it—the notion that action and contemplation are both means of reaching ultimately the same end, and that when the mind is enfranchised and the personality enlarged, one may do almost anything and not be soiled by the action: which is true, too, although thieves, liars, and murderers are not habitually the persons by whom this truth is vindicated. As for the rest, a curious mixture of beauty and uncouthness—especially the retention of the notion that Krishna himself, the All, is to be worshiped, propitiated, sacrificed before. How that lower side of godhood stuck! What inordinate human vanity, to require such servilities for the gods, our images! But enough: it is a good Scripture, and what meat it has is very nourishing indeed: I put it alongside the Sermon on the Mount.

I spent thirty happy years without active commitment to any orthodox religion. And I am still, I confess, very jealous of the Gods, and lay down all sorts of private conditions for my accepting their inscrutable intentions in contriving a universe constantly oscillating between Brahma and Kali, between creativity and catastrophe. But I can no longer deny the presence of the Gods, for I hear their footsteps on the hills, and see their faces mirrored in the waters! —Letter to Babette Deutsch. June 28, 1930

. . . May I say, before I forget it, that I like your pieces in The New Yorker: they have penetration without malice; and to remember to be human after one has thrust inside one's subject is almost the art of literature, if not in fact of life. This last year, or rather these last two years, have improved my own morals in this respect enormously: I have sinned as often and as copiously as a Dostoevski hero, and I think that at last I could get to the bottom of the most forbidding sort of character and yet fish up something which, if it would not redeem him, would bring him back within the pale of humanity: so perhaps I am at last ready to write novels and plays: and I can't pretend that I have ever been before. One can do everything with the intellect—that is what makes one so proud of it—except understand another human being. Well: here I am—and I hope I haven't piqued your womanly curiosity too much by mentioning my sins in such a lordly and offhanded way: one's worst enormities remain within, and it is only one's vulgar commonplaces of error and folly that turn into murders and suicides, treasons, infidelities, and betrayals.

Sophia is here, too, much refreshed by her trip, with a serenity that reminds me of the unawakened girl I first knew on The Dial: very dashing and beautiful and confident of herself, too. It was a good trip and a well-timed trip; for though almost every introduction she had missed fire, and there were all sorts of minor disappointments, she achieved all that we had both hoped out of the journey; and now, perhaps, we have broken our curious streak of misfortunes: although it is too early to whistle, and wise people don't whistle anyway. She is much pleased by what has happened to our little boy Geddes in the meanwhile, and is generous enough to admit that I had something to do with it: although the break itself was perhaps the only thing that was necessary for both of them, after their too long companionship on beds of misery: with all the harassing and bullying that goes with illness to make it worse. I enjoyed having him by myself very much: it gave us a new sense of intimacy, and even in the worst depths of my summer cold our relations were quite tolerable, although not without a little Spartan self-discipline on my own part. Having him so solely dependent upon me for the time, made me curiously anxious not to die at an inconvenient moment; amusingly enough, he was a little anxious about it, too, and kept on asking me who would look after him. At present we are a happy family. . . . —Letter to Babette Deutsch. August 16, 1930

. . . Apart from writing my book I have no events to record, no adventures, even in the mind; although after years of delicious effort, years which I would not for anything have shortened, I have finished 'The Guermantes Way'; and in less time than it takes me usually to read the Sunday newspaper, or so it seemed, I finished the now current volume of Jules Romains, who still maintains himself in my esteem, partly no doubt because he condenses the contents of so many hundred Sunday newspapers for me, but partly, also, because after the sociologist has returned with his report, and duly analyzed it, for the benefit of the busier members of the class who keep notebooks, the poet suddenly awakes and in the course of a brief chapter sets all the dry paper aflame, proving that the real use for all these paperoid preparations is after all to provide light for the eyes, warmth for the heart—those neglected organs.   —Letter to Babette Deutsch. August 6, 1936

. . . I have at last made a contribution to the paper where you are such a familiar star: I wrote an article for The New Yorker on Radio City. Oh these good editors! I respect them so deeply and they are so bothersome! They tempt one with their high rates, and by the time one has met them, debated with them, struggled with them, and come finally to a diplomatic understanding, one has spent enough time and energy to have written half a dozen articles for less competent and therefore more easily pleased editors! It has been fun, however, to see how their minds work: they really do know their business, and that is rare enough in any line of work to be enjoyed in itself. They have even asked me to do a Profile: but I have a preference for the full face, and have said No. —Letter to Babette Deutsch. June 2, 1931

. . . Amenia is more than tolerable: the hot spells are never impossible here, whereas Charlottesville was a miasmic pool of heat, and the kitchens in the University Commons gave off the horrid odors known only to cheap London fish restaurants. But my brief four days in the South gave me a truer picture of our country, or certain aspects of it, than I'd ever had before. The buildings of the University are marvellous: Monticello is in sight and aspect beyond one's most imperial dream, although Farrington, now a country club, has the better interior. It is all Mr. Jefferson, and Mr. Jefferson was quite as great a man as Virginia thinks he was. The Ranges, as his groups of buildings on each side of the central lawn of the University are called, form the finest piece of architecture in America: and heaven knows I have no love, ordinarily, for the taste of the eighteenth century. But he had an eye! The human scale of his arcade, his admirable monastic cells for students, his equally fine buildings which were once, under his plan, professors' residences and class rooms, are unequalled in America for plan and design. The site and the scenery constantly stirred and abetted the architect: I have not had more glorious views anywhere: and if this is my enthusiasm produced by muggy smothering July days, heaven only knows into what gibbering inexpressible ecstasy I would go if I had first seen the University and the surrounding region in October.

But the Southerners themselves are still exactly like the Old Regime in Russia as portrayed by Tolstoi and Chekhov: lazy, slow-moving, torpid, imperturbable, snobbish, interbred, tolerant of dirt, incapable of making effective plans or organization. Our handsome fraternity house had dirty beds in it, dreary walls, dilapidated furniture, an insufficient supply of pillows and towels, and bugs on the upper floor—not, happily, on mine. In spite of the preparations made for our coming, the human occupants had not been effectively moved out of our rooms: they hung on a day or two past their time, making our life uncomfortable. Six weeks in this environment would turn one, in sheer desperation, into a Connecticut Yankee. But I learned much in those four days that neither the historian nor the sociologist could tell me, things that require the immediate presence of one's eyes and nose. I will say nothing about the hospitality: it was *komisch*; but the chief point about it was that it handsomely took

175

down the conceit of four distinguished New York visitors, who, despite their personal modesty, had still secretly half a notion that they and New York between them were objects of some importance in the planetary scheme. Perhaps on *their* planet, my dear Babette; but certainly not in Virginia. . . . —Letter to Babette Deutsch. July 10, 1931

. . . As for 'Technics and Civilization,' it still goes: indeed "goes" is little better than Ogden's Basic English, for it pours, thunders, avalanches, tramples, and billows, knocking its poor author against the rocks as if he were shooting the Niagara, dragging him down to depths he had never suspected, whirling him through caverns measureless to man, scraping his buttocks against flinty facts and even more jagged theories, and in general knocking both wind and sense out of him, but at least leaving him with no doubt about the fact that he is living: for if Dr. Johnson vindicated reality by knocking his stick against the railing, how much more does one establish the fact of life by taking such a Niagara rapids journey! At the moment, I am just in the midst of proving, as an appendix to some remarks about War as a compensatory mechanism in an industrialized society, that the Class War, while real as a fact, is equally illusory and mischievous as a substitute for the realities of a genuine [internal] revolution: a point which will be misunderstood completely by Messrs. Calverton and Joe Freeman, but which is established, so far as I am concerned, by both logic and history—and what other props has man's judgment than those two? . . . —Letter to Babette Deutsch. August 3, 1933

The critics who look down their noses at Dickens, as even Virginia Woolf did—though she is full of characteristic Dickensian insights into the poor—simply envy his vitality and know they will never have more than a few drops of it, no matter how hard they exercise. The Dickensian gusto! —in another age and another country it would have made him a Rabelais. If Bulwer-Lytton was a 'lion in curlpapers,' Dickens was in fact a Rabelais in pantalets, a Victorian Rabelais, cut off in his writing from his sexual organs, indeed deprived, while writing, of the consciousness that they existed, but with all the other organs in the body patently quivering with eroticized energy and exulting in their activity. —Letter to Babette Deutsch. n.d.

. . . Your note touched me, dear Babette, because I have been through all this miserable trudging down the dusty rubbish-strewn streets of the past that you have been going through—if only because I am probably older than you, by at least a few weeks!—and I know that this nightmarish experience is not to be trusted. It is an act of self-punishment, out of all proportion to one's real offenses; an attempt at self-belittlement, in order to outbid the disparagements of indifferent critics.

There is no justice in this sort of biographic self-arraignment: it is as cruel as the punishments little children mete out to one another when they are handed over the privilege of self-government. Back of one's self-reproaches, looms the product of a vanity so colossal it disguises itself as humility: the assumption that one is completely responsible for one's sins and lapses, successes and failures! Neither is true: at best, one was a willing, sometimes conscious accessory of a multitude of external forces, visible and invisible. Yes: we faltered and we fell short: yet if we had proved stronger and more steadfast, it would still be true that we had sinned and fallen short. But as Rilke said in one of his letters, life would be wonderful even if it had held nothing more than this; and our very realization of our limitations is part of the wonder. —Letter to Babette Deutsch. October 2, 1960

Some day, if the world last that long, 'The City in History' will find a place on that very special shelf in American scholarship so far occupied in my library by only two books: George Perkins Marsh's 'Man and Nature' —famous in its day but quite forgotten even by geographers until I resurrected it in 'The Brown Decades'—and William James's 'Psychology.' The same combination of scholarly thoroughness, scientific insight, and palpable human experience. Let me whisper into your most private ear: *it is a masterpiece!* Yes: this is a large gobbet of self-appreciation even for an old friend to swallow. Perhaps you think that the ghost of Whitman has seized me? Since I am no longer a young man I've not his grand excuse—but then there's no Emerson to pat me on the back either! Perhaps it's good to let the Ego burst forth freely and unapologetically every once in a while, on the same principle that the famous medieval doctors of Salerno advised those who read their 'Regimen Salernitatis' to break wind, instead of bottling up the poisonous gases. One has to choose between embarrassing the company or preserving one's health! —Letter to Babette Deutsch. October 30, 1960

. . . I am against the complete works of almost anybody. Even Shakespeare would benefit by the dropping of a couple plays—no, at least half a dozen!—which have at best only academic interest. I have just come across an irritating case of the kind of flavorless reputation-stuffing that kills a man's good work. Years ago I resurrected the best architectural critic America has yet produced, the present writer not excepted, Montgomery Schuyler. Thanks to my efforts, the scholarly world, in no more than twenty years awoke to my discovery, and thanks to my good relations with Howard Mumford Jones, the Harvard University Press acted on my recommendation to reprint his classic work 'American Architecture,' published in 1892, when Schuyler was at the height of his powers. [In declining the office of editing and introducing this new edition I properly suggested that this job should be done by a younger scholar.] So what happened? The professors who undertook the editing of the book, dug up all the unimportant papers he had written, and buried his significant criticisms in a two-volume omnium gatherum which, by its very mass, also re-buries him. For this they will probably be advanced to full professorships and Schuyler himself will be demoted. Thus wags the world . . . —Letter to Babette Deutsch. January 1, 1962

Morally Cambridge is not an ideal climate for me, since, as in every university community, it is populated by too many people who, in Dante's words, are neither for nor against the good: belonging to that low circle in Hell set aside by Dante for academic minds. But apart from that, Leverett House is as near to Heaven as we can ever hope to get in a city; and it just happens that, in addition to enjoying its other virtues, we inhabit this term by far the finest apartment in Cambridge—one originally designed by the MacLeishes, with a commodious living room, big enough to hold a larger gathering than we'll ever invite, and a series of views from our many windows, so entrancing that they almost keep me from getting my work done, since eleven floors below us, we see the curving Charles, its ducks sitting on the water and sea-gulls swooping, and to cap it all three quarters of the sky, with sunrises on the east and the most magnificent sunsets, thanks to smoke pollution—the same that favored Turner!—on the West. We'll never be fit to descend to humbler quarters again: they are even better than the London apartment we used to have on the top floor of the Holfords' house, overlooking Regents Park. —Letter to Babette Deutsch. October 26, 1966

. . . Naum Gabo is really an extraordinary artist, as gifted and as pure as they make them. I've admired his work from the time I first saw a constructivist sculpture of his in 1923 at the Brooklyn Museum. The medium he works in is formidable—wire, glass, plastics, the materials of our current technology—so he serves me beautifully to make a point I wanted to emphasize in my Epilogue to 'The Pentagon of Power,' where I place one of his sophisticated modern constructions opposite archaic and primitive figures by Henry Moore, who makes another point. Do arrange to have him at your table for the Spring meeting of the National Institute next year: he'd love to talk Russian with Avrahm. (His wife, Miriam, by the bye, is a daughter of Bella Moscowitz, Al Smith's political mentor.)

. . . In a little while we hope to be sufficiently recovered to enjoy the good fortune we owe to 'The Myth of the Machine.' In a sense our cup not merely runneth over: it slobbers disgustingly. We are well fortified against poverty, disparagement, and rejection: but 'success' and prosperity offer a different set of problems, which we are quite unprepared to cope with. We are too old, thank God, to be corrupted by it; but if the book should be greeted as enthusiastically by the public as it has been by the publishers who have seen it, it may corrupt our grandchildren. Lord! we did ask thee for a *little* rain . . . And how ironic! Twenty years ago this recognition and reward might have made a real difference in our lives, perhaps leading us to buying a house in Cambridge or on Martha's Vineyard—or both! But then, I must also admit, it might have diverted me from writing either 'The City in History' or 'The Myth of the Machine': the three books on which my reputation will probably ultimately rest. . . . —Letter to Babette Deutsch and Avrahm Yarmolinsky. September 16, 1970

. . . I have, incidentally, become an admirer of Mark Van Doren's commentary on Shakespeare's plays, which I read for a second time while travelling. It is not exactly criticism in any orthodox sense, though perhaps it corresponds to what Spingarn meant when he tried to characterize 'creative criticism.' But I don't know anyone else who has gotten closer to the core of Shakespeare's mind, largely by dwelling on Shakespeare's very words and mulling over them: so, though Mark and I see each other too infrequently, a real bond has been established between us. —Letter to Babette Deutsch and Avrahm Yarmolinsky. October 31, 1971

. . . Nothing turns out to be more surprising about old age than Old Age itself; and I don't know if I have yet achieved the ability to embrace it that Henry James did when he faced death in his first heart attack: "Ah, the Distinguished Thing has come." (What presence of mind to be on the point of dying with the right phrase on one's tongue!) Having read Bernard Berenson's sere account of his day by day journey into Old Age, I have resolved to make no further reports of my own halting pilgrimage. Yet at times I am tempted to, if only to show whoever may look through my notes that I've been quite aware—and from a long time back—of all the disconcerting indications of being assailed by little demons, surreptitiously stealing familiar names, blocking well-trodden passages with blank walls, and even placing barriers across the stairs one climbs and lengthening the distance between one's shoulders and one's feet. But why double the misery by writing about it? Berenson's 'Diaries' tell everything! —Letter to Babette Deutsch. June 30, 1972

. . . We've just come back from Washington where I got the rare Hodgkins Gold Medal from the Smithsonian for services to the environment—plus a really gratifying encomium. Likewise I had the fun of appearing at a meeting of the new American Studies Association in a 'panel' on 'Lewis Mumford and the Future of American Studies.' The people who had at first consented to give papers all got cold feet and resigned, probably because they realized that they would have to confront the real Lewis Mumford and not the imaginary Lewis Mumford some of them had in the interests of 'objective' scholarship fabricated: so I had the floor more or less to myself, with Alan Trachtenberg of Yale and Suslow of Rutgers assisting, and I had a very good time demonstrating what a surprising fellow the genuine L.M. was, and how different were his ideas from those that had been imputed to him.   —Letter to Babette Deutsch and Avrahm Yarmolinsky. October 31, 1971

The publication of Lawrence Thompson's three volume biography, and even more the snide comments of some of the reviews of the last volume, have clarified my own judgments of Frost. Without denying any of his crotchets or moral contradictions, even in their most repellent aspects, I find that the current devaluations of his character leave the major evidence of his life—his poetry—obliterated by excessive attention to his shortcomings as a lover, a husband, a father, a friend. What was important to know about Frost's character, apart from his writings, could have been told, with no significant obfuscation or suppression in a single volume—leaving the reader to absorb and reflect upon what was worth remembering and treasuring: the poems. The problem of dealing with Frost both as a man and a poet is similar to that of appraising Dostoevski. Almost all that one needs to know about the worst side of Dostoevski, the epileptic, the gambler, the virulent reactionary, was fully exposed by him in the 'Notes from the Underground.'   —Letter to Babette Deutsch, n.d.

Christiana Morgan

As with Babette Deutsch, my correspondence with Christiana Morgan was part of a family friendship which included Sophia and our daughter

Alison. We met, possibly for the first time, at lunch in the Harvard Psychological Clinic, then on Plympton Street, where my new friend, Dr. Henry Murray, still the outstanding authority on the life and work of Herman Melville, presided. While a pale light from Christiana's special gifts is reflected in my letters to her, in conversation she betrayed, even more than in letters, some of the inarticulate passion of Mynheer Peeperkorn in 'The Magic Mountain.' But let me add here that Christiana, besides being a one-time disciple of Jung, skilled in the arts of vision, collaborated in the design of the Murray-Morgan Thematic Apperception Test, and became a psychotherapist in her own right. Our personal contacts were sufficiently infrequent and aloof to permit an easy intellectual intimacy without any emotional complications.

. . . Part of the miracle of our friendship is that we should be converging toward the same destination without having communicated a word to each other: both of us withdrawing, turning inward, digging into the compost of the past, preparing a bed for fresh seeds. The title of Silone's novel—disappointing as an imaginative work but somehow right in its direction—'The Seed Beneath the Snow' keeps coming back to me. The husk of our old life must rot away, and I suspect the winter will be a long one. But that only makes our present task more important. As long as we looked for an immediate part to play and hoped for early visible changes, we were bound to accept, as part of our going civilization, many things that we could not honestly try to assimilate and did not really believe in. Had the foundations been sound, this willingness to perform a modest function in the existing structure would have been sane and healthy.

. . . I fooled myself into thinking that the times were ripe for a profound change in our universities: I took the interest of my professorial sponsors in getting me to Stanford as an evidence of such a change; but it was at bottom, if unconsciously, something quite different: a desire to get the credit for such a change without effecting it: at lowest a desire for publicity. The fact is that the very perfection of the scientist's and the scholar's routine has made the university the last place in which to expect renewal. What they are looking for in our schools and colleges is something facile: a re-arrangement of courses, a new pattern for the curriculum that will use all the existing elements; without the least change of spirit and ultimate purpose on the part of those participating, whether teachers or students.

As I perhaps told you, the only person at Stanford who really grasped this fact was the new president, Donald Tresidder: another outsider like myself. Within a few years, if I do not mistake him, he will follow me, because he will find too few in the institution who are ready to meet this challenge.   —Letter to Christiana Morgan. May 25, 1944

. . . We are all being shaken loose from our old life, it seems to me, whether we like it or not; but only those who are brave enough to like it will be able to profit by this enforced detachment and turn it to their own best uses. If 'The Condition of Man' can serve any purpose at the present moment it should serve as a purgation: a spiritual symbol of an ordeal that must be accepted by our society if it is to map out a new road. Those who have rejected the book, so far, are those who want to buy their heaven cheaply, without too much personal effort. One of the reviewers reproachfully said that I was a strip-teaser: he was annoyed because I vanished behind the curtain before he had been given a glimpse of his final heart's desire: effortless salvation! I accept that description, but how sadly it reveals the weakness of our contemporaries! In their spiritual impotence, they think that the last word in satisfaction would be to *look at* the stripper's concealed Mount of Venus, forgetting that from my point of view, the next step is action, a step that turns a pathetic voyeur into a responsive and responsible performer. —Letter to Christiana Morgan. June 25, 1944

The difficulty of anyone's knowing old Geddes today is that he was primarily an oral teacher like Socrates; and so he was not at his best in his writing. I find that the young are usually deeply disappointed in Geddes when they try to read him, probably because what was excitingly new thirty years ago when I first read him has now become commonplace, thanks to the triumph of the very ideas for which he stood; thanks also, perhaps, to such use of them as I have made. If Geddes had published a little less and had died a little earlier I should have been tempted to mythopoetize his character and message, in somewhat the way that Plato deliberately did with Socrates, using his thought as a peg on which to hang my own ideas, before I was sure enough to make so great a claim for my own. There is a letter of Plato's still extant in which he reveals how deliberately he did this.   —Letter to Christiana Morgan. August 4, 1944

. . . I deliberately postponed 'The Condition of Man' till I reached the fullness of my maturity and had felt at least the first autumn frosts of old age, those frosts that come on foggy mornings before the hot sun rises again. By now I feel impelled to quicken the pace of my writing, lest I get too far away from the heat and passion out of which whatever wisdom I now have has been distilled. For the weakness of most moralists, philos-

182

ophers, and religious teachers is that they draw mostly negative conclusions from these data; whereas I want, rather, to indicate the positive incentives that previous systems have either left out or attempted too prudently to disguise.

My present tranquility and peace may be due, not to wisdom and balance, but mere hormonic inactivity: in which case I am in danger of forgetting too much! Thank heaven I have lengthy notes on my past life with which I shall refresh myself, like the notes taken by a famous French actor, described in Delacroix's Notebooks, in which he set down every gesture in order that he could renew his original inspiration when it had become too mechanical!   —Letter to Christiana Morgan. August 4, 1944

. . . My situation as either a professor or a writer is not good. I could crawl back to Stanford and enjoy such security and honors as go to a full professor with tenure. But I could not pretend to myself that there was any significance in my being there or that I would be fulfilling—as dear Geddes hoped I would, in a letter he wrote from Africa—a special task with post-war youth. My very presence there would make me give lip-service to an institution I regard as moribund in its present form, committed to its present purposes. And yet I want to be near the young now; above all near to those who have been through the war. I *have* something to say to them: something born out of a parallel though different experience, which will awaken more than an echo in them; and yet no university or college I know would encourage me or even permit me to have this relationship except under terms that would stultify it. Meanwhile my position as a writer is no better. I can still have my books published; but the leading magazines of the country now promptly turn down my proferred articles, not because they are inadequate, but because they challenge, inevitably, the assumptions on which their whole busy fabric has been erected; and even when the contradiction is obscure, the editors have eyes acute enough to sense it. . . .   —Letter to Christiana Morgan. December 4, 1944

. . . One way or another, dear Christiana, our minds still keep moving along parallel paths. For a great part of these last six months I have been studying Hindu philosophy and theology, from Yoga to Buddhism, feeling that I needed some deeper subsoil to support my reading of the Bhagavad Gita, as a person who reads only the New Testament might want to find out what its foundations in the Old Testament were. I find myself deeply attached to the maturity of their philosophical insight, which has measureless depths, and which found a way of expressing different levels of reality—something we began to differentiate successfully only after the invention of the microscope and the discovery of electricity and the phases of energy.

So, too, I have great respect for their psychological discriminations: we have discovered very little this last century that they had not at least touched on, sometimes penetrated deeply into, a long time before. Even their religious consciousness has a breadth that ours has lacked. More than any other religious system, perhaps, Hinduism has been all things to all men; and the various revivals that took place in India during the last century and a half have come closer to effecting a bridge between the East and West than anything that we have done. Spiritually, a religious soul like Ramakrishna—do you know his curious biography?—has a degree of generosity [to other beliefs and practices] one doesn't find even in Saint Francis. Even so, I find him personally as remote, as unattractive, as Dostoevski's Father Zossima!

The Hindu texts I have explored I find very difficult; and the translations are more than usually unsatisfactory; it would take a lifetime's effort to overcome this handicap, and even a knowledge of Sanskrit plainly is not enough to do so, because the translations reveal a sad lack of agreement on the part of the best scholars. Take the three aspects of existence, 'rajas,' activity; 'tamas,' inertia; and 'sattva'—what? With the first two there is a certain agreement on what they mean. But the last seems untranslatable: some scholars call it 'brightness,' and some call it 'equilibrium' or 'harmony.' I suspect that the idea that comes closest is conveyed by the word 'illumination,' meaning both equilibrium and the inner mystic sense of revelation that accompanies it. But no translation that I have used suggests 'illumination' as a possibility.

But while I have the greatest respect for the general philosophical acumen of Hinduism, I am shocked by its Sacred Cows, not just the literal cows but their unexamined premises. The inviolability of the caste system; the doctrine of recurrent births, which even Buddha did not slough completely off. How is it that minds as good as this could not see that neither of these postulates is as self-evident as they take them to be? —Letter to Christiana Morgan. June 25, 1945

The question Mrs. Coomaraswamy raised about your carving is one that I first threshed out in relation to Blake's symbolism. Almost every Romantic artist raises the same question. Even the second part of Faust, that product of Goethe's maturity, still swarms with symbols that are far from being self-explanatory, though he has plucked some of them out of the mythologies of the ancient world. Why is so much of Blake unintelligible? Why do his more formal poems, the very ones in which one feels that his mature mind attempted to say most, actually convey so much less than he probably thought he had? The answer is that he was compelled to create a whole world by private fiat; and to understand these symbols one would have to be present at their genesis; for even a verbal explanation would not suffice to recreate the experience out of which they grew.

That was an unfortunate obstacle but an inevitable one: creation is such a difficult and precarious matter that the great ones always rely upon common myths and legends, as Sophocles or Dante or Shakespeare did, so that they can give their best energies, not to creating the symbols, but to what life is to make of them. What Mrs. Coomaraswamy forgets, what the traditionalists ignore, is that the old symbols no longer hold any *mana*. The Romantic artists tried to find, in their brief private experience, some equivalent for what a whole culture had once discovered and formed in the process of its long growth. Their failure was inevitable; but their attempt was imperative. They had something fresh to say, and for lack of a common medium, a well-worn vehicle of expression, they could not say it; or, if they said it to themselves, they did not convey it intelligibly to anyone else.

There may come a time, perhaps it is drawing near, when these private experiences will coalesce and create a common mythos. Until that moment comes, we must mark time. The first purpose of all art, I am sure, is to clarify something in oneself; and the only way to do this is to get it out of oneself. But the second purpose is to share it and test it with others; for this clarification is incomplete until others participate in it and thus assure one that the precious experience was not an hallucination or a form of self-indulgence. The artist today is fortunate, as the traditional artist was, when the audience is already half-way in on his secret; when he can devote himself to doing something with the symbol, exploring its further applications, not just inventing it or re-stating it. Lacking this, his works are tied to his own lifetime, almost to his own autobiography; and maybe without the biography they would not be self-sustaining . . .

As for the problem of symbolism in general, you have sought to convey, in the form of art, and even of decoration, that part of your experience which is unspeakable; yet the question remains whether visual art can, in our time, do what music and literature do, or indeed, whether they have ever sought to do this in the past. New words can be coined by a poet; new rhythms created; even a new language and a new myth, up to a point, can be communicated by him; but it is precisely at the point where Blake begins to *portray* his new Gods, and where his poems pass into the realm of the visual, that he begins to be obscure and darkly undecipherable.

I have a parallel problem to solve for myself, dear Christiana, when I work on my new book; for desperately though the world needs a common faith now, I do not see that faith arising out of a return to Christianity or Hinduism or any other single 'ism,' no matter how freely we may seek to re-interpret it. Faiths or myths cannot be created out of whole cloth by conscious willing; and without stepping forth as a Messiah—a role for which both inexperience and a sense of humor unfit me—I must somehow conjure up a rational alternative which will lie midway between the cracked bottles of past orthodoxies and the hot molten glass into which one blows only one's own breath. . . . —Letter to Christiana Morgan. July 13, 1945

GOING BACK TO COOMARASWAMY. I regard all attempts to prove the littleness, the transience, or the insignificance of life, in relation to Eternal and Infinite Being, to be false to the facts of human experience. Suicide, even in such a seemingly rational and 'spiritual' form is no answer to the problems of life, because our human problems are precisely those that spring from life's shortness, its pain, its accidental defacements and destructions, its lack of assured justice or rational purpose or creative fulfillment, its failure to coincide with whatever dim cosmic or universal processes may envelop it. To me, the classic religious answers, even the most philosophical, are just a little childish; and I shall not rest till I have found better ones. . . . —Letter to Christiana Morgan. October 20, 1947

11: Speculations and Discoveries

Though even as a young man I never had the temerity to call myself a philosopher, no small part of my thought might be placed under that classic Greek rubric. But since the term philosophy has now shrunk mainly to characterize only academic studies in Logic, Epistomology, and Semantics, pride rather than modesty impels me to describe myself as a Generalist, though even a century ago Philosopher would still have been acceptable. While my qualifications as a specialist are attested by medals and awards and professorial affiliations in half a dozen fields, my characteristic achievements have come through breaking down the formal barriers between academic compartments, and drawing freely on whatever sources of valid knowledge were needed to deepen understanding or unify theory, experience and practice. None of these principles would have disturbed Aristotle, who was as much at home in discussing the nature of tragedy as in collecting and observing biological specimens.

In gathering the notes and extracts for these pages, I have been as much concerned with their biographical as with their intellectual interest. The imperfect, embryonic form of an idea tells something that may be hidden at later stages, for at times the gestation period is extremely swift; and some of my most original intuitions arose in the very act of writing this or that book, though the seed—as I have taken care to demonstrate—may have been dropped half a century before.

187

TIME AND BEING. The belief in time and movement and change is a commonplace to the time-minded man: change is the one thing he thinks is unchangeable—so complete and overpowering is the convention. But the convenience of time-keeping is greatly over-rated; and the people who practice it so faithfully that they lose the capacity for appreciating the fixed and the static and the immediate spatially related experiences cut themselves off from a good part of reality. I can conceive of a civilization, not lower in the scale of culture than the present one, in which respect for the clock and the calendar would be far this side of complaisant idolatry. In such a society, it would be looked upon as a waste of effort to bring out newspapers and magazines on recurrent dates, whether there was anything important to put in them or not; and no one would trouble to read the latest novels, copy the latest styles, or dismiss from consideration inconvenient ideas because they happened to be 'out-of-date.' One has only to outline a time-less society to see what a fine and agreeable place it would be: one can pick out, in one's own circle of friends, a few wise, serenely disposed people who conduct their existence very much on these terms—and one knows it is neither a low ideal nor an impossible one. Thoreau escaped this convention of time; so did Blake; so in their way did Dostoevski and Tolstoi—and is this not perhaps why their writings and the characters they created all seem 'contemporary'? Do they not live within that perpetual present in which the arts from the paleolithic caves onward have their being? —The New Republic. March 7, 1928

THE WORLD AS A WORK OF ART. We know the world we live in only as the environment of life. That there is an external universe, independent of life and indifferent to it is an assumption of Newtonian physics which is of great practical convenience: but it is an inference, and not an immediate datum, since every such datum demands the existence of an observer; that is, life. The universe as we know it implies not merely the interlinkages of organic life and all the sustaining conditions in the physical world, such as those which Professor Lawrence Henderson brilliantly demonstrated in 'The Fitness of the Environment': it also implies the developments of human history and prehistory. Our thought itself, our concepts, our grammatic structure, are the products of the multitude of human beings that came before us; and the existence of human society is a much surer fact of experience than the existence of Betelgeuse, or, for that matter, the whole physical universe—all of which is derivative and inferential, since it rests on the existence of human instruments like language, mathematics, measurements.

Instead of beginning with a portentous sterile physical universe, and finally discovering man, with all his aims and values, as a pathetic, ludicrous by-product at the end of it, let us begin with the human personality itself. The abstraction of an 'independent world' from the ego itself is the result of a long difficult process which begins in the cradle; and while this abstraction is a genuine aid to growth, the present convention of regarding the human personality as merely an insignificant fragment of that world is quite as false as the infant's original hallucination of creating milk or warmth out of the void merely by crying for it. We find ourselves, at the very beginning of our adventure, in a state of complicated interdependences which unite us not merely economically and spiritually with other men and societies, but to remote parts of the world and to physical conditions which were established long before human forms appeared upon the earth. Value and significance are the specific marks of human society: hence our task is not merely that of maintaining or reproducing the species, but of enlarging the domain of value and significance. —The Saturday Review. May 10, 1930

THE SCIENCES AND PHILOSOPHY. During the nineteenth century a curious thing happened in the world of thought: philosophy abdicated. The dominant philosophers of the century, the Comtes, the Mills, the Spencers, took their cue from science, and avoided inquiries which were not directly comprehensible in terms of science. So far as their philosophies still have significance it is chiefly because they sought to formulate the rationale of the scientific method. For them science and truth were synonymous; and because philosophy was not science it ceased, according to the prevailing conception, to be truth.

During the last generation, a great change has taken place in the realm of ideas. Partly under the influence of profound scientific minds, like Clerk Maxwell, Mach, and Poincaré, the limitations of science itself have been more clearly understood; its laws are approximations, its categories are practical conveniences, rather than insights into the ultimate nature of things: and as it becomes more rigorous in method, it is forced to exclude the complex and the anomalous. In short, the scientific picture of the world is as selective as the artist's picture; and just as the painter has to ignore in his symbol the change of colors and the movements of his forms, to say nothing of matters like odor and heat, so the scientist is compelled for his purposes to limit experience to those aspects which may be independently observed, quantitatively handled and repeated by other competent observers. "Evidence which lies outside the method," as A. N. Whitehead points out, "simply does not count."

Instead of looking upon a rigorous scientific statement as an exhaustive account of a phenomenon, we have at last come to recognize the clipped and conventional quality of such reports. As a result of this perception philosophy, beginning particularly with Bergson and Croce, has recovered a little of its own self-respect: for its claim is to deal with the totality of human experience, including the limited part of it which comes under the province of science. This change has not merely taken place among the traditional philosophers: it has been abetted by a series of scientific thinkers, who have turned the guns of science upon their own citadel: Eddington in astro-physics, Lloyd Morgan in biology, J. S. Haldane in physiology, Whitehead in philosophy, have shown the crudeness and the metaphysical dogmatism of Cartesian or Newtonian science —which hitherto had been taken by the positivists as another name for exact truth. 'The Sciences and Philosophy' and 'The Function of Reason' are both pertinent examples of the way in which philosophy is reclaiming the place which science so confidently pre-empted on the basis of its many successful pragmatic applications. —The New Republic. May 7, 1930

The fact that two events are contemporary does not establish a connection between them or make them part of the same social milieu. Thus the mechanistic conception of the universe, with its dead, imageless, inorganic world, and Baroque painting, with its great images and its powerful sense of the organic, in line as well as in symbol, were both visible in the same century. They were the products of different components in the social heritage; one was rising and the other was falling. The effects of the mechanistic conception were not fully visible until the nineteenth century; but the existence of Baroque art is no disproof whatever of the anti-visual, anti-organic results of mechanistic abstractions. To interpret any given stretch of history as all of one piece seems to me basically false. Every period has its historic dominants, so to say, and its historic recessives, to say nothing of its still active survivals. That is why a static cross-section of society—such as is implied in contemporary views—is always historically inadequate, because in the nature of things it centers attention upon the dominants, neglects the unpredictable mutants, and like any cross-section halts, or rather ignores, the flow of time. —RN. 1934

Man comes into the world an unfinished animal. What he makes of himself, by means of his culture, is quite as important as his original endowment. Without the continued pressure of his culture, from the moment of his birth, even his purely biological functions would lapse: he would acquire neither the upright posture, nor the free hands, nor the gift of speech. Man's nature, in other words, is only partly given: the better part of it is what has been achieved by ritual, molded by habit, shaped by precept, stirred by love, projected by dream, consolidated by habit and further experience. To be true to his own nature man must depart from the limited repertory of Nature. That break is more significant than all the ties which link him with his animal past. —From The Masks of Man (discarded manuscript). March 21, 1954

I have no private utopia: if I had one, it would have to include the private utopias of many other men, and the realized ideals of many other societies; for life has still too many potentialities to be encompassed by the projects of a single generation, still less by the hopes and beliefs of a single thinker. Unlike utopian writers, I must find a place in any proposed scheme for challenge and opposition and conflict, even for evil and corruption, since they are visible in the natural history of all societies; and if I nonetheless emphasize the sanifying virtues and point to more transcendental goals, it is because the negative moments of life take care of themselves and need no encouragement. One does not have to plan chaos and dissolution, for this is what happens when the spirit ceases to be in command. My utopia is actual life, here or anywhere, pushed to the limits of its ideal possibilities within the existing culture. So to me the past is as much the source of creativity as the future: and the vivid interplay between all these aspects of existence, including many events that cannot be wholly formulated or grasped or directed constitutes for me a reality surpassing anything one can imagine or depict by the exercise of rational intelligence or untrammeled fantasy alone. —Preface (1962) to paperback edition of The Story of Utopias

You cannot attempt to show that words are unimportant without demonstrating how important they are: for to make this demonstration you need words: and no other signs, in music or painting or mathematics or bodily acts will exactly convey that meaning. —RN. April 1966

SUPPOSE WE WERE ALL EQUILATERAL TRIANGLES. Accepting our basic triangularity, we could not conceive of any change, except that of becoming more or less of a triangle. We might think of becoming a bigger triangle or a smaller one, turning from an isoceles triangle to a scalene triangle, almost to the point of being flattened out; but the one thing that would seem indisputable to us would be that we could not keep our precious triangularity if we tried to cut any other kind of figure. Yet that would be a delusion; and it would be the kind of delusion that is brought about by a failure to conceive the role of love.

Let us endow two right triangles, absolutely equal in every respect, with the power to fall in love: that is, to delight in the constant presence of the other, and spurred by the desire to meet and mingle on the closest possible terms. The nearest that a triangle could get to connubial bliss with another triangle would be if 'he' superimposed 'himself' upon it, and in order that our identical triangles should not merge their identity completely, we will suppose that the apex of one triangle in the ideal state of their union would intersect the base of the other. At that moment a being unknown in the world of triangles will come into existence: a star. A quite remarkable star, with six points, and with an internal figure in a central position, holding the parts together: a hexagon. What is more, at the tips we will find that this union has begotten six little triangles, just like their father and their mother, only smaller. Mark that the lines and angles of the original triangles remain unchanged: yet in the combination they show new properties, unknown in a purely triangular world. In this scenario none of these little triangles would have existed if the big triangles had not 'fallen in love' and sought to merge their identities.

This parable not merely sums up the nature of emergent change, using existing components to make a radically different pattern or 'Gestalt': it also demonstrates, by the simplest of abstractions, the unexpectedly creative interaction that takes place in loving association! That association had its beginning at the very moment when the sexual differentiation into male and female began in the plant world, and was carried to a climax in the ostentatious sexuality of the flowering plants, long before vertebrates emerged.   —RN. August 27, 1956

Hannah Arendt's conviction, similar to Vico's, that man can know only what he creates, should have a different conclusion than that which she comes to. On her reading the real world is closed to man: what he makes of it is nothing more than a fresh picture of himself, with his limitations. What she forgets is that man himself is not extraneous to the universe: he is part and parcel of it, and so the self he seems to project is in fact an integral part of what he investigates. Therefore man's picture of the world, instead of being conditioned by him, is the very world that he seeks. Through his own personal and communal activities the inner and outer become demonstrably one.   —RN. March 20, 1967

For a long time I have played with two ideas about the origin of human speech, both so speculative that they must be classed as imprudent fantasies. One is that there may have been a phase, before man was wholly in possession of the gift of tongues, when he might have been afraid of losing this precious power. Primitive hominoids might have experienced anxiety over the possibility of dropping back into man's old inarticulate animal self. Hence the safeguarding of language may have begun even earlier—and have been more important—than the safeguarding of fire, and this might account for the persistence of the intricate formalisms of grammar among the so-called primitives. Slipshod speech and bold neologisms perhaps came only with security.

Against this hypothesis one must remember the ease with which early man, like the cave-bear worshippers, to say nothing of later primitives, identified himself with animals—as in many later forms of totemism, too. So if there was an anxiety over the possible loss of speech, it must have occurred at an extremely early moment, before man was yet quite sure of his new human self. *But, not strangely, this anxiety recurs with loss of names and words in old age.*

The other fantasy is concerned with the early appearance of cultures, Aurignacian and Magdalenian, where there seems a differentiation between a higher class of specialized magic workers, performers of sacred rites, and an underlayer of common men who benefit by their powers but do not share them. The great caves where paleolithic painting flourished were certainly not meant for mass assemblies: they were difficult to reach, tortuous, hidden, secret, in every sense 'sacred.' To crawl into the final sanctuary was in itself an ordeal, open probably only to the initiate or those about to be initiated. And this leads me to ask: Was the unique gift of collective symbol-making—with its signs, words, pictures, and ultimately mathematic notations and graphs—at first a restricted occupation? Did those superior minds which first discovered the use of abstractions, keep their knowledge to themselves, as being a supreme key to special powers that other men did not possess? Was this the reason for their studious maintenance of secrecy? Did they paint the likenesses of animals so as to get 'control' over them, or guard their ability to deal in language with events remote from the here-and-now world? Did the distinction between upper class and lower class speech, still present thousands of years later in many cultures, begin with a differentiation of symbolic thinking, exploring the inner life, from pragmatic utilitarian thinking, capable of dealing only with visible objects or events?

If so, this advantage through the mastery of symbolic abstraction would explain better than anything else the power that the Dominant Minority—at first kings and priests—has always exercised as a class not only on the basis of superior weapons but even more of superior knowledge—once largely fanciful and magical, now mathematical and rigorously scientific. The language of magic is always a secret language: so different from ordinary language that, as Malinowski complained, it cannot be translated. On this frail hypothesis many tempting further speculations open up: even the fact that in our own day, the acknowledged undermining of the Authority of the Roman Catholic hierarchy can be associated with the abandonment of Latin, their secret language, for the vernacular. With this their whole institutional apparatus now begins to fall apart.   —Letter to Erich Fromm. November 8, 1970

. . . I haven't been in touch with Alexander Marshak recently; but the point you bring up about the paucity of archaeological evidence and the difficulty of spotting it, even with a microscope, is a challenging one. What quiets my own doubts about one of his main discoveries, the paleolithic moon calendars, is that we are perhaps reading back into Paleolithic culture the physiological handicaps of present day society. For our eyesight has perhaps been seriously weakened by—among other things—the invention and constant use of eyeglasses, which are now increasingly needed even by young children. When in Italy, however, I noticed that some Italians could easily read print without glasses in a relatively dark room: this suggested how the old Roman bureaucracy could work in buildings without glass windows or full outside lighting, to say nothing of adequate artificial lighting. (And how much truer would all this be in the deep paleolithic caves lighted only by crude oil lamps.) Then, too, one of my German friends observed in Palestine that an Arab sheik could detect a horseman on the horizon minutes before he became visible to a European.

Conceivably, Aurignacian man could have made and seen scratches, using only his bare eyes, which we can see accurately only through a microscope. As for early man's not being interested in Astronomy, what is the Venus of Laussel doing with a crescent moon? For that matter, many animals, dogs and elephants, for instance, are conscious of the changes in the moon; and it may be that a preoccupation with the planets was one of the indications of Homo sapiens' increasing responsiveness to his whole environment, including woman's lunar periodicity in menstruation and pregnancy. Perhaps only superior minds concerned themselves with the position and movements of remote planets and stars; and that interest may have furthered their facility in making abstract notations about all repetitive and observable phenomena. Was this perhaps the cosmic source of their 'secret knowledge,' which gave a priestly minority in earlier cultures their special authority as representatives of the Gods?

If the powerful organic images of bison and deer were, as Leroi-Gourhan suggests, integral expressions of a primordial sex-motivated religion, what shall we say of the mysterious geometry manifested in abstract lines, 'graphs,' 'plans,' macaroni swirls? Were they not meant to convey information? Is this possibly not the earliest expression of quantitative scientific thinking, based upon measurable and repeatable phenomena in space and time? More important, perhaps, than Marshak's singular discoveries is the fact that, without purposely working toward this end, he has shown that the emergence of Homo sapiens was marked by the simultaneous appearance—and complementary interplay—of religion and science. That early union magnified and re-enforced the creative potentials of the awakening human mind. —Begun in a letter to Avigail Scheffer in Tel-Aviv. February 9, 1976

"Everything changes," our contemporaries say, "so we must not resist this process." But in this very proposition an absurd assumption lies concealed: namely, the belief that the system we have created, which makes change obligatory and inevitable, will not change! The postulate nullifies the conclusion. If this is true, then the system must obey its own laws, and there is nothing to prevent it from changing by resisting change— slowing down or even, on occasion, coming to a halt. —RN. March 12, 1965

MAN'S SELF-TRANSFORMATION. Sometime during the last million years— perhaps even far longer ago—a creature that was no longer an ape became identifiable as a new species, 'manlike' as we see him dimly from this distance, via a few bones and stones, but very far from being man. This creature became 'man' at a later but unidentifiable 'moment' when he became conscious of his animal state and took pains to alter it, to emerge from it, or at least to overlay it and remodel it. Was this event as mythical as the Fall in the Garden of Eden? Not quite. Man's earliest efforts at transformation left an unmistakable physiological imprint: for he acquired a face, mobile and expressive: a face capable of registering not merely changes denoting hostility or fear—like the bristling of hair, the retraction of lips, the erection of ears—but joy and love, friendliness and delight, in which the muscles around the eyes and mouth became capable of translating the inner message. Smiles and laughter, tenderness and tears, are the identifying marks of this new creature's social qualities: his gamut of visible emotions goes far beyond that of any other animal. Even before he had created transmissible signs or symbols the achievement of a truly human face, mobile, expressive, responsive, marks the replacement of the animal mask. The baby's first smile is a milestone on the road to becoming human.

But the second step, if equally remote and undateable, lay in the opposite direction: man sought an even more unmistakable way of renouncing his ancestral animal self; and his earliest success here came by way of cosmetic and costume, perhaps the oldest of all the arts, and the only one besides language practiced by both the most primitive and the most civilized peoples. The first creature who daubed his face with clay had found a quick way of changing his outward personality and establishing a new identity: he was no longer merely different from other animals, but different from other human beings whose tribe did not use this mark—who perhaps used the juices of plants to create another kind of mask. The changing of the color of the skin, the re-shaping of the skull or the nose or the lips or the ears, the scarification of the flesh—what are all these primitive practices but attempts by means of the mask to assume a new character, to make visible the inner changes that have created a special human identity? Body decoration, the arts of cosmetics and costume, are the oldest surviving forms of symbolic art, older possibly even than speech. When man appears on the stage of history, he is already an actor, a master of make-believe; one can even identify him by his make-up, before he refashions the natural scene or utters an intelligible word. This was not a passing phase of human development. Today statistics tell us that we Americans spend more on cosmetics than on public education. —From The Masks of Man (discarded manuscript). 1954

SUBJECTIVITY IN HISTORY. The notion that nothing in the past is worth paying attention to unless it has been inscribed on a stone, or recorded in a book, a photograph, a film, and assembled from a score of independent sources by a computer is one of the most dubious metaphysical assumptions of contemporary culture. Even in viewing the physical world with the most scrupulous efforts at accuracy in presentation and interpretation, we find that some of the most significant phenomena escape direct observation, or are lost in the welter of unrecorded experience. How much eludes the most scrupulous research! Yet we now have scientific evidence of the critical importance of trace elements, existing in infinitesimal quantities, in the adequate nourishment of the body. And though the chemical analysis of sea water is seemingly complete, fish kept in tanks of artificially imitated sea water will die.

In a similar way, our understanding of human history must remain deficient unless it treats individual experiences, chance encounters, singular events, as potentially no less needful for a competent and realistic appraisal of the human situation as the most voluminous collection of verified reports and documents. What historians still dare to call 'objective' history, what scientists call 'objective' science, is in the nature of things highly selective, however accidental or unintentional its shortcomings. What is open to record is inevitably a minute sampling, often a random sampling, of the dense, unrecorded and incalculable day-to-day actuality. To admit this buried subjective underlayer is the first step toward achieving objectivity. —From an unpublished lecture at McGill University, October 1974

THE MONASTERY AND THE CLOCK. Where did the machine first take form in modern civilization? There was plainly more than one point of origin. Our mechanical civilization represents the convergence of numerous habits, ideas, and modes of living, as well as technical instruments; and some of these were, in the beginning, directly opposed to the civilization they helped to create. But the first manifestation of the new order took place in the general picture of the world. During the first seven centuries of mechanization the categories of time and space underwent an extraordinary change, and no aspect of life was left untouched by this transformation. The application of quantitative methods of thought to the study of nature had its first manifestation in the regular measurement of time; and the new mechanical conception of time arose in part out of the routine of the monastery. Alfred Whitehead has emphasized the importance of the scholastic belief in a universe ordered by God as one of the foundations of modern physics: but behind that belief was the presence of order in the institutions of the Church itself.

The technics of the ancient world were still carried on from Constantinople and Baghdad to Sicily and Cordova: hence the early lead taken by Salerno in the scientific and medical advances of the Middle Age. It was, however, in the monasteries of the West that the desire for order and power, other than that expressed in the military domination of weaker men, first manifested itself after the long uncertainty and bloody confusion that attended the breakdown of the Roman Empire. Within the walls of the monastery was sanctuary: under the rule of the order surprise and doubt and caprice and irregularity were put at bay. Opposed to the erratic fluctuations and pulsations of the worldly life was the iron discipline of the rule. Benedict added a seventh period to the devotions of the day, and in the seventh century, by a bull of Pope Sabinianus, it was decreed that the bells of the monastery be rung seven times in the twenty-four hours. These punctuation marks in the day were known as

197

the canonical hours, and some means of keeping count of them and ensuring their regular repetition became necessary.

According to a now discredited legend, the first modern mechanical clock, worked by falling weights, was invented by the monk named Gerbert who afterwards became Pope Sylvester II near the close of the tenth century. This clock was probably only a water clock, one of those bequests of the ancient world either left over directly from the days of the Romans, like the water-wheel itself, or coming back again into the West through the Arabs. But the legend, as so often happens, is accurate in its implications if not in its facts. The monastery was the seat of a regular life, and an instrument for striking the hours at intervals or for reminding the bell-ringer that it was time to strike the bells, was an almost inevitable product of this life. If the mechanical clock did not appear until the cities of the thirteenth century demanded an orderly routine, the habit of order itself and the earnest regulation of time-sequences had become almost second nature in the monastery. Coulton agrees with Sombart in looking upon the Benedictines, the great working order, as perhaps the original founders of modern capitalism: their rule certainly took the curse off work and their vigorous engineering enterprises may even have robbed warfare of some of its glamor. So one is not straining the facts when one suggests that the monasteries—at one time there were 40,000 under the Benedictine rule—helped to give human enterprise the regular collective beat and rhythm of the machine; for the clock is not merely a means of keeping track of the hours, but of synchronizing the actions of men.

The clock, not the steam engine, is the key machine of the modern industrial and scientific age. For every phase of its development the clock is both the outstanding fact and the typical symbol of the machine: even today no other machine is so ubiquitous. Here, at the very beginning of modern technics, appeared prophetically the accurate automatic machine which, only after centuries of further effort, was also to prove the final consummation of this technics in every department of industrial activity. There had been power machines, such as the water-mill, before the clock; and there had also been various kinds of automata, to awaken the wonder of the populace in the temple, or to please the idle fancy of some Moslem caliph: machines one finds illustrated in Hero of Alexandria and Al-Jazari. But here was a new kind of power machine, in which the source of power and the transmission were of such a nature as to ensure the even flow of energy throughout the works and to make possible regular production and a standardized product. In its relationship to determinable quantities of energy, to standardization, to automatic action, and finally to its own special product, accurate timing, the clock has been the foremost machine in modern technics: and at each period it has remained in the lead: it marks a perfection toward which other machines aspire. Space, time, and motion, the ultimate categories of physics, were imprinted on the very face of the clock. Even 'miniaturization,' one of our most stunning technical triumphs today, was first achieved in the sixteenth century by reducing to the dimensions of a pocket watch the time-keeping function of huge cathedral clocks.

The gain in mechanical efficiency through co-ordination and through the closer articulation of the day's events cannot be overestimated: while this increase cannot be measured in mere horsepower, one has only to imagine its absence today to foresee the speedy disruption and eventual collapse of our entire society. The modern industrial régime could do without coal and iron and electricity easier than it could do without the clock.   —From 'Technics and Civilization.' 1934

Parasitism's Promises and Threats

Under the economy of abundance, even on the limited scale so far established in the United States, the huge bribe held out—of security, leisure, affluence—unfortunately also carries with it an equally huge penalty: the prospect of universal parasitism. Earlier cultures have had skirmishes with this enemy: Odysseus' scouts among the Lotus Eaters were so beguiled by their honeyed fare and dreamy ease that they had to be rescued by force. More than one emperor or despot discovered that permissiveness in the form of sensual inducements and enticements might be even more effective than coercion in securing compliance. Once established, the parasite identifies himself with his host and seeks to further the host's prosperity. Since parasitism has been widely observed in the animal kingdom, we have sufficient data to make a shrewd guess as to its ultimate human consequences.

Now megatechnics offers, in return for its unquestioning acceptance, the gift of an effortless life: a plethora of prefabricated goods, achieved with a minimum of physical activity, without painful conflicts or harsh sacrifices: life on the installment plan, as it were, yet with an unlimited credit card, and with the final reckoning—existential nausea and despair —readable only in the fine print. If the favored human specimen is ready to give up a free-moving, self-reliant, autonomous existence, he may, by being permanently attached to his predatory host, receive many of the goods he was once forced to exert himself to secure, along with a large

199

bonus of dazzling superfluities, to be consumed without selection or restriction—but of course under the iron dictatorship of fashion.

The final consequences of such submission might well be what Roderick Seidenberg in 'Posthistoric Man' anticipated: a falling back into a primordial state of unconsciousness, forfeiting even the limited awareness other animals must retain in order to survive. With the aid of hallucinatory drugs, this state might even be described by the official manipulators and conditioners as an "expansion of consciousness"—or some equivalent tranquillizing phrase that would be provided by public relations experts.

If proof were needed of the real nature of electronic control, no less a promulger of the system than McLuhan has supplied it. "Electromagnetic technology," he observes in 'Understanding Media,' *requires utter human docility* [italics mine] and quiescence of meditation such as befits an organism that now wears its brain outside its skull and its nerves outside its hide. Man must serve his electric technology with the same servo-mechanistic fidelity with which he served his coracle, his canoe, his typography, and all other extensions of his physical organs." To make his point McLuhan is driven brazenly to deny the original office of tools and utensils as direct servants of human purpose. By the same kind of slippery falsification McLuhan would reinstate the totalitarian compulsions of the Pyramid Age as a desirable feature of today's electronic complex.

The 'Big Bribe' turns out to be little better than the kidnapper's candy. Such a parasitic existence as megatechnics offers would in effect be a return to the womb: now a collective womb. Fortunately, the mammalian embryo is the only parasite that has proved capable of overcoming this condition once it has been established: the baby's birth cry triumphantly announces his escape. But note: once a human being has left the womb, the conditions that were there propitious to his growth become impediments. No mode of arresting development could be so effective as the effortless instant satisfaction of every need, every desire, every random impulse, by means of mechanical, electronic, or chemical equipment. All through the organic world development depends upon effort, interest, active participation: not least upon stimulating resistances, conflicts, inhibitions, and delays. Even among rats, courtship precedes copulation. Under this same meretricious canon of easy immediate success solitary masturbation has lately been suggested as superior to sexual intercourse and hetero-sexual love-making.

On this matter Patrick Geddes made some biological observations as early as 1885 that are still pertinent. In his 'Analysis of the Principles of Economics' he noted that the "conditions of degeneration in the

200

organic world are approximately known. These conditions are often of two distinct kinds, deprivation of food, light, etc. so leading to imperfect nutrition and enervation; the other, a life of repose, with abundant supply of food and decreased exposure to the dangers of the environment. It is noteworthy that while the former only depresses, or at most extinguishes the specific type, the latter, through the disuse of the nervous and other structures, etc. which such simplification of life involves, brings about that far more insidious and thorough degeneration seen in the life history of myriads of parasites."

The personality changes that will result—in many areas they are already visible—from an attempt to produce an existence that calls for as little thought and exertion and personal interest as possible, have still to be measured and appraised: yet the extremes to which this movement tends are now obvious: infantilism or senility. At some ideal future point the traits of infantilism will dissolve into those of senility without leaving a gap to be filled with anything that can properly be called a mature, self-directed, self-fulfilling life.   —From 'The Pentagon of Power.' 1970

CREATIVITY OF PLAY.   Play itself, though a trait man shares with diverse other species, often in courtship rituals as in the humming-bird's aerial dance, had a liberating effect upon every part of technological development, dynamic and static. Play, far more than necessity was the original mother of invention, and the first organizer of systematic communally shared work. The classic book on this subject, 'Work and Rhythm,' was written by the economic historian, Karl Buecher and published in 1896. It went through many German editions without being translated into English or altering the still common conception of all physical labor as a primal curse. But as I pointed out in 'Technics and Civilization' (1934) the radical importance of play—if only as a source of original technological ideas—is demonstrated by the fact that some of our most significant modern inventions, the telephone, the helicopter, the gyroscope, the motion picture, first appeared as children's toys; and that the earliest example of an automated factory was an Alexandrian toy working-model exhibited in a temple! Professor Cyril Smith, originally a metallurgist, has brilliantly carried this demonstration further; for he has shown that the earliest use of metals was *ornamental*: not only gold beads but iron beads were used in Egypt before iron was beaten into swords and plowshares. Hundreds of thousands of years earlier, a fragment of galena, a crystalline form of lead, was transported from a distance to the caves of Choukoutien in China: the esthetic fascination of these shiny cubic crystals preceded the first utilitarian exploitation of metals.

Man's release from the seasonal restrictions of animal mating, and his playful embroidery of human sexual activity, turned rutting into prolonged love play and promoted his facility in the rhythmic arts of singing and dancing and music-making, as Maurice Bowra demonstrated. But the full significance of man's emotional development in enlarging his total capacities for technological creativity, is still unacceptable to the more devout adherents of the Power Complex. Thus, the title of J. Huizinga's path-breaking book 'Play as the Basis of Human Culture,' was rendered by his shocked translator as 'A Study of the Play Element in Human Culture'—that century-old commonplace! The fact is that man's gift in creating images and symbols and patterns of movement and sound long preceded his ability to put these inventions of the mind to practical constructive uses. So the magnificent early Cave paintings antedated by thousands of years any comparable monumental buildings fit to house such high works of art. In short, expression precedes construction, even as the unfertilized flower appears before the seed. —RN. 1970

. . . Let me get back to what you say, dear Carlludwig, toward the end of your letter, about your sense of Humanity as the primary entity, and of the human scale as something to be transcended, since man has within himself a higher potential. This finds an answering chord in the work of Teilhard de Chardin, where in fact the Whole seems at the end to supersede the parts and to have no use for individuality or personality, still less any concern for their fulfillment, except as instruments of a higher ultimate unity. I wouldn't suppose that you would go as far as Teilhard in this respect. But even on your own terms may I not, as an outsider, refer to the wisdom of your Catholic Church on this very matter, though that wisdom has ironically been one of the prompters of scepticism, secularism, and protestantism! I refer to the way in which the concept of Divine Transcendence, through the Holy Trinity, has been mediated in the actual practice and ritual of the Church, by providing for a closer daily intercourse between earth and heaven, more intimate and affectionate, more akin to the pattern of the family and of the family's daily needs. Witness the intercession of the saints, as a means of approaching, in more visible and available form the sense of the Eternal which Christianity meaningfully introduced into human life. With the eye of the mind, the eternal becomes visible, as the city becomes visible when one rises in a plane high enough in the sky: and so, for me, each part of the city should convey, by symbol and allusion, sometimes by some institutional form or architectural expression, a sense of the whole (including humanity), just as the meanest parish church conveys the meaning of the mass and rep-

202

resents the more visible splendor of a great cathedral. But the lack of the human scale in the immediate environment presents difficulties even for those who know and feel that this is not the ultimate scale; that beyond this lies the monumental scale, appropriate to collective powers and communal rites; and beyond that still another scale, the divine, which cannot be clothed in visible form or represented by any tangible object, not even by the sun or the starry universe. Does this seem a far-fetched parallel? I would hardly dare to use it even in conversation, dear Carlludwig, with anyone but you! —Letter to Carlludwig Franck. October 14, 1962

. . . It is this easy familiarity with the science of your time, dear Carlludwig, that makes your critical examination of the current assumptions and dogmas with regard to the role of mind and purpose in evolution so effective—and so original. By accepting the postulates and methods of 'objective' science, you have been able to demonstrate in the scientist's own terms that he has been reluctant to recognize how far they stop short of coping with reality. In every chapter in which I have sufficient background to be able to follow your reasoning I find myself in substantial agreement, despite some slight differences in our vocabulary. And how effective you are in charging the scientist with anthropomorphic thinking, because he can think of 'purpose' only as some end consciously willed and carried out by man.

Even without your genius for abstract thought I discovered for myself that 'natural selection' was a fraud as a causative agent, since it did not account for the direction, the inner congruence, and the ultimate usefulness of the traits that are selected. George Wald, an excellent biologist with a mind unusually open to the data of religion, has thought to simplify the role of Evolution through Natural Selection by saying that it was a Book that was strictly edited but not composed by an Author. As if any such book ever existed or could exist! You and I both think that there is something in the organism, and for that matter in the composition of the original elements, that indicates an original set towards organization and what, at a much later stage, corresponds in some degree to human purpose.

My most fundamental difference with you comes, as you would suppose, in the ultimate religious chapters; for on your interpretation, God is present at every stage of cosmic and human evolution, so that no part of it can be considered as outside his scheme, from beginning to end; whereas for me, though a divine impetus may be there at the beginning, it gains force, coherence and sureness of direction only in the course of time, and yet, for the same reason, not merely remains incomplete, but may be subject to tragic setbacks. This, for me, is excellent justification for including the Devil and both the many negative and positive workings of chance in a graph of organic development! On this interpretation, the potentialities of biological and cultural evolution include predictable discoveries, happy surprises, and disastrous failures. Unless the apparent sequences of organic evolution, reaching on to man, are to be discarded for lack of solid evidence, what are we to make of all those experiments in the creation of species that turned out to be of no consequence—like, say, the whole race of insensitive giant dinosaurs with their minimal nervous system? Blind chance and blind purpose are both at work, overlaying 'God's purpose'! —Letter to Carlludwig Franck. Christmas Day, 1974

ORGANIC CREATIVITY. Recall Loren Eiseley's beautiful chapter in 'The Immense Journey,' about that turning point in organic development when the Age of Reptiles gave way to the Age of Mammals, those warm-blooded beasts that suckled their young. Eiseley pointed out that the Age of Mammals was accompanied by an explosion of flowers; and that the reproductive system of the angiosperms was responsible, not merely for covering the whole earth with a green carpet composed of many different species of grass—over four thousand—but for intensifying vital activity of every kind, since the nectars and perfumes and seeds and fruits and the succulent leaves dilate the senses, exhilarate the mind, and immensely increase the total food supply. Not merely was this explosion of flowers a cunning device of reproduction, but the flowers themselves assumed a variety of forms and colors that in most cases cannot possibly be accounted for as having survival value in the 'struggle for existence.' It may add to the attraction of a lily's sexuality to have all of its sexual organs displayed amid teasingly open petals; but the huge success of so many compositae, with their insignificant florets, shows that biological prosperity might have been purchased without any such floral richness and inventiveness.

Efflorescence is an example of nature's untrammeled creativity and the fact that the floral beauty we enjoy was not made for us and cannot be explained or justified on purely physical grounds is precisely what makes this explosion so wonderful—and so typical of all life processes. Biological creativity exists for its own sake: if survival were all that mattered, life might have remained in the primal ooze, or crept no further upward than the lichens. The capacity for self-transformation has not yet been expressed in any currently accepted biological doctrine, nor yet is it explained by the chemical instrumentality of DNA. But long before man himself became conscious of beauty, beauty existed in the endlessly varied forms and colors of the flowering plants. The selection and encouragement of these plants, quite apart from their possible utilitarian value for food, medicine, or clothing, was what gave man his first real glimpse, perhaps, of Paradise—for Paradise is only the original Persian name for a walled garden. The capacity for exuberant expression symbolized by efflorescence—this is the primal gift of life; and to consciously maintain it and guard it and expand it is one of the ultimate reasons for human existence. There are no mechanical or electronic substitutes for this kind of creativity. "There is no wealth but life." —Concluding address. Rockefeller University Symposium: Challenge for Survival. 1968

The Goods of Life

Most ethical and religious philosophies have sought to isolate and standardize the goods of life, and to make one or another set of purposes supreme and universal. They have looked upon pleasure or social efficiency or duty, upon imperturbability or rationality or self-annihilation as the chief crown of a disciplined and cultivated spirit. This effort to whittle down valuable conduct to a single set of consistent principles and ideal ends does not do justice to the nature of life, with its paradoxes, its complicated processes, its internal conflicts, its sometimes unresolvable dilemmas.

In order to reduce life to a single clear intellectually consistent pattern, a system tends to neglect the varied factors that belong to life by reason of its complex organic needs and its ever-developing purposes. Each historic ethical system, indeed, whether rational or utilitarian or transcendental, blandly overlooks the vital contradictions that are covered by rival systems: and in practice each will accuse the other of inconsistency precisely at those imperative moments when common sense happily intervenes to save the system from defeat. This accounts for a general failure in every rigorously formulated philosophic system to meet all of life's diverse occasions and demands. Hedonism is of no use in a shipwreck. There is a time to laugh and a time to weep, as The Preacher reminds us; but the pessimists forget the first clause and the optimists the second.

The fallacy of ideological systematizing is a very general one; and we can follow its ethical consequences best, perhaps, in education. Let us take an historic case, none the worse for being real: the childhood of Mary Everest, that extraordinary woman who eventually became the wife and helpmate of the great logician, George Boole. Mary's father was the devoted disciple of Hahnemann, the philosopher of homeopathic medicine; and he applied Hahnemann's principles, not merely to illness but to the whole regimen of life. Following strictly the master's belief in cold baths and long walks before breakfast, the system-bound father practiced upon his children a form of daily torture that drove Mary Everest into a state of blank unfeelingness and irresponsiveness. She hated every item in the strict routine; and her whole affectional and sentimental life as a young girl, in relation to her parents, was warped by it. The resentment she felt against this inflexibility and this arbitrary disregard of natural disposition is indeed still evident in the account she wrote at the end of a long life.

Believing blindly in the system, Mary Everest's father never observed what was happening to his beloved children in actual life: for the sake of carrying through the doctrine, he blindly disregarded the testimony of life and took no note of scores of indications in his children's conduct and health that should have warned him that he was working ruin. Every intellectually awakened parent who applied one or another of the rival systems in psychology and education that became fashionable during the last thirty years can testify out of his own experience, if he reflects upon it—or at least his children could testify—to the fallacy of over-simplification that is involved in the very conception and application of a system. Life cannot be reduced to a system: the best wisdom, when so reduced to a single set of insistent notes, becomes a cacophony: indeed, the more stubbornly one adheres to the abstract instructions of a system, the more violence one may do to life.

Actual historic institutions, fortunately, have been modified by anomalies, discrepancies, contradictions, compromises: the older they are, the richer this organic compost. All these varied nutrients that remain in the social soil are viewed with high scorn by the believer in systems: like the advocates of old-fashioned chemical fertilizers, he has no notion that what makes the soil usable and nourishing is precisely the organic debris that remains. In most historic institutions, it is their weakness that is their saving strength. Czarism, for example, as practiced in Russia during the nineteenth century, was a hideous form of government: tyrannical, capricious, inwardly solidified, severely repressive of anything but its own orthodoxy. But, as Alexander Herzen showed in his Memoirs, the system was made less intolerable by two things that had no lawful or logical part in it: bribery and corruption on one hand, which made it possible to get around regulations and to soften punishments: and skepticism from within, on the other, which made many of its officers incapable of carrying out with conviction and therefore with rigor the tasks imposed. In contrast, one may note in passing, the relative 'purity' of the present Soviet Russian regime serves to buttress its inhumanity toward those who would challenge any aspect of communist absolutism.

Thus a certain susceptibility to laxity, corruption, disorder, is the main thing that enables a system to escape self-asphyxiation: for a system is in effect an attempt to make men breathe carbon dioxide or oxygen alone, without the other components of air, with effects that are either temporarily exhilarating or soporific, but in the end must be lethal; since though each of these gases is necessary for life, the air that keeps men alive is a mixture of various gases in due proportion. So it is not the purity of the orthodox Christian doctrine that has kept the Eastern and Western Churches alive and enabled them to flourish even in a scientific age, but just the opposite: the non-systematic elements, seeping in from other cultures and from contradictory experiences of life: covert heresies that have given the Christian creed a vital buoyancy that seemingly tighter bodies of doctrine, like those of the Manicheans, have lacked.

Since the seventeenth century we have been living in an age of system-makers, system-appliers and what is even worse, system worshippers. The world has been divided first of all into two general parties, the conservatives and the radicals, or as Comte called them, the party of order and the party of progress—as if both order and change, stability and variation, continuity and novelty, were not equally fundamental attributes of life. People sought, conscientiously, to make their lives conform to a system: a set of limited, partial, exclusive principles. They sought to live by the romantic system or the utilitarian system, to be wholly idealist or wholly practical. If they were rigorously capitalist, in America, they glibly forgot that the free public education they supported was in fact a communist institution; or if they believed in communism, like the founders of the Oneida Community, they stubbornly but vainly sought to apply their communism to marital sexual relations as well as industry.

In short, the system-mongers sought to align a whole community according to some limiting principle, and to organize its entire life in conformity to the system, as if such wholesale limitations could do justice to the condition of man. Actually, by the middle of the nineteenth century, it had become plain that the most self-confident of the systems, capitalism, which had originally come in as a healthy challenge to static privilege and feudal lethargy, would, if unmodified by other vital social con-

207

siderations, strangle life: maiming the young and innocent who toiled fourteen hours a day in the new factories, and starving adults wholesale, in obedience to the blind law of market competition, working in a manic-depressive business cycle. As a pure system, capitalism was humanly intolerable. What has happily saved it from violent overthrow has been the partial absorption of the heresies of socialism—public enterprises and social security—which have given it some measure of balance and stability.

In short, to take a single guiding idea, like individualism or collectivism, stoicism or hedonism, aristocracy or democracy, communism or anarchism, existentialism or nihilism, and attempt to follow this thread through all of life's occasions, is to miss the significance of the thread itself, whose function is to add to the complexity and interest of life's total pattern. Today the fallacy of 'either-or' dogs us everywhere: whereas it is in the nature of life to embrace and surmount its contradictions, not by shearing them away, but by weaving them into a more inclusive unity. No organism, no society, no personality, can be reduced to a system or be effectually governed by a system. Inner direction or outer direction, detachment or conformity, should never become so exclusive that in practice they make a shift from one to the other impossible.

This skepticism of isolated systems is basic to my thinking; but it has another name: the affirmation of organic life. If no single principle will produce a harmonious and well-balanced existence, for either the person or the community, then harmony and balance perhaps demand a degree of inclusiveness and completeness sufficient to nourish every kind of nature, to create the fullest variety in unity, to do justice to every occasion. That harmony must include and resolve discords: it must have a place for heresy as well as conformity: for rebellion as well as placid adjustment—and vice-versa. And that balance must maintain itself against sudden thrusts and impulsions: like the living organism, our philosophy must have reserves of ideas and energies at its command, capable of being swiftly mobilized, wherever needed to maintain a dynamic equilibrium.   —From 'The Conduct of Life.' 1951

THE OPENING FUTURE. When we turn from the past to the future, we pass from memory and reflection to present observation and current practice and thence to anticipation and prediction. As usually conceived, this is a movement from the known to the unknown, from the probable to the possible, from the domain of necessity to the open realm of choice. But in fact these aspects of time and experience cannot be so neatly separated.

Some part of the past is always becoming present in the future; and some part of the future is already present in the past. Instead of thinking of these three segments of time in serial order, we would do well to take the view of a mathematician like A. N. Whitehead and narrow the time band to a tenth of a second before and the tenth of a second after any present event. When one does this, one understands that the past, the present, and the future are in that living moment almost one. Insofar as our minds become capable of drawing these three aspects together in consciousness over a wider span of time, we become capable of dealing with time in a more organic fashion, doing justice not merely to the succession of events but to their virtual coexistence in the mind through anticipation and memory.

Now part of the future we face has already been determined, and we have no control over it. To begin at the physical level, we are limited by the forces of inertia; at the biological level, by the facts of organic inheritance. At the social level we must reckon with institutional persistences which, if not so ingrained as biological structures, cannot be suddenly altered; even at the highest level of the human personality, memory and habit tend to keep our actions in a groove. We do well to reckon with these constant factors and their sluggish ways: if they fetter our creativity, they also tend to limit the possibility of disruption and chaos. For good or bad, a part of our future is given; and, like a Christmas gift, we must accept it gracefully, before we try to exchange it for something that fits us better.

We might, for example, in view of the special role that sexuality and love were to play in man's life, have wished that nature—sometime about the point when the structure of the frog was under consideration—had put the reproductive organs and the organs of excretion in different parts of the body. But we cannot hope that this fatal topographical mistake will be corrected. We have many similar commitments that carry over from the past. Some of us now wish, it seems, to feed the growing population of the earth with a synthetic concentrate; but if they succeed with the concentrate—I for one do not wish them well!—they will still have to furnish people with some bulk-producing jelly, as we do a sick person who has been on a liquid diet, in order to keep their bowels functioning; and they may even find it necessary, despite man's inordinate adaptability, to create some illusion of gustatory pleasure, lest the appetite for life itself should wane.

In calling attention to these constants, I am trying to emphasize what the French philosopher Raymond Ruyer, in his book 'Neo-finalisme,' characterizes as the fibrous structure of history. Just because of the nature of time, memory, and inheritance, we cannot make sensible plans for the future without doing justice to the threads and fibers that run through every past stage of man's development and will run through the future as well. In dealing with man's history, it is convenient to cut it off into stages and periods; so we speak as though the Stone Age were represented in our society only by museum showcases of axes and arrowheads. But the fact is that about two-thirds of the planet's population are still living under conditions that approximate those of a Neolithic village, certainly far closer than they touch those of a twentieth-century metropolis. And when the other day some of our colleagues said, almost a little contemptuously, "Don't let us go back to paleolithic society," I was tempted to ask them how far they thought they could express that idea without using one of the tools of paleolithic society, namely, language.

To sum up this point: the future is not a blank page; and neither is it an open book. The current notion that one has only to measure existing trends and to project, on a grander scale, the forces and institutions that dominate our present-day society in order to give a true picture of the future is based on another kind of illusion—the statistical illusion. This method overweights those elements in the present which are observable and measurable and seemingly powerful, and it overlooks many other factors that are hidden, unmeasured, irrational. In the second century A.D. an objective observer might well have predicted, on the basis of the imperial public works program, an increase in the number of baths, gladiatorial arenas, garrison towns, and aqueducts. But he would have had no anticipation of the real future, which was the product of a deep subjective rejection of the whole classic way of life and so moved not merely away from it but in the opposite direction. Within three centuries the frontier garrisons were withdrawn, the Roman baths were closed, and some of the great Roman buildings were either being used as Christian churches or treated as quarries for building new structures. Can anyone who remembers this historic transformation believe that the rate of scientific and technological change must accelerate indefinitely or that this technological civilization will inevitably remain dominant and will absorb all the energies of life for its own narrow purposes—pecuniary profit, predatory power, and parasitic leisure. —Concluding address at the Wenner-Gren Conference in 1955 on Man's Role in Changing the Face of the Earth

12: Expression in the Arts

As a New York boy whose home was always within easy walking distance of the Metropolitan Museum of Art and the Museum of Natural History, art entered my life too early for me to assign it a date, and visits with my Grandfather Graessel to both museums were an integral part of my boyhood.

My first real awakening to Modern Art did not come until 1915 when, in the Boston Museum of Fine Arts, I was dazzled by the dancing broken colors of Monet's canvases, and began making small water color drawings in the same fashion. Monet prepared me for the luminous Turner landscapes in the Tate Gallery. For me art in all its forms awakened or intensified my own experiences of actual life. The years I spent writing weekly art reviews for the New Yorker Magazine from 1932 to 1937 played an essential part in my emotional education which complemented my experience in love. What is more, I learned to read the hidden meaning of the artist's unconscious symbols—so often a prophecy of events that the artist is quite unaware of. No one can fully understand my 'Condition of Man' or 'The Pentagon of Power' who does not study the illustrations as intently as the text.

SYMBOLIC ARCHITECTURE. What hinders the development of a symbolic architecture, which will do for our own age what Chartres did for the thirteenth century, is, primarily, the fact that we live in a spiritual chaos. There are scarcely any values that a Catholic and a Ku Kluxer and an honest atheist, a scientist and a stockbroker, a Californian and a New Yorker hold together and deeply respect. For the sake of conventional agreement we have turned toward the past, particularly during this last

211

century, in order to conceal our own spiritual barrenness and timidity; but a formal rehash of the past, without love, faith, or understanding, has not even the virtue of self-deception. And we are not in much better shape now when we take the lowest common denominator of our life today, and attempt to worship the machine. We can, in a fashion, symbolize dynamos and airplanes, by structural forms that are subtle repetitions of these contraptions, but this is a crude and insufficient source of inspiration; for genuine symbolism is the translation, not of a fact, but of an idea. Eric Mendelsohn has designed a hat factory that has the outlines of a hat, and Raymond Hood has designed a Radiator Company Building which has the suggestion of a radiator; but neither of these efforts gives any hint as to how we shall build a library, a theater, or a school. One trembles at the prospect of a library in the form of a book.

For a while, it seems to me, our real salvation will lie in the steady pursuit of a vernacular.   —The American Mercury. June 1926

CONSTRUCTIVE FORMS. Well before I had begun deliberately to study architecture, painting, and sculpture in museums and books, I was conscious of the esthetic aspects of machines and machine products. One of my first contributions was a paragraph that was printed in 'Modern Electrics' in 1911, on the design for a sleeker model of binding post (brass standard), without the knurls and indentations that exhibit only the metal-turner's skill. So years before I had heard of Brancusi or Naum Gabo I was ready for their esthetic innovations. One of the earliest appreciations of the esthetic qualities of the machine was my 'Machinery and the Modern Style,' which came out in 1921, a few years before Le Corbusier's pioneer exposition 'Vers une Architecture.' If I was later to indicate that repetitive 'mechanical' behavior was an essential trait in all human culture, beginning with ritual, song, and above all language, long before any wood or stone tools, still less machines, had come into existence, my awareness of the esthetic aspect of machine products had likewise sunk in early, through direct experience.   —RN. 1969

THE BUFFALO WATERFRONT. Long tongues of water between wastes of open grass, with the grain-boats and the ore-boats adroitly maneuvered into the thin passages. These boats have clean decks, with the smoke-stacks in the extreme stern. Around the harbor stand the white grain-elevators, classic in their main forms, with fantastic chutes and passageways thrown across from one part to another high in the air. Nothing in the city except Wright's Larkin Building compares with them in simplicity and dignity. Beyond lie the steel works, with the iron ore and

212

limestone in mountains around them. The furnaces rusty and full of 'pathos.' Only two of them smoking.

On the other side of the avenue, parallel to the steel works which close off the lake-front, are the workers' houses, some of them standing isolated in the filthy cindery ground, others in even dingier rows: not a tree or a patch of vegetation anywhere. The whole effect is one of raw horror, accentuated by the flat waste of the landscape itself. (Different here from Homestead.) Wright's Larkin Building is superb: red brick, like his other Buffalo houses, with a handsome entrance. A reddish brownstone used for low ornament on upper stories. The interior white brick, fresh and spotless. Metal desks, designed by Wright; also badly designed metal chairs, painted. An absurd fireplace in the Reception Hall. A superb piece of monumental architecture—but now an empty temple to a dead god, doomed to sink into the industrial swamp around it. —RN. November 10, 1934

There is today one universal and accepted symbol of our period in America: the skyscraper. It came to us as a practical expedient: it has remained as a monument. When a small city wishes to show that it has an active Chamber of Commerce and a well-stocked Rotary Club it builds a skyscraper: when a university wishes to show that it stands for progress and big donations, it proposes to build a skyscraper: when a business man wants to express the pride of success or to advertise his product he builds a skyscraper: when, finally, a church wants to proclaim to the world that God and Mammon have, after all, a good deal in common, and that 'the Man Nobody Knows' was really a go-getter and a super-salesman, it builds a skyscraper. —Architecture. October 1928

If architecture was under the domination of painting in the Renaissance, there is a sense in which the reverse was also true: the painter himself became interested in spatial compositions unknown before in figure painting, but eloquently visible in architecture: so the vault and the apse dominate the figures in Giovanni Bellini's painting of the Madonna and Saints (with Saint Sebastian on the right) in the Accademia in Venice. Landscape, with its emphasis on distant views and prospects, plays a similar part in diminishing the importance of the figures and magnifying space as such: witness the marvelous painting by Basaiti—the Sons of Zebedee—where the figures are superb, yet only coeval with the bridge, the city, the rugged hills in the distance. In both cases, man is seen against his natural background and his urban milieu: no longer detached in the interests of his heavenly future. —RN. June 24, 1953

Form in building exists, not in a static, photographic view of the structure, but in the dynamic fulfillment of all its relationships. The impression upon the eye, though constant and important, is not the only effect of good architecture. To forget movement in relation to a building is to forget the essential difference between architecture and painting, and even between architecture and sculpture: for a building, unlike sculpture, is not so much a plastic mass as an envelope: the outer effect is rhythmically related and in part determined by the inner structure: indeed, the resolution of that double relationship is the very key to a positive work of architecture. A mountain, a pyramid, an obelisk, a statue may be seen from various angles and exposures: but, unlike St. Sophia, they cannot be approached from within. One may halt at any point to take advantage of the picture presented by the building: but the building itself is not a picture. Buildings conceived as pictures should never leave the draughting board. —This and two following paragraphs are from unpublished ms. 'Form and Civilization.' 1930–1931

BUILDING TECHNOLOGIES. Technically there is no end to the possible use of glass with a modern concrete or metal frame construction. But without social control there is as little benefit in the potential openness of the glass house as there is in the potential height of the skyscraper. For glass is not an end in itself: it is a means to sunlight, pure air, pleasant vistas. If, for lack of effective community planning, these things are not secured, if the houses are badly spaced and give no privacy, if the air is polluted by motor traffic, and if instead of gardens and parks there are only catwalks, garages, and parking lots the boldest of technical innovations may be no more than waste and lost motion. In fact, we may lay it down as an axiom that every collective economy, every labor saving device, every modern material or utility, tends to become a nuisance until it is collectively controlled and integrated into a new pattern. As an abstract invention, foisted on the market for financial gain, it merely adds to the amount of chaos our civilization is capable of producing. For lack of integrated patterns, the resources of modern technology have not been adequately applied to modern architecture. If we are to live in glass houses, we must abandon many other practices besides that of throwing stones. Does this not suggest that there is something wrong with the idea of glass houses?

When one dates the beginnings of modern architecture, not from the Crystal Palace or the Marshall Field Warehouse, or the Tacoma Building, or the Eiffel Tower, but from the Elizabethan period, one is taking into consideration the increased production of glass during this period. The result had a profound value for civilization: it not merely altered the

214

relation of window and wall in the design of a building: it also changed the internal plans and fittings, increased the possibility of hygiene, and above all, altered the outlook of the occupants. It is scarcely an exaggeration to represent the medieval mind by a closed wall and the modern one by an open window: what we have lost in defensive solidity we have gained in exposure to light. When the medieval man looked at the world through glass, he saw his own imagery: the virgin, the saints, the blue of heaven, the red of sacramental blood. But when a modern man looks through glass, while he may magnify the object he beholds, he takes the utmost care to maintain the purity and transparency of his medium, since he values it not for its own sake but for that of the object beyond. Human culture remains the essential medium.

THE OFFICE OF ART. In all but its most trivial and imitative forms, art is not a substitute for life or an escape from life. Even in the oldest paleolithic cave painting, the artist reveals more to us than the fact that he had observed the bison carefully, or that he venerated it as a totem animal: he also reveals, in the very quality of his line—in its selectivity, its sureness, its expressive rhythm—something even more essential about the nature of his own experience and culture. And if a dozen anthropologists had been observing and recording his life, they could not tell us more; indeed, in certain ways—the artist's 'secret'—they could not tell us half as much.

Or suppose we look at three nudes: by Cranach, Rubens, and Manet, the virginal wife of the Middle Ages, the lusty bed fellow and willing mother of the Renaissance, the cold, almost boyish courtesan of the nineteenth century. We find, in these condensed esthetic forms, three different ways of looking at the world, three different kinds of personality, three different philosophies: three cultures, not just three women. Art uses a minimum of concrete material to express a maximum of meaning. And if what we read into a Rorschach ink blot reveals our innermost nature, what do we not find and disclose about ourselves in the complex and deliberately evocative symbols of art?

Art is that part of technics which bears the fullest imprint of the human personality; technics is that manifestation of art from which a large part of the human personality has been excluded, in order to further the performance of work. No matter how abstract art is—and even in the most realistic convention every work of art is an abstraction—it can never be entirely impersonal or entirely meaningless. When art seems to be empty of meaning, as no doubt some of the vacuous painting of our own day actually does seem, what the painting says, indeed what the artist is

215

shrieking at the top of his voice, is that life has become empty of all rational content or coherence. And that, in times like these, is far from a meaningless statement.

Though the world we live in is constantly modified by our use of symbols, it has taken us a long time to notice the way in which symbols mediate all experiences above the level of our animal reflexes. Since the time of John Locke and David Hume we have tended to take for granted that our bare sense-data, rather than our symbols, form the solid groundwork of experience. But the brilliant researches of Adelbert Ames have experimentally established the fact that sensations are no more primary than any other aspect of experience: that they do not impinge upon us directly, but are always being linked up with the meanings and values and purposes of the organism, as established either in the general plan of life of the species, or in man's particular interests and needs, conditioned as they are by his history and culture. Once we recognize the part played generally by the symbol, in subjectifying and personalizing the world, we can understand the limitations of science and technics, since they are by intention an expression of that part of the personality from which emotion and feeling and desire and sympathy and love—the stuff of both life and art—have been eliminated.

Strangely, it is only in our own day that the work of George Mead, Ernst Cassirer, W. M. Urban, and Susanne Langer in philosophy has drawn attention to the constant part played by man's propensity to symbolize his experience; and in particular to the dynamic role of the esthetic symbol, in revealing man's nature and further modifying it. Our long neglect of the symbol, like our complete withdrawal of interest from the dream, was due perhaps to a cultural change that took place in the eighteenth century, through the naive rationalism and practical enthusiasm of the *philosophes,* led by Diderot. In his biography of Diderot, indeed, John Morley suggested that our devaluation of symbols was perhaps part of a more general shift in the intellectual climate; a turning away from an interest in words to an interest in things, from matters of value to matters of fact. This movement both resulted from the advances of technics and gave further encouragement to those advances; but, though it was hailed as a great emancipation of the spirit, we can now see that it actually involved a displacement of the rest of the personality and a disparagement of a good part of human life—that which has its source, not in external conditions and forces, but in the inner nature and funded historic experiences of man. In correcting this one-sided development we should not of course make the mistake of attempting to repress the impersonal, the repetitive, the practical, the technical; we should rather seek to bring these activities into working unity with other parts of the personality, for they have an important contribution to make, once they cease to exercise the one-sided dominion they now claim. —From 'Art and Technics.' 1952

Painting and music and the drama isolate and intensify experiences that occur in life fitfully, weakly, or in confusion. One looks at a landscape; the soughing of the wind through the trees, the distant murmur of water, the chirp of a cricket, the hum of an airplane overhead, share and divert —but sometimes intensify—the ecstasy of the eye. One experiences both more and less of the landscape. The full reality is neither music nor picture. The painter extracts the visual element alone: from that he takes away irrelevant details and recomposes it into a design having the maximum power as pure landscape: gone are the sounds, the human associations, the fatigue of one's muscles after the walk: here is the rarefied experience itself. One cannot recover this moment in life, though one return to the same spot a hundred times: the painter himself cannot recover it as actually experienced; but out of a hundred similar experiences, aided by the conventions of his art, he can create a symbol rich enough to recall and even magnify the reality. —RN. September 1929

The Graphic and Plastic Arts

THE BARLACH WAR MEMORIAL IN HAMBURG. This monument alone is worth a visit: a flat shaft that rises from a base below one of the most frequently used bridges. The German Ku Klux Klansmen have objected to the mother and child rendered in low relief on one side; their ground is that the figures look Slavic, a criticism even more absurd than the pious English outrage over the fact that Epstein's Madonna looked Oriental. What really troubles the Nazis is that the whole monument is so free from Bismarckian pomp and bluster; freer even than Tessenow's excellent interior of the war memorial in Berlin, with its metallic wreath and its top open to the sky. Barlach is a real *Nordgotiker*, essentially a hermit-artist, produced by what is still living in North Germany of the Middle Ages. In Lübeck, an hour away from Hamburg by train, one can see the first three figures of a series Barlach is doing; they occupy a special space in the old Katharinenkirche, now used as a museum. The strong Gothic interior, doubly strong by reason of the fact that it is painted a cold white, is just the right setting for Barlach's art; it needs the echo of that background to hold its reality, and to make one see that Barlach has not copied Gothic but *is* Gothic, perhaps one of the last creatures produced by that vanished world. —The New Yorker. October 8, 1932

FORMS OF JOY. Here is the Brancusi of old, the Brancusi whose new-born child and whose head of Mlle. Pogany once seemed so startling; and here is the new Brancusi, demonstrating that his secret lay not in the newness or unexpectedness of his forms but in his essential capacity as a sculptor to conceive new molds for our own experience. For he has continued his explorations of time and space and movement, of materials and textures and surfaces, and like some ancient deity he creates plastic forms—a rooster or a blonde metallic Negress—which have the effect of being new biological species.

If you can imagine a geometrical theorem that produces a smile, a machine shop that has become introspective, a lump of clay that displays adolescent ambitions to become a crystal, or two lovers who have dissolved into stone—if you can imagine any of these things, you are ready for Brancusi. If you cannot, you had better confine your explorations of the new world of form to the latest plumbing fixtures and electric gadgets; they are not so subtle and so human as Brancusi's sculptures, but they are a step in the right direction. "It's pure joy I'm giving you," says Brancusi in his brief introduction to the catalogue. "Don't look for obscure formulas nor for mysteries." The counsel is excellent. For the first effect of the show should be to make one clap one's hands and turn a few handsprings; the existence of so much pure imagination makes one feel young and innocent again. And part of Brancusi's own pleasure, I am sure, is a counterpart to that which one felt as a child on the beach when one finally succeeded in turning out a pail of wet sand in such a fashion that it would stand up and show no flaw. This elementary feeling for clean form and for the material in itself is one that we have almost lost today. Brancusi restores it to us, as he restores so many other parts of our deserted heritage. . . .

Craftsmanship and pure mathematics, the natural and the artificial, the living and the mechanical, the spontaneous and the calculated, primitivism as deep as a jungle fetish wedded to a rationality as coldly elegant and abstract as a demonstration in mathematics by the late Henri Poincaré—these are the ingredients of Brancusi's art. But heed him well! Do not look for mystery; look for joy and humor and the delight of being equally at home in every part of the world. —The New Yorker. 1933

THE OROZCO MURALS AT DARTMOUTH. As painting, as orchestration of emotion, as thought, as many-faceted symbol there is really nothing like it anywhere in America: so big and great and powerful that even the occasional weak spots—and there are a few—only seem to add vitality to the whole. And even technically, there is painting in it that cannot be beaten by anyone today. How can I describe the work to you? The Gods of Power and the Gods of Life are at work in Mexico. Horrible brutality on one side, and the great maize culture with the stone sculptures on the other. Science dawns there, too: a man with closed eyes reaching up into the black unknown. Quetzalcoatl, representing the spiritual life, comes to the Mexicans and promises to return: the priests of reaction, a black pyramid of defensive arms, retreat from him, as he is lost over the monstrous waters of the sea. At length the prophecy of Quetzalcoatl is wryly fulfilled: the Spaniard comes in his sable armor; and out of that springs—it is really an illustration for my book!—the Machine: the machine in its essence, orderly and powerful, disintegrating and dehumanizing, an altogether devastating image.

After that one faces the orderly North American sense of life, based on wheat culture, the town meeting, the individual homestead and barn, grimly dominated by the pioneer schoolmarm: this gives way to the mechanized, capitalistic culture symbolized by opened bags of gold, with two miserable capitalists slavering in the coins. But education shall save us? *Will it?* A living skeleton examines a bleached woman's skeleton, laid out in childbirth on a dissecting table, amid embryos pickled in bottles of alcohol, while a row of ghoulish figures in academic gowns with blind eyes preside over the event. They balance off against the monstrous priests of the Aztec ritual of death, who at least disembowel their victim, a live young man.

At the end of the room one beholds the apotheosis of war in one panel, with a Tomb of the Unknown Soldier as the final bitter result of the patriotism and propaganda and profits. On the other wall, the spiritual life, represented by the vultures that have stolen the Keys of Heaven. Finally: a burst of flame: a burst one is conscious of as soon as one enters the hall: that flame is the breast of Man: the spiritual life. Christ has risen and with a terrible axe he has cut down his own cross, has shattered the temples of Zeus and Buddha and Mahomet, and has obliterated all the dead creeds and moribund forms of living. —Letter to Catherine Bauer. February 17, 1934

Note: Both in 'Technics and Civilization' and 'The Pentagon of Power' I made use of Orozco's mural, directly influenced by the passages I have described. See Plate 25, The Academic Establishment, in 'The Pentagon of Power.'

THE 1934 SHOW OF STIEGLITZ'S WORK at An American Place comes in his seventy-first year; if anything, it is more positive and climactic than the exhibition of 1921. Stieglitz's head is now crowned with a vague, yellowish cloud of hair and the red vest has given way to gray; but the incredibly refined technique, the deep, relentless energy, and the steady vision of life are still there. Neither his friends nor his enemies have done justice to the man. One does not have to think of Stieglitz as a prophet to see that his work is prophetic, nor does one have to decide whether or not photography is an art to realize that Stieglitz is an artist who might under other circumstances have built bridges or written poems.

There is an astringent quality in Stieglitz that has escaped his admirers. He has been nourished by his hates as well as his loves; he has never cultivated that harmless good nature which is responsible for half the stupidities of American life. Stieglitz's demonic negations are part of his deepest vitality; they play the same part in his personality that the blacks do in his prints. As well think of Stieglitz without these dark elements as think of Melville without 'Moby-Dick' and 'Pierre.' I emphasize these personal qualities of Stieglitz because his photographs are not alone his work but his life.

In contrast to the restless cameramen of our time, Stieglitz does not go out of his way to get a print. He takes the world as he finds it; the grass at his feet, the sky over his head, the office buildings he sees from his apartment in the Shelton are equally good. Nature, Man, the Machine—these three form the major chords of his work; upon that triple theme he plays a bewildering infinity of variations. He does not look for subjects—'aesthetic' subjects, or 'photogenique' subjects—because his subject is life, and for him, as for Whitman, a blade of grass is a miracle. Some of the clever photographers who admire his technique even find him empty; but when they observe that he has nothing to say, they really mean that he says nothing they can copy. The secrets of his art are not in his camera, his papers, his developers; they lie in his mind. —The New Yorker. December 22, 1934

ALBERT PINKHAM RYDER. Not since Ryder's great exhibition at the Metropolitan Museum in 1918 have we had a better opportunity to see his paintings than this season. Farewell to the notion that Ryder was a painter with a single style or a single fixed technique. Here is pretty much the entire range and development of the man, or at least a synopsis of it: one passes from thin pigment to thick pigment and varnish, from the rapid brush strokes of 'Holland' to the sometimes miraculous, even enamel of the final period. And the change of interest and subject matter is equally remarkable.

Sweet adolescent commonplaces, done in soft autumnal coloring, are the marks of Ryder's earliest work. He begins with such feeble paintings as Christ walking with a shepherd's crook in the Garden of Gethsemane, or the 'Wayside Forge,' a reddish composition, marred by age and fire, that slightly recalls an inferior Blakelock. There is little in these early pictures save a certain delicacy of feeling, a certain timidity that keeps him from making gross and pretentious blunders. Such paintings somewhat excuse the judgement of Ryder's aunt, the good lady who advised the young aspirant to give up any hopes of being a painter. If that advice does not altogether damn her as an art critic, it shows that she was a poor psychologist. She did not know enough about her nephew to appreciate the depth and intensity of his feeling. So she could not guess that he would persevere with his art until his feelings became perfectly articulate, until it reached a pitch of perfection at which every stroke would reflect the quiet harmony and the deepening insight of his own life. . . .

There were weaknesses in Ryder's original equipment, and if those of technique diminished with time, others, derived from nature, like his festering eyes, which dreaded sunlight, remained. But no painter could have been less handicapped by the frailty of his natural endowments; he used every grain of his talents, and he knew how to harmonize what he was with what he might be. Ryder could not for his life have turned out a popular illustration of bathing or skating for 'Harper's Weekly,' as Winslow Homer did, nor could he have engraved a banknote with classic goddesses, like Walter Shirlaw. But he had qualities that more than made up for lack of the superficial brilliance one finds even in the juvenilia of Homer: he had an extraordinary persistence, and a no less extraordinary capacity for growth.

One finds Ryder at the beginning of this series of paintings little more than a child who has aspirations to be a great painter. One finds him at the end, after years of unfaltering discipline and devotion, a painter who, without losing the simplicity of a child, has actually attained maturity and greatness. His paintings belong to the nineteenth century; they belong to it like the tales of Hawthorne or Poe, the music of Wagner, or the poems of Baudelaire; and yet as paintings they are dateless: they are as far from the literalism of the realists, or the externality of the impressionists, as they are from the vapid sermonizings of the Watts and the Böcklins. Originality does not consist in avoiding the influences of history, tradition, and contemporary life, but in completely assimilating them and making them into new flesh and blood; and in this sense Ryder was surely one of the great originals of the nineteenth century.

Of all the paintings in the present show, perhaps the most precious to lovers of Ryder is his self-portrait. It is a small painting, glazed and reglazed without damage to the brilliant colors that glow under the surface, and the finish is remarkably without flaw. Here is Ryder in early middle life: fresh, sweet, even-eyed. Like so many other paintings of his, it has a lesson to teach our generation: the lesson that importance is not measurable in mere space—not in space in the headlines and not space occupied by the canvas on the wall. What counts in a little painting by Ryder is something which I trust I do not make more obscure by giving it a name: spiritual pressure, an unwillingness to be satisfied by the second-best, the half-finished, the unrealized. In the service of an ill-balanced personality, the pressure and grip and intensity one finds in Ryder's work would have made a financial Napoleon or a crazy political dictator; in the case of this harmonious soul, it made a great artist. —The New Yorker. November 2, 1935

In the nineteen-hundreds, two influences seeped into the American home and altered the attitude toward pictures. One of them was that of William Morris, who had observed that no one should ever possess anything he did not know to be useful or believe to be beautiful—a principle that obviously left most reproductions in limbo on both scores. The other crept in subtly at the very moment that the Kaiser was shouting about the Yellow Peril: the Japanese influence, brought to these shores by La Farge, Whistler, Fenollosa, and the French impressionists. It may also be, as a writer in 'Camera Work' once suggested, that the photograph, with its austere mountings, set an example for the style of decoration in other departments. One by one reproductions left the walls of the American home, sometimes to be replaced by original paintings, sometimes leaving behind a blank spot.

The same quality of mind that made the Japanese house anticipate in its method of design almost all that is best in modern architecture enabled the Japanese to develop a fine ritual for showing and enjoying pictures. Both Japanese precedents are, by some accident, closer to the practical needs and psychological insight of the modern man than anything the Occident can show by way of precedent. One may sum up the Japanese practice in three simple injunctions: Do not use pictures as permanent wall decorations. Look at one picture at a time. (If it won't stand up under this scrutiny, throw it out!) Change your pictures frequently. If these principles were generally observed, the presses of America might turn out millions of reproductions without hurting anyone; and until they do become popular, even original pictures should be kept in museums, if only to keep their owners from becoming weary of them. —The New Yorker. December 12, 1936

JOHN MARIN'S ROOTS. A while ago I stumbled upon Marin, that wrinkled, shaggy-haired Pan, in the Metropolitan Museum. He was looking intently at a little fifteenth-century Flemish primitive. When he turned around to me, he said, "Sometimes, when I am walking down Fifth Avenue, I say to myself, 'Marin, you are a mighty fine fellow, but do you know your job as well as those old boys did, and will your stuff last as long?'"

Marin belongs to that lonely, aristocratic band which includes Thoreau and Ryder and Frost—men who are not afraid to withdraw, to see what they see and to feel what they feel, though the world look somewhere else and think differently. Artists with large, copious social talents often show their best traits as readily at twenty as at sixty; the Raphaels in one age and the Sargents in another are more apt to spread themselves thin in maturity than to develop beyond their first intuitions. It is different with the lonelier type of artist. There is often a long period of conventional effort, of fumbling, of trying to "be like the rest," before the artist discovers his real sphere of interest and his appropriate method of attack. John Marin was thirty-five before he finally started on the road that led to the creation of the completely individualized paintings of his maturity—those paintings which are more like the work of the Chinese masters of the Sung dynasty than that of his European contemporaries.

The path of Marin's growth led through Whistler, but it went beyond the point to which Whistler, or even his Japanese exemplars, had carried it. Marin was to learn at an early stage the general truth expressed by the Chinese philosopher of landscape painting, Kuo Hsi: "If you wish to paint a big mountain, you must not paint every part of it, or it will not seem high." Similarly, in one of his earliest watercolors, that of a London omnibus, done in 1908, one observes the most typical of Marin signatures: the use of rectangular shapes—here timid and scarcely visible—to serve as a sort of dynamic internal frame for the central motif of the picture.

Up to 1910, if one may judge by Marin's etchings, he was at home in cities—the great culture cities of Paris, Amsterdam, Venice. At this point a break came in his work. It is marked by the effulgent rainbow lyricism of the scenes in the Austrian Tyrol, radiant and gay, with a rich blue which was to recur in more than one later picture. Then the return to America and the discovery of another kind of city, more uproarious in energy, but also more disturbing to the soul. From then on Marin became rooted in the land of his birth, and the roots sank deep. —RN. October 31, 1936

EVERY WORK OF ART HAS A HIDDEN MEANING, buried in the unconscious, that is often far more significant than the conscious message. So all the days I spent in the twenties and thirties, looking at paintings and sculpture, gave me a deeper understanding of contemporary civilization, especially of its approaching disruptions, than anything I found in books. Perhaps a single instance will suffice. In 1935 I briefly commented in The New Yorker on the work of an unknown painter, Alice Tenney: a newcomer, at least in New York. Of one of her canvases I said: "The V-shaped composition of the scene in the grocery store, with the green-faced grocery clerk and customers, might better have been reserved for a lynching." And presently the artist wrote me: "You said that I sometimes over-dramatized . . . Now strangely enough that picture which you mentioned in the same breath with a 'lynching' was *painted* also in the same breath with a lynching, so to speak. Previously to the 'Grocery' I had worked hard and long over a lynching picture, made lots of studies, etc., but never brought it to a satisfactory conclusion. I suppose all that work aroused a certain emotion which couldn't come out in the lynching because the picture was too weak but did find an escape in a stronger picture though of a less strong subject matter." —RN. 1935

Long before Dr. Sigmund Freud embarked on his career, a British esthetician, known apparently only to the late Professor George Saintsbury and myself, had written a book which began as a work of genius and rambled off into mediocrity. The author's name was Dallas and the book was called 'The Gay Science.' In this work, Dallas discussed the 'hidden soul' in relation to art, that being nothing more or less than an Early Victorian approximation of the unconscious. Dallas proved very ably, I think, to the discomfiture of all purely rational formulas for esthetic experience, that the quality which distinguishes a work of art is its pull and hold on the unconscious. What goes before this in design and manner of execution is by way of preparation; it can be analyzed. What follows eludes analysis; it must be directly felt or experienced.

Now, here lie precisely the attraction and the difficulty of dealing with the paintings of Georgia O'Keeffe. Every painting is a chapter in her autobiography, and yet the revelation is so cunningly made that it probably eludes her own conscious appraisal. As soon as one realizes that she is neither a botanist who looks at flowers through a magnifying glass nor a comparative anatomist who collects the skulls of the North American desert fauna, one is brought face to face with the real problem. What has she lived through? And what do these turkey feathers and bare hills and bleached bones convey in terms of one's own experience? One grants that her symbols are part of the scenery of New Mexico; but another artist in the same region might find nothing to paint but a railway train or a barroom.

Certain elements in O'Keeffe's biography were plainly visible in the paintings of the previous few years; physical or mental illness cannot be concealed. There was more than conventional symbolism in the dark crosses that stood out against the clear desert sky, and there was a bitter note in the pink rose stuck in the horse's skull. The painting in these pictures was still adequate, and there was even technical progress in her modelling of the landscape, but the work lacked the sense of sharp discovery that the earlier paintings had. One felt that the next word might diminish into that silence which is the artist's death.

The new show brings, for O'Keeffe's admirers, a resurgence of life and a resurrection of spirit. The epitome of the whole show is the painting of the ram's head, with its horns acting like wings, lifted up against the gray, wind-swept clouds; at its side is a white hollyhock flower. In conception and execution this is one of the most brilliant paintings O'Keeffe has done. Not only is it a piece of consummate craftsmanship, but it likewise possesses that mysterious force, that hold upon the 'hidden soul,' which distinguishes important communication from the casual reports of the eye. Here one notes the vast difference between those who are able to draw upon the unconscious, because they face life at every level, and the Surréalistes, who have been playing with the unconscious in the same way that a smutty adolescent might play upon a ouija board for the purpose of eliciting an obscene word. O'Keeffe uses themes and juxtapositions no less unexpected than those of the Surréalistes, but she uses them in a fashion that makes them seem inevitable and natural, grave and beautiful. —The New Yorker. January 18, 1936

VINCENT VAN GOGH. The religion he could not express through his ministrations in the church comes out in his pictures. It loses its mysticism and its certitudes about the after life: "No fixed idea about God, no abstractions, always on the firm ground of life itself, and only attached to that." Vincent's religion knows suffering because he has felt it in the toil and danger of the miners; it knows sacrifice because he has shared his last crust with people who habitually live on crusts; but at the bottom of it all is a simple, generous animal faith which gives up material happiness because it knows that the happiness of the artist or the thinker begins at the point where the more obvious modes of happiness are left behind. Near to simple folk, he feels in himself, no matter how brutal or petty they are, the strength of their lives: Gauguin, who is a sophisticated cockney, goes to Martinique, or to Tahiti, to discover what Van Gogh finds in his backyard.

Before Vincent can make his feelings manifest in his pictures, he has a long apprenticeship to serve: he is almost twenty-seven before he begins definitely on his new career, and although he follows it with magnificent persistence, there are obstacles enough in his way. What eventually becomes the 'style' of Van Gogh—firm, lean brush-strokes or quill strokes that are part of the design of the picture, a solidity of form, a palpable third dimension—discloses itself at the beginning only in the clumsiness that makes him inferior to the student who can copy surfaces with greater ease. Everyone doubts him; he needs a double share of courage not to doubt himself.

Now what was there remarkable in Van Gogh's life and art? What was remarkable was his capacity to absorb the most devastating experiences without losing his own vitality and faith. He achieved in sorrow and discouragement and ridicule and degradation what other men sometimes achieve out of health and fine adventure: one feels in his paintings and his letters that things went well with him, no matter how badly. This natural animal faith retreats sometimes in shipwreck and disaster, when men cling to phantoms whose existence they renounce in fair weather; but in Van Gogh it steadily gained strength. "For you, too," he writes Theo, "there will come a moment that you will know *for sure* all chance of material happiness is lost, fatally and irrevocably. I feel sure of it, but also know that at the same moment there will be a certain compensation in feeling in one's self the power to work."

Vincent van Gogh was a great lover of art: he loved Rembrandt, Corot, Ruysdael, Millet, Delacroix: but he was a poor critic of art, because he loved life more, and included in his embrace men like Luke Fildes and Frank Holl since they made up for him in human compassion what they lacked in color or design. No artist of his time was more fully absorbed in the thought of his own age: he read Dickens, Hugo, Zola, Michelet, Renan, Carlyle: and no one succeeded better than he did, I think, in escaping the limitations of his time and in reaching, in thought and art, toward a new generation which would be "able to breathe more freely." He purchased his faith, not cheaply, by day-to-day living. The miner, the peasant, the weaver, the prostitute, whose lives he shared, were all outcasts in bourgeois society; and he was an outcast, too. But Van Gogh knew what honest work was; and he lived by it; and if his pictures are still most talked about in salons and art galleries that irony is not without its parallels in history. I know scarcely a single figure since St. Francis, whose life lays such a hold on the imagination. If he lived tragically, he also lived to a purpose. The moral is incommunicable perhaps; but it lies open on every page of his letters.   —New York Herald Tribune Books. November 13, 1927

THE WORLD OF GOYA. As with Delacroix, one may look upon Goya as either the last of the princely line of Renaissance painters or the first of the new republican succession that otherwise began with Courbet or Manet. In any case, he was a giant. How many painters after Goya had so many important things to say and so many effective ways of saying them? Daumier and Van Gogh are perhaps his nearest rivals, yet neither of them quite had his immense technical span. . . .

In a sense, there is no Goya style; but there is Goya in all his styles; no other artist knew better how to adapt his method and his point of view to the subject. The result is that ultimate style in which the painter's individuality is so completely blended with the subject that it cannot be extracted as a separate mark. There are, of course, great painters whose style is easy to identify as soon as they appear on the scene; but there is a handful of even more consummate stylists whose individuality is too finely disciplined to leave such a coarse trail on the canvas: Tintoretto and Giovanni Bellini, for example. Goya belongs with the second group. One does not recognize his tricks first and then enjoy the painting; one enjoys the painting and then recognizes that only Goya could have painted it.

Marvelous as Goya's paintings are in range of expression, his drawings and prints are no less remarkable. The sepia washes, represented here by specimens from the Metropolitan's recently acquired album, are worthy to rank near Rembrandt's drawings. As for the etchings, in particular the 'Disasters of the War' series, the quality that made them odious to nineteenth century collectors only brings him closer to sound contemporary taste. Goya respected the reproductive process, and maintained the same even level in his first impression as in his last. He did not achieve a few good prints by way of a series of messy approximations. His combination of aquatint and etching gave him the same range in prints as in an original pen-and-brush drawing; and when lithography was invented, he quickly applied himself to it and demonstrated its serious possibilities. If only a few drawings, such as 'Crowd in a Park' or 'Foul Night' were left, one would still be assured of his power and reach.

The change in taste that has taken place during the last generation has given us a new insight into Goya's esthetic achievements, but the revival of Goya's fame is also due to the fact that our knowledge of the human personality and our experience of the series of catastrophes and mass brutalities that began with the World War have given us a new insight into his message. Brutality is no longer for us, as it was for the Victorians, something that exists on the edge of the jungle; it is something that may break at any moment into the parlor, in the form of a fascist squad or an aerial torpedo. What is peculiarly 'modern' in Goya is his combination of an intense realism and a high regard for fact on one hand, with an imagination that stops at nothing, and understands that nightmares can be realities and realities can be nightmares.

The Goya who drew the 'Caprices' and the 'Disparates' did not have much to learn about the murkier sides of the personality from Dr. Freud; he understood the character of our present psychoses—the fears, hatred, obsessions that keep men from acting sane and magnanimous and human. Only the most courageous of spirits could have faced both the terrors he found in his own consciousness and the brutalities he found in the world outside. 'God Spare Us Such Bitter Fortune' is the title of his drawing of a man showing a dagger to his wife and child. What the alternative was shows in the print called 'You Can't Look'—a group of victims shrinking before the points of massed bayonets, driven toward them by unseen soldiers. "The man," wrote Goya, "who shuts his eyes to the unsteadiness of fortune sleeps soundly amid danger. He can neither dodge impending harm nor make ready for calamity." Goya sought to open the eyes.

Love of life, love of women, love of the day's drama, all plainly vibrate through the work of this stormy, passionate, and tremendously intelligent man. During the latter part of his life, the catastrophes of war turned this love into an equally passionate hatred for all manner of frustration and cruelty and evil; instead of the Duchess of Alba, he shows us the butchered naked bodies of women, sprawling not in wantonness but in a last spasm of agony. One can say of Goya, as one can say of few painters, *he told the whole story*. And his horror and hatred are all the more terrible because none knew better than he how deliriously good life could be.   —The New Yorker. February 8, 1936

THE NEW GROPPER SHOW has left me with a desire to write him an Open Letter. It would go like this: "Dear William Gropper: Where have you been keeping this talent of yours all these years, and why have you not shown it more freely? When I put that question to you the other night, you said something about your skepticism about the value of painting under the present capitalistic order of society. I understand that feeling. For a while William Morris could be the idle singer of an empty day, but toward the end of his life his gorge rose. Today art is neither the honest day's work it was during the Renaissance nor the elegant, self-disciplined play that it might be in a society that knew how to extract leisure from the slavery of machines. Almost the only people who look upon painting as more important than a bathing-beauty contest or a cocktail party are those who would exterminate it altogether because they do not find the American flag in the right-hand corner of every canvas. So far, your skepticism and your scorn are both understandable.

"But if you mean that you can't take painting seriously so long as the state of the world is rotten, I think you are wrong. The world would long ago have become depopulated if lovers had acted on that premise. And Brueghel the elder might well have stopped painting had he realized that the century he lived in was ushering in that first development of large-scale finance capitalism, mechanized warfare, and militarized industry which was to sound the doom of the ways of life he depicted with so much spirit. No. The fact is that painting is as natural to man as the more primitive biological acts that preserve his existence. It began in the Aurignacian caves, and it will outlast the subway and the bomb shelter. Yes, the machine age itself.

"To create images, to play with images, to contemplate images, to share images are part of what it means to be human. Painting today, by reason of what it stands for, is both an act of protest and an affirmation. A protest against fear, routine, dullness, meaningless restriction—in short, the defeat of life—and an affirmation of what it means to be truly alive. Your own paintings have this quality of affirmation, the more because you have not kept your eyes off the vindictive realities that surround us. People cannot rebuild a rotten world unless they have a sounder and richer one inside themselves. Whatever exemplifies life assists in this process of growth and renewal. And those who have your gifts must have the confidence to use them." —The New Yorker. February 15, 1936

The other day, while I was prowling through the exhibition of the New York realists at the Whitney Museum—it was not the critics' preview—I became suddenly conscious of the other visitors. They were the sort of people you might expect to find at a fire, but never at an art gallery. There were groups of crisp, black-haired men, with cheeks like Westphalian hams, whom you might see dining at Cavanagh's or at Joe's in Brooklyn; there were shrewd horsey-faced fellows you'd more likely meet in the paddocks or the prize ring, judging limbs and shoulders, than in the midst of a collection of paintings. Politicians, real-estate brokers, contractors, lawyers—what were they doing here? My guess is that they were New Yorkers, pulled into the gallery by that dark, secret love for the city that New Yorkers hide from the world even when they brag about the city's wonders. And they had come to the right place, for the nine artists who are represented in this show,* through the work they did between

* Henri, Luks, Sloan, Glackens, Bellows, Coleman, Lawson, Shinn, and Du Bois.

1900 and 1914, loved the city too; not less, perhaps, because five of them came from the dingy, unexciting, provincial streets of Philadelphia as it was at the beginning of the century.

To their contemporaries these artists were tough babies. Four of them had got their training after art school doing sketches for the Philadelphia Press, and they all had the journalist's eye for news and human interest, and they weren't afraid of going off the old beats to find them. There had been genre painters of New York life before: men like J. G. Brown, who had painted bootblacks and gamins. But these figures had no more esthetic importance than a Horatio Alger hero, whose precise counterpart they, in fact, were. When Luks caught two little urchins dancing wildly, he didn't bother to change their clothes or wash their faces; he slashed their figures onto the canvas with a vigor begotten of his own delight. When in the 'Wake of the Ferry,' Sloan shows a lonely figure of a woman, standing partly exposed to the rain, looking out over the gray waters, he symbolizes forever the intense loneliness, as final as that of a deserted hermit on a Himalayan peak, almost everyone has known in the midst of crowded Manhattan. —The New Yorker. February 27, 1937

STORY OF AN ACROBAT. When the great Picasso show was assembled at the Galeries Georges Petit in Paris in 1932, one naturally supposed that New York would see it soon thereafter. But the next opening was in Zurich, where Dr. Jung beheld it and wrote a learned and amiable paper on its psychological significance: typical schizophrenic symptoms. After that Picasso came to Hartford, probably in search of the ghost of Mark Twain—who was also pretty schizophrenic—or the no less elusive corporeal self of the lawyer who wrote 'Le Monocle de Mon Oncle.' At all events, New York was treated like a tank town. It is only now, with two handsome and fairly exhaustive exhibitions on view, that Picasso and New York are on even terms.

Sooner or later, everyone will have to make a reckoning with Pablo Picasso, which means, in fact, that everyone will have to figure out for himself what the meaning of modern civilization was between 1900 and 1935. The man has not merely been a great artist; he has been a barometer, sensitively recording in advance the state of the cosmic weather. The symbols he used were not, perhaps, quite as clear as those on the dial, but even scientific barometers require interpretation.

From moment to moment, Picasso has recorded the go of things: sentiment, humanitarianism, primitivism, constructivist architecture, mechanization, the nightmare of war, the unreality of peace and sanity, above all the racked and divided minds of all sensitive men. These things occur successively in Picasso's paintings. Part of his paintings will survive

230

as art, great art; the rest will survive as history. Rarely does one find an artist of Picasso's dimensions who is so much both the victim and the master of fashion. His invention has been copious, wild, outrageous, and yet somehow inevitable. He has all the characteristics of a major artist except the capacity for consecutive growth. He has had many clever imitators and loyal followers, but the only person of talent in his generation in Paris who refused to be drawn into the Picasso circle was Pablo Picasso, his most envious rival, his most treasonable disciple. Most of his life has been spent escaping from his latest self.

It is customary to associate the experiments of the post-impressionists with the constructive theories of Cézanne—attempts to reconstruct esthetic order on a more logical basis. But this element played only a small part in Picasso's early development. Picasso's first paintings, at the Seligmann exhibition, show something strikingly different; he began, as a serious artist, at the point where Van Gogh left off when darkness gathered about him and the black crows flew over the dark-blue cornfields at Auvers. The Blue Period was a period of deep emotional response to the blues of life: poverty, wretchedness, chills and weariness and starvation. The 'Woman Seated with Fichu,' the 'Old Guitar Player,' and the 'Woman Crouching' are paintings to be hung in the same gallery with Van Gogh's 'Potato Eaters.'

A terrible sincerity, a deep sympathy, characterize most of the paintings of the Blue Period. This sympathy united him not only with the miserable waifs and wastrels he portrayed but with those other painters of the meek and the humble—Daumier and Goya, painters who were to be restored, at this very moment in history, partly because their images had at last bitten, like an acid, through the solid armor of the proud and the righteous. In this group of paintings, the 'Woman with a Crow,' done in 1904, strikes me as one of the supreme examples; the drawing of the elongated hand here is quite unsurpassable. In 1905, this note of despair, which could have led only to suicide, lifted. Picasso's palette changed, as browns and roses succeeded the blues, and his mastery of line disclosed itself in a series of nudes and harlequins whose beauty equals and sometimes, possibly, surpasses Degas. For a moment, Picasso was in poise. Note the 'Woman with the Loaves,' in which the bread she carries on her head rhythmically balances her breasts. Picasso's humanity was perhaps succored by gaiety and love—the charms of the body, the tender forms of children, the dream world of Harlequin and Columbine and the acrobats. Such nudes as 'The Toilette' and 'The Coiffure' are infinitely better than the ponderous vacuity of the columnar neoclassic matrons that ushered in Picasso's postwar phase.

After 1905 came the period of experiment; the 'Corsage Jaune,' begun in 1907, presents a new palette for Picasso, a palette composed of ashen grays and acidulous yellows and unrelenting blacks; and for the world it presents a new type of imagery. Art from the time of the Renaissance had rested on two important assumptions. If you knew enough about the appearance of an object, you would finally be able to embody its reality; hence measurement, hence perspective, hence natural color scales, and finally the movement from the studio to the open air. Likewise, if you knew enough about the physical reality, about the anatomical or constructive form, you would eventually arrive at a true order of appearances. Picasso renounced these assumptions. The inner and the outer world had for him no such connections as the classic painters assumed; to deform the image, to decompose the human body, to suppress external shapes—these were other paths to reality, a reality more akin to the physicist's or engineer's world than to the surface impressions of naive humanity.

From 1910 on Picasso became a byword, among collectors, for the audacious and the original and, above all, the incomprehensible; and perhaps Picasso was tempted to justify his reputation, or at least to live up to it—all the more because it may perhaps have touched his mordant Spanish sense of humor. At all events, Picasso became an international performer, a man whose gestures became fashions. His infinite variety of technical resources served only to set off the emptiness of his later spiritual experience; there is a close parallel here between the development of Picasso and that of James Joyce. The further he went away from the Blue Period, the more fashionable his tricks became, the more obvious it was that—as Hawthorne once said of another—he had cut himself off from the magnetic chain of humanity.

In some ways, there was genuine development—mastery of fresh realms of color. But among the audacious and amusing paintings of the last few years—the 'Nature Morte' and the 'Dame Ecrivante,' and vital, luscious paintings they are—there is nothing that I would place beside the 'Blue Boy' or the 'Femme au Peigne.' At the top, sheer genius; at the bottom, emptiness, sterility, a failure to find material sufficient to justify that genius. If this is a true picture of the man, it should be obvious why his paintings are, in their good and bad qualities, a portrait of our civilization. Another case of poverty in the midst of potential abundance.
—The New Yorker. November 14, 1936

Note: This was written before Picasso's art rose to 'the tragic sense of life' in the horrors of the Civil War. His art perhaps reached its ultimate height in the Guernica mural. But see the plate on Picasso's development, 'Drama of Disintegration,' in 'The Condition of Man' (1944).

The Course of Abstraction

Before going over The Museum of Modern Art's Exhibition of Abstract Art, we might clear our minds if we faced the fact that the abstractions of the present generation of painters offer no essentially new elements in art. To begin with, all painting and sculpture is abstract; even at its most realistic, it is a displacement of something that exists in life with a symbol that has only a limited number of points of resemblance. A sculptured head can smile, but it cannot wink; it can also live without the aid of a body and the usual apparatus for breathing and for digesting food. Every work of art is an abstraction from time; it denies the reality of change and decay and death. Only on a Grecian urn can a lover console himself over his inability to catch his mistress with the reflection that beauty and love will remain permanent.

Visual art, again, demands an abstraction from the four other senses. It belongs to a world where taste and smell and sound are absent, where touch exists by means of a visual counterfeit, and where (at least in painting) the movement of the observer and the many-sidedness of things are lost in a static image. The truth is that almost all that we call culture is based upon a system of abstractions; the signs of language and the symbols of art and religion are mere shorthand curlicues for the reality they indicate or express. The most fulsomely realistic genre picture of a country grocer's store in Kansas is closer to a geometrical form by Ozenfant than it is to the patch of life it seeks to imitate. The man in the street has been looking at abstract art all his life without realizing it. What he falsely calls realism is only a more familiar series of abstractions.

By nature, any single work of art is a thinning down of concrete experience. If this were its only characteristic, one would have to reject art as a weak surrogate for life, as the Philistine does—a tepid beverage, for people who are not strong enough to take life neat. But art makes up for its limitations by a series of special advantages. By means of abstractions, certain qualities of experience can be intensified. Divorced from immediate practical necessities, art can respond to experiences our daily duties usually shut away from us, and it can rearrange our perceptions and feelings in new patterns, more significant for us than life as we have actually lived it. In a period of social development, art can make us anticipate new experiences, and put us in a frame of mind to welcome them, as the sharp eye of a good hunter will pick out a bird in a faint stir of leaves, before it takes wing. It was in this fashion that the Renaissance painters, who invented deep-space perspective, and built it up on a strict

233

mathematical basis, prepared us for the visual background for our new conquest of space through maps and ships and rapid means of locomotion.

How does this apply to the development of abstract art during the last thirty years? As Mr. Alfred Barr has well shown in arranging the exhibition, that movement had many aspects, and the new abstractions pointed to many different modes of experience. But surely one of its main expressions was an attempt to symbolize in new forms the world in which we actually live, to call attention to those particular experiences that alter our spatial relations and feelings, and to represent, by means of the image, the same attitudes and perceptions that were being expressed in the physical sciences, in psychology, in literature, and finally in all the mechanical arts. So, far from being divorced from the currents of life, the abstract artists were closer to the vital experiences of their period than were the painters who kept to more traditional forms. The meaning of any particular painting was not always clear, nor were the efforts at expression always successful. But the connection between the image and contemporary reality was close.

The facts about abstract art have been obscure partly for the reason that artists, and the few critics who understood their aims, were more concerned with the formal and technical problems raised by these new abstractions than with their underlying content. In fact, in a revolt against banal illustration, the abstractionists even claimed that their art had no contents, except lines, surfaces, and volumes, duly organized; they attributed to paintings and sculptures the characteristics of architecture, without being able to supply either the rational uses of a building or the symbolic uses of a monument to justify their new organizations of form. They deceived themselves, these critics and artists. Their forms were sometimes undecipherable, but our initial inability to read their unknown language was no proof that it would remain meaningless once we had a clue to its word forms and vocabulary.

Take the derivation of the early Cubist forms from African sculptures. Is it not absurd here to overemphasize the form and forget the social milieu? This drawing upon Negro art for a fresh impulse was a sign of a new respect for primitive races and cultures that came in with the twentieth century. People began to realize that although the primitive African had not invented the steam engine, he had successfully expressed in his art certain primal feelings evoked by fear and death; likewise, he knew a great deal of essential lore about the erotic life, which the 'civilized' white had emptied out of himself, as Havelock Ellis's contemporary treatises on the psychology of sex were demonstrating. Remember, too,

234

the impending fear of war that ran in successive spasms through the peoples of Europe. In his admirable essay on Strauss's 'Elektra,' Mr. Paul Rosenfeld has pointed out how these terrorized mass feelings expressed themselves in Strauss's music, prophecy of the catastrophe to come. So with the rigid shapes, the barbarous heads, the deformed fragmentary images in the early Cubist paintings—the human body exploded on the canvas. Half a dozen years later, the war came, and those shattered forms were 'realized' on the battlefield.

I do not say that this is the whole story, for one may look at the Cubist's analytic dismemberment of form in still another way. The disappearance of the realistic image and the building up of a picture from a series of separate points of view have a scientific reference. This side of abstract art connects closely with Einstein's first theory of relativity, published in 1905: an announcement of a fresh way of looking at the world, in which the fixed station of the observer was no longer, as in Renaissance painting, taken as one of the main elements that determine all the lines in the picture. Do not misunderstand. Einstein did not produce Cubism any more than Cubism produced Einstein. They were, rather, both contemporary formulations of the same common facts of modern experience. Looking at it in this fashion, one may better appreciate Marcel Duchamp's original painting, 'Nude Descending a Staircase.' Plainly, it was an attempt to incorporate time and movement in a single structure. That picture is one of the masterpieces of the Cubist movement, although once it was one of the chief targets for mockery. Patently, such symbolism often failed to come off. Witness the comically feeble and pathetic painting 'Dog on a Leash' by the Italian Futurist, Giacomo Balla.

The next great contribution of the abstract painters was to prepare the eye more acutely for the new rhythms and the new spatial arrangements and the new tactile qualities of an environment that had been radically transformed by the machine. The engineer, in the course of the previous century, had often dealt with esthetic problems accidentally; occasionally he would even make esthetic decisions. But in the paintings of Léger, the sculptures of Brancusi, Lipchitz, Duchamp-Villon, and Gabo, there was a recognition of the fact that the machine had by itself profoundly altered our feeling for form. We liked hard things, finished things, accurate things, required less assurance of solidity, of static balance, and of symmetry, and found a fresh use for glass to symbolize that new world in which electric waves and light rays could pass through 'solid' bodies. The language of these new symbols has scarcely been worked out even now, but one cannot doubt its importance in projecting the new facts of our experience.

This aspect of abstract art led directly into the new machine arts and crafts, and one of the best features of the present exhibition is its demonstration of the effects of these new symbols upon typography, poster art, stage design, architecture, and furniture. —The New Yorker. March 21, 1936

A CONSTRUCTIVIST PIETÀ. Yesterday I got Gabo to show me once more his famous multiple-plane head of 1917: and he put it on a pedestal in a good light. I was glad he did so: for this time I saw, as I had never seen before, that in the right light this head was that of a Pietà, fully formed; and that by altering the angle of vision ever so slightly not merely the head but the shoulders moved.

Gabo had composed this, he told me, after his first visit to Italy; and he had intended that the head should express the composure and innerness that it actually does—perhaps unconsciously transposing to modern form some of the late medieval or early Renaissance images he had seen. He himself, however, does not remember exactly what took place in his mind when he constructed this figure: indeed, he had once asked his brother, Antoine, what had gone on then; and Antoine told him that he was intensely absorbed for months at a time, and had insisted how difficult it was to arrange the planes so that they registered equally on both sides. In some lights this head is merely a three-dimensional mask, astonishing but without human appeal. When, however, the shadows and highlights fall the right way, it is a grave but mobile human face. Yes! a Pietà: not an imitation but a re-creation.

Then Gabo showed me the stone piece he had just finished, an ovoid block with a rough form penetrating and interweaving with a smooth one. "I have a confession to make," he said with a smile: "I love working in stone. These other constructions"—and he pointed to a swirl of wires he had fabricated recently—"give me the same satisfaction only for a short time, when I am composing the image and putting it on paper: after that it is just hard work." (He thus answered a question I had always wanted to ask him: how he had the endless patience to string all the wires that make up so many of his pieces.) "But with stone it is different," he went on. "Though I have the image clearly in my mind before I begin, and there's nothing accidental about it, the whole thing is alive for me."

I made murmurs of admiration when he slowly turned the form around for me, but I could see that I had not said what he wanted to hear, for he went on to explain his purpose. "You see: I want to show in stone the difference between my kind of image and the ordinary one, which is bounded in space. For me there are many kinds of space *within* each object; and there is no single boundary, for the space inside is just as real to me as the visible space outside. Here," he pointed to the rough form, "you follow this form right into the object and see it come out again here. This is the new reality: even when one uses solid stone, one must not treat it as a solid; like all the rest of the world now, it is open and the inside is as real as the outside." —RN. September 7, 1963

SURREALISM AND CIVILIZATION. Is surrealism a passing fashion—or a new sphere of painting? Is it a variety of art or a metaphysical theory of the universe or a subversive political weapon or a series of practical jokes? Is it a meaningless revolt or a revolt against meaning? Or merely paranoia become playful? All these are weighty questions. One or two of them, incidentally, have something to do with art.

Usually, one of the easiest ways to place a movement is to ask where it began and who started it. Some say surrealism began with a group of young European exiles who sat in a café in Zurich in 1916, concocting a revolution in art called Dada (the art to end all art) at the very moment that Nikolai Lenin, a lover of the classics, was planning a revolution in politics. The two revolutions split at that point, but both were deeply in revolt against the heavy platitudes, the unctuous moralities, and the drab acceptances of the world of 'reality,' and they came together again in 1925, when everything fashionable had suddenly to prove its right to exist by showing that it was connected with Marxism. Most of the books and manifestoes that have been written on surrealism confine themselves to these Continental origins. They therefore neglect the wild surrealist element that has been present in American art and in American humor from the very beginning.

One of the great merits of the Modern Museum show is that it presents the immediate origins and achievements of surrealism against a broad background of fantastic and irrational art that goes back to the Middle Ages. Scarcely anything that has conceivably paralleled the present movement or contributed anything to it has been neglected by Mr. Alfred Barr: now a painting by Hieronymus Bosch, now a photomontage from the New York 'Evening Graphic.' The final result of such inclusiveness and exhaustiveness is that one begins to find surrealist images sticking out of every hole and cranny, and one loses sight of two or three of the great landmarks in painting that lead up to surrealism. These landmarks, though included in the show, are swamped in the weltering, dreamlike confusion of it. If I single them out, it may make the going a little easier.

The main divisions of surrealist art are distinct, but have a common foundation in the mind: the pathologically irrational, the comic, and the random unconscious. Each of these sides is in opposition to the conceptions and practical needs of everyday life; each of them stresses the private and the subjective and the whimsical, and belittles the public and the objective and the dutiful. The first, and at the moment the most engrossing, side of surrealist art begins with Goya. He etched a whole series of prints, called 'Caprices,' which for more than a century seemed only a perverse mystery to most lovers of art, prints with strange demonic figures in crazy attitudes, committing obscure follies. These prints seem to rise, like a miasma, from the murder and torture Goya depicted in the plates on the Horrors of War. Today, Goya's images recur too frequently in the photographic sections of the newspapers to be dismissed as 'unreal,' and it is perhaps no accident that a country that has known brutal irrationality in so many forms should have contributed so many leaders to the surrealist movement today—Picasso, Dali, Miró. If this were all there is to surrealism, one might justify Mr. David Gascoyne's beginning his 'Brief Survey' with Gilles de Retz and the Marquis de Sade.

The comic side of surrealism is familiar to the English-speaking world from 'Mother Goose' onward. "Hey-diddle-diddle, the cat and the fiddle," the Jabberwocky, the Yonghy-Bonghy-Bò, and the folk tales of Munchausen and Paul Bunyan have had their counterparts in an equally crazy folk art, like the china cat covered with flowers instead of fur in the present show. This part of surrealist art flourishes on the incongruous and the unexpected. It is at its best, in painting, in Dali's picture of the wilted watches, in those curious collections of objects that Roy assembles in his canvases, or in those marvelous montages of old woodcuts that Max Ernst has put together with such loving patience. One does not have to read Bergson's disquisition on the significance of laughter to enjoy this part of surrealism. Surely, the very worst compliment one can pay it, even when it is savage or sinister, is to greet it with a respectfully solemn face. If Goya contributed the sadistic nightmare, Edward Lear discovered the magical release of nonsense. (But surrealism has its practical side, too. It was a surrealist experimenter who had the courage to put sugar into a concrete mix to make it stronger.)

The last ingredient in surrealism is the unconscious. Ever since the Renaissance, painters have conscientiously been painting only what they could see with their eyes. "I don't paint angels," said Courbet, "because I have never seen one." But images of all sorts are perpetually welling up out of the unconscious: modern man, concentrated upon conquering Nature and piling up riches, penalizes daydreaming and forces these 'irrelevant' images back or keeps them from germinating; he has invented a score of contraceptives for the imagination, and then is surprised to find his life has become a sterile one. At night, however, the repressed images spring up again. These products of the unconscious are not necessarily sinister or macabre. In a more benign form, they took shape in the paintings and prints of Odilon Redon, as they had done in those of William Blake before him, and though Redon has had very little influence over the French, German, or Catalonian surrealists, the benigner unconscious activity he exhibited can be seen in the works of modern Americans like O'Keeffe and Dove.

If one judges surrealism by the esthetic and human values that lie outside it, a good part of it is rubbish; its value lies not in what it so far has found but in the fact that it has opened up the gallery of a mine which may, with more adequate tools, be exploited for more precious ore than that which has so far been brought to the surface. One of the most powerful and inventive of the European surrealists, Max Ernst, is only a moderately good painter; and if the earlier surrealist paintings of Chirico, spacious and noble in composition, still remain very fine, if Roy is always an admirable craftsman, and if Masson and Miró both have a graceful and deft touch, the quality of the paintings remains an incidental if not a negligible part of the whole movement. To judge the art fairly, one must realize that it is a symptom—a symptom of the disorder and brutality and chaos of the 'real' world; an attempt through disintegration—as in a Freudian analysis—to dig down to a point solid enough to serve as a fresh foundation. With all its praise of the irrational, there is method in the surrealist madness.

Until a generation ago, only soothsayers and ignorant folks believed in dreams. It took the genius of Freud to combine the ordinary consciousness of the neurotic with the ordinary dreams of the normal man, and to see that there was an underlying identity; *dreams meant something,* and in a sense, the more irrational they were, the more they meant. We can no longer go around pretending that the world is the same world it was before Freud gave us this clue. What we can see and measure and count is only a part of the picture. The complete picture is not so clear and not so orderly as the mind, for practical purposes, would like to have it.

This is one of the great commonplaces of our generation; and the proof is that it has made its way into literature so thoroughly that no one bothers there to call it surrealist. In Virginia Woolf's 'Mrs. Dalloway' the returned soldier, Septimus, is suffering from a psychoneurosis, and this is the way she describes his feelings: "He lay very high, on the back of the world. The earth thrilled beneath him. Red flowers grew through his flesh; their stiff leaves rustled by his head. Music began clanging against the rocks up here. . . . It cannoned from rock to rock, divided, met in shocks of sound which rose in smooth columns (that music should be visible was a discovery) and became an anthem, an anthem twined round now by a shepherd piping." Need I point out that one has only to transfer these images onto canvas to have a complete surrealist painting?

Anything that can be imagined is real, and nothing is so real as an obsession. In those words one might sum up the present attitude of the surrealists. Like every new school, they have wilfully lost sight of the historic reality which they wish to supplement or replace; they deny the orderly, the rational, the coherent, the visible. But what they are doing in fact is to widen the scope of reality. They are exploring foul underground caverns where one hears only the whir and whistle of invisible bats; they are holding the manacled hands of the prisoners in moldy dungeons; they are making their way, by touch rather than by sight, through slimy passageways that may bring them up to the surface of 'normal' life with a better comprehension of what lies beneath. Like the modern psycho-analysts, the surrealists have approached the normal by way of the pathological. That follows inevitably from the fact that the willing, wishing, urging, passionate part of man's life has been slighted, stifled, and even banished altogether in favor of practical routines. Distrusting the imagination, we let it sneak back into life only in the guise of fancy dress or an even fancier disease—just as many of us never get a real opportunity for pleasurable idleness until we find ourselves on our backs in a hospital, recovering from the birth of a baby or an operation for appendicitis.

But it would be absurd to dismiss surrealism as crazy. Maybe it is our civilization that is crazy. Has it not used all the powers of the rational intellect, all the hard discipline of the practical will, to universalize the empire of meaningless war and to turn whole states into fascist madhouses? There is more here than meets the eye. Demons, for the modern man, are no less real than electrons; we see the shadow of both flitting across the screen of visible reality. Surrealism makes us conscious of this fact, it arranges the necessary apparatus. Before we can become sane again, we must remove the greatest of hallucinations—the belief that we are sane now. Here surrealism, with its encouraging infantile gestures, its deliberately humiliating antics, helps break down our insulating and self-defeating pride. Even in perverse or sinister or silly forms, the surrealists are restoring the autonomy of the imagination. —The New Yorker. December 19, 1936

13: Literary Challenges

In grouping together the reviews, essays, articles, letters, random notes, verses—and even a dialogue!—that form this book, I have deliberately called attention to the fact that I am by profession a writer, and if I have written about other subjects than literature, I have done so in my special capacity as a writer. My 'Who's Who' biography says as much; but this has not prevented my being called an architect, a city planner, a sociologist, and even—a misnomer if not a final insult—an urbanologist. This narrow conception of my activities has perhaps arisen from the fact that many more people used to read my Sky Lines in The New Yorker, between 1932 and 1962, than have read my writings on literature and art, philosophy and religion. Yet since my generation, the generation of the Twenties, produced so many other fresh minds in literary criticism, from T. S. Eliot and Conrad Aiken to Paul Rosenfeld and Edmund Wilson, it is perhaps natural that my concern with buildings and cities overshadowed my contributions to literature. Here my reflections on 'The Golden Day' call attention to the whole movement in reclaiming the American literary past in which I played an active part, not least as co-editor of The American Caravan, from 1927 to 1936. These interests were more deeply rooted and enduring in my thought than many more urgent matters which I sought, as a responsible citizen, to grapple with. The Dialogue on Esthetics was one of a series I began in the hope of reviving this semidramatic confrontation of opposing views and ideas. But in the mid-Twenties, only Mencken and Nathan, the editors of The American Mercury, were hospitable to the classic form that Thomas Love Peacock and Walter Savage Landor had revivified. So, for lack of an assured out-

let, I turned away from the Dialogue. Who could have guessed that a generation later the Dialogue would be automatically restored as a labor-saving device, facile but undiscriminating, thanks to the invention of the tape recorder.

The Golden Day Revisited

When 'The Golden Day' came out just thirty years ago, it had one distinction that the passage of time has now deprived it of: it heralded a new attitude toward our classic American literature; for it singled out and attached a special value to the period it named. To recall this is to emphasize what a vast change has taken place in the study of the American past, and in particular in the appraisal of American values and forms during the last generation. In time, the affirmative revisions started by 'The Golden Day' were carried into the interpretation of the American contribution to architecture, painting, photography, landscape planning and urban design.

For those who are now immersed in 'American Studies,' the absence of anything like an appreciative attitude toward American literature and art before the present generation must seem almost incredible. But one need only scan earlier critical and historical texts in these fields up to the nineteen twenties to see with how many misgivings some of our greatest works of art were still regarded—or with how few misgivings they were disregarded. At the time 'The Golden Day' appeared, there were, so to say, no Vernon Parrington, no F. O. Matthiessen, no Constance Rourke, no Perry Miller, no Robert Spiller, no Makers and Finders Series, no full length studies of Emily Dickinson and William James, no five-foot bookshelf of Melville biographies, no fresh dissertations on Emerson, Whitman, Thoreau, Alcott, Poe, Longfellow, Hawthorne. Where today there is an overpopulated city of books there was then an almost virgin wilderness.

I set 'The Golden Day' within this almost empty frame with no wish to over-rate its importance: just the contrary, to explain why so modest a work could exercise the influence it actually did, from the moment when it drew such generous words from George Santayana as might easily have taken away a young writer's breath and his sense of proportion. That it did have influence, there is considerable public testimony to show, from the words of the late Professor Matthiessen on, to say nothing of many more intimate confidences. During the late twenties young people found themselves drawn back from Europe, as their forbears might have in response to Emerson's salute to Walt Whitman, because they suddenly realized that "unto us a man is born." In this case, I hasten to add, the man was not a person or a book, but a whole literature that had, up to the nineteen twenties, never been unreservedly accepted, even though individual contributions, Poe's, Cooper's, Longfellow's, Mark Twain's, to say nothing of Melville's and Whitman's, had become world famous. Until this moment, the American spirit had been kept in seclusion, like an illegitimate child, supposedly crippled, denied and half-starved by its parents, and rejected by the neighbors partly because of this very denial.

'The Golden Day' did not, it goes without saying, bring about this change. But just because it came at a propitious moment, it pointed to the new attitude and for a while possibly symbolized it. Before we Americans could recover what Mr. Van Wyck Brooks had happily called a "usable past," it was necessary to have a fresh sense of confidence in our own creativity, past, present, and potential; and this meant that we must accept some better criterion for our performance than its approximation to standard European models. It was imperative that we should, to begin with, cease our "ducking and deprecating" before foreign idols, and lift our heads, rather, to breathe the pure morning winds of the spirit that had once blown over Greylock and Walden and Cape Cod and fish-shape Paumanok.

Now this invigoration of our own natural hope and faith was what actually happened during the period, roughly, of my own adolescence, from 1912 to 1920. Who that was young then can forget that stir of excitement, when he first read the poems of Amy Lowell or John Gould Fletcher, Edwin Arlington Robinson or his younger peer, Robert Frost, or even, for that matter, John G. Neihardt and Vachel Lindsay? Who can forget the proud astonishment the young felt when Walter Lippmann's first book, his 'Preface to Politics,' appeared, or what fresh vistas opened up with Randolph Bourne's essays and criticisms, so firmly centered in our own country, yet exploring without embarrassment, indeed, with insatiable eagerness, as an equal among equals, the rest of the world? Van Wyck Brooks' voice, critical and admonitory, yet vibrantly confident, confirmed our own sense of approaching maturity: no one could say so many hard things about America as he then did who had not the impelling faith needed to resume in his own right the role of the "maker and finder." Though the first World War would blacken and blight the more tender buds, those whose minds were formed in the hopeful days before chaos dawned would, for the rest of their lives, still carry order—a human cosmos—in their hearts.

The novel, at this period, still lurched from the morass of sentimentality into an almost equally maudlin swamp of realism; yet even there, if one cocked an ear, one could detect a fresh note of high-spirited mastery: notably in an early book that was, alas! to become the high water mark of the writer's whole career. I refer to Ernest Poole's 'The Harbor,' a minor work that nevertheless took a special place in our imagination. For a while even the dry words of John Dewey, justifying our democracy by utilitarian and rational criteria, were, strange though it may now seem, part of that general sense of liberation: two leading critics of the new generation, Randolph Bourne and Waldo Frank, wrote appreciative estimates of his work. Before this, there had always been individual souls who had gone their own way and found their own heaven, no matter how solitary the path or unfashionable the destination: Hawthorne, Melville, Ryder, Eakins, Newman, Blakelock, Peirce, Emily Dickinson, Henry James; outcasts, recluses, exiles, leading lives of almost monastic devotion to their art. Indeed, when one sees Walt Whitman in his proper setting, must one not also put him, for all his bluff social manners, in this lonely group of "isolatoes," to use a telling word of Melville's? But now this alienation had ceased to be the destiny of the creative spirit: an army had gathered and was on the march.

For one decisive and altogether happy moment, these new forces, these new personalities, were mustered together in a new review, 'The Seven Arts,' a venture whose importance for all that was to follow cannot be gauged in terms of mere circulation or length of days. And even when 'The Seven Arts' passed out of existence in 1917, 'Poetry,' founded in 1912, 'The New Republic,' founded in 1914, and 'The Dial,' revamped in 1918 then refounded as a monthly in 1919, brought to a fresh focus new perceptions about the nature of the American experiment and the importance of the poet and the artist and the thinker, as a counterbalance to the over-valuation of the pioneer, the industrialist, the business man, the engineer, the representatives of a civilization plainly threatened with barbarism from within, precisely because of this naive over-valuation. Weaving through all these efforts was a precious thread, we began to think, the thread of the 'American idea'; though when, in due time, we faithfully traced that idea to its origins, we found it in Europe, and when we followed its consequences it became part of a much larger spiritual adventure than any complacent isolationist or 'Know Nothing' could take in.

The movement these reviews began was to go on in various other guises during the twenties, notably in that joint work of H. L. Mencken and George Jean Nathan, 'The American Mercury'; and perhaps I should not, out of modesty, neglect to mention 'The American Caravan,' a yearbook that owed its existence largely to the passionate convictions and hospitable esthetic interests of Paul Rosenfeld, benevolently seconded by Alfred Kreymborg and myself. This awakening to the challenge of our own scene on the part of a widely scattered group of American writers and artists gave each of us the support needed for developing our own individual powers. Though few of us had perhaps read Emerson on Self-Reliance, it was in the spirit of that essay and of the 'American Scholar' that we began to work. The days of our submissive tutelage in Europe were, for better and worse, over: this conviction formed the background for 'The Rediscovery of America,' to use the title of a book that Waldo Frank, one of the new leaders in letters, was to bestow on the movement, though for him a re-discovery in depth was even more important than the prospecting for surface ore easily carted away.

By 1925, at all events, the adolescent rebellion of the younger generation against our literary parents, and in particular against our aloof, ceremonious, seemingly solemn-faced grandparents, was over. Now that the break was definite and our independence established, it was possible for the young and the old to become friends, with delight and profit on both sides, as Frank Jewett Mather and Paul Elmer More were once so magnanimously to indicate to me. It was under these conditions that 'The Golden Day' was conceived in 1925, and born in 1926.

Now, it would be a lapse of scholarship, to say nothing of a moral blemish, if I were to say that 'The Golden Day' was the first book to usher in this grand revision of previous judgments and this instauration of the American past. The honor for that, even before Van Wyck Brooks' 'America's Coming of Age' (1915) and Waldo Frank's 'Our America' (1919), belongs to a work that antedated mine by almost half a generation: John Macy's 'The Spirit of American Literature.' This book, published first in 1912, and long available in the Modern Library edition, has achieved a kind of modest immortality; and deservedly so. Before Macy wrote, the American tradition in literature was a strangely meager and erratic one: the popular framed reproduction of Our Poets, which so roused the indignation of Van Wyck Brooks, included Bryant, Longfellow, Whittier, Emerson, Holmes, and Lowell; but Whitman rowed no oar in that galley. When Barrett Wendell, who gave one of the first courses, perhaps the only university course, on American literature at the beginning of the twentieth century, published his 'History of American Literature,' the balance of the text was poorly maintained and the tone of his judgment was often supercilious and even ill-bred. For him one sentence sufficed to cover all of Melville's work, and to damn him for "a career of literary promise which never came to fruition"; while he could find no better characterization of 'Crossing the Brooklyn Ferry' than that it sounded "as if hexameters were trying to bubble through sewage." These judgments were provincial in the worst sense of the word, like the comment of the bookseller in Dorchester who explained why she didn't keep the novels of their Wessex genius, Thomas Hardy. "You may think well of him in London, sir, but down here we have a different opinion."

Certainly it was to Barrett Wendell's honor as a scholar that he at least recognized the existence, and even the importance, of American literature; and that he explored its products more thoroughly than anyone else had done before. But it was nothing short of scandalous that he should not have applied to a Whitman or a Melville a more universal standard, which had brought them recognition from England, France, and Germany; for by 1900 even Henry James, who had once been so callowly—and callously—condescending in his review of 'Drum Taps,' loved to read Whitman aloud, and acknowledged to Edith Wharton that he was the only American worthy to be called our national poet.

John Macy's book was the first public rectification of a long series of provincial appraisals: singlehandedly, quietly but firmly, he established a new canon, which placed Whitman higher than Longfellow, Mark Twain higher than Harriet Beecher Stowe, and relegated to their position as minor writers people who had once been regarded as of major stature. So important was it to clear the forest of dead wood, so that one could get close enough to the big trees to climb them and measure them and gather their hoard of nuts, that there was a tendency, less in Macy than in those who followed him, to cut down some of the giants, too, especially if their immediate successors had crowned them with praise.

Macy's work was not flawless in judgment, for he left out Melville; but he escaped the later tendency to devaluate and debunk the great figures of our past: his omission of Melville was not a denigration but the revelation of a blind spot, singular in such a good Yankee as Macy, whose very forbears, notable among Nantucket whaling men, ought to have given him a family key to 'Moby-Dick.' John Macy's revaluation gave place, in the twenties, to a whole series of negative tributes to our classic writers; and in the case of shallower critics, professorial or popular, this attitude established a sort of inverse genteel tradition, which turned every sacred monument into a whited sepulchre. One of these humorless debunkers characterized a literary biography of the nineteen twenties as "the old-fashioned hero-worshipping sort of biography" because the biographer, after examining the subject's life with unsparing candor, still admired his work and respected his proud, battered spirit: the soul of Melville "standing alone, grim as a chimney when the house is gone."

It was no accident that the writer of that biographical study should have been myself, any more than it was that in writing 'The Golden Day' I should have proceeded further with the revaluation that John Macy had begun. No accident because, before I had read Macy or Brooks or Frank, I had embraced our classic past with as much youthful fervor—and that was not a little—as I had embraced the new poets and philosophers I beheld, from a distance, in Greenwich Village, at the Liberal Club on Macdougal Street, or at the lecture-teas given by the Intercollegiate Socialist Society when Harry Laidler and Louise Adams Grout presided over its destinies. It was precisely my sense of the present promise that made the past so vividly alive to me: the past as I heard it come forth from 'Leaves of Grass,' when I wandered with it in my knapsack over the Westchester Hills, or the past as I found it prophetically meshed in a future that had not yet dawned, in the Essays of Emerson, which I carried around in my middy blouse, in Cambridge, alternately with Plato's 'Republic,' during the summer and fall of 1918, when I trained as a radio operator in the U. S. Navy.

Even before that I had, fortunately, read a large part of Cooper, all the Leather Stocking Tales and 'The Pilot' and 'The Spy,' again and again; I was eight or nine when, happily, I began buying reprints on coarse gray newsprint, with bad type, in a sort of cloth binding for only ten cents: a week's allowance. And before I was sixteen I had, of course, read most of Poe and Mark Twain, too; indeed, Longfellow, Whittier, Lowell, Washington Irving, Poe, and Hawthorne, though not Melville, had been some part of our regular fare almost from the beginning in school. (Strangely, I find that despite the wholesale revival of interest in the American past, many of my present day students have often not made even a cursory sampling of these authors.) In Whitman and Emerson I heard the voice of close neighbors and friends; and by the time that Alfred Zimmern invited me to give a course of lectures on American literature at the new School for International Studies at Geneva, in the summer of 1925, I was ready to tell the world about both the old and the new. My qualifications for giving those lectures were certainly not those of a specialized scholar: who, indeed, apart from Carl Van Doren, William P. Trent, John Erskine and Stuart Sherman, had even modest claims to be called scholars in this field at that time? But I had a qualification that was at this point even more viable if not more valuable: I had *experienced* American literature; it was an integral part of my life, and indeed it had helped to shape that life quite as much as any more concrete day-to-day experiences.

I must emphasize the nature of this preparation, for it explains whatever may be good in 'The Golden Day,' even as it points, just as generously, to what is lacking. Neither in getting ready for these lectures nor for writing the book itself, a year later, did I do a long bout of reading, conscientiously filling in gaps in my knowledge. Though I made further notes, of course, most of these notes were reflections on matters that I had long been mulling over with no such direct end in view. Instead of reading new books to complete my knowledge of the author—at that time I had not, for example, read 'Pierre' or 'The Confidence Man' or 'The Blithedale Romance' or 'English Traits'—I re-read old ones, to refresh my judgment and deepen my insight. As a result, nothing went into 'The Golden Day' that I had not lived with for a long time and had not fully assimilated. This explains my unreadiness, which even now I do not regret, to pronounce judgment on my nearer contemporaries. What was involved was not the risk of being wrong, but the bad taste of intro- ducing a bright raw thread into a mellowed tapestry, or mixing this year's wine with an old vintage.

The fact that I had first given the substance of 'The Golden Day' in a series of lectures at Geneva was responsible for one of its distinctive features: its attempt to put our literature and our national experience in a more general setting, that which resulted from the breakdown of Euro- pean culture and the splitting apart of interests and activities and goals that had once been organically united. I still recall, with naughty plea- sure, the shock that my opening lecture gave my sophisticated European audience: particularly the effect of my polite demonstration that most of the qualities they loathed as "typically American" had had their origins in Europe. This was disarming the opponent and turning his weapon against him with a vengeance. But the book was already in its first draft before I discovered how, through the mere weight and importance of the work and personalities, I had concentrated on the period between 1830 and 1860.

That perception led me to change its original tentative title, 'Running Streams,' to 'The Golden Day.' The first title carried a suggestion of the old proverb, "running streams come clear." This in turn implied that ideas that had been muddy trickles at the beginning had, in the course of time, increased in volume and become clarified. But as I worked over the materials, I came honestly to doubt whether the work my contemporaries were creating, however excited I was by it, had anything like the central- ity and the depth that I found in the giants of the Golden Day. So I abandoned the first title and even departed from the chapter divisions in other parts of the book to emphasize the claim that I was making for this period, as in some sense a source and an expression of our highest creativ- ity: a unique moment in the American mind.

During the early spring of 1926, when I was writing the first draft of

'The Golden Day,' Van Wyck Brooks was writing his biography of Emerson. That book, when finally it was published, was to herald the change of attitude in himself which made possible the 'Makers and Finders' series. Brooks, through his immersion in Emerson, had suddenly fallen in love with our great literary ancestor and with this particular part of our past. The elation of discovering that we were, independently, striking out from different directions over the same territory, and were in our parallel movements well within sight of each other, gave a certain headiness to our correspondence during that period. Neither needed, at this point, to influence the other: we were simply held together in the same magnetic field.

In addition, certain changes in my own family life, above all our removal to a little hamlet in Dutchess County, where I was close neighbor to J. E. Spingarn, gave me a rural background not too dissimilar— and certainly no less rural—to that which Emerson and Thoreau had enjoyed. This included daily swims in Troutbeck Lake, much more of a pond than Walden Pond is, and rambles over hills and pastures more varied in contour and content than those around Concord. All this helped to give the book a kind of crystalline clarity, like the water from Troutbeck Spring, and from the mountain beyond, which of old used to be bottled and shipped to New York. As for Spingarn, he was a scholar and critic of rare quality: emancipated from pedantry by passion, imagination, and philosophic insight. Though I was never a disciple of Spingarn's in even faint resemblance to Thoreau's relation to Emerson, I enjoyed the stimulus of his challenging spirit: even his dark forebodings about the future, Melvillian in their grim unconditional willingness to face the truth, played a contrapuntal role to my own health and buoyancy, and gave me a firmer hold on reality: so that my debt to him, ultimately, in providing so much of the physical and the spiritual setting for 'The Golden Day,' was no small one. Even when we differed most about ideas and doctrines, we loved, in ever deepening communion, the quiet glories of our landscape, including an ancient oak that had probably stood in the neighboring hill pasture since before the coming of the first settlers to America. My own life at this period, then, brought me close to Thoreau, Emerson, Melville, and Whitman; and if any fragrance still hovers over my Golden Day, who can say if it blows from Concord or from Amenia?

This concentration on one period of American experience and culture may well be questioned. Certainly it carries with it the perils of worshipping a dead self, and if it provoked an uncritical adulation, or if only the hallowed dead were celebrated, I might well share the misgivings that others have sometimes expressed. But there was nothing strange or peculiar in the fact that America had passed through such a formative period: we had but repeated the experience of Athens in the fifth century, England in Elizabethan times, and Germany during that *Aufklärung,* which was also its own *Erwachen.* Nor is there anything strange in the fact that such an influx of creativity comes but once, or that whatever further developments in art and thought may take place, they cannot have quite the pristine quality that characterizes such a moment, giving to all its works a kind of resonance that cannot be reproduced later by any mere exercise of skill.

Those who wrote the great works of the Golden Day could not, of course, be sure that they or their contemporaries had succeeded; nor could they, even when they lustily heralded the dawn that was reddening the skies, be sure that their own cock crow had helped to produce it. Does it not often need the passage of at least two generations to clear up the doubt that originality, by reason of its very departures, leaves behind? Thirty years is hardly enough to silence the condescension if not total indifference with which contemporary critics too often treat the most significant work of their time. For Lowell, Henry Thoreau was only a cantankerous eccentric, so ungentlemanly as to protest fiercely against Lowell's bowdlerization of a sentence in an Atlantic article of his. But given sufficient psychological distance, the classic quality of the great writers of the Golden Day, their originality, their daring, their high creativity, could finally be recognized. By 1926, happily, that distance had at last been achieved. The present, without facing about, could at last embrace the past.

For playing a part in that general recognition, 'The Golden Day' could make a modest claim for itself, though the very nature of its leading idea was occasionally misunderstood or stubbornly rejected, even by those whose own views might seem closest to it. One critic characterized the book as a "crepuscular aubade," which may be translated as a "twilight serenade to dawn," and dismissed the dominant theme as a regressive exhibition of nostalgia. Nothing could in fact have been further from my intention, or from the mood in which I had written. It was only because the great writers of the Golden Day were still so magnificently alive, only because their work was still so nourishing, indeed so life-bestowing, that for some of us who had been brought up in an increasingly arid mechanical civilization, committed to a pragmatic instrumentalism if not to a purposeless materialism, the youth and freshness of the Golden Day were like citrus fruits offered to a crew suffering from scurvy. To draw on that source of nourishment did not drag us back into an irrecoverable past: it rather made us fit to go about the work of our day, as Thoreau and Whitman had gone about their own.

250

Yet this singling out of our five greatest writers, in the very act of correcting old distortions and injustices, was not free, perhaps, from the sin of perpetuating these errors in reverse. In measuring the great peaks of American poetic achievement, I neglected even in passing to make an estimate of the foothills; and that fact, if it established their lonely eminence, decreased their apparent height, as Pike's Peak, from the distance, seems less imposing alone than Mount Rainier, with its circle of lesser mountains that give one a better clue to its height. The fact that this was a lapse of art seems to me even more grievous than the fact that it was a defect of scholarship; for 'The Golden Day' was in no sense a factual survey of American literature, still less a close examination of individual works. Whatever merit it has comes from its interpretation and assessment of a literature already read and known. It assumes that the reader should have as full an acquaintance with the authors discussed as I had, and should be capable of correcting my judgments if I have erred, or of supplementing them if I have left anything important out of account. The emphasis is not on information but on evaluation: not on facts, but on forms and meanings: and in that sort of interpretation a significant sample may be more enlightening than the most exhaustive investigation. For me, a good book is a dialogue, and half of it is unwritten until the reader completes it. If that is true in general, it is preeminently true for such a book as 'The Golden Day.'

All too plainly, the book has flaws; but I do not count as one of the serious defects of this little study the fact that it concentrated on relationships and values, and sought to produce a unified image out of a vast welter of details. This method, one admits, did not become fashionable: quite the contrary, in academic circles it was often dismissed as superficial, if not somehow illicit, indeed, downright disreputable. Yet the need in every generation for performing this kind of inclusive generalized critical revaluation should be plain, for the mere piling up of details tends to obscure the design of the picture as a whole, thus making the smallest and least important part hold the eye so closely that one has no sense of the whole and no sense at all of relative values. This was not proper work for a specialist, but rather for one who, like myself, was dedicated to the complementary role of generalist. Those who would say, in response to this, "So much the worse for the whole" can hardly be within shouting distance of 'The Golden Day,' or, for that matter, any other work of mine; and unless they wish to lay themselves open to subversive doubts concerning their own pious certitudes, I should not commend the book for their perusal.

Well before the possibility of bringing out a new edition of 'The

Golden Day' arose, I had occasion to go through the book again, in preparing a course of lectures I offered from 1953 to 1956 at the University of Pennsylvania, under the auspices of their American Studies group. This course, called American Forms and Values, purported to go over much the same ground I had covered in 'The Golden Day.' It led me naturally to ask myself what, in the light of fresh scholarship or my own maturer judgment, I would change today. As concerns the special emphasis on the Golden Day itself I still found that I would diminish or reduce nothing; but that I would rather add and amplify, restoring for example a discarded fragment of the central chapter which had included Alcott; indeed that, even at the cost of blurring the original effect, I would enlarge the book in almost every dimension.

The most considerable change I would now make is one that I have taken the better part of a lifetime to formulate. This has brought me to a fresh interpretation of both the romantic and the mechanistic-utilitarian movements; for it seems to me that their coming together in North America created, for a brief period, a new kind of character, that which I have lately called New World man. (See 'The Transformations of Man,' World Perspectives Series: 1956.) Under this interpretation I would regard the march of the pioneer as an attempt, following the breakdown of a unified Christian culture, to find a new way out from the repetitive impasses of 'civilization' by making a fresh start on a more primitive basis. This effort, imposed by the very need to survive in the raw American wilderness, brought modern man face to face with the ancient realities of paleolithic and neolithic culture, on which the life of the indigenous Indians was based: in the New World modern man turned to the pre-civilized existence of the hunter, the trapper, the miner, the farmer, the fisherman and lived on this older level with a new intensity, as a conscious *release* from civilization—though fortified both with many civilized skills and with infiltrations of axial (Christian) morality.

Unfortunately for the ultimate success of this effort, the New World was opened with the aid of scientific and mechanical tools, from the navigation chart to the chronometer, from the rifle to the railroad; and in the pressure to conquer the wilderness and possess the continent with all possible speed, the mechanical side of New World man took precedence over the romantic side. So the new culture that the romantic writers, philosophers, painters and architects consciously aimed at, from Piero di Cosimo to Turner, from Rousseau to Emerson and Whitman, never had a chance to establish itself, though finally in the architecture of Frank Lloyd Wright the instinctual and the rational sides of New World man were symbolically united. Properly interpreted, it now seems to me, the rise and fall of New World man is a more significant drama than anyone has yet portrayed, though the pioneer himself was doubtless only partly aware of the significance of his actions and the implied goal of his efforts. There are a few hints of this interpretation in my chapter on the pioneer; but if I had fully understood the significance of romanticism, I would have included this as a fundamental side of the American mind in the first chapter, even though the image of a new kind of personality did not come forth fully until the nineteenth century, in the character of an Audubon and a Thoreau, in whom an unstable synthesis of the romantic and utilitarian elements was actually effected.

But to put this concept of New World man in its proper literary setting, with sufficient substantiating evidence, would demand something more than the re-writing of a few chapters: it would alter the whole perspective of the book. Above all, it would give more poignance as well as more significance to the pioneer experience, for there was, in this muffling of a unique opportunity, an element of wanton tragedy. The hope of making a fresh start in this new land explains the constant note of rebellion that underlies our greatest literary expressions: rebellion against the political state, against the caste system, against property, against religious ceremony and ritualism, even, in 'Huckleberry Finn,' against tidy routine and mechanical punctuality, as against every kind of cowed conformity. But in the very effort to escape the cumulative realities of the past, given in history and in memory, the pioneer chained himself to a present that had no concern for keeping alive the new values that he had experienced: so once he had conquered the wilderness he surrendered abjectly to the instruments that had made his conquest so swift—and his life so rootless. This whole aspect of American experience demands studious re-consideration; and if I ever attempted such a revision myself I could not confine myself to 'The Golden Day,' but would have to write a new book.

Even apart from this, the original framework called for reconsideration. Almost as soon as the book was out I was prepared to recognize that I had failed to treat the period after the Civil War in the same positive fashion I had treated the Golden Day: I had rather made its writers symbolic scapegoats for the crass evils of their period. Despite its sordidness, venality, and corruption, this era had remarkably continued to nourish original artists in every department. If its public vices deplorably weakened those who, like Mark Twain, were still susceptible to them— *pace* the shade of Bernard De Voto!—it also tempered the metal of those capable of standing up to the age and dissociating themselves from it, like Ryder and Eakins in painting, Sullivan and Root in architecture,

Emily Dickinson and Henry James in literature. In making mainly a negative presentation of this period I was following an unhappy precedent set by my older friend and mentor during the days of his own youthful dissidence. But Van Wyck Brooks himself was already purging himself of this error, in a profound change of spiritual polarity; and my failure to understand and sympathize with the writers of the post Civil War era was all the more flagrant, since I was myself living in a similar period.

This negative and occasionally somewhat querulous mood is what, if I were re-writing the chapters on the pioneer and post Civil War period, I would efface: not so much by deleting any particular passages as by surrounding my negative statements with more adequate appreciations.

That the creative minds of the Brown Decades were necessarily recluses, almost goes without saying: the cloister was a condition of their survival. Illness, testy recalcitrance, spiritual alienation were the price that they paid for their bare existence. Even if they raised their voices they could not be "heard" by their contemporaries; or, if occasionally heard, like Charles Peirce, they could not be understood. But note: the writers who seemed to remain most robustly in contact with their age, like Mark Twain and William Dean Howells, were perhaps in deeper retreat or more hopeless rebellion than those who, like Emily Dickinson, made themselves physically inaccessible. Mark Twain, instead of retiring from the raffish, money-ridden Gilded Age to save his soul, remained in it in order to pile the gilt on his own domestic life; and in the end that material gilt became the foundation—if I may pun about such a serious matter—of his spiritual guilt; for he ran away from his genius, and no man can look himself in the eye after doing that.

By denying his own responsibility for this act, Mark Twain earned, very properly, his own self-contempt; and to live at all, he had to transfer that contempt to an outside object, so that he projected it upon mankind at large. In 'What Is Man?' Mark Twain said: "None but Gods have ever had a thought which did not come from the outside." This renunciation of their own latent divinity, this submission to external pressures in confirmation of a failure to develop that which lay within, betrayed those who were committed to success: but it did not betray an Albert Pinkham Ryder, nor yet a Henry James. Their survival during this period of the flashy and the sordid was a more remarkable feat, morally speaking, than the development of a Thoreau or an Alcott in the earlier New England community. So when all the facts are faced, the high quality of the best work of the Brown Decades is even more remarkable than the almost effortless originality and génialité of the period that preceded it. My

254

failure to make more of this fact is one of the serious weaknesses, as I now see it, of 'The Golden Day.'

This new assessment of the post Civil War generation has, in turn, given me a better perspective on the work done by people who, with almost too-pointed emphasis, I had left out of 'The Golden Day': Whittier, Longfellow, Holmes: John Macy had taken a juster measure of these writers than I, in my high disdain of the obvious, was prepared to do. Happily time has scaled that particular cataract from my eye. How could I have been blind to the authentic indigenous note that is sounded in Holmes's entire series of Breakfast Table papers? Though this was plainly not the highest product of the New England mind, it still was a singularly original contribution. Did Holmes not make imperishable the homely urbanities of the oldtime American boarding house, that training school in psychological discrimination, with each individual the center of an unwritten novel: did he not, with his mixture of shrewd observation and worldly wisdom, create an image of our past as poignant and irrecoverable as that of the clipper ship and the covered wagon? True, the dapper little doctor could not appreciate Whitman and he was all too eagerly appreciative of the lesser products of his own wit, but that does not take away a whiff from the delectable odor of those Breakfast Table colloquies. That the Golden Day produced Oliver Wendell Holmes is in itself an important sidelight on the period.

Over my utter neglect of Longfellow, too, I would now smilingly do penance. In my reaction against my original disparagement I am disposed, perhaps, to be more appreciative than Macy was, even of those poems that made his popular place so assured. The fact that they were popular is a proof, better than the American free school or the free library, that the political democracy of the founding fathers had been able, in two short generations, to conquer the world of letters and achieve, if only at a low level, a universality that embraced other peoples. Walt Whitman saw the significance of Longfellow in that light; and it was snobbish presumption, if not worse, for a later critic to misread the lesson of Longfellow's popularity.

Plainly, many of Longfellow's most popular poems have little to commend them esthetically. But the person who can say this of the opening lines of 'Evangeline,' and of remarkably sustained passages scattered through that long poem, has no ear for their Homeric gravity, nor has he sufficient perception of the effect of the long ocean roll of those hexameters in making possible the great rhythms of 'Out of the Cradle Endlessly Rocking.' In the case of 'Hiawatha,' one must acknowledge that Longfellow's effort to use our native materials, treating the Indian as an active member of the spiritual community, could not satisfy either the literary taste or the anthropological knowledge of a later generation. But such experiments are not worthless even when they are failures: what Longfellow was thus saying and doing was, morally speaking, important to say and do. It was better to 'play Indian,' as children used to do before they aspired to the more primitive role of 'space-men,' than to shut one's mind and heart to all that we, the nonindigenous intruders, could learn from the primitive lords of this land. Here, as in Longfellow's early response to the cause of abolition, his moral sensitiveness was exemplary; and it partly offsets his tepid esthetic expression. It was our own failure as a people to follow the lead given by Cooper and Longfellow, in their appreciation of that great primitive heritage which we might have helped to keep alive, to our own benefit as well as that of the people we so wantonly neglected and despised—it was this, and not Longfellow's failures of realism that we should be critically aware of. Our Mary Austins and Paul Radins came all-too-late.

But Longfellow has other claims to our respect, as I would now interpret the development of the American mind. The first necessity of our spiritual growth was a breaking away from Europe: more especially, a weaning from the maternal teats of England. That necessity Longfellow himself quickly discerned and proclaimed, from the moment he delivered his Commencement Address at Bowdoin on Our Native Literature. In that examination of our situation he pointed out the absurdity of writing about nightingales in a country that harbored no such birds, or of falling back on foreign scenes and foreign experiences when we had our own to mind and master. It is, indeed, hardly an exaggeration to call that address the salutary opening, with special reference to literature, of Emerson's 'The American Scholar,' as Melville's essay on Hawthorne and his 'Mosses' and Whitman's 'Democratic Vistas,' are the peroration.

Up to a point the poet whose first published poem was 'The Battle of Lovell's Pond,' the poet who allied himself to the despised abolitionists shortly after Whittier and well before Emerson, who sought out the Indian, the early settler, the revolutionary patriot, the homely trades, for his themes, lived up to his own requirements—as well as Whitman's—for an American literature rooted in native ground. Here Longfellow, with Cooper, was the leader almost half a generation before 'Leaves of Grass,' 'Moby-Dick,' and 'The Scarlet Letter' were conceived. But Longfellow not merely sought to be fully at home in his own American world. He realized here, well before Henry James or Henry Adams did, how meager and provincial that world was: how much the American had lost, if not by committing parricide, then by running away from home; and how

256

useful his abandoned inheritance would be at his coming of age, so that he might start, with fuller equipment, on his own career. So, partly as a poet, but even more as a scholar, Longfellow performed an indispensable function: he restored to the American the riches that he had renounced, and the family estate he had vowed never to visit again. Once the American had cut his childhood tie to the Old World, it became necessary for the American writer to reinstate himself in the world once more, as Henry James and T. S. Eliot did: as an adult and an equal.

Admittedly, more colonial minds, servile or timid, who clung to the Old World, could get no benefit from Old World culture: the poetasters and connoisseurs who returned to Europe merely to raid its markets and old curiosity shops, and to store up, in a private museum, the loot they had brought back, were incapable of creative activity. My most astringent words about The Pillage of the Past still hold; for in fact, as Henry James himself pictured these people, in that decadent American, Gilbert Osmond, in the 'Portrait of a Lady,' their very taste and esthetic sensibilities had somehow become poisonous, and degraded their morals as well. So what I have said of Longfellow indicates in some degree what I would say, both in extenuation and in praise, of Henry James. What Longfellow sought to do, from 'Outre Mer' to his translation of 'The Divine Comedy,' became, in the stories and novels of Henry James, a source of potent creativity. There are moments when James's concern with the nonprovincial breadth of Europe was itself a provinciality: his almost morbid concern for the refinements of craftsmanship, kept him from appreciating the esthetic power as well as the human depth of Tolstoi; but in the end, it did not blind him to Whitman or Browning, as a more priggish Europeanism blinded Santayana. James's absorption in Europe, so far from being a defection or even a defeat, as Van Wyck Brooks often seems to suggest, was rather a necessary stage in our common development. What seem to me both esthetically and psychologically his maturest novels, 'What Maisie Knew' and 'The Turn of the Screw,' lose nothing by this absorption. If Hawthorne was an esthetician of sin, James was an esthetician of corruption; in fact, he turned the base common metal of the Gilded Age into gold. No one, not Henry Adams nor even Marcel Proust, gave a more detached report of the dissolution of the European spirit than James did; nor did anyone else, for that matter, give a more timely intimation of the dreadful shape of things to come. How prophetic, how universal an application, in the light of all that has happened since, seem James's perceptive juxtaposition in 'The American Scene' of "the family and the infernal machine."

This general widening of the horizon after the Civil War went hand

257

in hand with an intense absorption in the local and the regional. Here I particularly feel in 'The Golden Day' the limitations of my early reading; for this impoverished my interpretation of one element in American literature, the regional, where my own quick interest in geographic and cultural regionalism should have enabled me to make a positive contribution. Though much post Civil War regionalism was born of a nostalgia for past times and past ways, then being undermined by the forces of mechanical progress, it was also an effort at self-identification and individuation and self-actualization in which other parts of our land followed the early lead of New England. Perhaps the surest way to 'place' Mark Twain, and to center on the best he had to offer, is to regard him as emphatically a regional writer, never in his element, never capable of conveying his total sense of human existence, except in handling life along the Mississippi or in the even rougher Far West. In the local color writers the body and form of the country, region by region, at last became visible. New England, as usual, had led the way: for Hawthorne was the first to exploit these potentialities. With patience, attentiveness, reflectiveness, loyalty to something more than surface color and accent, durable works of art might have been achieved. But how easily these writers were drawn away: how quickly Mark Twain disobeyed his own precept, that one must write out of one's experience—he with his sentimentalized Joan of Arc and his Prince and Pauper, to say nothing of his Connecticut Yankee extravaganza, the most justifiable of his departures.

But in his proper role, Mark Twain was spiritually elder brother to Joel Chandler Harris, to Edward Eggleston, to Hamlin Garland, and to a group of New England women, Sarah Orne Jewett, Mary Wilkins Freeman, Louisa Alcott. The work that these people did was permanently valuable, though their technique—as in their stultifying pride in accurate dialect—might over-reach itself. The immense variety of our regional backgrounds, their very odor and savor, finally came through: without their listening ears, neither Carl Sandburg nor Robert Frost might so surely have been possible. The failure of these regional writers to establish a firm tradition, their too facile seduction by American success, itself poses an interesting problem. Whether the immediate loss of regional color can belatedly be restored by any activity of the intelligence, stemming from our regional universities, remains to be seen. In 'The Golden Day' I should at least have set the problem more clearly, instead of gliding over it.

As for other revaluations, to make them adequately I should have to do what I have firmly decided not to do: re-write the whole book, and in

258

particular to re-vamp my treatment of Edgar Allan Poe, Herman Melville, and William James, as well as bring forward Emily Dickinson. Yet I cannot withhold a word in reparation to Henry Adams; for his was a mind whose greatness smothers his moral blemishes—his arrogant humility, his cold superiority, even his ugly little streaks of anti-semitism. When one has said the worst about Adams, one must still admit that he, and he alone, had both the intelligence and the depth of intuition to see something that was invisible to most of his contemporaries: the disintegration of Western Civilization. What is more, he put his diagnostic finger on the very spots in politics, technics, and science, where the cancerous growth had begun to develop. Long before the scientists concerned were sufficiently roused from their sleep-walking routines to realize what they were in fact doing, Adams desperately tried to draw their attention to the more general transformations of society their discoveries were ushering in. He saw, if they did not, that the train of events set in motion by the accidental discovery of the Becquerel rays would, in time, threaten the structure of civilization, making "morality become police" and creating bombs of "cosmic violence."

At the time I wrote 'The Golden Day,' I was more conscious of the sociological imperfection of Adams's historic scaffolding than I was of the sound structure for which, willy-nilly, he had laid the foundations. In other words, I then shared the smug blindness of my contemporaries; and almost all that I said about Adams was not so much unjust as damnably irrelevant. Today, my contemporaries for the most part still remain indifferent both to Adams's warning and to the meaning of the present crisis in world civilization. If only because, being now awake, I can sympathize more fully with Adams's frustrations, I wish I had in anticipation done something like justice to Adams's most neglected side: the clairvoyance, as well as the scholarly historic insight, of his foreboding mind. Those who still condescend to Adams, as to a petulant amateur in science and medieval history, do not have the faintest insight into the world they are now living in. Their blindness to Adams's extrapolations derives from a more primal darkness: "invincible ignorance."

Such would be some of the emendations and additions to 'The Golden Day' I might, thirty years later, have made. But each phase of life has its own values and its own claims. I still can remember my intense resentment, as a child, when a competent old uncle, in all kindliness, would correct one of my youthful drawings with a sure touch that erased my own blurred lines. The 'improvements' seemed to me wanton and wooden, even if I envied the skill they showed. Since the lines of 'The Golden Day' are still sharp and clear, I fear that any sophisticated later touches of mine would only, in reverse, blur the whole effect, and make the book esthetically as well as historically worthless. In all decency, I would spare the young man who wrote 'The Golden Day,' that agony, and that well-justified resentment on finding his work defaced. If 'The Golden Day' is to remain alive, it will not be through a belated blood transfusion from my present self. For this reason, I have not changed a single sentence of the text. In a shifting world it is something at least to keep one's identity: that virtue this new edition still possesses. —Introduction to the Beacon Press paperback of 'The Golden Day.' 1957

Esthetics: A Troutbeck Dialogue

The corner of a library in a country house. The panel of books, the chairs and divan and table, the vase in the niche above the divan all sound the note of refined simplicity—no vulgarity, no helpless subservience to the interior decorator. The dominant colors in the room, blue, green, and yellow, are echoed by the cordials which occupy a small stand near the fireplace. With that fumbling over matches and glasses which is preliminary to settling down, the members of the group begin to distinguish themselves. They are: Charles Adams, Edwin O'Malley, Percy Scott, Ernest de Fiori, their host.

DE FIORI What do you say, gentlemen: shall we have a fire? The heating system in this house is excellent, but unfortunately our architect counterbalanced it by installing English casement windows, and after our walk this afternoon the November wind may feel a little raw.

ADAMS [*Politely*] It's really quite comfortable.

SCOTT This Alsatian quetsch is proof against November. It is the only efficient form of central heating.

O'MALLEY It seems warm enough now; but your American methods of superheating have weakened my resistance so completely that unless I am on the verge of perspiration I begin to think I have caught cold.

DE FIORI Well, suppose, we compromise on an—ahh—esthetic fire: just enough to give the inner feeling of warmth, rather than the physical effect. I see that Ellen has the kindling already laid. [*He draws a few billets from the woodbox, and Scott comes forward officiously with a lighted match.*] There! I am afraid Adams will not approve of such a fire. He will say that it is impossible to enjoy the esthetic effect without suffering the warmth.

260

O'MALLEY He is more of a moralist than that: he would say that one oughtn't to enjoy the esthetic effect without the warmth; whereas it is plainly a mark of aristocracy to keep the two things apart and to have your cake without eating it. Unless one is able to withdraw the esthetic emotions from practical life a civilized existence is impossible.

SCOTT I have always wondered what Adams's esthetic theories were. I have never been able to derive them, I confess, from your criticisms, Charles, although I enjoy your page perhaps more than anything else the 'Ancient City' prints.

ADAMS De Fiori has doubtless lighted the fire in order to smoke me out; but I don't think it's quite fair to fall on me so suddenly directly after dinner—especially after *such* a dinner. Besides, I really have no conscious esthetic theory: I recognize the esthetic interest as only one of a number of interests that are served in literature; and it doesn't seem to me the supremely important one that so many of you now make it out. My esthetics is implicit in my criticism, as is my philosophy or my psychology. I should like to use such a single canon as you, De Fiori, enjoy in your applications of Croce; but different kinds of literature seem to me to require different standards; and it is only in the realm of pure poetry that I find Croce's canon wholly justified. To dismiss the rest of literature because it is not pure poetry seems to me absurd.

O'MALLEY It's all very well to keep your esthetic from showing its bones through the flesh of your criticism: but my objection to your method, my dear Adams, is that you are not really interested in a piece of literature as such: you have always an ulterior interest in its background and you keep on asking yourself what sort of society this or that book will tend to produce. You are almost as bad as Mr. Paul Elmer More, who cannot even write about Plato without paying attention to the way in which his work may affect the Brahmins and *rentiers* of New England. The chief difference between you and More is that he has enough realism to pitch his social references toward a society which actually exists, whilst you, God forgive us, refer to an ideal community which has not yet come into existence, and in a country ruled by the *booboisie* has no chance of ever being a reality.

ADAMS [*Unruffled*] You object, do you not, O'Malley, to the fact that I believe that a community has a permanent self, made up of its best minds and embodied in its literature, as well as the shifting, temporary self which expresses itself in its daily actions and in the opinions of those who control it in the press and on the platform? I can't conceive what function you accord to literature, unless it is to embody that permanent self and make it visible. A work of literature as such has no value except to the bookworm or the pulping mill; it is only by association with human needs and desires that its values have any meaning.

DE FIORI My dear Adams: you mustn't confuse an act in the practical world with an act in the spiritual world. The values of literature lie entirely in the spiritual realm: they are independent of the society that has produced a work of art or that may be affected by it. What is it that makes the 'Divine Comedy' the glorious piece of poetry that it is? The theology? No. The picture of contemporary life, the attempt to redress the evils of the time? A hundred times No! What has preserved the 'Divine Comedy' for us in all its freshness is its complete fusion of imagination and feeling in an absolute poetic form. To judge the 'Divine Comedy' in terms of a rationalist theology like Voltaire's, for example, would be to miss all its essential beauties. That is why we must say to the critic—deal with the esthetic form by itself and prepare our minds to experience it: do not be confused by the ideas of the author, or by his *milieu,* or by whether his poem is likely to make us good or bad men; for in the realm of art these practical standards do not exist. A work of art is good or bad in terms of the author's own world. What was the writer's inner purpose, and how has he accomplished it?

ADAMS Your rule of judgment is satisfactory enough, perhaps, when it applies to a poem or a novel whose position is already established. But I don't see how it enables you to distinguish between—let me take an extreme example—between the Nick Carter detective stories and the 'Divine Comedy.' Some of the youngest critics are now rolling around helplessly in this very predicament. They have taken your esthetic counsel to heart; and they find that the author of Nick Carter perfectly fits his method to his materials, develops his theme with an unflagging logic, creates an independent world of his own, and affects them with an emotion which they call esthetic. By your criterion, De Fiori, I don't see how you can ask more of these stories as literature: from the standpoint of Pure Form they are perhaps more perfect than the 'Odyssey.' [*De Fiori makes a gasp of protest.*] Don't you see how childish it is? The esthetic value of literature is inseparable from its intellectual and moral value: your 'esthetician' is as grotesque an abstraction as the Economic Man of political economy: he is a spiritual Robinson Crusoe. The little Italian boy Samuel Butler told about, who thought that "Hey diddle-diddle, the cat and the fiddle" was the most beautiful poetry he had ever heard was a prince of estheticians; and if literature were concerned only with pattern and form Gertrude Stein would have a higher place than Sophocles.

SCOTT   Our position is not reduced to quite the absurdity you seem to think, Charles. In the universe of esthetics there are the nebulous particles of Nick Carter and the comic strips as well as the suns and planets and fixed stars; and we only say that the qualities which make Nick Carter a good piece of work at its level are what make 'Madame Bovary' a supreme work of art on another level.

ADAMS   That is all very well; but there must be a world by which the critic measures the relative importance of these self-begotten planets and particles; and this world, it seems to me, is necessarily broader than the world of esthetics. In the abstract universe of Pure Art, Edgar Poe might be a very great figure indeed: his cold metallic verses are like the notes of some thin brass instrument which admirably echoes the plutonian tears he drops over the graves of his impalpable maidens. Well, I respect Poe as a literary critic; but I have never read a single line of his poetry which could be put along-side Tennyson's 'Ulysses' without turning out to be mere pasteboard and tin-foil; and that is because Tennyson, for all his shaky philosophizing and moral squeamishness, had encompassed the realities of this world, he had lived imaginatively in a land where lovers are disappointed or suddenly happy, where children are begotten and men face the tragedy of growing old, whereas Poe remained always emotionally immature, and growth and decay and all they carry with them were left permanently outside his world. In painting, Albert Ryder had the same kind of imagination; but it was humanized and became great. An esthetic which tends to place Poe above Tennyson because of the 'purity' of Poe's poetry is a new sort of bowdlerism: it has an animus against the natural smut and obscenity of life—without which no work of art has ever endured.

O'MALLEY   Before you know it, my dear Adams, you will be telling us to read Sainte-Beuve again, and will lead a popular crusade under the banner, Back to Taine! I thought all this had been settled years ago. Literature is simply one thing; and life is quite another. Civilized people prefer to live in the world they have created themselves, rather than in the 'real' world, where boobies become great states-men, and men who cannot tell the difference between a sonneteer and a charioteer become the leaders of armies. If we must have commerce with the real world, let it be through the offices of slaves and servants; it is only on those terms that culture is possible. If De Fiori's theory compels him to accept Nick Carter, yours would force us to say a good word for Harold Bell Wright!

SCOTT [*Aside to O'Malley*] You are the most reckless sociologist of us all, Edwin: in the act of divorcing literature and life you have proclaimed a dozen contentious principles which would weld them together. Your aristocracy is as factitious and imbecile as anything else in the world: it makes no provision for the best getting to the top.

ADAMS [*Firmly, getting back to the argument*] I am not sure that "Back to Taine!" wouldn't serve my intentions excellently.

DE FIORI Really, Adams! The race, the age, and the *milieu!!* The cumbrous analysis of the climate! the manner of eating and drinking! the form of industry!—in short, the consideration of everything but the work of art itself! You surely don't ask us seriously to bring back all these impedimenta again?

ADAMS Yes and no. The means by which Taine approached English literature now seem to us irrelevant, because the fashion has changed, and it isn't done any more; but my point is that Taine's judgments, his esthetic judgments if you will, are extraordinarily just and penetrating. Moreover, I have a confidence in them that I don't at all feel with Croce when he discusses Walter Scott or Shakespeare, or, for that matter, when he discusses the work of any writers except his fellow countrymen, such as Ariosto and Dante, where his esthetic values are ballasted by all the knowledge he unconsciously draws on about Italian manners and psychology.

DE FIORI I protest: you don't appreciate Croce. Have you read his essay on Corneille?

ADAMS I bow to your knowledge, but I must maintain my point. If you miss the context of a work of art you miss its overtones: you miss the things that every contemporary experiences just because he is on the spot. The core of a great piece of literature is some universal human experience; but the core is surrounded by the pulp and skin of circumstance; and if we would reach it we must penetrate these things. When either the critic or the writer aims at form alone he becomes empty and meretricious. People have criticized 'Moby-Dick' because it is formless and full of irrelevancies; but the truth is that the irrelevancies are an essential part of its form, and had Melville attempted to reduce the bounds of his universe to the scene required for a slick story of the sea, that universe would not have been the multitudinous and terrible thing he sought to create.

DE FIORI [*Becoming the host in order to dissipate the slight sense of strain that has entered into the discussion*] And what do you say to all this, Scott? Have you become converted to Adams's creed?

SCOTT Indeed, I am in a difficult position. It is a personal convenience with me, indeed almost a necessity of existence, to disengage myself from the robust tangled world that Adams tries perpetually to draw us back to. I prefer to consider esthetics as a world apart; and my own esthetic, with certain modifications, is akin to yours and Croce's —and perhaps O'Malley's. Yet, after all, criticism must also be judged by an esthetic standard; and I feel that Taine and Adams have the better of us! They are much more interesting, on the whole, than, say, Gourmont and Croce, although their interest in art seems so much less single-minded—so much more, if I may use the word in a neutral sense, polluted with the things of this world. I think, of course, that an esthetic judgment is the final judgment about a work of art: if it is bad esthetically, its good intentions, or the amiable character of the author, or its excellent tendency, will not raise it an inch in stature. Once the judgment is formed, however, there is little to be said about a work of art; and it is too easy to rest satisfied with dialectical clichés—form, pattern, movement—which the weak critic applies indifferently to the greatest and the least. Esthetic criticism cannot elaborate the final judgment; it can only lead up to it. Adams, it seems to me, is not averse to reaching the same goal; but he does not fasten on it consciously. Confident that he will sooner or later reach an esthetic judgment, he concerns himself with the views he encounters on the road.

ADAMS You are a very welcome ally, Scott. My mind does not run to dialectics, and you have put my position in a much clearer light than I had seen it in myself—and I brush away your compliments as too palpably friendly. In turn I will admit that the method I practice is full of dangers: the by-paths are numerous, and in one's forgetfulness of the goal one may sometimes get lost in the thickets of psychological analysis or in mere biography. But I see that De Fiori still has a bolt or two up his sleeve: I fear my ordeal isn't over.

DE FIORI I feel that our minds haven't really met yet; and I find it hard to maneuver my own into position. You are quite right, Adams, in condemning the sort of critic who talks about style as if it were a veneer which could be laid on a work of the imagination; and I regret to say that in spite of Croce this purely practical side of literature—the mechanics, as it were, of expression—is being treated by some of the younger men as though it were the essence. An interest in style, in this sense, is as foreign to esthetics as typography; both exist in the realm of the practical. I would also admit that the mind that is purely concerned with art rarely rises to the level of art: it is a sort of fungus which feeds upon its own substance, whereas the true artist sends his roots deep into the soil of morality, of industry, of the practical and ethical life. The artist draws on this soil for nourishment: but the work of art rises above it and is so essentially different in character that by no examination of the soil and seed could one predict the strange shape and beauty of the flower, which is art itself. The observations and concepts of the practical life may enter into the work of art; but, entering it, they cease to be observations and concepts: they become inseparably part of the poem or drama itself. People have tried to draw the maxims of political government or a view of the universe from Shakespeare's plays. But what folly! In their artistic office, these maxims and views are embodied in Hamlet, Lear, and Julius Caesar; but they are thus no longer useful as philosophy or political sagacity; if we are interested in these things we must read Aristotle and Machiavelli. This was the paradox about art that Plato could never grasp: how Homer could speak about navigation without being a sailor, or about wisdom without being a philosopher. The artist seemed to Plato a charlatan, because he pretended to discourse with authority upon a hundred actions and experiences without having a practical grasp of any of them. The explanation of this paradox, of course, is that the artist portrays the imaginative truth of navigation or war or philosophy; and this truth remains authentic and real as long as one lives with the artist in the world of esthetic. Even Bernard Shaw, who so often has been misled by a practical interest in movements and ideas, recognizes this distinction when he puts into his prefaces the overflow of thought that has not found an esthetic channel for itself in his plays. The goal of the artist is not to be a theologian, a social reformer, or a friend of humanity: the goal of the artist is to create a work of art, and the only question for the critic is—has he created it, and what is its esthetic merit? Esthetic criticism does not use the same terms to interpret the 'Æneid' as it does to describe Walter Landor's chaste Greek fables in verse; but in both cases it dwells upon the floral rather than upon the terrestrial aspects of the work, and it leaves the latter to the pedants and philologists. The Greece of Landor and the Greece of Theocritus are, in so far as Landor and Theocritus are both true poets, the same Greece—a Greece of the poetic imagination. That Landor's happens to be the result of a

Greek revival, which turned English country houses into temples and resulted in some excellent translations of Plato and Aristophanes, whilst Theocritus' Greece was the fields he saw and the culture he shared—that, I say, is a practical accident, and it does not concern the critic. . . . But forgive me, gentlemen: one is never so much the pedant as when one attacks pedantry, and similarly I find that I am never so earnest as when I am doing battle with Adams! I apologize if I have turned an argument into a lecture. It is more than ten years since I was Professor De Fiori, but it is not easy to shake off the practices of one's guild.

O'MALLEY Oh, don't apologize: you have reduced Scott and myself to the abject imbecility of pupils who have the mingled pleasure and fear of seeing one of their schoolmates flogged; and I have so long felt uneasy at having no defense against Adams's criticism of the country in which I have chosen to live, or against his covert contempt for the sort of literature in which I am interested, that I am quite content to settle back in these cushions and cry, Hear! Hear! More power to you, De Fiori: I see that I shall have to read Croce after all in order to have the pleasure of agreeing with him.

SCOTT [Hastily turning to Adams] There speaks the voice of envy, Charles. Let us thank heaven, however, for the miracle that reduces O'Malley to silence, and get back to the discussion.

ADAMS I find myself so much in agreement with what you say, De Fiori, about art that it seems a little ungenerous and pedantic to dwell upon what you don't say; and yet this, I think, is one of the chief differences between us. To begin with, I can't accept the Crocean divorce between the practical and the esthetic or ideal: it is a dialectical subterfuge, and its sole effect is to embarrass criticism with tautologies. Soil, seed, plant, and flower are one in life, and I would take the metaphor over bodily and say that they are one in literature: cut the flower away from the plant and it soon ceases to be a flower. Art can grow and reproduce and scatter its seeds in the hearts of men only when the conditions in what De Fiori dismisses as the practical life are favorable. The good critic is therefore a gardener who pays attention to all the conditions that environ the production of a work of art. It is only when he has secured the best possible conditions in his own community that he is free to taste and enjoy, and to lead others to this pleasure. By reducing criticism to esthetic commentary you do not necessarily further the aim of art: you may merely further the method of dialectics. If you will forgive me for saying so, De Fiori, I find nothing in Croce except an interesting critic of criticism: his appreciation of Shakespeare is singularly barren and banal. Croce's method, perhaps, enables him to avoid the dialectic pitfalls into which Frank Harris fell headlong when he wrote his study of 'The Man Shakespeare'; but it was Harris's book, and not Croce's, that sent me back to Shakespeare with a fresh set of perceptions and appreciations which, so far from being external, added to the intrinsic enjoyment of the poetry itself. From my point of view, Harris's criticism is better than Croce's. And, as I said at the beginning, I feel that the esthetic element in literature is over-rated. Literature, after all, is an avenue to many different experiences; and I sympathize with the English critic who complained that Mr. Leonard Woolf had praised the esthetic success of 'A Passage to India' without once saying that it was at the same time a profound study of Indian life! The true critic, it seems to me, must concern himself with the whole life of the mind, and in life, all the qualities that go into a work of art interpenetrate and mingle.

DE FIORI Ah! we have made a brave effort to meet, Adams: but I fear we are back again at our original positions, and are as far apart as ever. We use different words and we talk about different things. I daresay we share equally in the fault.

SCOTT [*Concealing a yawn*] Precisely! Discussion never gets one anywhere; at most it shows more clearly where one stands. I see you have an esthetic theory, after all, Adams: its only trouble is that it sets too low a value upon esthetics.

DE FIORI I do not mean to be abrupt: but do you realize, gentlemen, that it is three o'clock? What do you say to a night-cap of Scotch? —American Mercury. November 1924. Troutbeck Leaflets, No. 3. 1925

Note: Though the original dialogue took place at Troutbeck three years earlier, it is a fair recapitulation—without notes—of our discussions. De Fiori is of course, J. E. Spingarn, O'Malley is Ernest Boyd, Adams is Van Wyck Brooks, while Percy Scott is more Clarence Britten, my old Dial friend, than I, who secretly lurk behind both De Fiori's and Adams' opinions.

On Literary Styles

I have read and re-read your letter on my literary style at intervals throughout the day, dear Van Wyck, immensely stimulated by part of it, encouraged by another part, made full of contentious thoughts by another, and finally, downright startled by one of your suggestions, so much so that I rubbed my eyes and wondered whether you could be saying what you seemed to be saying, and if so, how this could be? But whatever my reaction to it was, your counsel was disarming—how could it have been otherwise?—and such frankness as you expressed was the proof of our friendship, which I shall try to deserve by equal frankness on my own part, as I continue the discussion.

Let me begin by dealing with the problem of style; for I think you may have misunderstood something that I said about the style of my later books as compared with the morning freshness of 'The Golden Day.' I do admire the ease, lucidity, and pith, the apparent effortlessness, of that book, just as I would admire the body of a beautiful young athlete, aged twenty, and compare my own present form unfavorably with it. But the grace of youth, good in its day, is not necessarily to be desired in middle age, which in its strength and toughness and hoarded experience has other virtues. This, it seems to me, applies to literature as well as to bodily organs. There are parts of 'Technics' or of 'The Culture of Cities,' a smudgy paragraph here, an overlabored thought there, or a too facile technical vocabulary in another passage, which call for improvement: some of this was due to fatigue at the moment of writing, or to a desire for brevity even at a sacrifice of beauty. Those passages I shall be zealous in correcting when I come to revision.

As for the style of the series as a whole, it seems to me to be, like every genuine style, a natural and proper expression of the contents. If it is complex, it is because the thought is of the same nature, not wilfully, but because a multitude of different themes cannot be woven together without achieving a certain complexity of form—just as a symphonic form is more difficult to follow than a melody carried by a single voice. The difficulty lies less in the writing itself than in the nature of the thought. Many people who declare that I am "unreadable" really mean that I am "unthinkable"—and by that they mean that they have no desire to follow my thoughts or at least not enough patience to do so. People who are sympathetic to what I am saying and prepared to go along with the thought often characterize as plain spoken and even brilliant the very passages others look upon as obscure and dull; and I think that in time much of what I have said will seem elementary and obvious to a generation better prepared for the thought itself.

To have achieved a different style with these books I would have had to approach the whole series with a different intention: that of making it a purely literary work of art along the classic lines that you commend. Whether I should have done this is an arguable matter, and I will discuss it with you presently. But by the choice I originally made, I addressed the series to those who had some learning and 'background' in the fields covered, who were at home in the realms of science and philosophy as well as literature, and who yet lacked certain elements of humanist discipline that I, by reason of my varied heritage, could bring to the subject.

Writing for such an audience it was inevitable that my language should be a little less 'pure' than it would have been if addressed to the cultivated general reader alone: some of the technical words for example are excusable only as masonic high signs, telling those who know the literature that I am familiar with their subject and have read the same essential texts as they have. But is this altogether a defect in the twentieth century?—even though some of the new words will wear thin quickly and vanish! If a writer is to win over to his cause those who are hostile, because of their specialized learning and narrow interests, he may well try to close the gap between him and them, provided he doesn't thus make himself unintelligible to the general reader. Where I have in fact been unintelligible—and I don't doubt you could finish such places—I have, on my own terms, sinned . . .

But now, as to the nature of the book itself, since this is the true determinant of style. The books in this series have affiliations with the more traditional writings in these various fields; but they resemble still more closely a new kind of writing that grew up first in the nineteenth century: a species represented by 'Moby-Dick' and by William James's Psychology, in which the imaginative and the subjective part is counterbalanced by an equal interest in the objective, the external, the scientifically apprehended. This is no shallow fashion; and my recourse to science is not merely an attempt to make people believe what I say, by backing it up with scientific statements, as you suggest.

Far from it. What lies behind the new method is the conviction that personal experience and personal intuitions, however sound, do not carry full weight until every effort has been made to square them with what William James called "hard, irreducible facts," meaning by that results that have proved valid in experience for all sorts of different observers, *partly in consequence of the application of the scientific method.* I would not say that this is altogether a new attitude or discovery: Aristotle had it in his writings, though he had to do the original work in science as well, before he could use it as a confirmation of his own intuitions. But this combination of personality and individuality with impersonality and collective research is what, it seems to me, characterizes the best thought of our time; and though it demands a mighty effort in the thinker—and perhaps an equal effort in the reader—the results promise well and will ultimately justify themselves by their effect on larger issues.

You are wrong, however, dear Van Wyck, when you suggest that what offends you in my style is the result of my reading scientific books too exclusively "for years." My reading has *not* been of this one-sided kind; the only period when I was immersed in scientific writers (as a result of my interchanges with old Geddes) was back in the early twenties, when my style, because of my more simple and superficial methods, was much closer to the moralists whom you advise me to imitate! The question, then, is whether my purpose in writing my major series, for a relatively limited audience was unsound? Perhaps it was, but my own justification would be that, if one has new thoughts to express, one had better get them out in some form, even if only a handful of readers understands them entirely in all their complexity and depth, than to seek to avoid complexity and depth in order to satisfy the many—thus leaving the few without the best one had to give them. This, at all events, is the assumption on which I have written these books.

What your counsel does for me is to make me ask whether, now that I have accomplished this part of my intellectual mission, the time may not be at hand when I should alter the pattern and seek more direct contact with a larger body of readers. This is a very timely question for me because, as I may have told you, my next book will probably be on Love and Marriage; and though inertia might lead me to handle the theme as I handled the other books, a fresh decision might create quite a different kind of book. (There was a moment when I thought I could handle 'The Conduct of Life' as a poem!) So in one sense, though I reject so much of what you say in criticism of my style, to another part I am deeply receptive—and in both cases grateful.

Perhaps I have said enough by now to show you why I don't regard your remedy, a bath in the ancient and modern moralists, as a "cure" for what seem to you defects in my style. But it may be that there are fundamental literary differences between us as to what constitutes a good style. And my first answer would be that, since style is organic, no single style is a good one for all occasions; from which it follows that a style that is too definitely that of the humorist or the moralist, the literary man or the scientific man, because it contentedly hugs its own limited boundaries, is a handicap to expression. Though I have not pleased you by my efforts, I have never been unconscious of style or careless of it: I have sought, rather, to find the right mood and accent and rhythm for each new book. For that reason a pamphlet like 'Men Must Act' is different in style from 'The Culture of Cities,' written a little earlier, and from 'Green Memories,' where, returning through the subject matter itself to youth, I recovered quite naturally the properties of 'The Golden Day': a fact that must, unless I err, keep you from damning the style of my later years, as if it were cast in a single mold. For me the single mold is the sign of a bad style—even if the mold itself was, for one particular purpose, a sufficient one. You passed over 'Green Memories' in your essay, I think; yet at least from the standpoint of *style* it deserves consideration.

. . . But there is still another reason why I found your prescription to read the moralists a strange one, dear old friend. Whom on earth do you think I read every day of my life? And whom did I read attentively and exhaustively, day after day, in preparation for 'The Condition of Man' and 'The Conduct of Life,' for a period of six or eight years? Perhaps I am incapable of profiting by them sufficiently; but though I never expect to leave off reading them, there is nothing fresh for me to get from Plato, Aristotle, Lucretius, Epictetus, Marcus Aurelius, Confucius, Lao-tze, and the rest of them; while except for a few Frenchmen, like La Bruyère, I know the latter-day moralists from Montaigne on equally well. What I have gotten from them and found usable is distilled, for the most part, in 'The Conduct of Life'; and all that you are doing in suggesting another book on morals is to demand that I write 'The Conduct of Life' over again, in another form! It was at that point that I raised my eyebrows. They are still aloft . . . —Letter to Van Wyck Brooks. January 22, 1952

14: Modern Biography

These reflections on the nature of biography were a later overflow from the writing of my study of Herman Melville, and took account, too, of some of the things I had learned in contemplating my own life during the period that followed. Though this essay came later, it leads, by way of Vossler's study of Dante, into the notes I have grouped under 'Melvilliana,' and opens the door wide on the crucial events in my own personal life which, it turned out, were to reconstitute and energize all my later work, beginning with 'Technics and Civilization' in 1934—the first volume of 'The Renewal of Life' series. Dante's passionate but Platonic love for Beatrice has no parallel in my own life; but Karl Vossler's exhaustive study of the life and work of Dante furnished a timely demonstration, for me, of the way in which, given enough time to sift all the evidence, one can do justice to the whole man. Thus both Dante and Melville are necessary links in the story of my own life.

The Biographer's Task

The writing of the old-fashioned biography was a relatively simple matter. The subject was a homogeneous unit, an individual. He had been born at a certain date, had gone through this or that experience, and on dying had left behind two invaluable things: a set of papers and letters and a well-modeled clay mask called a 'character.' To sift the papers, to put the letters in order, carefully expunging words of questionable taste or opinions which were not 'in character,' and to cast a bronze effigy from the clay mask—this was the main task of the biographer. In an excess of piety he would often gild the bronze head; but it was a rare biographer who, like Froude, questioned its correctness or sought to present an image closer to life; and his contemporaries repudiated such skepticism with horror, even when, as was the case with Carlyle, they had reason to admit its truth.

The task the modern biographer has chosen is so much more complex than that of his predecessor that one does not wonder that there are timid critics who are shocked by the dangers it presents, and who loudly proclaim that the whole duty of the biographer is to verify and set down 'the facts.' What they mean by facts are such data as the old-fashioned biographer uncritically used. But this demand is a good deal like that of the simple-minded moralist who believes that all the ethical dilemmas of life are neatly solved by obeying the injunction to be good. What *is* good? What *are* 'facts'? What relation do they bear to the life that they punctuate? By what principles are the facts themselves to be selected and ordered? The hard-boiled exponent of 'facts' offers no answer to these questions, because he is not acute enough even to ask them.

Let us first dispose of the notion that the facts of a life, the recorded sequence of events, are the sole business of the biographer. The facts of any life are the sum total of its experiences in living; they comprehend all that the subject has ever seen, felt, sensed, touched, heard, remembered, or otherwise encountered. Plainly, then, no one-to-one relation can exist between a life and even the most exhaustive biography; indeed, no one has even been able to know his own life in this fashion. It would need another super-Boswell, serving as a recorder from moment to moment, to set down this experience; and at that, a good third of it, what transpired in sleep and dreams, would be pretty well lost to the observer.

The nearest approach to this complete kind of biography has been, perhaps, the autobiographical notes of a Montaigne, a Samuel Butler, an Emerson; but even here it is the conscious, intellectual life that is chiefly portrayed. In introspection and reflection our experience is inevitably foreshortened. Did not Joyce take a whole volume to describe even a day in the lives of Stephen Daedalus and Bloom? Try as we will, we cannot grasp more than a fragment of the totality of our living, for to grasp the whole would be to live the whole over again, and that would require another lifetime. By force of circumstance, then, all biography is selective; it is based, not on all the facts, but on such facts as seem, from one standpoint or another, to be significant.

But there is another difficulty that dogs biography. Like the book of evolution as Darwin once so graphically described it, most of the pages have been lost and what remains is barely decipherable. There is no necessary connection between the important events of a life and the records of it that have been preserved in memory, in documents, in memorials, or in living testimony. The biographer must compose his life of what he has, just as the archeologist must restore his temple or his statue with such fragments as thieving time and careless men have left him; but fate often ironically leaves him a well-preserved leg and a dismembered torso, while the head, which would supply the main clue to the body, is missing. Hence, in addition to the purposive selection exercised by the subject himself and by the biographer in making use of such materials as are left, there exists a purely external selection dominated by chance, which cuts across the evidence in an arbitrary fashion. To correct for such distortions the biographer must be an anatomist of character: he must be able to restore the missing nose in plaster, even if he does not find the original marble. It will not be the authentic organ; but it will help cement the face together. To make such restorations the biographer must be a historian as well as a student of the individual; he must know, at a given moment, in a given habitat, what would be the probable color and shape of a missing part. If he have no clues, the good biographer, when he leaves such a detail out, will at least call attention to its absence.

There is, however, a favorable side to this lack of major data that so often confronts the biographer, and this is the fact that to a sufficiently perceptive eye no datum is altogether insignificant: in understanding a civilization, a rubbish heap may disclose as many important things as a palace, and the mere débris of an individual life may take one farther into the core of it than the most outstanding events. A chance letter written to a friend on the eve of a marriage may be a more significant clue to the marriage itself than all the testimony that contemporaries who observed the marriage will bring forward. This eye for the little, this fine sense for infinitesimally small quantities, this perception of the significance of the insignificant, is one of the distinguishing marks of modern science, and the minerals and vitamins in diet have their equivalent in the writing of a modern biography. Perhaps the most expert user of such data in America is Mr. Thomas Beer: his Stephen Crane and his Mark Hanna both gain in psychological richness by reason of his uncanny perception of the value of stray bits of evidence that usually remain below the threshold of most biographers' consciousness. If in part this method is derived from science, or rather has developed parallel to science, it has been reinforced and amplified by the work of such a novelist as Mrs. Virginia Woolf. It implies a respect for events that do not stand high in the conventional scale of importance.

But in addition to the essentially fragmentary nature of the data of even the most completely documented lives, there is still another difficulty in writing a modern biography. We can no longer be content with depicting the shell of outward events, with using merely those materials which were open to everyone's inspection. There is a partly independent, partly autonomous, partly unconditioned inner life that must also be examined and revealed; and much of this inner life is as obscure to the subject himself as it is to the person who seeks to understand him. Long before Freud, an able English esthetician named Dallas, in a book called 'The Gay Science,' had called attention to the importance of what he called "the hidden soul," and before him Emerson had said, Tell me what your dreams are and I will tell you what manner of man you are. But the notion that the hidden life of the unconscious, welling up in dreams, obscure impulses, secret promptings, was coeval with the more orderly forms of waking consciousness and partly conditioned them did not make its way very speedily into biography. Novelists like Meredith boldly dealt with such phenomena long before the biographer dared to handle them.

And no wonder; it complicates the biographer's task enormously. The old-fashioned individual, that creature of reason and sobriety and deliberation, was like the Newtonian universe; the 'new' individual, on the other hand, is as difficult to conceive and to explain as is the modern universe of physics. For the sake of practical convenience, the biographer, like the working engineer, is sorely tempted to limit his investigation, so to say, to Euclidean space and Newtonian motion; but to do this he must ignore the fact that his subject now, in certain relations, behaves like a moving particle, and in certain others like a wave—now he is a rational being, and now an explanation which should assume his continued rationality will throw the entire picture into the most spotty kind of confusion. The new subject of biography has both surface and depth. The biographer who is not aware of this unconscious element, who does not seek to penetrate it, or, worst of all, who deliberately ignores all the special data that it heaps up, is guilty of ignorance or childish cowardice; and when he exhibits this cowardice under the cloak of sticking closely to objective facts alone, he is adding error to his original weakness, for a dream or a fantasy is as much an objective fact as a bag of gold or a blow on the head.

The courage to resort to this inner world, and to that remoter part of it, the unconscious, in order to interpret the objective facts of a career was displayed in American biography by Mr. Van Wyck Brooks in 'The Ordeal of Mark Twain.' Brooks sought in the inhibitions, the constraints, and the terrors of Mark Twain's boyhood for a key to his later mediocrity and frustration, despite the eminent talents he obviously possessed. Brooks's analysis of Mark Twain's inner development has been challenged by Bernard de Voto, who professes to find the whole clue to Mark Twain's life in the frontier environment in which Mark Twain spent his early days: but unfortunately such a broad environmental explanation does not account for the fact that the same forces which produced the amiable Mark Twain also produced the diametrically opposite and no less typical character of Ambrose Bierce. And the point is that even if in detail Brooks's psychological analysis of Mark Twain is subject to correction, the effort itself was fruitful. It is better to make mistakes in interpreting the inner life than to make the infinitely greater mistake of ignoring its existence and its import.

If our overt and conscious life were the simple expression of the hidden and unconscious impulses, one might, without forfeiting anything except the primitive richness of experience, accept a careful exposition of the first as a sufficient symbol of the second. But unfortunately the conscious and the unconscious are only fitfully in harmony; frequently they are in conflict and elements that are unresolved in action and expression are thrown back into the unconscious and assume disguises there, or, in the reverse direction, they escape from the dark into the light, like a prisoner from jail, by being concealed under the petticoats of an apparently naive impulse. One cannot help seeing the excessive purity of Dickens' heroes and villains as a relief from the intolerable complexity of his own moral dilemmas, caught as he was, in his relations with his wife's sister, between his own impulses and actions and the strict Victorian code upon whose observance he had built up his vast reputation as a writer of 'Household Words.' Life, as he knew it, had no such whites, no such blacks; and his novels were emotionally adolescent because he could not, in print, face the man that he was or disclose the realities of life as he knew it. Because of the importance of the hidden life in interpreting the fullness of any character, there is a natural tendency, upon the part of those who espouse this method to use men of letters for their subjects; for, unlike the statesman or industrialist, limited by external affairs he dominates, the writer projects his subjective life in letters, poems, novels, plays, and however great or elaborate the disguise, the essential materials are there.

One of the earliest, as well as one of the most daring, of all such attempts to read from the objectified fantasy, the play, or the poem back into the life that produced it was Mr. Frank Harris' study 'The Man Shakespeare.' This biography exhibited at the same time the dangers of the method, for it can be used with impunity only when the biographer's guesses and interpretations can be backed by a body of independent data, not derived from the works of art, which must serve—intermittently if not constantly—as a means of checking up these excursions into subjective events. The complexities are baffling; the dangers are inescapable. But it is merely a prejudice of thought to believe that clearness, accuracy, and certainty have any necessary connection with truth and reality. While the biographer must aim at all these things, he must likewise acknowledge data which introduce an obscurity, a confusion, a certain number of unresolved contradictions, into his final portrait; and a biography which loses internal unity by reason of these unassimilable facts may be in closer accord with the actualities of life than a tidy narrative cut in one piece.

There has been still another outcome, for biography, of this desire to build up a four-dimensional character, in which the hidden motives and the devious passages of the inner life will be dealt with as zealously as the more obvious events. The removal of the moral mask has become one of the main tasks of the school whose most distinguished exponent was the late Lytton Strachey. In this biography the point lies in the contrast which is deliberately created with the old-fashioned biography. Strachey took a 'noble' life like Florence Nightingale's, an 'adventurous' life like Chinese Gordon's, and sought to show the essential nature of the naïve impulses that often lay sealed in the apparently consistent and harmonious envelope of the public character.

In Strachey's original essays in biography there was obviously a certain *Schadenfreude* in poking open the stuffed reputations of the Victorian deities and in applying the tiny candle of rational analysis to their waxen nobilities. But Strachey was too good a biographer to lose sight of the realties of the life itself, and in the single case of Queen Victoria it is notorious that he came to scoff and remained to pray, or, at all events, to sympathize and to understand. Strachey's many imitators, unfortunately, saw in his ironic method of examination only an instrument for increasing their own self-esteem and that of their generation. Seeking to deflate—their word was "debunk"—the extravagant reputations of the past, they often completely neglected the realities upon which they were founded. Besides, they lost an important clue. The mask itself is as important an aspect of a life as the more devious tendencies it conceals. To tear off the mask and to throw it away was a little like tearing off the face of a clock on the hypothesis that if one wanted to tell time correctly one must get nearer to the works; it abandoned the very part of the instrument that recorded the action of the works.

And again, the a priori notion that all noble attitudes were false, the notion that anger was unreal if one could explain it physiologically by the release of adrenalin, or that love was imaginary if it were also related to the functions of the hormones and the glandular system, prevented the lower type of biographer from understanding the integration of a character or the development of a harmonious life out of the original welter of animal impulses, instinctive desires, projected wishes, and purposeful abnegations and controls. So that, paradoxically, the attempt to strip off the moral mask usually led, not to a clear reading of the character, but to the building-up of a sort of negative moral mask, as artificial and arbitrary as the one that it replaced—or rather more so, because the original mask was a work of art produced by the subject himself and it bore his own veritable imprint. This misconception of the task of the modern biographer is so common today that one recent biography was characterized by a professor of literature as an "old-fashioned hero-worshiping biography" merely because the author, though he had revealed unsparingly all his subject's weaknesses, had nevertheless preserved a sentiment of respect for his character and his achievement!

The biographer's task, plainly, is neither to praise nor to blame, neither to glorify nor to deflate. His business is to approach as closely as possible the life he is describing, to take advantage of the psychological distance that time and a different frame of values give him, and thus to make explicable the inner and outer events that formed the character, shaped the destiny, and made the life significant either to his own contemporaries or to us or to that timeless society which includes past, present, and future generations. The ultimate result is necessarily selective, as even the purest mirror or the most faithful photograph is selective—if only because the size of the picture and the distance from the image place a direct physical limitation upon what can be shown. But if the biographer has worked well, the biography will be a concentrated symbol of the subject's life; and even forgotten or concealed events will be implied in those that are presented.

There is one final thread that enters into the modern biography, and this is the society and the landscape in which the subject moved; for, like all forms of life, he was in part a creature of his environment, and characteristics which might seem specific and distinctive if taken alone become generic and communal if considered in relation to a particular place or tradition. The relation of the personality to the social milieu is perhaps one of the most delicate tasks set before the modern biographer; for the temptation to explain specific traits or events by references to large general influences is as often as not a disguise for laziness or psychological incompetence, and this mars the interpretations of even such a great critic as Hippolyte Taine. Even the most solitary character, a Leopardi shut up in a castle, a Hawthorne confined to a Salem house which he leaves only at night, takes in, almost out of the atmosphere, traits, attitudes, interests, and beliefs which mark him as a product of his society and his age—and of no other. One of the soundest and most effective reconstructions of a geographical and social environment was that in Carl Sandburg's description of the Prairie Years of Lincoln: he not merely explained Lincoln but gave the quick, immediate taste of his life.

To create a real character and to portray him against a mere conventional background of painted canvas and makeshift stage props borrowed from a local costumer is to falsify every word and gesture of the character himself; for what is living derives from the continuous interaction of an organism with its environment, or rather, the actual person with his entire world. To neglect the environment is just as bad an error as to forget the organism in which its forces are momentarily concentrated. But the term "environment" must be taken in its widest sense. It means not only the soil itself, but the people living on it; not merely teachers, family, friends, but the economic class, with its special array of traditions, hopes, and prejudices; not merely the physical scene, but the social heritage of ideas, and that more diffused subjective environment which I have elsewhere called the 'idolum.' So that, finally, the ontogeny of the individual's becoming crosses the phylogeny of his species; and the good biographer, who wishes to seize and penetrate a particular life must also be a historian conscious of the entire fabric in which this life, no matter how great, how original, how significant, is only a minor figure in the pattern. To achieve such complete knowledge, to arrive at such an exhaustive interpretation, is to aspire toward an unattainable goal. But the modern biography will fulfil its purpose to the extent that the biographer is aware of the depth, variety, and complexity of his task, and moves forward along the various roads I have indicated. —The English Journal. January 1934

Dante as a Contemporary

Dante Alighieri seems at first blush the most distant of poets. Homer's world, with its fights, quests, brazen deities, capricious doxies and strong vain men, is so near it can easily be dished up as a popular novel. Horace makes his bow in the newspaper columns; and Hamlet in modern dress might be a young man under the care of a psychoanalyst. The things that separate us from Horace's Rome or Shakespeare's London are decorative and topographical, in great part; and with one step of the imagination we surmount them.

Dante is not so easily approached, for he belongs to a different spiritual organism, and we might visit his Florence a score of times, and saturate ourselves with the physical images of his contemporaries and their buildings, without penetrating the body of which he was so typical and potent a member. His world had a dimension which even the most orthodox can now keep before himself steadily only by a rigorous effort: it had the dimension of eternity, and its rapid, brawling, turbulent life was dwarfed by the shadow of another world. Life was, at best, a dying, and death, even for the damned, was the beginning of one's essential career.

The credulous marketwomen of Verona who believed that Dante could descend at will into hell, and pointed to his smoky complexion for proof, exhibited, but scarcely exaggerated, the closeness of the natural and the supernatural during the crowning years of medieval culture. The realm toward which Dante's vision was directed in 'The Divine Comedy' had been described with the same sort of authority that now convinces us of the existence of electrons or the efficacy of germs in producing disease; and no one suspected in his time that the body of dogma upon which it was founded could be successfully assaulted, or, what is even more serious to the orthodox, could simply be ignored. Life existed, for Dante, within a vast Necropolis: to understand the Hereafter, and to portray it, was an immediate and objective task.

When one has said this much about Dante and his times one realizes that the breach between him and the modern reader is so great that the intuition of his poetry, though always the surest approach to his mind and spirit, is not enough for real comprehension. If 'The Divine Comedy' is to mean something more definite than music, or music accompanied by pictures, we must make ourselves contemporaries of Dante. Is the effort worth making? Assuredly; not merely because we shall enlarge our enjoyment of poetry, but even more, perhaps, so that we may understand ourselves. Foreign travel gives one a perspective upon one's home; and there is no country today whose customs and modes of thought are so strange as the Eternal Realm in which Dante lived and moved.

Fortunately for us we have a Virgil to guide us through this labyrinth, a scholarly Virgil, Karl Vossler, whose monumental study of 'The Divine Comedy' has just been translated into English. The American title of his work, 'Medieval Culture,' is an accurate one, for Dante was the creative embodiment of the entire culture that preceded him, and that culture, we now perceive, had its roots deep in the ancient world, its notion of heaven and hell being derived from the Persians, its idea of the Logos, the immanent principle of order, being Greek, while its historic acceptance of a redemptive Messiah was, of course, Jewish.

How Dante came by all the materials that enriched his mind and personality is the first or proximate object of Vossler's study; what Dante made of these things in his great poem is his final goal. His discourse sweeps, with epic reach and breadth, toward these two ends. After all the weak outlines and simplifications the last decade produced, it is a great joy to embrace a work of real scholarship which is also a living synthesis. Of very few books can one say, with even a faint touch of justice, that to read them is the better part of an education, and yet this work of Vossler's deserves such a description, if any single work deserves it. The crucial problems of philosophy, religion, ethics, politics, the outlines of ancient and medieval literature, the origins of modern language and poetry, the psychological penetration of the poet's task and character, and, finally, the explication of 'The Divine Comedy' itself are brought together in an impressive unity.

Too well do we know the kind of minute scholarship which, like the mole, turns over the ground so exhaustively and raises such a prodigious molehill that the living plants under which it has burrowed are left uprooted and lifeless; that scholarship which aridly fulfills itself in the preliminaries of investigation and never by any chance reaches or appreciates or infects anyone else with a love for the work it has chosen to expound. Mr. John Jay Chapman in his ingratiating study of Dante, has wisely railed against such tedious intrusions, saying: "The truth about religion and the fine arts can only be expressed in terms of religion and the fine arts." It is such an order of truth, no barren, extraneous erudition, that Karl Vossler displays in his 'Medieval Culture.' He comes to Dante by a hundred different paths, and each of these excursions has an independent import; but the supreme interest of all is Dante and 'The Divine Comedy,' and once he reaches the poem he casts aside the impedimenta that have been so useful on the journey.

How is one to summarize the richness of Vossler's study? It begins with a comparison of Dante and Goethe, which may well be placed alongside Mr. Santayana's perspicuous essays, and goes, with apparently effortless mastery, into all the conditions and dilemmas of medieval thought, life and ideality. There is no way to convey Vossler's achievement except to say that he makes one a citizen of Dante's world; doing this, he prepares one for that tumultuous and passionate experience of life whose molten stream, not free from the scum of personal animus, was finally poured into the rigid mold of 'The Divine Comedy.' Vossler does not arbitrarily separate 'ideas' from the poetry, or 'structure' from intuition; 'The Divine Comedy' becomes, under his interpretation, a resolution of all these discrete elements, Dante's life among them, into a final whole.

One cannot, however, too often repeat that the unity which the Middle Ages boasted and which Dante supremely exemplified existed most visibly in art, and only partly in the conglomerate experience of daily life. It is in the dead Middle Ages of our ignorance or obtuseness that the Realists always triumph over the Nominalists, that the Thomists uniformly defeat the Averroists, and that orthodoxy prevails over paganism and heresy. In the actual Middle Ages, even at the peak of its unity in the thirteenth century, the clash of forces was constant and relentless, and the victory of any particular set of them was more than doubtful. Men sought for a common ground in custom, action, creed; but the facts were slippery, and the very man, Dante himself, who absorbed the most diverse elements of his culture and presented us with the completest image of his age was for his contemporaries a defeated and discredited man.

The only doctrine that remained unchallenged in those troublous times was the unconscious dogma of art. Forms changed throughout this period; but the belief in form remained. It is this belief that has been attacked in modern times, partly as a result of the necessary effort to wreck and get rid of old forms which stand in the way of new achievement, partly because the new achievements themselves are so often quantitative in nature. We have lost faith in the formal powers of the mind, not, as some suppose, because our universe is too difficult to grasp, but because we lack the inner principle of order. If the author of 'The Divine Comedy' does nothing else for us, he should restore our belief in the efficacy of the mind. For his world, a world which we now enter with such difficulty, was formed by the imagination over a period of more than two thousand years, and while mountains melted away and cities sank beneath the dust that world retained its contours and its actuality. Even today, though Dante's supernaturalism is at odds with all our fundamental concepts—its necrology being the precise opposite of our biology—his universe keeps it shape: millions of people, not themselves Roman Catholics, are nearer to Dante in habit of thought than they are to Bergson, Whitehead, Geddes, Freud, Einstein.

If Dante's world was palpably not eternal, it nevertheless had a different quality from the helpless evanescence and formlessness which is the characteristic mode of thought and life today—that harried 'journalism' which threatens us as much in the laboratory and the studio as on the streets. Until the constructions of our own minds and the works of the imagination seem as valid to us as the ideal body of his life did to Dante, we will not, one may say pretty confidently, be able to impose direction upon the mere flow of life, or order upon the chaos that surrounds us. Our form cannot, of course, be Dante's; what he stands ready to give us is his faith in its existence.

We shall not appreciate Dante's triumph if we think of his period as a fabled time of harmony and unity, established in an outward world, such a period as he himself dreamed of under the Roman imperium. Dante's wholeness was not an external thing that existed as an image exists on a wood-block before it is duplicated in a print: it was rather the outcome of a long struggle of conflicting forces and beliefs. Medieval society was constituted like a great French cathedral—load, thrust, tension, counter-thrust, living, pushing, acting forces, all pitted against each other so as to produce a stable fabric. Such equilibrium as the society had was a dynamic one; it implied constant effort.

If Dante is a classical writer, as in every sense he surely is, it is not because he begins with a heavenly harmony, but because, by dint of an imperious will and a splendid talent, he finally achieves it. Let no one be deceived by current academic fatuities as to the nature of classicism: this Dante wrote in the midst of an almost paralyzing discomposure. Politically, he was at war with the Pope and his party, and on the losing side: his domestic life was bleak and probably unhappy, married as he was to a woman who belonged to a family he hated: exiled from his native city, he wandered, full of scorn and bitterness, through the minor courts of Italy, meditating too long and too often on things which were altogether of this world, and quite beyond his personal power to rectify.

Out of this strife and personal frustration, not out of serene fulfilment, his poem arose: it was from the abyss of his soul's darkness, perhaps made more keen by remorse over past sins and mistakes, that he beheld the inner illumination of his star. But, unlike minor poets and petty romanticists, his fantasy was something more than the covert elaboration of pangs and grudges. On this point I agree with Professor Vossler and not with Mr. Chapman, for whom Dante is supremely the type of Solitary Egoist, and 'The Divine Comedy' itself a *journal in time,* forerunner perhaps of Amiel and Maurice de Guérin. Dante poured into his poetry all those diverse streams of thought, from Plato to the Provençal troubadours, which constituted his culture, to say nothing of the warm, homely images of landscape and daily toil which he stored up on his solitary walks and journeys. So completely did he enrich his poem with the spiritual heritage of his time and his country that his spites and vanities and weaknesses are transcended by that greater Ego which he at the same time expressed.

Such a man, such a culture, may seem to be a tissue of flaws and failures; and yet because they have aimed at something full and rich and whole, they have power to endow us with life. Dante gave his age a common territory in the imagination, the true meeting ground of all our partialities and diversities. What existed, diffused and contradictory in life, became crystallized, purified, hard as a diamond, brilliant as its reflected blues and yellows. Popular fable and scholastic metaphysics, political intelligence and ideal hope, Italian patriotism and human magnanimity, all had their place in his supernatural universe; and in that universe all the warring forces of medieval Italy responded to a common emotion.

Dante left nothing out of the picture; certainly he left out no antagonisms, lusts, heresies; but, on the contrary, he used them stone by stone in his final structure. That structure itself was defined with mathematical exactness: the stanzas of three lines, the three divisions of the Hereafter, the thirty-three cantos, and the completion of each part with the final symbol of spiritual illumination, the star. With all his architectural sense of form, however, Dante made no attempt to limit the contents of his poem or to elevate his figures into barren abstractions. As in the cathedral, the gargoyles and obscene or ludicrous images are as much a part of the whole as the saints and the angels: the mud is there as well as the eternal bath of light. That is true order, for it rejects nothing; and that is true ideality, for it transmutes everything, not by glozing dogmas, but by conveying them onto the plane of the imagination.

By examining the stuff that pours into Dante's poem, we can convince ourselves that another Divine Comedy will not be produced in our own day by those who dream tepidly of such a humanism as may be achieved, without further experience or strife or effort, in the decorous isolation of a classical college. Dante the municipal ruler, Dante the technician, familiar with the construction of public works, if not the designer of them, Dante the amateur artist and friend of Giotto, Dante the diplomat, the author of 'De Monarchia,' are as necessary to the composition of this poem as the youthful follower of Cavalcanti and Folquet of Marseilles, or the student of St. Thomas Aquinas. Before the poet can create a work which will be approved by later academic critics, he may, perhaps, have to live a life from which they would shrink, smugly horrified. It was not the studious disciple of the inner check who discovered that the perfect hell for Paolo and Francesca would be an eternity of dovelike rapture: Dante must have known what a week of such a hell was like.

Vossler puts this point with admirable clearness and finality. "But for his pride and ambition, Dante would never have plunged into politics; but for his sensuousness, he would never have found Beatrice. His love, however, molded him into a religious man, his political struggle made him a moralist. Without *luxuria* and *superbia*, no 'Divine Comedy.' It is because he is a complete man that his virtues are so indissolubly linked with his vices."

The main subject of Dante's poem, the fall and redemption of mankind, as exhibited in every phase of the human personality, from utmost baseness and slavering animality to the illumination of beatified love, would have lost its power to hold us today had Dante merely given expression to medieval theology. It is because Dante included all the varieties of human experience, natural, cultivated, deformed, transcended, that his poem is still an enrichment of human experience. The sugared supernaturalism of a minor poem like Rossetti's 'The Blessed Damozel' is as antipathetic to Dante's imagination as the raw realism, untouched by ideal relations, of some of Zola's novels of the middle period. Indeed, that breach between the empirical and the transcendental schools which marks the literature as well as the philosophy of the nineteenth century, with a few grand, germinal exceptions, resulted in illusions far grosser and essentially far more superstitious than those Dante exhibited. Dante's Inferno, Purgatory and Paradise existed, when all is said and done, in a place that is still accessible to us: the human soul. By showing us his dilemmas and picturing to us the eternal fate of his contemporaries Dante is also, by parable and example, showing us ourselves.

No: it is not alone Dante's supernaturalism that erects a barrier and embarrasses our approach to his vision. The thing that has kept his achievement remote is that, though his world was one of strife and conflict and on the brink of dissolution, it formed and embraced a whole culture; while ours, during the last three hundred years, has been split into fragments. While the Asiatic and the European now wear the same clothes as the American and ride in the same motor cars, we have no common ground in the imagination: it is only in practical methods and in the governance of materials that we are one. If Dante put a pinnacle on medieval culture, the most that the wisest can say in our own day is that they have got down to bedrock again and are exploring our rotten foundations. Contrast 'The Divine Comedy' with our characteristic works of art! 'Ulysses' and 'The Waste Land,' for example, do not gather the living elements in our culture into new organisms: they are themselves shards in the débris of a demolished building. Our most valiant efforts to build anew—and no one doubts the *valor* of Mr. Eugene O'Neill—are little better than the attempts of mimicking children to build a new temple with chance blocks, fit only to compose dolls' houses.

The completion, the perfection, which Dante attained in 'The Divine

Comedy' may lie beyond our reach; but the audacious effort itself is a challenge. The poet who would resolve our chaos will be as deliberate as Dante. He will not order experience by turning away from it and renouncing it, as our academic humanists advise; but, confronting it, absorbing it, dominating it, he will convert it with implacable will into the materials and symbols of art. To achieve this, even decently to fail at this, he will have to be a poet, but such a poet that men will mistake him equally for a scientist, a technician, a philosopher, a statesman. For our age will have its own culture and unity, and even now, playing over features that are in slumber, one begins to detect the mood of its dream. In such potent embryons as 'Faust,' 'Moby-Dick,' 'Leaves of Grass,' 'War and Peace,' our own imaginative synthesis begins to take form and grow. In its naturalism it will have a place for all nature, including that which is ideal and directive; and though it will show the supernatural world of Dante in reversed image, it will be nearer to his art, I think, than it will be to the lesser poetry and philosophy of our immediate past. Dante seems distant now, not because we have left him behind, but because he strides on ahead of us. Almost all the dogmas he consciously believed in have crumbled or are crumbling. But the dogma of art remains, and it is our star. —New York Herald Tribune Books. April 7, 1929

15: Melvilliana

With the publication in 1926 of 'The Golden Day: A Study in American Experience and Culture,' my work attracted the attention of readers and editors not concerned with my earlier books on utopias or architectural history, and George Santayana's generous praise of that book, coming out of a blue sky, made more than one editor aware of my potential capabilities as a literary critic and possibly a biographer. In 1927 John Farrar, then with Doubleday, Doran, suggested that I write a study of Herman Melville. Until then my interest in Melville had fastened mainly on 'Moby-Dick'; for as yet Melville played no formative part in my life comparable to that of Emerson, Whitman, or Thoreau. But in drawing close to Melville the modest literary study I had agreed to write turned into a more searching inquiry into his whole career: a task at once hastened and handicapped by my need for an early financial return. My exploration of Melville's life brought to the surface problems, pressures, bafflements, and emotional cross-currents of my own similar to those I was probing in Melville. More even than Dostoevski, he made me aware of the moral ambiguities that all the great poets from Homer to Shakespeare body forth in their mottled heroes and their villains of both sexes.

The publication of my 'Herman Melville,' though it was a Literary Guild selection, came in the first year of the Great Depression; and both my philosophic outlook and my handling of his dark life story met at first with a dubious reception. But Melville, no less than Dante, brought me close to the underlying realities of human experience, and released me from the current faiths of my generation; counteracting our too hopeful liberalism, our glib futurism, our pious belief in the progressive solubility of all human problems through science and technology. Not the least reward of my interest in Melville was that it formed the basis for my friendship with the dean of Melville scholars, Dr. Henry A. Murray: a physician by training, a rigorous scientist by faith, a psychologist by vocation. Though I was never included in the ranks of academically accredited Melville scholars, my lifelong interest in Melville was ironically capped in 1977 by my being made an Honorary President of the Melville Society.

HERMAN MELVILLE'S LIFE AND WORK WERE ONE. A biography of Melville implies criticism; and no final criticism of his work is possible that does not bring to it an understanding of his personal development. The exotic elements in Melville's experience have usually been overstressed; the fatality and completeness of his withdrawal from the contemporary scene have been exaggerated; the incidental rocks and rapids and whirlpools have diverted the critic's attention from the flow of the stream itself. It is with Herman Melville's strength and energy on the spiritual plane that I shall chiefly deal. He lives for us not because he painted South Sea rainbows, or rectified abuses in authority in the United States Navy: he lives because he grappled with certain great dilemmas in man's spiritual life, and in seeking to answer them, sounded bottom. He left the clothed and carpeted world of convention, and faced the nakedness of life, death, energy, evil, love, eternity: he drew back the cozy hangings of Victorian parlors, and disclosed the black night outside, dimly lighted with the lights of ancient stars. Had he been a romantic, he would have lived a happy life, buttering his bread with feeble dreams, and swallowing down his regrets with consolatory port: he who wishes to escape the elemental stings of existence need only grasp the outstretched hands of his contemporaries, accept the subterfuge goals they call success in business or journalism, and shrink by means of a padded physical apparatus from the thorny reality of human experience.

But Melville was a realist, in the sense that the great religious teachers are realists. He saw that horsehair stuffing did not make the universe kinder, and that the oblivion of drink did not make the thing that was forgotten more palatable. His perplexities, his defiances, his torments, his questions, even his failures, all have a meaning for us: whether we renounce the world completely, affirm a future transcendence in heaven, or, like Walt Whitman, embrace its mingled good-and-evilness, our choice cannot be called enlightened until it has faced the gritty substratum

Melville explored. Melville left a happy and successful career behind him, and plunged into the cold black depths of the spirit, the depths of the sunless ocean, the blackness of interstellar space; and though he proved that life could not be lived under those conditions, he brought back into the petty triumphs of the age the one element that it completely lacked: the tragic sense of life: the sense that the highest human flight is sustained over an unconquered and perhaps an unconquerable abyss.
—From 'Herman Melville.' 1929

. . . I had no qualms when I wrote you as to what you would eventually say about Melville; but I am reassured over the fact that you see him as a real twin to Whitman, and so absolve me from my bad conscience at having to leave behind me at my death a work I badly wanted to write but never could get around to doing. That you were disgusted by the rhetoric of 'The Confidence Man' is more than understandable. That unreadable book was a product of his madness, not a wild product like 'Pierre,' which has also a great deal of brummagem eloquence in it, along with the masterly kind, but a product of dull deliberation, an *intentional* satire, written with only sand and thirst for inspiration, full of private King Charles's heads, among which was an accusation against his wife for being, as he falsely imagined, unfaithful, and for wanting to put him in an asylum, as indeed she doubtless was advised to do. The book is definitely a pathological document. I alluded to some aspects of this in my study of Melville, but Murray has brought to light more data on this period which make my interpretation conclusive.

Melville sent the book to his Uncle Peter, with an affectionate or at least graceful dedication; but Uncle Peter never cut its pages: indeed, they were not cut until I did so in the Rare Book room of the Public Library in 1927! Maybe you remember that I spent a whole chapter examining Melville's poetry, giving as favorable a verdict as I then dared: though A.E. reproached me for wasting any time on it. But I find that, on going back to it, it is better than I remembered, in many places: somewhat dated because of the inversions and strained rhymes; but often at least as good as Thomas Hardy's, both in style and in content. I will be curious to see what you find in it for yourself when you go over the ground. Maybe our final title to greatness will be the fact that we are the sole living Americans who have read Clarel from end to end! What you say about Whitman's deliberate naturalness can be applied to his poetry, too: certainly it was full of conscious artifice, consciously bardic, with an avoidance, more often than not, of that prosy naturalness which Wordsworth achieved in his blank verse. The influence of Yvor Winters has begun to pervert the judgment of a whole generation of our young professors of literature, if not a lot of other students too; and your influence is needed to redress the balance. Fancy a book like Esther Shepherd's on Whitman even getting a publisher—and worse than that, getting *my* publisher, with the aid of my friend Cap Pearce at that. —Letter to Van Wyck Brooks. September 10, 1944

ONE THOUGHT ABOUT ETHAN BRAND STILL TEASES ME, though it seems to have escaped the eyes of Melville's recent interpreters. Before Melville went down to New York to finish off 'Moby-Dick,' he told Hawthorne he had just been reading 'The Unpardonable Sin.' This probably occurred too late to cause that drastic alteration in the original manuscript which Olsen posits: but may it not have caused Melville to accentuate the alienation motif in Ahab, though he proclaims himself in that letter on the side of feeling?

And if there is no possibility of Hawthorne's conception of Brand having influenced Melville's conception of Ahab, then it raises an even more critical problem for students of American literature: and that is how two such deeply contrasting temperaments as Melville's and Hawthorne's should have both turned up, within a few years of each other, with the same type of hero: two intellect-begotten Ishmaels. Are not Ahab and Brand both Modern Man; and is not the Atomic Bomb his final progeny—even though in 'Moby-Dick' Melville was optimist enough to provide a 'happy ending,' namely someone left to tell the tale . . . —Letter to Henry A. Murray. June 22, 1947

My little criticism of Melville has turned into a ponderous book. I had only to read all of Melville's works, especially his later poems, to see that what you suspected in your Freeman review of Weaver was true: Weaver had been misled completely, overlooked the material for the last thirty years of Melville's life, which was lying around in buckets and bushel baskets, and created, instead of a man, a romantic tailor's dummy—making of Melville the very South Sea 'character' that would have nauseated him. I am happy to be able to report that Melville had at least twenty years of peace and three years, at the very end, of fulfillment: wistful and sad he may have been at the end, but not bitter or harassed. The book as it stands will have equal parts of biography and criticism, 'Moby-Dick' being the peak that dominates the parts that taper away on each side. I have based all my interpretations of Melville so far upon his own words, just filling out here and there with extraneous data; but in August I shall go up to Edgartown for a couple of days to consult

Mrs. Metcalf about her grandfather, and possibly see some Melville memorabilia. As for the rest: the days will be Melville, Melville, Melville, till at last I can say "Done." —Letter to Van Wyck Brooks. July 2, 1928

Note: A rare letter, for between 1925 and 1931 our correspondence almost ceased; though during Brooks's trying mental illness I remained in close touch with his wife, Eleanor Stimson Brooks.

. . . The Melville books you sent came last week, dear Harry, and I plunged right into your Introduction to 'Pierre' and read it through in two sittings. Reading it, I had the sense of being present, in a fashion that would be impossible in real life, at an interminable series of psychoanalytic sittings which had somehow, as in a dream, been speeded up sufficiently to avoid the tedium which must accompany such treatments. That is one of those mysteries I've always wanted to be party to; and here you have made it public, in a fashion that is altogether enthralling. Your literary judgments seem to me impeccable; and dispose, forever I hope, of those blear-eyed scholars who, because they think no one will perhaps bother to find them out, have treated 'Pierre' as an unqualified masterpiece. If there are any residual differences between us it would only be in minor matters; or over the fact that, when I wrote my book, I was overreacting against Weaver, whose judgments I did not respect and whose manner I did not like; so, in interpreting Melville's weaknesses and his illness I was inclined to put the best possible face on every dark incident. Even now, my own 'superficiality' has saved a good part of Melville for me; while your autopsy of Melville is so thoroughgoing that even the Last Trumpet would hardly suffice to bring the various organs and parts together again.

The worst of it is that I must agree with your dissection, as I follow your demonstration, organ by organ; for no one has gotten closer to Melville than you have. But in the very act of penetrating the hidden layers of Melville's being, you followed his own method in apprehending the universe: so that your natural disenchantment with him, finally, springs from the same root as his disenchantment with the world itself. It is only on the surface, perhaps, that any life holds together and can stand up under inspection; if one goes far enough in one's analysis one is left with a hot shower of sub-atomic particles disconcertingly unlike a man. The fact is that Melville's inwardness is frightful to behold; and 'Pierre,' which reveals so much of it, is like a living man with his entrails exposed. Perhaps the most necessary agent for holding a human character together is the skin: once that is penetrated in too many places, once too large a patch of it is burned off, the creature dies.

So much in Stubb-like defense of my 'superficiality': for which, like Stubb, I probably deserve a kick in the rump from Ahab! But you couldn't have written anything more appropriately stimulating to my own thoughts, at this particular stage of my work, when I am dealing with the Nature of Man and with what, under heaven, may be done about it. —Letter to Henry A. Murray. June 29, 1949

. . . You are partly right about my treatment of Elizabeth Melville: but I sympathized with her, and didn't minimize her difficulties, which were often overwhelming. Melville was outraged by her calling in Oliver Wendell Holmes to decide whether he should be put in an asylum and for a while could not forgive her. This comes out in 'The Confidence Man.' (The fact that Holmes was a fellow-writer *and* a neighbor must have made it more galling to Melville.) He also had neurotic hallucinations about her infidelity. I left this out because the evidence was based on unverifiable family tradition. Their belated reconciliation [recorded in some of his last poems] was what counted. But *all* writers' wives deserve pity and charity, dear David: yours and mine, too! —Letter to David Liebovitz. March 11, 1963

LÉGER AND MELVILLE. I would as little think of associating Fernand Léger's name with Melville's as with my own: but the fact is, he told me, that he had read my book on Melville almost as soon as it came out, and he had first come upon Melville's books, as a young man, in Joseph Conrad's own library. The first night he had stayed at Conrad's house in England—I suppose at Rye—he remarked on his discovery to Conrad, and Conrad said: "I am glad you found his books: they have had a great influence on me. But not in the way you might think: not as a writer of the sea; no, I don't care especially for 'Typee' or 'Omoo,' or even for 'Moby-Dick.' But it is as a profound psychologist and metaphysician that I admire him, as a writer who touched the depths of the human situation, and who understood the darkest facts about the human character. As for me, I do not love the sea: I hate it. I do not write about the sea but about something quite different: the ships that defy the sea and the relations of men who are bounded by the ship."

Léger's words cut deep; and I think I have repeated what he said at our one and only meeting fairly faithfully. How much would I have given to have known all this while I was writing my Melville! Even now it is precious; and Léger's own comment, coming from an artist, is hardly less so; for he feels, as I do, in contrast with a friend of his who had done an allegorical study of Melville, that the symbols in a work like 'Moby-Dick' are not as definite and limited as most interpreters make them out: that Melville realized their meaning *after* he had written, and that he had not, like a bad artist, chosen them beforehand and then looked for material to serve as illustration. Only a minor writer would do that. . . .

Léger and I got on famously and I was happy that in writing my Corcoran Lecture I had alluded to his work spontaneously, and in a favorable way. He is a strange creature to look at, with brown poppy eyes, and hair so obviously dyed red that, till one looks closely, one takes it for a shockingly dressed wig. He has been living in America for the last few years, 'at home,' as he told me, because for him America is an 'abstraction.' He is both an artist and an intelligent mind, with much broader interests than I should have guessed. —Letter to Henry A. Murray. January 26, 1954

Melville's Marital Plight

In 1856, while Melville was in Italy, there happened an event, obscure, mysterious, obliquely narrated, and published only at the end of his life, which gives us a further clue to his character and experience. Knowing Melville's habits of composition, one is fairly sure that some objective fact lies beneath the surface of the verse called 'After the Pleasure Party': all the more because he published the poem only after he had reached the serenity and safety of old age. That these verses were not merely the product of untethered imagination one suspects, too, because their theme, remorse and bitter regret after renouncing a passionate experience, is underlined by the words of another poem, 'Madame Mirror':

> What pangs after parties of pleasure,
> What smiles but disclosures of pain!

This long poem, 'After the Pleasure Party,' stands out with particular boldness because it contains the only direct references to his own sexual turmoil that one finds in Melville's entire work, except for haphazard and unimportant incidents—or the plainly fictitious events in 'Pierre.' It is a faint and intricate clue; but one must not neglect it.

"Melville pictures a paradisiac garden in Italy: the upland falling behind the house, fragrant with jasmin and orange blossom, the white marble of the house itself gleaming between the lanes of austere trees, the green terraces falling in gentle cataracts down to the starlit Mediterranean Sea: a place of beauty and an hour of balm 'after long revery's

294

discontent.' The pilgrim, dusty with travel in barren lands, revels in the sensuous peace. He is not so completely the pilgrim, so thoroughly the hermit, that his heart is entirely his own: on the contrary, it is out of a desperate dryness and loneliness of soul that Melville is suddenly beset by such temptations as the hermits of the Thebaid found in the desert.

"We have no image of the woman who walked with Melville through these green walls, under the starbright sky: he himself tried, in the years that followed, to forget 'the glade wherein Fate spun Love's ambuscade,' tempting him to flout pale years of cloistral life and 'flush himself in strenuous strife.' We do not know if it was she who repulsed him, as 'the shore repulses the hungry billows, tired of the homeless deep,' or whether it was a resistance within himself that wrecked and scattered the impulses that were driving him against the warm object of his desire: but we know that, flushed perhaps by wine, and stirred by the fragrant spring night, sex asserted itself again in Melville: the 'dear desire through love to sway' came over him, and when he found himself baffled, attempting to rule his passion yet not able to reign, neither conquering the woman herself nor the passion she had awakened, he was aware of a dreary shame of frustration. Blocked in his highest powers of thought, in his career as a writer, Melville found himself equally defeated—and perhaps by the same cluster of images—in that other citadel of personality. Bitterly he cries: 'And kept I long heaven's watch for this, contemning love, for this, even this?'

"There is the cry of the passionate man who in his marriage had kept to the letter of his pledge, and yet found himself struggling against its spirit—struggling and yet paralyzed. The sudden opening of passion, which had begun at lunch this day, as the guests of the house, like the ladies and gentlemen in the prologue to the Decameron, had lain about in groups on the grass, this passion, deepening in a secluded glade under the Mediterranean night, had pulled Melville off his lonely throne. In dream he was a king, perhaps a lonely king—an idiot crowned with straw! That gust of passion had brought enlightenment: the fires in him were banked, not dead: but it left him bereaved. He shrank from the consequences. In this enlightenment he remembered and magnified other incidents on his journey: the barefoot peasant girl in Naples who had climbed up the hills near the wheels of his carriage and had given him the sudden impulse to fire upon her the petty hell within his own bosom. Hers was a wily innocence, and one can only vaguely guess at Melville's memories when he exclaims: 'The cheat! On briars her buds were strung. . . . To girls, strong man's a novice weak.' All this became part of his 'sad rosary of belittling pain.'

"Melville might seem to others, in opaque moments might seem to himself, a pale, scholarly man, immersed solely in things of the mind: but what a caricature that apparition was of the actual man! The pallor did not mean he could not feel the sun when it shone upon him: 'the plain lone bramble thrills with Spring as much as vines that grapes shall bring,' and when this mood was uppermost, how gladly would he throw his arms around some 'radiant ninny,' the first glad, willing girl he might meet, and buy the veriest wanton's rose—'would but my bee therein repose.' If only he could remake himself, or free himself from this disturbance, this void tormenting urge, this feeling of disunity, this being but half of a mismatched whole: surely, there was some archaic blunder, some rank cosmic jest, in the state that made the single self incomplete and yet set all the odds against the possibility that selves who matched should meet and mate. This was part of Melville's disillusion. The hot impetus he had felt in that fine Italian garden promised an ultimate reward no more than his marriage, equally fervid and romantic at the start, had brought him. And yet—and yet—perhaps this temporary impulse was an impulse to act upon, whether it had any cosmic justification or not: the turbulent heart and the rebel brain did not satisfy themselves so easily with abstract reasons.

> 'For Amor so resents a slight
> And hers had been such haught disdain
> He long may wreak his boyish spite,
> And, boylike, little reck the pain.' "

—From 'Herman Melville.' 1929

The Taste of New England

On winter days alone one finds New England.
Brown slush creeps from South Station toward the India Wharf,
The bromine State House dome blends with the fog;
Upon the sullen muck, the powder-sprinkled newness of the snow, like
    sugar on burnt hot cross buns,
Dissolves again. The taste of brown grits in the mouth.

Brown is New England's color: the brown of sunburnt barns on Vermont
    hills,
The reddish brown beneath kelp-tangled rocks that thrust against the sea;
Umbers, cedars, bistres, coffees, chocolates, cinnamons;

The brown of sandalwood from India, Cuba's mahogany, and milo from
  Hawaii;
The brown of rotting wharves at Newburyport and Gloucester;
Brewed tea, tarred hemp, brown kegs and bean pots, smoked fish and
  tarpaulin;
Brown coils of rope, the spider brown of fishing nets; froth brown of
  turbid rivers in spring flood;
Brown tastes, acrid with spice or smoke; the tanner's brown at Lynn,
  butternut smears upon the hand;
Brown bacon rind, brown cider, plowed meadows, brown russets that
  outstay the fall;
The moss-brown velvet of the tidal flats; brown oak leaves that scrape
  against a sodden sky.
Pull off New England's shroud! White is for surfaces alone—white is for
  coverlets and icing.
Dissolve the genteel paint; scour the wood until you find the grain!
Beneath the mask you'll come upon the dark New England,
Dark as a face that's sailed around the Horn and blistered under the
  equator.
That's it: the sumac brown; the Fairbanks House and Hawthorne's Seven
  Gables;
Richardson's Sever Hall, his shingled house on Brattle Street, his earth-
  brown libraries;
The smoke-charred soul of Melville standing alone, grim as a chimney
  when the house is gone.

Here is a proper home and what is more a destination;
This is what makes one hunger for the walnut-bitter hills
And poke around the tunnelled root cellars of old farmhouses,
Where, at winter dawn, a pin of light between the rocks
Shines like a sun.

—The New Yorker. February 27, 1943

16: Amor Threatening

Lines Traced Under an Image of Amor Threatening

Fear me, virgin whosoever
Taking pride from love exempt,
Fear me, slighted. Never, never
Brave me, nor my fury tempt:
Downy wings, but wroth they beat
Tempest even in Reason's heat.

Herman Melville

Dantean Prelude

In October 1930 I became thirty-five years old: not quite midway, as it has turned out, in the journey of my life. At this point, like Dante, "I found myself in a dark wood where the straight way was lost, verily in a wild and rough and stubborn wood," where phantom monsters and teasing nymphs lurked. But, again in Dante's words, "to treat of the good I found there, I will relate the other things that I discovered."

During this period, though I had more than one glimpse of both Inferno and Paradiso, I was destined to endure a longer period in Purgatorio; for which purgation and release from sin I was to be ultimately rewarded, not by Dante's vision of supernal beatitude, but by a wide-awake return to the common earth, where heaven and hell and all that lies between are, in varied measure, everyone's daily portion from cradle to grave. Up to this point, one part of my nature had been largely untried and unformed: even as a writer, until I wrote my study of Herman Melville, I had never pushed myself to my limits. And by the same token I had never let my nascent intimacy with any of the attractive young women who crossed my path draw me away from Sophia or take possession, except in fleeting daydreams, of my waking life.

In finding my way out of this dark wood, Dante's vision of good and evil was of more use to me than Freud's psychoanalytic insights, much though I had learned from the whole movement of thought that began with Freud's 'Interpretation of Dreams.' Admittedly I was repelled by many aspects of Dante's theology, particularly his adherence to the Christian interpretation of Divine Justice, with its dogma of eternal punishment for unforgiven earthly sins and an eternity of vacuous bliss for the virtuous or the truly repentant. For all that, my own experience helped me to accept his poetic presentation of the Inferno, the Purgatorio, and the Paradiso as a true picture of mankind's historic experience and daily life. And in the end, it was through my open-eyed participation in the Divine Comedy of human existence that I was able to pass beyond the limitations of my own character, and even more of the culture which had formed me.

The first expression of this profound inner change came in the pages of my 'Herman Melville,' and soon after it took form in an essay I contributed to a series in The Forum on 'What I Believe.' Once my eyes had opened, I could at last face the accidental misfortunes, the paradoxical disparities, the conflicting loyalties, the irrational contradictions in my own conduct—as harassing but inescapable aspects of all human experience. As Emerson astonishingly observed in 1851—yes! Emerson in 1851—"In living one swims through seas strewn with wrecks, where none go undamaged. It is as bad as going to Congress: none comes back innocent." Having reached this point, I was not merely strengthened and toughened enough to face the worst that life might offer, but was more ready than I had been earlier to seize and embrace with open arms life's unexpected blessings, whatever the risk—even though these departures more than once threatened the stable structure of my marriage and broke the smooth life-curve I had so far actually followed.

This belated breaking up of the somewhat cramped and restricted mold of my adolescence of course exposed me to the outside challenges, the open temptations, and the laming mischances of maturity. Yet this transformation penetrated and illuminated every part of my being, and gave me the courage to explore other fields which my contemporaries had neglected, and to open up human potentialities that the contemporary axiom of automatic and inevitable progress had sedulously dismissed. This, as Professor Eddy Dow has perceptively pointed out, was my 'Passage to India'; and its effect on my mind compensated for the painful tensions and ruptures which, as in childbirth itself, accompanied the emergence of a maturer self. As Emerson again put it in 'Uriel,' "Evil may bless and ice may burn."

Superficially, there was no parallel whatever between Melville's life and mine. Even at the points where we touched, such as our experiences of the United States Navy, I had hardly more than a spectator's passing glimpse of the ordeal he had gone through in every part of the ocean, in all kinds of weather, doing his part as able seaman from the fo'casle to the maintop. And temperamentally we were even less akin. As an only child I had received all the love I could make use of, and even in the most disheartening periods of my adolescence, I never felt myself an Ishmael. Though the poverty and the deprivations of my growing years had been almost as bleak as Melville's they did not have the same humiliating effect, nor was I even in retrospect embittered by them. Nor, finally, did every gate of opportunity seem to me "barred by golden keys," as they did to Melville when he was forced to sign on a whaler.

In our literary careers, however, Melville and I were closer together and more fortunate. We both found an easy entry into the literary circles of our time, at almost the same moment in our lives; for older men, like Evert Duykinck and Hawthorne for him, and like Robert Morss Lovett, Van Wyck Brooks, John Macy, J. E. Spingarn, and Frank Jewett Mather for me, had gone out of their way to perform all sorts of tactful and helpful offices: moved possibly as Alvin Johnson sweetly put it in response to a letter I wrote him on his ninety-fifth birthday, because they had already discerned in my work "the savor of originality."

All through my writing of Melville's biography, my own naturally buoyant temperament was uppermost: so much so that it proved a handicap to my interpreting Melville's frustration, despair, bitterness, and satanic rebellion against his unchosen lot. During the period of writing, my own sanguine disposition kept me from tunneling into the black inner core of my subject: wherever possible I minimized his covert identification with Ahab or the threat of his actually sharing the impulses he described in "mad Ahab." Yet scarcely had I finished the final draft than I found myself in the same state of exhaustion that Melville was in after his struggle with the White Whale. What is more, I felt myself being sucked down helplessly into the same whirlpool, unable to overcome the unconscious forces that were threatening to drag me to the bottom. This was the Cape Hatteras of the soul that Melville had prophetically warned about earlier in 'White Jacket.' More than once during this period his words came back to me:

"But, sailor or landsman, there is some sort of Cape Horn for all!

300

Boys! beware of it: prepare for it in time. Graybeards! thank God it has passed. And ye lucky livers, to whom, by some rare fatality, your Cape Horns are as placid as Lake Lemans, flatter not yourselves that good luck is judgment and discretion: for all the yolk in your eggs, you might have foundered and gone down. . . . "

Despite our profound differences, I felt that I had found in Melville a brother spirit, temperamentally closer to me in certain ways than Emerson or Whitman or Thoreau: and when I confronted the crisis of his life that almost unseated him, the crisis which had developed in the act of writing 'Moby-Dick,' when he first became aware of the riled depths of his unconscious, I began to suspect that there was a deeper parallel. Possibly his sexual development and his marriage provided a clue to his own self-bafflement and therewith an admonition for my own future course of life. Melville's brief encounter with his relaxing and tempting Polynesian maiden, Fayaway, had possibly broken the crust that had covered an erotic volcano. And even when, after his brief sojourn with the Typees, he effected his physical escape, he still carried the image of Fayaway with him, an image that did not fade like a dream; for according to legend Melville's own sketch of her lovely body for long flaunted itself on the mantelshelf of Arrowhead, his Berkshire home. Failing to cope with his early erotic promptings or to understand later the effect of his repressions, Melville revealed his even deeper torments and frustrations in 'Pierre,' the book that followed 'Moby-Dick.' By the time he wrote 'Pierre' he was indeed at the mercy of his unconscious; and in submitting himself to its wild promptings he turned his own story into a flagrant melodrama, so crude that one scholar has sought to cover up its florid rhetoric by characterizing it as a satire on obsolete romantic affectations.

From my reading of Melville's life I read a lesson for myself; and as the months passed, with my book finished, I found myself ever closer to the mood in which Melville, in far deeper desperation, had written 'Pierre.' Melville's shattering experience, as symbolized there and later in 'Bartleby,' served as a warning and spurred me to follow another way than that which caused him to wander for the next decade or two through the bleak waste land of tormented chastity and self-renouncing loyalty.

While I was pondering Melville's dilemma, one part of me was beginning consciously to come to grips with my own. During that year, Blake's lines, "Damn braces, bless relaxes," competed in my mind with another gnomic saying of his: "Sooner throttle a babe in its cradle than nurse an unacted desire." All my post-adolescent defenses and disciplines were breaking down.

Toward the end of the summer of 1929 on a sudden panicky return from Geneva, I became more fully aware of the state I was in and the decision I still hesitated to make. And at that moment I earned the characterization of the sage one finds in the seventy-first book of the 'Tao Te Ching.' "The sage is not a sick man; and it was because he saw sickness as sickness that he ceased to be sick." In a verse I addressed to Melville on finishing the biography, I pictured my relation to him, 'a sick man,' as that of a nurse, watching by his bedside, tending him through the fever that brought him almost to death. In that office, I poured my sunlight upon him, only to find myself being swallowed up by his blackness, falling with him into chasms no light of mine could ever penetrate. Before that vigil was over, I wrote, "the weakened nurse became the patient: I watched the fever take possession of my bones." But now, I too had reached the crisis that precedes a recovery.

This is how things stood in the spring of 1929, when my 'Herman Melville' was published. And that half-written verse was completed not on paper but in my life.

The Human Comedy

After 1929 three young women, besides Sophia, successively played active but different parts in my maturation. Here I shall confine the account to my relationship with Catherine Bauer, for this in the more reserved and muted form of friendship persisted to the end of her life. Catherine's challenging mind, particularly during the first two years of our intimacy, had a stimulating and liberating effect upon my whole development. In effect, she played the part of Hilda Wangel in Ibsen's play: the voice of the younger generation, bidding the Master Builder to quit building modest, commonplace houses and to erect instead an audacious tower, even if, when he had reached the top, he might fall to his death.

Catherine and I became acquainted in the fall of 1929, the year my 'Herman Melville' had appeared in the spring. She was then in charge of advertising at Harcourt, Brace, my new publisher, and we were drawn together—at first rather slowly and warily—by our common interest in modern architecture. But even before this, she confessed later, it was her reading of 'The Golden Day' in Paris in 1927 that had then re-enforced her own wavering impulse to return to America. From the beginning, then, we were excited by each other's minds, and plunged and leaped in a sea of ideas like two dolphins, even before our bodies had time for another

302

kind of play. It was the overflow and intermingling of both impulses that provoked the stream of letters that deepened our relationship. They were often quite long letters, even though we might have spent hours together the day before. In being drawn toward Catherine I was approaching a person whose intellectual and emotional qualities made her almost the direct opposite of Sophia; and this difference went equally deep in the contrast between their physical characteristics; for Sophia's almost classic Graeco-Oriental beauty was the antithesis of Catherine's definitely Germanic cast. Catherine was a type I had never been attracted to, the type one finds in the paintings of Lucas Cranach the Elder: with the same high forehead, the small turned-up nose, the soft body curves, the blonde hair of the medieval Germanic woman, though spiritually there wasn't a touch of the medieval woman in Catherine. Certainly, to serve men dutifully and bear children was not her central purpose in life, however gamely she might in time do both.

Not strangely the contrast between Catherine and me was even sharper; for she felt close to the Renaissance painter, Bronzino, whom she had studied at Vassar, while my favorite painter of the same period was Paolo Veronese, he who had magnificently presented both Sacred and Profane, both Faithful and Unfaithful Love. Alike by native temperament and experience Catherine and I were opposites, almost enemies. But our erotic intimacy enabled both of us to profit by this polarity; and this, I can see now, broke through some of the limitations in my own character and experience, and helped release energies needed for the work I was at last ready to do.

What's Wrong with Utopia

Utopias rest on the fallacy that perfection is a legitimate goal of human existence. They mistake the points of the compass for alternative destinations and real cities, forgetting that North and South point to equally barren wastes, and that East and West inevitably meet. In fact, fixed points and ideal directions are of practical use only because they cannot be achieved. Humanity would starve in utopia as it would starve at the Poles; for a good spiritual diet must contain a certain amount of phosphorous, iodine, and arsenic, although they are poisonous if taken in large quantities. The problem of evil is to distribute the poison in assimilable amounts.

When I was younger neither evil nor ugliness had any part in my view of a desirable, or even acceptable, world. I conceived that the mission of intelligence was to stamp them out. I sought perfection and without knowing it embraced death. If my search had been a little more effective I would have killed myself through an excess of virtue: for the virtuous son would have strangled the faithful lover: the faithful lover would have strangled the growing man: the growing man would have been stunted by his inhibitions and would have shot himself or written 'The Modern Temper.' I was saved, if indeed I am saved, by the immitigable presence of error and vice, by sufficient amounts of miscalculation, self-deception, and blackguardism. As soon as I was strong enough to take an honest look at myself I discovered that I was neither so virtuous, so faithful, nor so inhibited as I had made myself out to be.

Conclusion? Damn utopias! Life is better than utopia. . . . —Letter to Catherine Bauer. July 1930

Note: This conviction, already latent in 'The Story of Utopias,' thenceforth threads through all my writings: indeed a whole chapter, 'Life is Better than Utopia,' has a crucial place in 'Faith for Living' (1940). Despite this evidence many people persist in calling me a Utopian.

ON AMATORY AMBIVALENCE. It's such a relief to me . . . to have admitted at last to myself that it's painful, but possible, to love two girls at one time—and to do injustice to them equally. It's only through being separated from both of you, at equal distances, for six weeks, that I have been able to discover for myself how curiously little sexual excitement has to do with it—except as a natural ingredient like conversation or any other medium of intimacy.   —Letter to Catherine Bauer. July 1930

All talking about oneself, all strict accounting of one's motives and impulses and actions, even if set down in a diary, sounds priggish. I have been doing a lot of this lately, and I know. Very well: but one must go ahead and do it just the same—not as a habit, but in times of doubt, conflict, fresh decisions.   —RN. 1930

SOPHIA SAILED IN THE FOG OF EARLY MORNING bound for Bremen, but, though not without mutual tenderness, there were three thousand miles between us even before she stepped on the gangplank. It seems very queer, and I feel as if I had put a couple of cultures in test-tubes, and had washed my hands and noted down the date, and then gone about my own work, knowing that it would be a couple of months before one could tell if the experiment proved anything. And meanwhile there was nothing to do, but just mechanically note down the changes every day. It is very queer indeed; and if I began to explain the why of all the queerness, I should presently be telling you the story of my marriage. I might be the better in the meanwhile for a more impersonal confidante with a short memory and a sympathetic ear, for whom I could just pass in review the last ten years of my life. Amy Spingarn won't do; and the Charlotte of 'The Little Testament,' who *would* do, is now so distant both by marriage and miles that she is impossible: so I will have to write to myself if it really gets bad. Not that my thoughts are tangled: they are quite plain. Something that was dim in the past has become sharper: a hundred things about me that I had never let myself feel or observe have passed over the threshold of consciousness. How much even a fairly honest person conceals from himself or just turns his back to! Yet I don't regret the concealment either; for until I met you there was no conceivable alternative.   —Letter to Catherine Bauer in Berlin. June 19, 1930

"EVERY MAN OVER FORTY IS A SCOUNDREL." I now well know the meaning of that saying of Bernard Shaw's which puzzled me when I was eighteen. *He is!* and the scoundrelism begins to develop around thirty. I can already feel a lot of good horny callouses on my spiritual anatomy. Frank Jewett Mather did a handsome and generous review of my critique of Humanism in The New Republic in March, and when I wrote him an equally handsome letter, he confessed to an unhumanist kinship with what he calls my neo-romanticism, saying that he felt that the greatest difference between his generation and mine was the fact that his own was "consistently hypocritical." It was a nice confession from the old boy; and it really says so much.   —Letter to Catherine Bauer. July 9, 1930

Both Sophia and I have had a good winter, perhaps the best we have had in four or five years, despite the fact that this last year has been for us a period of intense and painful spiritual housecleaning—during which we have opened all the dusty closets of our marriage, emptied out the drawers we had kept under lock and key, and run the vacuum cleaner over apparently immaculate surfaces, only to find them covered with dust and bacteria.

We have been married for ten years; Sophia is now thirty-one and I am thirty-five; and I have observed that this is a critical period in the lives of a great many of our married friends and acquaintances. What happens so often is that the woman begins to yearn again for romance, at least a release from her deadly household routines; or more sharply perhaps, dreams of a more satisfying kind of sexual experience with another lover. The man, on the other hand, though not past romance, still less past roving, begins to look around for sympathetic intellectual companionship with a woman, closely bonded by erotic intimacy. At such times the many genuine ties formed in marriage get temporarily loosened, sometimes permanently disrupted.

We are in the midst of this situation now. In a superficial way I have of course been on the brink of being 'in love' more than once, but until recently have always withdrawn when there seemed the slightest chance of the relationships' being close enough to disturb my marriage. But last year has been different. And Sophia and I and the other girl have been struggling for a year to face the whole business honestly and see what could be made of it. More than once I have remembered with a bitter smile Jung's example; but it is of no use to me. —Letter to Henry A. Murray. May 12, 1931

ON A TONSILLECTOMY. I have written this letter to you so often in my mind that it is already stale, like a manuscript that has been revised too often, however lovingly; and I shan't be able to give you half the sense of adventure and horror. The sticky New York days before the operation: the increasing sense of calm and relief when the day finally came: the amusement of lying in a hospital bed, quite healthy and ruddy-brown, and of seeing how easy it was to accept all the little details, the winding sheet, the turban, and that sort of thing: then alone in the operating room for five minutes, blankly looking with a blank mind at a blank ceiling: the appearance of a lovely blonde nurse, sweating like a waterfall under her costume and one's sense of delight at finding the right level with her in the first thrust: watching oneself go under the ether, feeling the numbness, looking up at the doctor, hearing the nurse say: "Are you putting him under so soon, doctor? We were just beginning to get acquainted." (Nice girl!) And so here it comes . . . But I see that I haven't given you half the fun of it. There was Sophia, for example, with her experiences of being curetted [after a miscarriage] if that's how one spells it, wondering when the nurse was coming in to *shave* me; and then there was the dim, muzzy state of awakening, when I was sweet and impish, and asked Sophie if I had called her by the right name. But what is the use of having a highly disciplined imagination? I had anticipated a dozen different eventualities: a hemorrhage, post-operative pneumonia, choking, a blood transfusion, a funeral in Woodlawn, even going so far as to picture a highly touching meeting of you and Sophie, each of you being for the moment very much of a gentleman and trying to conceal from the other how much I loved her. I thought in fact that I had canvassed all possible misfortunes and catastrophes, and that nothing could surprise me; but I had forgotten one thing: one's throat for almost five days actually hurts. That was a surprise, and I felt like a little child who discovers for the first time that he lives in a cruel universe, where candy melts and fire is hot. . . .

But there were so many things I wanted to tell you about the hospital, and most of them alas! have almost vanished, but I recall the fact that the nurses, for one, had very trim buttocks and were younger and fresher than I remembered them from previous visits, and very prompt and efficient, too: that is, prompt always, and efficient up to the point of not losing their modesty; for who could predict, in this modern and rationalized age, that the technique of giving a male patient a bath and an alcohol rub should—shades of Odysseus and Nausicaa!—include every necessary part of his body except his genitals—with the result after four days of heat that I acquired some nameless and fortunately only temporary itch, all for lack of soap and water and a woman's soothing touch! —Letter to Catherine Bauer. September 28, 1930

POST-OPERATIVE FANTASIES. At one period in bed, being very dull and having no one to amuse me, stirred by a smugly self-righteous advertisement of a sanitary toilet paper, I began to compose a series of howling good contraceptive advertisements, anticipations of the day when they should come forth, like Kotex and Sanitissue, from their devious concealment. If only I could remember all those ads! One of them was for Puella Pessaries, by the makers of Kleinert's Dress Shields (the House that has Protected Women for Half a Century); and another was a historical ad, with a picture of Monsieur le Colonel Condom, Comte de Roquefort, pacing up and down the terrace of the Chateau Roquefort, and deciding that he must preserve the honor of the woman he loved. But how? Then the great idea comes! He calls for his housekeeper . . . and so on. Then there was the solid middle class ad, very practical, of a father and a mother and two children: a balanced family seated in front of a very bad three-colored fire. "Do not endanger their safety and comfort: take no chances! In case of failure, we pay the Hospital bills." And then there were the diaphragms in five colors, to match Milady's underthings; and much, much more, all the details of which—and it was all in the details of course—I have unhappily forgotten. —Letter to Catherine Bauer. September 25, 1930

Though when we met I was concerned far more with letters and philosophy than with housing and architecture, I did, consciously or not, have something to do with your descent into social statistics, figures, responsibilities, housing research, and political propaganda; and now that you are up to your neck in it, hating figures, hating housing, hating me, it is only too obvious that this is the last thing I had in heart or mind when we met. What was your attraction? Why, naturally, the fact that you were so coldly and completely indifferent, so wayward, so irresponsible, so unconcerned with the weal of the world, so completely egoistic and self-absorbed, such a monster of aloofness and such a mistress of playful irresponsible estheticism. Even your amorous response had the cool disengagement of a spectator, viewing a new artist with an open mind. —Letter to Catherine Bauer. June 7, 1933

[LETTER FROM CATHERINE BAUER TO L.M. . . . *The brilliant suggestiveness of 'The Golden Day' simply must be fulfilled in the richness of your new series of books. And the implications mixed into the early book as to what a study of the present and future should be are really terrifying . . . I should think you'd get stage fright every time you think of it. But you will do it. Won't it be nice, some day, when all the nasty little housing statistics and all our complicated train rides and all the distracting comforts and discomforts, prejudices and passions of wandering around in Europe and America—having died a natural death and been buried— won't it be nice when they suddenly rise again in the form of real experience and indications of ultimate truth and significant slices of life, and force you willy-nilly to write the best book that's ever been written on the nature of that complicated phenomenon, living in the twentieth century and after.*] —September 1, 1932

Note: This letter came as a happy climax to the strains and conflicts that marred our intermittent meetings in Europe that summer. But long before this I had written: "Lovers are often closest at the moment of parting."

KARL MARX IS AN AMAZING WRITER, or rather two writers. One of them is the abstract dialectician, juggling with the same empty counters as the businessman or the commercial economist, and trying to convince himself, against his own better judgment, that he can make them mean something, because he can keep six metaphysical balls in the air at one time, instead of two or three. There was never an absurder spectacle than that of a man attempting to lay the foundations of a revolutionary economics in terms of abstract values, divorced from their vital relationships, and reduced to the state of merely pecuniary magnitudes. He is able to describe, in tortuous detail, the whole process of capitalistic exploitation and production; unfortunately not a word of it would apply to a system that renounced pecuniary profits and abstract labor hours as a basis for exchange and distribution.

But the other Marx is a grand fellow: a man who directly or by absorbing a great deal by osmosis from Engels—who was in the cotton trade and knew industrialism from the inside—has a sense of actual processes, a reading of human character, and historical imagination, a capacity to see into the details of social intercourse: in short a sociologist of the first water, full of hate and admiration and disgust and humanity, quoting Shakespeare and Horace and Diodorus Siculus, and god knows whom else, and slang-whanging the people he dislikes with the same pithiness that Carlyle had in 'Past and Present.' Marx the pure Ricardian economist was merely a Talmudic student who had got locked up by accident in the Stock Exchange one night and had mastered the whole set of capitalist rules and procedures before they opened the door next morning. But Marx the sociologist is Carlyle and Ruskin and Veblen and Sombart pretty much all in one: no wonder Sombart acknowledges his immense debt to him.   —Letter to Catherine Bauer. June 28, 1933

. . . The book ['Technics and Civilization'] has become gigantic, but the more one puts into it, the more empty somehow it gets: or rather the holes become more visible, as when one blows up a child's balloon the flaws in the rubber become clearer with every extra inch it is distended. This monstrous work is but the sketch of the book I want to write: the very touch of failure that already hangs on my words as they reach and snatch after the thoughts that elude me is perhaps in another sense the best pledge of success. When at last one knows anything well one realizes how vastly one is ignorant and how "life is not long enough to know antimony." [Robert Boyle, 'The Skeptical Chymist.'] As one really gets on with one's knowing one leaves one's little limitations and one's easy acceptances, and begins to touch the bottom of things—as one becomes, if in minute amounts—godlike, one realizes that one lacks alas! the most important qualification for godlike knowledge—namely, an eternity to acquire it in! . . .   —Letter to Catherine Bauer. June 4, 1933

. . . There are parts of 'Technics and Civilization' that will, though I have fact upon fact at my command, be hard for contemporary scholars to accept; for instance the section on the future, in which I suggest that we have now reached a point where the machine is about to dominate the organic, and when, instead of simplifying the organic in order to make it mechanical, we will begin to complicate the mechanical in order to make it organic; for the reason that our skill, perfected on the finger exercizes of the machine, will be bored with a mere repetition of the scales and suchlike imbecilities, and we will set ourselves something harder to accomplish. Frank Lloyd Wright has used some of the words I have used and perhaps has, in the depths of his mind, similar intuitions. Oscar Stonorov, curiously, expressed the same general set of ideas on a walk last Sunday, pointing out how feeble and inadequate our best mechanical construction was alongside the hollow tubing and the perfect joints of some of the grasses that were growing by the roadside; and he said in addition that the latest advances in the airplane in Germany were made not by analyzing mathematical aerofoils in wind tunnels, but by going back to the duck, one of the strongest of fliers, although one of the weakest of gliders, and analyzing its motions in flight as a basis for mechanical reproduction. All this will be terribly hard for the old-fashioned machine-minded specialists to accept for they naively regard the automatic machine as the goal to which all creation moves. —Letter to Catherine Bauer. July 2, 1933

. . . Yesterday, at Spingarn's invitation, I went to Troutbeck Lake, where Joel is secretly entertaining a secret conference—placarded by signs all along the road: "This way to the Amenia Conference: Amenia Conference 1 Mile!"—of young Negroes, thirty-three of them, chiefly between twenty-five and thirty-five years of age: the coming leaders of the race. I got there in time to partake of the excellent camp dinner and discussion: both were good. Despite the fact that Joel, by a hitch in his arrangements, had to house all of them in one huge tent, and despite the fact that they had no mattresses on their beds, no place except the lake to wash in, and no place wherever to shave in—"Fortunately," said one of them, "our race is supposed to be the least hairy of the three great divisions of mankind"—you never saw such a lot of jolly, hearty, strong, confident, chaffering, good-natured people anywhere, swimming and playing baseball, even though it rained, and having a two hour discussion in the afternoon, even though it wasn't provided for in the program.

Then came dinner, and a keen discussion afterward. They were all, these young doctors, professors, lawyers, librarians, tussling with the eternal dilemma of all intellectuals today: how to be a communist without wilfully swallowing the fierce ignorances, the blind hatreds, the wilful dogmatisms of the orthodox revolutionists who are preparing for a final pitched battle between communism and capitalism—if they are not providing a rationalization for the even more ferocious hatreds and brutalities of fascism. Even those on the left, even as you and I, are caught by the predicament of not wanting to sacrifice everything for a cause that may easily dissolve and be replaced by its opposite in the course of the battle itself. It is a little like the dilemma of a follower of Lucretius in Rome, who wanted to have the personal faith and force of Christians without accepting the stultifying articles of organized Christianity. I am curious to see how these young Negroes and Negresses will answer it. —Letter to Catherine Bauer. August 20, 1933

Note: Perhaps I should explain that J. E. Spingarn, my friend and neighbor at Troutbeck, was one of the founders of the National Association for the Advancement of Colored People, and was actively concerned with equalizing their rights and opportunities as citizens with all other Americans. Though he did not in the least share the communism of W. E. B. DuBois, the outstanding leader of the Negro intellectuals, he admired the quality of his mind. Spingarn was tireless in pressing the case for racial equality upon his Dutchess County neighbor, Franklin Roosevelt; but he died in 1939, before the ideas discussed at the Troutbeck Conference had begun to take effect.

I suppose it needs turbulence and unhappiness and release and a dozen other exalted or dreadful ingredients before one is ready to write such magnificent prose as your description of the weather in Maine in your second letter. You have never done better, and I know no one except Virginia Woolf who could have approached it: indeed, you have just that extra touch of abandon which she, perhaps reacting against Ruskin, sometimes lacks, to the impoverishment of the reality which would naturally provoke it. When you let your emotions and your thoughts run out to the end of your finger tips, instead of your packing them in their overflowing richness into some tight little bag inside you which won't contain them, there is simply no one around who can touch you. —Letter to Catherine Bauer. September 14, 1933

. . . Sophy was almost as conscious of your charm last night as I was. When we left Clarence's she said: "Drat your friend Catherine! I hate her—because I really like her so much and I can understand why you do, too. There is something about the curve of her mouth and the delicacy of her neck that almost brings a lump in my throat." —Letter to Catherine Bauer. November 25, 1933

YESTERDAY GEORGIA O'KEEFFE'S EXHIBITION OPENED. Cary Ross eyed me suspiciously in the hall and said ominously: "You'll have a surprise." (Has he a suspicious eye? Does he always look ominous?) But the only surprise of it was to find how good she was originally; for one of her first two drawings—not the one Stieglitz regards as Sacred, but the other— was in some ways as good as anything she has done since. Although Stieglitz put a few of the weaker and more metallic paintings on the walls, the show is strong: one long, loud blast of sex, sex in youth, sex in adolescence, sex in maturity, sex as gaudy as 'Ten Nights in a Whore-house' and sex as pure as the vigils of the vestal virgins, sex bulging, sex opening, sex tumescent, sex deflated. After this description you'd better not visit the show: inevitably you'll be a *little* disappointed. For perhaps only half the sex is on the walls: the rest is probably in me. . . . —Letter to Catherine Bauer. January 30, 1934

. . . At last I have read Colette. Just the sort of novel for either of us to read: an egotistic male, a playwright, who takes his little girls as they go but still loves his wife: also his secretary, who is witty and sophisticated and intelligent. Like you she is an ashen blonde, too; and his wife, an older woman, who is large and dark-skinned, doesn't mind his trifling love affairs, but resents the secretary, whom she really likes. I shall burn the book in the furnace! But I have discovered the secret of Colette's power and influence. Instead of saying: "She had an impulse to embrace him and he fondled her," she says: "She drew his arm around her waist and he played with her breasts." Always the exact physical description instead of the abstract bowdlerized image. The other secret, the thing that makes American best-sellers every year, from 'The Bridge of San Luis Rey' onwards, is that various characters drop enigmatic and 'pro-found' remarks on life and character, which sound exciting and mean exactly nothing. . . . —Letter to Catherine Bauer. 1934

A JUNGIAN ANALYSIS. Coming from reading Jung's privately published talks in one of his seminars, full of interesting self-revelations and ex-posures, I have the best example in the world before me to think clearly about us and our little difficulties: all the more because I chortled with delight, again and again, at finding that Jung and I had reached by different paths a very similar philosophy, so that sections of my essay in 'Living Philosophies' might have been inserted in Jung's talks, and no one have been the wiser. It all began with this long quotation from Jung . . .

"Just so with a man about his books. He does not want to tell of the secret alliances, the *faux pas* of his mind. This is what makes most auto-biographies lies. Just as sexuality is in women largely unconscious, so is this inferior side of his thinking largely unconscious in a man. And just as a woman erects her stronghold of power in sexuality, and will not give away any of the secrets of its weak side, so a man centers his power in his thinking and proposes to hold it as a solid front against the public, particularly against other men. He thinks if he tells the truth in this field it is the equivalent to turning over the keys of his citadel to the enemy. But this other side of his thinking is not repellent to a woman, and

312

therefore a man can usually speak of women as belonging in general to two types, the mother and the hetaira. The hetaira acts as the mother for the other side of men's thinking. The very fact of its being a weak and helpless sort of thinking appeals to this sort of woman; she thinks of it as something embryonic which she helps to develop. Paradoxical as it may seem, even a cocotte may at times know more about the spiritual growth of a man than his own wife."

This gave me, to begin with, a very sharp image of you and me: you, the only one to whom I have ever shown the very first draft of anything I have written, the only one to whom I have completely let down my intellectual as well as my emotional barriers. I had seized you and appropriated you in just this relation: and you had accepted the seizure and appropriation because it fitted the person you had been and wanted to be; for it was not entirely as a jest—was it?—that you have accepted the label of the 'Mistress type' from that girl at college. —Letter to Catherine Bauer. July 25, 1931

TO RETURN TO US. Six relations will not cover everything. You forget the relation of the feminine part of my ego to your intellect: it is a pure mother relation, and I can watch this development with a pride and selflessness which would make the great abnegators of fiction seem ruthless ideologists. The test of this was really my reaction to your winning the Fortune prize: there wasn't, so far as I could touch bottom at all, the faintest grain of jealousy in my feelings, nothing more than a wisp of regret at not having my summer handsomely solved by the possession of an unexpected thousand dollars; and that had nothing to do with you. But of course there is a danger in that very mother relation . . . As long as I can remain to a certain degree aloof, I cannot merely give you all I have, but I can face with a certain nonchalance the day when, if you are intellectually worth your salt, you will leave me: when you will have taken from me all that can nourish you and when, in order fully to break away, you will have to slay me and turn your back on me. The instrument of this release and this reintegration will almost certainly be another man: and no matter what the extent of your emotional and physical attachments to him might be, the affair, or the series of affairs, might easily prove disastrous to the rest of our relationship. If I did not respect your mind it wouldn't matter: or rather it would be legitimate for me to play upon the feminine side of you as hard as I know how, and to keep you and win you back by those sure and dastardly methods. That would be the natural masculine response. But there is the mother side of me that wants to see you grow, that knows that my part in your growth will not be fully successful until the painful moment when you rise up and leave me finally comes: that realizes, in addition, that you must sow your intellectual wild oats all over the place, and that if you were content with less you would not be worth as much attention and effort as I have actually given. —Letter to Catherine Bauer. July 28, 1931

MY FALLING IN LOVE WITH YOU prevented you from having still another brief superficial 'affair': you had your first taste of the real thing. Consciously or unconsciously, as time went on, we wove a hundred threads of faithfulness and domestic familiarity into our encounters. You never guessed at the beginning—did you?—that I would awaken in you the kind of unfashionable desire for stability and continuity which goes with marriage? That produced a serious problem for both of us. Before you knew it, you were in love, too, and had reluctantly to face the fact that my marriage with Sophia exerts a gravitational pull which no passing comet can overcome. Whatever your secret hopes then, our frustrating jaunts about Europe in 1932 showed how irreconcilable were our egoes, our respective pasts, our habits of work, our personal loyalties, our thinkable futures. In revenge for our mutual disappointments then, you crowned our European trip by turning yourself into a full-fledged Housing Expert; and all your thwarted love life, in both its permanent and its roving aspects, has gone into producing a book on Modern Housing. No wonder you are sober, depressed, alarmed—and cannot even get on with your book! In the meantime, a vigilant but somewhat malicious Providence has punished me equally by removing from sight and mind and intimate contact the girl I once fell in love with. I call for you in the stillness of the night, and what do I hear? The percentage of vacancies in *Laubengang* apartment houses in Germany as compared with cottages. Where is my lost Eurydice of the winters of 1930–1931, she who had no social conscience, and who never felt guilty, defensive, inadequate, possessive—or tempted by marriage? And which of us now feels most deserted? —A pastiche of letters to Catherine Bauer, written between 1931 and 1934

[LETTER FROM CATHERINE BAUER TO L.M. . . . *There is of course a deep conflict here between us. On the one hand, your intensity, your idealism, your inherent feeling for perfection or nothing, your fine esthetic sense of the* form *and single strength of love—love made up of a sum of things but still an identity in itself, not to be chipped off, not to be experienced unconsciously in ups and downs, in offs and ons, without being ruined!—these are the* very things that *I admire most, respect most, love most, and yes,* need *most, in you. A capacity for such feeling in*

314

myself is the biggest, the most priceless thing, you have given me. You gave me perhaps the first intimation I ever had of what incorruptibility *means. On the other hand (alas, for I am still myself) I simply cannot help feeling that the girl does not exist, could not exist, who would not make you feel that she had failed you, every now and then. Perhaps it is true. Perhaps it is just the price you pay for having fallen in love with an opposite.*] —July 12, 1933

Note the strange paucity of modern terms to describe the nuances of extra-marital devotion. The word 'mistress' for a "woman who is loved and courted by a man" dates, my Oxford dictionary tells me, from 1509; and the last of ten definitions which realistically characterize a mistress as "a woman who illicitly occupies the place of a wife," is described as "late medieval." This sets her relations definitely apart from the historic attributes of a courtesan, a prostitute, or a modern promiscuous woman open—thanks to contraceptives—to temporary liaisons outside or inside marriage. The medieval definition properly conveys the notion of both parity and continuity. Just because of the mistress's constant presence and sustained rivalry in the mind of the lover, both wife and mistress are exposed to much the same tensions, the same jealousies, the same hopes for continuity; and both feel at critical moments the same sense of being deceived, callously flouted, or deserted. In truth the pressures of love in both cases—apart from the presence of or the desire for children—may be almost equally great; and to the degree that both relations are, in their different ways, self-sustaining the man likewise is distracted, apprehensive, driven to subterfuges, emotionally pulled apart. Noel Coward, seemingly a shallow fashionable dramatist, showed a more profound insight in his 'Brief Encounter' than Ingmar Bergman in his 'Scenes from a Marriage.' —RN. 1976

I have written a dozen different letters to you: all imaginary, and not one in the least degree like this. What were they all about? The arthritic pains of love: severe twinges of jealousy: all as mysterious as those changes in the joints which turn nice young ladies into cripples overnight. How to cure them? Medical science has no answer. The seven serious letters I wrote you all said this: When you get tired of me and want to go somewhere else or to someone else, say it quick, and be ruthless; and we will both be happier. The five comic letters said I know quite well that when the fatal time comes the chances are that neither of us will be able to recognize it until we are badly lacerated; and we will blame the stiff joints and the pains for our separation instead of recognizing the fatal antecedent symptoms. But jealousy, I think, fares better if one at least can hope for ruthlessness and decision: for Japanese rather than League of Nations tactics.   —Letter to Catherine Bauer. February 28, 1933

AFTER A QUARREL. As for having anything 'out' with me further in connection with our ecstatic sun-and-thunderstorm afternoon in Maine, no! not a word! We have spent a good part of the last year, certainly the worst part of the last year, in performing surgical operations upon our emotions: we have taken the stomach out and washed it, we have short-circuited duodenal ulcers and anchored floating kidneys, we have removed gall-stones by the bucket and replaced them with more liquid and pervasive forms of gall: we have taken out healthy appendixes and attempted to awaken flagging hearts by overdoses of adrenalin. In short, by now we are pretty well eviscerated, and the only possible thing I can think of to prevent us from putrefying is to rediscover the secret of Egyptian embalming, and to douse our insides with mummy powder. So to the sarcophagus and the tomb, Miss Cleopatra Bauer and Mr. Amenhotep Mumford! It is the sort of hell you both deserve: desiccated, impotent, eternal. Our egos are both comic. [Possibly a Freudian slip for cosmic?] If mine is at any moment more *exorbitant,* yours is more *continuous:* so they balance up; and the times when we really hate each other are those when they are *both* active and cancel out love.   —Letter to Catherine Bauer. September 14, 1933

And so today, Catherine dear, you are packing: putting things into boxes, and throwing oddments in desperation into corners, and consigning the boxes, with here and there the tags of our life together, to a moving van and a dark room somewhere, where the dust will filter slowly through the fine cracks, and you will not recollect their going or their past existence until another moving day comes, when you will open them, and be more conscious of the dust than of this book, those letters, or that picture which will be covered by it. And here we are both of us on your moving day, on your going away day, surrounded by the broken crockery of that once so handsome bowl decorated with the intertwined figures of Lewis-and-Catherine. Where is the Major's Cement? Shall we mend it for utility? —put it all together again, trying to forget, in the interest of preserving a fine antique, genuine Greek!—*hetaira* and all—that the sexual organs of both figures are missing, and parts of the once embracing arms? Or shall we not bother about putting the fragments together? Shall we just collect the scattered pieces and put them separately in little glass cases: each a perfect fragment, but without unity or relationship: a fragment called wit: a fragment called mind: a fragment called sex: even a fragment for some part of the Museum farthest from a window, called Architecture and Housing? Or will you call in the janitor and tell him this broken crockery was something not worth the packing, and will he please clean it up after you go; for the five o'clock Philadelphia Express is leaving in thirty minutes, and you must call a taxi. At all events, waving good-bye, bitter, ironic, teasing, mocking—and also beneath that, if not so visible to you at the moment, understanding and loving—*here I am!* Are you there too? Have you just gone on a vacation or have you emigrated for good to another land? It may take half a dozen years before either of us is quite sure of the answer.   —Letter to Catherine Bauer. May 31, 1934

A FINAL EXPLOSION.   Ever since getting your letter Wednesday I have been living in a different world. It is like waking up on a battlefield on a clear morning in spring: there is a corpse hooked over a fence and half an arm with a clenched fist is lying next to one's coat, and there are a couple of burned holes in one's pants: so that there is no doubt that something ghastly has really happened; but this fact only increases by contrast the intense innocence of the blue sky and the sound of a song sparrow bursting in the thicket. One's throat is sore, too, so probably one shouted a great deal during the battle, and one can scarcely move one's right leg. And yet the mere fact that one can call out "Hello" and move one's left leg becomes, on this spring battlefield, an astonishing blessing. And that is how I feel. Now . . . You have come back. Not really come back, of course, but come back at least inside of me.
P.S. Since the smoke of battle is clearing, I may tell you, mayn't I? how *much* I enjoyed that letter of yours in which you said I was the cream in your coffee. It was a perfect declaration of love. I remembered that you never took cream in your coffee, and that you always said that it spoiled it for you . . .   —Letter to Catherine Bauer. July 29, 1934

NOTE ON CHARACTER. SOPHIA TO ME: In some ways you are the most exasperating man—because you are so sweet and good—and so absolutely ruthless.   —RN. 1936

BETWEEN FRIENDS. . . . Queerly, in the midst of these last terrible five months, the most sinister in some respects that I have lived through, part of me has remained completely unscathed: I have been conscious of a happiness and a satisfaction in all that makes domestic life sweet that I had never experienced in any such fullness before. What complex brutes we are! No mere stream of consciousness method will ever quite depict the co-existence of incompatible layers of self, and the changes that take place in their position and involvement as one keeps on living. One thinks of oneself as a country under a firm monarchy, dominated by a single set of laws, where the only events that matter happen in the capital: whereas actually we are a federation in which a bandit chief may temporarily exercize more power than the throne, in which different races live side by side, sometimes quarreling, sometimes in amity, and in which extremes of prosperity and poverty, of happiness and sordid disorder, may co-exist even more flagrantly than they do in the streets of New York and London . . . —Letter to Babette Deutsch. May 31, 1936

Amor Embracing

"Looking back on our life," Sophia wrote, while I was in the midst of revising the first draft of 'Amor Threatening,' "I'd have nothing changed, if I could live it over again, except our Geddes's death and whatever in the world's affairs and in our lives made Alison's childhood tense and difficult. But I could accept your having been in love with other women. I don't believe a blameless life is a good life."

I was not surprised by those words; but they led me to read to her for the first time a passage from my unfinished novel, 'Victor,' which I had begun in 1939; for there the wife, though drawn from a quite different imagined model, was already speaking in Sophia's proper person, as I had come to know her and, in a graver sense than in my youth, to love her. Here it is:

"One grows, my love; but never reaches any moment
Of finality, except in death: perhaps not there!
We keep on growing, growing and sometimes shrinking
But not the way we planned. Just like the garden:
Never finished, never quite in order or full flower:
Never safe from worms or drought or sudden frost.
Our marriage is imperfect: yes, and always will be!
I'll never be the girl you wanted
Or sometimes thought you had!
Even our children are a little strange as well as dear:
As if two other parents had begot them.
You're almost all I want, you darling:
But I could do without your guilty conscience
Or guiltier efforts at atonement by taking on
My household tasks—you call it 'cooperation'—
Don't you? Just like a male!

Let's not add up the score: how can we now?
Your wanderings hurt me: yes! And yet I took them
Easier than you could take my small distractions.
Sharing your pain I kept your gleam of ecstasy:
Feeling your ecstasy I shared its sharpening pain
And watched you grow
From fragile, propped-up sapling, tautly wired,
Into a tough, free-standing, time-weathered tree
With many deepening roots and reaching branches
Entangled in my own,
And so we've grown together though never one—
Not trimmed in artful shapes that curb
All expectation of further growth.
. . . If only you and I could hold this blissful moment—
Too soon I know you'll draw within yourself,
Leaving me alone while seeming to be close—
Or Peggy will come bouncing in between us,
Jealous as a child can be of parent lovers:
And so the spell will break: we'll move apart—
Two sudden strangers, who have never met!
And I shall wonder if you really care for me!
More likely you'll dig up some time-bleached jealousy,
Like a dog who keeps his buried bone
For gnawing when the meat is scarce.
Black moments, frigid days, dark premonitions—
These are just as much a part of being loved and loving
As endless opportunities for perfect orgasms.
You men are all perfectionists:
You seek in life what one can only find in art,
Forgetting that love on a Grecian urn
Is not a pledge of utter bliss but Death.
Lifeless perfection's not for me.
Give me the wine, bad years and good,
And don't forget the ferments that help turn
The grape's raw juice each season into headier blood:
Even the lees will tell us when it's time
To fill the flask again with younger wine. . . .
Now kiss me and be off with you!
But come back soon, for I'll be waiting."

—From 'Victor': rough draft of an unfinished novel. 1939

319

17: Letters to Yillah

Yillah—my private nickname for Josephine Strongin—flits in and out of these pages between 1925 and 1942, as she flitted in and out of my life, and still hovers occasionally in my consciousness. We met in Geneva in 1925, when she was sixteen, accompanied there by an older friend and mentor, Lily, who performed some now forgotten task at Zimmern's newly opened school. Delicate, shy, starry-eyed, she was like some newborn Ariel, with her heart visibly palpitating beneath her dress. She was already writing poetry: quite astonishing in its originality, which she read to me one afternoon sitting on a bench in the Promenade des Bastions. It was as if a counterpart of Emily Dickinson had suddenly come to life in suburban Richmond Hill. She was so fraily childlike that she awakened a feeling of parental protectiveness in me which overlay all our future relations. Happily, it was her mind, not her barely pubescent body, I fell in love with. Her earliest poems were breathtaking, and some of her sonnets, published in The American Caravan, likewise deserve a place in any American anthology. Though our correspondence continued on a less tense note after 1944, when as a patient she met the Richmond surgeon who became her lover and husband, even my sparser letters thereafter were preserved in the sealed portfolios she had designated for return to me after her death. That took place in 1969.

. . . Your poems astonished and delighted me, dear Josephine, as much on re-reading them as they did when you read them to me two years ago. Yesterday I showed them to Kreymborg and Rosenfeld, and although we had finally closed the pages of the Caravan we shall open them to the extent of putting in two or three of your very best. We created The

American Caravan just to give such an opportunity; and you should have seen Paul's and Alfred's faces whilst we were reading your poems aloud. I am not competent to judge your musical abilities, but I know that you have a rich literary prospect before you—if you'll work hard, keep your head, and avoid like the devil all the people who will want to 'take you up' and make much of you (for their own ego's sake) as soon as they find you out. If this involves avoiding me, too, I can't rationally complain . . . Yes, I am talking like a dusty old uncle, Josephine, only because I want to reinforce your own instincts, not because I suppose you lack them. I salute you, as Emerson did Whitman, at the beginning of a great career. Dare to grow up!   —To Josephine Strongin, February 27, 1927

. . . The days pass, and most of them I spend with Herman Melville. Occasionally I find some strange, oblique glimpse of you in Melville: in Pierre's sister, and in Yillah, the creature in Mardi that the stranded seamen wander from island to island seeking to capture. Yillah is, I think, your right name: not that I know who she is, or what she means in Melville's parable: but you are she.   —To Josephine Strongin. December 5, 1927

Josephine: you are a precious and unexpected girl. As the summer waned I had given up hope of ever hearing from you, and now you break the silence with a sudden fling of bounty. I've read the sonnets again and again; and I am greatly delighted and reassured. Shall I confess why? I had faith in your coming development; but I thought that perhaps this period of transition out of sheer girlhood would be a hard one, and that for a while your verse would suffer . . . But you have gone on, and all my uneasiness, all my cautious lack of optimism are as nothing. You have done well to impale yourself upon the sonnet: it is a sort of measure of one's inward control, and once liberated here there is scarcely any mood or mode of expression that isn't open. Your sonnets are beautiful: Ever since I read it I have been repeating "I cannot call the day a darker name than Day." But I mustn't pick out all the lines that have affected me, lest you fancy I have responded to them in snatches, and not as parts of a whole. One ought to be mute when one is happy; and I cannot add anything, really, to the fact that your sonnets have made me very happy. —To Josephine Strongin, on The American Caravan stationery. October 6, 1927

. . . Oh! happiness—I don't know whether I am happy or not; or rather, I have discovered that happiness is not the thing that interests me; since the best moments, the remembered moments, the ones one can return to and make something out of, are those that were too sharp and terrible to be embraced at the time; whereas the 'nice' moments are forgotten, and almost as meaningless, as this morning's breakfast, which was nice, too, and no doubt necessary—only it doesn't mean anything. There is one kind of happiness I do prize: but it isn't happiness, it is rather a sort of physical poise, when one's hand is steady and one's eyes bright, clear, and there is nothing but wind and sunlight inside of one. But that is a physical sort of happiness, it is that of a keen animal, and it has nothing whatever to do with one's relations with other people. When they come in, one gets, not happiness, but tension—or—snap!—no tension, and then the relation is over. Balance? Equilibrium? Yes; the balance of the dancer and the equilibrium of the spinning top, which seems motionless because it is in perfect motion, one part playing off against the other in a terrific battle of equal forces. And yet sometimes balance and equilibrium come a little too easily: the old suit fits too well. Then one must deliberately break out of the cage that one fits into so perfectly, lest it become a coffin. But I think I know the mood in which you write: in the midst of it, all tangible things seem a mirage, which one forever is reaching one's hand out to grasp—and forever failing to reach. Wait: and something else will happen, too: life will become all foreground, and you will only have to put out your hand to touch your uttermost desires—and that will be tantalizing, too; and you will long for the mirage you couldn't reach. Do you want to know what I most regret about my youth? That I didn't dream more boldly and demand of myself more impossible things; for all one does in maturity is to carve in granite or porphyry the soap bubble one blew in youth! Oh to have dreamed harder! . . . —To Josephine Strongin. December 5, 1927

. . . As for Melville, I have not yet plunged into him: I feel like a diver on the edge of a high diving platform, ready for the exhilaration, but a little afraid of it. All the people who have so far touched the 'madness' of Melville have been the feeble-mad sort themselves; whereas it takes strength to feel the strength of Melville's madness, which at bottom was not madness at all, in the medical sense, but a tragic insight into a destiny without bottom. Happiness, I think, lies on the surface: it lies in the arts, in love-making, in all the sports that take one out on the sea or up into the mountains: in being a parent or a gardener and watching things grow: in feeling confidence in one's professional technique, whether it be sweeping a street or writing a sonnet: but when one plunges under the surface all these buoyant things disappear, and the farther down one gets the more cold and dark it seems: and the more oppressive space feels. Melville could not stay on top; had he been able to do this, he would have remained, very possibly, among the Typees in the South Seas; but he could not even rest happily with his wife and children; one by one he stripped away from him all the things that make a happy man, until finally he had not even his own courage in adventure to buoy him up. I don't think that his was a road to follow; but it is a road that one must be aware of and reckon with.   —To Josephine Strongin. January 29, 1928

. . . You were right in your criticism of my Melville biography: there is much of me in it, but the material itself was not created by me, and I was cut out by nature and circumstances to do something other than comment upon other men's work—however able or pertinent the commentary may be. I have always known that: but I have kept this impulse patiently in check, for I plan to do something larger, more terrifying, than the ordinary novel or play, and one must use a good part of one's life in the mere absorption of nourishment before one is ready for such a task. It is in this manner that you must consider the books that I have so far written, and the one or two more I may have to write, before I am ready to kick over the traces, and gallop forth in my own right, without bit or bridle. One should write poems about love while one is young, and still learning: but one can't write epics then, for an epic demands a mastery and a control large enough to manoeuvre an army or dig the Panama Canal. Now, at last, I feel that the vital years for me are approaching: and I am ready for the plunge. In five years, ten years, we shall see the results. In the meanwhile I am happy; and happy not because things are going well with me: they never went worse than this winter: but because I can stand on top of them and bear them down, whether they go well or ill. When I was a little boy my nurse used to call me His Little Royal Highness, and I am afraid that such early suggestions must have fostered my pride and made it enlarge; it took me years to lose the royal habit of expecting the world to wait upon me and attend to my wishes, and now that I have become reasonable about such things, only the lure of pride, which the Romans called—how much more adequate it sounds!—*superbia*, remains. It is not altogether a lovely quality. Dante had it to the full, and he is an odious person; but a quality that is dreadful at a dinner table may be marvellous in a work of art, and it is so in 'The Divine Comedy.' What a furious and rich work that is! I am reading it at last in an adequate translation, Melville Anderson's, and though I reject the whole conception of the universe on which it is based, the marvel is that so much remains. A man: a life: a culture: they may be a tissue of defeats and failures, but so long as they have aimed at something beyond, which is full and rich and whole, they endow us with life. . . . —To Josephine Strongin. March 27, 1929

. . . Every once is a while some larger idea rises before me, and I walk around it quietly and look at it and say to myself: Yes, I'll return to you in a little while, and then we shall see! Patience! I am not ready for you yet. I have done a little consecutive reading, slow, at my own pace; and that is a great pleasure. The first part of 'Swann's Way' entranced me; and I said to myself, Ah! I have kept away from Proust too long; this man reincarnates one as a Frenchman, just as Tolstoi does as a Russian, and every hour one spends with him lengthens one's life by a year. True: as long as he kept to the little provincial society of Combray. But Paris and Swann left me with a brackish taste. A marvellous picture of jealousy, and even at times of love, but tedious in the way that obsessions are tedious, and beneath it one felt the sourness and boredom of French society, despite its cultivation, refinement, finesse, intelligence; that sense of perpetual *un*youthfulness which makes one say to oneself as one walks along the Boulevard des Italiens: Thank Heaven I am an American! If I had to live here, I would become a whiff of anarchy, yes, a hurricane, and blow it all away! —To Josephine Strongin. June 23, 1929

[Josephine and her husband, Alfred Leiserson, dropped in on us a little while ago: the first time I had seen her since her marriage. She looked like a very frail and swaggery young unicorn that had been dressed by Bergdorf Goodman: panting with fear and excitement: oppressed by the chores of domesticity: delighted, I gathered through no open word, by the sweets of connubiality; and in general, though she still has the alarming habit of fainting suddenly, was not merely happy but in the mood for work. And she kissed me, too—for the first time I hasten to add—with a confidence in her own powers rather than a belief in mine. At all events, the strain of being a literary uncle to a tremulous virgin was over, and we were very nearly equals. —To Catherine Bauer. July 31, 1933]

. . . The days pass, the months pass, almost the years pass; and I have not heard from you. But I have heard about your errant body from Babette and thought of you often. Some of the thoughts must have reached you: they didn't need letters for wings. The last two months have been benign for Sophy and me; we have rested and breathed slow and rested again. I can stand a lot of doing nothing; it agrees with me; I was made for it; I am already, by that token, one who looks forward to Eternity. How nice it will be to know one has a million years ahead of

324

one before supper: the book will fall from one's hands as one's eyes close and a smile appears on one's relaxing lips, as in a pleasant dream; and when one wakes up there will be another million years before one has to brush one's teeth. Geddes rides a brown and white mustang and carries a rope lariat and swears and flourishes a cap pistol: he is Geddes. I am a patient gardener, and my Italian squashes and Chinese cucumbers sing a hymn to the Lord. Sophy, as usual, is an Earth-Goddess who originally came from Tartary. Can you, will you, won't you join us for a few days? Won't you and Alfred at least spend another night with us? —To Josephine Strongin. March 3, 1934

GLIMPSES OF HAWAII. . . . There is no privacy outdoors at the ocean's edge, save in the shadow of the palm trunks. Everyone may walk along the sea wall or wander through anyone's yard: privacy is a luxury which even the rich can scarcely keep for themselves: how would a Hawaiian get fish to spear, how would he manage his surfboard, unless the ocean front were open to all? The library that goes with the house is a treasure: it represents the stale and undiscriminating selection of two generations, filled with now comical books that once were literary events: with such surprises as a life of Michelangelo in two volumes, not J. A. Symonds', and the works of Shakespeare in duplicate, and Holmes's 'Elsie Venner,' a novel I have always meant to read and so am now reading. I have the services of a secretary who comes at eight in the morning when I beckon her; I hold conferences; I meet the fabulous monsters who play polo, collect Ming statuary, and govern the pineapple and sugar plantations: sometimes in their homes, sometimes at a golf club that nestles under the bare hills. And I utter sociological platitudes with an air of innocent profundity: I say "Ah yes!" more often than is good for my soul, and I say, "This beauty still intoxicates me," at breakfast, luncheon and dinner—and *still mean it*. The sharp heathen voluptuousness of the island has me in its grip. —To Josephine Strongin. August 8, 1938

. . . Melville spends a whole chapter in 'Moby-Dick' dwelling on the nature of Delight; and now I can add a paragraph or two to all he could say about it. I have packed the tiny phial of ginger perfume I picked up in Hawaii to send away to you; and now that it is irretrievably wrapped I begin to wonder if it is really ginger and not pikaki or carnation or some other Hawaiian scent, and I doubt if it can even faintly give you a sense of the dark woods beneath the jagged mountains on the windward side of Oahu where, stumbling over stumps through an ancient forest, near an old Hawaiian temple and sacrificial ground, I came upon the ginger plant, growing with all the lusty strength of canna: heavy stems, broad leaves, sweet rank odor, heavy and pungent, like some anesthetic invented to allay the pains of thwarted lovers. If you had popped out from behind the great dark mango trees, when I first saw the ginger wild, I should not have been surprised: a month of browning would make you a fine *wahini* in the native style, without their unprovocative over-ripeness. —To Josephine Strongin. November 2, 1938

. . . About the enigmatic face I find in the mirror: that demands a long poem, called The Barber's Looking Glass. It is the barber's chair that really is the one continuous thread in a man's inner life: every two or three weeks he beholds his face in the mirror for half an hour: that visit has a concentration, a holy intentness about it, that is almost as good as prayer. And visit by visit the face changes: the anxious eye of the adolescent, the merry eyes of the young man in love, the sober eyes of the struggling worker, the face now plump with complacency, now lean, sometimes even haggard: a white face, a red face, a greenish face. I want to put that all down sometime: the story of a whole life could be told in terms of those punctuating images. The changing face in the mirror would play against the counter-image of the barber: now a Greek, now a German, now a cockney in London, now a man from Peoria in Honolulu, and the barbers' stories would thread in and out of the main theme, although one would have to take liberties with fact there, since barbers, who are still known to low comedy as loquacious fellows, have now become as silent as Vice-Presidents of a bank passing on an application for a loan. It is a very masculine story, of course: the male's fateful periodicity, as he watches his face becoming transformed, perhaps disfigured or distorted by life—and as time goes on, *de-faced*. My talent is probably not equal to my conception: so you will have to guess my poem . . . or write it!   —To Josephine Strongin. December 1, 1938

. . . What a moral universe we live in! It is a great gambling house with only one rule that must be observed by all the players—*No cheating! You will positively be detected!* That perhaps is the ultimate wisdom for all of us, dragged forth from the bitter years.   —To Josephine Strongin. February 3, 1939

. . . Work is a man's spine, and if that isn't straight and firm he cannot even relax in bed! A very remarkable Englishwoman once wrote something about this with more general reference. She was Mary Everest Boole, the wife of the great Cambridge logician, a man whose genius was so original that the prudent University still dares not publish his papers because they *seem* so mad. She said that one's ultimate moral victory was to be able to relinquish that which one wanted most at the moment of actual possession! Musty words! And yet the one time in my life I consciously did this I had a feeling of triumph that no other moment has ever brought me.   —To Josephine Strongin. November 3, 1938

Note: Mrs. Boole became for Josephine the cold incarnation of all the marital loyalties and duties that kept her passionate demands and expectations from being fulfilled.

. . . During the last two days I have been drunk—drenched with sunlight, drunk with fatigue, that sweet weariness which follows a whole day spent in getting a garden in order . . . But it is a great relief from the bleakness of the winter: to say nothing of the bleakness of talking, as through a megaphone across the Hudson River, to the girls at Barnard and Smith. Somehow, we never were in the same room, those girls and I. I saw their faces: they looked at mine—and I might have been maundering over the radio between the National Cheese Program and the Fluffy Shaving Soap Hour. At Dartmouth it was a little better. I delivered three or four talks that were probably as good as anything I had ever done: including one on Van Gogh in which I was seized by his demon and spoke like the vehement inarticulate Mynheer Peeperkorn. I saw old Meiklejohn again, whom I had not met for ten whole years, since my visit to Wisconsin, which he remembered in acute detail. He has the face of some keen Lancashire mummy, a little dried but not showing the effect of age, with alert eyes, still young with wonder; and I met Eugen Rosenstock-Huessy at last. Rosenstock is a little compact man, by vocation a philosopher, with blue eyes, a soft, almost Viennese face, and squat legs slightly bowed, legs that might belong to a groom, an ex-jockey, or a professional riding master. [Actually, he loved horses, gloried in mastering them, and used to ride horseback to class.] He, Meiklejohn, and I all agreed on what a liberal education needed most—work! Daily renewal and companionship in actual physical work. So we got along famously. Rosenstock founded the first German labor camps, for educational purposes, students, farmers, mechanics all together. Six years later Hitler turned them to baser military uses.   —To Josephine Strongin. May 3, 1939

. . . Murray and I were talking of the New Englanders who turn an impassive face to death and show no grief; and what they don't show presently vanishes from them. But such a loss, said Murray, should be returned to, not put aside, not forgotten. And though we had taken opposite sides at first, for I had praised the heroism of New England mothers in an infantile paralysis epidemic, quoting Van Wyck Brooks, I remembered, in agreement with him, how Robert Frost had sat too firmly upon his hot temper, his passion, until now I suspect it is not available for expression: hence the staid epigrams of his old age. —To Josephine Strongin. February 21, 1939

. . . The weather has been wild and fitful, like everything about our lives today: yesterday, in noonday sun, the thermometer registered 92 and I walked out in my leather jacket without a hat, and saw a bluebird, while the snow melted into torrents and lakes formed on the surface of the fields. Today I should not be surprised to meet a polar bear on an ice-floe, floating down the Webutuck. The skies, the temperature, the dubious choice between woolens in many forbidding folds, and sheer inviting nakedness is symbolic of the course of our friendship. At a distance of four hundred miles from you I am always reaching for wool and feeling the shivering ripple of flesh, or imagining flesh and confronting wool: so perhaps we had better talk about two other people! —To Josephine Strongin in Richmond, Virginia. Winter 1940.

. . . After my talk at the anti-fascist meeting in Emerson Hall I had my first chance to meet Salvemini, the Italian historian, a little pudgy near-sighted man, with a gray complexion and a gray beard that makes him look like an Etruscan Silenus. I like Salvemini. He had a fine addition to propose to my anti-fascist measures. "Your demands are too heroic," he said. "Let us begin with something simple. We will solve the problem of where to put the fascist refugees by a simple proposal: exchange them for the fascists who are now here!" I agreed: *Excellent!* His conversation is full of memorable, half-true epigrams; as for example his definition of an Englishman: "One who is clever enough to look stupid enough to appear honest." Or his saying: "The English are really an exceptionally honest people: more so than any other. If in the rest of Europe eighty per cent of the people are honest, and twenty per cent are liars and crooks, in England ninety per cent are actually honest. Unfortunately the remaining ten per cent are all politicians." —To Josephine Strongin. February 13, 1939

. . . That there were large bounties of passionate love in you, Jo, enough to turn water into wine and feed all the guests at Cana, I always knew. The mischief is that you can neither contain your love within your present bounds, nor let it flow freely, since no outlet short of another life as ready and open as yours is big enough to receive it and hold it. And what have I to give you? Only a fraction of a life already narrowed and concentrated on my work: A life filled and preoccupied by marital attachments and civic concerns: already turning away from disturbing personal intimacies, perhaps prematurely—as if age were coming early to all of us in times like this—in order to give my undistracted energies to that which may help quicken the mood of creation in the world again—without which we all die. . . . That is why Sophy and the children remain so steadily in my mind; and that is why, if your love for me were only the overflow of a happy life, as mine is for you, we could give more to each other. But I won't pretend, as you tried to pretend to yourself last year, that there is any short way to live through such a love to the point of satiation, so that you might then fling it out of your life like a squeezed orange. A little is no substitute for all.   —To Josephine Strongin. March 24, 1939

. . . Nature has backed up my admonitions about your tired heart before I had time to even utter them. The heart! the heart! Today it is the weak spot in all those who are truly alive: the very mail that brought your letter this morning brought another from my dear friend Walter Curt Behrendt, at Hanover, to tell me that he had been in bed for the last fortnight with a heart attack. The Egyptians were right: the heart is the seat of the soul: the first point of attack, the very outpost of the battle line, in a world where brutality is uppermost. Only the hard-hearted, with the turtle's pulse and the fish's coldness, can survive on their own terms today. The rest of us must look to our hearts, and woe to us if our hygiene is complicated with love!   —To Josephine Strongin. June 1, 1941

. . . To parallel your life a little closer, Jo, Sophia and I "went to a party," too, when Borgese had a birthday and invited us over to his summer place in Smithfield. Your little goblin Neilson was there, with his wife; and Thomas Mann and his wife were up for the briefest of parental visits in addition: so perhaps you think I am going to tell you about the meeting of four great minds, and of all the jewels that dropped from the creator of Joseph, who always—did I ever tell you?—carries with him the indefinable aura of a true German prig, an aura conveyed best by the tone of his voice: just a touch of fussiness and unction, like the German rentier I met once on a train going from Zürich to Innsbruck, who meticulously put on a pair of elegant silk gloves as soon as he entered our compartment. I did have a few brief snatches of conversation with Mann, not about Joseph or Hans Castorp but about Shakespeare. We agreed that he was a very great writer! More, that he had pre-figured the entire modern world. Mann had just been to a dress rehearsal of Macbeth and was struck by its contemporaneity. But what a difference, he observed, there was in the ruthless monsters of Shakespeare's day! with what speed they were seized with remorse! and with what sensitiveness they reflected upon their wickedness!

We had cocktails; and the giver of that party either had a demon in him or suffered as much from the effects of gin as you did from Bourbon: at all events, there was a wild look in Borgese's eye, and though Mrs. Neilson has likewise a devouring ego, too long suppressed by the pedantic leading strings of Smith College and the competition of the most beautiful and loose girls in America, it was nothing to Borgese once he was started. And it needed only a little to prompt him to a tirade: just Mrs. Mann's somewhat favorable interpretation of a broadcast from the Vatican! Then a torrent poured forth, an avalanche, which foamed around the herb-roasted filet of beef, poured over the artichokes, thinned the sauce Béarnaise, and diluted the champagne. It needed only one thing to become a geyser; and this was the fact that at one point the great Mann somewhat tactlessly remarked, like a character in one of his novels repeating a pat line, that in every Italian there was something of an actor—indeed, a touch of the *buffone*, Mann added, as if to be sure that the insult was properly pinned in place and would stick.

The geyser exploded. History was summoned to become a tidal wave of refutation. Was Dante a *buffone?* Was Michelangelo a scalawag of an actor? And what finally was Mazzini—an empty strutter? There was no need for Borgese to bring in Borgese: Mazzini was close enough, for, now that I know Mazzini better, I realize that the best parts of 'The City of Man' are pure Mazzini, and all the better for that. The refutation was complete enough to silence an even greater writer than Mann and a more heroic warrior; but unfortunately it did not silence Borgese; and so, in the course of the evening, he refuted his own unanswerable arguments by holding the center of the stage, by haranguing and soliloquizing, by bringing forth both question and answer, and, having provided the dinner, he also provided all the speeches at this more than platonic symposium. He was magnificent; but only as one is magnificent when one is drunk or infuriated or mad: the kind of magnificence that embarrasses the spectator when it occurs and should embarrass the subject of it for weeks later on.   —To Josephine Strongin. November 13, 1941

. . . By some freak of fate I am at this moment writing about Rousseau's central place in Romanticism. He and Thomas Mann's Joseph are the two bêtes noires of my life: they are the stalking caricatures of my extra-marital love life, and will be enough to make posterity wonder if I had any love life, in or outside marriage. Yet who was so powerful in his weakness as Jean-Jacques? Just because he had an inflamed penis that made sexual intercourse too painful, he courted his ladies instead of throwing them abruptly on the bed; and if he never got around to the final act of love-making, he made a whole generation of women recognize how their more ready lovers had been neglecting them: he made visible tenderness and friendly intercourse the rival of copulation. —To Josephine Strongin. November 13, 1941

. . . I came up here a little jaded, fighting a cold but so changed did I become with the first whiff of spring air and the friendly faces of the station master and the grocer and the taxi driver that I almost feel as if half a year rather than half a day separated me from this morning in the city. The house was so friendly, too: shabby, the paint scraped away on woodwork and floor, dust, misplaced books, dead wasps under the window and live wasps crawling over it, the musty smell of winter and mouldly papers, yet bearing layer upon layer of my past life: full of that sense of time, precisely because of the frayed edges and the battered ends, which Virginia Woolf interpreted so poignantly in 'To the Lighthouse.' (A pang stabs me; for maybe this place, like the Professor's house, will be deserted in the course of the war; and rain and snow and wind will work upon it, too, without even an old scrubwoman to fend them off.) The very commonplaceness of this old farmhouse, the ordinariness of its site and its views, are all just what they should be, our life being what it is. This is not some magnificence I dreamed of, plotted for, and finally achieved; but a place I came upon as one may come upon an inn when the day is over and the hour to stop for the night has come. Whatever comeliness our home may have is what we have given the house and the land out of sheer neighborly intimacy. —To Josephine Strongin. April 30, 1942

. . . You asked about 'Lady Chatterley's Lover'—*lover*, not lovers, you naughty girl! And alas! I must confess that I don't possess a copy, though I read it soon after it came out, and know that I meant to get a copy when I was in Paris in 1929. I can't remember who loaned me my copy; but I have a pretty keen recollection of the book itself, and of the impression it has made on the various girls I know. Unless I am mistaken, it will have far less for you than you perhaps fancy. As a novel it is a feeble work indeed; for Lawrence loads the dice by giving Lady Chatterley not only a cold husband, equivalent to Anna Karenina's Alexander in Tolstoi's novel, but one who had become incapacitated for sex through a war

331

injury. That makes it easier for her to accept the gardener who woos her, but it removes the tension within Lady Chatterley—heavens! I can't remember her given name!—between the repressive side of her nature, the side that would keep close to convention, duty, family obligations, class differences, sublimation, and the part which craves expression and complete sensual fulfillment. In that very tension lies half the drama of marriage and half the excitement and delight in love. Lawrence removed the tension by making the simple gardener, whose name I also forget, who takes pride in his sex and awakens Lady Chatterley's pride in hers: consciously adding to their physical intimacy little ceremonies like bedecking her Mount of Venus with forget-me-nots, and teaching her the coarse, blunt, earthy, sometimes very ancient words for the sex organs and acts. Releasing girls from their verbal inhibitions about acts of love was a necessary step in returning to a more elemental and healthy attitude toward sex itself. —To Josephine Strongin. April 30, 1942

. . . Daily the Amenia house grows emptier, Jo: one by one our roots are being pulled up: by now we have disencumbered ourselves of our Lares and Penates and wander around like ghosts, unable to leave the spot but no longer attached to it. In a few days we must set out for Stanford. All but our physical selves have flown: what is left is querulous, impatient, edgy, waiting for the moment that will make our state real through the final act of doing. The house is empty and I am empty, too: I am no longer here and I am surely not anywhere else . . .

This moving away has been a big job, not in the mass but in the thousand cluttering details that have attended it. (It had better be for a long time, or the sheer futility of it will be brutal!) For one thing I have put my private papers in order: such ironic order, too, with Beryl in the oldest file, along with my juvenilia, above Helen, who is next to Catherine, who jostles Alice, who attempts to freeze out the indomitable Jo, the latter too precious and too voluminous to be entirely frozen out by anyone. And above them all stands Sophia, proudly alone, filling an entire drawer: still Winged Victory! What a Westminster Abbey of Love that is! Though each is shrouded in a series of manilla envelopes, I foresee fights, anarchies, disruptions; but you, being the only one who is not wholly a ghost, have the edge on the dissolving shades of my past. Old Geddes, venerable and Hebrew-prophetic, pronounces a lofty curse on all of you, and then proceeds to fall into a muffled soliloquy on the importance of sex in life and the divinity of Aphrodite! —To Josephine Strongin. August 28, 1942

18: From a Family Album

Not the least significant of my Random Notes are those devoted to our children, Geddes and Alison—named after the naughty wench in the Miller's Tale!—supplemented as these are by the letters Sophia and I wrote to each other during my frequent absences, or notes which Sophia independently made and preserved in her own files. Without these notes to true up our vague or spotty recollections, it would have been impossible for me to write 'Green Memories.' Though we never made these observations systematically, they came forth spontaneously in times of crisis—birth, illness, parting—or in days of delight we sought to engrave deeper in our consciousness. When in 1940, writing 'Faith for Living,' I stressed the re-birth and deliberate culture of the family, I was speaking from our own time-weathered experience, as I noted later in my introduction to Kenneth Beame's pamphlet on keeping a 'Family Log.' Like any other young parents, we shared our pride and joy in our young all too fully in letters to older friends—somewhat naively, somewhat smugly we realize now, after having received many equally lengthy letters from later generations of young parents! Instead of being a regression in our present 'instant culture,' this conscious replenishment of family ties, practical and sentimental, still seems one of the most promising immediate means of combatting the total disintegration of human society— already manifest in the idiot anti-art of our time.

Our boy, Geddes, who is now three years old, as the result of his mother's tactful interpretation of his dim questions and puzzlements knows more about biology than I did at twelve: he not merely knows the sequence of seed, shoot, plant, flower or fruit, and seed, by participating in the garden; but he also has bridged the gap to mammals and knows that all animals grow from seeds, and that the mammals carry the young inside of them. This is a genuine farming district; and there is no difficulty in providing the boy with illustrations and experiments. At three years, the sexual interest is awake and active, and this seems to us a much better period to establish such knowledge and relations in a plain simple way than a later time in childhood when self-consciousness and shame make the business of asking questions and answering them much more difficult, and when one may say far too much, if one does not err on the usual side and say far too little. And emphatically, this is a matter for a mother, not for a teacher; for the time to get these matters settled is when the query is dawning, not when the school schedule allots time to it. —Letter to Victor Branford. August 22, 1928

. . . [Geddes] was playing he was a horse this morning, and the horse was looking after the two little baby birds (Sophy and me). I said that I had never heard of a horse taking care of birds. But he answered: "Yes: this is a horse with wings: it's Pegasus." . . . He has an enormous interest in living creatures, mice, moles, fish, insects, as well as the barnyard creatures, and will spend half an hour at a time following an ant about: in short, he has a distinct bent toward following his namesake's footsteps! . . . —Letter to Patrick Geddes. August 26, 1929

There was a moment when at the age of four, Geddes's very self pops out in a letter Sophia wrote me in 1929, when I was again in Geneva. "Our young son was really too amusing to be, the other night. Right after supper Mother and he were singing Yankee Doodle together, he very deep and loud. He explained this was because 'all the people could hear him sing and they'd come round to listen.' When no audience showed up he was slightly at a loss. He felt himself to be in fine form and evidently thought it a shame to waste such good singing. So he announced he was going to the Glintenkamps, to sing to them. Off he marched, shoulders hunched up and arms stiffly swinging, very sober, all by himself. I followed at a discreet distance to make sure he made no stops on the bridge. As I drew near I heard a brave voice calling on the Glints to appear. When no one was forthcoming after several attempts, with arms straight at his side and head erect, the little troubadour stood there in the pathway in front of their house and very solemnly and profoundly sang Yankee Doodle from start to finish. It was all done so simply and earnestly, with such faith, I found my eyes tearing as I watched. He was

so steadfast and so solitary there in the garden in the twilight . . ."
—From 'Green Memories.' 1947

Little Geddes has had a good winter so far. I must tell you the latest story about him. Sophy found him one afternoon dancing up and down, his face distorted, and she asked him, a little frightened, what on earth was the matter with him? "I am a soldier," he explained, "and when soldiers can't go to war, they dance madly!" —Letter to Patrick Geddes. January 27, 1930

. . . The life up here is very healthy: we have lived off our own garden since the end of June, and we plan to have an even richer one, both floral and vegetable, next year. Little Geddes, at six, is a good gardener: his first move after breakfast is inspection of the vegetables in his own plot, and he hoes it and weeds it assiduously. He has a sharp eye, and can identify the plants he knows in even their young or withered forms. The horsetails and the clubfoot moss grow in different places up here: the first is familiar to him, but the second we had never discovered till the other day. Geddes looked at the segmented stem and said: "This is just like the horsetail!" In the lake, he is a little porpoise: he taught himself this summer to swim, dive, and float, and he has no more fear of that element than he has of the land. In addition, he is a passionate fisherman and has a pretty good anatomical knowledge of the fish he catches. In short, he is in many ways a credit to you as well as to his parents! —Letter to Patrick Geddes. September 6, 1931

Just this morning, discussing with Sophia the imminence of our cat's having kittens, Sophia remembered an episode that should have gone into 'Green Memories'; for it introduced Geddes, when he was nine or ten, to the process of birth and the fact of motherhood. Our Sunnyside cat, when she was about to have kittens, plainly demanded Sophia's company and insisted that Sophia stay with her during the whole ordeal. The way she got Sophia to be with her was to stand in front of her, and look at her, meeowing, and as soon as Sophia noticed her she ran toward the cellar stairs. When this had been repeated a few times, Sophia took the hint and followed her to the cellar. She then went into the box that Sophia had prepared for her; but when Sophia started upstairs again she ran after her, and mewed piteously until Sophia consented to return. This happened on a Saturday, and Geddes spent a large part of the morning watching the process of birth, fascinated; and since he had plenty of

335

experience with animals, having already skinned them, if not killed them, he was not in the least upset by the physiology of it.   —RN. March 26, 1963

Green Memories

THE KITCHEN—WHAT WENT ON THERE. Perhaps the best thing about our farmhouse in Leedsville was that it had a large old-fashioned kitchen, with a pantry that served as a secondary workroom for messier jobs. Its low crumbled ceiling was patched with puddles of ancient plaster; near the two windows facing south was a large deal table, painted daffodil yellow; and the walls were a lighter yellow that stood out against the gray woodwork.

The fittings of the kitchen changed from time to time; but the main thing about it was that it was spacious and many activities besides cooking went on there; for here is where the loot of Geddes's trapping and hunting would be piled; here is where, in winter at all events, he might—especially before his room was enlarged—play dominoes or chess with John; here is where he tested his traps, wound his fishing lines, greased his boots, or just lounged about and chatted with his mother. To some of the houseworkers who came and went during the next few years, Geddes's affairs seemed an intrusion; but, at least till he was fourteen, the kitchen was the great common family domain, and it could not have served its purposes if it had been planned for cooking alone. Mark that, you economical architects and you close calculators of costs per cubic feet!

Geddes had scope in this kitchen. His traps and gear hung on the hooks by the door; his guns nestled in the corner; his school books would be tossed on the window sill while he dashed out, with his shot gun, to "paste" some derisive crows. Sophy gave him plenty of leeway in puttering around: my desk still has a paperweight, now precious and venerable, consisting of a little wooden boat carved by Geddes in the kitchen, its interior being a lead weight he had melted down on the stove from old foil and sinkers and poured into it. Much that Geddes and his mother had in common, apart from temperament, was bred of the intimacy that grew out of this working relationship, with her baking or cooking while Geddes painstakingly cleaned his gun, or scraped the stretched skin of a muskrat. Naturally, cooking did not make the room less attractive to a growing boy. The aroma of pies, cakes, icings, cookies, hung over the house; on baking days, there would be bowls to lick, too.

Yes: the kitchen and its products played no small part in Geddes's growing years. We used to broil steaks and chops over the open fire in the dining room; for Geddes and I both held, against Sophy, that they needed to be charred; but the kitchen remained the center of our actions and our affections: indeed, one could not pass from one part of the house to the other without going through it. No good architect could have planned the place so badly; but from a family point of view, no good architect would have had imagination enough to make such a happy, sociability-provoking blunder.

The best moments of life are usually unplanned for, indeed unplannable. The most one can do in designing a house to further intimacy and family living is to allow enough space to have one occupation take place beside another, so that people will meet spontaneously even when they are not drawn together by a common job. What is wrong with too sedulous a division of labor is simply the fact that it divides people. If the room is large enough, a family won't get in one another's way. Geddes's gear sometimes piled up too heavily and overflowed too copiously into the kitchen; but Sophy, wiser by instinct than I am, was always ready to sacrifice neatness and order to spontaneity and good fellowship, at least this side of sheer chaos.

GEDDES'S BEING USUALLY A YOUNGER BOY among older ones made him something of a solitary in relation to his age group and perhaps put him under a special strain. After he had knocked around the country on his own, and had perhaps seen more of the seamier side of life than was good for him, on both his Florida trip and the wheat ranch in the Northwest, Geddes felt himself "too old" to be thrust back into the company of more stay-at-home high school kids; so at times he brought upon himself an extra twinge of loneliness. At this time, he was actually longing for more human companionship; but he had a shyproud way of waiting for others to make advances to him.

Certainly Geddes reacted against the notion, so dear to educators during the last generation, that there is a duty to achieve a sort of smooth conforming acceptance, adjusted to the group's requirements whatever they may be, creating no 'situation' because of a failure to fit in with the group's pattern. Those who accept this ideal have an easy time of it, becoming Romans in Rome or Nazis in Nazidom, as readily as they might become joiners, go-getters, or smoothies in a land where nonconformity has, in these latter years, been set down as the cardinal sin. People who take what is going, who make no demands of their own, often feel a certain self-righteous indignation toward those who choose a thornier path. But Geddes's inwardness, though it often hurt and baffled him, was the mood out of which original, self-sustaining personalities develop:

from such as they come the new forms of life. Geddes was rarely to have a smooth or easy time; but hardship, pain, frustration, alienation produce their own kind of reward. "Character everywhere," William James wrote, "demands the stern and sacrificial mood as one of its factors." We never shared the anxiety of Geddes's teachers about his nonconformity; we would even, perhaps, have to accept their reproach if they said that our own attitudes had something to do with fostering it. But Geddes was social enough when the situation demanded it.

Once in Geddes's early teens, after talking about what the boys he had known at the City and Country School were going to do that summer, his mother asked Geddes if he would not perhaps like to go to camp. He was outraged at the idea; and his mother said, in self-defense: "I thought perhaps you might like a change from your usual mode of living. Lots of boys like camp: they have fun in group activities and games."—"I can't understand your need to be surrounded by *mobs*," Geddes answered.

Among his elders, Geddes's manner usually had an inbred courtesy, full of tactful deference that was charming to watch, because it was so deeply part of his nature, not put on for show; the very bend of his shoulders sometimes expressed his attitude. He was sensitive to the needs and feelings of others: once when in the rush of packing, his mother wanted to pass on a pair of his overalls to a neighbor's child, though it needed to have a hole patched, he sharply reproved her and insisted that she withhold it altogether, so as not to humiliate the lad, unless she was ready to mend it. Sometimes he might be impatient, quick-tempered, and even overbearing; but this sense of what was due to human dignity was with him from the earliest years. So he had no difficulty in getting on with the people he rubbed up against in the Army. Far from being upset by the coarse and rough types he might meet there, he understood their good points and read what they were really saying through the smoke-screen of obscenity which served only to cover up their acute malaise and discomfort. He understood how some of the men in his company could honestly weep with sentiment over the pictures of their wives or children, though they had spent weekend leave with a prostitute. "The great thing about the Army," he once said earnestly, "is that you could line up eight million of us soldiers, four million on each side, and every man would have something in common with the man opposite him and be able to talk freely to him right off. That's something that just wouldn't happen with eight million civilians."

From 1938 onward, there was a mounting tension within our household, as Sophia and I sought, with gathering determination to rouse our

338

friends, our neighbors, and where possible a wider public, to take the measures needed to combat actively the mephitic "Wave of the Future" which seemed about to engulf the earth and wipe away, as if it were sand, every human landmark. Our intentness on this task as citizens often made us too anxiously busy to be good parents. "Children and world crises don't mix!" Sophy exclaimed in a letter of June 1941. "I never dreamed I would find myself almost resenting the time I must give to listening to Geddes's confidences or assuring Alison her dolly is beautiful." We envied a little those who could still serenely plan picnics and set out new plants in their gardens. We could not. Yet the best of the young sometimes shared our concern. In the delirium before his untimely death, Geddes's young cousin, Conrad Fleisher, had said—these were his last words—"I dreamt I was a strong man flying over China to help the Chinese against the Japanese." That was in 1938 and it was part of Geddes's background.

Geddes had one tantalizing glimpse of Heaven, a visible, palpable Heaven: the five weeks he spent in Hawaii. We went there in the summer of 1938, that ominous summer when the storm that was to overtake Geddes's whole generation was already piling up on the horizon; and the experience remained, all in all, one of the most vivid and rewarding episodes in his life. Sometimes, during the long three weeks when Sophy lay in the Queen's Hospital with virus pneumonia, I was inclined to doubt the decision that had brought me back there to write a report on the planning of Honolulu's parks; but I had only to look at Geddes's eager face to have my doubts vanish. From the moment he heard about this jaunt, our first large adventure as a family, Geddes—his mother reported—had been riding high, and Alison, in tune with Geddes's gaiety, went around the house singing: Glory, glory, Honolulu!

We were lucky enough to rent a house on Kalakaua Avenue, fronting the ocean, separated from the sea wall by a lawn of sparse needlelike grass. We were about half way between Diamond Head, where our new friend Lester McCoy lived, and Waikiki, where Geddes was to spend most of his days, swimming and mastering the surfboard. Our house was made of weather-blackened boards, with white trim; and though it had been built too early to have any of the graces of modern architecture, its wide porches and its spacious rooms, as dark as the outside boards, had that combination of openness and shade which is so necessary under the tropical sun; and its sordidly comfortable furniture, with its Morris chairs and battered bricabrac, its alcoves and recesses, its wide stairs to the meagerly furnished upper rooms, gave it attributes that paralleled our Leedsville home. In the yard, hibiscus bushes and a lone papaya tree grew; but on the ocean side we were sentineled by a group of palm trees, slanting away from the house, whose black fronds, delicately waving and whispering in the moonlight, sent shivers of delight up and down our spines.

The first night, as we watched the moon's path on the smooth sea from the second story lanai Sophy said: "It would be worth traveling all this distance just for this, even if we had to go back tomorrow morning." That exclamation brought an ironic reward not a day but a week or so later. Before leaving Amenia, Sophy had battled with a serious strepto-coccus infection in her throat; indeed, she had done her packing alone, while still weak with fever; and she was the victim of a singularly obtuse physician who should never have encouraged her to start, at such an early date after recovery, on her long journey. So she was never quite up to scratch physically, at any point in the days we had in Honolulu, though characteristically she tried to conceal her weakness and laugh it down. I hardly dare to think how entrancing that trip would have been for us as a family if she had only been in health. As it was, Geddes, I am glad to say, suffered least from her disability. We had arranged his days so that he could spend most of his time with a surfboard at Waikiki, sometimes not even coming back for lunch, but getting hot dogs and coca-cola on the beach; and he threw himself into that routine with boundless zest, frequently coming home so exhausted, indeed so battered, that he would, of his own accord go to bed half an hour or more before his usual bedtime.

Yet for Geddes those were good days. Regularly at six-thirty he and I would slip from our pajamas into our bathing trunks and go down to the sea for our dip, a dip in that calm ocean, smoothed by the coral reef, whose temperature at every hour of the day or night was just right for swimming in. Neither of us would have gone without those morning swims, with breakfast afterward on the lanai, looking out to the ocean, often watching the white steamers of the Matson line gliding offshore toward Honolulu harbor, just at the time we would be finishing break-fast. Higuchi, our Japanese man-of-all-work, would have breakfast ready by 7:15 and, beginning the day with papaya or fresh pineapple, rather than with orange juice, somehow set us more in tune with the incredibly lovely landscape around us; for by the time we were at breakfast the sun would have risen full above the waters and changed the gray sea into stretches of pure emerald or sapphire or amethyst.

At night, when I went to the hospital for the third visit of the day to Sophy, Geddes would stand by Alison and even see that she got to bed properly on evenings when her Japanese nurse, generously loaned us by our other new friend, Harry Bent, went off duty. Geddes did all this with a patience and a good will, with a sympathy and an understanding, that helped piece together the ragged patches of anxiety formed by the divided and distracted life I was leading. He was on easy terms with the Japanese children of the household, particularly with Tatsumi, who was younger than he, and Asami, who was older; and he had also made the acquaintance of some haole boys in a nearby house whose father boasted a yacht. Asami would give Geddes pointers on the handling of a surf-board, and little Tatsumi would demonstrate how one climbed a palm tree; and they would all feast on the coconuts that Tatsumi shook down. The art of climbing a curving coconut trunk with bare feet is one all the native young Hawaiians have mastered; and Geddes was not satisfied until he could imitate them, right up to the top, where the footing was narrowest and the ascent steepest.

The Polynesians are great fishermen, and in Hawaii, Geddes quickly found out, he was in his element. He promptly acquired a pair of wood-framed underwater goggles, a pair of Japanese sandals for walking on the sometimes jagged coral bottom, and a native fishing spear of the kind that is released by a spring: a weapon that fascinated him. I took him more than once to the Japanese fishing tackle shops on the waterfront; and he acquired such a collection of hooks, leaders, sinkers, lines, and soochee (for leaders) as he had hitherto only dreamed of. On one of our shopping expeditions—which sometimes included a leisurely Chinese lunch together—Geddes also acquired a pair of Hawaiian swimming trunks, and, as a special reward for all his helpfulness at home, a blue silk shirt with a flying fish pattern, also in the native style. He was always proud of that shirt, reserving it for his best occasions, and then wearing it a little defiantly, for it was still "irregular" in the East.

Those days when Sophy lay in danger, very close, before the crisis came, to death, brought Geddes and me together as perhaps we had never been before: no longer just father and son, but two Men of the Family, standing shoulder to shoulder, and bearing our common respon-sibilities. Just as our earlier sense of comradeship is attached for me to the sense of us walking home along the Leedsville road, after a hunt, with my arm around his shoulder, singing, "We are pals, best of pals," in a hearty voice, both of us off key; so this later feeling was crystallized for both of us, I think, in two experiences we shared together.

One of these experiences was a tropical storm that sprang up the second night Sophy was in the hospital. Along toward one or two in the morning the doors began to bang and the wind and rain swept through the upstairs lanai, where Alison was sleeping: so that I had to carry her from her outdoor bed to one in my own room. Prowling around the house, to lash down whatever else was loose, I found that Geddes, wakened by the lightning, the wind, the violent cannonade of thunder, had gotten up, too. There was still an unaccountable banging downstairs, where everything should have been tight; so we went down together to investigate and we found ourselves, at last, by a swinging window in the special pantry where flowers were arranged. Enormous tropical cock-roaches clicked and scurried over the floor in front of the flashlight and we forced ourselves to look sharp, so as not to place our bare feet too near a tarantula which might also be there. Each of us felt, at that moment, a touch of the eerie, a touch of the terrible, in which our helplessness before Sophy's plight was mingled with our helplessness in the face of nature; and we instinctively drew together.

The other episode occurred toward the end of our stay. Sophy had at last taken a turn for the better; indeed, she was slowly on the mend; and Dr. Nils Larsen, her physician, a suave, reassuring man, with a taste for the rugged in sport, invited me and Geddes to go with him one Saturday afternoon to his ranch on the leeward side of the island, which we reached by way of the Pali, whose windy, literally breathtaking vistas, had excited us before. The ranch was up in the hills; and on the way up we encountered a water buffalo, driven by a native, who muttered threateningly when I unthinkingly took a snapshot of the beast. A mixed party of young campers had stayed overnight at Dr. Larsen's shack; and they joined us. The nearer we got to the ranch, the more deeply we became immersed in the primitive, though the immense cactuses in the foreground had certainly never been seen by the original Hawaiians. Geddes and I had been to the Bishop Museum together and had heard an old Hawaiian woman there talking about the potency of Hawaiian medicines, when handled by a proper Kahuna, who knew the spells, or even one as skilled in herbs and magic as herself; one was, in fact, never far away from the aboriginal world of magic, the world of Kahunas and Shark Gods, of stone altars deep in the jungle, the world that Melville had revealed in Typee.

Not far from Larsen's place the guavas were growing wild, and we had a "snowball" fight with soft guavas. We passed through a bamboo forest, where the trees grew so close we sometimes had to wedge our way between them; and we went through groves where the flower of the wild ginger saturated the air with its sweet musky perfume; finally we came to a steep hillside, where Dr. Larsen had found, or developed, a ti-slide, a slope at an angle of at least sixty degrees, perhaps steeper, down which the adventurous might slide, sitting on a wide green ti-leaf held front and rear, which was supposed—that was the theory at all events—to absorb some of the friction. It was a wicked breakneck course that caused my stomach to turn over when I looked at it; and I had some anxiety, not wholly unfounded when I remember the rest of the trip, that Geddes might break a leg, if not a neck, in that exciting pastime. Geddes took to the sport gamely, though he jolted his spine so hard when he hit bottom that it gave him a headache that night; but better still he enjoyed the waterfall slide we came upon in another part of the ranch, above a pool set in brown volcanic rocks. I have a snapshot of him and the other children by that pool which recalls the idyllic scenes John La Farge tried so hard, half a century before, to capture.

Best of all, however, we stumbled by accident on a Hawaiian feast, which an elderly Negro-Hawaiian, mated to a Chinese wife, was about to celebrate. The old man, half-drunk, was as hospitable as he was loquacious; he and a Chinese friend were about to open the earthen bake oven, or imoo, in which they had been roasting a young pig; and when he unwrapped the ti leaves that surrounded the pig in classic fashion, he insisted on treating us to a generous helping of the pork. This was not the Polynesia of Herman Melville; but somehow it was still close enough to it, it was sufficiently filled with the same *mana*, to satisfy both Geddes and me. We agreed later that we had never tasted such succulent pork, with a special flavor that no other manner of preparing this meat ever gave it; nor did we forget how the meat had been seasoned by the oratory of the old kanaka, discanting on the fabulous prowess of Kamehameha the Great and the sad lot of the conquered Hawaiians ever since.

"Kamehameha, he great man; he make Hawaiian great. Now Hawaiian got nothing. Haole, he come; haole take everything away from Hawaiian. Missionary, he get land. Japanese, he get money. Hawaiian"— here he kicked one of the hot stones that had surrounded the meat— "Hawaiian get rock. Poor Hawaiian!" The old man shook his head sorrowfully and his dark face shriveled into a maudlin grin.

Though we put Hawaii behind us, we consciously prolonged its reverberations and echoes. When Sophy was decorating Geddes's room on Bleecker Street, next year, she found stuff for curtains with a Hawaiian palm tree and hula-girl design, which pleased him; and the old Hawaiian records that Harry Bent sent us, those records with the deep gentle bass voices and the high male falsetto, melancholy songs like Wiliwili Wai, became Geddes's favorite music, good for what they were, but good, too, for the memories they evoked. They are almost unbearable for us to listen to now: Geddes's Aloha indissolubly mingles with the plaintive melody.   —From 'Green Memories: The Story of Geddes.' 1947

Hawaiian Goblin Market

Come buy! Come buy!
Beads from Hawaii:
Bright yellow shells
Tiny bright bells
All the way from Hawaii,
Where palms sweep the sky
And coconuts grow
Beneath the rainbow.
Come buy-a, come buy-a
Pineapple, papaya,
Mango and guava:
Jasmine vine, banyan tree:
Taro patches by the sea:
Red and pink hibiscus:
Hawaiians without whiskers,
Coral reefs, ginger leis
Purple seas, golden days.
Come buy, come buy
This necklace from Hawaii:
A birthday kiss will do:
But better make it two!
Ride a surfboard, spear a fish,
Torches for a birthday wish.
Bring pikake and poi
To add to your joy:
And take this yellow lei
May it last you for aye:
May it quicken memories
Of Trade Winds, rustling trees,
Diamond Head, perfumed bed:
Hoarded glimpses of Heaven
For Alison at Seven.
Don't sigh: you may buy
Still more beads from Hawaii:
Be bold but not reckless
In wearing this necklace:
For this is your Birthday:
May it ever be a Mirthday:
Yellow shells and red earth-day.

344

Aloha to Alison!
And now my little mele's done.

—Beads for Alison's Birthday. April 28, 1942

Yesterday I went out with Alison looking for wild strawberries on the hillside half way to the lake. On the way back Alison said: "I don't believe I went strawberry picking with you a little while ago. Maybe it was a dream; maybe everything is a dream. I only believe what I see." It was very unexpected; but plainly her mind at six, in its candid innocent way, has been facing the philosophical problem of the relation of knowledge to reality: and she had arrived at a sort of moment-to-moment sensationalism, worthy of Hume, with a touch of Berkeley! —RN. June 10, 1941

I wonder if, in the strain and upset of our departure for Stanford in 1942 I ever recorded an incident connected with Alison's going that remains fresh in my mind, though I found that Alison had completely forgotten it, and Sophy had done so till I quickened her memory, when I recalled it the other day. On the last night that September, just before Alison was going to bed around eight o'clock, the three girls of the village, Margaret and Alice Duffy and Susanne Farley, perhaps with still another Farley, appeared in the twilight just below Alison's window and softly chanted:

Farewell to Alison! Farewell to Alison!

They had been admirably trained to sing in chorus by the teacher of our little one-room Leedsville school, Mrs. Kane, and their voices were so soft and tender and haunting that they have stayed with me ever since, as a perfect expression of human feeling, possible only in the intimacy of such a hamlet, such a human environment. As they sang, their voices became fainter with each line, and it had the effect of a benediction, in the same fashion that taps has when it is blown by a good bugler. —RN. February 20, 1950

Sophy had longer and even deeper hours with Geddes on the motor rides they took together, to and from Amenia, when we lived in New York, or up to his schools in Vermont. These rides covered the period from fourteen to seventeen. When he was old enough to drive, they would take turns at the wheel, and the closed car was their cell. In its intimacy each would talk, in time, of what was closest to his heart. They would come home with an account, perhaps of the snow and ice that they had battled together; they would recall with keen delight the feathery mist they had seen in the hollows, or the young lambs skipping over twilit pastures in spring. But more than what they did and saw was what they shared with each other, in a phrase, in a story, in a sudden gesture of understanding or a halting confession: what Geddes said about his own goals, his ambitions, his secret hopes, the kind of girl he went around with, the kind he noted at school, the kind he expected to marry: what a family ought to be and what one owed to them.

Often, too, their talks would turn to religion. If Geddes never lived to achieve any ultimate and sustaining faith, at least one of a rational order, he never lost interest in the subject itself: the mystery of life, the even deeper mystery of the universe, fascinated him; and though he rejected the easier answers, he returned persistently to the questions themselves. By the time Geddes was sixteen he had found in Buddhism, in the conception of moral self-restraint and an ultimate Nirvana of release, something that corresponded closest to his own intuition of life. I daresay that the noble atheism Gautama originally propounded met Geddes's own requirements at this time. His difficulty, his mother recalls, was that "he could not apply logic to the concept of God, because God was a finite conception, yet, if there was an infinity, and if God was the creator of all things, then it was illogical to suppose that the creator was less than his creation: God and Infinity seemed mutually incompatible to him."

[I got back from California in 1941 in time to write some doggerel for Geddes's birthday, while Alison, following the custom of our young German helper, Hildegard, had introduced into our household when Geddes was eleven, got up early to decorate his place at the breakfast table with hollyhock flowers, because they looked like hibiscus from Hawaii. My worst enemy will hardly suspect me of vanity if I put down our family sentiments on this occasion:]

For Geddes on His Sixteenth Birthday

Sixteen years have come to stay
So let us celebrate this day
When Geddes legally can shoot
At woodchucks and not care a hoot
For what some snooper might report.
Now is the time to shoot a rocket
And fill with gold his careless pocket.
So here is fifty for a car
And may it take you near or far,

Up hill or down, through mud and mire
Without a scratch or punctured tire.
May all your rides be full of fun
From green Vermont to Oregon.
And if you're touring with a lass
Be sure you don't run out of gas.
You're old enough to steer and shoot
And work for pay, you dear galoot:
So jump right in and drive ahead
And choose your course and keep your head:
And don't, old chap, for goodness sakes,
Step on the gas when you need the brakes.
Sixteen years at last are here:
May life get better year by year;
And if our love and hope will do it
You'll get more ripe than greenish fruit.

Love, true love, shone in Geddes's eyes that June, in 1942 when Martha
came up for a weekend. Lust is something that even fleas and lice know,
as the old German theologian said, but "love begins when one wants to
serve another." Love had come to Geddes: to serve Martha, to make life
sweet for her, to show himself worthy of marrying her, were his underlying preoccupations for the better part of the next year. It was this love
that at last aroused him to the necessity for making a go of it in his
studies, so that he might enter college and establish himself in a vocation
that would enable him, eventually, to support both of them and have a
family. He felt that a true marriage must be one between equals, and he
could not respect himself unless he were intellectually on his future wife's
level. That is a formula for converting a roughneck into a scholar.

Over all our heads hovered the knowledge that this year at Stanford
might be our last winter together as a united family. That colored many
attitudes and decisions. Though we disapproved of Geddes's going off to
a roadhouse on the Highway for drinks after a movie on Saturday night,
particularly when, as at first, he did this alone, picking up what companions he could find, and though we had serious discussions with him
occasionally about this or that dubious item in the adolescent code, we
had decided to drive the parental nag with a very loose rein. When
Geddes was only four or five years old his mother, with a mother's concern and a mother's intuition, had predicted that he would have a
troubled life and might, before he arrived at peace, break every com-
mandment in the Decalogue, to test it for himself before accepting it; but

that, in the end, all that was fine and generous in him would triumphantly come to the surface, the purer for having been tested in the fire. That prophecy we were often to remember; and every day that year brought its last terms closer to fulfillment.

Some of Geddes's letters, to Martha written from Stanford in the winter of 1942–43, have allusions to our discussions at the dinner table. In one of them he observed: "I just got done with my dinner and the post-vittle talk was as usual most interesting and enlightening. My father has some very great advantages for me. If I don't know more about Civilization than his Humanity students by the end of this year, I shall be very surprised. I'm really getting to know my social history as well as an awful lot about biology. Where the guy picks it all up is beyond me, but it's there for the asking which is just what I have been doing." Another letter, written in the dumps, told about a futile day which "didn't even have one of my usual post-meal discussions with Dad." In still another letter to Martha he was more excited (and more flattering) still: "Oct. 20 . . . It's ten P.M. and I had no intention of writing you tonite—but this life is getting to be too damn much for me. I've just finished talking with my father again, and this time we brought the usual bio-scientific talk up and through the realm of human behavior and its biological origins. And frankly things are getting too drastic in this line for me to cope with. The last thought that was left me was, that the human organism has practically finished its biological metamorphosis and in the future will have to confine itself to changes perpetuated through the mind alone. I haven't stated myself in full, as this would take pages and pages, but the basic idea is positively astounding to a person who, almost all his life, has believed in biological evolution as the basis of continued life. You have no idea how much I want to talk this over with you and get your opinion on it. I feel as if I had just been hit hard and landed in another world."

I found out today just why democracy is capable of really working in this country at least, and probably in the world. I don't think anything has ever showed me as much as the people who I worked with this afternoon. When I came on the job at one there were over a dozen ranch and farm owners waiting in the warehouse in which we mix the grasshopper poison. Some men had always worked—some hadn't for twenty or thirty years. Some believed in the poison, most of them didn't, but they worked all of them; they worked till their shirts stuck to their backs. It made an impression on me, just the fact that people who did not believe in a thing would work; went right out and helped because their neighbors *might* suffer if they didn't. A lot of them were skeptical as hell, but it still didn't

348

prevent them from helping those who were not. They didn't sit on their fences and laugh at "those damm fools." They gave; they didn't hinder.

I don't know whether I've conveyed the impression I meant to, but I hope you can see what I mean. It was pure co-operative spirit put into practice. —Letter from Geddes to Martha Binswanger. 1942

For us the best part of coming back to California was that in the middle of January [1944], just in time as it turned out, Geddes managed to get a furlough and spend eight precious days with us. If anyone was ready to profit by army discipline it was Geddes. Now all the loose parts are firmly fitted together, and he has achieved a degree of self-control, personal direction, and integration that I would regard as admirable at any age level; to say nothing of his reaching it in the middle of his nineteenth year. He has made the external discipline an internal one: has taken the war and its duties seriously, and has already turned himself into a skilled infantryman, with an expert's rating in the rifle and the machine-gun. (Along with his external toughening has come a deepening of internal gentleness, compensating it.) His division, he has just written us, will be sent overseas, possibly within the next month. Short though our days together were, they seem doubly short now that we realize that we will probably not see him again, at best, until after he has seen combat. He has had a shorter preparation for combat than most of the men of his division, and though everything he has done has been to expedite his entry into active service the suddenness of this move was a shock to us—and perhaps even to him. It gives a certain fatefulness to every letter that passes between us: a need to hide one's anguish and make more visible and palpable one's love. —Letter to Christiana Morgan. February 12, 1944

This morning Alison (aged twelve) said to Sophy: "You know, one must take people as they are; you can't change them over to your way, except a very little. It's like guiding a horse: if the horse wants to go in a certain way, you've got to give in to him a little in order to keep control at all; you can't check him altogether without paying attention to what he wants. When it comes to a political discussion in class, I will argue all day to try to convert someone to what I think are the right views. But you can't do that with a person's character; you've got to accept that, and then approach it in such a way that, without giving in to them, you learn how far you can go along with them without being untrue to yourself." I wasn't present; so I am only paraphrasing Sophy's account; but both of us were struck by Alison's psychological maturity. —RN. August 16, 1947

349

The family conversation tonight, at a late supper, turned to religion, prompted by Sophy's asking me why I had taken to reading 'The Book of Job' aloud. We talked about the difficulty of reconciling a just and loving God with the undeserved misfortunes, to say nothing of horrors, that often overtake people. Sophy pointed out how hard it was to accept the notion that a world so full of unreason could be fundamentally reasonable: that required, she thought, absolute faith in God. Erica and Alison both took an active part in the conversation; and I brought forward the conventional theological answer; that man's finiteness could not encompass what an infinite power had created. To make this a little more understandable I said: Suppose you were a cell in an organism; about all that you would know about the creature of which you were a part was that immediately under your nose. Some chance blow or scratch might harm the cell and all its neighbors, or bring about their death; and that would seem, inevitably, to be a great grief and miscarriage to the cells concerned; but the body itself might hardly be aware of the tiny scratch; and so long as it went on living no permanent damage would be done to it. Erica put forward the case for the individual, his right to happiness; but Alison, who had caught the point, said eagerly: "But you can't defy God, Erica: He is what He is. Like the cell, you must accept your place in God and take what comes your way. But"—turning to me—"it's hard to think of man as being so small and helpless." I quoted Pascal's observation: "Man is a reed, but a thinking reed"; and she rose to it at once. "Oh, I like that," she said. —RN. August 15, 1948

Last night Sophy was reflecting on the quality of Alison's mind, as evidenced by the books that she reads. Alison [aet. thirteen] has a special love for Chesterton's 'Father Brown' stories, and as Sophy pointed out, one must read through a great deal of mature comment and philosophy merely to follow the thread of a Father Brown plot. Her favorite among Chesterton's writings, is 'The Man Who Was Thursday,' which she read just the other day. The whole story gave her a poignant delight: "It's the best mystery story of all," she exclaimed. With all the little leftovers of childhood, like her unconscionable dawdling over meals, she still has, as the dominating part of her, an exceptional quality of self-possession, maturity of insight, and intellectual keenness. Just last night Alison began commenting on a picture of Winslow Homer's we had seen at the Metropolitan Museum last October: 'The Returning Soldier.' "The thick ripe field of grain," she pointed out, "makes the loneliness of his homecoming seem all the greater." The picture, its feeling, its meaning, as well as its image, had more deeply imprinted itself on her mind than on that of

350

either Sophy or me. She had liked Botticelli, whose reproductions she had come across in the Phaidon book about his work; but once she had come across El Greco she lost her heart to him completely. Matisse, especially in his still-lifes, seems to her empty and superficial, though she likes his figures against their complicated arabesque backgrounds. That sort of taste and feeling informs most of her judgments. —RN. January 31, 1948

We were talking at table about our house at Stanford; and Alison said: "You grownups don't know how wonderful that back garden was; it had all sorts of secret paths a child could follow and pretend to get lost in. Every child should have that kind of place to play in. Eveleth and I used to make believe it was fairyland. We didn't believe in fairies; but Oh! we believed in Fairyland. It was different from the hard cruel world; you got your wishes in Fairyland. Erica and I believed in Fairyland, too, for a long time; we would get on that little blue rug on my floor, the soft heavy one, and go around the room on it; when we were on the rug we were safe from witches. You see, we believed in witches, but not in fairies." Afterward Sophy remembered that when the girls went to bed they had to have their covers arranged just so, and lie very still, if they were to float to Fairyland. —RN. April 12, 1947

Yesterday at 1:00 P.M. President Truman gave his second inaugural message to the Congress; and in the evening part of this was repeated on Edward R. Murrow's program, to which Alison listened. She was very much interested in both his manner and his words; though we didn't discuss the speech at much length. But when Sophy went into her room, half an hour after she had gone to bed, to see about her windows, Alison half-woke herself enough to say drowsily: "Lincoln was a genius; but President Truman is just a plain courageous man doing what the people want him to do—and I think it's wonderful. You know he's a real American, just a haberdasher who worked his way up to be President; and he makes me awfully proud of our country." —RN. January 6, 1949

For Alison, on Her Sixteenth Birthday, 1951

Rise daffodil! and greet your lady:
Rise trillium, tulip, and hepatica!
Sing robins, thrushes, springtime peepers!
Awaken, relatives and neighbors
Rise ye woodland nymphs from Attica!

With festal toot if not with tabor:
Let birthday shouts defy the rain
And bid the sun to shine again.
In swampy haunts, now dank and shady,
Skunk cabbage, April's flag unfurl!
(Blow wind! to keep that perfume back.)
Come rabbit, chipmunk, woodchuck, squirrel:
Come forward and salute your lady!
That she no creature's love may lack
We'll deck her fingers, bind her wrists
With honeysuckle, periwinkle,
Instead of pearls and amethysts:
With flowery stars her hair will twinkle.
For sixteen years the startled earth
Has leaped in spring to hail her birth.

To form this paragon, this minx,
Miranda, Portia, Ariel
Were poured into a single mold
Along with Homer's nonpareil:
A stranger creature than the Sphinx
Is she, our own and April's child:
A dozen maids rolled into one—
This darling poppet Alison:
This trilling bird, this budding flower,
This dark and dappled sky, storm-wild,
This seething flood of unspent power
This mixture of the springtime season:
With shyest beauty sharpest reason.

We utter proud parental cheers
To celebrate your vernal years:
We bless the time you had your way—
As usual without a fuss!—
And came in April, not in May!
We bless you most for choosing us.
We bless your eyes, we bless your face,
We bless your wisdom and your grace.
We've but one wish for you, you elf,
You faun, you sprite, you faery-fay:
Each birthday and each other day
                    Just be yourself.

19: Hopes and Forebodings

The threat of a Second World War—actually a resumption of the 'unfinished' First World War—roused more sensitive and prescient minds, between 1920 and 1940, to seek positive means for avoiding another such catastrophe. But the inertia of past errors carried over into future calculations, even though at the end of the nineteen-thirties the possibility of harnessing the atom for military purposes had—thanks to the success of the cyclotron at Berkeley—become an open secret. Unfortunately such a deep scar had been left upon the nations of Europe by the futile mass butcheries that masqueraded as military strategy in the 1914–1918 war, that people in every non-totalitarian country had become passivists, if not pacifists: no government in the nineteen-thirties dared to take the necessary steps to circumvent or resist totalitarian aggression.

Faith for Living: 1930

At the age of eight I believed in the omniscience of my teachers and the power and glory of the United States. When I learned that Brazil had a greater area than my own country, I felt that geography was an indignity, and if the facts could not be disputed, we ought to annex Brazil.

At fourteen, I believed in a very personal God who helped me usually to get good marks in my examinations, and in the offices of the Protestant Episcopal Church of America. This belief remained with me at least two years, until I discovered to my horror that the priest had a way of going through the prayers rapidly, as if he wished to get the day's job done. In an excess of piety, I left the church and fell into the arms of Spinoza. God was in me and I was in God, but the sky from that time on was empty!

When Europe went to war, I was eighteen, and I believed in 'The Revolution.' Living in a world choked with injustice and poverty and class strife, I looked forward to an uprising on the part of the down-trodden, who would overthrow the master class and bring about a regime of equality and brotherhood. In the subsequent years I learned the difference between a mass uprising and the prolonged spiritual travail and creation of a more organic transformation; politically, I am no longer naive enough to believe that any militant uprising can change the face of the world. But I have never been a Liberal, nor do I subscribe to the notion that justice and liberty are best achieved in homeopathic doses. If I cannot call myself a revolutionist, it is not because the current programs for change seem to me to go too far: the reason is rather because they are superficial and do not go far enough.

My principal quarrel with the Russian communists, for example, is not so much over their ruthlessness in achieving the new order, as over their acceptance of half the fallacies of the mechanistic system of thought which happened to be dominant when Marx formulated his revolutionary dogmas. This Communist ideology subordinates all human values to a narrow utilitarian scheme, as if production had no other end than pro-duction, and the result is a caricature of both society and the human personality. The orthodox communist has not escaped the mechanistic prison by taking possession of it and assuming the duties of jailer; nor does the jail look more inviting when it is called a Proletarian Palace.

It is a new life I would aim at, not simply a new balance of power. Such a life would leave less of the present world standing than Soviet Russia has left.

My naive original beliefs in one's country as the sole home of the saintly and the elect, in some institutional embodiment of Christianity, and in a dramatic transformation of a sordid present into a beatific future were common, in various proportions, to most members of my generation. They constituted our system of working values through the greater part of childhood and adolescence.

Some of us have remained fixed in these attitudes: manhood finds them still measuring the size of the United States Navy against that of its nearest rival, or, in more refined moments, comparing the value of our poetry or technology to that of some other country—as if there existed any rational purpose today which was not common to men of different regions and did not depend upon their continuous cooperation and inter-course. Some of us still talk about revolution, without altering our inter-ests or occupations in the smallest way to accomplish it; while others of us are still seeking, in psychoanalysis or the latest reports of molecular physics, our God.

What has happened to my original belief in 'my country'? What remains of it is no longer a disguise for my childish egotism. To enjoy one's own region, to feel attachment to some particular landscape and way of life does not demand that inverted form of patriotism which consists in a blind resentment against what is foreign and an intense desire to extirpate it. As a New Yorker—aware of the procession of ships up and down the Bay, seeing strange faces, hearing strange voices almost every hour—I am much closer to Europe than to Oregon. This is natural and seemly. What is unnatural is the political theory which would disregard these real loyalties and attachments in an effort to create a uniform grade of cannon fodder for the next war.

To confine human association to the political state, or to make membership in that state the highest good, is like trying to put an actual landscape that stretches many miles toward the horizon into a wooden picture frame. Cultures cannot be isolated; they grow by perpetual intercourse across the boundaries of time and space; without cross-fertilization they are sterile—sterile and sour.

As an expression of the will to power, the sovereign state is an enemy of culture: its only significant purpose is to preserve justice and liberty among its constituent cities, regions, associations, corporations. This purpose is not furthered by patriotic taboos, fortifications, tariffs, frontiers, and an everlasting parade of the instruments of war. 'My country' is the common territory of all men of good will. As for the actual soil, I agree with Nathaniel Hawthorne when he said that New England was about as large a patch of earth as he could feel any natural affection for.

Well, just as my childish pride in the United States has been transformed into a more comprehensive grasp of society and culture, so my parochial religion and my sanguine social faith have, without disappearing as a nucleus, undergone a profound change. How shall I describe the results? One's deepest faith cannot be expressed. As Walt Whitman put it, the best cannot be said; the best is that which must be left unsaid. Whatever I can say will be only a faint symbol of that deeper urge of life, that rationality beneath all reasons, which bottoms one's existence.

An adequate faith ought to harmonize one's actual scheme of living, one's conscious reflections, and the inner go of the self; while it faces the evils of existence, it should recognize and consciously multiply the goods. What are these goods? Where does one find them? What attitude must one bring toward them?

Most of the ethical philosophies of the past have sought to isolate the prime goods of life, making pleasure or efficiency or duty or imperturbability the chief end of the disciplined and cultivated mind. Since no one goes through the world unhurt, and since violence and injustice often have the upper hand, many of these systems have sought by a sort of supernatural bookkeeping to redress the evils of existence in another sphere. To seek pleasure, or happiness, or immortality, has been the goal of these faiths; if not now, then hereafter.

No such single goal seems to me legitimate or even desirable. The fact that sunshine is good does not make the Sahara an ideal place to live in. Instead of beginning with such factitious ends, and reproaching the universe because it does not fully serve them, let us rather begin with the nature of life itself.

One begins with life; and one knows life, not as a fact in the raw, but only as we are conscious of human society and use the tools and instruments society has developed through history—words, symbols, buildings, grammar, logic, science, art. Life considered apart from this milieu is merely an abstraction of thought. One begins with a world of human values and purposes, and only as a result of persistent inquiry and experiment does one reach such a useful concept as that of a dissociated 'physical universe,' considered as self-existent and separate from these organic accretions.

The vague stir and strength within us, which we associate with the beat of our hearts or the expansion of our lungs, requires for sustenance a whole solar system, merely to maintain such elementary conditions as the heat of our blood. And similarly, the crudest social existence implies the effort of untold generations of men to differentiate foods from poisons, invent tools, create symbols and expressive gestures. Individualism in the sense of isolation is merely a spatial illusion. The more self-sufficient an individual seems to be, the more sure it is that, like Thoreau at Walden Pond, he carries a whole society in his bosom. This fact applies equally to nations. Both physically and spiritually we are members one of another; and we have never been anything else, although the callosities of ignorance and egotism have sometimes made us insensitive to this condition.

Life, then, implies these manifold cooperations, and the finer life becomes, the more complicated is this network, and the more highly conscious does one become of it. Goethe once declared that the sources of his thought were so numerous that one who traced them out would find it difficult to attribute any originality to him; and since Goethe's honesty was equaled only by his pride, one may take his witness as final. The business man who fancies he has made his own fortune, or the inventor who imagines he has the sole right to his invention, is merely ignorant of his sources. The individual contribution, the work of any single generation, is infinitesimal: the power and glory belong to human society at large and are the long result of time.

This is the philosophic justification for communism, and since it coincides with the practical reason for communism—namely, that every human being requires approximately the same amount of air, water, clothing, food, shelter, with small differences to allow for climate and the type of work—the political institutions of society should be arranged to establish this minimum basis of life, differentiation and preference and special incentive being taken into account only after the security and continuity of life itself is assured. This is my elementary political faith; it corresponds roughly to Plato's.

The task of organizing a basic communism is not an easy one. Special societies, like monasteries and armies, have often achieved a rough measure of it; but the real difficulty is to apply it to the community at large and still preserve those delicate volitions and those intense individual interests which are an incentive to creative activity. One of the first moves in this direction is obviously to alter by example and education the current scheme of values. In our present society, pecuniary prestige comes first; life and the values derived from living exist on sufferance.

While a basic economic communism [now called 'Social Security'] would extend to the whole community the decent household practices of sharing, which seems to me a necessary measure of justice and practical statesmanship, one need not therefore hold, with an older school of revolutionary thinkers, that the evils of life are solely the work of an ominous capitalist class, or that they are entirely economic in origin and would be abolished under a more equitable regime.

On the contrary, I have no more notion of abolishing evil than I have of abolishing shadow in the world of light. Fourier's crazy belief that the ocean itself under a harmonized social order would turn into lemonade, and Spencer's picture of the future society as a sort of polite eternal Sunday afternoon, are merely exhibitions, as it were, of an unfathomable shallowness. Evil and good are phases in the process of human growth; and who shall say which is the better teacher? Illness, error, defeat, frustration, disintegration, malicious accident, all these elements are as much in the process of life as waste, nutrition, and repair. The very forces which, if triumphant, would destroy life are needful to season experience and deepen understanding.

Observing this, the popular religions of the past have celebrated almost solely the negative aspects of existence. But, in release from their superstitions, one must not commit the opposite error of neglecting the role of evil and forgetting its value. Customs and actions we habitually call good have large capacities for mischief: who does not know the charity that poisons the giver and the purity that offends common decency?

Similarly, the evils of life have a certain capacity for good; and the mature person knows that they must be faced, embraced, assimilated, and that to shun them, or innocently hope to eliminate them forever is to cling to an existence without perspective or depth—a child's picture done in pretty chalks, charming perhaps, but only that. Like arsenic, evil is a tonic in grains and a poison in ounces. The real problem of evil, the problem that justifies every assault upon war and poverty and disease, is to reduce it to amounts that can be spiritually assimilated.

This doctrine is just the opposite of certain 'optimistic,' life-denying attitudes and habits of mind that have become popular during the last three centuries: particularly, the notion that comfort and safety and physical ease are the greatest blessings of civilization, and that every other human interest—religion, art, friendship, family, love, adventure—must be subordinated to the production of an increasing amount of 'comforts' and 'luxuries.' Believing this, the utilitarian has turned an elementary condition of existence into an end. Avaricious of power and riches and goods, he has summoned to his aid the resources of modern science and technology. As a result, we are oriented to 'things,' and have every sort of possession except self-possession.

Today it is only a fortunate minority of spiritually wealthy people, together with a handful of "the undeserving poor" (to use Doolittle's epithet in 'Pygmalion') who have any notion of the true uses of leisure and who are not bored or frightened by the mere prospect of achieving it. By putting business before every other manifestation of life, our mechanical and financial civilization has forgotten the chief business of life: namely, growth, reproduction, development. It pays infinite attention to the incubator—and it forgets the egg!

Now the end of all practical activity is personal culture: a maturing mind, a ripening character, an increasing sense of mastery and fulfillment, a further integration of all one's powers in a social personality; a larger capacity for intellectual interests and emotional enjoyments, for more complex and subtle states and self-stimulation of mind. Arrested personalities look back with regret to some temporary fulfillment in youth, as Mark Twain looked back to the happy adventures of Huckleberry Finn. Developing personalities accept, without impatience or regret, the next stage in their growth; by the time they are mature, they have no difficulty in putting away childish things.

Growth and culture imply sustained activity and periods of leisure sufficient to absorb the results of this activity, using it to enrich art and manners and personality. The Athenians were quite right in believing that these things could not be achieved by anyone who was forced to spend the entire day in some spiritually deadening or physically exhausting task in the shop or the countinghouse. Jesus-ben-Sirach came to the same conclusion, and Emerson finally gave up long hours of work in the garden because the toil robbed him of ideas. Most of us who have enjoyed both manual work and contemplation would agree with Patrick Geddes when he says that two hours of physical activity—whether in work or in sport—are all one can profitably use in a day devoted to the humane arts, and that the hard-working laborer who has any mental life left at the end of his day is nothing less than a prodigy.

The practical moral to be drawn from this is that servile labor—even if it produces 'comforts' or tempting luxuries—should be minimized to the utmost, and that leisure must be distributed more universally in the form of a shorter working day, instead of being permitted to exist as the penalizing burden of 'unemployment.' Without leisure there can be neither art nor science nor fine conversation, nor any ceremonious performance of the offices of love and friendship. If our boasted Machine Age has any promise for culture, it is not in the actual multiplication of motor cars and vacuum cleaners, but in the potential creation of usable leisure. But so long as 'comfort' and not life is our standard, the Machine Age will be impotent.

All our higher activities are curbed by the present alternations of excessive toil and short periods of sodden release. The fact that the majority of people go to the theater, for example, at the end of a long working day explains in good part the quality of the drama they demand; in a state of physical fatigue, they are unable to experience the deep or subtle emotions that the great dramatists or composers call forth. Except for an occasional musical festival for the leisured, like those at Salzburg or Glastonbury or Bethlehem, there has been little opportunity in our civilization to experience art under conditions which permit sensitive enjoyment, to say nothing of complete rapture.

And if painting and poetry have so meager a role in the life of modern people, one might sufficiently account for it by the fact that they demand responses which few people are able to give at the end of a working day—or for that matter, a working week. There is no proof whatever that the capacity for art and thought is smaller today than in the thirteenth century or the fifteenth; but the conditions favorable to this capacity belong to only a handful of specialists and dilettantes.

What applies to the contemplative arts, applies equally to the arts of action: the dance, gymnastics, and above all, perhaps, to sexual intercourse. Without leisure, freshness, energy, they lose their inner impetus, and must be excited to activity by the rivalry of athletic matches, by the negative stimulus of ill health, or by preliminary bouts of strong liquor.

Yet all these arts are quite as central to life as the most beneficent instrumental activity. In so far as many primitive communities have maintained the arts of action in a more consistent and whole-hearted way than our Western civilization, we need not boast too loudly about our advantages; for our 'progress' has not been unmixed with lapses and regressions in matters that are far more important to our welfare than the production of cheap pig iron.

Instead of the one-sided practical activity fostered by the ideals of the utilitarians and the working out of modern technology, with its intense specialization, I believe in a rounded, symmetrical development of both the human personality and the community itself. Economics would play a part in that development, but it would not dominate it.

The two ages of human achievement that stand out for me are those of fifth century Athens and fifteenth century Florence; and both of them were, effectively speaking, the work of amateurs, who, by a symmetrical development, gave to each aptitude a quality which years of separate specialization would in all likelihood never have produced. That specialization leads inevitably to efficiency is a specious argument; for as there is, in Ruskin's words, no wealth but life, so there is no efficiency except that which furthers life. Moreover, this argument takes no account of the mountains of useless, arid work that are accumulated under our present habits of specialization; and it gives to this practice the sole credit for gains which are due to quite another modern technique, namely, cooperative intercourse and association.

The metaphysical case against specialization is even more overwhelming. We live in a world where no single event exists by itself, but, on the contrary, is organically conditioned by its entire environment, physical and human. If one attempts to deal with any little segment in isolation, one is dealing with a figment; and one begins to know a little about the things which are closest to one's interest only when one traces out their interrelationships with that which may, apparently, lie far beyond. While abstract analytical thinking is one of the great *practical* achievements of the race, it is misleading and mischievous unless it takes place in a life-oriented human culture.

How are we to achieve this? By heaping together in a vast mechanical accumulation all of our specialized researches? By attempting to boil all knowledge and practice down into popular outlines? Alas! no: the result of such an arithmetical addition of specialisms would merely be another specialism. While a schematic synthesis may be a help to orderly thinking, the place to achieve organic unity primarily is in living itself, in encompassing all the activities that make a full life.

We must experience at first hand manual toil and esthetic ecstasy, periods of routine and periods of adventure, intellectual concentration and animal relaxation. We must know what it is to be a cook, a tramp, a lover, a digger of ditches, a parent, a responsible worker. In this way we shall be exploring our environment and exploring the possibilities of ourselves in relation to the personalities around us—instead of shrinking, after a preliminary skirmish or two, into a sort of war of attrition with life, seeking to achieve a maximum of safety and comfort in the dugout of some specialized interest, and viewing the horizon with the aid of a periscope.

Such a complete mode of living must inevitably carry over into each special situation: only a vicious system of mis-education can prevent it. By ceasing to live in isolated compartments, one avoids the delusive habit of treating the world in this manner, and one approaches each event with an intuition of its wholeness—as not primarily physical or biological or economic or esthetic, but as all of these things together in a certain unique combination. Temporarily, as a practical convenience, one will not be afraid to use the method of analysis to the utmost; but, weighing, measuring, calculating, decomposing, we shall still be aware of the dynamic whole in space and time with which we started, and to which, enriched by the process of analysis, we must ultimately return.

My faith, for its full consummation, must be embodied in a community. But how shall I describe it? This life does not exist in any single phase of the past, although every great civilization in its best moments gives more than a hint of it and plenty of guarantee against its being fantastic and beyond reach. Here and there it may be said to exist in some living person, or to be embodied symbolically in a poem or a novel, such as 'Moby-Dick,' 'War and Peace,' or 'The Magic Mountain.' If one were founding a church, instead of summing up one's intuition of life, one would include in the calendar of saints a Blake, a Goethe, a Whitman. And while among men of science this faith has cohered more slowly, partly because the pattern of research has been set by seventeenth century physics, it gets rational support from science and today would include scientists like A. N. Whitehead, J. S. Haldane, C. G. Jung.

For me the confirmation of my intuitions came first through acquaintance with Patrick Geddes, whose long life spans the service of many sciences, from biology to sociology, and many types of activity, from that of the speculative philosopher to the planner of cities. Geddes showed that a conception of life, unified at the center and ramifying in many interrelations and comprehensions at the periphery, could be rationally lived; that it had not been outmoded by the age of specialization but was actually a mode that might, through its superior vitality and efficiency, supplant this age; that one could practice in one's own person, in the germ, a type of thinking and feeling and acting which might ultimately be embodied, with fuller, deeper effect, in the whole community; that, even on the crude test of survival, a life that was organically grounded and pursued with a little courage and audacity had perhaps a better chance than the narrow goals and diminished possibilities of our dominant civilization. My utopia is such a life, writ large.

To be alive, to act, to embody significance and value, to be fully human, make demands that are difficult of achievement. Who has not his dead hours, his moments of apathy or disintegration—and who persists, for any long period, in being half the man he is capable of being? These goals are none the worse for being difficult. They come at least within the realm of possibility; and, pursuing them, one arises early and smells the dewy air of morning, or, at night, one sinks with a good conscience into one's bed, as one may hope to sink, without bitterness or a vain sense of disappointment, into one's grave.

If a religion be that which gives one a sense of the things that are worth dying for, this community with all life, this sense of a central purpose in oneself, inextricably bound up with the nature of things, even those accidents and brutal mischances that are so hard to assimilate—this faith may be called a religion. For a good lover knows when to embrace, when to conquer and when to renounce; and he who loves life well will not grudge the surrender or fail to recognize the appropriate moment for it. Life must be measured by the capacity for significant experience, and not by power or riches or length of days. —The Forum. November 1930

Our Present Dilemmas: 1930

There are times when one spends perhaps a whole day, vaguely conscious that one has been through all its details before. Was it in a dream, was it in the imagination, was it in activity? I have had this feeling during the last year, and upon analyzing it I find it has to do with a series of decisions and purposes that came more or less to a head about ten years ago. The deflation of the war and the deflation of our recent 'prosperity' were not altogether dissimilar events: each left behind a sinister aftermath of hunger, terrorism, disillusionment, fatal resignation.

Upon looking through some old papers the other day, I found the fragment of a novel I had begun in 1917—it was called, in pointed irony, 'A Soldier's Testament'—and discovered, certainly to my own surprise, that I had anticipated the letdown that the war was to bring, and that I sought to find some way of carrying into the later years the élan that before 1915, my generation had known. The novel is still a fragment on crumbling yellow paper; but the letdown came; and I remember well the series of watchful calculations that determined the course that I set in the dozen years that followed. Was that course a reasonable one? Can it still be pursued in 1931? Perhaps the answer is not the same to both questions; but they are closely bound up.

Let me recall the scene that I confronted in 1919. I had been in training in the regular Navy: it was, in essentials, the same Navy that Melville pictured in 'White Jacket' almost three generations before. But the Navy had, during the war, one characteristic that set it off from the mass of civilians: it was not, so far as I came into contact with it, manned by hysterical and demented people. One could admire German seamanship in the Navy without being immediately arrested as a Hun; one could refuse to subscribe to a Liberty Bond—a sturdy handful of us did!— without being written down as a traitor. So I remember with pleasure all the useful work I accomplished during that year in the Navy. I read Emerson's essays on chow line and studied 'The Republic' carefully during the influenza epidemic. In the odd hours that were free from routine, I did a study of housing and community planning and drafted a long essay on the subject. I faced the cold bright world of February 1919 with accumulated reserves of energy, and no sense whatever that my whole generation was already painfully skidding downhill. The armistice had not been signed, and it was still possible to think, at least to hope, that the world had been 'saved for democracy.'

During the next six months, the original momentum, acquired before the war, carried us all along: but sinister habits, generated by the war or given a full rein then for the first time, rose to the surface. The Department of Justice, under A. Mitchell Palmer, kept on with that series of vindictive violations of civil liberties which, to this day, make the defenders of law and order more suspicious to decent citizens than undisguised crooks and cutthroats. The historian who seeks a clue for Mr. Wilson's loss of prestige will err greatly if he does not take into account the domestic infelicities of his war and post-war administration. In New York, in the summer of 1919, my colleagues on The Dial were hailed before the Lusk Committee and examined under strict oath of secrecy about the radical activities of the paper. This same committee discovered with horror that the works of Karl Marx and Bernard Shaw could be purchased in ordinary bookstores, and that large groups of people believed that the economic and political basis of the country should be changed—as if a nation that supported Palmers, Burlesons, Archibald Stevensons, and Lusks [read McCarthys and Nixons] were not in an enviable and permanent state of perfection!

But while these depredations of law and order were going on, it was still possible to gather encouragement elsewhere. In the face of foreign opposition, the Red Armies in Russia were successfully combating the reactionaries under Denikin: the able young engineers one met [at The Dial], men like Captain Otto Beyer, were in favor of shop-committees and management-sharing in the factory, as well as a more rational and equitable system of distributing the product. So, too, economists like Veblen had left the Government administration in Washington convinced that, had the war only lasted a few years longer, the superior efficiency of a socialist organization of our national resources, under the control of economists and technicians instead of financiers, would have been shown. The I.W.W.s had not yet been extirpated; their profane songs still echoed in unexpected places; and even the strong conservative unions, not yet tempted by the bait of Florida land speculation, were intellectually alive enough to listen sympathetically to such a hopeful American translation of the English guild idea as the Plumb Plan.

Thorstein Veblen was not alone, in the summer of 1919, when he looked forward to an early collapse of the financial system and to the institution of a more socialized method of production in the United States: but he was ten years ahead of his time, at least in the negative side of his prediction; and before 1919 was over it became apparent that the expectation of salvaging any positive benefit from the war was gone. The Treaty of Versailles had been signed; and our country, with a perversity that has become characteristic of its foreign policy, certainly during the last ten years, accepted the indefensible part of the treaty and renounced the one hopeful element that remained, the League of Nations.

Wilson made a gross strategic error in binding the Treaty and the Covenant together. Those of us who were against the treaty, opposed the League, too, because it seemed merely to be an instrument for bringing more power back of that inequitable and unworkable arrangement. The two instruments have not proved to be quite as closely bound up as Wilson would have had them be; and the League, though still feeble, and still too often merely a convenience of the big powers, has certainly turned out better than we expected. But the United States can claim no share in this development. On the contrary, our arrogance, our bad manners, our self-righteousness, and our downright imperialism make us one of the first nations that should be bound over to keep the peace.

Now the only valid reason for our entering the World War was to ensure a decent peace. We failed in this; and we failed in creating better conditions in the twelve years that have followed. Indeed, the chief boast of our present administration is a Naval conference which has sanctioned the expansion of the American fleet to a level that was undreamed of before the war: a sanction which, though only permissive, and in this sense a sop to our childish sense of prestige, has been taken by those in favor of war as mandatory. Those of us who watched the development of the Army and the Navy after the war in the United States need not be surprised at this turn. The support of the Chemical Warfare Division; the refusal to sign the League Covenant abolishing the use of poison gases in warfare; the shameless distribution of bonuses and loans to all able-bodied veterans; and finally, the use of a large air fleet to dramatize the delicious terror of an impossible invasion—a dramatization accompanied by large scale propaganda in favor of war over the radio—all these events show how little sincerity there has been in our governmental professions of good will. To stand for peace only on our own terms, to adhere to the common decisions of other nations only when they happen to coincide with our own interest or our own sense of self-esteem—these are the marks of stultifying belligerency.

We are among the most belligerent of the larger powers. That we attempt to veil this situation with fine counsels to other nations to lessen their land-armaments and to accept our tariffs and our immigration discriminations in a humble and contrite spirit only makes our offensiveness more odious. But our present development existed in the germ in 1920. It looked then as if an out-and-out militarist, General Leonard Wood, might get the nomination for the presidency: it even seemed for a moment as if this might be the stepping stone to a dictatorship: who could tell? When one was setting one's course, the likelihood of witnessing an even more ghastly war than the past one was a constant possibility.

That likelihood is still here. The situation for peace is almost as precarious today as it was in 1919; it is certainly much worse than it was in a world so comparatively unorganized for war as was that of 1914, that innocent world, without passports and visas, without compulsory military service in the United States and England, with no greater instruments of destruction than the siege gun and the rifle, with populations that were still largely unregimented and with even an unorganized and somewhat independent press—not completely tamed to organized falsehood by official propaganda! That was an innocent world indeed. *Let us not make the mistake of thinking we are still living in it.*

As it turned out, our hopes for social justice were as badly deflated as our hopes for peace. Among the things one had to reckon with ten years ago was the fact that a large social revolution, which had once, by peaceful methods, seemed so imminent, had within almost a few short months ceased to be a reality. This was not due to the wave of prosperity: it will be remembered that this did not begin until 1922; and in 1920 and 1921 the greater part of the population was in an acutely miserable state. The lack of housing accommodation in our big cities was scandalous: it was scarcely possible to obtain quarters of any kind, and what few leftovers remained were run down and expensive. In fact, it was only by letting down the salutary tenement house regulations in New York, permitting the doing over of old-fashioned dwellings into apartment houses without sufficient fire safeguards, that the situation for the middle classes was eased. No one who had been conscious of the poverty and distress and lack of amenity that attended the housing of the greater part of our population could think for a minute that it had been removed; what was gone in 1921 was the hope for a speedy remedy. We saw by the example of Russia that the ruin of the existing system, with all its inefficiency and injustice, and the building up of a more adequate substitute were two different matters.

Meanwhile, in America, the Socialist Party, which in 1916 had seemed so vigorous and formidable, suddenly melted away; some of their slogans had been taken up by the more progressive members of the conservative parties, who favored government ownership of waterpower rights or of railroads. What remained lacked force, conviction, and point: socialism had become an empty formula. The trade unions were waning, undermined by their complacent antagonism to ideas, by their distrust of the intellectual, to say nothing of mere go-getting and bribe-taking and racketeering on the part of many of the leaders. If their absence left deplorable conditions for the unskilled unorganized workers, their presence was far from a guarantee of utopia.

In our political and economic life, no pressure of ideas remained. The great abstractions of the eighteenth and nineteenth centuries suddenly became ghosts. People might still call themselves Republicans, Democrats, Socialists, Single-Taxers, Trades Unionists; but in the United States you could not, from their actions, tell them apart. The period of 'normalcy' had begun. There were oil wells to be stolen, stocks to be promoted, graft to be picked up, flimsy houses to be built, motor roads to be laid, vacuum cleaners and radio sets to be sold. In the great excitement of pursuing these concrete symbols of affluence the impoverished conditions that surrounded the mean lives of the greater part of the population were forgotten. One's contemporaries even dared talk about 'prosperity'; and toward the end of those fat seven years the 'Duty to Consume' began stridently to be preached—a premonition of the disaster that was to come.

Let me sum up the conditions I faced during the years immediately after 1918. I lived in a world committed to war, a world subjected to intermittent tremors of collective animosity and hatred, a world still organized into belligerent states, girdled with fortified frontiers and supported by armies and navies and air fleets: a world where the principal resources of modern industry—petroleum, rubber, lac, coal, steel, vanadium—were unequally parcelled out and sought for by nations still clinging to their outdated notions of independence and sovereignty. This was a world where every important activity operated on an international scale except an international organization for political control.

At any moment this latent warfare might actively break out. My old master, Patrick Geddes, had characterized this posture of civilization as Wardom (not unconscious of tieing it with whoredom), and what we called war was not a new aspect but merely its old active phase. The first time that I heard a radio blare in the public square of a little European city, Geneva, I knew that another war would be accompanied by such a terrorism of the mind as was unknown in the previous one, except at moments perhaps in the trenches. One had only to combine the threat of an air attack on an unfortified city with the announcement that could be made over the radio to see that the instruments of hysteria and collective psychosis now at the disposal of governments were more dire than ever before. Our own War Department, like every other government, no doubt, had a blacklist of pacifists and radicals: on the outbreak of war they would be rounded up and imprisoned or shot. The chance of an intelligent man's surviving would be small: smaller still that he would survive with his intelligence. The machine had regimented us too well. War contracts with manufacturers were already signed; doubtless war propaganda and war lies were already manufactured, too, with a blank space left for the name of the particular enemy who was to be vilified.

In the light of these observations, what conclusions could one draw, what course could one plot? The conclusion that I drew for myself was that the situation demanded, not specific attacks on specific evils and specific points of danger, but a wholesale rethinking of the basis of modern life and thought, for the purpose of eventually giving a new orientation to all our institutions. In this situation, it might be more important to contribute a new philosophical idea than to prevent a battleship from being launched or oppose an effort at territorial aggrandizement: for the latter, at best, was a matter of bailing water out of a leaky boat with a spoon, while the essential need of the time was to create a more seaworthy boat than that we were afloat in. There was always the risk that any large-scale revision of purposes and institutions would be arrived at too late. In one's ears rang Schiller's ancient aphorism, "Whilst philosophers debate, hunger and love are settling the affairs of the world." In fastening on tangible, concrete objectives, in not being satisfied with purely abstract interpretations and ideal directions, the ordinary man who had taken the first choice and grasped at some positive end, however limited and little, had been right. The reason that our gas-filled idealisms had been so suddenly deflated after the war had been due to their own limitations: they mistook the abstract compass points for actual goals that we were trying to reach, forgetful of the fact that if all one seeks to do is to travel toward the magnetic North one reaches in the end only a waste of ice. Or else they took some limited portion of reality, like the overthrow of the capitalist economy, as equivalent for the general re-orientation of life, not realizing that no alteration in the means would be significant or even feasible until it was coupled with new ends and objectives.

The two countries where political ideas had not suddenly rusted away were Italy and Russia: both had been faced by concrete situations that demanded a concrete solution, even when that solution contradicted the philosophy with which the ruling group started out. In each of these countries, moreover, there had been an attempt to rethink the entire basis of life, not merely to alter some special set of institutions: religion, education, philosophy, even recreation had been affected by communism, and however much the immediate economic situation engrossed the government's efforts, communism at first did not lose its positive direction toward larger goals.

Why then, one may ask, did not either a fascist or a communist program appeal to me? The answer is that both these ideologies carried with them a large part of the errors and vices of the civilization which they had set out to combat. Communism, with its limitations on free intelligence, with its dogmatic adherence to Hegelio-Marxian formulas, with its distrust of pure science, with its notions of forcible indoctrination, with its apotheosis of the machine process, had powerful elements in it which were as life-denying as any in a so-called capitalist system: indeed, they both sprang from the same common sources in the seventeenth and eighteenth centuries. Both fascism and communism tended to deify the State; both of them denied the actual autonomy and authority of other corporate groups such as the university, the city, the church, the professional association, the industrial organization; both ideologies tended to be at their maximum of effectiveness in a state of war, a fact which is supported by the curious way in which the peaceful efforts to consummate the Five Year Plan in Soviet Russia have been accompanied with devices of dramatization derived from war. Skilled and loyal workers are called 'shock troops,' and the various industries are referred to as the

368

coal 'front' or the steel 'front,' while the population is keyed up to a continued sacrifice of the barest decencies of life by a constant appeal to the heroic mood—alternated with threats of savage reprisals.

Soviet Russia even in peace was what the United States had come close to being in times of war; and the reason was that the underlying ideals of both countries had been derived from the same source. It was these ideals, this mechanistic plan of life, this absolutist ideology of the Power State, that seemed to me the largest sources of our present evils. Nothing less than a complete philosophic and social reorientation would promote a more satisfactory social order.

The breakdown of our present system of production, the worldwide depression, the threats of war, war between the big states, war between the capitalist nations and communist Russia, the impoverishment and dire distress of vast masses of people, while wheat clogs the grain elevators and even the price of butter and eggs tumbles to new low levels—all these things increase the tension of our days, and lead to a feverish demand to "do something." Edmund Wilson, one of the ablest of our literary critics, voiced such a demand in a ringing article in The New Republic last winter: an article that reached its climax, after a picture of the sordid and futile and desperate state of current society, with a demand that we "take communism away from the communists."

This article gained wide attention; it called into existence a number of earnest responses, all of which recalled, in one way or another, those hopeful expectant days of 1919; but neither the original essay nor those that served as commentary, it seemed to me, took sufficiently into account the fact that our remedies are as much under suspicion as the dire diseases we would like them to exorcise. To take communism away from the communists, or even capitalism away from the capitalists, we must have a much deeper and firmer critical grasp of the whole human situation, and we must have a definite plan of action, capable of being worked out, step by step, in our daily personal life and our institutions. It is not merely a matter of appropriating catchwords or starting parties: it is a matter of altering the entire basis upon which our present venal and mechanistic and life-denying civilization rests. This is not a task for the next five years, but for the next five hundred.

The Two Germanys: 1932

On Saturday I came to Lübeck, thinking to leave here today (Monday) and go on to Berlin. But the town is entrancing and I wasn't in it half an hour before I decided it would be a good place to sit down for a few days and think. It is crowded, but surrounded by parks and water and green spaces; and by walking twelve minutes in any direction one is out of it. Stonorov's friends here speak perfect English and are very, very hospitable—not realizing perhaps that the cosmopolitan Stonorov is already so Americanized that he treats me like a long-lost brother and eternal friend on the basis of one lunch we had with Clarence in New York: plus an hour's conversation on the boat. How I wanted you at a concert of modern music Saturday evening, all the people present looking like the portraits and holy pictures of their ancestors hanging in their churches: honest, homely, stiff, decent faces: protestantism incarnate. On Sunday, with Dr. Vermehren, I climbed up into the organ loft at the Marienkirche to see the same organ that Bach's master, Buxtehude, had played two hundred years ago: still perhaps the best organ in Germany.   —Letter to Sophia. May 2, 1932

There was a fussy little man in the compartment from Zürich to Innsbruck: he wore gloves, used a monocle, had dapper little legs in golf stockings, and a round, pursy, well-fed red face. His manner at first seemed affected and over-solicitous: he recommended parts of Switzerland for their 'herrliche Landschaften' with repellent unction. But during the last two hours of our trip we talked steadily, and he proved unexpectedly enlightening. He had been with Mackensen's army in Poland, and at the end of the war he was a commandant at Constanza. In the meanwhile he had had all the 'children's diseases' of the war, had got a bullet through his skull, which came out in his cheekbone, had been near to death and blindness through the subsequent blood poisoning and when he was returned to service he had been gassed! His finest memory was of a walk he had taken through the hills of Bulgaria at the end of the war. (He was, at the end, in the secret service, for he had a fine memory for faces and could understand Russian and Bulgarian.) He said he had always been infuriated, as a youth, by the Old Boys who gathered together periodically to jabber about the war of '70; and everyone had said then that *they* wouldn't talk about this war, after it was over; but somehow it kept coming up now! Nowadays he could not look at any kind of marmalade: he had had to live on it and moldy bread that even the horses rejected, for weeks at a time.

"I am a patriot and a nationalist," he said, "but I must tell you this: it is a good thing Germany lost the war! A few months before the end we were afraid we might win, and we knew it would be bad for us if we did. The discipline, the respect for the uniform, were unbelievable. If Germany had won, we would have had to stand at attention when we wanted to mail a letter!" I told him I had seen 'The Hauptmann from Köpenick.' He said: "*That* was the temper of Germany before the war. It has changed now except perhaps in Berlin. We were too proud of our discipline: we felt that the rest of the world was completely inferior." This would have sounded pretty convincing, even if I had not read Thomas Mann's 'Betrachtungen eines Unpolitischen.' —RN. June 1, 1932

AT SALZBURG, en route to München, a healthy, good-looking man around thirty-five came into the compartment. I was puzzled to make him out. His face, red and round, seemed to belie the intelligence in his eyes; and the illustrated newspapers he was reading gave me no clue at all. Was he a country squire? I could not place him; so an hour passed before we fell into conversation. I began it by asking him whether we had not passed the Chiemsee; then somehow we began to discuss the state of the world, and I was amazed to hear from his lips the same liberal sentiments I had heard from the porter in Basel, the drug clerk in Vienna, the genteel business man on the way to Innsbruck. Actually we got into politics by first discussing fish and fishing—trout and salmon in Lapland to be exact. An one point he said that he lived in Berlin for a few months in the winter for the sake of spiritual companionship, and that the rest of the year he lived in a village near Salzburg. This made it seem he might be a writer, so finally I told him that I was a writer, and he said he was one, too. Then I wrote my name on a card. He asked me if I had seen 'Der Hauptmann von Köpenick.' I said I had in Lübeck. He said he had written it. Instantly I felt Carl Zuckmayr and I were 'friends.' —RN. June 9, 1932

Note: Zuckmayr's play was a satire on German militarism and officialdom. The Captain from Köpenick is a down-and-outer in Berlin who gets hold of the military uniform of an infantry captain, and on its authority alone commandeers a squad of soldiers and for a brief while exercises undisputed authority.

UNSENT LETTER TO DR. FRITZ SCHUMACHER, ARCHITECT AND CITY PLANNER, AS OF 1933. You probably do not remember the first time I met you in June 1932. I called at your office in the Hochbauamt, in the company of a young Russian. Our friend Frau V. had arranged the meeting. We talked about the abandonment of the International Exhibition that had been planned to take place in Köln in 1933, the city whose inner quarters you had replanned. I told you how enthusiastic some of us in America had been over Dr. Ernst Jäckh's program for that Exhibition; how it made me feel personally that Germany, rising out of the defeat of the last war, had assumed the leadership in Western Civilization and was about to bring together and fuse into an organic whole all the fragmentary aspects of the modern world.

That enthusiasm was, alas! misplaced: but in 1930, when the program was printed in Die Form, it was still possible to think that people like you and Jäckh and the leaders of the Deutscher Werkbund were truly representative of Germany: that you were its actual leaders, and not the polite disguise for quite another kind of leadership. When my friend Walter Curt Behrendt was still the editor of Die Form, I used to contribute to that paper: and I still have my old back numbers. Just the other day I refreshed my memory by re-reading the program of the New Era Exposition.

"What does the idea of a 'New Era' mean?" asked Dr. Jäckh. . . . "The 'New Era' is an organic result of the development of a century, the conscious experience of the continuity of the most decisive century of discoveries, inventions, and transformations of form. To represent the totality and unity of such a 'New Era,' to make it palpable, to develop it avowedly and credibly, is the aim of the International Exhibition of 1933, which points to the future. We are convinced that Max Scheler, the philosopher, was right when he characterized the epochal significance of our times as the beginning of a new era. "The geometric order, in which every extensive transformation of matter and man lies, at the beginning of which we are standing, can scarcely be overestimated . . . It is not only a transformation of matter, circumstances, institutions, the fundamental ideas and form of the arts and nearly all of the sciences, it is a transformation of man himself, of the character of his inner construction, in body, instincts, soul and spirit; it is not only a transformation of his actual being, but also a transformation of his standards. . . .'" —From Letters to Germans in 'Values for Survival.' 1946

Just yesterday Phyllis Ackerman, Arthur Pope's wife, told us of having been the guest in 1936 of the Max Warburgs in Hamburg. They had taken her in sometime in the middle thirties, after she had broken her paralyzed leg through falling. During a dinner party one night there were ominous sounds in the square outside the house, which everyone pretended to ignore. When they retired to the drawing room at the front of the house, they found that a mob of Nazis were parading around the place with torches, singing Nazi songs, and making threatening gestures: so Warburg, drawing the curtains, said: "Let us watch the show from the top story, where we can't be seen."

All the guests followed their host up to the great bathroom on that floor, where, by lying on the sill of the high window they could look down into the street. The sky was growing darker and the crowd was getting more frenzied: finally, they began moving toward the gate in front of the Warburg place; and it seemed that in another moment they would burst through it and work their will upon the mansion and its inhabitants. (Warburg had thoughtfully told Phyllis to have her American passport in her hand.) "That," he said, "should keep them from doing anything to you." Just at the moment when it seemed the whole party was doomed, a flash of lightning followed at once by a peal of thunder, broke from the sky; and a sudden downpour of torrential rain made the crowd scatter and run. The guests got down from the shelf, straightened up, and began to breathe freely again. "That," said their agnostic host, "was the voice of Yahweh. For the moment we are saved." —RN. September 7, 1963

TO FRAU V. IN LÜBECK. . . . I cannot guess what has happened to you, dear Frau V., since August 1932.

It is easier for me to picture what happened to Rosa Bitberg, that lovely sixteen-year-old Jewess, who was your daughter Else's friend: she who was your house guest and who played all sorts of silly parlor games with us that last night in Lübeck, as plump as a well-ripened peach, as friendly and innocent as a kitten. I can picture Rosa's fate because I know what your countrymen did to millions of Rosas all over Europe. Wrapped in the security she enjoyed in your household, finding out too late that the people she had called her fellow-countrymen had transformed themselves into Hitler's trained beasts, criminally obedient to his every command, Rosa probably did not escape.

Even the friendly living room of your villa outside Lübeck, with its gray porcelain stove, its Bechstein piano, and the painting by Carl Hofer on the wall, held a hint during that gay evening of what was in store for Rosa. For you had another guest, a clever sharp-tongued man, polished and worldly, the editor of Der Querschnitt: a man very much at ease in the cosmopolitan world of Paris, London, and New York, was he not? He was full of both salty stories and poisonous opinions. Something that I said about politics started him, to my surprise, upon a long tirade against the Jews: a tirade as violent as it was prejudiced and untruthful, and no deference to you or your Jewish guest caused him to soften his opinions or to curb his tongue. Finally you could bear it no longer: you turned to him and under your breath said indignantly, "Schändlich!" [outrageous]. Presently you found some excuse to interrupt him; perhaps it was then that we began to play charades.

At the time, my wife and I were still too innocent of the forces working below the surface of German life to attach to this incident the significance it actually had. But in the years that followed it dramatized all that was happening to Germany, and all that set it off, step by step, act by act, from the rest of the world. The rudeness and the mocking brutality of the editor of Der Querschnitt was not a reflection of the state of mind of the down-and-outs who followed Hitler for the sake of a handout: it was the cultivated deformity of an otherwise keen and active intelligence.

Every country has a 'lunatic fringe': people filled with irrational hatred for any idea or any way of life but their own; people who, because of their ignorance, their frustration, or their mental derangement boil over with prejudices against other races, or other nations. We have such people in America; but except in a few backward areas they remain at the periphery of our political life and our culture. One did not expect to find such opinions and attitudes as the editor of Der Querschnitt expressed in a person of his general culture. You had made me forget, dear Frau V., by your own warm humanity and your own clarity of mind, how deeply this strain of irrationality went all through German life.

When the Nazis came into power, the avowed prophet of barbarism, Oswald Spengler, scornfully observed: "This was no victory: there was no opposition."

. . . I remember the anxiety in your eyes during that spring of 1932; I laid it then to some private worry or some personal frustration; but now I wonder whether you then felt premonitions of what was about to happen. We discussed D. H. Lawrence together, do you remember? You had seen him or had actually met him in Italy and had read some of his novels. As a prophet he had a certain advantage in his observations on Germany; for his wife was a von Richtofen, and he had visited Germany before 1914 as well as after the war. His Letter from Germany was written in 1924, though it was not published in the New Statesman in England till after the Third Reich had, by its final appearance, justified his intuitions. One year after he wrote that letter the Pact of Locarno was signed, and everyone took for granted that a new era of good feeling and understanding was under way: the year that your dishonest and disastrous inflation policy was brought to an end, having accomplished only half of what its German sponsors secretly sought to achieve, since while it canceled your internal debts it did not free you—as your reactionary politicians and financiers had hoped—from your reparation payments. All these facts only make Lawrence's prediction more remarkable. Lawrence wrote, in 1924:

"Germany, this bit of Germany, is very different from what it was two and a half years ago, when I was here. Then it was still open to Europe. Then it still looked to Western Europe for a reunion, for a sort of reconciliation. Now that is over. The inevitable, mysterious barrier has fallen again, and the great leaning of the Germanic spirit is once more eastwards, towards Russia, towards Tartary. . . . At night you feel strange things stirring in the darkness, strange feelings stirring out of this still-unconquered Black Forest. There is a sense of danger. It isn't the people. They don't seem dangerous. Out of the very air comes a sense of danger, a queer, bristling feeling of uncanny danger.

"Something has happened. Something has happened which has not yet eventuated. The old spell of the old world has broken, and the old, bristling, savage spirit has set in. The war did not break the old peace-and-production hope of the world, though it gave it a severe wrench. Yet the old peace-and-production hope still governs, at least the consciousness. Even in Germany it has not quite gone.

"But it feels as if, virtually, it were gone. The last two years have done it. The hope in peace-and-production is broken. The old flow, the old adherence is ruptured. And a still older flow has set in. Back, back to the savage polarity of Tartary, and away from the polarity of civilised Christian Europe. This, it seems to me, has already happened. And it is a happening of far more profound import than any actual *event*. It is the father of the next phase of events. . . .

"And it looks as if the years were wheeling swiftly backwards, no more onwards. Like a spring that is broken, and whirls swiftly back, so time seems to be whirling with mysterious swiftness to a sort of death. Whirling to the ghost of the old Middle Ages of Germany, then to the Roman days, then to the days of the silent forest and the dangerous, lurking barbarians."

All that Lawrence prophesied in that letter has come to pass in our time: indeed, it had begun before Lawrence observed it, for what the masses of men felt in their souls was already declared in the self-conscious doctrines of a Moeller van den Bruck or an Ernst Jünger or an Oswald Spengler, who provided new symbols for everything in the German soul that was dark, repressive, and alien to the life of the rest of the world. There were plenty of outward signs of this change before 1933 if one had the sense to pay attention to them. The election of Hindenburg as second President of the Republic in 1925 showed which way the wind was blowing: a symbol of a re-established continuity with all that was archaic and backward-looking in Germany: its worship of the army, its obedience to the Junker caste, its gift for political Machiavellianism in the style of Frederick the Great. Did not this man who first betrayed the

Monarchy find it no less easy to betray the Republic that had put him into power? Both times he had the supreme satisfaction of justifying his Judas-like career under the guise of Duty.

Yes: your countrymen turned toward their barbaric gods, from Wotan to Wagner; that is, they turned back upon what bound them to the rest of the civilized world: they enslaved themselves, willingly, joyfully, in order that they might more effectively prepare for the enslavement of mankind. But it was only a Lawrence who felt in the political air of 1924 "a sense of danger, a queer, bristling feeling of uncanny danger." While we still thought of your Wandervögel as youths in rebellion against the old Germany, with its strictness, its harshness, its personal tyranny, he recognized this youth movement for what it was: an uprising, not against Germany, but against civilization.

Meanwhile, if you are alive, do you still live in Lübeck, that city whose Seven Spires once rose above the flat meadowland and heath, reminding its burghers of the time when the Hansa cities had not only been rich and powerful, but free; when they were not only self-governing cities, but cities in an economy and a polity that stretched from Bergen to the Holy Land? The towers of your beautiful city are no longer seven: the richest of your memorials has been bombed, an inevitable retribution for the forces of evil which your own fellow citizens in their stupidity, in their slavish exaltation, helped set in motion. It is the world's loss as well as your own. The Lübeck I once visited and lost my heart to I shall never see again. It has vanished for both of us as hundreds of other places and monuments have vanished, from Coventry to Canterbury, Bayeux to Leningrad. Those terrible scars unite the victors and the vanquished.

Do you remember the walk we took along the Landstrasse toward Travemunde, that April afternoon, when the wind from the Baltic whipped against our faces and gave just a touch of color to the tip of your tip-tilted Cranach nose? We talked about the earthy humor of Ernst Barlach's sculptures, and how he had brought back into modern Germany the very spirit of the old Northern Gothic: the spirit of Brueghel, without the under-current of nightmare in some of Brueghel's works. And you said then: "The nightmare may still come. You know the Nazis hate him and they want to remove his war monument in Hamburg."

You were right. The nightmare came, and one of the first things the Nazis did, along with the burning of the books, was the removal of Barlach's tender monument of a mother and child, because, they said, it wasn't Aryan. By that they meant that its humanness was more visible than its Germanness; and in this they were right. That spirit of nihilism, which denied the human, that spirit which "worked for the extinction of mankind," as Ludwig Klages said, has been successful.

376

The Menace of Totalitarian Absolutism

We do not know if Western society is now in the midst of its death rattle or its birth throes. But we do know that an old dream is dying, and some of us believe that a new dream, a new picture of human possibilities and fresh motives for human action, is taking shape. And meanwhile, since the new dream does not yet govern men's actions and indeed exists concretely only in the most fragmentary forms, we realize that our civilization as a whole faces a severe threat. The forces of physical destruction and mental disintegration released by the massive technological equipment of modern states and empires threaten alike the conquerors and the conquered. The only peace held forth by the future is the peace of death.

"Nothing is so savage," Aristotle observes, "as injustice in arms," and injustice in arms is the very essence of the class suppressions and the imperialistic conquests that are being waged by the more backward ruling classes throughout the world today. And whereas the barbarian who brought an end to Roman civilization had a conviction of strength but no strength of conviction, fascism has been preceded by an intellectual advance guard of fantasies and rationalizations and dogmas—a specious system of social psychology, like Pareto's; a Prussian drillmaster's version of history, like Spengler's. Partial demonstrations of intellectual strength (for no one need deny the abilities of Pareto or Spengler) have systematically prepared the way for neurotic simplifications of human conduct, inordinate collective ambitions and perfectly infantile forms of communal savagery.

No intelligent person can in the present situation forget the parallel between our own state and that of Roman society at the end of the fourth century. But that lesson may be read in two ways; and the final outcome need not necessarily be a sense of futility and defeat. Every known civilization has faced, at some period of its existence, the specter of Necropolis. Sometimes this specter occurs at the end of a cycle of striking cultural activity and achievement, and is the natural terminus of a long life, honorably lived. Sometimes it occurs in the midst of such a cycle, as a result of some terrestrial misfortune or social catastrophe. In Provence, after the Albigensian crusade, or in Rome, during the period when papal power shifted to Avignon, or indeed throughout Western civilization when the Black Plague struck its ugly blow in the fourteenth century, such a relapse temporarily took place. But the corpus of civilization, though left with a broken frame, permanent scars, and splinters of steel too deeply imbedded to be removed, nevertheless recovered. Spengler, when he speaks gloatingly of the final phase of paralysis and brutality and death, forgets that his 'final' phase often occurs in the 'springtime' of civilization—and need not prove fatal.

But if one wishes to make the parallel between Roman civilization and our own a nightmare, one need only read Gibbon and then turn one's eyes from the pages of the book to the street outside. As Rome's civilizing energy went downhill, power came more and more to rest, not on intelligence and consensus, but on the force of arms and brutality. Already we of the Western world have seen the spectacle of a handful of gangsters, armed with machine guns, terrorizing and exacting tribute from a whole industry, in broad daylight and in the midst of populous cities—whose officers the gangsters themselves partly control. So, too, we have seen political parties, organized on gangster principles, paralyzing a modern state in a fashion that recalls the early work of the Vandals: again we have seen these parties attempting to terrorize by swagger and promise of unlimited brutality the somewhat more civil polities in Western Europe that surround them.

These are all plainly the phenomena of degradation and decay: physical power and fear become the sole binding forces of a society when it loses the last remnants of more human ideals and more rational collective goals. But against these forces we still have energies at work that move in the opposite direction: plus active intelligence for which one can find no counterpart in the Rome of the fifth century A.D. For one thing, we have deeper stores of sheer biological vitality; for another we have a body of socialized knowledge and able technical practice, and all that further skill in social cooperation for which our scientific and industrial achievements have set a pattern, whilst the Romans, to the end, were hopeless empirics, who attempted to run a vast empire with a system of accountancy whose mathematics were so clumsy they could not be applied to the management of a country store. —The New Republic. November 27, 1935

20: The Fateful Decade: 1935-1945

No notes of mine are adequate for conveying the personal tensions and struggles, the political decisions and indecisions, the desperate hopes and the ignominious betrayals, the cowardly moral retreats and the heroic sallies, counter-attacks, and sacrifices that characterized the years after 1940. Those years left an increasingly sinister trail over the world's later life; for what seemed a victory and a vindication of the democratic cause turned out during the next decade to be a proof of A.E.'s dictum: "Man becomes the image of the thing he hates."

Even alert citizens who had reacted intelligently to the calculated assaults and atrocities of the totalitarian dictatorships—Communist, Fascist, Nazi, Racist or Ultra-Nationalist—were unable to rouse their countrymen in time to make voluntarily the only choice open to them after 1939—a readiness to accept the lesser of two evils: armed resistance or supine submission. That choice was made for us Americans, not by the United States Government but by the Axis powers.

In the military action that followed I was disqualified by age, occupational training, and health to play even a minor part. Because of my remoteness from the strains and sacrifices of war, I sought to offset my incapacity for active service by attempting to clarify the immediate tasks and the ultimate issues of the war in a succession of articles, lectures, and books, beginning in 1939 with an appeal for immediate action, 'Men Must Act.' This was followed in 1940 by a book written in the urgent three weeks after the fall of France: 'Faith for Living,' a work that served as a more timely message for the British than for my more insulated

379

countrymen. Two other books, 'Values for Survival' in 1946, and 'In the Name of Sanity' in 1954, record some of my efforts to meet this ongoing crisis. Many of their pages bear the marks of wartime apprehensions and emotional stresses: all that may remain of value in them now was perhaps crystallized in 'Green Memories,' 1947, the story of our son Geddes, killed in combat in 1944.

National differences of opinion about the necessity for actively turning back the totalitarian 'Wave of the Future' brought about many grave breaches and ominous silences even among old friends and colleagues; but some account of these personal divisions and later re-unions await my Autobiography. Meanwhile, this bare introductory note must serve as substitute.

Timely Symposium on War, 1935

Question 1: What will you do when America goes to War? This question is too abstract to permit me to give an unqualified answer. What war? When? For what purposes? Between the passive phase of war, under which we now live, and its active phase, I recognize only a difference of degree. In general, I oppose war because of its imbecility, its absence of human purpose, its brutalization of life, its abject failure to achieve reasonable goods, and its futile simplification of all the conflicts and real issues involved in life in communities. In so-called times of peace I fight this war animus; and I shall continue to fight it when war breaks out—even if the war itself be the lesser of two evils, and even if the issues compel me, momentarily, to participate in the war. I am no absolute pacifist: it is neither the waste of war nor its toll of death that appalls me, but the fact that this waste and these deaths come to no purpose, by reason of the very technique of fighting and its special behavior patterns—no matter how just and rational the cause seems at the outset. War is always a losing fight even when it is a just one.

Question 2: Will your decision be altered if Soviet Russia is an ally of the United States in a war with Japan? The entrance of Soviet Russia on the side of the United States would not sanctify American imperialism for me, as against Japanese imperialism. On the other hand, the support by the United States of Soviet Russia, against a demented Japanese militarism which threatened the accomplishments and ideals of Soviet Russia would certainly make me more favorably disposed to the war. In any case, however, my duty as a writer would remain the same: namely, to remain sane, to think clearly, to correct emotional distortions and patriotic biases, and in general to see to it that the fight did not lead to the enthronement of the Hearsts and the Brass Buttons and the 'patriotic' setting up of a permanent military political organization, namely Fascism. Outside of giving aid to Soviet Russia in a serious crisis I cannot detect a single rational reason for a war with Japan. Our present belligerent policy must be reversed. There is nothing fated and inescapable in this conflict.

Question 3: Would a prospective victory by Hitler over most of Europe move you to urge U.S. participation in opposition to Germany in order to prevent such a catastrophe? Certainly I would favor United States participation; indeed the menace seems to me great enough at the present moment to warrant the collective institution of a blockade on all war material and on all raw materials indispensable for armament. This would take the guts out of Germany's present bellicoseness before Hitler is sufficiently armed to fight. A preventive international blockade—not of course including foodstuffs—would probably save millions of lives within the next decade. The failure to apply it is due to the fact that all the other big states of the world differ from Nazi Germany only in degree: they are unwilling to face applying a measure which might—as in the case of Italy with Abyssinia—be applied against them. —L.M.'s response, *When America Goes to War: A Symposium, Modern Monthly. June 1935*

Note: This symposium was published in V. F. Calverton's Modern Monthly in June 1935. The answers came from a wide range of American intellectuals, none of whom, save me, advocated taking positive measures against Hitler. But in a similar canvass of a group of American labor leaders, published in the July issue, there was a more alert and realistic response to the impending crisis, and a greater readiness to take action.

We must meet this week, with Edmund Wilson, dear Waldo, and discuss the Call for a Writers' Congress you sent me: meanwhile I want to tell you briefly why I will not sign it. To me it is a pretty sad document: as dead and uncreative as the radical movement itself in America has been these last ten years, and beneath this deadness and uncreativeness is a laziness in thinking that amounts to dishonesty. The program that is offered is based upon six points, all of them negative: beginning first of all with an injunction to fight against imperialist war and defend the Soviet Union! In the name of what is the fighting to be done? Answer: in the name of an incipient proletarian revolution. In the form that this revolution has taken in Russia, and that it takes even more in the stale formulae derived from that revolution, I do not believe in it. Too many mistakes were made in the course of that revolution, and later incorporated as a form of orthodoxy, to be of service in an American movement. At the present moment, a revolutionary movement does not have to protect Russia against the capitalist nations: it has to protect itself equally against the tactics and the assumptions, against the forms of autocracy that have been developed there—and against the notion of creating by force alone what cannot be produced by intelligence and persuasion. Except by physical means, you cannot fight fascism in terms of the Russian Revolution. Their social and political tactics are now identical, even though their class and economic bases are dissimilar. Beneath both movements is a profound disrespect for human life, for the autonomy of the personality and the group, and for the basic liberties of civilized existence. . . . —Letter to Waldo Frank. January 6, 1935

Note: Unsent because repeated orally the next day.

. . . I trust you are back in stride with more to show for the last few months than I can. At least you have not been spending your time in aimless Pullman cars, like a Thomas Wolfe hero, have not been dispersing yourself in unimportant lectures to vacuous people, have not been showing, as I have, latent capacities for mob oratory in addressing groups on War and Fascism. One is damned in one's work, not by the cohorts of Satan, against whom one is on one's guard; but by all the little Children of Light who bait one with their good intentions and make one surrender one's proper virtue in the interests of *their* virtue, as if, in the long run, that could be more important. Henceforward, I shout to the heavens, I shall deliver no more lectures on behalf of good causes: I am the good cause that denies the need for such lectures. Avaunt! importuning world! Back to my cell. . . . —Letter to Van Wyck Brooks. April 12, 1935

ISOLATIONISM AND WAR. War was probably further from the consciousness of Americans during the late twenties than it had been at any other period of their history. They agreed that they didn't like it, and so they preferred not to think about it. As a people, they had participated in the First World War with an emotional heartiness that now seems astounding: some passionately, some vindictively, most of them hopefully, thinking that it would prove, in fact, a 'war to end war.' Even Dr. Charles Beard then had the moral insight to advocate that the United States take part in the fight directly after Germany's invasion of Belgium.

But from the spring of 1919 onward, pacifism and cynicism flourished together. Few indeed read the signs of the times as keenly as our neighbor, J. E. Spingarn, for they were unable to recognize the truth of his judgment that their irresponsible and unconditional pacifism was in fact preparing the world for extremer butcheries and more systematic enslavements than man had ever before encountered. Those of our countrymen who did not take comfort out of the unadulterated wishfulness of the Kellogg Peace Pacts, took refuge in isolation: this time, they said to themselves, the United States would stay out of it. We would pull up the gangplank, cut loose from the rest of the world, and drift around in our own hemisphere, 'protected' by our palpable disinclination to fight, 'protected' by our own unreadiness and moral spinelessness, 'protected' by our contempt for the principles of international law and order, ready to retreat from justice if we could not gain our point easily. We renounced war for ourselves, but we accepted no responsibility for restraining those who in fact espoused war. We did not believe such people could exist. No wonder the dictators laughed openly, and spat.

That attitude cut deep into our whole national life. It helped create the state of civic rottenness in which gangsters flourished, bullying the sheepish business men, blackmailing the law-abiding, controlling whole industries, dominating states and cities, their police departments and their courts of justice, under the general principle of appeasement; for this pacifism found it more tolerable to allow the gangsters to exercise their powers, shooting those who got in their way, bribing and looting with a free hand, than to risk physical danger and to challenge their right to take over. Almost every city had its little Hitlers and Mussolinis: we watched them rise, as we watched Hitler himself rise, passive if not indulgent, tolerant if not amused. Isolationism became our narcotic; and we increased the dose lest we become aware of our moral degradation. Most of our countrymen achieved this condition in a high state of self-approval, with the sanction of their popular leaders in politics, in journalism, in education. A whole army of debunking journalists and cynical professors, in the name of the academic virtue of objectivity, weakened in their students and disciples every trace of moral judgment, every potentiality for action, every capacity for active choice. That corruption bit deep: more than a residue of it is still at work.

This was the world in which our son's generation grew up. Even the cold disillusion brought on by the panic of 1929 and the depression that followed did not awaken us Americans sufficiently to face the painful realities of our day. Paradoxically, our country was never so isolationist as it became in the nineteen thirties, when airplanes were beginning to girdle the globe in every direction, and when a dictator, with the courtesy of the radio, could instantly pour his poison into the ears of the peoples he had set out to enslave, with the consciousness that he would find them ready to absorb every drop of it, so long as they could absolve themselves, by their very acquiescence, by their 'open-mindedness' as it was

383

called, of the necessity of making a stand and risking their properties or their lives. If the secret motto of the twenties in America was 'purposeless materialism' that of the thirties was 'effortless security.'

Some of us awakened from this nightmare of paralysis and moral emptiness more quickly; some more slowly; many never awakened at all; but few indeed were those who could boast that they had never been asleep. —From 'Green Memories.' 1947

A country like Germany or Soviet Russia with only one party and one voice is a danger not only to the rest of humanity, but to itself: if that was not clear in Soviet Russia before 1930, it should be clear now. It is the totalitarian nature of Soviet Russia, taken over directly from Czarist and bureaucratic Russia, not this or that special mistake in policy, certainly not the quarrel between Trotsky and Stalin, that has brought about this catastrophe. Where dissent is a crime, treason becomes a patriotic duty. And under a regime of repression the rulers inevitably create a race of crypto-revolutionaries who may easily become as disintegrated as the pathetic figures that are now on trial. Who knows but that the very prosecutors, ferociously carrying out Stalin's purge, are not also crypto-revolutionaries, Azeffs of the left? Stalin himself, in his dual capacity of Lenin-Hitler, may have the most mangled psyche of all: one does not kill all one's old comrades without either being a madman or becoming one. —RN. 1936

. . . It is for lack of some vivid sense of what life is worth living for that the revolutionary cause has gone astray: its courage wasted, its hopes deflated. I do not listen to the Trotskyites, for their speech bears the same accent as their Stalinist enemies. But I believe my eyes and I was frankly horrified by the architectural exhibition that the U.S.S.R. has been showing in Detroit. Nothing that Trotsky could say against Stalin's regime is half as eloquent as the self-confession of this architecture: the same bastard classicism that the financiers and imperialists of Nineteen Hundred in America conjured up as emblem of their power. Only one thing was more sickening than these dead forms: the dishonest apologetics that accompanied them. The whole show stank; alongside it, Napoleonism, coming in the wake of the French Revolution, had a noble vitality. My nightmare now, which I scarcely dared confess to myself a year ago as even a possibility, though in my heart I knew it existed, is that Stalin's Russia and Hitler's Germany and Mussolini's Italy may form a block. Perhaps the chief obstacle to this, the only thing we can count on, is Hitler's invincible, demonically inflated irrationality. A pleasant thought . . . —Letter to Waldo Frank. January 10, 1938

An atmosphere of foggy unreality hangs over current discussions of peace. Most of the proposals to keep war from coming to America are noble and high-minded and humane; but they have one serious defect: the world on which they are based no longer exists. The proposals are dated 1938; but the premises remain those of 1928.

This failure to keep up with events may prove almost as fatal as the events themselves. For we are now confronted with a worldwide political phenomenon, fascism, whose deeply malignant character and cancerous spread have changed every problem of civilized political existence. Peace-loving people are still trying to make themselves believe that fascism is not what it seems and that fascists do not mean to do the things they actually do. Such people even hope, by some show of affability, by some economic bribe, to transform the very nature of the evil that threatens to engulf us all. Surely, these people say to themselves, turning away from the latest fascist barbarity in the morning paper, the world cannot be so bad as that; or if it is for the moment, it cannot long remain so.

But the world *is* as bad as that: what is more, the skies threaten to become much blacker before the clouds lift again. Those who persist in closing their eyes to the vicious forces that are now deliberately attacking our civilization are the victims of unprofitable hopes and palsied wishes. Hating war, they are preparing themselves and their countrymen to endure something far more hideous than war: the 'peace' perpetrated by fascism. . . .

To seek to get along with fascism on the democratic principle of 'live and let live' is to open the way for a more complete fascist conquest. Whatever strength fascism has lies precisely in its pathological condition: its predisposition to suspicion and hatred, its violent paranoia, its readiness to exalt the maimed ego through collective sadism and murder. Every form of dishonesty, torture and violence is justified by the fascist if it promotes the advantages of the state; every form has already been used by the German Nazis and the Italian Fascists and the Japanese militarists. The bestial torture of political victims in concentration camps, the piratical sinking of defenseless cargo boats, the pitiless bombing and strafing of innocent civilians are merely the objective symbols of this philosophy of government. It is not a new philosophy: what is new to the modern world is that it is now unchallenged and unchecked. —A Call to Arms. The New Republic. May 18, 1938

This is the end of a restless harrowing week whose anxiety all the world shared. On the last day of the international crisis, before the declaration of war, I hung over the radio, with few intermissions; between eight-

thirty and four. The tension was unbearable: the fear of war and the fear
of that retreat which would be worse than war were not resolved till nine
o'clock Sunday morning, when the news of Chamberlain's announcement
came over the radio. I recalled the days of my own past when in August
1914 I walked along Riverside Drive one morning and said to myself:
"This finishes my career." Then I remembered the deadly years of disillusionment that followed the Versailles Treaty; and I wondered what
beam of hope would be left the younger generation—no matter what
happened. The final treachery that opened the way for Hitler—expected
by me but a cruelly unexpected blow to millions of decent people—was
the agreement between the Brown and the Red Bolsheviks. It was hard to
say which was worse; the agreement itself or the apologies that were
made for it by the Communist faithfuls. —RN. September 1939

As for sogginess, that is the state of the world. Not to be in trouble or
pain at the present moment, not to feel baffled and empty, is to be
outside the experience of our generation and therefore inhuman. I almost
feel a little guilty when I find myself enjoying a free day, as it occasionally comes to one. On the other hand, I smile too, when I catch myself, as
I did the other night, pleading earnestly, zealously, for—guess what!—
law and order! Twenty years ago those were the tags of a reactionary;
and one did not suspect then that they were, like most conservative
sayings, the leftovers of an earlier revolution: that of the seventeenth
century, which, faced with the caprices and uncertainties and terrors of
despotism, opposed to these political vices the concepts of law and order:
the first stop beyond despotism!!

We have lived to see strange things. —Letter to Thomas Beer.
October 31, 1939

During the last fortnight, I have been settling down to that long communion with other books which is part of the incubation period on my
own. . . . I am still excited by our return to the city, and I wander around
the streets, peering at the faces and attempting to read them, as I might
if I were in a strange city in Europe for the first time: I feel that I have
much still to learn; and that at any rate, every sight, every person, every
building, has something fresh to say. It would be marvelous, in a mood
like this, to begin the preparation of that interpretive book on the development of New York I once planned to write; but that was a task that
beckoned before the evils and catastrophes of the times began to press
upon me; so, with a sigh, I put it aside; and instead I have started to
flounder about the vague literature of a subject that won't be fully defined

until I have succeeded in writing about it; which means that I am reading practically everything about human life, from books on psychology and costume and medicine to the 'Imitation of Christ' or the 'Paradise of the Heart.' It is really great fun, if anything can still be called fun in a civilization that shows so many signs of disintegration. . . .

As you know, I never completely despair; just last night, facing a wealthy Philadelphia audience—the Fairmount Park Art Association—telling them that civilization could not be saved unless they were willing to resign most of their status, their privileges, and their wealth, instead of losing everything in the general onslaught of barbarism, I met with an unexpected reaction. One of the audience challenged me to name a class that had ever voluntarily resigned its privileges anywhere; and when I cited the abolition of serfdom in Russia by the aristocracy, and the renunciation of the much more complete power of the Samurai in Japan, the audience loudly applauded!! There is always a ray of hope flickering somewhere through my mind; but certainly the treachery and moral obliquity of our time has reached the point of producing in me an almost physiological nausea.   —Letter to Van Wyck Brooks. December 19, 1939

. . . An inertia as massive as that of America is not to be overcome in a few days; and I fear that if things go badly for the English and the French—and I don't see any ground for thinking that they are going well, when it is obvious that they are being opposed by the combined force of Germany and Russia, and the latent force of Italy—it will be too late for us to do anything effective, unless we have been getting ourselves ready, intellectually and morally, a long time in advance. A last moment intervention, as in the first World War, may prove as disastrous, in its final results upon peace, as our first was: an outburst of unconditional idealism, followed by an outburst of unconditional disillusion. And the thing that needs emphasis now is that there is neither health nor safety for us alone: our fate is bound up with the world's, and all men are our brothers.

Maybe I am vehement on the subject now, out of all reason, because I feel deeply my own guilt during the past twenty years, when despite my extreme skepticism of the totalitarian tyranny that was being built up in Russia, I said nothing and did nothing to counteract it, because 'Russia was Russia.' I made the mistake of thinking that Russia would work out its own salvation, and must therefore be protected from hostile criticism: forgetting that a poisoned political system transmits its infection, by subtle carriers, all over the world. Compare the timid brutalities of

387

Mussolini before 1925, with his arrogant villainies afterward, and the absolutely unscrupulous violence of Hitler after that. Russia, with its contempt for democracy and its open persecutions, had made the path easier for these later dictators. I feel now, if I was oblivious to it then, that our only chance for salvation consists in moving to create a universal society based on a common set of human ideals: a society wider than Christendom, and big enough to contain all the creeds that war within it. —Letter to Van Wyck Brooks. February 10, 1940

Today, dear Van Wyck, I put the final touches on my resignation from the contributing editorship to the New Republic. The reasons that prompted me to do this are very much like the reasons that make me wish to wrestle with you, like Paul with the men of Corinth, over your heretical belief in isolation. For it is a heretical belief for you to hold: it denies all the things that make you what you are and that make all your thoughts, not just a gift to your countrymen, but to the world. How can we be isolated? Men are suffering by the million in Europe; our whole civilization is likely to perish there. Whole patches of Europe are already dead; the flesh is covered with gangrene; the putrefaction and the poison will spread.

I would not bother to remind you that our physical isolation is gone; that Berlin is closer to New York than Boston was a century ago; nor would I awaken a very legitimate fear over what may happen to us *if* Hitler wins. No: the real reason to be concerned is that humanity cannot be divided off into isolated parcels: for good and ill we belong together; we must live or suffer together. We Americans are not the Chosen People, precious though our own historic experiment was, unique though some parts of it have been. If we withhold ourselves in this crisis, we shall only create that philosophy of insane national pride and self-adulation out of which fascism grows to fuller stature. By fostering this attitude we will make the pacification of the world impossible, for a true world organization, without serious sacrifices of privilege and power on our part, just as much as on the part of the British Empire, would be impossible.

I know as well as anyone the insufferable attitude of the English toward other peoples; I know their long series of crimes and blunders in fulsome detail: the horrors of the cotton industry, the iniquity of the Opium War, the human desecration in the Sepoy mutiny, the terrible brutality of Amritsar: symbols of a score of other acts not so easily remembered. But if I take England at her worst, in her rule in India, and if I add to it every crime, brutality and deprivation she has inflicted on her own workers and peasants, I still see in the English, taken as a whole, the unmistakable signs of a civilized people that is capable of self-correction and self-improvement, and that even in India has created by her own example, her own ideas, the very power that is capable of challenging her regime. To remember the terrible crimes and blunders that England and France committed in the remote and the recent past seems to me a stultifying attitude today; for crimes a thousand times worse are being committed by the Nazis. —Letter to Van Wyck Brooks. February 1, 1940

. . . These are perilous days; and I still cannot share the optimism that people continue to express: from Churchill's original exultation over his belief that Norway would turn out to be Hitler's Spain, it has all seemed premature and therefore hollow. There is neither enough imagination nor enough audacity in England—nor yet perhaps the means to carry out either—to make one confident that they will come out on top in this crisis. Of fine animal courage there is no lack; but the essential mediocrity, the deep fifth-ratedness, of the British governing classes is coming out: they are not on their toes; and what is worse they now lack that animal sense of danger, so necessary to our survival today, which I wrote about in my New Republic article. Well: I relieved my feelings by resigning from the Artists' Congress: the Stalinists had not merely forced through a resolution in favor of complete neutrality, but, even more significantly, instead of boycotting the Fascist art exhibition at Venice this spring, they gave their members permission to exhibit there: fascism being now, viewed by the Party Line, 'a matter of taste,' as they put it in Moscow. If Germany should be victorious in this war, the Stalinists will be our fifth column, acting in harmony with the Nazi Bundists and the Coughlinites: and the sooner we are prepared for that eventuality the better. The only fault I have to find with your 'Chart for Rough Water' is that even you are optimistic in thinking we have five or ten years before any physical danger will threaten us from Europe, for we will be lucky if we have as many months. . . . —Letter to Waldo Frank. April 16, 1940

. . . About your plan for an Ecumenical Council, dear Jo, to bring order and wisdom back to the human race. Borgese—did you read his 'Goliath'?—shares your poetic idea; indeed he anticipated it by almost a year, for last March he broached to me the notion of creating a Council of Wisdom, consisting originally of Antonio Borgese, Thomas Mann, and Mumford—now extended to a few less worthy names!—which should meet periodically and issue reports and pronouncements on the state of the world. He has been working on it steadily. Unfortunately the atmosphere of Chicago caused it to take on somewhat grandiose proportions, so that he scared the necessary financial backers away by talking of a million dollar foundation and a huge secretariat, as though we were to become a private League of Nations; but there is still a chance that he may, within a month or two, call a first meeting. You have conceived something more heroic; and I am sure something more heroic, and more desperate, is needed: but alas! you must not deceive yourself into thinking that this in itself is an *alternative* to the coming years of mental strife and physical struggle. . . . To hold such hopes now is to out-Chamberlain Chamberlain. Where you are right is in thinking that successful resistance to barbarism will be empty and meaningless unless in the meanwhile we summon together all the forces of mind which must otherwise be paralyzed by the very act of fighting, as they are paralyzed in fever by the body's struggle for survival. . . . —Letter to Josephine Strongin. February 1, 1940

First 'City of Man' Conference: May 24–26, 1940

After Hitler's first ominous triumph in Poland and the Netherlands in 1939, a number of people hitherto unconcerned with militarist Germany's program of conquest and enslavement in Europe, drew together spontaneously in little groups for the purpose of awakening their countrymen to the threat that Hitlerism and Stalinism then posed to democratic (representative) government. Possibly the first of these groups to combat American isolationism was William Allen White's Committee to Defend America by Aiding the Allies, soon followed by Herbert Agar's Fight for Freedom Group.

Even before 1935, G. A. Borgese, the Italian scholar and poet, then a professor at Smith College, sought to bring together a group of representative intellectuals, who would pool their wisdom and exert their authority to make clear the issues democracy now faced. Borgese, indeed, dreamed of formulating measures which might forestall or circumvent the worldwide totalitarian threat. Before this proposed group even had a name, Hitler had taken the initiative, and when we met in May 1940, Borgese's original conception was already obsolete, and the ensuing split of our committee into militants and pacifists showed how quixotic his original hopes were. Both our strength and our weakness were well revealed in our first and only publication: 'The City of Man,' which bears Borgese's unmistakeable stamp. What these groups perhaps did was to

*make America's possible participation in the struggle against Hitler open
to discussion—though until the Japanese drew the United States into the
war, with Hitler's incautious backing, England might have been as overwhelmed and humiliated as France was, without stirring the United States
government to throw our military weight on England's side. What was
remarkable about all the awakened groups of which I was a member is
that they were made up of people with the most varied backgrounds,
temperaments, vocations, and political beliefs. One such informal body,
which met monthly in 1941 at the Century Club, brought together characters outwardly as incompatible as Rear Admiral Standley, Walter
Wanger, the film producer, Henry Luce, the progenitor of Time and Life,
and Maury Maverick, the arch Texan—all bound momentarily by the one
insight most of our countrymen lacked: a sense of the immediate danger
to political freedom all over the world, should the Berlin-Rome-Tokyo
Axis extend and consolidate its conquests.*

G. A. Borgese called our conference to meet in Atlantic City at the end
of May—which turned out to be the fatal days when France fell into the
hands of the Nazis. . . . There were twelve of us in all, barring William
Benton, the advertising executive who was there by courtesy of his financial support. Antonio Borgese, with his swarthy Sicilian skin, his beetling
brows, his protrusive underlip, quietly dominated. He has a voice that is
usually strong and sonorous, but sometimes caressing: always speaking
with eloquence, in the ironic vein of Settembrini in 'The Magic Mountain,' but no windbag. At the extreme opposite pole was Robert Hutchins: tall, urbane, boyish looking; keen but supercilious, rational and
outwardly reasonable, but shallow: an unawakened isolationist.

Thomas Mann, grave, genial, aloof, a little shy still because of his
English, was silent most of the time: but his deep feeling in the reading
of his paper on democracy impressed everyone: at one point he could
hardly keep back his tears. He had, as a sort of shadow, brought to the
conference at his suggestion a tall, stoop-shouldered, pipe-smoking intellectual named Hermann Broch: outwardly an Austrian Sherlock Holmes,
a brilliant mind, but given to manic-depressive changes; now full of noble
hopes and indignations, now saying that the dynamic Nazis were better
than the isolationist democracies. At one point Broch asked me, in German, to convey to our colleagues his belief that the United States must
itself become a 'totalitarian democracy' in order to defeat Nazi totalitarianism—a proposal I buried in silence.

Another Central European was Hans Kohn: a heavy-set man, with a
kindly pasty face, an earnest pessimistic air. He talked volubly, but with

great dialectic skill, real insight, well-supported arguments, and unshakable moral conviction. Kohn despaired of the international situation. Some of his comments on our political unreadiness were penetrating. He believes that Charles Beard's attempt to justify his isolationism by debunking the valid reasons for participating in the First World War had done much to undermine our will to resist the present Nazi assault on all democratic institutions. And in addition, though himself a Czech, he holds that American political traditions and doctrines had been undermined by the large-scale migration since the eighties from the politically most backward parts of Europe.

At the opposite pole was Gaetano Salvemini, with his snub-nosed, Socratic head. He has a squeaky voice, a bubbling humor, an able rationalist mind; ebullient, vehement, sometimes almost grotesque. Herbert Agar, a lean, self-contained man, with a low voice, had none of this European vehemence: he shares this trait with Lloyd Garrison from Wisconsin and Yandell Elliott from Harvard; but in his quiet reserved way Agar was one of the most forceful personalities there. Then there was President William Allan Neilson of Smith College, now over seventy; still admirably alert and hopeful: not perhaps an original mind, but a highly intelligent one, his judgments salted by a quiet humor.

I have still to describe the blue-eyed Reinhold Niebuhr, with his bald head, the most Dürerlike of our whole group. He was our seraphic doctor, and only a certain looseness in the flesh of his face kept him from being the handsomest man there. He was usually the first to take the floor after each introductory statement, and he spoke with an excessive inner pressure, too rapidly for the fullest effect, but still impressive. Myself I cannot describe with objectivity. But all of us were at our best during the first day's discussions, tense days because of France's plight. At the beginning our minds met in a series of personal affirmations and discussions, superior in moral texture to those of any other group I had ever worked with. The tragic decisions we were all facing, as gravely as if we were the responsible political leaders, lifted our spirits to the highest plane: a plane well above our private egoisms, vanities, or ambitions. At first it even seemed we should achieve a consensus.

But the next day, when we began to discuss Borgese's plan that the Conference make a joint declaration on behalf of democratic principles, it turned out that our financial sponsor, William Benton, an advertising magnate, would perform the classic role of him who held the money bags. Before our morning discussion could approach a point calling for a resolution, Benton intervened to express his opposition to Borgese's half-outlined proposal. He told us flatly that we were all insignificant (read 'unpublicized') people: he even suggested—in the presence of Thomas

Mann!—that none of us was as capable of composing an effective statement as were the advertising writers he hired. This unexpected assault, in the middle of our deliberations, was as Neilson later characterized it to me, exactly like a Nazi dive bomber breaking up a gathering of civilians going about their business. Benton's face should have prepared us for the part he was playing: the face of a doomed character in Dante's Inferno, uncolored by spiritual activity.

Borgese at first covered up his shock over Benton's proposal with a masterly display of Italian courtesy and irony, professing to accept, without reservation, Benton's characterization of our incompetence and unworthiness. So that morning we went on with our discussions, led by Niebuhr, as if no interruption had occurred.

In the afternoon session, Borgese was to present in detail his suggestions for our future activities. After some sound remarks by Hutchins on the need for creative thinking rather than "re-search," and by Salvemini, approving Thomas Mann's moving declaration of the day before, Benton again claimed the floor before Borgese had a chance to present his ideas or unfold his plans. This time Judas grew bolder: he suggested that we give up any idea of a general declaration on behalf of threatened humanity. Again he stressed our futility and unworthiness; for he spoke, it turned out, for the handful of liberal isolationists or pacifists among us who flatly rejected the militant conclusions our discussions had brought forth.

I looked down the table at Borgese, sitting in profile, and saw that he was sunk. I wrote him a note while Benton was still talking: "Save the Committee at any cost: we will pay our own way." When Benton had finished speaking Borgese handed me a note: "You must take over. I will not say another word."

In a blistering counter-attack I rejected Benton's effort to narrow Borgese's wide-ranging conception. Later Salvemini said to me: "Mumford: you were heroic but terrible!" But when Borgese came to see me in New York the day after we adjourned, he said: "I cannot use words to thank you for your support yesterday, because one does not thank the bird because it flies." At the end, happily, much of Borgese's original proposal was salvaged: an agreement to publish a broad, general declaration, summoning all the latent forces of world democracy to save humanity from a malign totalitarian victory. Borgese, Agar, and I were appointed to draft it: and we projected another meeting in July to pass upon our work. —RN. May 28, 1940. [Shortened.]

A second conference took place in July in Sharon, Connecticut, near my own country home, and gave its approval to the statement, written largely by Borgese, entitled 'The City of Man.' But truth compels me to confess that the Chicago advertising magnate's estimate proved correct. Our little book sold perhaps eight or ten thousand copies, and at best re-enforced the convictions of a minute number of the already awakened minds. Of this, and the many similar efforts that followed, one must still use the sad words attributed to Confucius near his death: "The Phoenix does not fly."

Tensions and Anxieties

The following items expose the tensions between the hopeful isolationists and the realistic activists, which divided friends and households and close colleagues.

MAURY MAVERICK. A stubby man with a pot belly and blobby blue eyes. He talks in a blustering, he-mannish sort of way, exaggeratedly, self-consciously Texan, but humorous and sincere. He made an interesting confession about his life. He had been in the Army during the last war and had two months of front-line fighting in the Argonne offensive. Chunks of flesh were torn out of him by shrapnel. When his son was a boy he asked Maverick about this and when he learned that the Germans had done it, the boy wanted to get back at them. "'No, son,'" said Maverick. "'That's all in the past. We mustn't think about getting even. The Germans are good people. We must work for peace.' So I went around like a goddam fool, bleating about peace and neutrality, telling people they mustn't fight for Morgan, Mellon and Mills, and the sons of bitches in Wall Street. Now my son is nineteen, and he believes in peace and is against the draft and he won't believe me when I tell him I was plumb crazy and we've got to fight now. I always thought I was a hard-boiled American, but when I read about the English now I find tears in my eyes. Jesus Christ! And I never believed in religion and all the goddam truck before, and now I am all for Jesus, too." —RN. September 20, 1940

All through this last year, I have had one recurring dream: it has taken many forms, but the content is always the same. I am in England, sometimes on the continent; and I suddenly become aware that my family is in America—though sometimes Sophy is with me—and I must try to get home. I make feverish efforts to engage passage; I find my way to the

394

booking office over bomb-torn streets; sometimes I get on the ship; but always I have a sense of suddenly being trapped: of having undertaken lightheartedly a visit that turns out to be my doom. The other night I had a variant of this dream: this time I was caught in a fascist country, Italy, and though I had been permitted to enter freely, I could not get out; in fact, was turned over to the mercies of the fascist police. My fate was not in the least lightened because I had fallen in love with the city of Rome: not the real Rome but a curious modern Rome concocted in sleep. The contents of the latter dream were provided by an admirable article written by Bernard Shaw for Look, against the bombing of all cities, in which he had said that Rome was the one city of the world which every civilized man felt was his home. —RN. July 21, 1941

. . . If one man deserves the world's gratitude for rescuing it from the Nazi 'Wave of the Future' it is Churchill. But Churchill's strength lies in his connections with the past: this very historic sense helped evoke and restore England's greatness at the moment she desperately needed it. Unfortunately, the seeds of the future are not in him, and his very readiness in dealing with the hard problems of the moment has robbed him of the ability to think of a different kind of future. With Churchill's imperialist principles, Roosevelt's utter lack of principle, and Stalin's ruthless contempt for any arrangement that does not re-assert and re-enforce the power that is concentrated in the Kremlin, I see little immediate hope for laying the foundations for a better international structure. Whatever is done, it will take decades and generations to work out the terms of an essentially peace-willing world order. But bad leadership may postpone even the beginning by giving play to the truculences and antagonisms that are generated in the very act of fighting; and by their cowardice and their false 'realism' they may increase the moral devastation and disillusion and social disintegration. —Letter to Frederic J. Osborn. October 24, 1943

Repeatedly, I've had it in mind to write you, dear Babette, after receiving your pamphlet, 'Only the Living.' Few of us can summon up the words needed to give reality to the condition the world now faces—and you succeeded. Our emotions have almost been nullified by the scale of our present evils, for we cannot apply the same words to the wrecking or annihilation of a whole people that might move us in response to a railway wreck: the two horrors are incommensurable. So we remain speechless, and presently we become emotionless, without mental pain or compassion—and then helpless, by reason of this inner failure. I have commented on this disquieting fact in my book: comparing what has happened during the present war with the worldwide protest that went up over the mere sequestration of a single man, Henri Pirenne, the Belgian historian, during the First World War.

What you say about the divisions among the Jews themselves of course applies to all the nations. It was this general internal division in every country that enabled fascism to flourish and that permitted the present war to break out; it is this that has prevented the democratic forces from inventing a political strategy capable of energizing our belated military efforts. Instead we are using our arms with the same ferocity as our enemy, imitating him in his errors and insanities like our futile attacks by air on cities and civilians, and we are so unawakened to reality, so inwardly divided, that our behavior has aroused no general public criticism, except in a roundabout way, with allies against this or that man, this or that minor oversight or error. Borgese is right: our leaders have not espoused the Common Cause: so our only strategy is the common slaughter. —Letter to Babette Deutsch, with a few minor amplifications and emphases. December 6, 1943

The combination of technical expertness and moral hollowness that Roosevelt showed in his manipulation of the convention [for his fourth Presidential renomination] runs all through our society; it undermines the work of the many good men who struggle for something more coherent in the execution of their various offices and duties, and it brings to the top, too often, those who have Roosevelt's infirmities, his essential division of mind, in an aggravated state. Back in 1933 I called him Mr. Facing-Both-Ways; and the tragedy of his three administrations is that he has never been able to make a clean choice, or do a good deed without undermining it at the same time. The New York Times did well to remind us the other day that in the very year he delivered the splendid speech on quarantining the aggressors, he also signed the Neutrality Bill, which succeeded only in quarantining the United States and making it incapable of facing its tasks. Roosevelt has already done enough good things as President, to earn the undying gratitude of his country: that I think is clear. But he has already shown such a fatal weakness in handling our international relations, combined with impenetrable complacency and cockiness, that he is likely to leave behind him as many curses as blessings. —Letter to Van Wyck Brooks. July 25, 1944

WAR AND THE HUMANITIES. One of our Humanities students at Stanford said to me the other day: "We have decided that the main trouble about our education is that our parents and teachers fed us with fairy tales; they taught us that we lived in a world where everyone had a right to be happy, and where he would certainly achieve happiness if he managed to get a sufficient income. That kind of philosophy isn't very useful to us now, when we have to say good-bye to our lovers or our husbands whom we've just married and may never see again. We suspect that this fairy tale kind of happiness never was real in the first place; now it seems a cheap five-and-ten-cent-store substitute for something harder and better, harder to get and better worth keeping."

This student came to me when my introductory course on the Nature of Man was over and said she would have to leave, because she was married and expected to have a baby in a few months more. "Before I came here to study," she said, "I was a disheartened and cynical girl; I could not see any meaning in the war and I couldn't see any meaning in life, either. I even resented the fact that I was going to have a baby, for my husband was going to be torn from me in a few months—he is a lieutenant in the Navy—and he might never see me or the child again. He had a fine career in business before him when we married; and I hated the war for breaking that up, too. Now," she went on, "I don't feel that way any more: this course has made me understand what we are fighting for. At last life has some meaning for me, and you ought to hear me argue with the officers and wives back at the station, trying to make them understand some of the things the Humanities have made me see so clearly. My husband is on my side now; the others have a long way to go. But I haven't told you the best thing I got out of the course: I am *glad* to have my baby, whether my husband comes back from the war or not. I have something to give the child now, and if my man dies he won't die in vain."

Some of you will perhaps say in your hearts, if you are too polite to utter your words openly, that no academic institution can hope to be faithful to the great tradition of the university, the disinterested pursuit of knowledge, if the proudest boast of its new Professor of Humanities is that he has made a young wife ready to accept the responsibilities of motherhood. So I hasten to add that the contents of the course had nothing specifically to do with the prenatal mental care of mothers or the morale of soldiers' and sailors' wives. But who can study the nature of man in all its manifestations, its animal inheritance, its historic social roots, its personal and communal choices, its many unplumbed potentialities, without having a better grasp on his own life, a better insight into his own duties, purposes and opportunities?   —From the First Annual Conference of the Stanford School of Humanities. May 1943

I find that the shock of Roosevelt's death clarifies my judgments about him; but does not make any essential revisions. He was great as a symbol: his *being* was always on a higher level than his doing. The quality of his voice in his first inauguration speech did more for the country than the actual political measures he fostered. In a sense, he was a better *king* than prime minister. He had the magic touch and presence; and this quality transcended his tragic errors in action.

My chief consolation from his death at this moment is the thought that the qualities that made him great may be enhanced by his going: what he stood for may gain now that he himself no longer stands in the way of his own better vision. He was too divided a man ever to win a clean victory: his magnificent physical courage, perhaps unparalleled in our time except in actual warfare, was never equalled by his moral courage. The chances are that he would have fumbled and compromised the organization of peace far more pitiably than Wilson did. —Letter to Van Wyck Brooks. April 14, 1945

A week ago we were waiting to find out if the Japanese had agreed to surrender. The President was scheduled to speak to the nation at seven o'clock; so we delayed dinner, and I said to Sophia: If the news is good, let us open a special bottle of wine. When Truman announced the surrender, I found myself choked; and after it was over, and the National Anthem was played, with all of us, that is Sophia, Erica and Alison, myself, and my Mother, standing at attention, I embraced the two children; Sophia embraced Mother; and then Sophia and I embraced. They sat down again to listen to Prime Minister Attlee's speech; but I fled outdoors, into the fields and over to the gravel pit where Geddes and I used to test our guns, weeping as I had not wept since the news of Geddes's death came. Then I skirted the river, as he and I had often done, and sat down near the place where we had once had a cornstalk blind, for getting near the ducks. I ate no dinner that night, and needless to say, we drank no wine.

At half after eight Sophia went down to comfort Margaret Duffy; and I stayed in the living room alone, listening to the raucous sounds of celebration that came in over the radio from city after city. Meanwhile, the children of the village organized an impromptu celebration of their own; for a great load was lifted off their hearts; and they marched from house to house, singing and making noise, as they usually do on Hallowe'en; though next morning Alison exclaimed that this was much better. At seven-thirty a caravan of autos, perhaps twenty cars, led by the village fire engine, passed the house honking; some of the cars had American banners waving over them. —RN. August 21, 1945

Looking back on the last fifty years, it is curious how often our present situation appeared to many people in the form of nightmares and forebodings, even before there were visible reasons for disquiet. I am not thinking merely of Wells's prophecies, although 'The War in the Air,' and 'The World Set Free,' both a decade before 'The Shape of Things to Come,' certainly show him to have been a good diagnostician. (No: prognostician is the word. His diagnoses were often amateurish!) But just the other day I came upon a very good book by C. B. F. Masterman, 'Condition of England,' published in 1909, which, in the midst of that prosperous and peaceful Edwardian world, asks whether Britain and Europe are not on the verge of disintegration: whether their securities and prosperities may not presently be swept away in an upsurge of primeval violence. It must have looked like very dyspeptic writing in the first decade of this century; but today it sends the shivers up one's spine by reason of its almost prescient accuracy. —Letter to Van Wyck Brooks. December 6, 1945

21: Death and Wartime Grief

Until the present age the lowering shadow of death was never absent from human consciousness; and the expression of grief over death had an accepted and honored place in every life. But we of the Western world, particularly we Americans, have lately turned our backs on death: even many Christians and Jews who perform some of the traditional rituals of mourning in church or synagogue, hardly permit even a temporary break in their daily routines. I have often speculated over the reasons for this flat banishment of the very thought of death. Is it because our prevailing 'instant culture' deliberately cuts itself off from the living past? Or is it because, despite massive efforts at repression, the daily imminence of violence and death in our lives poisons our happiest moments; so that in sheer self-defense we anesthetize our feelings in advance. But he who has not accepted death or lived with grief has not fully encountered human experience—as I was to find for myself only in middle life. Hence I dare here to explore publicly my own responses, mostly in poems, despite their imperfections. These personal expressions properly terminate in my description of the Memorial to the innocent citizens massacred by the Nazis in the Cave Ardeatine in Rome. That Memorial links our own Dark Age to the nearby crypts and catacombs out of which Christianity triumphantly emerged.

Yesterday a small parcel came from the Army's distributing depot in Kansas. Within it was a small manilla envelope; and out of it came the following items: two rusty cigarette lighters, a cheap automatic pencil, a dozen fragments of paper money, including a part of a ten dollar bill, grimy pieces of paper marked with sweat and blood; a combat rifleman's badge (a silver rifle on a blue field with a wreath), an Italian Theater ribbon with a bronze star in the middle, the ribbon stained with blood, his social security card, preserved by scotch tape, three little photographs, one of Ann, one of Sophy, and one I had taken of Geddes on his last visit, with drawn eyebrows and troubled eyes. All this was found on Geddes's body; it tells little and it tells much. These were the last tokens of his life; and all that one shall ever know, beyond conjecture or fantasy, of what his death was like. —RN. June 30, 1945

A Word to Those in Danger

We are all old, cankered and old before our time;
Grizzle-aged in youth: mummy-old in the prime.
Calloused with evils our skins cannot shed;
Tear-grimed are our faces: cleansed only the dead.
Racked with the effort to live through the day:
The weak dare to linger: the strong do not stay.
Flogged into hard action unquickened by dream
We claw the black air, far off the beam.
We have lost all our gear—radar, compass, and chart:
Over is under and close is apart:
The seconds are years, for no landing's in sight:
Far off the beam we may crash in the night.
Rise higher! rise higher! our safety lies there:
Now jump from the blind craft and trust to the air!

—The Saturday Review. October 21, 1944

At Parting

My son is dead. If I am sage
I'll follow on his pilgrimage.

He loved life well while life was free:
Safety he spurned, or bended knee.

His was the task of lonely scout,
To spot the foe or smoke him out.

Death kept him silent company:
Dark tutor of maturity.

The fear of God stood by him then:
He learned to love his fellow men.

"We live by helping one another:
In combat every man is brother."

So, long before his work was done,
He was the father, I the son.

Now he lives on: in action sage.
His was the final pilgrimage.

                           —The Saturday Review. March 10, 1945

. . . Many things have made me think of you, dear Christiana. You were one of the few people with whom I could bear, even in the imagination, to share my thoughts and feelings about our son's death. And now your letter shows that you alone have divined the inward change that follows the death, or rather the unfulfilled life, of one's son. There are sons who, by circumstances or a natural disposition, inherit their father's position and carry on his work. But there was nothing in my experience or my reading to give me a clue to what is now happening in me: the desire on my own part, though handicapped by years and incapacity, to carry on young Geddes's work; to bring into the world, or if not into the world at least into my own work, the clear, unconditional self-reliance, the brooding intensity, the incorruptible firmness that he showed even in the brief course of his own life and might have put to so many more proofs had he lived even a dozen years longer. —Letter to Christiana Morgan. December 4, 1944

My analysis in 'The Condition of Man' of the effect of death, grief, and daily anxiety in providing a medium for Christianity to grow in was good as far as it went, but it did not go far enough. It needed the actual experience of grief to give me a new insight into the effect of this emotion on the sexual life; to understand how it drives sexual energies back into the unconscious, as the coming of winter drives the sap down to the roots of a tree. The Christian emphasis on chastity, therefore, was not merely a revolt against Rome's overblown sexuality; it was also the natural revolt against the body's pride and the body's delight which comes with deeply felt grief. The very blood disappears from the surface of the body; and the limbs are stiff. The cry of Edgar in 'King Lear'—"Poor Tom's a-cold"—is the cry of the grief-stricken. In this desolation overt sexual acts lose meaning, and because of grief, perhaps, more than for any other reason, love leaves its snug instinctual nest and seeks anyone who needs succour. —RN. December 18, 1944

. . . There are great problems in form to be solved in doing such a memoir as 'Green Memories,' for the burden of my tale is a sad one, not only at the end but even at the beginning; and yet one must at every page do justice to the vitality, to the high spirits, to the undauntedness that was Geddes, too; and one's saddest mood must be flecked with humor, the humor that was his. Moreover, to make it *his* book, I must go to school at his knee; for the words themselves must be as sinewy, and the telling as laconic, as his own. So I must curb myself to an austerity of expression that was native to him, not to me. —Letter to Christiana Morgan. January 13, 1946

A HAUNTING DREAM. The other night I found myself sleeping restlessly. Then I had a dream. In it Sophy called from another room, at the telephone: "It's Geddes. He wants to speak to you." My agitation over this announcement woke me up and I remained awake from two-thirty till almost five o'clock in the morning. A few nights before I had had another dream about him. He was in the midst of combat: swimming in the water, his mission was to make fast a boat to a landing place, and he did the backstroke magnificently and swiftly in the act of carrying this out. Somehow, I was a spectator; and as he came out of the water I came over to him and said, relieved both that he was safe and that I was able to embrace him: "Darling: you don't know how much I *admire* you." He murmured the few embarrassed deprecatory words that Geddes would have mumbled on such an occasion. Then he went into the water again. The enemy fire was heavy and he kept his head under most of the way. And then I heard a voice saying, as if reading from a book: "This time, when his head came up, an enemy sniper, who had aimed where he thought he might be, finally hit him." Those words roused me from sleep. —RN. April 10, 1945

. . . It was good dear Harry, to have from your own lips confirmation of what I hoped would be your ultimate response to 'Green Memories.' Your original opposition was nothing compared to Sophy's; for in the act of writing the book matters that had been 'settled' and buried for years rose again to the surface of our lives, and the deep temperamental differences between us, too, became actively separatist. Yet I don't know which contributed more to the book; her direct aid, which was of course immense, or her opposition. Certainly the book is a far better one than I could have produced without the dialectic struggle that ensued with you and with Sophy. If I transcended some of my own weaknesses in the act of writing it, it was because of that struggle. So if you are pleased with the result, you may give yourself some of the credit, too: as you unsuspectingly did when you asked who said of Geddes that he had "an all-or-nothing quality." Who but you? —Letter to Henry A. Murray. November 16, 1947

. . . AS FOR OUR ATTITUDE TOWARD GRIEF, that is a fundamental matter which goes down to the very roots of the differences between Ananda Coomaraswamy and me: not between our two selves alone, but our two cultures. The quotation that I liked best of all, among those he sent me, was his own: "Every meeting is a meeting for the first time, and every parting is forever." That is profoundly true. Likewise, I think one should live every minute as if it were one's last; and I remember too how at nineteen I answered my own question, "What would you do if you were told that you were doomed to die in six months?" by saying "I should go on doing exactly what I am doing now." On that he and I are one. In bringing up young Geddes Sophia and I always had in mind old Geddes's dictum, which was likewise Emerson's, that our child's life should be good here and now, and not merely in preparation for a future that might never come: 'being' mattered to us as much as 'becoming.'

But I do not feel that one can be liberated from grief except through the experience of grief, any more than one can be liberated from love-blindness except through the experience of love. Nor should one try to; for death is no more a deception than parting is. The sense of loss deepens one's feeling toward the life that once existed and makes it present again; and the greater the feeling of loss, the fuller that present becomes. I feel alien toward all efforts, Hindu, Buddhist, Stoic, Christian, which attempt to avoid disruption and pain by washing the dark spots out in the ocean of eternity. The dark spot ceases to be real when it is treated in that fashion; but at that moment he who wears the stained garment loses precisely that which gives meaning to his very temporality. So, too, I am not in the least consoled by the thought of immortality in any of its offered forms. When one says good-bye to a person for the last time, it is but a mocking balm to know that they will be 'alive' and active forever in some remote corner of the cosmos. Their here-and-nowness is the reality that is being taken away. —Letter to Christiana Morgan. November 18, 1946

Though there is scarcely an hour of the day when the image of Geddes does not pass through the mind, or become the object of thoughts, affectionate or regretful, proud or bitterly self-reproachful, I now rarely dream of him. Night before last, however, he came into my dreams and seemed to hold them most of the night; it was like a long visit; and when I awoke two feelings mingled in my mind: how wonderful to have been with him so long, and how terrible to lose him. Those conflicting feelings stayed with me throug! the day. He had come back, maturer than ever, but gay and outgoing in every fashion: the report of his death had been false. 'Green Memories' was already written; so there was some doubt in my mind as to what ought to be done, by way of providing an explanatory ending; a doubt which gave way to a debate over whether I should tell Geddes about the book or not. It turned out that he would have to go back into combat again, so that made me decide that he should see the book, in order to understand the depth of our feelings about him; but even before I did that, I was able to convey to him, in so many words, our tender and overwhelming love; and he reciprocated it with the same degree of feeling. We planned a climb together; we spent a day or more in each other's company; and it was such an overwhelming relief to have him back with us once more! The reality of it, the intensity of it, was far solider than any usual dream of mine: this was not a tenuous illusion of the senses, to be corrected swiftly on waking, but a real visit; all the more real because of the indications of further growth, maturity, acceptance of life, in his own attitude. As such the dream was a blessing; but all too soon it was snatched away, and I still feel bereft, almost as bereft as if he had really come back home and then gone off again into the zone of danger. —RN. February 2, 1948

'GREEN MEMORIES,' I am confident, will slowly make its way, even though the booksellers have refused to stock it and the book review editors have grudged it space for review. One of the curious offsets to this neglect was an offer from Hollywood to put 'Green Memories' into a film, four offers to be precise. Though we gave a flat 'No' to all of them, Hollywood being what it is, I was happy to realize that there was enough of the generic and the common in the story, which seemed to me so very special and private as I told it, to tempt the movies to make a bid for the book solely on its merits, and not because it had attracted public attention or sold well. You will not be surprised perhaps to know that some of the best responses to the book have come from the younger generation; particularly from men who were in combat and who still grieve for their dead comrades, but have not found, in America, anyone who would understand or share their grief. —Letter to Christiana Morgan. December 25, 1947

For Those Bereaved in War

Death comes to every household:
One day he bore a message for you:
Maybe the station agent's helper
Brought you a yellow envelope—
His eyes shifted away: you understood:
His fleeing back dismantled hope.
You were quiet; all your hoarded fears
Went scattering like white skeletons:
This fear was flesh and blood.
"Our son was killed in action." Hold Fast!
The numbness and the silence will not last.

Death comes to every household:
Let the tears melt the stone within your breast:
Give your grief to the sunlight, mother;
Let it blacken the cloudless day;
Let your empty womb utter its final agony:
Do not mock the dead with a stoic mask.
Let your sobs, father, be as a woman's cry.
Let your tears mingle, husband and wife,
Let the bitter water fall:
This is the end of your waiting:
The last message of all.

Death comes to every household,
Not for a visit but for a long stay.
Make the guest room ready; get the blankets aired:
See that the old clothes are stowed away.
But remember! Death is a disturbing guest:
Unbidden, he will join you at table,
Drawing up the empty chair:
Or he will claim the dark fireside nook
Where your son—how lately he was there!—
Would curl up with the comics or a book.
Death will prowl through the hall
While the family is sleeping lightly:
You will face him at breakfast and face him nightly.

Death comes to every household:
More ruthless to the dooryard trees

Than the autumn winds: his breath will freeze
The tender flesh to brittle rock.
He leaves you, mother, at the edge of a chasm,
Hands holding vacantly a half-knitted sock,
Swaying above a darkness you dare not fathom:
Time will be emptier than a handless clock.
Your house no longer stands on the crest
Of the hill, but far down the slope:
The sun will come later in the morning:
The days that bring certainty have ended hope.

Death takes the household to the battlefield:
How did he break the body's living wall? . . .
Come pelting in a spray of leaden rain?
Or roll in a grenade, like a fumbled ball
At your son's feet: extinction or slow pain?
Was the lad dragged in an undertow—
Battered and sore—or riding the crest,
Like a surf-rider, headed for shore?
Or was he relaxed, unsuspecting, sober,
Remembering the startled pheasants and the taste of dawn
On the frost-hung grass in October?

No matter how Death came! He came.
Your son handled the package he brought
And guessed its contents without opening it.
You have a lifetime to read the giver's name
And mark how well he wrought.
Dunkirk, Gettysburg, Thermopylae
Left nothing braver for a memory
Than some nameless open field
Where the young, eager to live their unlived years,
Tempered to fight it out and not to yield,
Held fast—and yielded all
Hoarding their courage for Life's final call.

Death comes to every household:
Remember your son's works and his days
And his acts! Remember his earnest lines—
"Don't worry about the grimness of it all:
Of course it's rugged: but the guy who stays
Can take it. Your job's to keep the country straight.

Fighting is a young man's game. That's sharing fair
I say, but you must pull your weight
And bear our burden till we've had a rest.
You'll never taste the peace we've almost won
If you relax just when *our* fight's begun.
I've seen enough by now to know the score:
The way the front line soldier faces life
Is *what* we're fighting for."

Death beckons us—the old Schoolmaster:
He rings the bell to call us in from play:
He taught our sons life flowers in disaster
When fighters give as lovers give and take,
Withholding nothing that their buddies lack;
Dividing the last ration in their can
—Or giving up the chance of getting back.
Our sons looked soberly into the Master's eyes,
Following his demonstration step by step.
Unless we learn that lesson their sacrifice
      Will bear no fruit.
Unschooled, unscathed, the living will forget.
The lingering presence of the maimed and dead
Alone may give us strength to rise.

—Twice a Year. Winter 1945

Memorial of a Nazi Massacre

One of the oddities of the post-war period in Europe is that none of the new buildings is half as impressive as a scattering of sober-eloquent war monuments to the dead. Though architecture seems now to be in a period of internal contradiction and indecision, the older schools of sculpture have, at the end of forty years of experiment, produced public works of great vitality and distinction, in which the original purpose and program of the various new movements have been carried to a significant conclusion by Ossip Zadkine, by Naum Gabo, by Jacob Epstein. Usually 'war memorials' deny the sentiments that prompted their construction by sculptural platitudes as emotionally unconvincing as they are esthetically banal. But there is more esthetic life in this Roman monument, dedicated to the dead, than there is in most of the recent multi-storied housing developments, dedicated (supposedly) to the living. If anything today seems emptily grandiose, it is not the monument but the big slab apartment house.

The Cave Ardeatine, sometimes misnamed the Fosse Ardeatine, is less known than it should be, for it lies outside Rome, along the Appian Way, just beyond one of the most famous Christian catacombs, and the tourist is not so likely to stumble upon it as he is upon the fountains of Bernini. Moreover, a reticence about treating this sad memorial as a mere spectacle doubtless keeps the Romans from listing it as a show place.

The three hundred graves in the Cave Ardeatine, the final focus of this monument, are still visited by relatives and friends of the slain victims, bringing flowers to the dead where they lie under their heavy concrete canopy. In retaliation for a wartime Partisan ambush of a detachment of German soldiers, the Nazis rounded up three hundred Romans at random in a public square—the young and the old, the destitute and the comfortable, the amiable and the inimical—and took them to one of the caves that honeycomb the hills of Rome. There they machine-gunned their captives; then, perhaps appalled by the thought of the effect this massacre would produce on the populace, they concealed the bodies by the simple expedient of blowing in the roof of the cave with the same notable technical ability they have applied to other forms of extermination.

To give honorable burial to the dead, and to remind us, in today's Purgatory, of the Inferno they had passed through, this monument was conceived, after the war, by a team of five architects and landscapists, and two sculptors. The names of these artists should be perpetuated, for they brought to the task not only skill and esthetic discernment but a human sensibility that is foreign to many contemporary artists, seemingly bent on capturing the incoherent noises of pre-human unconscious processes, as if recorded in a decapitated brain, severed from heart and guts, from feeling and meaning. The sculptors are Mirko Basaldella, who wrought the wide bronze gate at the entrance to the cave, and Francesco Coccia, who did the figures that stand above the entrance; the architects and landscapists are Nello Aprile, Cino Calcaprina, Aldo Cardelli, Mario Fiorentino, and Giuseppe Perugini. The dead may well be grateful to them for the clarity of their feeling and the forthrightness of their interpretation.

On the road leading to it, this cemetery—for that is what the monument is—is first announced by a wall of brown volcanic stone that rises gradually to a height of fifteen feet at the entrance. This serves as both a visual boundary and a retaining wall for the lower part of the hill over the cave; in addition, the great flat field stones that compose this wall form a dark, rough-textured base for the three white marble figures, about twice the human scale, that stand just inside and above the entrance—three victims bound together back to back. The effect of these figures in the sunlight is of a silver horn above the brooding beat of a bass drum. The rightness of this contrast diminishes one's disappointment in the figures themselves; the absurd costume of modern man, baggy and formless, is hardly redeemed by the naked torso of one of the figures. Only a master could have risen above the tepid realism of this sculpture without losing the pathos and tenderness that were a necessary part of the artist's intention. Except for Ernst Barlach and Jacob Epstein, one might look in vain for a modern sculptor capable of doing justice to both the formal and the emotional elements of such a monument. But if the detail is weak, the concept is sound: so well placed is this vertical accent, so just is the scale, that the figures, almost in spite of themselves, match up to the rest of the design as an organic part of the composition. The whole, by its unity of spirit, has turned the transient victims by way of art into enduring victors.

The entrance gate is at the inside corner of a right-angle indention in the wall, and this achieves the double purpose of creating a pocket of parking space beside the road and indicating the point of entry. The bronze gate in which, at one side, a small door is set, strikes, even more definitely than the sculpture, the opening note of the martyrdom here recorded; the jagged pattern of the heavy rods that are interlaced to make the gate gives a feeling of the inimical, of the bound and the chained, without forfeiting the language of abstraction or the function that an entrance must serve. Basaldella's achievement here is a firm one. Entering, with the sculptured figures hovering above one on the left, one crosses a broad, irregular open area, paved with small stones and edged by grassy slopes planted with laurels and cedars, toward the high opening of the cavernous passage to the site of the massacre. The two cedars near the entrance and the rich green ivy that covers it perhaps unduly soften the austerity proper to the whole design; the landscape gardener's natural desire to overcome by plantings the desolation of the bare slopes seems at odds with the expressive grimness of the rest of the composition.

But once one has crossed this open space and entered the cave beyond, all is circumspection and restraint—the interior has been kept rough and dark, with only covered lights of shoulder height to guide one over the earthen floor and through a long, high passage that terminates in a humble chapel, from which another and equally dark passage takes one back to the entrance and to the sunken burial ground to which the bodies of the victims have been removed. The chapel is, like the Pantheon in

Rome, open to the sky, but its utterly artless simplicity says more than the Pantheon in all its grandeur. For here is where the roof of the cave was blasted by the Germans to bury the victims, and the sudden exposure to the air and light stabs one, by contrast to the enveloping darkness from which one has just emerged. At the rough edges of this high opening, grasses and bushes have taken hold; when I made this pilgrimage, the petals of wild roses were fluttering downward through a shaft of sunlight, and that accidental contribution of nature deepened one's sense of the coldly calculated violence and horror that had been committed here.

In designing the cemetery itself, architects of less imagination might have been tempted to say, in stone or sculpture, what is unsayable. But these artists were wise enough to let the dead have the last word: their building is in the most elemental of forms—an oblong, horizontal slab of concrete, gigantic in scale, without a touch of molding or lettering to relieve its surface. That slab stretches flatly over the graves, which are arrayed in a wide, low chamber with dark stone walls. The dead are banked in double rows, enclosed in seemingly solid granite, each stone coffin separated by a narrow channel from its neighbor, the tops of the double rows slanting gently upward to form a low-pitched gable. The space beneath the roof is unbroken by columns, and the sole illumination is the daylight that enters through the crack, apparently not more than a foot high, that separates the walls and the roof. The starkness, the pervading gloom, the oppressive monotony of the composition are relieved only by the contrast in texture of the wall, the rough concrete ceiling, and the pitted granite surface of the graves, with their bronze wreaths and the names of the identifiable dead.

In this cavelike structure, one is not merely alone with the dead; one is close to their final moment of agony. So far from making that moment easier for the visitor, the architects have sought to intensify it—though their desire to keep the whole space free of votive offerings has been humanely ignored, and now bouquets and vases of flowers provide a tender contrast to this solemn moment of encounter. Here the severity of truth chastely curbs any kind of esthetic glorification. Mere pictures and words cannot do justice to such a monument; one has to go through the experience, in its contrasts, in its eloquent omissions, and even to repeat the pilgrimage, observing its cumulative effect on oneself, to feel the depths of the artists' imagination and the quality of their execution. This is like the descent into hell in ancient times as practiced by the Mystery religions, a descent followed by a promise of redemption as one returns to the daylight world. To say that the passage through the Cave Ardeatine is unforgettable is merely to say that art has done all it can do to bring the dead back to life in the very place that gave their life its tragic significance. —From 'The Highway and the City.' 1963

Consolation in War

Happy the dead!
If we do ill
They will not know we lied.
Happy the dead!
If we do well
Their death is justified.

—The New Yorker.
November 25, 1944

22: Britain in 1946

During the Second World War my Scots friend, Alexander Farquharson, aware of the salutary effect that my 'Faith for Living,' had made on the British in the early part of the war, wangled an invitation to me from the British government to come to England as an observer and reporter, under the auspices of his Institute of Sociology. Our Department of State, perhaps nettled by my criticism of American policy vis-à-vis Pétain's and Darlan's subservient cooperation with the Nazis, then refused to give me a passport. But Farquharson persisted, and early in 1946 he succeeded in arranging a grand tour of Britain, not to build up morale—that was no longer needed—but to bring a breath of outside air to discussions of post-war housing and planning. For this the favorable British reception of my 1938 book, 'The Culture of Cities,' had paved the way. Unfortunately I was too preoccupied, then and later, with the problem of inciting a public demand for bringing atomic energy in every form under rational worldwide control, to write a full report of that visit. These scattered notes nonetheless may tell something to those who can read between the lines.

THE QUEEN MARY BOASTS WAR MEMORIALS carved in wood. Dot, Betty, Mary, Lib—these are some of the names carved on her teak rails when she was a troop-ship, along with the name of the carver. Was this not a self-made Roll of Honor and public monument to themselves and their loves which our men left behind? Some of the paired initials have hearts encircling them. One of them, incised deeply, is that of Ralph Hilms of Marshville, N.C. 1945; and another, enclosed in a rectangle, is KRUPA—

Dec. 42: July 45. Shouts of triumph! *We have come through!* —RN. June 6, 1946

TALKS WITH TWO TECHNICIANS ON THE QUEEN MARY. Both of them are practical internationalists. One of them was my cabin companion, a Scotsman named McLean. He is a chemical engineer who turned to personnel management; from the fact that he made some reference to soap, and stayed in Cambridge, Mass., I gather that he is with Lever Bros. He was interested in the racial problem in America. There are all races and nationalities in his laboratory. Recently they took in a Negro Ph.D. because he was so good. He finds Scotch nationalism a little absurd. When he recruited workers for an aviation plant during the war, the Scots workers, he found, usually began their application by saying: 'I am a Scot,' as if that were their most important qualification. He told them that no Englishman would ever mention his nationality. —RN. June 6, 1946

Farquharson was telling me how people behaved during the Blitz. It became the tradition in London that the Mayors of the Boroughs should go to the scene of the bombings and show themselves, if not actually to take part in the work. "But in some places," said Alick, "it turned out that the people in charge, though not cowards, were men of straw. They were unable to rise to the emergency, and power would go to someone who really grasped the situation and could deal with it—a policeman or a Non-conformist Minister. Mere routine efficiency, which carried people through their ordinary day's job, was not enough. Something else was required to meet the unforeseen." —RN. June 11, 1946

This afternoon I discussed with Farquharson whether the different social castes in Britain could, as a result of the war experience, be more closely mingled in neighborhood units. Alick's opinion was No. The war had at various moments brought them together under pressure, but the broad lines had held. There was a St. John's Unit in the Fire Service: working class! There were two Red Cross Units: middle and upper. Disraeli's Two Nations were still intact. —RN. June 13, 1946

My day began at the Goring Hotel in London with a talk with William Watson of Oriel, Cambridge, ex-flying major, who stayed for an hour and a half—very rewarding to me—telling me about the temper of the working people in Scotland and England, for he himself belonged to them, being indeed a Communist. He had spoken at public meetings from the

414

time he was fourteen. "You are the Karl Marx of this generation," he said to me. [Not true, but pleasant to hear!] "The Universities aren't what they were. The blues used to go in for sport alone; if a man was interested in books, he was a sissy and wore pink pants. We fellows aren't afraid to be both. I am a boxing blue myself." He is a trim, spunky little fellow: did over two hundred missions in the air. I could hardly let go of him; but I had a luncheon appointment with Sir Montague Barlow at the Athenaeum.

The meeting with Sir Montague was a happy disappointment. Almost at once he identified where I lived, for he recognized it as the habitat of the South Amenia Barlows, a farming family whom he had spotted as members of his clan. He had been described to me as old and pompous; but he looks no more than sixty-five, at most seventy, though he confesses to being almost eighty; and I didn't find him in the least stuffy. He is a Tory, he confessed, with left leanings. He has visited America often; and told me a story about Sam Gompers and J. D. Rockefeller, Jr. This was on the eve of the steel strike of 1919. Rockefeller held out for a company union. Gompers said that meant a strike. After Gompers left, Rockefeller turned to Sir Montague for advice. Barlow, answering Rockefeller's objection to a walking delegate coming from the outside, said to him: "But if you had a dispute with your men, you'd expect your accountants or your lawyer to accompany you to a conference, wouldn't you?" Yes, of course. "Well, they come from the outside, you know: why shouldn't your workers have the same right?" Rockefeller couldn't see it; and fifteen years later, when they met again, he still couldn't see it. —RN. June 25, 1946

Note: Barlow, later called Sir Anthony Montague-Barlow, was Chairman of the important parliamentary commission on urban and industrial decentralization, which laid the foundations for the New Towns Act of 1947: a landmark in urban planning along the lines first laid down by Ebenezer Howard's project forty years earlier for the first Garden City, Letchworth.

At every turn one becomes conscious of the holiness of custom. Every morning I eat porridge; every afternoon and evening drink beer; every lunch and dinner I have soup; and you should see the smirk of quiet satisfaction on the face of the head waiter at the Malvern hotel when he approaches me and says: "The usual, sir?" I never dare disappoint him: I hold fast to the usual; and that gives him the feeling that I am a man to be trusted.

This accounts for much in English life which has changed far less than one had imagined, viewing it through the Blitz and blast of the war.

The quality that saved them was not imagination but tenacity; not adjusting themselves to the circumstances but getting their cup of coffee at eleven and tea at four in the afternoon in spite of everything. Again this is subject to local correction; for if the old life survived anywhere, it was in this part of the country. What the war has done is to restore English self-respect! Their life has been tested and they have come through. They even have accepted with satisfaction the innovations that were made with respect to children's feeding: for example, giving children orange juice and currant juice at the Health Stations, thus compelling a visit and enabling the health officers to check up on the children's development. One of the people at the party told of meeting his wife coming home with eighteen eggs in her basket; which he viewed with pleasure, since he had not seen any for some time. "Not so fast," she said, "seventeen are for the child; one for me; and *none* for the male head of the household. . . . —Letter to Sophia. June 15, 1946

SCENE: County Hotel lounge, Malvern.

OLD DOWAGER [*in embroidered black coat, passing before me on her way back from the window*]. It's raining again. Just like yesterday. We didn't come here for *this!*

MYSELF [*soothingly*]. But did you see the marvellous rainbow before dinner?

DOWAGER [*indignantly*]. The same as yesterday! All thick and thundery —*just like the world!*

MYSELF. Oh quite!

One could have transferred her into any British comedy of manners without altering an inflection. —RN. June 1946

. . . At eleven I went to King's Cross Station to drop my bags; so I still had almost an hour before an appointment made by Osborn to meet him for the Garden City lunch in my honor at the Connaught Rooms, off Kingsway, at twelve o'clock. That walk through Bloomsbury, our old part of the city, gave me a greater sense of the extent of the devastation than my brief visit to the St. Paul's area the day before: air raid shelters sprouting out of the grass in crescents, iron railings down around Russell Square, bullet holes in unlikely walls, all gave one a sense of the ubiquitousness of danger and damage, wherever one might have been. I got to the Rooms on time, only to find that Osborn didn't arrive till 12:20. That gave Lord Lytton and me ten minutes together alone; so we withdrew to a private dining room and sat down for a talk. He is an old-

416

fashioned English aristocrat; the kind you imagine, lean, white handle-bar moustaches, self-possessed, well-preserved, courteous; and when I met Lady Lytton she turned out the classic opposite number, too, well-preserved, still charming, once extremely beautiful, a touch of her girlhood still shining through. Presently we returned to a crowded dining room and I stood around talking. English people have a way of not introducing their neighbors, even if they know them, which is slightly embarrassing; but I managed a brief chat with a whole series of people, an Australian Commissioner, who knew all my books, Lord Harmsworth, John Rothenstein, the director of the Tate, and—guess who!—our Stanton Catlin, now in UNRRA, who had flown over from Germany that morning to attend the luncheon. At table I was sandwiched between Lord Lytton and Lord Horder, the King's physician; and I managed to have some very good talks with both of them; but I can't report that in full except verbally. Lytton, after proposing the King's health—after which it is proper to light up cigarettes, though not before—Lytton introduced me in a very warm and appreciative speech; and I, though I had been so terribly tired the day before, and was unable to concentrate on what I was going to say, managed to reply with a fair degree of grace and warmth: "Quite emotional," said Osborn later; though that tells as much about him as about me . . . —Letter to Sophia. June 29, 1946

IN OXFORD on Saturday night I dined with A. L. Lindsay, the Master of Balliol, in the Senior Common Room. The invitation came through Dr. Bell of Coventry, who has the title of the Bishop's Messenger. Bell is a man of about my age, with a tanned, leathery face, boyish in its cast; and his beliefs and attitudes are those of a Tory country squire applied without modification to current morals and religion. What his thoughts were came out by indirection in a discussion of beauty. He didn't believe that people should be permitted to say that they liked jazz better than Beethoven. They should be told, by God, that Beethoven was better and there was something wrong with them if they didn't like it. He put the case in such a crass form as to spoil the crumb of truth in it. We chatted over sherry and met some of the students who ate with the Master. Then the Master came in, very affable, with a perpetual glint of humor in his eye, holding the center of the conversation and keeping it in hand: full of reminiscences, anecdotes, jokes. The talk after dinner was exclusively Oxford; at least it stayed close to the family circle. I took no part in it, though it amused me, if only because it removed some of my old private embarrassment over our parallel university provincialism in America. Farquharson remarked later how typically Oxford this was: the invisible

417

social walls, the limited horizon, the incuriosity about the outsider, the genial triviality. Only at the end did I venture to introduce the subject of the atomic bomb; and then we had twenty valuable minutes of serious political discussion with the Master. —RN. July 1946

One of the British girls in uniform shyly rose at the Sociological Institute's discussion meeting at St. George's Hall. Her face was a delight to watch: her mouth had a wonderful mobility and sweetness; her voice was delicate and musical; her smile played over her whole face. She spoke with great earnestness about the need for education and the need for educating the teachers who were to do the educating. She wanted them to know 'the decent things,' 'the fine things,' 'the nice things.' She wanted them to be able to think. She felt that it would take two generations to work the change needed. Not so much for her thought, as for her winsomeness and loveliness through which her fine feelings and hopes became visible, she was wonderful to behold and to hear. Her inarticulateness gave her words an extra depth. In short, she was, to perfection, an ethereal embodiment of England: Shakespeare might have imagined her. —RN. July 28, 1946

In England, the English feel me almost to be an Englishman—at least a New Zealander! In Scotland, when I ordered whisky with plain water, Macaulay—the good man from Glasgow whom I met at the Town Planning Institute—felt I was a Scotsman and was a little disappointed when I said there was no Scots blood in me. The two Irish planners at the Edinburgh Conference, whom I talked to for a few moments afterward, felt that I was an Irishman, and were delighted when I said I had corresponded with A.E., had read the Irish Homestead long before it became the Irish Statesman, and had been looked after as a child by a nanny from Youghal. They felt I didn't need further preparation to understand Ireland. All these encounters have made me feel more American than ever, in the sense that I was living the substance of Whitman's poems, particularly of course the 'Salut au Monde.' So much for American isolationism! —RN. July 20, 1946

Newsom, an Education Officer who works among the coal miners, told of an old Northumberland miner, who was showing him around his village. The miner pointed to the old schoolhouse and said: "I used to go to that school, until I was twelve, and went down to the pit, as eager as the lads today to go to the cinema. There would be a Shakespeare, a Milton, or a John Stuart Mill in my satchel then, and I loved them." That man, added

Newsom, was taught by a teacher steeped in the humanities. The modern teacher, who praises the twentieth century, has no liking for noble literature, and the students of that teacher line up for the cinema and have no live interest in anything except the comparative charm of the film stars. Which had the better education—the old miner or his grandson? —RN. July 29, 1946

The chambermaid in Oxford who came to make up my bed today was the first English servant I've met to drop the mask of servility and be herself; but of course it turned out that she was an Irishwoman; indeed, her name was Margaret Duffy; a blue-eyed, buxom woman, with reddish hair, and a very Victorian-looking figure and face, soft lines, and sad, sometimes indignant eyes. We started talking about the hot weather, which she didn't like; it was hard enough to get on with the work without the heat, and nothing decent to put in your mouth to eat, and not enough of it. I said things were bad in America, too, and she asked me who makes them bad, but the same people that caused the war, and that got all the people killed fighting it, when they might have stopped it, as you'd stop a mad dog, if they hadn't Heiled Hitler, wanting him to go after Russia for them. They were afraid of Russia, the first country to put Socialism into practice; and a young air force man was saying the other day, Why wouldn't Russia cooperate? and she asked him when had we ever cooperated with Russia? You and your kind, she said, are always blackening the place; but there are two hundred million Russians who don't seem to make any complaint about it. She saw that I was sympathetic, and so she went on.

She was full of contempt for the English, for they were so smug, and for the upper classes, for they were so selfish, they only loved themselves, and they were bored stiff, for no one could be any good if they loved themselves. She never loved herself and never had any reason to: but she wouldn't take things lying down, like the English did; she was Irish and when things were bad, she'd fight. She told these fussy old creatures, no good to anyone, what she thought of them and their life; just a lot of useless drones they were. Did I ever hear of the Duchess of Leinster; she was the American girl that married the Duke; and one day—she was at the Dorchester House then—the Duchess had rung for service; but being busy answering another one of those rich men, who always want everything prompt and quick, she hadn't answered the bell promptly and the Duchess had complained to the housekeeper. She went to the room and instead of apologizing she called the Duchess down. You said I refused to wait on you and I couldn't refuse, because I never saw you before this, nor you me. Then she tried to apologize, when she saw I wouldn't knuckle under to her, and said it was all a mistake. Next day she asked me what part of Ireland I was from and said what a fine people the Irish are. She isn't married to the Duke any more; she bought him with her money; but that's the way with them, they have no loyalty and no faith, and they don't stick to each other in marriage, like decent people. They have the best of everything and they don't know what to do with it. People say that the Communists here are bought by Russian money; but I never talked to a Russian in my life, nor had any of his money; but I've seen what I've seen, and I've formed my own opinions. It's a hard life for the likes of us, but someday it will be a better one—though not if those B's can help it.

So she went on. She was querulous and complaining, yet upstanding and decent; above all quick-witted and sure of herself. She was no one's fool. Such a relief after the servility or the stoniness of the usual English servant. Even the porter at the County Hotel, who dropped his mask for a moment when I gave him one of the food packages Sophia had sent, so that he even mentioned his wife and his family, resumed the mask again when I came back after a week.   —RN. July 14, 1946

MANCHESTER. Fortunately I have a room with a bath in this incredible hotel, the Midland, model I am sure for Arnold Bennett's Grand Babylon Hotel; and luxuriated in a bath in a tub so big that if one lost one's grip—fortunately, there are side grips!—one might drown. The tub is in an enormous bathroom, lined with marble, though the flush toilet is the old-fashioned kind that sounds like Niagara Falls when it works. After soaking for a quarter of an hour is that fine bathtub I emerged a new man; and set out, at seven-fifteen, to a banquet at the Town Hall. It was my first banquet with a *Lord* Mayor: up to now they have sent deputy mayors. Today I went about the city with the City Surveyor, a keen, hard-headed fellow (Roland Nicholas) whose planning I admire. Manchester itself is a dismal black hole; but the day was far from being a black one; and lunch with some of the municipal Councillors, at the hotel here, proved to be an enlightening affair. Most of the people there, except the Municipal Health physician, were Conservatives, and their good nature and fairness, in meeting the Labor criticisms or in putting forth their own, gave me a taste of what is really the strongest and soundest element in British political life. —Letter to Sophia. July 17, 1946

At the Garden Cities Luncheon, where I received the Howard Medal for my services to the movement, I had the good fortune to be seated next to

420

Lady Lytton, whose husband presided. Lady Lytton is still a beautiful woman, and lively in conversation too; and she dropped more than one good story about the way people behaved during the Blitz. She explained that dinners were always served early during this period; and when she went out to dine she had a compact with her servants to return home as soon as the warning wail was heard, to stay with them in the cellar. One evening she left dinner halfway through and went out in the empty street, almost in despair after a few minutes because no taxi had come along. Finally, an old cab lumbered up, and the driver asked her, a little gruffly, where she wanted to go. When she told him, he hesitated a moment, and then said almost rudely: "Get in!" and they drove off in silence by a somewhat erratic route. Puzzled by the driver's surliness she felt she should apologize for keeping him out with the bombs blocking their way. By this time, they had reached her door, and as the driver took her fare he said: "You didn't think I was afraid, ma'am, did you? I takes the old bus out every night. Me own house was hit and me old woman was done in; and the least I can do now is 'elp other people get 'ome safe. Wot I say is Shikespeare was right. 'The coward dies a thousand deaths: the 'ero dies but one.'" RN. June 1946

. . . I FIRST MET FREDRIC WARBURG and his wife Pamela in New York in the thirties, when he was still an editor at Routledge's, and had persuaded them to publish my 'Technics and Civilization.' When Warburg set up his own firm, my 'Culture of Cities' served as a mainstay during the war, though a whole edition was destroyed by a German bomb early on. So it was natural that he should set up a dinner party for me; and that in 1946 the one gala feature of the meal should be a fresh salmon, a delicious fish that happily accompanied me at every formal dinner. Either then or later Pamela told me how she managed to get that scarce fish: she had bespoken it long before, informing the fishmonger that she had an important American guest coming. When she entered the shop that morning the owner proceeded to take out the prize and prepare it for her; at which another woman who was there became indignant and said: "You said you had no salmon: what do you mean by giving it to this woman?" "You've no call to complain, ma'am," the fishmonger said. "When the Blitz was on, you ran off for a safe place in the country; but Mrs. Warburg stayed right here in London, even when the buzz bombs was falling all over the place; and many's the time when Mrs. Warburg and me 'ave laid under the same table together. The best is none too good for her, any time I have it! . . ." Pamela has always been a dashing attractive woman, the most feminine of theoretic feminists: so I can't resist another story of hers. The buzz bombs did indeed fall anywhere, any time of the day; and one day as she was walking home through Regent's Park a bomb exploded near her and she found herself knocked flat on her back right next to a young soldier. She was dismayed when she emerged from shock, not because her whole leg was exposed—but worse!—there was a runner in her stocking.   —RN. July 1946

The English, dear Harry, have received me as well as I ever hope to be received anywhere; and on one or two occasions, with a very un-English depth of visible emotion on their own part. They have taken me in so completely indeed that I find myself, against my own volition, meeting them half way on little things like manners and pronunciation—even occasionally, to my horror, tone—just to narrow the gap that is already so small. But live here permanently? Never! The thought never had entered my mind before coming here; and if it had, it would have vanished on almost the first day. I am still a foreigner in this society; and much though I admire parts of it and love other parts of it, I could never identify myself with it: at least not more than I could with France, Poland, Italy, or any other foreign country whose citizens made me feel at home.   —Letter to Henry A. Murray. July 1, 1946

23: Personal Sidelights

The attempt of this sheaf of notes is to catch in passing odd aspects of the subject's personality which he might evade or suppress in the more deliberate composition of a biography because they seem too egoistic or too trivial. A more informative group of similar notes could probably be assembled from letters intimate friends have written me, in sentiments ranging from admiration to exasperation and reproof. But I must leave the task of choosing and developing these snapshots to some more patient and objective witness.

CONFRONTATION WITH MY OWN IMAGE. The other night I had a good long look at myself in Amy Spingarn's motion picture of the picnic I wrote you about: I saw the thing twice, and was scarcely aware of the existence of another person in the picture except when they inconveniently blotted me out. It is a little weird to see oneself moving through time: it turns one's Euclidean mirror self into a strange Einsteinian paradox. My first thought was: how foreign I look! How little Americanized that face! And those unconscious gestures that always seem to me so utterly negligent: they look studied, as though I had acquired a style for the movies. This happens even on parts of the film where I had no consciousness whatever of being taken. How easily my worst enemy might think I had made it my business to cultivate those little tricks: how strange to think that they evolved themselves somehow, from within, so many of them, at all events, as were not consciously cultivated during the narcissistic period of eighteen to twenty-three. I confess that I want to see thousands and thousands more feet of myself, just to learn a little better from an 'objective' or behaviorist angle what I am like.

What a galaxy of 'I's' I find! There is the composite 'I' that I know: an altogether chimerical monster, impossible to describe: god, beast, child, shadow, three-dimensional solid, superimposed upon each other to create the illusion of a man. Then there is the 'I' that I gather from other people: a variable and amorphous I, now cynical, now worldly-wise, now practical, now shrewd, now capable, now charming, now stubborn and obstreperous, now vain and masculine. The illusion and the reflexion modify each other, yet somehow the real and continuous self escapes. So I pick up a book I have written, and discover a third 'I'—in most respects the best of them all, harmonized yet fairly complete: 'reality' with its best foot forward. Finally, there is the 'I' that I am capable of becoming: the 'I' that haunts me, reproaches me, dogs my steps on solitary walks, tugs at my coat when I am about to lurch into ditches—the 'I' that once in a great age I have the sense of measuring up to—for a moment—but no more. As the hours pass the situation changes, and the composition of the 'I's' alters. If it were not for the relatively stable physical solids that underlie it, the whole ego would be an incredible phantasm much more wry and tangled than the most elaborate dream.   —Letter to Catherine Bauer. September 7, 1930

By the middle of spring I shall settle down to my autobiography, which attracts me more and more as I contemplate the richness of my data, despite my seemingly unadventurous and humdrum life. The kind of autobiography that tempts me most, alas! is that which could not be printed in my own lifetime; and though I put part of this into a novel in verse, which I began in 1939, I can neither continue that effort nor yet start a different novel on the same general lines—nor yet transpose every-thing into a more prayerful Augustinian confession. I've goaded myself to write a wholly honest and self-revealing autobiography: a task so difficult that I don't think anyone has ever achieved it, least of all Rousseau; while the man who perhaps went nearest to openness, Havelock Ellis, suc-ceeded only in writing a dull book which by its very honesty ruined the image of himself that he had happily created, and painfully damaged his reputation as a master of erotic experience—at least among those who, like myself, persisted in reading it. All in all it is a hard choice; but as in most big choices it will probably take care of itself, and will defy my more conscious decisions as boldly as 'The City in History' did, when it pushed me, much against my will, into the field of ancient archaeology, which I had intended to glide past in the most superficial way.   —Letter to Stearns Morse. August 3, 1961

424

. . . Eleanor Brooks very decently read off the palm of my hand the night before last. Looking at my right hand, which represents the original endowment, she said: "It is the hand of a man with modest talents who, if he followed the lines here indicated would have had a smooth and happy life. And here," she said, turning to the left hand, "are lines that show that you have sacrificed your happiness by erecting a series of purposes and goals, which will give you a more interesting life, but a more difficult one. In early middle age there is a serious break: maybe jealous cliques work against you, maybe a woman enters, I can't say: but after a period you go beyond it. This line indicates the affections: there are various women in your life; but although they mean something to you, they do not mean enough to deflect you from your purpose."

To this I add: Eleanor knows too little about me, and seems too lacking in intuitive flashes to make me believe she invented this out of her head or out of hearsay. And of course it is all 'superstition'! Still, it may happen that this superstition is exactly the same as the old-wives' interpretation of dreams seemed, until the subject was reopened by Freud. But how remarkably correct both as biography and character analysis! —Letter to Catherine Bauer. July 25, 1934

THE TRICKINESS OF BIOGRAPHY. This morning I was talking with Sophia about the tortuous job a biographer would have in interpreting my life. I was an only child, and since I spent too much of my time in adult company, I was sometimes a lonely child. I resented the hours in Atlantic City that I had to spend watching the stockmarket boards in a broker's office: likewise even the mornings spent listening to band concerts, which usually bored me, on the Steel Pier. Perhaps the latter spoiled me for music, as Whitehead confessed that the systematic study of 'King Lear' at school had spoiled that play for him. Yet for all this I did not feel deprived, nor did I feel in any way peculiar, or 'out of it,' for I was accepted by my playmates and schoolmates as one of them, despite my good marks and my docile 'deportment.'

On current biographic theory, I should have felt as alienated and as desperate as, say, Rainer Maria Rilke; but the fact is I did not. Even at Stuyvesant High, where I was younger and more 'gentlemanly' than most of the entering freshmen, the same thing held, though I was thinner and weaker too. Although a few of the boys in my freshman year hit on the L. C. of my original initials [Lewis Charles] and teased me by calling me Elsie, that didn't get under my skin; and I was too innocent to even guess, until long after, what one of the nastiest boys meant when he gloatingly pursued this feminine allusion further. I had no sense of 'being out of it,' still less persecuted. No need to take my word for this. In my junior year I was one of the cheer leaders at High School games, and in a canvass for the 1912 yearbook I was voted the most popular member of my class.

In the Navy it was much the same, though by that time I was more consciously aloof and had a need for being off by myself, especially on our rare overnight weekend leaves—reading in the Redwood Library at Newport or going for lonely walks. One of my younger shipmates at Cambridge, I remember, at some pause in our day's routine during the worldwide influenza epidemic, was driven by something I had said to remark: "Hell, Mumford, you're different. When the brass pass along some damfool order, we grumble and raise hell; but you just ask yourself: 'I wonder what they mean by that, or what's back of it?' You never get mad the way we do."

This detachment might have proved dangerous if it had been accompanied by feelings of personal alienation, by buried grievances, by inner uncertainties; but as a matter of fact it helped keep me on my own course. The disruptions of adolescence were due, not so much to my social situation as to an unbalance between my swelling sexual urges, my invalid's regimen, and my inhibitions against having any premature commitment in love that might hamper my vocation as a writer. —RN. December 1963

I awoke from a dream this morning, a dream about mice, and found these words on my lips, taken from the dream: "The mice wrote many books about themselves: the archaeology of mice, the biology of mice, the anthropology of mice: they went into everything. But when they came to the elephant they could only say: It is a large animal." —RN. May 8, 1940

BRIEF ENCOUNTER. Last night, during my lecture at the Royal Institute of British Architects, the face of a responsive young woman singled itself out even while I was speaking. At the end, as I was passing out of the hall, I saw the same face again: a wide oval, healthily colored, smiling and animated, capping a slim body. In the corridor, while I was being ushered to the President's car that would take us to his dinner, I saw her once more. This time we frankly looked at each other, as if we both wanted to speak. It took a little while to assemble the official party: so once more I saw her standing outside. This time we looked more boldly at each other: by now we both knew we were interested. Before I dove into the car, I turned to her once again, smiling, and she, still loitering, smiled openly back, as pleased as I was. As the car drove off, our eyes met for the last time and with a bashful quick gesture she waved 'Goodbye.' She was so healthy, so lovely, so spontaneous and natural that I felt cheated by our peremptory separation when we seemed on the brink of meeting. Of meeting *only?* It had already gone beyond that! Never before had I so quickly 'fallen in love' with anyone or met with so quick and complete a response: recognition, communion, courtship, declared love, tension, and final separation, all in the wink of an eye. What is more, I felt that she had experienced this encounter precisely as I did, and knew it for what it was: a sudden glory too perfect to be prolonged or repeated. Even a brief note from her next day would have spoiled it. She knew that too! —RN. London. June 8, 1946

In the act of widening my whole cultural horizon after 1930—I never lost sight of my original ties with my own country or with the rural environment of Dutchess County, where we established our second home, as an unwavering beacon to call us back no matter how far away we wandered. During the next twenty years I became acquainted with sections of the United States I had never even casually visited before, from Wisconsin to California, from New Hampshire to North Carolina; and even spent almost two months in Hawaii. So at the very point where I was turning away from 'American Studies,' I was still exploring my own country more vigorously than ever before. But wherever I travelled, whether in America or in Europe, I never went as a tourist; for always I had work to do, as a lecturer, a visiting professor, or as a scholar gathering material for my next book. Moreover, during the post-1945 years, when I was digging deeper into the beginnings of human culture and reinterpreting man's whole development, giving primacy to language and art rather than to far later utilitarian artifacts, I was also writing fresh estimates of Frank Lloyd Wright, Audubon, Emerson, Thomas Eakins—the last three of which are included in 'Interpretations and Forecasts.' —RN. 1972

. . . Before I had begun systematically to study architecture in museums and books and cities, I was conscious of the esthetic aspects of machines and machine products. One of my first contributions, a paragraph that was printed in 'Modern Electrics' in 1911, was on the design of a sleeker model of binding post (brass standard), without the knurls and indentations that exhibited only the metal-turner's skill. Years before I had heard of Brancusi or Naum Gabo I was ready for their esthetic innovations. One of the earliest articles on the esthetic qualities of the machine was my 'Machinery and the Modern Style,' which came out in 1921, a few years before Le Corbusier's extensive pioneer exposition 'Vers une Architecture.' If I was later to indicate that 'mechanical' repetition was a fundamental trait of all human culture, beginning with ritual, song, and language, long before any specialized stone tools, still less machines, had come into existence, my awareness of the esthetic aspect of machine products had sunk in early, through direct experience.

At no point in my life have I ever wished to be a professional architect or a planner, though more than once the invitation to give disinterested criticism and practical advice has been hard to resist. Still, it is possible that at some deep level of the unconscious I have not accepted this divorce from active responsibility and participation without a certain inner resistance. Two of my essays in imaginative writing, a drama, 'The Builders of the Bridge,' 1927, and an unfinished novel in verse, 'Victor,' seem to challenge my exclusive commitment to a writer's lonely life. For in the play, Jefferson Baumgarten, is an engineer and, the son of a great engineer; while the chief character in 'Victor' is an architect whose partner bears a patent resemblance to my friend, Henry Wright. Still, it is a diametrically different character in the play, Robert-Owen Benns, a philosophic artist, who represents the dominant side of my personality; for after the Bridge has been triumphantly completed and dedicated, leaving the now exhausted engineer empty and desolate, it is Robert-Owen, the artist, who utters the last word. "You reached your goal this time, Jefferson. Next time attempt something you can't reach." —RN. n.d.

Just a week ago, around five in the evening, Sophy called me in from the garden where I had been working to answer the telephone. "Montgomery, Alabama, wants to talk with you," she called. "Oh," I said airily, and without thinking, "that must be the Air Force wanting me to come down to give a lecture." Until then they had never invited me or been in touch with me on any occasion, though in 1947 I lectured on the Social Consequences of the Atom Bomb at the Army War College and later at the Naval War College in Newport. Nothing could have been further from my mind than this offer. But when I answered the phone I found myself talking to a Colonel Shapiro, who in fact asked me whether it would be possible for me to go down there and give a lecture. They would even send a bomber up to fetch me! What could have prompted them I can't imagine; and since I am out of sympathy, to speak mildly, with their whole strategic conception, I said "No." But he was reluctant to take my answer; he said they had been trying to get hold of me so often.

428

Since none of these efforts had ever come to my attention, I conclude that they must have *discussed* inviting me once or twice. —RN. June 1954

. . . How often I am tempted to stop writing altogether and settle down serenely to the daily round of a gardener! I have already renounced New York, as Saint Jerome renounced Rome—and for the same reason. But he had an advantage over me, in that he had the company of a regiment of fellow-Christians, daily growing; whereas except for a bare handful of old friends I feel completely isolated, in an unfriendly, if not actively hostile world—which I respond to, I am afraid, with equally cold unfriendliness. This of course is only a passing, if recurrent mood: and it vanishes quickly, as it did the other day, when a lovely young Broadway actress, Nan Martin, who was introduced to me after my lecture at Wooster, told me that my books had become dog-eared through her constant re-reading of them. At that moment, as you can guess, Saint Jerome forgot he was seventy and found himself mockingly teased by fantasies more befitting Bernard Martin, aet. 30! —Letter to Babette Deutsch. May 4, 1966

Probably no two marriages are alike in their climaxes and fulfillments; and just as some people prefer autumn to spring, or winter to summer, there are marriages that were frost-nipped in flowering time and show the perfection of their efflorescence only shortly before winter comes. A marriage may begin well and end in alienation; or it may be almost uprooted in a devastating pre-autumn storm only to bear fruit triumphantly the next summer. If people more generally realized these facts—and therewith realized that a marriage equally rich in every season is an exception—they might face the bad periods more cheerfully and be more patient. —RN. March 16, 1953

The Sunday newspaper told of the death of Esther Johnston who used to be head of the circulation department in the New York Public Library. She came there in 1924 the obituary said and from the first we had a nodding acquaintance. When only a handful of people turned up for my New School lectures in 1924—she must have been one of them—she marshalled a sufficient number of students, many from her staff, to make it possible for me to give the course the following year. I owe much to her: but I doubt if I ever properly expressed my gratitude to her. The photograph the New York Times published was very much the face I remember: sweet, self-assured, sensitive. She and Laura Bragg of the Pittsfield Museum both 'recognized' me when I was still a young man, with only a few books behind me; and in a quiet way they played the part of guardian angels. How lucky I was in their unobtrusive friendship. Happily a few years ago I had occasion—again because she had suggested me for a lecture—to thank Miss Bragg, who was back in Charleston once more. She was related, I suppose, to the famous Confederate general.   —RN. January 22, 1968

Two weeks ago I underwent a Rorschach test. The man who gave it was Caesar Finn, once a musician, now a professional psychological tester. You know the test: a sort of quick psychoanalysis; and it has been refined to such a point in the course of twenty years that about half of it can be graded mechanically, without any special interpretation by the tester. I found the results illuminating, not because they told me anything that I didn't know, but because by this apparently trivial and mechanical means —one's responses to a series of blots—they told me so much that I *did* know about the buried parts of my life, that they gave me a little extra confidence in their flattering interpretations of my more public self. "Very superior, beautiful balance of the intellectual, the emotional, and the practical; almost equal balance of introvert and extrovert." In short I have been unwittingly projecting *myself* in the concept of the Balanced Personality, whereas I have always regarded this merely as an ideal goal I have naturally fallen short of.

The test wasn't done for my personal benefit. At Columbia, a group of specially chosen people, from Eleanor Roosevelt and myself to Eisenhower and Einstein are also getting this test. But the interpretation of the dream symbols in the analysis was even more revealing; for the analyst really got on the trail of some of the more devious and hidden elements of my life, before he had gone beyond the third blot! Three things that he said clinched the diagnosis for me, though all of them were disturbing. First: a block between my outer life and my inner life which ✓ reduced my actual output of creative work. My potential creativity, on the record, was a third more than my actual productivity. Second: though there were no visible anxieties whatever, there was a heavy load of depression which might reach suicidal depths. [This was three years after our son's death.] Finally, a failure to resolve the conflict between the pragmatic scientist-intellectual and the artist-philosopher in me. This raises the possibility that the latter side, which at times I had slighted, was really my major one.   —Letter to Catherine Bauer Wurster. August 30, 1947

. . . Sometimes I wish I had a small, neat, tidy mind, that could isolate a small section of a big problem, treat it by itself, reduce it to half a dozen parts, still smaller and more isolated, and then let it go at that. The writing of such a lecture would be easy and what is more I would have a sense of getting somewhere. But I am struggling with the hardest possible kind of material for the human mind to grasp or formulate, that of a change in the total pattern. I think it is an important task for our time; but whether one tries to walk around it or to see it from the air, it is difficult to focus on and describe. Did you ever stumble across D'Arcy Thomson's book on 'Growth and Form' in which he puts a particular fish form, say, within an ordinary system of Cartesian coordinates, and by changing the angle, he derives, by changes at every other point in the system, a neighboring species, seemingly quite unlike it? I am looking for such a system for formulating a total change in societies, like that leading from pre-Christian to post-Christian society, or from our own order to the one that may follow it. To do so in words, without such graphic aid as D'Arcy Thomson summons, is extremely difficult; but once one has started thinking in this fashion it is as hard to go back to any simpler method as it is to go back to checkers after one has mastered chess. Only I haven't mastered this particular game: far from it. . . . —Letter to Catherine Bauer Wurster. January 16, 1947

VOCATIONAL DECISIONS. . . . You ask how I came to decide to be a "writer on historical-sociological subjects," and whether my mentors envisaged such a career. The fact is that I never decided: life made the decision for me. Do you remember Samuel Butler's note about this?—that a man may well decide what color of tie or what kind of suit to wear, but when it comes to anything big, like choosing a wife or a career he'd better leave the decision to providence. I reached the goal which *now* seems deliberately chosen by elimination. My earliest *decision* was to be a newspaper reporter, but I never got beyond a copy boy. Then I thought I would be an academic philosopher, but ill-health threw me out of college and kept me from working systematically for a degree. Then I wanted, or rather all along I wanted, to be a novelist or a playwright, and I almost succeeded in the latter effort before I was thirty, and kept on writing plays until I was thirty-two. One successful stage production might have confirmed my dedication to the theater, but it never quite came and I lacked the temperament to battle Broadway or Hollywood. If I had had an overwhelming ability I doubtless wouldn't have been daunted; but actually I was emotionally too immature, before I was thirty-five, to have been anything but a clever, superficial fellow, like Bernard Shaw.

So I could go on. What really prepared me for my career was a negative decision: I didn't want to be a specialist. In this Patrick Geddes's encouragement and example fortified me, and my own naturally diverse interests made the way easy. Nothing pushed me in any one

431

direction, and that is what finally gave me "squatters rights" to the broad field I now occupy. Happily I had no academic ambitions—in university harness I would have been frustrated or have committed intellectual suicide. In short, my path was an uncharted one. There were no short-cuts; I followed the currents of life where they took me. Fortunately in 1915 I came into a small inheritance which helped me to endure a long apprenticeship and many rejections without actually starving. Soon after the money was gone (1923) I had 'arrived'—or at least could keep my head above water.   —Letter to F. J. Osborn. October 17, 1963

Note: For other personal reflections and confessions, see 'The Letters of Lewis Mumford and Frederic J. Osborn: a Transatlantic Dialogue, 1938–1970.' New York, 1972.

The other night I dreamed I was walking out of a city, along a wide span of railroad tracks, such as sometimes precede the entry into a big station. The buildings of a great metropolis, big and small, orderly and dis-orderly, rose at one side of me; but the tracks stretched out illimitably in the distance. I was alone, and the tracks themselves were deserted, for no train of any kind passed. After a while I began to wonder, since there was no wall between me and the city, how far I would have to continue before I would find a road leading up from the tracks to the city, such as that which I thought I must have entered by. I had not reached the end of this pilgrimage before I woke up, still with a sense of the weariness and desolation of my track-walking.

Next morning I told the dream to Sophia; and she, who has unusual gifts for interpreting dream symbols, immediately translated it. The road, with its many tracks, was the book I was writing, whose end was not yet in sight: but of which I have shown signs of growing weary. My being alone naturally increased my weariness. Once she had given me the clue I saw how well it worked out in particulars: down to the fact that the many parallel tracks, which I could cross freely, were all the different but parallel fields that I have attempted to take in in order to explain man's development in relation to technics; while the railroad system itself was of course an ideal symbol of technology: though the absence of machines and its human emptiness threw a light of my own historic interpretation. —RN. December 19, 1965

About a week ago I had one of those rare dreams one is grateful to remember. I was looking at a large picture, almost a mural, but done in oil: a painting by Picasso, though in style it did not bear the slightest

432

resemblance to his work; for while the theme was abstract, or at least non-representational, it was brilliant in color and rich in texture. I was so entranced with it that I kept on exclaiming to my companions: But see how it is painted! *Every square inch of it is painted!*—as if this were the highest possible praise, though these words were unable to give the full measure of my delight. I told Sophia about it at breakfast next morning, and the memory of it pleasantly colored the day; indeed it still somehow lingers, though the image itself has disappeared. In the very act of putting this down, I realize that perhaps my unconscious was talking to me about my book, and encouraging me to go on with it, even though there were many more square inches of it to be painted.   —RN. January 25, 1966

For the past year, and perhaps for longer, I have been dreaming about death. I became conscious of this a few weeks ago, when I found myself in a dream swimming in the sea, far from land, not panicky, but knowing it would be a long pull before I reached shore. What made this dream even plainer was that Artur Glikson, my younger Israeli friend who died a year ago, was swimming alongside me: he was about fifty when he died. My unconscious identifies him, I suspect, with young Geddes, who would now be over forty. Then I realized today when I awoke from another dream I have had recurrently in many forms, that this dream too was about death; for it had to do with a long and unusually frustrating railroad journey, of a highly fantastic kind; and two of the people in the dream, a young woman and my mother, have long been dead. This railroad journey is the final journey before me: full of uncertainties and delays and difficulties—as in the fact last night that my mother had come aboard the train, but did not know I was on it, and I could not for some reason go to the rear of the train where I had seen her get on, to tell her I was there, too. My unconscious seems more concerned about my death than my waking self is. No wonder Bergman's 'Wild Strawberries' has so much to say to me.   —RN. October 12, 1967

Emerson quoted Isaiah on the Egyptians, when he visited Egypt in 1873: "It is their strength to sit still." Perhaps there is some of the Egyptian in me. If my work survives, it will be because I never joined the fashionable scramble or looked elsewhere for support than on the seat where I sat. —RN. January 21, 1960

Fantasia on Time

Slip the reel into the rack, wind up the played-out film! Let beginnings be
    endings; let skeletons be enigmatic eggs!
Reverse the irreversible; let age deflate to youth and youth look forward
    to nonentity.

Mark how gray stubble darkens, how the flesh fills out the languid calf,
The pain-dulled eyes awaken to expectancy.
How quick the adolescents unlearn their letters, sheathe defiant frowns,
    recover their bloated infanthood
Until, leaving a stifled shout behind, they retreat into the womb
To disappear forever nine months earlier with the orgasm that fades out
    into an early tremor of flesh
Beneath a lover's hand.

Dead men now levitate in coffins and return to sweaty beds whose creases
    unrumple before the sick arise to cautious health.
Thunders of war become the fainter thud of marching men;
Wild shot returns, unerring, to the cannon's mouth; trenches refill with
    earth made innocent again;
Cathedrals geyser upward from powdered stone to permanence;
Unknown soldiers recover their dog-tags of identification and achieve
The utter anonymity of a nameless being
Before they lose it for a second time at the baptismal font.

The daily bread, uneaten, turns back to yeast and flour, revives into
    green shoots that down-pierce the earth and so retreat to seed.
An airplane, winging rearward for a landing place, hits the runway,
    dismantles into sticks and wires, becomes once more a sketchy mind-
    thing, part hunch, part hope, part blueprint,
Part fanatic leer that vexes sleep with billowing motions in unfettered
    space.

And so it goes; the coal, consumed as heat, dispersed as gas, and dumped
    about as ashes, funnels downward into black clumps beneath the
    crannied earth,
Sear newspapers rise up again from libraries and moldy cupboard
    shelves, from scrapbooks, from rubbish heaps, from walls in mountain
    cabins, from the muck of cesspools,
To resume once more their pitiless serenity as trees.

434

The parted reunite; the dwindling friends recover intimacy; the wanton
     wife relapses into faithfulness, the husband reflates from boredom to
     unpunctured adoration;
And so the years diminish—diminish and recover clarity.

Slip the reel into the rack and wind it back again;
Let the past return upon itself. Reverse the years!
Then youth's at hand once more
And all that's worked toward our undoing is undone.
The cone of light sharpens the blackness that enfolds our images:
The sound track, returning to gibberish our pompous affirmations,
The plot itself, unravelling to threadlike ends
—All now unite to send us hurtling back
Through shrinking minutes, hours, days, lifetimes till we reach the point
     where credits are assigned and origins obliquely cited
Whereat the celluloid will rip and leave cold silver light to shine
     embarrassment
Upon our certainties as to the authorship.

                                             —The New Yorker. December 30, 1939

24: ABC of De-moralization

Power. There must be a relation between power
and probity . . . We seem already to have more
power than we can be trusted with . . . Except
to better men the augmented science is a new
chemic experiment of the quickest poison.
  —Emerson. The Journals. 1848

*Only a handful of people, mainly scientists, reacted adequately to the
situation produced by the explosion of the first atom bomb. Among them
the names of Leo Szilard, Harold Urey, Norbert Wiener, Linus Pauling,
and Max Born deserve to be specially remembered. As a student of
technological history—or even earlier as a reader of science fiction—I was
not unprepared for this devastating feat. Had not Jules Verne capped
his long series of scientific fantasies with a novel whose central character
had invented a super-bomb which could destroy the world? And coming
nearer, had not H. G. Wells in 'The World Set Free'—a novel I had read
serially in the English Review in 1913—depicted the destruction of a
great city by a single bomb? Rutherford's assistant, Frederick Soddy, in
his 'Interpretation of Radium' (1920) had not only exposed the lethal
potentials of nuclear energy, but had warned that to avert the fatal
misuse of such power, hitherto unthinkable, the entire social structure
would have to be radically altered.*

*During the next ten years small groups of conscientious people
initiated political and economic measures to bring nuclear energy under
the control of a world authority. But hardly had the first steps been taken
when the Cold War between the United States and Soviet Russia broke*

out. Once the Russians exploded their hydrogen bomb, this Cold War turned into a smoldering Hot War, an equally deadly War Game in fact, in which the side that produced and stored the greatest number of nuclear bombs and bomb-carrying rockets and submarines could at any moment claim a temporary victory on points—provided that neither by accident nor design did the game turn into the reality it was supposed to avert. So early in the fifties it became plain that a strategy for controlling nuclear weapons alone had become futile.

Of all the essays and papers I wrote on this subject, I have singled out two: one on the immediate atomic threat, and one on the all-embracing final threat of unidentifiable and uncontrollable ABC Weapons. The first article, on the social effects of the atom bomb, was published in 1947 in Air Affairs, a short-lived quarterly under the editorship of William Pardridge. The earliest response to this came from Lieutenant General Grunther, while he was still head of the Army War College in Washington. He invited me to give a lecture in the special Atomic Energy Course for Senior officers, for which my paper in Air Affairs was required reading.

The second paper, on 'The Morals of Extermination,' needs neither updating nor apology. It was one of the first attempts to fully expose and challenge the almost universal moral debasement that followed the rise of totalitarian dictatorships—Soviet Russian, Fascist Italian, and Nazi German—after the First World War. All temporizing efforts to establish comity and peace between hostile nations on the basis of political and economic agreements had become a mockery after 1943, in view of the secret research led by the United States to create alternative weapons— atomic, bacterial, and chemical—to achieve 'Victory' by unrestricted extermination. This article, after it appeared in The Atlantic Monthly, was widely circulated by small independent groups and individuals.

Listening to the six o'clock broadcast the night before last, I heard Quincy Howe announce that a single atomic bomb had been used by our Air Force to obliterate Hiroshima: a whole city. This was the first announcement that the terrible weapon had been perfected. My immediate reaction was one of almost physical nausea: the power it places in the hands of the human race is too absolute to be entrusted to them; and the very fact that we used the bomb is a proof that we were neither intelligent enough nor morally sound enough to be in charge of this weapon. Yesterday I devoured both the Times and the Tribune for details, and

437

learned that there had been a race between the Germans and the British and ourselves to perfect this horrible instrument; that the Germans had failed, probably, for the providential reason that they had exiled as Jewish enemies some of the very physicists who were farthest along in atomic research.

The description of the first tryout of the bomb—only three weeks ago—was hair-raising; and apparently the military authorities who had sponsored this weapon were allowed to put it in use against Japan without any further check upon their plans. The cocky response to this dire weapon on the part of President Truman was that it will 'shorten the war.' Apparently, he did not stop to consider that it might also shorten the existence of the human race. The press was more sober than the President: the editorial comments, for the most part, recorded awe and fear, mingled with efforts to find compensation in alleged peacetime uses of this atomic energy.   —RN. August 8, 1945

THE ATOMIC BOMB has altered overnight the entire international picture. The presence of this new source of energy makes every other form of military power, and every claim based on it, negligible. Nothing will be proof against a suicidal anxiety except an absolute submission to a universal standard of humane conduct: a morality built on new foundations to repair the world we have devastated during the last thirty years. If the 'Great Powers' on the Supreme Council are in their senses, they will promptly convene the nations of the world and beg to be 'bound over' to keep the peace: they will give themselves up, as a dangerous maniac would, in a lucid moment give himself up, in order to be put safely in an asylum.   —RN. August 8, 1945

GENTLEMEN: YOU ARE MAD!   We in America are living among madmen. Madmen govern our affairs in the name of order and security. The chief madmen claim the titles of general, admiral, senator, scientist, administrator, Secretary of State, even President. And the fatal symptom of their madness is this: they have been carrying through a series of acts which may lead eventually to the destruction of mankind, under the solemn conviction that they are normal responsible people, living sane lives, and working for reasonable ends.

With stony sobriety, day after day, the madmen continue to go through the undeviating motions of madness: motions so stereotyped, so commonplace, that they seem the normal motions of normal men, not the irrational compulsions of people bent on total death. Without a public mandate of any kind, the madmen have taken it upon themselves to lead us by gradual stages to that final act of madness which may corrupt the

438

face of the earth and blot out the nations of men, possibly put an end to all life on the planet itself.

These madmen have a comet by the tail, but they think to prove their sanity by treating it as if it were a child's skyrocket. They play with it; they experiment with it; they dream of swifter and brighter comets. Their teachers have handed them down no rules for controlling comets; so they take only the usual precautions of children permitted to set off firecrackers. Without asking for anyone's permission, they have decided to play a little further with this cosmic force, merely to see what will happen at sea in a war that must never come.

Why do we let the madmen go on with their game without raising our voices? Why do we keep our glassy calm in the face of this potential catastrophe? There is a reason: we are madmen, too. We view the madness of our leaders as if it expressed mankind's traditional wisdom and common sense: we view them placidly. Our failure to act is the measure of our madness. —Introduction to Gentlemen You Are Mad. The Saturday Review of Literature. March 2, 1946

Nuclear Futures

> 'Tis the time's plague when madmen lead the blind.
> —'King Lear.' Act 14, Scene 1

The social effects of atomic war cannot be dealt with outside space and time: where, when, and how the war takes place will condition the purely physical results and their social consequences. Hence no single projection of a curve that represents the present known factors will suffice. For the sake of reducing the problem to manageable proportions I shall take two constants: the atom bomb itself and a state of chronic non-cooperation between the political powers. On this basis, I shall make a series of alternative assumptions as to the time, the duration, and the destructiveness of the atomic war itself.

First Assumption: The atom bomb is used by the United States against a single power before any other power has an equivalent means of retaliation.

As soon as one makes this assumption, one also lays down certain other conditions. One of them is that the object of such an attack would be Soviet Russia and that the purpose of it would be to safeguard the United States from an unwelcome surprise of a similar nature. On this assumption the Lilienthal plan for safeguarding the production of atomic

439

energy has not yet been put into effect: fear has therefore risen that Russia has been stalling for time and perhaps will soon be at the point of being able to meet our challenge of atomic supremacy halfway.

Unfortunately, the success of such a preventive war depends upon the military element of surprise: hence the assumption of an undeclared war must also be made, which means that the military forces have taken it upon themselves—as part of their 'sacred trust' of safeguarding their country from attack—to make the political decision, possibly with the advice and consent of the President, but not with the open authority of the Congress. The necessity for secrecy finds additional justification in the fact that, no matter how steadily political relations between the two countries might deteriorate, it is unlikely that such an attack would have sufficient popular support in advance to sanction a cold-blooded declaration of atomic war. After the attack has taken place, the proofs of its 'necessity' can be easily brought to light: the 'finding' of an atom bomb, supposedly planted by the enemy, in the heart of Washington or New York; or the reported encountering of an imaginary fleet of Russian bombers, halfway across the Atlantic, as the first strike against the enemy is made.

By hypothesis, the first act of this atomic war is unbelievably successful: every plane finds its target and every bomb reaches it; so that some 36 Russian cities with populations of over 200,000 each are wiped out, in all about 18,000,000 people; and the obliteration of certain other strategic cities of smaller dimensions, removes another 7,000,000: 25,000,000 persons in all. The first newspaper headlines to herald this unprecedented success would undoubtedly read: "Red Menace Removed Forever!" But the elation of victory is presently succeeded by a sense of frustration: for, assuming the present deployment of Russia's military forces, the atomic victory is not at once followed by an unconditional surrender. The United States has done its worst; but it has not yet done enough. Though theoretically wiped out, the Russian Government proceeds to make an effective response to the situation by moving its armies in force to the periphery of Europe and Asia, taking these areas under its protection and summoning them to unite against this Yankee imperialism which has butchered twenty-five million innocent people and plainly is bent on bringing the whole world under its barbarous dominion.

Russia's response takes time; but the fact that Russia's major cities all have been wiped out does not prevent this response from taking place; nor does the wiping out of Russia's military potential prevent her from falling back upon industrial Asia and Europe to serve as arsenal. So, far from the menace of Russian domination being settled, the whole case has in fact become more difficult. Just as in the past the drying up of the grasslands pushed the Mongols and the Huns onto the periphery of the continents, so the radioactivity in the destroyed areas, and the fear of further attacks, will set in motion a great mass migration. Though millions will perish on that trek, millions more will reach their destination and mingle with the non-Russian population. Even if the supply of atom bombs is inexhaustible, there is no military answer to this situation. Shall further instruments of extermination then be used to back up the atom bomb? Bacterial warfare perhaps? Not if we hope to follow up our victory anywhere in Eurasia. The large-scale use of a DDT or the spraying of radioactive materials on the land might lead to unparalleled starvation within the Russian domain; but the impulse to adopt these grisly methods must take account of another fact: the growing moral recoil.

In spite of a complete suppression of free discussion over the origins and justifications of this war, in the newspapers and on the radio, a steadily deepening moral reaction has taken place: the very unwillingness of the President and the military authorities to submit to any examination of their case only increases the general sense of suspicion and guilt. The usual justifications for suppression in wartime are now lacking, for, according to the propaganda issued by the military, the enemy has been wiped out, and the war is all but over. Suspicion and misapprehension grow, however, when an act is presently passed to raise an armed force of ten million amphibious and airborne soldiers for the invasion of Europe and Asia. Even those who had joyfully accepted the atomic victory pause at this next step. Instead of a cheap war, the one-sided atomic war has turned out to be a costly one: instead of a swift war, it promises to have no termination at all. In a country with the territory and population of Russia, even wholesale extermination is still not total extermination. To complete the illusory quality of this victory, and to give it an extra touch of irony, the danger of atomic retaliation has not altogether been removed, for Russia can now look to the willing aid of European and Asiatic scientists: so the main purpose of the attack is, in this event, nullified. Meanwhile, so many links in the process of human co-operation and human understanding would have been destroyed by the very manner in which the attack was carried out, that any hope of bringing about peace and order for centuries would be fantastic.

Second Assumption: War itself does not break out until each of the two chief powers, the United States and Russia, possesses a large stockpile of atom bombs, and by hypothesis, the stockpile of the United States is many times that of Russia.

By the time this war breaks out, certain precautions against surprise have already been taken: every package and crate of goods in international trade is rigorously inspected, not only for radioactive materials but for other mechanical components of the atom bomb, and all direct air travel between continents has broken down: the outlying islands have become halfway stations, and any foreign plane found beyond these points is shot down on sight without warning. Nonintercourse between countries has reached the point where even diplomatic relations between Russia and the United States have been broken, because of the suspicion on each side that the conventions of diplomacy are only a thin disguise for an espionage organization. After a succession of feints and withdrawals, war breaks out on both sides, with or without an accompanying public declaration; for by now the impossibility of publicly declaring war in advance has been accepted in the United States, along with a renunciation of various other essentials of the democratic process. For all the superiority of the United States in number of atom bombs, our absolute losses are greater because, thanks to the surviving premises of free enterprise, our dispersal has been less effective.

In both countries, the military establishment, because of its reasonable degree of dispersal, is more intact than the civilian population; but despite the piling up of stores and weapons in the prewar period, the United States forces, precisely because of the technical refinements of their weapons, suffer more quickly than the more primitive Russian organization from the total disorganization of industrial and social life which follows the destruction of urban centers.

On the edges of the old metropolises, life reverts swiftly to a preindustrial level. With forty million people dead in these centers—a few survivors perhaps remember this was General Groves's original estimate —and with no hospital or medical services capable of taking care of the maimed and wounded, the Army is faced with the burden of relief and reorganization, if its own security is not to be ultimately threatened. 'Mercy deaths' add to the total holocaust. But the war is not yet over. From bombproof shelters, deep in the Ural Mountains, Russia launches new supplies of atom bombs. This settles down to a war of attrition, which is also a war of nerves. All forms of international intercourse cease throughout the planet; and unfortunately most of the plants for creating synthetic substitutes for natural products located in distant parts of the world have been destroyed; so there is no way of offsetting this loss. In the 'island cultures' which appear in the less threatened parts of the world, there is a deliberate relapse into primeval ways: in some places, machines are attacked and disemboweled, and in others they are allowed to fall into complete neglect: in any event, they are treated as symbols of man's decadence, of his will-to-extinction. Free curiosity, invention, innovation, become taboo; and life resumes the repetitious round of tribal society, weighted down by fears even heavier than those Nature alone once occasioned.

Third Assumption: Atomic war does not break out until a sufficient time has elapsed to bring about the atomic armament of the greater part of the civilized world. Not two countries, but at least twenty, are involved in the atomic armament race: Africa, Asia, South America all contribute their quota of suspicion, fear, terrorism, and death.

On this hypothesis, certain other events may reasonably be predicted: namely, a vast increase in the production of atomic energy, possibly a decrease in the size and weight of the apparatus itself, and even, thanks to the extraordinary concentration on physical research, the utilization of commoner elements hitherto impervious to atomic disintegration. But to keep the prospective horrors within the bounds of the commonplace, I shall not posit the release of atomic energy among the lighter elements. Because of the secrecy that everywhere surrounds atomic experiment, there is much guesswork about the work of rival powers and little diffusion of scientific knowledge: indeed, to guard against diffusion by code and cryptogram or any other kind of indirect exposure, all scientific publication is classified as top secret; and even puzzle magazines and comic magazines are not allowed to leave the country in which they are issued—a precaution that followed a terrible leak through what seemed an entirely innocent channel. Though all this tends to retard atomic investigation, a national concentration of scientific resources on atomic physics and its adjacent spheres in mathematics and chemistry has partly counteracted this tendency.

In every other department of life, there is a slowing down of creativity: worse than that, an active regression. Life is now reduced to purely existentialist terms: existence toward death. The classic otherworldly religions undergo a revival; but even more, quack religions and astrology, with pretensions to scientific certainty, flourish: the tension and anxiety cause even atomic scientists to take refuge in one or another of the new cults. The young who grow up in this world are completely demoralized: they characterize themselves as the generation that drew a blank. The belief in continuity, the sense of a future that holds promises, disappears: certainty of sudden obliteration cuts across every long-term plan, and every activity is more or less reduced to the time span of a single day, on the assumption that it may be the last day. To counteract this, a cult of the archaic and the antiquarian becomes popular: the Victorian period is revived as mankind's Golden Age. Suicides become more frequent, especially among those carrying the weight of responsibility in science and military affairs; and the taking of drugs to produce either exhilaration or sleep becomes practically universal.

In this situation, secrecy gives rise to suspicion and suspicion to uncontrolled fantasies of betrayal and aggression. Despite the most rigorous immigration barriers, despite the almost complete cessation of foreign travel, rumors that the Communist party has access to the secrets held by other countries, put even the most remote minor officials under the constant surveillance of the FBI; only to encourage the further suspicion, as the ranks of the CIA swell to the dimensions of a considerable army, that Communist influence has also penetrated the CIA. No man trusts his neighbor or dares speak to him freely. Research that turns out to be sterile is regarded as a possible manifestation of treason: those involved in it are purged. Mistakes, failures to achieve production schedules, slips of the tongue, all lead to further purges: the new Police State can take no chances. Internationally, an apparent stalemate is reached, because the perfection of an indiscriminate weapon of attack has been followed by the policy of an indiscriminate retaliation on all suspected enemies.

In the threatened atomic war, as in a riot, people will claw and club their neighbors because they have no means of identifying the real culprit and no means of isolating their reaction to him. At first, that universal danger is a restraining influence; but as tension mounts, this becomes the medium for a psychotic outbreak. We will suppose that an atomic explosion takes place either by accident or by deliberate intention; both are definitely possible, and in the very nature of the case, the facts themselves can never be determined. Perhaps a single unbalanced person is responsible for what happens; perhaps a group on the top levels, secret admirers of Hitler, neo-Hitlerians in fact, have decided that the moment has come to establish national supremacy, even if half the world, and half the nation itself, are therewith exterminated. This lights the fuel for a widespread holocaust, one even greater than that originally feared, for meanwhile one or more countries involved has found a way of retarding atomic explosions so that they come not in a moment but in waves of increasing duration: the blast effect is small but the gamma rays are far more effective. Before the world's atomic stockpiles are exhausted more than half the population of the planet has been killed; and by reason of this high order of radioactive saturation, changes take place in the weather and in the balance of vegetable, animal, insect, and bacterial life; so that the food supply is not sufficient for the random hordes that remain. Death by starvation, or by the drinking of chemically poisoned waters even at points distant from the contaminated areas, slowly destroys more than three-quarters of those who remain.

Now, for the first time in history, the disintegration of civilization takes place on a world-wide scale: no 'island cultures' are left to carry on the old processes, even at a reduced level. Within a generation, mankind will enter an age so dark that every other dark age will seem, by contrast, one of intense illumination. Even the animal survival of the species may for long hang in balance. The trauma left on the human psyche will be far worse than that from any previous fear or terror, even the melting of the icecaps. Surviving man will repress his higher functions, not merely his curiosities and his mechanical skills, but his powers of abstraction and symbolism, as threats to his life: he will revert to a stage just this side of the idiot level, a creature of low cunning, focused on the immediate and the concrete, seeking safety in repetition and order, in respect for taboo, ruthlessly killing every variant from this norm, partly losing the use of language itself in his desire to control fresh departures. This will be all that remains of *Homo sapiens*. He will survive as an animal with the merest remnant of his intelligence, by eliminating every other capacity that identified him as human.

On this Third Assumption, the damage to the environment might be so complete that man would not have even these diminished alternatives. For if the lower orders of life remained, variations in bacterial enemies, to say nothing of transformations in the human genes, might result in the production of diseases and deformities which would wipe out the surviving members of our species. If that happened, there would be no further social deductions to draw.

Fourth Assumption: Atomic war does not break out at all. But meanwhile, for at least a century, in every part of the earth it remains a constant threat; and the response to this threat is made only in those departments that can be controlled by individual non-cooperative states. The adaptation is complete.

On this hypothesis, the manufacture of atomic weapons has not resulted in indiscriminate violence, destruction, or wholesale extermination; indeed, the very universality of the terror, which almost guaranteed non-resort to war under the Third Assumption, has resulted in something that could be called, in a purely formal sense, peace, and this indefinite suspension of hostilities seems likely to last as long as the total danger that now confronts mankind. Is this, then, the Atomic Golden Age? Let us look at it more closely.

It would be needlessly repetitive to describe results already touched on in the Third Assumption; but in the course of a century certain trends, already visible under those conditions, are carried to their logical conclusions. As the danger presses, the plea of the insurance companies and businessmen to hold population in the old centers is first met in the United States by the building of extensive underground shelters and new subway systems. But in New York City, because of its rocky terrain, this process proves too costly to carry through, and that city is the first to be abandoned: its Atomic Age population dwindles to something less than 100,000. At first the Federal government assumes the entire municipal debt and grants a subvention to private owners on a basis of half their assessed values; but this proves too heavy a load, and in engineering the compulsory exodus from the big cities an elaborate pension system is worked out to compensate the still dissatisfied property holders. The nationalization of banks and insurance companies is only the first of many more desperate measures to distribute losses. Taxes continue to rise to a point that nullifies financial success; and as soon as the top salaries in the bureaucracy become greater than the maximum net income from private ownership and management, all the earlier advocates of free enterprise become eager for state ownership and flock into the government, where power and privilege are now concentrated.

Presently, the development of the atomic earthquake bomb, capable of penetrating thirty feet of solid concrete and exploding within the earth, makes it plain that any sort of concentration, even underground, is a military liability. Hence the sporadic dispersal of population, which has been taking place, first of all, with military equipment and personnel, gives way to a large-scale effort, using every resource of government, to decentralize and deconcentrate. Under this dispensation, the advocates of the Linear City come into their own. I will not make the picture too grim: let us assume that people continue, where possible, to live and sleep in houses above ground; but all who can afford the luxury, have provided against 'the day' by purchasing from the government the standard underground shelter, like the week-end cottage of an earlier day; and the rest of the population has bunks assigned in the underground dormitories. Meanwhile, factories, administrative buildings, schools, in fact almost all collective structures are distributed underground, forming underground road-towns, connected by a transcontinental subway system. While in many parts of the country the problem of securing a water supply is readily solved by tapping only underground sources, the likelihood that radioactive materials would be used by an enemy to destroy surface crops and cattle makes it necessary to build up great hydroponic underground farms. Unfortunately the costs are far greater than those of sur-

446

face farming: another item that demands huge subsidies and in turn still higher taxes. With falling productivity in almost every part of the industrial mechanism not connected with atomic warfare or security, the individual standard of living falls, too; and there is a growing tendency among people to desert their posts in the underground collective life in order to scratch for a bare, self-centered, insecure but adventurous living on the surface. That breakdown automatically cuts off the 'new pioneers' as they call themselves from every form of social security and pension, and from protection in case atomic war breaks out. When this movement shows signs of becoming a mass reversion to irresponsible primitive life, the government rounds up and shoots every deserter.

Meanwhile, the Constitution of every country is altered, where necessary, so as to give complete control to the military caste. Included in this caste, also in uniform, also sworn to perpetual secrecy, are the scientists and technicians responsible for atomic production and anti-atomic defense. Even on the highest levels, the means of creating secrecy—the fragmentation of information and knowledge—prevails. The Chief of Staff who is also head of the Central Intelligence Agency and ex officio Dictator—though in the United States still called, by courtesy, President —appoints his own successor; for he has the key by which the jigsaw puzzle of guarded knowledge can be put together. The military caste not only takes over the function of government: it likewise exercises rigorous control over every department of education: at no point can individual initiative or individual opinion be tolerated. By the age of twelve, youths who score high in their aptitude tests are set aside for further training in technological and scientific research along increasingly narrow lines laid down by atomic warfare and its accessory arts. No evasion is possible. Other lines of research are progressively neglected, and, for lack of contact and cross-fertilization of ideas, the quality of research in the physical sciences themselves falls off.

By skillful conditioning, ensured by the centralized control of publication and expression in every form, backed up by constant espionage on conversation, this state of affairs is characterized as freedom, just as the military dictatorship is promoted as the ultimate expression of democracy: one for all and all for one. To make this pill palatable, certain benefits and perquisites are at first bestowed on the mass of workers, who at this stage still have organizations capable of striking; but these privileges are soon canceled out by the actual depletion of real wages and decent living standards, and by the time the workers realize this, they no longer have the means of uniting or even communicating, to register their grievances. Long before this dictatorship is perfected, travel and intercourse between countries has practically disappeared: the police state has become the prison state, and even the jailers do not know what the weather is like on the other side of the prison wall, though many ingenious efforts are made to plant secret agents in other countries.

Because of the all-enveloping quality of the danger, every thought, every action, every plan becomes subservient to the requirements for ABC warfare. Will this fear of a total catastrophe lead to the traditional indifference of the peasants who cultivate their crops on the slopes of Vesuvius? The answer is No, for the peasant's life is free from fear precisely because he continues to do what he always has done, whereas every precaution taken to avert atomic disaster shuts the door to some cherished aspect of normal living and concentrates even the most remote parts of the personality on one theme alone: Fear. The steady increase in atomic destructiveness reaches a point at which everyone realizes that enough potential energy has been stored to destroy all the living spaces of the planet: so as time goes on, the fear becomes more absolute, and—with increased isolation—the prospect of finding a way out diminishes to zero.

These conditions—as unfamiliar to the experience of the race as the atom bomb itself—must lead to grave psychological disruptions. We can posit the familiar forms of these regressive reactions: escape in fantasy would be one: purposeless sexual promiscuity would be another: narcotic indulgence would be a third; but perhaps the most disturbing result of this cutting off of the personality from the normal sources and outlets of development would be the frequent outbreaks of catatonic trances; complete resistance to the demands of outward life. Like Bartleby in Melville's story, such people would in effect say, "I know where I am," and have nothing further to do with life. But if the libido were turned outward instead of inward, paranoiac manifestations would probably be universal: suspicion, hatred, systematic terrorism would break out at every level, followed by rounds of murderous violence. In short, the disorders of personality exhibited by the Nazi elite would not merely become universal: they would, if possible, be magnified, though the worst sadism might sometimes be disguised, as with the Nazis, as responsible scientific experimentation with live subjects.

As tension continues to mount, millions of people working below ground begin to show other signs of chronic psychological maladjustment for which the current psychological conditioners attached to the General Staff have no adequate answer. Rumors of something more lethal than the atom bomb, impervious to every known means of defense, begin to spread through the catacombs and warrens of this civilization. An epidemic of influenza of a new virulent type creates a fresh wave of terror, because it is suspected to be the work of an unseen and unidentifiable enemy. Hitler's real secret weapon, people say, is at last perfected. A 'Let's Die Above Ground' movement begins to spread. Something like a collective attack of claustrophobia breaks out in more than one country almost simultaneously: workers drop their tools and roam around the surface in predatory bands. The very troops who are brought to the surface to combat this subversive movement in more than one case become the victims. Still, no country as yet dares make a wholesale atomic attack. Peace reigns: the rigid peace of death.

On the Fourth Assumption, not a single life has been lost in atomic warfare; nevertheless death has spread everywhere in the morbid violence of anticipation, and civilization has been almost as fatally destroyed as it would be under the Third Assumption.

For what is civilization? Civilization is the process whereby a part of mankind threw off the limitations of a rigid, static, tribal society, increased the range of human cooperation, communication, and communion, and created common instruments for the continued development of the personality and the community. The basis of civilization lies in the fact that energies that were once devoted almost exclusively to physical survival eventually reached a point at which an increasing part of them could be devoted to man's higher functions. Instead of submitting to brute necessity, man altered his environment, he remolded his own patterns of living, he created goods and values, purposes and meanings, in short, a common social heritage that other men could share over ever wider reaches of space and time.

When secrecy, isolation, withdrawal, and preoccupation with mere physical survival dominate in a society, civilization begins to disintegrate: in the end, the capacity to become human is arrested, if it does not actually disappear, because the very meaning of human life lies in the fulfillment of values and purposes that issue out of past continuities and are directed toward an ever-developing future. Otherwise, the social order becomes a prison and existence therein is punishment for life. That is why the Fourth Assumption turns out, in some ways, to be the most horrible of all; nothing less than the living death of humanity. —From 'In the Name of Sanity.' 1954. *First published in Air Affairs, March 1947.*

. . . About my Atomic Energy lecture at the National War College. Probably I was so awed by the super-confidential envelopes I received from them when they sent a transcript of my unwritten speech that I didn't tell you half enough about what I said. I did *not* advocate industrial and urban decentralization as a palliative in atomic war: I never have said that and never will. But I pointed out that the future during the next ten years was highly uncertain from a military point of view; and that if there was not enough mutual trust and cooperation among the nations to achieve World Government, almost anything might happen, and the Armed Forces ought to be ready for that X. If they over-prepared for atomic war, Russia might dump troops by parachute and ship on our West Coast, and we would have nothing to come back at them with, without annihilating our own people. Whatever preparations you make, I said, should be such that they would still make sense even if we shook hands with Russia next year. Then I quoted you to show the extent of our need for new housing, and urged the Army to use what influence they may have now to see that the housing is put in the right places, instead of piling up the risks in big cities, the natural targets for a limited aerial attack. . . . F. J. Osborn, who later saw some of the War College people, reported that they had been stirred up by my argument. If I surprised you by invoking the Army in my last letter to you, it was perhaps because they seemed so much more rational and businesslike in their attitude than the timid tabbies who have been governing the housing and planning movement.   —Letter to Catherine Bauer Wurster. December 15, 1947

THE PERVERSIONS OF POWER.   By bitter experience we should know now that a gross enlargement of power may present man with temptations that did not plague him when he was strictly subservient to Nature: indeed, all previous concentrations of power, even in the relatively small amounts that have been placed in the hands of individual despots and emperors, show that the human soul is subject to special strains and temptations when man oversteps nature's restrictions and breaks through his own traditional curbs. Under such conditions, so far from man's becoming godlike, it is with great difficulty only that he keeps from reverting to the bestial and satanic. Typically, the end of the mighty Nebuchadnezzar was both a moral and a mental breakdown.

Dostoevski placed his fingers on this perversion in his 'Notes from the Underground.' His narrator in those letters points out that Cleopatra loved to thrust golden pins into the breasts of her slaves and took pleasure in the cries of her victims; and, granting the existence of a mechanical world in which science has ordered all things and reduced life, apparently, to a simple mathematical equation, he asks: "Is there anything which dullness might not lead men to devise? For instance, out of sheer boredom, golden pins may again be inserted into a victim's breast." Can anyone who has followed the reports of the German extermination camps say that Dostoevski's insight was not profound? As for the increase of man's physical power to cosmic dimensions in our own time, this threatens both to magnify man's insolent pride and to increase the scale of his destructiveness in relation to his own species. —From an unpublished lecture series at the Pacific School of Religion, 1948

The other night we had a colloquium at M.I.T. in which I took part, along with Norbert Wiener, another physicist, Bernard Feld, and a complacent fathead who was the chairman. The subject was 'A Moratorium on Technology'; and it turned out that Wiener, viewing with alarm his own cybernetic monsters, who now threaten to know more than the people who control them, and may take things into their own hands, is just as alarmed at the compulsive productivity of our scientific technology as I am—though because of his original part in developing electronic 'brains,' he tended to steer the whole discussion into that alley alone. "The more intelligent we make our computers," he exclaimed, "the less subservient they will be, and the more independent will their actions be of our own wishes." —RN. December 11, 1959

NOTES FOR A LECTURE AT LEVERETT HOUSE. The world of 1914 summed up in the title of three books: 'The Age of Innocence': 'The Age of Confidence': 'The Century of Hope.' *Innocence:* evil in all its forms, war, arbitrary power, random violence, torture—gone forever. *Confidence:* There is no problem that human reason, aided by science, could not solve. *Hope:* Progress is now continuous and inevitable, in laws and institutions as well as technics. The new is by definition better. When Fascism claimed to be the Wave of the Future, this faith in the religion of progress tricked many pious souls.

My problem is to explain how the world of 1914 became the world of today, whose leaders have proved by their plans and their actions that they have seen nothing, understood nothing, learned nothing, and repented of nothing; and who now interpret 'progress' as license to commit on a planetary scale all the collective errors and sins and crimes of their historic predecessors. The shock experienced by our age is summed up in the life and work of H. G. Wells: his many hopeful books and essays were based on the assumption of endless scientific and technological progress. But note his underlying anxiety. His writing career opened with a profoundly pessimistic futurist book, 'The Time Machine,' and ended with a senile wail of despair: 'Mind at the End of Its Tether.' So much for the promise of Progress! —RN. Cambridge. 1965

CONCERN OVER FUTURE ENVIRONMENTS. Many of us have become over-sensitive about the disappearance of this or that zoological or botanical species. Yet this in itself is not necessarily an evil. Should we mourn the passing of the hairy mammoth or the saber-toothed tiger? Don't forget that some of our most important food plants have disappeared precisely because they have been domesticated! But there is nonetheless a reason for our overtenderness and apprehension, for we know that *all life is now threatened*. In our concern for the whooping crane we are at once sym-bolizing and furtively concealing a far deeper anxiety—namely the pro-spective extermination of the human species. The public silence on this larger subject is strange, and *our own silence in this conference is even stranger*. We have been gathered for four days and have discussed many things. But has anybody said a word about the fact that the leaders in the Pentagon, if they become even more committed to nuclear strategy than now, may destroy the major habitats on the planet? That we have not said a word about this threat, that we have acted as though it were non-existent, is fantastic. —Closing Statement to conference on Future En-vironments of North America. 1966

The Morals of Collective Extermination

Since 1945, the American government has devoted the better part of our national energies to preparations for wholesale human extermination. This curious enterprise has been disguised as a scientifically sound method of ensuring world peace and national security, but it has ob-viously failed at every point on both counts. Our reckless experimental explosion of nuclear weapons is only a persuasive salesman's sample of what a nuclear war would produce, but even this has already done sig-nificant damage to the human race. With poetic justice, the earliest victims of our experiments toward genocide—sharing honors with the South Pacific islanders and the Japanese fishermen—have been our own children, and even more, our children's prospective children.

Almost from the beginning, our investment in nuclear weapons has been openly directed against a single country, Soviet Russia. In our gov-ernment's concern with the self-imposed problem of containing Russia and restricting by force alone the area of Communist penetration, we have turned our back on more vital human objectives. Today the political and military strategy our leaders framed on the supposition that our country had a permanent superiority in nuclear power is bankrupt, so completely that the business probably cannot be liquidated without seri-ous losses.

This situation should give us pause. While every scientific advance in nuclear weapons and intercontinental missiles only widens to planetary dimensions the catastrophe we have been preparing, our leaders still concentrate the nation's efforts on hastening these advances. Why, then, do we still listen to those mistaken counsels that committed us to the Cold War, though our own military plans have wiped out the possibility of war itself and replaced it by total annihilation as the only foreseeable terminus of the tensions we have done our full share to produce? By what standard of prudence do we trust our lives to political, military, and scientific advisers who have staked our national existence on a single set of weapons and have already lost that shortsighted gamble, whether they become desperate enough to use these weapons or remain blind enough to believe that they can conceal their flagrant misjudgments by not using them? Every day that we delay in facing our national mistakes adds to the difficulty of undoing them.

The first step toward framing a new policy is to trace our path back to the point where we adopted our fatal commitment to weapons of mass extermination. This moral debacle, it is important to remember, was not a response to any threat by Russia or by Communism; still less was it imposed by Russia's possession of similar weapons. Actually, the acceptance of deliberate unrestricted human extermination antedated the invention of the atom bomb.

The principles upon which the strategy of extermination was based were first enunciated by fascist military theorists, notably General Douhet, who believed, like our own Major Seversky, that a small air force could take the place of a large army by confining its efforts to mass attacks on civilians and undermining the national will to resist. This reversion to the vicious Bronze Age practice of total war was a natural extension of fascism's readiness to reintroduce terrorism and torture as instruments of government. When these methods were first carried into action, by Mussolini in Abyssinia, by Hitler in Warsaw and Rotterdam, they awakened horror in our still morally sensitive breasts. The creed that could justify such actions was, we thought correctly, not merely anti-democratic but antihuman.

In the midst of World War Two a moral reversal took place among the English-speaking Allies, such a transposition as happened by accident in the final duel in 'Hamlet,' when Hamlet picks up the weapon Laertes had poisoned in advance in order to make sure of his enemy's death. The fascist powers became the victims of their own strategy, for both the United States and Britain adopted what was politely called "obliteration bombing," which had as its object the total destruction of great cities and the terrorization and massacre of their inhabitants.

By taking over this method as a cheap substitute for conventional warfare—cheap in soldiers' lives, costly in its expenditure of other human lives and in the irreplaceable historic accumulations of countless life-times—these democratic governments sanctioned the dehumanized techniques of fascism. This was Nazidom's firmest victory and democracy's most servile surrender. That moral reversal undermined the eventual military triumph of the democracies, and it has poisoned our political and military policies ever since.

Civilized warfare has always been an atrocity per se, even when practiced by gallant men fighting in a just cause. But in the course of five thousand years certain inhibitions and moral safeguards had been set up. Thus, poisoning the water supply and slaying the unarmed inhabitants of a city were no longer within the modern soldier's code, however gratifying they might once have been to an Ashurbanipal or a Genghis Khan, moral monsters whose names have become infamous in history. Overnight, as it were, our own countrymen became such moral monsters. In principle, the extermination camps where the Nazis incinerated over six million helpless Jews were no different from the urban crematoriums our air force improvised in its attacks by napalm bombs on Tokyo. By these means, in a single night, we roasted alive more people than were killed by atom bombs in either Hiroshima or Nagasaki. Our aims were different, but our methods were those of mankind's worst enemies.

Up to this point, war had been an operation conducted by military forces against military targets. By long-established convention, a token part, the army, stood for the greater whole, the nation. Even when an army was totally defeated and wiped out, the nation it represented lived to tell the tale; neither unarmed prisoners nor civilians were killed to seal a defeat or celebrate a victory. Even our Air Force, the chief shaper of our present policy, once prided itself on its pin-point bombing, done in daylight to ensure that only military targets would be hit.

As late as the spring of 1942, as I know by personal observation, a memorandum was circulated among military advisers in Washington propounding this dilemma: If by fighting the war against Japan by orthodox methods it might require five or ten years to conquer the enemy, while with incendiary air attacks on Japanese cities Japan's resistance might be broken in a year or two, would it be morally justifiable to use the second means? Now it is hard to say which is more astonishing, that the morality of total extermination was then seriously debated in military circles or that today its morality is taken for granted, as outside debate, even among a large part of the clergy.

More than any other event that has taken place in modern times this sudden radical change-over from war to indiscriminate collective extermination reversed the whole course of human history.

Plainly, the acceptance of mass extermination as a normal outcome of war undermined all the moral inhibitions that have kept man's murderous fantasies from active expression. War, however brutal and devastating, had a formal beginning and could come to an end by some formal process of compromise or surrender. But no one has the faintest notion how nuclear extermination, once begun, could be brought to an end. Still less can anyone guess what purpose would be accomplished by it, except a release by death from intolerable anxiety and fear. But this is to anticipate. What is important to bear in mind is that atomic weapons did not bring about this first decisive change; they merely gave our already de-moralized strategy a more effective means of expression.

Once extermination became acceptable, the confined tumor of war, itself an atavistic pseudo-organ, turned into a cancer that would invade the blood stream of civilization. Now the smallest sore of conflict or hostility might fatally spread through the whole organism, immune to all those protective moral and political restraints that a healthy body can mobilize for such occasions.

By the time the atom bomb was invented our authorities needed no special justification for using it. The humane pleas for withholding the weapon, made by the atomic scientists, suddenly awakened to a moral crisis they had not foreseen while working on the bomb, were automatically disposed of by well-established precedent, already three years in operation. Still, the dramatic nature of the explosions at Hiroshima and Nagasaki threw a white light of horror and doubt over the whole process; for a moment a sense of moral guilt counteracted our exorbitant pride. This reaction proved as short-lived as it was belated. Yet it prompted Henry L. Stimson, a public servant whose admirable personal conduct had never been open to question, to publish a magazine article defending the official decision to use the atom bomb.

The argument Mr. Stimson advanced in favor of atomic genocide—a name invented later but studiously reserved for the acts of our enemies—was that it shortened the war and saved perhaps more than a million precious American lives. There is no need here to debate that highly debatable point. But on those same practical, 'humanitarian' grounds, systematic torture might be employed by an advancing army to deter guerrilla fighters and to blackmail the remaining population into accepting promptly the torturer's terms.

That only a handful of people ventured to make this criticism indicates the depth of moral apathy to which our countrymen had sunk in less than a dozen years. Those who used this illustration, however, were not surprised to find that the French, themselves the victims of Hitler's carefully devised plans of torture and mass extermination, would authorize the use of military torture in Algeria a decade later. Our own country had forecast that depravity by our national conduct. This conduct still remains without public examination or repentance, but, unfortunately, retribution may not lie far away. Should it come, Civil Defense estimates have established that it will at once wipe out forty million American lives for the one million we once supposedly saved.

Let us be clear about cause and effect. It was not our nuclear weapons that committed us to the strategy of extermination; it was rather our decision to concentrate on the methods of extermination that led to our one-sided, obsessive preoccupation with A B C weapons. Even before Russia had achieved a single nuclear weapon, we had so dismantled our military establishment that we lacked sufficient equipment and munitions to fight successfully such a minor action as that in Korea.

The nature of our moral breakdown, accurately predicted a half century ago—along with the atom bomb—by Henry Adams, can be gauged by a single fact: most Americans do not realize that this change has taken place or, worse, that it makes any difference. They have no consciousness of either the magnitude of their collective sin or the fact that, by their silence, they have individually condoned it. It is precisely as if the Secretary of Agriculture had licensed the sale of human flesh as a wartime emergency measure and people had taken to cannibalism when the war was over as a clever dodge for lowering the cost of living—a mere extension of everyday butchery. Many of our professed religious and moral leaders have steadily shrunk from touching this subject; or, if they have done so, they have naively equated mass extermination with war and have too often given their blessing to it, for reasons just as specious as those our government has used.

It is in relation to this gigantic moral collapse that our present devotion to nuclear weapons and their equally atrocious bacterial and chemical counterparts must be gauged.

When we abandoned the basic moral restraints against random killing and mass extermination we enlarged the destructive capacities of our nuclear weapons. What was almost as bad, our pride in this achievement expressed itself in an inverted fashion by our identifying our safety and welfare with the one-sided expansion of our weapons system. Thus we surrendered the initiative to our instruments, confusing physical power with rational human purpose, forgetting that machines and weapons have no values and no goals, above all, no limits and no restraints except those that human beings superimpose on them.

The one thing that might have rectified our government's premature exploitation of atomic power would have been a public assize of its manifold dangers, even for wider industrial and medical use. As early as the winter of 1945–1946 the Senate Atomic Energy Committee made the first full inquiry into these matters, and the physicists who appeared before this committee gave forecasts whose accuracy was fully confirmed in the tardy hearings that have just taken place before a joint congressional committee. Almost with one voice, these scientists predicted that Soviet Russia would be able to produce a nuclear bomb within five years, possibly within three. On that basis, the nations of the world had three 'safe' years to create through the United Nations the necessary political and moral safeguards against the misuse of this new power.

There was no salvation, the more alert leaders of science wisely pointed out, on purely national terms. Naturally, Russia's totalitarian isolationism and suspicion made it difficult to arrive at a basis for rational agreement, but our own sense of holding all the trump cards did not lessen this difficulty. All too quickly, after the Russian rejection of our 'generous' but politically inept Baruch proposals, our country used Russian hostility as an excuse for abandoning all further effort. Even before we had openly committed ourselves to the Cold War itself—a now obsolete pre-atomic military concept—our leaders preferred to build a threatening ring of air bases around Russia rather than to pursue with patient circumspection a course directed toward securing eventual understanding and cooperation. So the difficult became the impossible.

As late as 1947 the situation, though grave, was not yet disastrous. Our very mistakes in turning to mass extermination were capable, if openly and honestly faced, of leading both ourselves and the world back to the right path. Up to then, our totalitarian weapons system had not yet consolidated its position or threatened our free institutions; the organs of democratic society, invigorated rather than depressed by the war, had not yet been enfeebled by official secrecy, repression, suspicion, craven conformism, or the corruptions of absolute power, shielded from public criticism. Meanwhile, unfortunately, the strategy of mass extermination, which did not bear public discussion or open assessment, was rapidly taking shape.

For a brief moment, nevertheless, our leaders had seized the moral initiative, though they were handicapped by ambivalent intentions and contradictory goals. Our contribution to organizing the United Nations, though it had been originally proposed by the United States, was as cagey and inept as Russia's, for the frustrating Council veto was an American conception. Under a more imaginative leadership two other, admirable American proposals came forward, UNRRA and the Marshall Plan. Both these agencies had great potentialities, for at first we had the intelligence to offer their benefits even to Communist countries.

Had we followed these efforts through, they might have permanently increased the whole range of international cooperation. In wiser executive hands, these initiatives would not have been prematurely terminated. Rather, they would have been employed to reduce world tensions and to win general assent to a program for giving all nations the prefatory exercises in magnanimity and understanding essential to the re-establishment of moral order and the control of our demoralizing weapons. But even in their brief, limited application these agencies did far more to fortify the assisted nations against oppressive Communist dictatorship than all the billions we poured into NATO and SEATO to build up futile armaments for wars neither we nor our allies were capable of fighting. Witness our long series of backdowns and letdowns: Czechoslovakia, Korea, Vietnam, Poland, East Germany, Hungary, Egypt.

In our commitment to the strategy of extermination, under a decision made when General Eisenhower was Chief of Staff, the United States rejected the timely warnings of the world's leading scientists and the common counsels of humanity. Instead of holding a series of world conferences in which the dangers of nuclear energy could be fully canvassed, not alone by physicists but by thinkers in every threatened field, our official agencies deliberately played down these dangers and used every available mode of censorship to restrict the circulation of the knowledge needed for such an appraisal. In this obstinate desire to exploit nuclear power solely for our national advantage, our government relied upon insistent publicity and indoctrination to build up a false sense of security. Instead of regaining our moral position by ceasing the reckless experiments whose mounting pollution justified a world-wide apprehension, we flatly denied the need for any such cessation and allowed Russia, after it had come abreast of us, to take the moral lead here. Even at a recent United Nations conference, which clearly demonstrated the dangers, our own representatives helped vote down the Russian preamble to the conclusions of the conference, which called for a cessation of all further nuclear testing.

To explain this obstinate commitment to the infamous policy of mass extermination one must understand that its side reactions have proved as demoralizing as its central purpose. Within a bare decade, the United States has built up a huge vested interest in mass extermination—in the weapons themselves and in the highly profitable manufacture of electronic equipment, planes, and missiles designed to carry them to their destination. There are tens of thousands of individual scientists and technicians engaged in nuclear, bacteriological, and chemical research to increase the range and effectiveness of these lethal agents, though we boast we already have a stockpile of nuclear weapons capable of wiping out the entire planet. There are also corporate bodies—the Air Force, the Atomic Energy Commission, the Central Intelligence Agency, not least great industrial corporations and extravagantly endowed centers of research—whose powers and presumptions have been constantly widened along with their profit and prestige. While the show lasts, their careers depend on our accepting the fallacious assumptions to which they have committed us.

All these agents now operate in secret totalitarian enclaves, perfecting their secret totalitarian weapons, functioning outside the processes of democratic government, immune to public challenge and criticism or to public correction. Whatever the scientific or technical competence of the men working in this field, their sedulous restriction of interest and the limited conditions under which they work and have contact with other human beings do not foster sober wisdom in the conduct of life. By scientific conviction and vocational commitment they live in an under-dimensioned and distorted world. The sum of their combined judgments is still an unbalanced judgment, for moral criteria have, from the start, been left out of their general directives. Some have even used their authority as scientists to give pseudo-scientific assurances about biological defects that no one will be able to verify until half a century has passed. Furthermore, in matters falling within their province of exact knowledge, the judgment of these authorities has repeatedly proved erroneous and mischievous.

All this should not surprise us: neither science nor nuclear energy endows its users with super-human wisdom. But what should surprise us is the fact that the American nation has entrusted its welfare, safety, and future existence to these imprudent, fallible minds and to those who have sanctioned their de-moralized plans. Under the guise of a calculated risk, our nuclear strategists have prepared to bring on a calculated catastrophe. At some unpredictable moment their sick fantasies may become unspeakable realities.

Even now our experimental explosion of nuclear bombs, at a rate of more than two for Russia's one, has poisoned our babies' milk, upset the delicate ecological balance of nature, and, still worse, defiled our genetic heritage. As for the possibility that nuclear weapons will never be used, our children in school know better than this every time they are put through the sadistic mummery of an air-raid drill and learn to 'play disaster.' Such baths of fear and hostility are gratuitous assaults against the young, whose psychological damage is already incalculable; their only service is to bar more tightly the exits that would permit a real escape.

There are people who would defend these plans on the grounds that it is better to die nobly, defending democracy and freedom, than to survive under Communist oppression. Such apologists perhaps exaggerate the differences that still exist between our two systems, but they err even more seriously in applying to mass extermination a moral standard that was defensible only as long as this death was a symbolic one confined to a restricted number of people on a small portion of the earth. Such a disaster, as in the bitter-end resistance of the Southern Confederacy in the Civil War, was still relatively minor and temporary. If the original resolve to die were in fact an erroneous one, in a few generations it could be corrected. Nuclear damage, in contrast, is cumulative and irretrievable; it admits no belated confession of error, no repentance and absolution.

Under what canon of sanity, then, can any government, or any generation, with its limited perspectives, its fallible judgment, its obvious proneness to self-deception, delusion, and error, make a decision for all future ages about the very existence of even a single country? Still more, how can any one nation or sovereign state treat as a purely private right its decision on a matter that will gravely affect the life and health and continued existence of the rest of mankind?

There are no words to describe the magnitude of such insolence in thought or the magnitude of criminality involved in carrying it out. Those who believe that any country has the right to make such a decision share the madness of Captain Ahab in 'Moby-Dick.' For them Russia is the White Whale that must be hunted down and grappled with. Like Ahab in that mad pursuit, they will listen to no reminders of love, home, family obligation; in order to kill the object of their fear and hate they are ready to throw away the sextant and compass that might give them back their moral direction, and in the end they will sink their own ship and drown their crew. To such unbalanced men, to such demoralized efforts, to such dehumanized purposes, the Nuclear Powers have entrusted our lives and the very survival of mankind. To accept their plans and ensuing decisions, our own countrymen have deliberately anesthetized the normal feelings, emotions, anxieties, and hopes that could alone bring us to our senses.
—The Morals of Extermination. Atlantic Monthly. October 1959

. . . Probably the most difficult thing, dear Catherine, about coping with the problems of our Age is that it is next to impossible to convince healthy people like yourself that there is anything fundamentally the matter with our 'normal' habits and institutions. The desperately sick and the neurotic might come flocking to my banner all too easily, on the same terms that they would follow any charlatan who recognized their state and promised some sort of remedy for it. Now the healthy people, even in a time as bad as this, still constitute a great majority; and it is these healthy people I am after.

I remember my own reactions more than twenty years ago, when Spingarn told me: "Mumford, you think your liberal and progressive world is going to last forever; but mark my words: you'll see the time when tyranny and torture and slavery are revived in this world." I said to myself, "Poor man, he's sick and everything he looks at reflects his sickness." I was right in my diagnosis of my friend: he *was* sick. But he was right, too, as it turned out; because his sickness made him sensitive to phenomena that I, at the time, was too healthy either to notice or correctly interpret. —To Catherine Bauer Wurster. January 17, 1950

OPEN LETTER TO PRESIDENT LYNDON JOHNSON. The time has come for someone to speak out on behalf of the great body of your countrymen who regard with abhorrence the course to which you are committing the United States in Vietnam. As a holder of the Presidential Medal of Freedom, I have a duty to say plainly, and in public, what millions of patriotic fellow citizens are saying in the privacy of their homes. Namely, that the course you are now following affronts both our practical judgment and our moral sense.

Neither your manners nor your methods give us any assurance that your policy will lead to a good end: on the contrary, your attempt to cure by military force a situation that has been brought about by our own arrogant, one-sided political assumptions cannot have any final destination short of an irremediable nuclear catastrophe. That would constitute the terminal illness of our whole civilization, and your own people, no less than the Vietnamese and the Communists, would be the helpless victims.

In embarking on this program, you are gambling with your country's future, because you have not the courage to discard a losing hand and start a new deal, though this was the magnificent opportunity that your election presented to you. Your games theorists have persuaded you to play Russian Roulette. But you cannot save the Government's face by blowing out our country's brains.

From the beginning, the presence of American forces in Vietnam, without the authority of the United Nations, was in defiance of our own solemn commitment when we helped to form that body. Our steady involvement with the military dictators who are waging civil war in South

Vietnam, with our extravagant financial support and underhanded military cooperation, is as indefensible as our Government's original refusal to permit a popular election to be held in Vietnam, lest communism should be installed by popular vote. Your attempt now to pin the whole blame on the government of North Vietnam deceives no one except those whose wishful thinking originally committed us to our high-handed intervention: the same set of agencies and intelligences that inveigled us into the Bay of Pigs disaster.

Instead of using your well-known political adroitness to rescue our country from the military miscalculations and political blunders that created our impossible position in Vietnam, you now, casting all caution to the winds, propose to increase the area of senseless destruction and extermination, without having any other visible ends in view than to conceal our political impotence. In taking this unreasonable course, you not merely show a lack of "decent respect for the opinions of mankind," but you likewise mock and betray all our country's humane traditions.

This betrayal is all the more sinister because you are now, it is plain, obstinately committing us to the very military policy that your countrymen rejected when they so overwhelmingly defeated the Republican candidate.

Before you go further, let us tell you clearly: your professed aims are emptied of meaning by your totalitarian tactics and your nihilistic strategy. We are shamed by your actions, and revolted by your dishonest excuses and pretexts. What is worse, we are horrified by the immediate prospect of having our country's fate in the hands of leaders who, time and again, have shown their inability to think straight, to correct their errors, or to get out of a bad situation without creating a worse one.

The Government has forfeited our confidence; and we will oppose, with every means available within the law, the execution of this impractical, and above all, morally indefensible policy. There is only one way in which you can remove our opposition or regain our confidence; and that is to turn back from the course you have taken and to seek a human way out. —San Francisco Chronicle and St. Louis Post-Dispatch. March 3, 1965

Address on the Vietnam Holocaust

On behalf of the American Academy of Arts and Letters, and its parent body, the National Institute of Arts and Letters, I once more bid you welcome to our annual spring ceremonial. Traditionally this ceremony, with its bestowal of honors, prizes, and awards, has an air as festive as the spring itself. And since this is the last year I shall have the honor to serve the Academy as President, I have a special reason for desiring that this occasion should not be marred by any somber or discordant notes.

But, as the ancient Greeks well knew, one cannot escape the grim Fates or the evil Furies when they are pursuing a man or a people. And I cannot artificially manufacture an atmosphere of joy for this meeting, when under the surface of our ritual a rising tide of public shame and private anger speaks louder than my words, as we contemplate the moral outrages to which our government, with increasing abandon, has committed our country.

Last year, when we met here, the pain of an unhealed grief, occasioned by the assassination of President Kennedy, still gnawed at our hearts. And this year an equally ominous black cloud, also the symbol of unpredictable and irrational violence, hangs over our own land and people, even as it hangs over the peoples of Vietnam and the rest of Asia, threatening the lives and prospects of our own younger generation, staining the good name of our country, and violating the peace of the world.

Now, on such grave national issues, institutions like ours have no special license to express an opinion, even if we had any mechanism for formulating a common judgment and recording our reasoned convictions. So, in what I say to you now, I speak on my own initiative alone, without consulting a single other member, addressing you and my colleagues not as President of the American Academy of Arts and Letters, but as a private citizen, appealing to our common love for our country and our concern to keep alive the traditions of democratic responsibility that are threatened by the high governmental agencies whose patently erroneous judgments are now magnified by a panicky commitment to even grosser errors of policy and strategy.

I would gladly remain silent, if one could do so and maintain one's self-respect, and keep faith with the generations that are still to come. But those of us who are devoted to the pursuit of the arts and humane letters, have a duty to oppose any assault upon those basic moralities that alone have preserved mankind's common heritage from the aggressive egoism and the presumptuous national claims that so often undermine the prudence and common sense of those who exercise political authority. And we have a special duty to speak out openly in protest on every occasion when human beings are threatened by arbitrary power: not only as with the oppressed Negroes in Alabama and Mississippi, but the peoples of both North and South Vietnam who must now confront our government's cold-blooded blackmail and calculated violence.

463

At this moment I would be untrue to the best traditions of our country, the proud home of a Jefferson, an Emerson, a Thoreau, a William James, if I remained discreetly silent and encouraged you, too, to close your eyes and your ears to the realities we must now face. To find a proper setting for the moral issues before us, I go back to the words that Emerson uttered more than a century ago, in the Ode inscribed to W. H. Channing; and I quote:

> But who is he that prates
> Of the culture of Mankind,
> Of better arts and life?
> Go, blindworm, go:
> Behold the famous States
> Harrying Mexico
> With rifle and knife.

Even while I was speaking the last three lines, many of you must have been mentally bringing them up to date by saying to yourselves:

> Behold the famous States
> Harrying Vietnam
> With poison gas and napalm bombs.

All our government's unctuous professions of reasonableness and peacefulness and restraint have been undermined by the incontinent actions it has taken, and by its constantly repeated threats to widen the scope of its destruction and extermination unless its conditions are met.

The abject failure to date of both the political and the military policy we have been pursuing in Vietnam is only a first installment of humiliations and human losses that now loom ahead of us, as long as the government stubbornly holds fast to the invalid premises upon which it has been acting. By what legal or moral code has the United States a right to exercise political authority or military coercion in a distant foreign country like Vietnam? Obviously we have no more reason to have our will prevail in Vietnam than Soviet Russia had to establish rocket bases in Cuba; and if Russia could liquidate that blunder and withdraw under pressure, our own country can do the same in Vietnam—and all the better if the pressure come, not from an outside power, but from our own citizens.

The United States, even if it were governed by wiser minds than those who have fabricated our present policy, cannot be and never can become a self-appointed substitute for the United Nations. In the very act of asserting such high-handed power, the United States has done more to rehabilitate totalitarianism and to corrupt responsible democratic government, than the whole communist movement—which has recently showed happy signs of disintegration—could hope to achieve by its own efforts.

The flagrant absurdity of the official American position can be easily demonstrated by applying Immanuel Kant's criterion for judging the effect of a proposed action by asking what would follow were it taken by everyone as a universal rule. What would happen, indeed, to human intercourse at every level if each political creed, each religion, each nation, each government, acted as if its word alone were law, not merely within its own sovereign territory, but in every country that was small enough to be bullied, and sufficiently weak and friendless to be threatened with ultimate extermination without fear of our provoking equally decisive retaliation? This behavior does not exhibit the "decent respect for the opinions of mankind" that our forefathers showed when they founded this country. To behave in this fashion is to build a cell of moral isolation: hated and shunned by all self-respecting peoples.

Twenty years ago, our country reached the height of its authority and influence by generous acts of succor to the starving, war-torn countries of the world. In helping to create the United Nations, in fostering the great UNRRA organization which fed and clothed our neighbors in Europe and Asia, finally in carrying out that most imaginative of all national acts, the Marshall Plan, whose economic aid we had the wisdom at the beginning to offer even to the communist countries, the United States laid the foundations for a United World. Ours was then an authority and a power that no other nation had ever before earned or exercised. Yes: that was, internationally speaking, our finest hour.

Instead of building on that massive foundation of good will, foolish men allowed the invention and exploitation of nuclear weapons to foment delusions of grandeur based on their supposedly absolute power; and as a result of our growing preoccupation with this kind of power a vast network of secret agencies, armed with secret weapons, prepared with secret plans, have committed our country to a strategy and a policy whose dehumanizing effects, though visible from the beginning, are now being nakedly exposed. As a result, from the heights of effective power that our country had achieved, by evoking the admiration and gratitude and even love of other nations, we have now descended to the depths of political and military impotence; and still more sinister depths of demoralization already yawn beneath us.

The whole world has reason to fear such leadership and unite against it; and our own citizens have perhaps even more to fear, for this is the first time in our history that a victorious presidential candidate has dared to carry out the odious policy that caused his rival to be rejected. One may well question the value of a democratic election when confronted by such a totalitarian outcome.

Our plight today is all the more grievous because it is so unexpected, and because it finds us too stunned to react against it with all our force. President Johnson, indeed, by courageously reversing his earlier position on Civil Rights, gave us reason to hope that he would show equal strength and moral fiber in extricating our country from the sticky spider-web of political illusions and military miscalculations that originally had entangled us, so arbitrarily, in Vietnam. In his handling of the Civil Rights issue, we had reason to be proud of a President who showed the very qualities of passionate moral conviction and statesmanlike command of the means that the extravagant Vietnam fiasco demanded for its rectification. Were the President miraculously to undergo a similar conversion in international affairs to the way of justice, mercy, pity, and peace, he could—even at this dismally late moment—halt the escalation of error and terror to which he has obstinately committed our country. One magnificent act of human decency on the part of our elected leader—without threats or bribes—confessing the government's errors and renouncing any one-sided achievement of our aims, would make it possible to find a human way out. And there is no other exit than a human one from the present situation.

Such, ladies and gentlemen, is the grave threat that hangs over our country today: such has been the moral betrayal our more humane traditions have suffered: such are the dark forces that threaten all of us who seek, in Emerson's words, to promote the culture of mankind through the "better arts of life." Unless each one of us now seizes every possible occasion to speak out, the barricaded minds in the Pentagon and the White House may take our silence for consent, as the other nations of the world will take that silence for cowardice and self-betrayal, if not total democratic corruption.

In conclusion, I find myself turning once more to those closing lines in Shakespeare's 'King Lear': lines that haunt me and yet fortify me, with their sinister illumination of all that those of us who have lived through this last half century of war, terror, starvation, and extermination must feel, even though our own lives, by some accident, may have had more than their share of happy fulfillments. These lines should awaken, above all, our tenderest forebodings over the fate of the young, who in Shakespeare's words, may "never see so much or live so long." In departing from the natural order of this Academy ritual and the natural affabilities that go with it, I have honored those final words in Lear:

> The weight of this sad time we must obey:
> Speak what we feel, not what we ought to say.

Had I said less, I should have been false to my vocation as a writer and my duties as a citizen. —Address as President of the American Academy of Arts and Letters. May 19, 1965

25: The Human Heritage

At an early stage in my studies on the relationship between technics and social change, I found that I could not understand many contemporary institutions and activities without tracing them back to what often proved very remote, sometimes prehistoric, events. Unfortunately much of our thinking today in technocratic circles is being done by one-generation minds bedazzled over our immediate successes with nuclear energy, moon-shots, and computers—however isolated these feats are from the total historic culture that made them possible, and from man's many non-technological needs, projects, and aspirations which give meaning and value to the whole process.

Naturally those who think this way do not thank me for pointing out that their so-called Industrial Revolution did not begin in the eighteenth century; that on the contrary the 'new wave' in Western technology began as far back as the eleventh century; and that the invention of the mechanical clock in the fourteenth century did far more to advance modern science and technics than the steam engine or the automatic loom. For the clock, on its very face, unified our whole conception of time, space, and motion, and laid the foundation in its exact measurements by standard units for the astronomical-mechanical world picture that still dominates our minds and our daily activities.

Despite later reinforcements from scholars like Bertrand Gille, Georges Friedmann, Fernand Braudel, and Leroi-Gourhan this revision of the standard technological scenario has not yet been widely accepted. So it would be presumptuous on my part to look for a more favorable immediate reception for the even more radical revisions I shall proceed to summarize. For I propose to widen the historical perspective suf-

468

ficiently to present a more adequate picture of the relationship between technological progress and social change and human development. Instead of celebrating the further expansion and acceleration of post-eighteenth century technology, on the lines which have ultimately led to the power system that now governs our lives, I shall endeavor to restore a more life-favoring ecological and cultural equilibrium. And so, far from taking the conquest of nature and the elimination of any recognizable form of man as the inevitable consequence of technological progress, I question both the value of this one-sided conquest itself and its inevitability. Not least, I seek to expose the irrational factors that have led modern man to forfeit those essential expressions of human creativity that do not conform to the unlimited quantitative requirements and inordinate pecuniary ambitions of the dominant power complex.

The Primacy of Mind

My point of departure in analyzing technology, social change and human development, concerns the nature of man. And to begin with I reject the lingering anthropological notion, first suggested by Benjamin Franklin and Thomas Carlyle, that man can be identified, mainly if not solely, as a tool-using or tool-making animal: *Homo faber.* Even Henri Bergson, a philosopher whose insights into organic change I respect, so described him. Of course man is a tool-making, utensil-shaping, machine-fabricating, environment-prospecting, technologically ingenious animal—at least that! But man is also—and quite as fundamentally—a dream-haunted, ritual-enacting, symbol-creating, speech-uttering, language-elaborating, self-organizing, institution-conserving, myth-driven, love-making, god-seeking being, and his technical achievements would have remained stunted if all these other autonomous attributes had not been highly developed. Man himself, not his extraneous technological facilities, is the central fact. Contrary to Mesopotamian legend, the gods did not invent man simply to take over the unwelcome load of disagreeable servile labor.

Man's chief technological inventions are embedded in the original human organism, from standardization to automation and cybernation: automatic systems, indeed, so far from being a modern discovery, are perhaps the oldest of nature's devices, for the selective responses of the hormones, the endocrines, and the reflexes antedated by millions of years that super-computer we call the forebrain, or neopallium. Yet anything that can be called *human* culture has demanded certain specific technical traits: specialization, standardization, repetitive practice; and it was early man's positive enjoyment of playful repetition, a trait still shown by very young children, as every parent knows, that underlay every other great cultural invention, above all spoken language. This utilization and development of the organism as a whole, not just the employment of man's limbs and hands as facile tools or tool-shapers, is what accounts for the extraordinary advances of *Homo sapiens*. In making these first technological innovations man made no attempt to modify his environment, still less to conquer Nature: for the only environment over which he could exercise effective command, without extraneous tools, was that which lay nearest him: his own body, operating under the direction of his highly activated brain, busy by night in dreams as well as by day in seeking food, coping with danger, or finding shelter.

On this reading, before man could take even the first timid steps toward 'conquering nature,' he first had the job of discovering, controlling and utilizing more effectively his own organic capacities. By his studious exploration and reconstruction of his bodily functions he opened up a wide range of possibilities not programmed, as with other animals, in his genes. Strangely, it took André Varagnac, a French interpreter of the archaic folk remains of neolithic culture, to point out only recently that the earliest mode of a specifically human technology was almost certainly the technology of the body. This consisted in the deliberate remodelling of man's organs by enlarging their capacity for symbolic expression and communal intercourse. Most significantly, the only organ that continued to increase in size and weight was the brain. By this close attention to his body, even primitive man at a very early moment placed his automatic functions under some measure of cerebral intervention: the first step in conscious self-organization, rational direction, and moral control. The mind of man is his own supreme artifact. And out of his most highly developed organ, the brain, all his specifically human artifacts, beginning with words, images and graphs, have emerged.

Long before man had given stone tools the form of even the crudest hand-axe, he had already achieved an advanced technology of the body. These basic technical achievements started with infant training; and they involved not only repetition, but foresight, feedback, and attentive learning: learning to walk, learning to control the excretory functions, learning to make standardized gestures and sounds, whose recognition and remembrance by other members of the group gave continuity to the whole human heritage. Not least man learned to distinguish to some degree between his private subconscious dreams and his shared waking realities;

470

and as the forebrain exercised more authority he learned, likewise in the interest of group survival, to curb his blind destructive impulses, to diminish overpowering rage and fear, to inhibit demented fantasies and murderous aggressions, and to superimpose social responsibility, moral sensibility and esthetic delight upon random sexuality. Unless man had mastered fear sufficiently to be able to play with fire—a feat no other animal has dared to perform—he would have lacked one of the essential requirements for the survival and spread of his species, since fire enormously increased the number of foods and habitats available for both paleolithic and neolithic man.

The point I am stressing here is that every form of technics has its seat in the human organism; and without man's many artful subjective contributions, the brute materials and energies of the existing physical world would have contributed nothing whatever to technology. So it was through the general culture of body and mind, not just through tool-making and tool-using, that not only man's intelligence but other equally valuable capacities developed. Almost down to the present century, all technical operations took place within his organic and human matrix. Only the most degraded forms of work, like mining, which was reserved for slaves and deliberately treated as punishment, lacked these happy educative qualities. Today at last we are beginning to measure the loss we face through our present efforts to remodel the human organism and the human community to conform to the external controls and objectives imposed automatically by the power system.

This leads me to a second departure from technocratic orthodoxy. How is it that modern man since the seventeenth century has made technology the emotive center of his life? Why has the Pentagon of Power, dominated by the conception of constant technological progress and endless pecuniary gain, taken command of every other human activity? At what point did the belief in such technological progress, as a good in itself, replace all other conceptions of a desirable human destiny? To answer this question I have had to trace this power-bent aberration back five thousand years to its point of origin in the Pyramid Age. But first I would call attention to its modern expression in a sign that once greeted the visitor at the entrance of a World's Fair celebrating "A Century of Progress." That sign said "Science discovers: Technology executes: Man conforms."

Man conforms indeed! Where did that strange categorical imperative come from? How is it that man, who never in his personal development conformed submissively to the conditions laid down by Nature, now feels obliged at the height of his powers to surrender unconditionally to his

471

own technology? I do not question the fact itself. During the last two centuries a power-centered technics has taken command of one activity after another. By now a large sector of the population of the planet feels uneasy, deprived and neglected—indeed cut off from 'reality'—unless it is securely attached to some part of the megamachine: to an assembly line, a conveyor belt, a motor car, a radio or a television station, a computer, or a space capsule. To confirm this attachment and make universal this dependence, every autonomous activity, once located mainly in the human organism or in the social group, has either been wiped out of existence or reshaped by training and indoctrination and corporate organization to conform to the requirements of the megamachine. Is it not strange that our technocratic masters recognize no significant life processes or human ends except those that further the expansion of their authority and their magical prerogatives?

Thus the condition of man today, I have suggested in 'The Pentagon of Power,' resembles the pathetic state of Dr. Bruno Bettelheim's psychiatric patient: a little boy of nine who conceived that he was run by machines. "So controlling was this belief," Dr. Bettelheim reports, that the pathetic child "carried with him an elaborate life-support system made up of radio, tubes, light bulbs, and a breathing machine. At meals he ran imaginary wires from a wall socket to himself, so his food could be digested. His bed was rigged with batteries, a loud speaker, and other improvised equipment to keep him alive while he slept."

The fantasy of this autistic little boy is the state that modern man is fast approaching in actual life, without as yet realizing how pathological it is to be cut off from his own innate resources for living, and to feel no reassuring tie with the natural world or his own fellows unless he is connected to the power system, or with some actual machine, constantly receiving information, direction, stimulation, and sedation from a central external source, with only a minimal opportunity for self-motivated and self-directed activity.

Technocratic man is no longer at home with life, or with the environment of life; which means that he is no longer at home with himself. He has become, to paraphrase A. E. Housman, "a stranger and afraid" in a world his own technology has made. But in view of the fact that during the last century our insight into the organic world has been immensely deepened, indeed revolutionized by the biological sciences, why do we still take the Newtonian 'machine' instead of the Darwinian 'organism' as our model, and pay more respect to the computer than to the immense historical store of knowledge and culture that made its invention possible?

472

Since my own analysis of technology begins, not with the abstract physical phenomena of mass and motion, but with organisms, living societies, and human reactions, I do not regard such conformity as anything more than an institutionalized mental derangement, one of many errors that the human race has committed while straining to improve its condition and to make use of powers and functions it does not even now fully understand. Within the framework of history and ecology one discovers a quite different picture of Nature, and a more hopeful view of man's own countless unexplored potentialities. Biology teaches us that man is part of an immense cosmic and ecological complex, in which power alone, whether exhibited as energy or productivity or human control, plays necessarily a subordinate and sometimes inimical part, as in tornadoes and earthquakes. This organic complex is indescribably rich, varied, many-dimensioned, self-activating; for every organism, by its very nature, is the focal point of autonomous changes and external transformations that began in the distant past and will outlive the narrow lifespan of any individual, group, or culture. What is now accepted and even exalted as 'instant culture'—the beliefs and practices of a single generation—is in reality a blackout of collective memory, similar to what takes place under certain drugs. This bears no resemblance at all to any recorded human culture, since without some of paleolithic man's basic inventions, above all language and graphic abstractions, even the latest scientific discoveries of this one-generation culture could not be kept in mind long enough to be described, understood, or continued beyond their own ephemeral lifetime.

On this interpretation the most important goal for technology is not to extend further the province of the machine, not to accelerate the transformation of scientific discoveries into profit-making inventions, not to increase the output of kaleidoscopic technological novelties and dictatorial fashions; not to put all human activities under the surveillance and control of the computer—in short, not to rivet together the still separate parts of the planetary megamachine, so that there will be no possibility of escaping it. No: the essential task for all human agencies today, and not least for technology itself, is to bring back the autonomous attributes of life to a culture that, without them, will not be able to survive the destructive and irrational forces that its original mechanical achievements generated. If our main problem today turns out to be that of controlling technological irrationalism, it should be obvious that no answer can come from technology alone. The old Roman question—Who shall control the controller?—has now come back to us in a new and more difficult form. For what if the controllers, too, have become irrational?

Invention of the Megamachine

What then was the origin of the Victorian notion that science and technology, if sufficiently developed, would replace or happily demolish all the earlier phases of human culture? Why did 'progressive' but still 'human' minds, from the eighteenth century on, think that it was possible and desirable—indeed imperative—to wipe out every trace of the past, and thus to replace an organic culture, full of active ingredients derived from many ancient natural and human sources, by an up-to-date manufactured substitute, devoid of esthetic, ethical, or religious values, or indeed any specific human qualities except those that served the machine? By the middle of the nineteenth century this belief had become a commonplace. Progress meant, not humanization, as in the earliest technology of the body, but mechanization; with bodily efforts becoming more and more superfluous until they might either be eliminated, or at best transferred, in a limited way, to sport and play. Was this the inevitable effect of the 'Industrial Revolution'? And, if so, what made seemingly liberated minds embrace so fatalistically the 'inevitability of the inevitable'?

My own generation, I confess, still accepted readily—all too readily —this faith in the redemptive power of science and technology: though not, I hasten to add, with quite the fanatical devoutness of a Buckminster Fuller or a Marshall McLuhan today. So, when I wrote 'Technics and Civilization' more than thirty years ago, I still properly stressed the more beneficent motives and the more sanguine contributions of modern technology; and though I gave due attention to the ecological depredations of the earlier paleotechnic phases, I supposed that these malpractices would be wiped out by the further neotechnic improvements promised by hydroelectric power, scientific planning, industrial decentralization, and the regional city. Still, even in 'Technics and Civilization,' I devoted a long chapter to the negative components which, so far from disappearing, were already becoming more demonic, more threatening, and more insistent.

Some twenty years later, in a seminar I conducted at the Massachusetts Institute of Technology, I critically reviewed this early interpretation, and found that the chapter I had devoted to the negative aspects of modern technology would have to be expanded. While much of the current praise of industrial rationalization was, up to a point, sound, this had been accompanied by a negative factor we had not dared to face—or had mistakenly attributed to Fascism or Communism alone. For during the last half-century, all the concealed symptoms of irrational behavior had suddenly exploded in our faces. This period witnessed not only the unparalleled destruction wrought by two global wars, but the further degeneration of war itself into deliberate genocide, directed not against armies but against the entire population of the enemy country. Within a single generation, less than thirty years, thanks to purely technological advances, from the airplane to napalm and nuclear bombs, all the moral safeguards mankind had erected against random extermination had been broken down. If this was technology's boasted conquest of nature, the chief victim of that conquest, it turned out, was man himself.

With these massive miscarriages of civilization in view, I tentatively put to myself a decade ago a question that I did not ask publicly until I wrote the first volume of 'The Myth of the Machine.' "Is the association of inordinate power and productivity with equally inordinate hostility, violence, and destructiveness, a purely accidental one?" This question was so uncomfortable to entertain, so contrary to the complacent expectations of our technocratic culture, that I cannot pretend that I eagerly searched about for an affirmative answer. But fortunately, at that moment I was making an intensive study of the whole process of urbanization, that which Gordon Childe called the Urban Revolution, as it took place in Egypt and Mesopotamia toward the end of the Fifth Millennium before the Christian era. Digging mentally around those urban ruins, I discovered an extraordinary complex machine which turned out, on analysis, to be the first real machine, and the archetype of all later machines. This artifact had for long remained invisible, because it was composed entirely of highly specialized and mechanized human parts. Only the massive constructive results of its operation remained visible, not the formative ideas and mythical projections that had brought this machine into existence.

What Childe called the Urban Revolution was only an incident in the assemblage of the 'Megamachine,' as I chose to call it. Please note that the superb technological achievements of this gigantic machine owed nothing, at the beginning, to any ordinary mechanical invention: some of its greatest structures, the pyramids of Egypt, were erected without even the aid of a wheeled wagon or a pulley or a derrick. What brought the megamachine into existence was not an ordinary invention but an awesome expansion of the human mind in many different areas: a transformation comparable only to that which took place when in a far more distant past the structure of language and abstract signs had advanced sufficiently to identify, interpret, communicate, and pass on to later generations every part of a community's experience.

The decisive tools that made this machine possible were likewise inventions of the mind: astronomical observation and mathematical notation, the art of the carved and the written record, the religious concept of a universal order derived from close observation of the heavens and giving authority—the authority of the Gods—to a single commanding figure, the king, he who had once been merely a hunting chief. At this point the notion of an absolute cosmic order coalesced with the idea of a human order whose rulers shared in its god-like attributes. Then both the machine and the Myth of the Machine were born. And therewith, large populations hitherto isolated and scattered could be organized and put to work, on a scale never before conceivable, with a technical adroitness whose precision and perfection were never before possible. Small wonder that those divine powers were worshipped and their absolute rulers obeyed!

In unearthing this invisible megamachine I was not so much trespassing on the diggings of established archaeologists as flying over them. So far I was safe! But my next move, in equating the ancient megamachine with the technological complex of our own time, caused me to push into heavily defended territory, where few competent colleagues have as yet been willing to venture. This is not the place to summarize all the evidence I have marshalled in 'The City in History' and 'The Myth of the Machine.' Enough to point out that the original institutional components of the Pentagon of Power are still with us, operating more relentlessly if not more efficiently than ever before: the army, the bureaucracy, the engineering corps, the scientific elite—once called priests, magicians, and soothsayers—and, not least, the ultimate Decision Maker, The Divine King, today called the Dictator, the Chief of Staff, the Party Secretary, or the President: tomorrow the Omnicomputer.

Once I had identified the megamachine, I had for the first time a clue to many of the irrational factors in both religion and science that have undermined every civilization and that now threaten, on a scale inconceivable before, to destroy the ecological balance of the whole planet. For from the beginning, it was plain, this Invisible Machine had taken two contrasting forms, that of the Labor Machine and that of the War Machine: the first potentially constructive and life-supporting, the other destructive, savagely life-negating. Both machines were products of the same original myth, which gave to a purely human organization and an all-too-human ruler an absolute authority derived from the cosmos itself. To revolt against that system, to question its moral validity, or to try to withdraw from it, was disobedience to the Power Gods. Under very thin disguises, those gods are still with us. And their commands are more fatally irresistible than ever before.

476

Since the original labor machine could not be economically put to work except for large-scale operations, smaller, more serviceable and manageable machines of wood and brass and iron were in time invented as useful auxiliaries to the Invisible Machine. But the archetype itself persisted in its negative, military form. The army and the army's 'table of organization' was transmitted through history, more or less intact, from one large territorial organization to another—the army with its hierarchical chain of command, with its system of remote control, with its regimentation of human responses, ensuring absolute obedience to the word of command, with its readiness to impose punishment and inflict death to ensure conformity to the Sovereign Power. Not only does this power system break down human resistance and deliberately extirpate the communal institutions that stand in its way, but it seeks to extend both its political rule and its territorial boundaries; for power, whether technological, political, or pecuniary, recognizes no necessary organic limits.

The real gains in law, order, craftsmanship, social cooperation and economic productivity the megamachine made possible must not be belittled. But unfortunately these gains were reduced, often entirely cancelled out, by the brutalizing and dehumanizing institutions that the military megamachine brought into existence: organized war, slavery, class expropriation and exploitation, and extensive collective extermination. In terms of human development, these evil institutions have no rational foundation or humane justification. This, I take it, is the basic trauma of civilization itself; and the evidence for it rests on much sounder foundations than Freud's quaint concept of a mythical act of patricide. What is worse, the hallucinations of absolute power, instead of being liquidated in our time through the advance of objective scientific knowledge and democratic participation, have become more obsessive. In raising the ceiling of civilization's constructive achievements, the modern megamachine likewise lowered its depths.

Technological Exhibitionism

The parallels between the ancient and the modern megamachine extend even to their fantasies: in fact, it is their fantasies that must first be liquidated by rational exposure if the megamachine is to be replaced by superior and more human types of organization and association based on personal initiative and mutual aid. In the religious legends of the early Bronze Age, one discovers, if one reads attentively, the same irrational residue one finds in our present power system: its obsession with speed and quantitative achievements, its technological exhibitionism, its bureaucratic rigidity in organization, its relentless military coercions and conscriptions, its hostility to autonomous processes not yet under control by a centralized authority. The subjective connection between the ancient and the modern megamachine is clear.

All the boasted inventions of our modern technology first erupted in audacious Bronze Age dreams as attributes of the Gods or their earthly representatives: remote control, human flight, supersonic locomotion, instantaneous communication, automatic servo-mechanisms, germ warfare, and the wholesale extermination of large urban populations by fire and brimstone, if not nuclear fission. If you are not familiar with the religious literature of Egypt and Babylonia, you will find sufficient data in the Old Testament of the Bible to testify to the original paranoia of the Power Complex in the dreams and daily acts of the gods and the kings who represented that power on earth.

Just as today, unrestrained technological exhibitionism served as proof of the absolute power of the monarch and his military-bureaucratic-scientific elite. None of our present technological achievements would have surprised any earlier totalitarian rulers. Kublai Khan, who called himself Emperor of the World, boasted to Marco Polo of the automatic conveyor that brought food to his table, and of the ability of his magicians to control the weather. What our scientifically oriented technologies have done is to make even more fabulous dreams of absolute control not only credible but probable; and in that very act they have magnified their irrationality—that is, their divorce from ecological conditions and historical human traditions under which life of every kind, and above all conscious human life, has actually flourished. The fact that most of these ancient fantasies have turned into workaday realities does not make their present and prospective misuse less irrational or less hostile to Life.

Do not be deceived by the bright scientific label on the package. Ideologically the modern power complex, if measured by the standards of ecology and humane morality, is as obsolete as its ancient predecessor. Our present technocratic economy, for all its separate inventions, lacks the necessary dimensions of a life economy, and this is one of the reasons that the evidences of its breakdown are now becoming frighteningly visible. We have abundant biological evidence to demonstrate that life could not have survived or developed on this planet if command of physical energy alone had been the criterion of biological success. *In all organic processes quality is as important as quantity, and too much is as fatal to life as too little.* No species can exist without the constant aid and sustenance of thousands of other living organisms, each conforming to its own life-pattern, going through its appointed cycle of birth, growth, decay, and death. If a feeble, unarmed, vulnerable creature like man has become lord of creation, it is because he was able deliberately to mobilize all his personal capacities, including his gifts of sympathy, group loyalty, love, and parental devotion. These gifts ensured the time and attention necessary to develop his mind and pass on his specifically human traditions to his offspring.

For remember: man is not born human. What has separated man's career from that of all other species is that he needs a whole lifetime to explore and to utilize—and in rare moments to transcend—his human potentialities. When man fails to develop the arts and disciplines that bring out these human capacities, his 'civilized' self sinks, as Giambattista Vico long ago pointed out, to a far lower level than any other animal. Since the megamachine from the beginning attached as much value to its negative components—to success in war, destruction, enslavement and extermination—as to life-promoting functions, it widened the empire of absurdity and irrationality. To face this built-in irrationality of both ancient and modern megamachines is the first step toward controlling the insensate dynamism of modern technology.

Let me cite a classic example of our present demoralizing conformities. Observe what a distinguished mathematician, the late John von Neumann, said about our current addiction to scientific and technological innovations. "Technological possibilities," von Neumann said, "are irresistible to man. If he can go to the moon, he will. If he can control the climate, he will." Though von Neumann expressed some alarm over this situation, I am even more alarmed at what he took for granted. For the notion that technological possibilities are irresistible is far from obvious. On the contrary, it is a historical fact that this compulsion, except in the form imposed by the original Bronze Age model megamachine itself, is limited to modern Western man. Until now, human development was curtailed severely both by archaic institutional fixations and backward technological practices, conditioned by magic hocus-pocus. One of the chief weaknesses of traditional village communities was rather that they too stubbornly resisted even the most modest technical improvements, preferring stability and continuity to rapid change, random novelties, and possible disruption. As late as the seventeenth century an inventor in Rostock was publicly executed for designing an automatic loom.

What von Neumann was talking about was not historic man in general, but modern Western Man, Bureaucratic Man, Organization Man, Post-historic or Anti-historic Man: in short, our compulsive, power-obsessed, machine-conditioned, contemporaries. Let us not overlook the fact that when any single impulse becomes irresistible, without regard to past experience, present needs, or future consequences, we are facing an ominously pathological derangement. If von Neumann's dictum were true, the human race is already doomed, for the governments of both the United States and Russia have been insane enough to produce nuclear weapons in quantities sufficient to exterminate mankind five times over. Is it not obvious that from the outset there has been a screw loose in the mighty megamachine? And have these paranoid obsessions not increased in direct proportion to the amount of political and physical power the system now has placed in the hands of its leaders?

How is it then, you may ask, that earlier civilizations were not destroyed by the persistent aberrations of the power complex? The most obvious answer is that their destruction repeatedly did take place, in most of the twenty-odd civilizations that Arnold Toynbee's 'Study of History' examined. But in so far as these power systems survived, it was probably because they were still held back by various organic limitations: mainly because their energy, in the form of manpower, was until recently derived solely from food crops; and though sadistic emperors might massacre the populations of whole cities, this killing could be done only by hand. Even in its palmiest days the megamachine depended upon the self-maintenance of man's small, scattered, loosely organized farming villages and feudal estates, whose members were still autonomous enough to carry on even when the ruling dynasties were destroyed and their great cities were reduced to rubble.

Furthermore, between the power technics of the megamachine and the earlier organic, fertility technics of farm and garden, there fortunately persisted until recently a third mediating mode of technics, common to both the urban and the rural environments; namely, the cumulative polytechnics of the handicrafts—pottery making, spinning, weaving, stone-carving, building, gardening, farming, animal breeding—each a rich repository of well-tested knowledge and practical experience. Whenever the centrally controlled megamachine broke down or was defeated in war, its scattered members could re-form themselves, falling back on smaller communal and regional units, each transmitting the essential traditions of work and esthetic mastery and moral responsibility. Not all the technical eggs were then in one basket. Until now, this wide dispersal of working power, political intelligence, craft experience, and life-supporting communal practices happily mitigated the human disabilities of a system based on the abstractions of power alone.

But note: our modern power system has annihilated these safeguards, and thereby, incidentally, endangered its own existence. Thanks

480

to its overwhelming success in both material and intellectual productivity, the organic factors that made for ecological, technological, and human balance have been progressively reduced, and may soon be wiped out. Even as late as 1940, as the French geographer, Max Sorre, pointed out, four-fifths of the population of the planet still lived in rural areas closer in their economy and way of life to a neolithic village than to a modern megalopolis. That rural factor of safety is fast vanishing, and except in backward or underdeveloped countries, has almost disappeared. No competent engineer would design a bridge with as small a factor of safety as that under which the present power system operates. The more completely automated the whole system becomes and the more extensive its centralized mode of communication and control, the narrower that margin becomes; for as the system itself becomes more completely integrated, the human components become correspondingly depleted, disintegrated and paralyzed, unable to take over the functions and activities they have too submissively surrendered to the megamachine.

Judged by any rational criteria, the modern megamachine has poor chances of survival. Though everyone is now aware of its mounting series of slowdowns and breakdowns, its brownouts and blackouts, its depressions and inflations, these failures are ironically the results of the power system's very success in achieving high levels of production. Technologically speaking, the old problem of scarcity of food or goods or valid knowledge has been solved, but the new problem of over-abundance has proved even more disconcerting, and harder to remedy without radically revising all the sacred principles of the Pentagon of Power.

The ancient megamachine worked, we now perceive, only because its benefits were reserved for a restricted, privileged class, or a small urban population. The modern megamachine, in order to universalize its methods and goals, now seeks to impose unrestricted mass production and mass consumption upon the proliferating populations of the entire planet. But it should now be plain that without deliberate human intervention, vigilantly imposing thrift, moderation, humane restraint upon the whole business of production, consumption, and reproduction, this affluent society is doomed to choke to death on its waste products. The only resources that can be increased indefinitely are those that nourish, energize, and expand the higher functions of the mind.

Happily, in recent years there has been a sudden, if belated, awakening to the dire human consequences of our unquestioning devotion to technology's expansions and extensions. Who can now remain blind to our polluted oceans and rivers, our smog-choked air, our mountainous rubbish heaps, our sprawling automobile cemeteries, our sterilized and blasted landscapes, where the strip miner, the bulldozer, the pesticides, and the herbicides have all left their mark; the widening deserts of concrete, in motor roads and car parks, whose substitution of ceaseless locomotion for urban decentralization daily wastes countless man-years of life in needless transportation; not least our congested, dehumanized cities where health is vitiated and depleted by the sterile daily routine. With the spread of biological knowledge that has gone on during the last generation, the meaning of all these ecological assaults has at last sunk in and begun to cause a general reversal of attitude toward the entire technological process, most markedly among the young. The claims of megatechnics are no longer unchallengeable; their demands no longer seem irresistible. Only backward Victorian minds now believe "you can't stop progress," or that one must accept the latest devices of technology solely because they promise greater financial gains or greater national prestige, or greater scope for the bureaucratic and military elite.

Though there has been a general awakening to the negative goods— or "bads" as Bertrand de Jouvenel calls them—that have accompanied the explosive technology of the twentieth century, most of our contemporaries still hold stubbornly to the naive belief that there is a purely technological solution to every human problem. Hence the elaborate build-up, since 1945, of rocket projectiles to intercept nuclear weapons at a distance, as if this could promise any substantial control over the self-imprisoned minds that had, in the first instance, sanctioned these weapons. Such minds are open to the same kind of anti-social psychotic impulses we find spreading in many other groups. If we seriously mean to control the megamachine, we must now reverse the process that brought about its original invention, and bring back to all its human agents—not merely its leaders—the necessary self-confidence and moral discipline that will make them ready to intervene at any point where the power complex threatens human autonomy, to challenge its purposes, to reduce its automatic compulsions, to restore and further cultivate the missing organic components of the human personality.

Unfortunately, our recent consciousness of the physical pollution and degradation of the environment that has taken place during the last three centuries, and with alarming swiftness during the last three decades, is still mainly confined to visible environmental results and bodily illnesses and injuries. But we must be equally conscious of the mental pollution and cultural desecration that results from the imposition of our uniform electro-mechanical model on our many-layered cultural heritage. Not least we must realize the massive damage done by our own special cultural products—the mass production of printed matter, of pictures, of films, of scientific and scholarly papers no less than the daily outpourings of the mass media. All this has done as much to degrade our minds as our physical conquests have done to degrade the planetary habitat. The excess storage of insignificant information, the excess transmission of unnecessary messages, the passive submission to the constant symbolic bombardment by images and sounds of every sort, culminating in the nerve-shattering extravaganzas of amplified electronic 'music' are fast reducing even our genuine cultural achievements to an agglomeration of astronomical dimensions that will be inaccessible to the mind. No system of condensing this bulk or retrieving its separate items will do anything but add quantitatively to the chaos.

Envoy

The end of this long paper is obviously not the place to canvass and carry further the positive measures needed to reverse the accelerating forces of technocratic disintegration. Certainly it is not in extensive cosmonautic explorations of outer space, but by more intensive cultivation of the historic inner spaces of the human mind, that we shall recover the human heritage. In a sense, all my major books, starting with 'Technics and Civilization,' the first volume in The Renewal of Life Series, have been attempts to understand the repeated miscarriages of mind that have limited the highest achievements of every historic civilization. My maturest interpretation of the archaeological and historic evidence will be found in three successive books: 'The City in History,' 1960, 'Technics and Human Development,' 1967, and 'The Pentagon of Power,' 1970.

Fortunately, at least one reputable anthropologist has clearly perceived the implications of this interpretation of the basic role of man's unique symbolic artifacts in technics and in human development. By the terms of his rejection of these views, he has willy-nilly given support to my description of the modern power complex. I refer to the review of the first volume of 'The Myth of the Machine,' published in 'Science' by Professor Julian Steward. "The thesis of this book," Steward noted, "has inevitable practical and political implications for the contemporary world. If two million years of cultural evolution results from man's mind, rather than from the imperatives of technology, man is presumably able to devise a better society. If on the other hand, economic, social, and political institutions are inevitable responses to mass production and distribution, to what extent can the human mind, or reason, reverse or deflect these trends?"

If this second option were indeed the only one open, technics as practiced under the guidance of positive science today would have precisely the cosmic status attributed in the Sumerian King List to the institution of Divine Kingship. Like the sacred Powers of Kingship, our technology must have been "handed down from heaven." If so, not man but the Gods would be responsible for its existence, its devastating power, and its ultimate destination—namely to take over and supplant all autonomous organic and human activities. On such terms, the megamachine, eviscerated of all latent human attributes except such traits as may have been implanted in the human genes, would have absorbed all the attributes of Godhead. In the end human beings would be reduced, in Teilhard de Chardin's ominous words, to mere 'particles'—specialized cells in a megalocephalic brain.

I am indebted to Professor Steward for having restated, as the solid foundation of current scientific orthodoxy, the ancient religious Myth of the Machine. *Quod erat demonstrandum.*

Note: This paper was first published in Technology, Power, and Social Change, Charles Thrall and Lerold Starr, Editors, Lexington, Mass., 1972. A revised version for the Rome World special Conference on Futures Research, entitled Technology and Culture, was published by the IPC Technology Press in England in 1974.

26: Excursions Abroad

I have been chary of drawing on my many Travel Notes, since the trips that were personally most rewarding offered too little time then or afterward to record satisfactorily what I had seen and felt. I regret that I have no adequate record of my 1956 trip with Sophia; for that turned out to be a modest version of the sort of triumphal tour that a famous actor might make at the end of his career; but the round of hospitalities and honors, from Rome to London, left no space for recording the day's excitements. Our 1967 journey, however, was even more eventful and delightful; yet again, though it gave no opportunity for jotting down notes about people and places, I nevertheless succeeded, while my memories were still fresh, in giving the flavor of those climactic days together in the 'Reflections' that largely fill this chapter.

NEAPOLITAN DIGGINGS. 'You may; therefore you must.' This gratuitous *nonsequitur* is the mischievous fallacy of our time; it accounts for the fact that every technological permission has been turned into an irresistible collective compulsion—usually, no doubt, because the new technical facilities can be exploited at a profit. So, comically, though this age has ceased to believe in human progress, it clings with almost hysterical tenacity to the Victorian faith in technological progress as the only means left for human redemption and salvation. When anyone reasons against the multiplication of nerve-shattering supersonic planes or the wider spread of mind-smudging psychedelics, he finds himself branded by these old-fashioned minds as a traitor to civilization.

During an otherwise pleasantly somnolent voyage to Italy on the

Michelangelo, these thoughts came back to me through the insistent presence of the loudspeaker, whose dreary melodies followed one all over the vessel, even to the solitude of the top sundeck. It's all very well to say that the Italians like noise, but why pick on the Italians? It would be more correct to say that noise likes us, for no radio, no television set, no loudspeaker can be quite sure of its technological success until it has dominated our human consciousness or at least has cunningly infiltrated into our unconscious. Theoretically, the loudspeaker can be reduced in volume or turned off. But the very name we have given this instrument makes people feel that its essential nature is being flouted unless it inundates the air with sound, and as for turning it off, that would mean making a human decision for a purely human end—which is in itself a heretical departure from the mass religion of our age. The electronic priesthood will not stand for that kind of impiety; with one voice they proclaim, on behalf of their mechanical and electronic gods, "You may not reject us, you must not turn us off, and, above all, you may not try to escape from us." Perhaps that is why the young are so desperately scrambling for the nearest exit, though, ironically, the main route they have chosen only leads back to the same prison. Result: a world yawningly empty of human meaning and purpose, a Happening whose studious disorder reinforces our sterile mechanical and electronic routines by serving as a seemingly animated counterpoise.

The glories of the Bay of Naples were a standard theme for the nineteenth-century traveller, but were they not a little overrated even at that period? Give me the entrance to the Cherbourg mole, after passing the Channel Islands, especially in the pre-1940 days, before Cherbourg had become industrialized, or—even more exciting—the harbor of Plymouth, both during and between its perpetual showers. As for the approach to Venice by sea, what could be more heavenly—yes, *heavenly* —on a sunlit day when the buildings dance with color? The 'blue Mediterranean' must exist, but it's just my bad luck never to have seen it when the water could compare with the greens and blues of the Pacific around Honolulu.

Not that I feel sour about Naples. Great men have lived and flourished there, or thereabouts, from Thomas Aquinas to Giambattista Vico and Benedetto Croce, and who could be sour when, before he had reached land, he received a radiogram informing him, to his utter surprise, that "the friends of Bruno Zevi" would be on hand at the pier to receive him and his wife? B. has a gift for assembling fine friends, and we recognized each other—no doubt because we were all professors—with singular ease. But after our first embraces, the deadly handicap of being tongue-tied in an unfamiliar language nipped the blossom of friendship before it could open, for grown men can't keep on embracing and smiling amiably all day, like so many infants or idiots.

For long I have felt that, as travel increased, we should be well advised to postpone seeking a common spoken language, colored as it will inevitably be by the native tone, rhythm, and pronunciation of the speaker. Rather, we should concentrate on devising a truly universal language of gesture, unmarred by indigenous vocal peculiarities and deliberately limited to essentials. Even a hundred such signs, ranging from 'Where is the toilet?' to 'I love you,' would do more to promote cultural understanding, to say nothing of ease in travel, than a battery of Berlitz schools. Now, Naples is famous as the *Urheimat* of this gesture language among Western peoples. According to tradition, much though Neapolitans love to talk and shout and sing, they can dispense with words as long as the 'speakers' are visible enough to follow each other's mobile faces and hands. So I came to Naples with a mental note to observe my proposal in this favorable milieu. But what a disappointment! I heard plenty of talk on the Via Roma, but I sought in vain for gestures, with or without words. Apparently the radio, which has leveled so much of our oral communication, has helped likewise to destroy gesture. The only place where this language survives is among motorists, for even the streamroller crawl of Naples traffic would be impossible without the give-and-take of gesture between driver and driver, to say nothing of driver and pedestrian; without it, the man on foot would be mangled at every turn.

Alfred North Whitehead once observed that the use of foreign travel is to "show familiar things in unusual combinations," and perhaps the most useful object lesson in Naples is to show that the motorcar—which our countrymen once thought of as an essentially American achievement—has everywhere reached a point of congestion and futility equal to our own. This must terminate finally either in an explosion of insensate aggression or, even more effectively, in an explosion of laughter over our common folly in sacrificing all the benefits of urban life for mobility and speed. Or, rather, for the purely abstract *idea* of automobility and speed. For the more mobile we become the more fixed and unvaried becomes the environment; and the greater the number of cars on streets, roads, and speedways, the less time we have for anything except travel. What stationary mobility! Strangely, the thing that really protects the pedestrian in Naples is the fact that Neapolitans, though they, too, may adore speed, are not at heart aggressive drivers, as are the British; even on temptingly straight stretches, like the Via Partenope, along the waterfront, they are reasonably watchful of the pedestrian and, given a chance, are ready to yield—that ultimate courtesy of the road. In contrast, British drivers are ruthless. If every Englishman's house is his castle, on the King's Highways he acts as if he were a king. When I got to London, the automobile clubs were making an impassioned protest against a Ministerial decision to experimentally reduce the speed on highways to a mere seventy miles an hour. Not infrequently I have been driven at eighty miles an hour along twisting and turning two-lane English country roads, with not even a shoulder between the road and the thick hedges and trees. My British friends—why did I almost write "fiends"?—were quite incredulous when I told them that the highest speed permitted on ordinary roads in my own state is fifty miles an hour, and that neighboring Connecticut favors forty to forty-five, and has lowered the accident rate by imposing it.

In lingering a few days in Naples I had two conscious objectives— one was to take another look at the Pompeiian collection in the National Museum, and the other was to visit Herculaneum. After playing second fiddle to Pompeii for more than a century, Herculaneum—sealed in a mass of baked clay, not just covered with ashes, like Pompeii—has only in recent years been given a modicum of the attention and the energy necessary to excavate its all too well-preserved treasures: doubly guarded, in fact, because the present-day urban slum of Resina squats on top of the site, and its inhabitants must be removed in order to reveal the ancient town below. As is usual on expeditions of the sort, Sophia and I were the victims of the kindliness and zeal of our friends. I prefer to make the first visit to such a site unaccompanied—to take in as much as possible with my untutored eyes alone, without extraneous explanation. But nowhere have I yet succeeded in doing so when even a hint of my intentions has reached my friends. Now, by a series of polite misunderstandings and frantic telephone calls, my wife and I again found ourselves seeing an ancient ruin in the worst possible way—with the aid of an official tourist guide. The only thing we managed to do alone was to go there in a taxi, and even that was a disappointment, for Herculaneum, unlike Pompeii, does not lie in the open country, among vines and olive trees, but is close to the sea, and by now the spreading slums of Naples have filled the entire four miles between the ruined town and the teeming city.

The excavations are impressive, but I lost count of the number of

488

times the guide triumphantly exhibited still another platter of lava-baked beans or loaf of petrified bread. At all events, the demonstration happened often enough to blur my impression of the villas and the workshops, and the tunnels that have been opened farther under the cliff. I did not get a satisfactory impression of what it was all about until I reached Rome and was given Jay Deiss's recent book on Herculaneum. Despite inadequate funds, the new archeologist in charge, Dr. Giuseppina Irelli, has been pushing into fresh territory and has revived interest in this site. Only a small fraction of the city has so far been exposed—just the chin, as Mr. Deiss observes, not the head. Obviously, this is one of a hundred sites that might make good use of the billions of dollars our government spends annually in giving extravagant handouts to the moon-rocket and arms industries in order to make the policies of the White House more credibly incredible. These funds could be more profitably spent in deepening our knowledge of the past and lengthening the historical perspective of our rocket-happy barbarians, in the hope of preventing them from letting their well-publicized plans for nuclear eruptions turn the whole world into another Herculaneum.

Italy is of course filled with Etruscan and Roman and Greek ruins and monuments, and more keep coming to light, thanks partly to aerial photography. Greek buildings, notably those at Paestum, are often better preserved in Italy and in Provence than in their homeland, just as the classic Greek nose and chin (neither, incidentally, very appealing to our modern taste; indeed, distinctly adenoidal) can be seen in southern Italy, whose Greek colonies remained, in isolation, till the tenth century A.D. Where, in fact, can one get a better impression of a Greek theater than on the hillside at Fiesole? But what has most strikingly come through, over the centuries, from Roman civilization is its old sense of scale—the spaciousness that is necessary for handling large crowds of people, which McKim deliberately imitated in the old Pennsylvania Station in New York, and the serenity that follows this scale when it is brought into aristocratic domestic quarters.

POMPEII. There is not a city of a million population today that is as copiously served by baths, theaters, markets, gymnasiums as was the little provincial town of Pompeii, which probably held at most thirty or forty thousand inhabitants. Proportionately, our modern metropolises are poverty-stricken when it comes to providing the essential organs of urban life. A theater goer in Pompeii could reach home on foot after the performance—faster, often, than an American in a similar crowd could find his car and get out of the parking lot. And did this insignificant little town not boast such fine murals and mosaics that the great museums of the world have eagerly competed for these treasures, while great Rome, sucking into her maw the art of Greece, Asia, Africa, and Spain, had nothing better to show? Not that Pompeii was utopia; the point is that it was just a little provincial town, with the usual number of slaves, whorehouses, and lovesick youths scrawling messages on the walls in public places. But even the slaves must have eaten honest bread, for it was made of wheat ground in the bakery's own mill just before the loaves were baked. Pompeii still taunts us with its genuine wealth, proportionately far greater than opulent Rome's—that true birthplace of mass culture and its latter-day counterparts. Even the apt whorehouse murals, showing the more classic modes of the thirty-nine positions, were not vulgarly obscene. Characteristically, the tradition of the Pompeiian graffiti has remained over the centuries, too. In the Trastevere quarter in Rome I stumbled upon a contemporary message on an otherwise blank wall: "*Fa l'amore, no la supresa.*" I doubt if that plea owes anything to Freud; it sounds more like Ovid.

Views from the Villa Aurelia

AT HOME IN ROME. In May of 1967, we were guests in the Villa Aurelia, once Garibaldi's headquarters, now a part of the American Academy in Rome. This building, though not an old one, is as spacious as Ditchley House, beyond Oxford, where Churchill took refuge during the war, when Chequers was too obvious a target for the Germans.

I have never felt happier than in our perfectly proportioned bedroom at the Villa Aurelia, with its high ceilings, its serene spacing of walls and windows, its handsome traditional oak doors—dating in design, but not in manufacture, from the sixteenth century—to say nothing of the breakfast tray that the smiling, buxom maid, Giana, brought promptly each morning, gay with flowers and fruit, aromatic with fresh coffee. This, I said to myself, is exactly what Henry James pictured in 'The Great Good Place.' For once, I was actually living in that Good Place—all beautified, as James put it, by omissions. The best modern architecture would have nothing better to offer. Nor was I disturbed, as one too often is in modern rooms, by the architect's officious effort to call attention to himself by regimenting the furniture in Miesian formation, by taking the backs off chairs, by inventing forms that only an acrobat can get out of gracefully, or, finally, by discarding furniture altogether so as not to lose the drawing-board purity of his vacuous design. There was no such esthetic dictatorship about this room; it had its own life, so to say, and let its inhabitants have theirs without further fuss. When a building is finished, the architect should be buried, as it were, in the walls; one should not find him nudging one or grimacing at one when one is eating dinner or making love. The greater a work of architecture, the more anonymous should be its final effect—and so, inevitably, the less dated. Ideally, one should feel not the petty ego of the creator, or the cultural idiosyncrasies of a particular period or people, but a large, more universal spirit, borne out of mankind's long experience, which simply speaks through the architect. Today, architecture is too often strictly a public-relations art, and the success it seeks is a success of advertising and salesmanship. Too many modern buildings are designed to be photographed, not lived in.

But it is not merely the old Roman scale that has remained; look at the color of the walls or the courtyards of the tenements in Naples, for are not these courtyards survivals of the ancient atrium, around which the rooms were grouped? Now they serve as domestic parking lots, and without the extra space they offer there would be narrow streets in Naples where no car could turn around, or even get out of the way of one coming from the opposite direction. Pompeiian Red may not originally have been an outside wall color, but the local variations of this hue— muted vermilion in Naples, a burnt orange in Rome, and many different shades of red, orange, and yellow in other cities, or in different spots in the same city—are what give Italian façades a character of their own.

Doubtless, bad parts of the ancient Roman tradition have survived, too, but the good parts are worth conserving and enjoying.

CRISIS IN ROME. My main purpose in coming to Rome was to receive an honorary doctorate from the Faculty of Architecture of the University of Rome, but my underlying motive was to meet old friends and compare notes with them about the state of the world. The University courteously allowed me to pick the date for my *laurea*, but I chose it badly for the second purpose, since the state of the world that May was too distracting for connected conversation. For one thing, the students of Italy, like the young everywhere, have been in a yeasty state, not merely demonstrating against their professors and rejecting traditional values and traditional studies but rejecting the leaders of the past generation who staged an earlier revolt. The ten-year-old mind, now so common in science and scholarship, is spreading everywhere, and it takes the form of asserting that no one has anything to learn except what has happened in his own brief lifetime, within his private field of vision, as amplified and distorted by mass media.

In Italy, the revolt has even taken physical form: In the courtyard of the School of Architecture at Naples I had seen tables strewn about, thrown out by the students. Since my writings identify me as a hoary if recalcitrant member of the older generation, there may have been some uneasiness about my appearance at this ceremony, lest my presence or, even more, my speech of acceptance rouse a demonstration. But the only thing the students openly challenged was the Latin citation that accompanied the honor; they found the Rector's Neapolitan accent funny— as I did, I fear, when I discovered that my given name had been Latinized into Aloysius. The United States Information Service had provided everyone with a mimeographed translation of my address, and delivered it in English to an attentive and respectful audience; the effect was rather better, it seemed to some of the listeners, than a simultaneous translation with earphones, and infinitely preferable to a sequence of translations, sentence by sentence or paragraph by paragraph. My stand against Washington's policy and strategy and ill-disguised intentions in Vietnam may have accounted for their sympathetic response, and even my deliberately Tennysonian ending may have appealed to the students: "Come, my friends, 'tis not too late to seek a newer world." At all events, no Coca-Cola bottles were thrown at me.

Meanwhile, the Near East crisis had come to a head, with its premonitory anxieties and its even more horrible anticipation of a doom hanging not only over Israel but over the whole human race, thanks to the studiously cultivated insanity that passes for high strategic policy within the political and military think-tanks of the great states. What did an honorary degree matter on such a threatened planet? And how could the usual enjoyments of food and wine, of animated conversation, of views from the Janiculum over the Tiber and the spreading city have any meaning in a world where meaning itself was perhaps on the point of vanishing, along with all of man's other works? During the tense, ominous days before Israel's swift victory, when it seemed as if Israel would be quietly thrown to the Arabs by the 'Great Powers,' as Czechoslovakia had once been handed over to Hitler, no one could talk freely, because what we were secretly thinking about was the unthinkable.

Ten years before, our friends the Bruno Zevis—he is the editor of L'Architettura—had given a huge party for us in the big garden of their house on the Via Nomentana, and we remembered it as a party that would forever overshadow all other such occasions in its intellectual vivacity and its fluttering gaiety, since people had come from all over Italy for it. Now, "in occasione della laurea honoris causa," as the invitations read, they sought to repeat that festive performance. But uniqueness is unrepeatable. The invitees came—those who were not prevented from coming by official duties—but the crisis was overhead, underfoot, and in the depths of our souls, like the weather, which had become cold, windy, threatening rain, and we huddled under the trees near the house for warmth and mutual support, instead of spreading out over the garden. The grim moment flowed backward in our minds over the past and forward into the faceless future: the First World War, the Turkish massacres, the Second World War, the Soviet concentration camps, the Nazi extermination camps, 'strategic' (extermination) bombing—Warsaw, Rotterdam, London, Coventry, Hamburg, Dresden, Tokyo, Hiroshima, then Korea, Vietnam, and more civilian extermination. And now the Near East.

No wonder the younger generation loathe this world and find no good whatever in it; they have known nothing else, and it is easy for them to believe that there never has been anything but fraud, hypocrisy, malevolence, and violence. And yet the crisis brought out many of the old decencies, the old moralities, the old heroisms that have enabled the human race to survive both natural and man-made catastrophes. The declared sympathies of the Italian people were overwhelmingly on the side of threatened Israel while it still seemed that Egypt was about to impose Hitler's 'final solution' upon the Jews. And in Switzerland, my Swiss friends told me later, something had taken place that had been unimaginable before this moment: the high school students, never given to demonstrations, had marched in public to show their solidarity with Israel. To be footloose in Europe at such a moment gave one a peculiar sense of guilt, as if one had chosen this occasion to desert the human race. The effect of these repeated crises is to make the normal enjoyments of life mockingly unreal, or, if not unreal, offensive to one's sensibilities.

VENETIAN ENCHANTMENT. Venice called us once again, and for a few days we bathed in its mellow sunlight. At the end of May, the tourist traffic was not yet at its heaviest, and the pedantic drone of Baedeker in German was not as loudly authoritative in the Piazza San Marco as it usually is. This is too late a day to talk about the glories of Venice, still less to explain why I follow Ruskin in regarding the Ducal Palace as one of the perfect works of architecture in the world. Nor am I tempted here to repeat why I believe that the six neighborhoods of Venice, with their workshops, markets, and *trattorie*, with their minor parochial subdivisions, and with their heavy industries established in separate zones or islands—like the glass industry of Murano—still present a workable model for contemporary planning, quite apart from the fact that by its variety, its functional efficiency, and its beauty Venice makes hash of our own Jane Jacobs' naïve anti-esthetic dogmas on planning.

We had a room with a balcony on the Grand Canal, opposite my favorite Venetian view—of the Santa Maria della Salute, not far from the old, turreted Customs House at the point. For the view alone I would rate the hotels along this strip of the canal above the more famous hostelries that command the open waterfront. The Santa Maria is Baroque design at its extravagant best—as lively and adventurous in construction as the best medieval work. It must have been my anticipatory pleasure, approaching it by foot on Sunday morning, that made me, quite by error, toss a silver coin to a squatting beggar woman, instead of a coin of baser metal I had in the same pocket. But the squawk of stunned delight that she uttered as we walked away, which made me realize my mistake, more than compensated for my careless gesture. I can't remember ever having produced so much happiness so cheaply.

It is easy to dismiss Venice as a museum piece, a tourist trap, a moldering remnant of a beautiful but too often sinister past, and there is plenty of ground for all these judgments. Venice, which was built on piles, is physically threatened not merely by rotting foundations but by periodically rising floods, which seem to be getting worse. But as the historic core of the province of Venetia it is far from being outmoded, since, on the nearby mainland, there is a large and growing industrial complex, whose very prosperity, indeed, threatens Venice as it has always been. Already there have been silly proposals for filling up the canals of Venice and turning them into motor highways—something that would cause Venice to lose its immense distinction as a town perfectly designed for pedestrians and capable of surviving comfortably even if every gondola and gas launch except the boats bringing in vegetables, flowers, and fish were banished.

What Venice needs is neither motorways nor high-rise slabs but a systematic renovation of existing buildings with an opening up to daylight and sunlight of its foulest slums. The turning of the old *palazzi* into hotels has long provided for the needs of the wealthier visitors, and with a sufficient supply of capital a much more thorough piecemeal rebuilding would be in order. Nevertheless, the city is still alive, as a cultural center in its own right. (I don't refer to the Biennale!)

IN THE HOME OF JUNG. The *rapido* from Milan to Zurich is a superb modern train, one of a whole fleet in Europe that makes one realize what sublime idiots our own countrymen and the English have been in allowing their railroad systems to be dismantled by railroad executives and transportation 'experts' who seem to have got all their training in junkyards. But seven hours of rail travel from Venice had left us that night aching for bed, and it was a shock, when we reached our hotel, to find that despite two confirmations and a deposit the desk clerk had neglected to enter our reservation in the book and that every room in the house was occupied. The efficient Swiss! The night clerk stuttered and cringed, and, suppressing our indignation, we waited in grim silence for something to be done. He finally offered to find a hotel in the neighborhood and promised us that a room in his hotel would be ready by noon next day. So we followed the porter carrying our overnight bags up a steep street to a nearby 'hotel,' actually a folksy Swiss restaurant specializing in Swiss dishes and yodelling for a tourist trade; the bedrooms were apparently an afterthought. We were tired and wanted only to get to bed, but the next few hours were a comic nightmare of such ineptitude that it gets funnier every time I think of it. For the clerk who showed us to our cramped room was much too proud of its uniqueness to let us go to bed. First he pointed to a bulky chest in a corner, covered with frilled chintz, and, sweeping the cloth aside, showed that it was really a refrigerator, already stocked with mineral water, Coca-Cola, whiskey, and champagne (with their prices listed on the door). "Thanks, but we'd like to get to bed at once." "Ah, the bed! But look." And he demonstrated. "See, I press this button." And up came the head of the bed. He pressed another button, and the foot of the bed was raised, too. It was, in short, the latest type of motorized hospital bed, and he was so proud of it that it was wicked of me to deflate him by saying dryly, "We prefer it flat; *we want to go to sleep.*"

In a few minutes we were ready to try the bed, noting, this hot night, that it still boasted that final absurdity in bedding—the old-fashioned Central European puff, too short in winter, too hot for any other season. But there was a knock at the door and a waiter entered bearing a tray laden with cold cuts, bread, salad, and coffee. We said crossly that there had been an error; we wanted only to go to sleep. But the waiter insisted; we *must* have ordered it, the room number was unmistakable. Since we had barely finished our dinner before the train pulled into Zurich, the thought of food at this hour, in our state of fatigue, was repellent. We almost pushed the man out of the room, wondering if the guilty clerk at our first hotel had ordered the repast as a gesture of apology. Again we prepared for sleep, but the heat of the night—augmented by the heat emitted by the refrigerator, and magnified by the noise of the revellers and the kitchen staff below—thwarted us. The heat and noise supplied the penultimate comic touch; the ultimate one came next morning when the waiter brought in breakfast. His first move, after laying down the tray, was to open the refrigerator. "You did not drink anything last night! . . . You would like Coca-Cola for breakfast, then?" We would not like Coca-Cola at any time, or any Veuve Clicquot for breakfast, either. I could see the waiter's face say, 'They are not American!'

That was our introduction to Zurich, but once we escaped this den of folksy modernity, everything went well. Our room clerk, in atonement, assigned us the finest room in the house—a corner one on an upper floor, with a view up and down the Limmat and over the lake, the swans and the *Faltboote* gliding on the river, and, below, an outdoor public balcony for dining. Yes, it really was an excellent hostelry. As for the error of the room clerk, that was cleared up by one look at the sweet-faced, dreamy young man who had made the mistake. He was obviously a poet; even a mediocre vocational counsellor could have told him he had no qualifications whatever for keeping a reservation book in a busy hotel.

In Zurich I was the guest of the Jung Institut, and I gave a couple of talks at that center. This hospitality was evoked by a long review of Jung's autobiography I had written in The New Yorker a few years ago. While Jung's disciples in New York had severely criticized my review—on the ground that it failed to do justice to his work, especially because it brought out the likenesses between him and Freud, rather than their usually overemphasized differences—many of those who had worked with him closely in Europe were delighted by my analysis. One of his colleagues, Dr. Jolande Jacobi, felt mistakenly I had come so close to him that I must have undergone an analysis at his hands. We took part in a commemoration meeting, held on the sixth anniversary of his death, in 1961, in a community room not far from the Institut. The occasion brought together those who knew him too well to worship him and those who worshipped him too well to know him, but it also presented the living image of the old man himself, in a British documentary film I had not seen before—a well-conceived and well-rendered dialogue in which the cultivated European and the shrewd peasant, now long past life's storms, came through in the friendliest partnership. Let me add parenthetically that the term 'peasant,' which had seemed derogatory to some of the American admirers of Jung when I used it in my review, happens to be the highest compliment one can pay to a Swiss.

As with any other great figure, Jung's life and thought were full of contradictions, some of which he transcended in the act of living, some of which were never resolved. As for his ambivalent attitude toward the Nazi movement, which at times seems to have carried him along with its exultant dynamism, and his equally ambivalent attitude toward the Jews, there is something further to be said, though only those who were near to him can say it. Jung was reluctant to admit that his failure to take a stand against Nazism indicated a certain sympathy with its ideals, if not consent to its sadistic practices, but in the end, under pressure from old colleagues who had been affronted by his conduct, he acknowledged his blindness. Only recently I came upon a letter of Jung's, dated 1933, to a friend of mine, now dead. That letter decisively cancels out Jung's

496

uneasy exculpation. Strangely—perhaps not so strangely!—this vital document is not included in the published volume of Jung's letters, though another to the same person, Christiana Morgan, is there. Certainly Jung chose an unfortunate moment in the thirties to dwell on the peculiarities of the Jewish psyche, just as Dr. Carleton Coon chose an unfortunate moment lately to bring forward his hypothesis that the Negroes as a race were late arrivals on the human scene. And certainly, too, Jung never denounced Fascism or Nazism as vehemently as he had denounced Russian Communism, though the terrorism and inhumanity systematically practiced by both systems were patent from the start. Jung does not stand alone. More than once I have been shocked, since the Second World War, to discover that some of the most internationally minded Europeans I know of—humane, deeply cultivated men, not shameless barbarians—had stultified themselves by their sympathetic attitude toward Hitler and Nazism. And did not the gentlemanly Harold Nicolson, who redeemed his early allegiance to Mosley's Fascism by joining the small band that before 1939 actively opposed submission to the Nazis, proclaim himself frankly an anti-Semite?

That corruption is not yet over. Indeed, the stultification has now taken a more subtle turn in A. J. P. Taylor, the Oxford historian, who has fabricated out of whole cloth a mild, sensible, almost genial character, a sort of German Neville Chamberlain, whom he has the incredible impudence to call Hitler. Taylor's Hitler is just an ordinary patriotic statesman who couldn't possibly have meant the things he shouted and wrote, or have perpetrated the ghastly deeds that he conceived and brought to pass. Alongside this seemingly equable but insidious reworking of the evidence by a trained scholar, Jung's political sins during the overheated thirties seem venial.

Doubtless there are moments in every life at which people do or say things, confidently, brazenly, rashly, that, when they look back later, seem crazily out of character—at least morally or intellectually indefensible. But there was another conflict in Jung's life that still teases one, because to the end he remained silent about it and pronounced no judgment on its success or failure. This was his relation to the two women who occupied a central position in his life—his wife and his mistress, who was also a close colleague at his clinic. What was peculiar about this dual attachment was that it was open, that it was maintained on principle, and that it endured. Did Jung at the end still regard this as a new sexual pattern, a happy complementary union of both constancy and change, or did it turn out to have the same tensions, strains, jealousies, desolations, bitternesses as more conventional departures from marital fidelity? If this duality were easy to maintain, one could hardly explain the number of murders committed both in fact and in fantasy in order to shake loose from either the wife or the mistress.

I found myself unexpectedly confronted with this unresolved question one evening when, to collect my wits before the lecture, I took refuge in a little office at the Jung Institut. On one wall three large photographs stared at me. To the left was an elderly woman with a strongly modelled face, slightly grim, almost formidable—not the placid young mother I remembered in an earlier family photograph. In the center was Dr. Jung, in ripe old age but still with the inner vigor he had shown in the film. The third was a somewhat younger woman, finely modelled, self-possessed, slightly disdainful about the mouth—more the face of a pure intellectual than Jung's: Toni herself. The wife, the man, and the mistress. How I wished, as I looked from one to the other, that I could have made at least one of them talk! When Jung himself, in his autobiography, said that one can make no judgment about one's life, he was perhaps protecting his own ego—or was he just saying that the emotional storms he had lived through could not, even for such a bold navigator as himself, bear cool review and appraisal once the living moment was past? Either way, I remain dissatisfied, for I would have liked him to answer a single question: Would you follow the same plan of life again?

Crotchet Castle and Wild Wales

On a summer visit to Britain, I spent ten days in a roughly triangular journey that took me from London through Birmingham into North Wales, then by way of Manchester to Edinburgh. I came back through Durham, whose cathedral, embedded—like the fortress it was—upon a rock, is as fine an example of grand architectural form married to its site as can be found anywhere. On this journey, my architectural discoveries were all quite incidental and unplanned, though occasionally my hosts took a hand in them. By good luck, it turned out that these discoveries cast oblique illuminations over many of the major architectural and planning problems of our time.

Going to and from Wales by the routes I took, one passes through the classic wastelands of the early industrial period, with their scorched-earth landscape, their slag heaps and coal tips (so mountainous that they seem geological formations, not man-made accumulations), their begrimed rows of workers' houses, set in a clutter of factories—the whole scene exhibiting diagrammatically all the typical mistakes of the begin-

498

nings of industrialism. After years of helpless acquiescence, efforts are now being made to absorb these mountains of debris into the urban landscape; the efforts range from levelling the heaps with steam shovel and bulldozer to coaxing grass and even trees to grow on their inhospitable slopes, but the process of accumulating soil and humus is a slow one. One of my brief halting places was Eccles, near Manchester, and the home of the delicious Eccles cake, which, like the Bath bun, is at its best in its native habitat. Wandering about one of Eccles' Victorian suburban estates, I was struck by the fact that the ruling classes, even when they commanded plenty of land and money, had not known how to use these resources to produce a pleasant environment for themselves any more than they had for their workers; at best, they had made an art of ugliness and a virtue of the grime they shared with their poorer neighbors.

But here comes the architectural paradox. This blasted environment has produced over the generations no small number of people whose moral and intellectual qualities have been of a superior order. For it was in this kind of setting that the Rochdale weavers founded the great Consumers' Cooperative movement, by applying Christian principles to marketing, and built up a huge, ramifying organization that set a pattern for later chain-store economies under capitalist management. Here, too, the weavers of Manchester upheld the cause of the North during our Civil War, though they themselves were starving for lack of Southern cotton to weave. One of the oldest problems in human development, the relation of moral qualities to esthetic forms, of goodness to beauty, hits one between the eyes here—far harder than it hit Plato, in an environment much richer in handsome bodies and well-formed buildings. The moral order and the esthetic order should not be congenitally incompatible, for they presumably have the same parents, but, like jealous offspring, they are often contentious and unresponsive to each other, and in the old industrial conurbations of England—'conurbation' is now a favorite English word for the endless scrambled urban sprawl—this aloofness sometimes comes close to downright hostility. As often happens, nature saves the day, for a sudden splash of color will now and then redeem this urban wasteland, especially the color of purple lupine, growing wild along the railroad cuts, as the goldenrod grows in our own country. The lupine followed me all over England, brightening the most depressing railside views, but my awareness of the rhododendrons was even stronger. If their splendor in June has been sufficiently appreciated and described, I have not stumbled upon the written passage that says so. In England, rhododendrons seem to thrive everywhere, but they are at their overpowering best, and in all their possible varieties, in a place near the country house where I stayed in Wales. The place is Portmeirion, an artful and playful little modern village, designed as a whole and all of a piece, on a peninsula close to the sea, and the rhododendrons.

Portmeirion is a fantastic collection of architectural relics and impish modern fantasies. The entire village is the work of the Welsh architect Clough Williams-Ellis, whose book 'England and the Octopus,' more than thirty years ago, was the opening gun in a fresh campaign to overcome the devastating ugliness that was spreading again in the motor age, as it had spread in the earlier railroad age, over the small historic towns and still verdant rural areas of Britain. Williams-Ellis was resuming and following through the pioneering work done by William Morris two generations before; and as a result of a sharpened public conscience about both the natural landscape and historic buildings, a whole series of public trusts and national foundations are now addressing themselves to this task, taking over ancient country inns and running them well, opening country houses and castles to public inspection, preserving ancient monuments and works of art—in short, reversing the policy of contemptuous and ruthless destruction that the old ironmasters and millowners regarded as a happy emblem of progress. At long last, even wild areas that had been deemed fit only for mining, quarrying, or for exploiting hydraulic power have been turned into national parks. So sensitive has England become over the quality of its landscape that the Electricity Board does not site a row of pylons to carry its high-tension wires without calling in its eminent architectural consultant, Sir William Holford.

In these efforts, Clough Williams-Ellis has had a hand; for he acquired and held a large part of the magnificent Welsh landscape that is dominated by the peaks of Snowdon until Parliament followed his lead by turning the area into a national park. As an architect, he is equally at home in the ancient, traditional world of the stark Welsh countryside and the once brave new world of 'modern architecture.' But he realized earlier than most of his architectural contemporaries how constrictive and desiccated modern forms can become when the architect pays more attention to the mechanical formula or the exploitation of some newly fabricated material than to the visible human results. In a sense, Portmeirion is a gay, deliberately irresponsible reaction against the dull sterilities of so much that passes as modern architecture today. If Williams-Ellis's work is more traditional in its echoes of old forms than the nursery-book novelties of Le Corbusier's chapel in the French town of Ronchamp, it is nevertheless prompted by a similar impulse, which does credit to both architects: to reclaim for architecture the freedom of in-

500

vention—and the possibility of pleasurable fantasy—it had too abjectly surrendered to the cult of the machine.

The nineteenth century owners of Portmeirion's site were responsible for the great plantation of rhododendrons for which the place is famous, but this weird forest of them is very much in the Williams-Ellis vein, as if by anticipation. The landscape of North Wales was new to me, and its bare hills, its dark outcroppings of slate and granite, its stone walls and stone farm buildings, its compact villages, also of stone, whose minute squares and open spaces relieve an otherwise oppressive sobriety and grimness, brought a shock of delight to me; and the roadsides, with their stone fences to keep in the sheep, are edged with spiky pennywort and magnificent dark green nettles, almost twice as high as our own breed. My visual experience was sharpened by my eating, on the first night, green nettle soup and Welsh saddle of lamb, both delicate and delicious regional dishes. The rearing, barebacked mountains of Wales, which finally plunge into the sea, must be counted among the most noble landscapes in the world; they have the starkness and almost the capacity to lift one to a super-mundane level that the landscape of Delphi has; indeed, one might even call Snowdon Wales' Parnassus, which would be proper only in a country that still does homage to its bards and orators, where every countryman still speaks in a soft singsong, as if verse were more natural than prose. In their usual callous manner, the Nuclear Gods have chosen this almost untouched part of wild Wales as the site, only a dozen miles from Portmeirion, of one of the great temples in which their priests will perform their dangerous even though seemingly innocent cosmic rites—a power plant that forms a vast, desolate pile, already half finished, which not even the talents of Sir Basil Spence, its architect, will be able to make acceptable to the eye.

To efface that image of desolation, one turns again to Portmeirion for communion with an older pantheon of earth gods in the rhododendron grove. The rhododendron bushes here often attain the height of trees, and in June they are bursting with multicolored clusters of blossoms. Here one stumbles along narrow paths, through almost impenetrable thickets and dark tunnels filled with purple light, tripping over twisted roots, battling with writhing stems, until the tangle suddenly ends on a cliff that discloses the sea. Nature has taken over this human plantation and turned it into a magnificent display of the savage energy of life itself, with its continued growth and efflorescence—perhaps our last hopeful symbol of deliverance from the death-oriented institutions, the suicidal strategies, and the dehumanized routines of our age. —The New Yorker. July 6, 1968

For Sophia, on Her Seventieth Birthday

"Never come the day that sees us old,"
Ausonius of Bordeaux wrote his young wife.
He had his wish, poor man! She died too soon
And stayed forever young. But you and I
Have spanned—what grace!—a fuller life:
For half a century we've faced together
Love's changing seasons, from tight-lipped buds
To sultry flowers, from crinkled leaves
To ice-glazed twigs, and back again
To leaping shoots and startled burgeonings.
And now we've found delight that only age
Can know: those bird-bright winter days
When cardinals feast on scattered seeds
Above the snow, more sweet than summer fruit.
Oh yes! my wife, my mate, my love, my friend,
"The day that sees us old" has strangely come.
At seventy time stops, and all our life
Becomes the living present, joined closely
In a seamless web that knows no end.
The less of age is more: for that give thanks!
My birthday gift for seventy is all our past
And all our days to come, bound fast
By love: sharing the storm-tossed raft that was
And is our life, defying wintry weather
And wind-whipped waves that slap our creaking planks:
Our saving hope and final prayer
To cling together
Still loving, fiercely one, unto the last.

—Amenia, New York. October 8, 1969

502

27: Myrtle and Forget-me-nots

These critical portraits of two old friends are only a token of my debt to a large, diversified "escort of friends" some of whom, like Thomas Beer, Paul Rosenfeld, Benton MacKaye, Henry Wright, Clarence Stein, and Artur Glikson I have already written about elsewhere, though not always to my satisfaction. More than once I have sought to round out the sketch of Van Wyck Brooks that I had already done for my Autobiography; but when I put it alongside Van Wyck's more extensive and generous survey of my work, it seemed all too brief, almost grudging; so instead I must refer the reader to our published letters to get the flavor of our relationship. Again, with Paul Rosenfeld, I feel the inadequacy of my public appreciation of his qualities as a literary critic, in Mellquist's symposium, 'A Voyager in the Arts.' There are still other close and dear friends, like Walter Curt Behrendt and Naum Gabo about whom I have hardly written at all. But the fact that the two major subjects chosen deserve to be better known gives a special reason for their being more adequately represented.

J. E Spingarn: The Scholar as Activist

No one could write an adequate account of American letters during the first thirty years of this century without discussing the work and influence of Joel Elias Spingarn. Yet it is only now, a whole generation after his death in 1939, that the first preliminary estimate of his achievements has appeared. We owe a debt to Professor Van Deusen for having undertaken this delicate and exacting task. His brief sketch, interweaving biog-

503

raphy with criticism, has a clarity often lost in a more exhaustive study. And one may praise this book further by saying that even when it exposes the weaknesses in Spingarn's early manifestoes, with their sweeping rejection of the traditional canons of criticism, it would have earned the approbation of Spingarn himself, who was too good a critic to overlook his own shortcomings.

In the 1920s every American critic from Irving Babbitt to Allen Tate reacted to Spingarn's challenge consciously or unconsciously: Spingarn enjoyed the notoriety of being a writer whose essays were freely discussed without being read; yet some who originally opposed him, like Professor Norman Foerster, were decent enough later to acknowledge their debt to him—if only for his pointing out the importance of Benedetto Croce. But surely few scholars ever gained such a large reputation on the basis of such a small output of books and papers. If not the proverbial *Homo Unius Libri*, Spingarn was substantially a man of only three books: the scholarly classic of his youth, 'Literary Criticism in the Renaissance,' which appeared in 1899, when he was twenty-four; 'Creative Criticism,' first published in 1917 and enlarged in 1931; and his singularly Melvillian poems which came out in 1924. In addition, he edited two collections of critical essays; and in one of them, 'Criticism in America,' he gallantly gave representation even to such an unworthy opponent as Professor Stuart Sherman—he who had questioned Spingarn's right to be considered 'American' because of his affiliations with the Italian Croce and his "sharp Semitic intelligence."

In all, Spingarn's writings seem a mere feather for tipping the scales in his favor. The mystery of his inescapable influence is not cleared up by examining the actual contents of his books; for what such a study discloses is less Spingarn's originality as a thinker than the ingrown provincialism of his American adversaries, who treated—as if it were an outrageous attempt to undermine the foundations of scholarly knowledge, political responsibility, and moral discrimination—his traditional defense of the activities of thought and imagination as the source of all that can be called a truly human life.

Viewed dispassionately Spingarn's critical iconoclasm was essentially an attempt to restore the primacy of the mind and do justice to the creative activities of the human spirit. Yet so completely had the positivism, the pragmatism, and the utilitarianism of post-seventeenth-century thought taken possession of Western scholarship that this effort to unify the inner and the outer world had indeed become a heresy, and gave Spingarn the reputation of being an irresponsible iconoclast. Going through Van Deusen's outline of Spingarn's whole life and work, one discovers that there was a potential leader who never fully developed, but who was arrested at a critical moment by ambitions and hopes that brought his university career to an end. Instead of exerting the influence of his incisive, powerful mind to become one of the first of the university activists, he became, in effect, one of the first of the rebellious dropouts.

Van Deusen's study has made it necessary for me to re-examine both Spingarn's philosophy and my own relation to him as a friend and fellow critic. We first met as members of the group that Harold Stearns had brought together in 1921 to compose 'Civilization in the United States'— the prototype of what turned out to be a long and increasingly boring series of symposiums, now being automated and mass-produced by means of the tape recorder. The essay Spingarn contributed to that book, Scholarship and Criticism, was one of the best—and by best I mean maturest—of his essays, to be placed alongside his Appeal to the Younger Generation, published in the Freeman in 1922. Despite a twenty-year gap in our ages, we edged slowly into friendship, and, surprisingly, he soon invited me, along with Van Wyck Brooks and Ernest Boyd, to a more intimate symposium at his country house, Troutbeck, in the Dutchess County hamlet I was soon to make my summer home.

That weekend at Amenia gave me the materials for a 'Dialogue on Esthetics,' which was first published in The American Mercury in 1924 and a year later became Troutbeck Leaflet Number Three. Looking over it recently, I was amazed to find how much of Spingarn's essential views of the nature of art and the function of criticism I was able to pack into that discussion, as well as my own early reactions to his and Croce's dialectic formulas. Apparently my equable exposition satisfied even Croce, for in a review in Critica he pronounced it *"fine e elegante."* Though I was always put off by Croce's tortuous Hegelian rhetoric and felt that Spingarn shackled his own thought when he conformed to it, this did not keep us from having many keen discussions of our respective positions.

Partly under Spingarn's influence I spent the better part of a year plowing through the formal literature of esthetics, from Edmund Burke, Coleridge, and the Wisconsin philosopher Bascom—whom Spingarn had independently unearthed—to Schiller, Santayana, and Croce. In this I was perhaps as much under the influence of Tolstoi as of Spingarn; and like Tolstoi in 'What Is Art?' I was put off by the esthetically irrelevant nature of most of this literature, though this did not bring me any closer to Tolstoi's one-sided moralism than it did to the theoretical esthetic isolationism of Spingarn's first expositions of 'The New Criticism.'

Spingarn's book 'Creative Criticism,' which included the original manifesto of 1910, 'The New Criticism,' was subtitled 'Essays on the Unity of Genius and Taste.' At what crepuscular critical seance, one asks oneself now, did those ancient ideological ghosts come forth? Unfortunately, until the 1920s, Spingarn's critical discussions were dogged by his effort to use an undefinable idea, genius, to give substance to an equally undefinable idea, more useful in cookery than in criticism, taste. Yet if one substitutes the terms 'creativity' and 'esthetic appreciation,' one sees that Spingarn was making a salutary effort to widen the scope of American criticism and overcome its genteel taboos: he sought to open the windows once more to the fresh air that Emerson, Margaret Fuller, and Whitman had long before brought in.

Spingarn's position can perhaps be most easily understood as the precise opposite of Henry Adams's surrender to the dominant forces of his age. If anything was unreal, Adams observed, it was the poet, not the banker: it was thought, not the things evoked and shaped by thought. Against Adams's meek abdication of the spirit, with its arbitrary separation of all mundane activities from the formative powers of the human mind, Spingarn's whole life was a continued protest. Unfortunately, Spingarn's scholarly training as a critic induced him to put these large issues within the banal framework of orthodox criticism, which had rarely absorbed the energetic attention of first-rate minds. Viewed biographically, Spingarn's effort to promote the new criticism may be explained as a first effort to throw off the harness, especially the bit and bridle, of the kind of scholarship for which he had undergone a sedulous training. Paradoxically, his own passion for perfection in whatever task he attempted—see his thirty-six-page bibliography for Vossler's 'Medieval Culture'—had made him the very model of the kind of scholar he had come to despise: one who aimed at easy targets in order to be sure of hitting the bull's-eye.

In his first polemical manifestoes Spingarn fastened on the domain of esthetics as the most neglected domain of criticism. While ultimately he demanded for the critic the right to play freely with all the inner resources of the human mind, he sought to release criticism from those arbitrary moral prescriptions and practical concerns which if taken seriously would stultify understanding the artist's expression; and in the same way Spingarn sought to emancipate criticism, at a lower level, from thematic analysis, piddling textual rectifications, supposedly 'objective' historic data that explained away whatever was significant or original in the artist's inner life, because it had no insight into any kind of innerness.

What Spingarn characterized as the new criticism was a mood and a method that would bring the critic closer to the 'madness' of the artist in his primal act of creation. To say that enjoyment, appreciation, and esthetic discrimination must precede any kind of intellectual or moral judgment seems hardly a revolutionary proposal. Who except the pedants could regard that as a threat to anything but pedantry itself?

From this elevated but not dangerously dizzy position Spingarn unfortunately jumped impulsively into a critical ditch, or rather two ditches. He held that the central office of the critic was to re-create the work of art, not in the impressionist's sense of merely recording the adventure of the critic's soul before a masterpiece, but in the sense of representing in purified esthetic terms the original performance. Spingarn never explained on theoretical grounds, why such a recapitulation was necessary or valuable: for why indeed should the critic linger over what the artist had already done except to prepare the ground for a more illuminating judgment? This kind of tautological replication in philosophic terms is what makes Crocean criticism an obstacle rather than a help to esthetic insight.

By Spingarn's criterion there was nothing for the new criticism to say about a work of art except to affirm its esthetic presence. Croce himself did not stop there, for Croce said: "There is no human thought that does not demand and expect to be perfected, enriched and modified by subsequent experience and reflection, and there is no book, no matter how great, that ought not to be read in a critical spirit." A decade after Spingarn's attack upon the academic establishment, he expressed the same sentiments in his manifesto to the younger generation.

Yet in one sense Spingarn's statement is beautifully true. Every work of art must be re-created again and again in order to be savored and understood. But that is the function of the reader—of generations of readers—not the critic, though no critic worth his salt will attempt to make an appraisal of any original work unless he has gone back to it at intervals, to efface his own preconceptions and come closer to the meaning and intention of the artist. This vital relationship between the creator and the appreciator was put once for all by the sculptor Naum Gabo when he said that every work of art is by its nature incomplete, that is, only half-created, until it has been finished by the beholder. Essentially it is the reader, the viewer, the auditor who performs the office that Spingarn reserves for the critic.

Spingarn had more than a glimpse of this doctrine, which would transfer his conception of criticism to the reader or viewer, in his essay Creative Connoisseurship. That essay, which gives the essence of Spingarn's critical theory, has been largely overlooked, while his polemic half-truths have been given undue emphasis; even Spingarn himself failed to carry it far enough to alter the center of gravity in criticism itself. The reasons for this neglect are quite obvious. Such a simple, nonacademic prescription seems little less than an insult to the over-zealous mind. Who could write an acceptable Ph.D. thesis or get professorial advancement on the basis of such limited activity? Yet Spingarn's effort to restore the creative approach to criticism miscarried in a peculiar way, for unintentionally he gave support to the kind of scholarship he was challenging. When translated into orthodox academic terms, Spingarn's new criticism fostered a quite different approach: one that elevated the critic above the creator and replaced the artist with the leaden-footed scholar, a specialist in semantic, symbolic, and rhetorical esoterica.

Once this canon was accepted in scholastic circles it became an offense to approach a work of art directly. Since the critic knows better than the artist what he has achieved, why should the reader bother with the original work at all? The ultimate creator turns out to be the critic. As a result students today are carefully trained to read everything that has been said about a work of art, but to keep a safe distance from the original creation itself. In substance this transposition of functions gives to the academic commentator the role occupied in medieval religion by the saintly intercessor, by whose aid alone one could hope to approach the throne of God (genius). Ultimately this has led to further perversion of criticism, whereby a population explosion of fake geniuses has come about—people who have no visible justification for being called artists except the *ipse dixit* of critics who tailor elaborate verbal clothes to cover their subject's brute nakedness, or rather, his esthetic nonexistence.

In confining the critic to purely esthetic perceptions Spingarn curiously overlooked an excellent argument for his own belief in the "unity of genius and taste": the fact that in the very heat of creation the artist himself is at every moment making corrections, critical revisions, and extensions that further clarify his expressions. Proverbially the artist's severest critic, if he is an artist at all, is himself. But were the artist too conscious of his necessary function, too detached, too judiciously cold, he would be paralyzed. So in the end he must leave the reader and the critic to later amplify the work in a more detached judgment. When Hawthorne pointed out to Melville the rich symbolic meanings of 'Moby-Dick,' Melville was properly grateful for this insight. But if he had begun with the symbolism fully worked out in advance, he would have turned the whole fable into a wooden academic exercise.

Neither the artist himself nor his critic can realize what the artist's purpose actually was until to his splendid surprise he views the final work. Perhaps the simplest way of explaining why Henry James, who had impeccable critical detachment, was inferior in creativity to Tolstoi or Dickens was that he knew all too well, and too deliberately, what he was doing: there was too much method and too little madness. In a decade before the great Freudian insights into the role of unconscious processes had become familiar, Spingarn proclaimed that 'madness' was an essential prerequisite to effective esthetic expression. Carried away by this valid perception, he overlooked the fact that the capacity to assimilate experience and give it coherent intelligible form is what distinguishes art from scatter-brained private fantasies.

Spingarn's original error of limiting the significance of a work of art to its esthetic aspect alone caused him out of sheer exuberance to amplify Croce's dictum that all art is expression. He went farther and proclaimed that all expression was art. On such an assumption art itself can no longer be identified, still less appreciated or judged; and Samuel Butler's little Italian lad, who thought that "Hey diddle diddle, the cat and the fiddle" was the most beautiful poem in the world, would be justified. Thus in emptying the esthetic and moralistic rubbish out of scholarly attics, Spingarn came pretty close to destroying the house of art itself.

Strangely there is an early poem of Spingarn's, later called 'Art, a Nightmare,' which even suggests that Spingarn himself once was visited by a demonic impulse to work precisely that destruction. But by the 1920s Spingarn was sufficiently detached from scholarly embroilments to have recovered his own intellectual balance: so he reminded the younger generation—though still in pure Crocean terms—of the importance of discipline, tradition, moral responsibility, rational judgment.

Certainly Spingarn would have shuddered over the later extrapolation that all expression is art could he have foreseen the infantilism of Pop Art and the mindless evacuations of the anti-artists. But often a critic's errors, by provokng further thought, turn out to be almost as important as the firmest truth; and on rereading Spingarn's 'Creative Criticism' I find myself asking many fresh questions: such as how it comes about that some of the greatest works of art—take 'The Iliad'— would be devaluated by a purely esthetic judgment; and how is it that some of the weakest theoretical conceptions of art have not prevented critics like Taine from making extremely keen esthetic judgments? Witness his early appreciation of Stendhal. To understand the contradictions in Spingarn's theory of criticism one must, I find, defy his own strict principles and see how far his failure to develop his great capacities for scholarship must be related to his own personal development.

As I read Spingarn's life, his audacious manifestoes were directed not against fallacies in criticism but against the entire academic establishment as such. His colleagues at Columbia did not have to read between the lines of 'The New Criticism' to perceive that Spingarn, though himself a paragon in exhaustive scholarly research, did not like professors or pedants, and did not admire their finished products. His one chef-d'oeuvre in this genre sufficed him for a lifetime. His reason for rejecting the academic establishment was that it did not by and large produce admirable men, still less mature minds capable of actively meeting the social, political, and moral demands of modern life. The ideal scholar in the new 'objective' style was one who had deliberately submitted to spiritual castration: only an insignificant part of the whole personality could function, because both 'madness' and 'courage' were lacking.

The truth is that Spingarn had in his mind broken away from the whole academic establishment and was itching to leave it long before he used President Butler's peremptory dismissal of his colleague Harry Thurston Peck as an excuse for challenging the university authorities in his own person with sufficient rancor to bring on his own withdrawal. In taking a stand against Butler, Spingarn found himself backed by hardly even a handful of supporters. The passivity—if not poltroonery—of the faculty only made his decision easier. Plainly, academic routine did not produce the kind of 'manliness' Spingarn valued: for him courage belonged equally to the soldier, the poet, and the scholar; and as he left the university he flung at his colleagues the verses that contain the bitter line: "Seven hundred professors and not a single man."

Though his ignominious dismissal from Columbia was galling to Spingarn, he did both Butler and the faculty too high an honor by accepting as final and total his severance from academic life. This resulted in his seeking in the life of action the qualities he found lacking in academia. In this mood he ran for political office, he trained at Plattsburgh to be a military leader, he devoted himself more heartily than ever to the cause of the Negro, he exercised his talents as an editor of Harcourt's European Library, he sought, as a country gentleman and a follower of Theodore Roosevelt, to invigorate a nascent country-life movement, and in the end he devoted himself to horticulture and became a world authority on clematis.

But his complete immersion in these 'extraneous' activities was nothing less than desertion to the enemy: to have been true to his own philosophy, which raised the life of 'theory' above that of practice, his duty was to apply both his imagination and his militancy to the reconstruction of the university, which, as then and now constituted, has little

510

use for original minds unless they sham dead. As a scholarly activist, but not necessarily as a fully harnessed professor, Spingarn might have used his personal economic independence to demonstrate what was lacking, and to utter challenges which those within the academic walls could venture to do only at some hazard to their future careers. Who was in a better position than Spingarn to play a leading part in this movement? Who had better earned the right to attack pedantic formalism, spiritless drill, subservience to institutional pressures from business and government?

Had Spingarn risen to that opportunity, he would not have been alone. William James had recently uttered his diatribe against the Ph.D. octopus; Thorstein Veblen was soon to attack the Higher Learning; Patrick Geddes in Britain was calling for the "University Militant." What I am saying, I suppose, is that when Spingarn withdrew from the university it was still open to him to become another Nietzsche, another Charles Peirce, another Whitehead: to demonstrate by his own example the meaning of creativity, not only in literature or painting but in every realm that the mind could reach. This would have been deeply in accord with his own philosophy, namely, that "all true idealism rests on the assumption that inner and outer reality are indissolubly intermingled in the realm of the spirit." Though Van Deusen has made a fine start in explaining Spingarn's later activities and evaluating them sympathetically, it remains for still another biographer to review more fully the various personal pressures and public events that turned Spingarn away from the one field where his own example—his 'madness' and his 'courage'—might have produced a decisive effect.

At the critical moment in his life, when Spingarn turned thirty-five, he made the fatal decision, prompted both by rebellious ambition and Dantean pride, to leave behind him the career in which, whether he went back to the university or not, he seemed destined for eminence. This decision in turn brought on many conflicts and inner tensions that manifested themselves in disabling illnesses, surgical interventions, and in a fading of élan and drive—all of which one would hardly have anticipated in the man whose photograph at this age remains vibrant and radiant with that vital energy which Blake called delight. Despite a succession of disappointments and physical setbacks, Spingarn's friends all through the twenties kept on hoping for his return at least as the challenging leader of thought he seemed cut out to be.

During that decade, Spingarn, emerging from his last serious illness, even played with the idea of establishing at Troutbeck an informal School of Wisdom, surrounded, at least in the summer, with kindred spirits. Still later, in 1931, when he accepted Alvin Johnson's invitation to deliver a series of six lectures at the New School, his friends still hoped he would resume his career as writer and scholar, if not as a tethered university professor. But that effort proved a final disappointment. He had anticipated, I suspect, an overwhelming ovation on the part of the young; but his audience was neither as large, as young, nor as eager for his message as he must have hoped. Though the lectures were taken down stenographically, the depth of his disappointment can be gauged by the fact that he never could be tempted to revise them. Only one lecture, Politics and the Poet, was sufficiently worked out to be published in The Atlantic Monthly in 1942.

In the end, the impression left by Spingarn both as a scholar and as a man calls to mind that produced by one of Edwin Arlington Robinson's enigmatic heroes: proud, reserved, saturnine, but smolderingly passionate. One hardly needed his own confession in verse to know that he had explored more than one dark circle in Dante's Hell. For those who knew him, Spingarn's inner greatness outshines his achievements and leaves behind a sense of unused potentialities: potentialities that, if they had been even partly realized, might have altered the academic institutions that had no place for his kind. Yes, he was, both in theory and practice, one of the first of the university activists; and his life, properly understood, should remain a call to the many succeeding generations who could well use his defiant courage, his sharp intelligence, and his many-sided grasp of the world around him. Van Deusen's modest monograph has made it possible for a coming generation to get closer to him than ever before.   —The New York Review of Books. March 23, 1972

Waldo Frank: The Ego and His Own

Today the name of Waldo Frank is almost unknown in his own country. But half a century ago Frank seemed to many of his contemporaries one of the most vital literary figures of his generation, then rivalled only by Van Wyck Brooks. His was a robust spirit, in tune with his age, eagerly exploring new paths in the novel, the drama, and in criticism, testifying by his presence to that general upsurge of creativity which brought back to the twenties the self-confidence that Emerson and his contemporaries had expressed almost a century earlier.

Before Frank was thirty he had come to the fore as co-editor of The Seven Arts, interpreting the spiritual ferment that was working no longer in Europe alone but in Our America. In confirmation of his American fame Frank was welcomed as a colleague and a potential equal by the leading writers of Europe, from James Joyce to Romain Rolland and Jules Romains, the Romains whose "unanimism" permeated Frank's 'City Block.' As early as 1926 his 'Virgin Spain' was widely accepted as a classic interpretation of Spanish culture by the Spanish-speaking world, beginning with the Rector of the University of Salamanca, Miguel de Unamuno. Though Frank's own countrymen have undervalued this work, the intelligentsia of Latin America have continued to admire it.

Who could have guessed, after such a swiftly mounting career, that this rocketlike reputation at the height of its trajectory would lose its momentum and plummet erratically to earth long before its energies were used up. But so it happened. During the last quarter century of his life Waldo Frank felt himself disdained and ignored by his countrymen, and during the final years no publisher would even consider his fiction for publication. When he died on the ninth of January, 1967, he left behind the manuscripts of two novels, the voluminous diaries he had kept all his life, and his still not quite completed autobiography. Though the present memoir presents one of the most illuminating pictures of the period that I know, and has even greater value as a personal confession, this manuscript went begging, even when offered to publishers who had brought out Frank's earlier work.

For most of Frank's contemporaries after 1950 he was no longer a star but a dead planet, almost invisible even by the reflected light of other stars. Critics who had either ignored or disparaged Frank's current work did not hesitate to dismiss him as "unreadable." Whether he is in fact unreadable the reader of this memoir will find out for himself: but certainly he, who had prided himself on being one of the avant garde, was no longer fashionable. This anticlimax was not the temporary fading out of a reputation that so often follows a writer's death. Established writers, even great ones like Goethe or Hugo, or popular ones like H. G. Wells and Arnold Bennett, often become 'unreadable' or rather invisible in their old age, like pictures that have hung too long on the same wall. But Frank met a worse fate, for while still alive, still productive, he vanished from the scene. Without dying he ceased to exist as a literary presence in his own country, though he still kept his Latin American readers. He had become too obscure even to be attacked.

This would have been a harsh outcome for an author whose writings were less significant than Waldo Frank's. But no matter by what standards one may rate Frank's work, such total indifference was not only unkind, it was unjust. If any proof were needed to show that Waldo Frank was still indeed a writer to be reckoned with, this autobiography should suffice. Though it is not an exhaustive work, and though it hardly does justice to his genuine achievements, the fact that Frank exposes and assesses his own errors and weaknesses, sometimes with scarifying objectivity, gives the true measure of the man. This memoir, backed by the testimony of his major books, should re-establish him as one of the important writers of his generation—the generation that includes J. E. Spingarn, Van Wyck Brooks, Paul Rosenfeld, Sherwood Anderson, and Frank himself at one end, and Ernest Hemingway, Scott Fitzgerald, William Faulkner, and Edmund Wilson at the other.

My task here, as I conceive it, is not to make a fresh evaluation of Frank's literary achievements, but to throw a light on them with the aid of his own belated discoveries about himself. This is a genuine problem, and it admits of no facile answer. How is it, I have often asked myself, that such an abundantly endowed personality, such a well-seasoned mind, at home in the literatures and religions of the world, such an active participant in the intellectual and political turmoil of our times, should have left on his own generation such a faint and often distorted impression of his genuine talents? If my claims for his work as a whole are not just the indulgent inflations of a friend, how is it then that they must be made at all? Though Frank and I had known each other for almost forty years, I lacked the inner clue to his fate until I read this memoir. Until then I was almost tempted to say of Frank, as he did of Simón Bolívar: "The more I delved into the man the less sense I had of understanding him." Fortunately Frank himself has provided in this confession, with unsparing honesty, all that anyone needs for understanding. What remains baffling is that he himself seems to have been unable to use this self-knowledge in guiding his own development.

The only satisfactory answer for me takes the form of a paradox. Perhaps Waldo Frank's greatest handicap was that he started in life with so few handicaps, or to speak more accurately, with such a surfeit of advantages. At birth some wicked fairy played the sinister joke of giving him a magnificent largesse of natural abilities, supplemented by all the cultural furniture that an upper middle-class household, well-stocked with books and music scores, free from importunate financial pressures or obsessions, accustomed to European travel, could afford. Everything that a youth of the highest potentials needed for his education and maturation was at hand for the asking—everything, that is, except hardship, deprivation, resistance, natural difficulty. Frank himself, even as a youth, seems to have been uneasy over this economic favoritism: and in fantasy, he took the side of the deprived and the subordinate—as in the incident he tells of the carpenter who was kept waiting in the kitchen while the family finished its leisurely dinner. Though spurred by his democratic convictions he later made many separate gestures of sharing the lot of the underdog, he never in fact flew far from this well lined bourgeois nest.

Our generation is only beginning to realize fully the perils of the Affluent Society, now that great masses of the population have a share in mass-produced abundance. But this is a peril that ancient aristocracies have often confronted, and what is worse, succumbed to. Many of Frank's convictions and much of his conduct could not be interpreted fully until the same trails—the same inordinate expectancies, the same demand for instant compliance—were magnified in the imperious conduct of the younger generation today. In following Frank's account of his childhood and adolescence, I find myself concluding that the surfeit of gifts and opportunities he enjoyed from the beginning coddled his exorbitant ego and kept him from making the best use of his many native capacities. At sixteen an immature novel of his was even accepted for commercial publication; only the prompt intervention of his family prevented that embarrassing 'success.' More such restraints and rebuffs might have seasoned his talents.

Part of Waldo Frank's affluence was organic and innate, the expression of a sturdy body and an active, highly sensitized brain; so even as a child his cultural precocity matched his material advantages. As a boy of ten or twelve he had passed beyond Dickens and was already reading Tolstoi and Balzac, and as a senior in high school he refused to attend the required course on Shakespeare because he felt he knew Shakespeare better than his teacher. (When he was older, I might add wryly, he transferred his sense of superiority from his despised teacher to Shakespeare himself.) That characteristic act of juvenile insolence deprived him of his high school diploma, but did not prevent him from entering Yale. There he had a brilliant scholastic career, being graduated with an M.A. as well as a B.A., with an Honorary Fellowship to boot. Who could doubt that his was a mind of the highest calibre: self-propelling, audacious, original?

Somewhat small in stature, though compact, as a youth Frank counterbalanced both his size and a kind of feminine sensitiveness with a show of defiant energy; and to the end of his life he was protected by an almost incredible naiveté from understanding the impression he made on others by his innocent assumption of superiority. To put it bluntly, on the evidence he himself offers, in early adolescence Frank was dominated by a mythical sense of his bodily self, or rather of his penis, contemplated in erection while floating in his bath, as the very center of his personal universe—a universe he actually named 'Waldea.' In all our intercourse he never mentioned this central motif to me, any more than Jung related to anyone his own comparable phallic dream. But the fact that Frank returns to this image at the end of his memoir offers a central clue to his personality, and above all, to his repeated failures to take into account and come to terms with the experiences of other men. If the cosmos was already within Frank, as he deeply believed, what else did he need?—except the willingness of his countrymen to acknowledge this myth and do homage to the ruler of 'Waldea.' Once Frank's authority was accepted, once this revelation stirred the masses, then what Frank conceived as the 'deep revolution' would take place.

Here again Frank's most serious defect sprang from his remarkable gifts: not alone his early intellectual maturity and his overabundant talents, but his unabated, seemingly uninhibited, sexual energy. Unfortunately his sense that he possessed magical powers which might transform the world, a sense he shared with a long succession of religious prophets, major and minor, undermined his ability to work with others or command their unreserved loyalty. 'Waldea' cut him off from reality. In a sense Frank secretly anticipated the rebellious London University student, by scrawling on his private wall: "I want the world and I want it now." As a result, Frank did not even get that part of the world to which his actual achievements entitled him.

Many exceptional minds achieve their growth in a spiritual cocoon, unconscious of their special gifts until ready to break forth. That is their good luck, the luck that both Whitman and Melville enjoyed. But young Waldo could not help being aware of his many genuine talents and gifts. As if to confirm this sense of himself, he came under the spell, he tells us, of Max Stirner's once famous book, 'The Ego and His Own,' which was translated into English at a critical point in Frank's adolescence: 1908. Though he mentions this book, Frank unfortunately does not appraise its influence upon him, perhaps because it only confirmed and reinforced an ego that was already tumescently visible. Yet even his friends would admit—and who sooner?—that the most trying aspects of his personality could be summarized in that title, 'The Ego and His Own.' Just because Frank's original endowments were so large, the demands of his ego became correspondingly inordinate, and the more his ego was slighted or denied, the more visible homage it demanded.

On this matter, Paul Rosenfeld's criticism, timely though emotionally somewhat ambivalent, might have helped release Frank's creative potential if Frank had not armored himself against criticism by seeing in Rosenfeld's analysis only hostility and envy. With full foreknowledge of how he was endangering their friendship and with many misgivings which he confided to Sherwood Anderson, Rosenfeld seized the publication of 'The Dark Mother' to analyze Frank's central weakness. "Don't think for a moment," he wrote Anderson, "that I wrote this merely because of the failure of the D.M. If I thought the failure of the D.M. merely a fluke, an ill chance, I would let the book pass unnoticed. But I perceive something at the base of the faulty esthetic of the work that is the very devil in Waldo, in me, in everyone. I hope to hit it wherever I catch sight of it. I hate it in myself, and give everyone the right to point to it whenever they spy it. . . . I have got to break that false circle Waldo has drawn about himself . . . the circle that forbids anyone to be frank with him about his work, and that threatens everyone who dissents with excommunication."

Unfortunately Frank's early successes stood in the way of his reducing the ego's demands to more reasonable proportions. He found himself at the top of the mountain without having been toughened in a slower, harder ascent by scrapes, falls, freezing winds. Success came to him too quickly and effortlessly, in every possible form: money, adulation, countless erotic adventures, flattering publicity. And much as he might despise popular journals with large circulations, it was there that, right into the thirties, he found receptive editors and a mixed audience that was no less responsive than those who attended his lectures. Such early acclaim may handicap a young writer far worse than twenty years' indifference; for thereafter any failure to gain the same measure of approval becomes a major misfortune, a sign, as Frank felt after the publication of his uneven collection of essays, 'Salvos,' of public neglect and alienation.

But even more than popular acclaim, Frank needed the recognition of his peers, and his patent efforts to achieve this too often evoked skepticism, if not suspicion. Regrettably the premature appraisal of his writing by Gorham Munson, in a book published in 1925, when but a single major work of Frank's—'City Block'—had appeared, had an effect like the exposure of an embryo to X-rays: it helped to bring on the leukemia that eventually vitiated his literary reputation. Frank did nothing to block this exposure; indeed, in his desire for early ackowledgment as one of the great writers of his generation—which he potentially was— he helped to nourish doubts about his genuine achievements and even perhaps to foster an unfair revulsion against his whole work.

Though at the outset I promised myself to write about Frank's life without discussing his literary work, I shall not be able to carry out this intention; for where else does one come closer to the essential being of a writer than in his mode of expression? Frank's early choice of words and metaphors provoked unfavorable criticism and eventually evoked the pat response I have noted, that he was 'unreadable.' How far was this reaction justified? Frank shared with many writers of his generation, long before unintelligibility became the badge of avant-gardism, the effort to freshen language by dissociating words from their traditional context and creating meanings through shattered metaphors: witness James Joyce and Boris Pasternak. In his early novels he sometimes strained too hard to embellish commonplace events with a bizarre prose. This, as Chekhov kindly tried to show young Gorki, was not originality but fake poetry.

As a boy, Frank had fallen in love with Edgar Allan Poe and admired the least admirable part of Poe, his pretentious use of esoteric words. Frank tells us that he then would observe at the dinner table that he was too 'lustrums' old, or that his hair was too 'planturous' to be combed. In time he came to write in his best moments a strong, supple prose; but he never entirely mastered the childish temptation to trot out an unusual word. Bittner points out that he ruined a whole passage in 'The Invaders' by needlessly inserting the strange word 'inspissate.' But in his best work after the twenties, this trick does not often intrude. He shook off these Poesque gewgaws; so it was his ideas, not his words, that the more hostile critics found hard to swallow. But since only those who were capable of thinking on the same plane as Frank were equipped to criticize effectively his vision of life and the program of action that he sought to derive from it, it was easier to dispose of his ideas by pointing to occasional verbal idiosyncrasies.

Obviously, most of the traits that I have noted are common in some degree to all artists and writers. Though Robert Frost's efforts to establish himself as the poet of his generation were more private, they have the same unpleasant characteristics; for it is only a rare Shakespeare or a Bach who dares to stand aloof and let his work speak for itself. But in Frank the claims of his ego had a retarding effect on the efflorescence of his extraordinary talents. As to his original gifts, all his friends—Adolph Oko, Roderick Seidenberg, Alfonso Reyes, Reinhold Niebuhr—could warmly bear testimony. Certainly he was one of the best educated men of his generation: no other contemporary I know of had read more widely, had reflected more deeply, had ranged so far in travel both at home and abroad, had encountered such a wide variety of people, both distinguished and humble, or had lived with so many different types, often on intimate terms—on a Wyoming ranch, among the populist farmers of Kansas, among French intellectuals on the Left Bank of the Seine, or even, once, in a prison cell with a low-grade Communist politician.

Not only was Frank an eager explorer of cities, landscapes, and cultures, but he had disciplined himself to record his day's experiences every night in his diary, and his outward explorations mingled there with inner probings of his personal life. What perfect training for a novelist! one instinctively exclaims. But here again Frank's life presents contradictions. For his finest qualities as a writer came forth, not in his novels, but in his perceptive interpretations of other cultures and ways of life: not merely Spain and Latin America, but Russia, Israel, and Cuba. Even in old age he was eager to explore China when invited to speak there at the Walt Whitman celebration.

In this brief sketch I cannot attempt to separate the tangled skeins of Waldo Frank's life. At best I can only point to the problems that a new generation of critics, beginning with Professor William Bittner, has now begun to explore. Central to any appraisal is the philosophy that consciously underpinned—and alas partly undermined—his entire work. Two large themes, with religious foundations and political consequences, dominated Frank's whole career. One was his personal mission, addressed to restoring the individual's sense of cosmic unity and personal commitment: a unity that, on his historic analysis, had been lost with the breakup of the 'medieval synthesis' in Western Europe. This belief in his special mission was secretly attached to his juvenile Waldean myth; for though he ostensibly sought love and personal union he also carried with him a Stirnerian demand to satisfy the ego on his own terms, without concern for the interests or feelings of other people.

Frank's innate sense of being one of the elect was flatly opposed to his conscious democratic sympathies; but unfortunately it went far deeper and led him, as he himself ruefully recognized at the end of his life, to nourish fantasies as private and as high-flown as Don Quixote's. Who but Frank could for a moment have supposed that by aligning himself with the party Communists in the thirties he could convert them, overnight, from orthodox Marxist Stalinism to the more religious 'Waldean' concept of the 'deep revolution' founded on the expression of the whole personality? This quixotism hampered both his personal relations and his social hopes, and in the end, without a Sancho Panza to bring him down to earth, it left him lonely and abandoned without even the solace of his utopian dreams.

The other dominant theme, present from Frank's youth too, was his desire for union with God. To feel that God or the cosmos was within one and to surrender utterly to it was, on Frank's readings, the key to human salvation. This openness to transcendent realities that cannot be put into words or rationally explicated gave Frank a vivid understanding of the historic function of religion. That mystic sense was so lacking in his generation that many who still considered themselves religious and regularly attended church or synagogue utterly lacked it. In believing that the mystery of life was an essential aspect of its meaning Waldo Frank was on firmer ground than most of his own intellectual generation. This partly accounts for their total rejection of him. To the popular pragmatists and rationalists, the very word mystic was anathema: they held that the ultimate mysteries would either be explained—that is, devaluated—by science or erased by the advances of technology. Thus Frank was separated from his contemporaries by one of his positive virtues: his concern for meanings and values and perceptions above and beyond those which the here-and-now world admits. As a result of this breach, his religious conceptions never received the rigorous criticism they deserved. For had Frank's contributions here been taken seriously, he might have become conscious of the fatal isolationist streak in his interpretation of the 'Great Tradition.'

In his boyhood Frank had identified himself with a cat he encountered, as part of the same cosmic whole: a profoundly Hindu conception of cosmic unity, which Emerson had put to perfection in his poem, 'Brahma.' But for a man who had such an intuition of unity, Frank's philosophy was a singularly Western one: what he called the Great Tradition was essentially the Western tradition, or at least that part of the Western tradition which had taken form about the Mediterranean, mainly in Palestine, in Egypt, Greece, and Rome. Frank's fixation on that Great Tradition was, to say the least, one-sided, since upon a mere count of heads it excluded about half the human race. Strangely Frank seemed untroubled by the fact that this was far from being a universal solution, even if by some miracle the 'deep revolution' he sought could be brought about. This was a flaw that ran through all Frank's thinking.

But the errors of an original mind are often more fruitful than the truths of a more limited one; and by understanding the background of Frank's thought and seeing into what he sought to do, one has a more comprehensive insight into vital problems affecting the whole future of mankind, not merely the intermingling of the races but the marriage of cultures and the efflorescence of personalities, than one would otherwise have. Let me here confess my own debt to Frank's earnest concern with the most central area of life, that of religion. It was partly by wrestling with Frank's passionate metaphysical convictions, which I could never make my own, that I opened the way to an answer more satisfactory to me—one that, as Emerson had put it, includes the skepticisms as well as the faiths of mankind

The issues that Frank raised in book after book are the essential issues of human life: they deal with its meaning and value, and question all those institutional routines and ideological fixations which limit man's consciousness and his potentialities for further growth. That Frank wrestled with these problems at a moment in Western history when even the Churches, in the main, had lost sight of them or had lost faith in the standard solutions is more significant than the fact that Frank's own answer was inadequate.

The contrast between Frank's ego-dominated energies and his vision of social justice and personal love brought exacerbating inner conflicts, and those conflicts were never to be resolved, even in the period of self-criticism and personal humility that marked the last decade of his life. To judge by his quotations from his own diaries, he was engaged in endless moralistic battles with himself, nagged by a persistent sense of guilt. This self-examination started early, for when his own conduct brought his first marriage with Margaret Naumburg to an end just at the moment when, with the birth of their first child, he confessed to himself his readiness to accept the joys and obligations of fatherhood, he realized that he had not only failed in marriage but cheated himself. But even this realization did not cause him to alter his course: "The supreme sin," he told himself, "is not to be able to forgive yourself."

That self-absolution was naive. With Frank's deep understanding of Christianity, with his admiration for Thomas Aquinas, he surely should have remembered that the only way to earn forgiveness is to repent and change one's ways. Like the defiant high school boy who forfeited his diploma rather than apologize for or alter his conduct, Frank chose to feel guilty and not to repent. So too, though in time he regretted his unkind portrait in The New Yorker of his English professor, William Lyon Phelps, who had greatly stimulated and nourished him, he reprinted it later in a book. Even worse, he held up to scorn in 'Salvos' a popular poet who, on Frank's own interpretation, was not worth his attention. Though he felt rejected by his countrymen, it was only belatedly that he realized, in his description of his relations with the Washington Square Players, how ready he had always been to scorn their values and reject their advances. Frank needed comrades and colleagues of equal gifts to give body to his own vision, but what he actually sought was disciples who would accept his "total commitment to either revolution or revelation." On those terms he was forced to disparage even his best friends because they did not share his peculiar commitment, though by excluding the rest of the world he crippled and ultimately excluded himself.

Little though Frank's contemporaries appreciated his true worth, they were nevertheless justified in their sense that there was a discrepancy between his professions and his actions. Toward the end of his life he became bitterly aware of this disparity, one long ago acknowledged in the famous words of St. Paul. But despite Frank's critique of empirical rationalism, he pinned too much of his hope for personal improvement on new techniques for achieving 'wholeness,' especially that based more or less on the therapeutic exercizes of Matthias Alexander which had attracted John Dewey. Though the book in which he elaborates this prescription, 'The Rediscovery of Man,' has like the earlier 'Rediscovery of America' many pregnant passages in it, this mode of 'salvation by posture' proved on his own pathetic confession an imposture, for it had not operated successfully in his own life. In asking for a quick personal remedy Frank was, in opposition to his own valid insights, denying both the complexities and the depths of anything worthy to be called a good life, for such a profound transformation demands a lifetime of effort, without any promise, apart from moments of grace, of some final consummation. Alexander's sword could not sever *that* Gordian knot. Only in 'Waldea' could the collective transformation Frank passionately sought be achieved.

So once more we come back to the struggle between Waldo Frank's expansive genius and his insistent, self-defeating ego. In his youth, Frank explains in this memoir, he had made a covenant with God to give up "the expected rewards of an author, money (Kipling), disciples (Tolstoi), World Fame (Hardy, Meredith, Shaw) in order to search for Truth." But this was a brazen self-deception: in his heart he had given up none of these rewards. To judge by his actions, Frank valued money, disciples, and fame almost as much as Ernest Hemingway did, though less blatantly. Yet the means that he took to achieve these ends only put them further away, so that he became toward the end of his life what he had called the hero of his first book: 'The Unwelcome Man.'

The allusion I have just made to Hemingway would have shocked Frank, but it is more than a haphazard reference. Looking at Stieglitz's portrait of young Waldo Frank in the frontispiece of Gorham Munson's study, the intense innocent face, the intent eyes, the fierce black hair, the bravado moustache, one realizes that he was physically a smaller counterpart of the younger Hemingway I met once at one of Rosenfeld's soirées. From a literary standpoint, the two were of course diametric opposites: Hemingway's marvellous ear for the spoken word, his studious underemphasis, his affectation of a limited vocabulary in which "good" served as a stand-in for all other adjectives and adverbs—this was the opposite of Frank's strained, overflorid early prose, in which buildings or furniture often showed more life than the human characters.

In actual life, however, there were many points of resemblance between Frank and Hemingway. Both were wilful men, both were restless for physical adventure, both failed in their early marriages, and above all, both were licensed egoists in the old-fashioned nineteenth-century style. Not least, their early triumphs kept each—though in different ways— from fulfilling his potentialities; so at the end each was sunk in black despair. But the fact that Waldo Frank could nevertheless face his life and expose his weaknesses with the candor he shows in this memoir, gives him a large margin of superiority over Hemingway in moral courage.

As for physical courage, Frank had that too, in more than usual measure: he was equal to facing the blows of the posse that ran him and his fellow-investigators of a coal strike out of Harlan County, Kentucky, back in the thirties: he was equal, too, to flying over the Andes in an early single-motored plane, to standing up to the Fascist thugs who laid him low with a blow on the head in his apartment at Buenos Aires, and, not least, early in the twenties to exploring the South, with Jean Toomer, disguised as a fellow–colored man and accepting the indignities that the Negro endured. This courage wore perhaps the armor of innocence; he did not believe evil could befall him. Yet after one has reckoned with Waldo Frank's egotism, one must remember this heroic side of him which nobly offsets it. Whatever his need for public appreciation, he never boasted of these heroic encounters, still less attempted to capitalize on them. And in this respect, too, he stands as a man in happy contrast to Hemingway.

If I have been as unreserved as Frank himself is in appraising his life, it is because, after due allowance has been made for all the idiosyncrasies and faults that alienated so many of his contemporaries, much of Frank's work actually remains admirable: full of luminous perceptions, challenging interpretations, vibrant calls to further thought and action. If Frank felt himself in his own words a Jew without Judaism and an American without America, it was partly because he had by his own efforts transcended these limitations and become a true man of the world. Not alone was he at home in all the new movements in the arts, realizing that the modern world had disclosed social and esthetic values no earlier culture had been aware of. To counterbalance this he had a special sense of older treasures that the modern world was, to its own loss, ignoring or brutally destroying. These values he found through repeated intercourse with the fundamentally primitive peasant cultures of Latin America, with their vivid emotional responses and erotic expressions. And it was here, I suggest, that Waldo Frank made his unique contribution. On this matter the verdict of his ranking Hispanic contemporaries deserves to be taken seriously; and if Frank had at an earlier point fully understood his own gifts, it is in this realm, I believe, that he would have concentrated a major part of his energies.

In making this judgment I am in effect depreciating Frank's novels; and that would have grieved him; for he regarded his imaginative fiction as his central life work. Let him then speak for himself. "I was not a politician, not an economist or a preacher; I was a poet. My method was simply to tell stories that revealed—within the heartbreak, within the dark and terrible mystery of being born and of living—that joy which is the presence of God made known beyond knowledge."

Yes, that was his conscious intention. And if he had indeed achieved it in his fiction, he would now rank with Gogol, Dostoevski, and Tolstoi. But as earnestly and sympathetically as one may read Frank's novels, this joy is just the redemptive quality one fails to find in them. That note one finds in Tolstoi's description of the mowers in 'Anna Karenina,' and one finds it again in Father Zossima's deathbed injunctions in 'The Brothers Karamazov': some of it pervades all their works. But despite Frank's effort to impart this divine joy through his fiction, the place where it naturally arises, organically and magnificently, is in his imaginative representation of other cultures: pre-eminently in 'Virgin Spain,' in 'South American Journey,' and in his biography of Bolívar.

Now it is in Frank's major works, where he himself is least visible, least seeking to manipulate events and experiences in order to reveal his ultimate philosophy and plan of redemption, that the poet comes out and his true virtues as an imaginative writer, as a kind of lyrical anthropologist and historian, rise to the surface. In this realm Frank has few American rivals, and for any comparable gift one must go back to writers like de Tocqueville and Taine. In these books Frank actually comes close to what he dearly wished to achieve in both his life and his novels: the surrender of himself to a movement of life that transcends his personal limitations. What Frank saw, felt, grasped, understood of the elemental Hispanic world completely absorbed him; and he surrendered himself to it like an imaginative lover who, by his very self-effacement, gives more of himself to the object of his love.

Though I regard Frank's interpretation of nations and cultures as offering the best evidence of his special gifts, there are other works that have stimulated and challenged me, and may still do so to later readers if only as mementoes of past historic occasions and now buried hopes. These begin with 'The Rediscovery of America' and come to a climax, as a further summation of his conscious philosophy, in 'The Rediscovery of Man.' In between lies his timely and often cogent 'Chart for Rough

Water.' If Frank's autobiography sends the reader back to these books, he will not, I promise, come away empty.

But enough! Far more important than anything I have been able to say in this Introduction, by way of either appreciation or negation, are Frank's own reflections on the whole course of his life: for this memoir, written in the loneliness of old age, while inwardly battered to the point of almost suicidal despair, exhibits such an access of self-knowledge, such desperate candor about his human misjudgments, his political naivetés, his Quixotic fantasies, as few men dare to display even at the height of their powers. In his latter years Frank had in fact achieved a humility and an honesty that should disarm all petty personal hostility. Here, as repeatedly in his latest letters to me, his grief over the cold indifference of his contemporaries mingles with a remorseful wonder over whether the fault may not in fact have been his own.

Looking into his own heart, Frank plainly did not find "the whole and integral man" who was to "create the fertile revolution." Both had turned out to be mythical projections, disappearing below the waves with the sinking continent of 'Waldea.' For consolation he turned to the image of Don Quixote, whose heroic illusions would still be needed to quicken the ass's pace of the multitude of sober, down-to-earth Sancho Panzas.

Too late Frank had acquired the self-knowledge that might have altered his whole career and earned for him in his own generation the place that his redoubtable talents originally promised him. It had taken a lifetime of experience for him to understand that though he might have "the egoism of the martyr" he had utterly lacked "the shrewdness of the saint." He realized in these final hours that his bravest ambitions had been thwarted, his most generous social hopes had been betrayed, his prophetic announcements had remained unheeded: in short, his cosmos had fallen apart and his God had deserted him. Yet out of that funeral pyre of Waldo Frank's ego, a living writer arose; the brave man who in his last days wrote this memoir of his life. —Introduction to 'Memoirs of Waldo Frank,' edited by Alan Trachtenberg. University of Massachusetts Press. Amherst, 1973

On Receiving an Honor in Literature

A citation always has something a little ironic about it. It's as though one were listening illicitly to one's obituary. And to speak frankly, I'd rather be dead than listen to my obituary. But in another sense, this is a resuscitation, a coming back to life again. When I learned from Felicia Geffen that I was supposed to make a formal written response, I quailed at this. As you see, I have no notes here. So I began to play in a fanciful way with various ways of making such a response. How would Emerson have made it? What would Henry James have said? And I had a wicked thought, which I scarcely dare disclose here to my quick and intelligent colleagues! I remembered the mock humility of Henry James's reply to Walter Berry when Berry presented him with an utterly ornate and impossible sort of dressing case. Poor James shrank so, he said, in the presence of this "article," this *procédé*," which he scarcely dared name; he said it was so far above the poor shabby hold-all which he ordinarily used in travel that really it was too much for his humble station. Well, one can overdo that! and one mustn't question the judgment of one's superiors.

Then I thought of another equally wicked sally—how Melville in his old age might have greeted such a medal. I remembered that he had written a little poem called The Flowering Aloe, about the Century Plant which blooms only once in a hundred years, meaning that finally this poor old pathetic plant, Herman Melville, had at last flowered. He hears the plant saying to the roses that used to scorn him when they passed, "accounting him a weed": *"See, I am in flower now!"* That didn't seem quite modest enough for an occasion like this! So I recalled something that happened once when Frank Lloyd Wright asked my wife and myself to lunch at the Plaza, and showed us for the second or third time the collection of medals he had been given in Europe. Admittedly, Wright was a self-confident man, full of bounce and audacity, yet he was—not too secretly—proud of these medals. Then we went down to lunch, and as we were walking through the corridor, along came two waiters rolling a big round table-top. Wright stopped, clapped his hand to his forehead, and said in mock amazement, "What! *another medal?*" And at this point my old guide and mentor, Emerson, disposed of both Wright's cockiness and my own qualms, for I heard him quietly whisper: "The day will come when no badge, uniform, or star will be worn."

But alas! since I've worked unusually hard over the book that's coming out next year—harder than I like to work—in my weariness I was obliged to put all these playful thoughts behind me. I certainly had to put away any notion of writing down beforehand what I was going to say. And I felt a little hesitant—regretful, almost ashamed—to come here as unprepared as I actually am. What on earth could I possibly say on this occasion? Standing here now, still at a loss for words, I suddenly remember that just five years ago I opened our Spring Academy meeting, and Mr. Kennan, who was then President of the Institute, conducted the rest of the meeting when I was through with my part. Today, once more I am standing on the same platform. Mr. Kennan is now President of the Academy, and I am closing the meeting. It took a little courage on the part of the Academy, I would say, to give me a medal at this late day, and to ask me to appear again on this platform, since the affairs of the world have grown much grimmer, much more sinister than ever. We Americans are all of us still involved in the atrocities that have been committed in our name by our Government and its Military Arm. We have witnessed this moral debacle, and by our silence, in so far as we have been silent, we have sanctioned it and taken part in it. And then I said to myself: But this has already been said. *I said these words here in 1965*. What I said is in print. I would not add a word to that address, even though the times have steadily grown worse. I would not take away a single word. And the fact that I said all this at such an early date absolves me from saying anything further now—except the simple sentence which I meant to begin with: Thank you for the honor you have given me.   —Acceptance of the Gold Medal for Belles Lettres and Literature of the National Institute of Arts and Letters. 1970

Call Me Jonah!

Friends and Colleagues: I don't know how to face this bestowal of the National Book Award. With all my due preparation for this event I'm now left speechless. And yet this literary honor, the National Medal for Literature, is in many ways the climax of all my earlier honors: nothing less than the celebration of my Golden Jubilee. Some fifty-odd years ago, my wife and I got married. Those fifty years have left a mark on everything that I have written. When I spoke to a large audience in Dublin, the summer before last, the Chairman in introducing me said: "I am happy to say that Mrs. Mumford, too, is here with us tonight, and you will be interested to know that they recently celebrated their Golden Wedding." And the whole audience broke into applause; they were so surprised that two Americans could live together that long!

Then I realized a little while ago while putting together some essays and reviews of mine, that this was the fiftieth anniversary, too, of my being a writer of books. My first book, 'The Story of Utopias,' (which I wouldn't recommend to anybody!) is still in print. It came out in 1922. Dr. Dubos and I might have a private fight about my 'Utopianism' later on. But that's not for this occasion.

Facing my fifty years as a writer of books, I put together a book of my own, a quite new book, though composed entirely of published material. A real book, not just a collection of scattered essays, but a highly organized assemblage of 'Interpretations and Forecasts' from 1922 to 1972. About those interpretations and particularly about those forecasts, I can only repeat what I have said more than once to my wife: "I would die happy if I knew that on my tombstone could be written these words, 'This man was an absolute fool. None of the disastrous things that he reluctantly predicted ever came to pass!' Yes: then I could die happy."

You see what's happened to my well-prepared 'impromptu' talk! It is already turning into something quite different; and in order to stress that, I am tempted to add some seasoning to Dr. Dubos's eulogy, and perhaps also to Senator McCarthy's remarks. Grateful though I am to both speakers, I am going to give a brief but quite different account of the man in front of you. To begin with, his name is Jonah. This places him as one of the minor prophets, not to be mentioned in the same breath as Amos or Isaiah. Jonah has become one of my favorite books in the Bible, though he figures in my personal life, not as a character to imitate, but as an admonitory figure, exposing my failings, taking me down when I am too elated by some minor success, jeering at my most acute forecasts.

This private Jonah is of course quite different from the stock character still visible in folklore. You know what Jonah stands for in the mind of the ordinary man today. The popular conception of Jonah is principally that of a bringer of bad luck. If anything goes wrong, Jonah is to blame for it. Jonah is that terrible fellow who keeps on uttering the very words you don't want to hear, reporting the bad news and warning you that it will get even worse unless you yourself change your mind and alter your behavior. What can people do with such a nuisance? Well, what happened to Jonah when he took the ship from Joppa? And why to begin with did he want to escape from Nineveh? Because he was fleeing from the voice of the Lord. Jonah did not want to tell the people of Nineveh, that mighty metropolis, what the Lord commanded him to say. *"If you go on this way you will be destroyed."* So Jonah abandoned his mission and fled as fast as he could for a distant port. But once at sea a violent storm arose, and everyone on board cursed Jonah for bringing bad luck to the ship. Then the crew threw him overboard, and he was swallowed by a whale. There the straightforward account of events takes a fresh turn, and the whale now becomes an important part of the story; for it turns out that the whale was sent by God to succour Jonah. What must have seemed to Jonah to have been desperate bad luck turns out in fact to be his salvation.

At this point something very strange happens in my own imagination. First I begin to identify my own life with Jonah's, and then Jonah himself turns into the whale, not the Biblical whale but the whale in Herman Melville's stormy sea drama, 'Moby-Dick.' What kind of a whale is this transmogrified Jonah? Does he resemble Moby-Dick, that tortured monster of the deep? No: not closely; for he is plainly no Leviathan. Perhaps he is nearest to the Right Whale, another species of whale that Melville describes. The human term for the Right Whale would be the Righteous Whale. Strangely the very day this notion came to me I had been reading a passage in Samuel Butler where he said: "If a man doesn't want to destroy his reputation entirely for the future, he mustn't be right too often." My identification with the Right Whale, or to put it more honestly, the Righteous Whale, exposes an unpleasant temptation every prophet must guard against: the temptation to remember how often he had been right.

Closely related to the Right Whale in my imagination is still another species, the Narwhale. If any of you know German you will appreciate this identification. In German 'Narr' means fool; and the Jonah-Whale is a fool whale, an idiot whale. That is an understandable aspect of Jonah: he ventures to defy prudence and common sense, to point to evils that people have learned to close their eyes to, and blurt out truths they are trying to hide from themselves. Anyone who has something new and important to say must be brazen enough, self-confident enough, to out-face those Ibsen called the 'compact majority,' who will regard his readiness to speak out as a proof that he is either crazy or an 'Enemy of the People.' Only a fool would be vain enough to suppose that what he alone says now will some day seem important, no matter how many people reject it, or how scornfully they continue to dismiss it. So much for my private transformation of the story of both Jonah and the Whale.

But there is a more telling version of this singular story in 'Moby-Dick': the classic interpretation of Jonah's moral dilemma that one finds in Father Mapple's sermon. In that parable the whale has not the slightest importance. The important fact is that Jonah, who was a dedicated prophet, had heard the voice of the Lord, and in a cowardly panic ran away from it. He didn't dare to deliver the awful message he got directly from the Lord's mouth. Jonah fled from Nineveh as far as he could, and almost welcomed being buried in the belly of the whale; that, at least, got him out of his unwelcome duty to admonish the people of Nineveh about changing their ways.

This betrayal of his mission as a prophet is what Father Mapple properly denounces and castigates in that most magnificent passage. I have read his words aloud again and again, and each time the sermon gets better and better. It teaches something we must all learn if and when Truth calls us. For what is the lesson of science? What is the lesson of religion? Whenever Truth commands us, we must obey it and utter it aloud whether our friends and neighbors and countrymen like it or not.

There is a special lesson in the Book of Jonah which Melville chose to pass over. It comes out only at the end in Jonah's petulant complaint to God. This querulous conversation contrasts unfavorably with that incredible earlier dialogue Abraham had with God over the terms on which Sodom and Gomorrah, those cities of violence, bestiality, and hardcore pornography, might be saved from God's wrathful destruction. In a wonderful scene, a perfect example of Oriental bargaining, Abraham gets God to admit that perhaps these cities would be worth saving if as few as fifty righteous people could be found there. Agreed! But if not fifty, what about forty? If not forty, then perhaps thirty? And so, finally, by wheedling and needling, Abraham gets God to promise that those cities might be saved if as few as ten decent people could be found there. To their honor, it is plain that neither God nor Abraham wanted these cities destroyed, whether the majority repented of their sins or not. If a saving remnant could be found—that no doubt is where we get the phrase 'a saving remnant'—even Sodom and Gomorrah could survive.

Jonah comes off badly in comparison with the wise and wily old Patriarch, who didn't set out to be a prophet. Jonah actually feels let down by God because God didn't carry out his threat any more than he had punished Jonah for having failed the first time to deliver his message, but gave him another chance. In effect, God made a fool of Jonah by acting more mercifully than Jonah had guessed he would; and the people of Nineveh had made a double fool of him by tearfully repenting of their sins, from the King down. No wonder Jonah feels so humiliated that he wants to die. Jonah's monstrous error was to imagine that he knew in advance how badly both the people of Nineveh and God would behave.

In the final passage of this account it is plain that God had no more confidence than had Jonah that the people of Nineveh would permanently change their ways; but he was touched by at least their public remorse over their violence and villainy. That was something: so perhaps in future the garbage would be collected more regularly and officials would blush when they took a bribe or broke a law. That was all God seems to have expected from this proud city of six score thousand people—and here I quote—"who could not tell their right hand from their left." The moral need not be spelled out. Woe to the prophet who confuses his own voice with the voice of the Lord and who thinks he knows in advance what God has up his sleeve!

530

Now you know why I have told you this story. In a sense it is the story of my life, because I am much closer to the mythic Jonah in all his ways, not least his temptations, than I am to any utopian dreamer. If anything, I am an anti-utopian, who knows that a blessing repeated too often may become a curse, and that a curse faced bravely may become a blessing. I wrote a whole chapter in one of my earlier books, 'Faith for Living,' entitled "Life Is Better than Utopia." Long ago John Ruskin taught me that "there is no wealth but life." So long as consciousness remains up to the point where it is obliterated by bodily injury or intolerable pain, life is, as Henry James once said, the most precious thing, one might say the only precious thing, we truly possess.

That is the sort of man who is talking to you tonight: neither a pessimist, nor an optimist, still less a utopian or a futurologist. And now, at the end, I want to say an almost unsayable thing, to record the depth of my thanks for what you have done on this occasion—to express my gratitude, not alone to those who are here, not just to those who have sung my praises, or who have bestowed this award, but also to those nameless voices coming from the distance and the deep, when I was entombed in the belly of the whale. Their response to my words has given me the faith to struggle out of that darkness and rise up into the sunlit air again. In the name of Jonah, the Biblical Jonah, Melville's Jonah, my private whale of a Jonah, and above all God's Jonah, I thank you. —December 13, 1972

Index

540

Perugini, Giuseppe, 409
Pétain, Henri, 413
Phelps, William Lyon, 521
Philosophy, 26–27, 34–36, 93, 187, 355–56; and science, 189–90
Photography, 219–20, 222
Picasso, Pablo, 20, 230–32 and n, 238
Pirenne, Henri, 396
Plato, 26, 31, 49, 117, 182, 272, 357, 499; 'Phaedrus,' 41; 'Republic,' 247, 363
Play, 201–02
Plotinus, 17
Poe, Edgar Allan, 242, 243, 247, 259, 518
'Poetry,' 244
Poincaré, Henri, 189, 218; 'Science and Hypothesis,' 117
Poland, 390, 453, 458
Police, 13, 71
Polo, Marco, 478
Pompeii, Italy, 489–90
Poole, Ernest: 'Harbor, The,' 244
Pope, Arthur, 372
Portmeirion, Wales, 500–01
Power, 9, 193–94, 450–51, 469, 471–73, 475–84; and nuclear weapons, 437, 465
Pre-1970 Ecology, 29–32
Primacy of Mind, The, 469–73
Primitive man, 196
    and art, 188, 193, 202, 215, 229, 473
    and language, 193–94, 470, 473
    organic development of, 470–71, 474
Progress: and science and technology, 6–16, 451, 468, 471, 474, 482, 485–86
Proust, Marcel, 257; 'Guermantes Way, The,' 174; 'Swann's Way,' 324
Psychoanalysis, 104, 299, 430

'Querschnitt, Der,' 373–74

Radin, Paul, 256
Radio, 103–04, 365, 367, 383, 487
Ramakrishna, 184
Redon, Odilon, 239
Regional planning, 106–08
Religion, 26–27, 32, 84, 173, 183–84, 195, 202–04, 207, 233, 346, 350, 353, 477–78
Rembrandt van Rijn, Paul, 226, 227
Renan, Ernest, 226
Renewal of Life series, 16–17, 273, 483
Revolutions, 354, 382, 384
Reyes, Alfonso, 518

Reynolds, Sir Joshua, 77
Riehl, Wilhelm Heinrich: 'Natural History of the German People,' 104–05
Rilke, Rainer Maria, 177, 425
Robertson, Will, 55
Robinson, Edwin Arlington, 243, 512
Robinson, Frederick B., 50
Robinson, Geroid, 57–58, 80, 87
Robinson, James Harvey, 51
Rockefeller, J. D., Jr., 415
Rodin, Auguste, 20
Roentgen, Wilhelm, 3
Rolland, Romain, 513
Romains, Jules, 174, 513
Rome, Italy, 490–91; ancient, 377–78, 490
Roosevelt, Eleanor, 430
Roosevelt, Franklin D., 50, 311n, 395, 396, 398
Roosevelt, Theodore, 510
Root, John, 253
Rosenfeld, Paul, 162, 163, 235, 241, 245, 320–21, 503, 514, 516–17, 522
Rosenstock-Huessy, Eugen, 327
Ross, Cary, 311
Ross, Harold, 37
Rossetti, Dante Gabriel, 286
Rothenstein, John, 417
Rourke, Constance, 242
Rousseau, Jean-Jacques, 10, 11, 97, 252, 330–31, 424
Roy, Pierre, 238, 239
Rubens, Peter Paul, 215
Ruskin, John, 10, 102, 309, 311, 360, 493, 531
Russell Sage Foundation, 112
Rutherford, Ernest, 72, 436
Ruyer, Raymond: 'Neo-finalisme,' 209
Ruysdael, Jacob van, 226
Ryder, Albert Pinkham, 220–22, 223, 244, 253, 254

Sabinianus, Pope, 197
St. Louis Post-Dispatch, 462
Saintsbury, George, 224
Salvemini, Gaetano, 328, 392–93
Sandburg, Carl, 258, 280
San Francisco Chronicle, 462
Santayana, George, 93, 242, 257, 282, 288, 505
'Saturday Evening Post,' 170
'Saturday Review, The': as source, 189, 401–02, 439

542

544